Oxford Dictionary of
Quotations by Subject

Susan Ratcliffe is an Associate Editor for Oxford Quotations Dictionaries. Her previous publications include the *Little Oxford Dictionary of Quotations* and the *Oxford Dictionary of Phrase, Saying, and Quotation.*

Oxford Paperback Reference

The most authoritative and up-to-date reference books for both students and the general reader.

*forthcoming

Oxford Dictionary of

Quotations by Subject

SECOND EDITION

Edited by SUSAN RATCLIFFE

OXFORD
UNIVERSITY PRESS

Great Clarendon Street, Oxford OX2 6DP

Oxford University Press is a department of the University of Oxford.
It furthers the University's objective of excellence in research, scholarship,
and education by publishing worldwide in

Oxford New York

Auckland Cape Town Dar es Salaam Hong Kong Karachi
Kuala Lumpur Madrid Melbourne Mexico City Nairobi
New Delhi Shanghai Taipei Toronto

with offices in

Argentina Austria Brazil Chile Czech Republic France Greece
Guatemala Hungary Italy Japan Poland Portugal Singapore
South Korea Switzerland Thailand Turkey Ukraine Vietnam

Oxford is a registered trade mark of Oxford University Press
in the UK and in certain other countries

Published in the United States
by Oxford University Press Inc., New York

First published 2000 as *The Oxford Dictionary of Thematic Quotations*

Second edition published 2010

British Library Cataloguing in Publication Data
Data available

Library of Congress Cataloging in Publication Data
Data available

Typeset by Interactive Sciences Limited, Gloucester
Printed in Great Britain
on acid-free paper by
Clays Ltd, Bungay Suffolk

ISBN 978–0–19–956706–5

10 9 8 7 6 5 4 3

Introduction

Nearly a hundred years ago, the French writer Anatole France said 'When a thing has been said and well said, have no scruple: take it and copy it'. The American dramatist Wilson Mizner expanded on the theme: 'If you steal from one author, it's plagiarism; if you steal from many, it's research'. This book collects together the words of many authors, from ancient times to the 21st century, and arranges them by subject to provide a quick answer to the question 'what's been said about this?' Some of the quotations are serious and profound, others witty or frivolous, but whether old or new, all have topical relevance to the issues of today.

It is now ten years since the first edition of this dictionary was published, and the text has been fully updated. More than 1,200 new quotations have been added: some are classics from the past which have gained new prominence, while others are freshly coined, and may or may not outlast their fifteen minutes of fame. A new feature is the inclusion of nationality and occupation with the author details for every quotation. Twenty-five new subjects have been added. Some, such as **Banking**, **Iraq War**, **Nine-Eleven**, or **Thrift** relate to current events, while **Babies**, **Birthdays** and **Retirement** are more personal. Other new subjects include **Chemistry**, **Design**, **Disasters**, and **Wisdom**.

New quotations from the current century range from American president Barack Obama's campaign slogan 'Yes, we can' at **Achievement** to Jamaican athlete Usain Bolt on his success at the **Olympic Games**: 'I just blew my mind. And I blew the world's mind'. Singer Victoria Beckham has a different thought on **Exercise**: 'I'd love to go to the gym, but I just can't get my head around the footwear'.

Many of the 'new' quotations are very old, but still true today: it is two thousand years since Seneca said of **Adversity** 'Fire is the test of gold; adversity, of strong men', and five hundred since Cervantes said of **The Body** 'Every tooth in a man's head is more valuable than a diamond'. A little later Samuel Johnson wrote of **Children**: 'Allow them to be happy their own way, for what better way will they ever find?' while Henry James' views on **Relationships** are widely quoted 'Three things in human life are important. The first is to be kind. The second is to be kind. And the third is to be kind'.

As always, one of the most enjoyable features of a dictionary such as this is the buzz of contrasting voices: John Lennon revealing 'It's not fun being a genius. It's torture', Albert Einstein suggesting that 'Imagination is more important than knowledge', James Dyson on **Business**: 'Making money from money should be replaced with making money from making', the Victorian novelist Elizabeth Gaskell on **Fools**: 'I won't say she was silly, but I think one of us was silly, and it wasn't me', and the unlikely thought of American president Herbert Hoover: 'All men are equal before fish'.

Many more lively and interesting quotations can be found simply by dipping into the text, but some practical notes may be useful for those seeking specific information. The *Oxford Dictionary of Quotations by Subject* is arranged by alphabetical order of subject, and within each subject the quotations are arranged in alphabetical order of author name. Dates and brief descriptions are given for each author, as is a source for each quotation. Contextual notes are supplied where this may be necessary to understanding the quotation. Cross references are also provided from the subject headings to other subjects where related quotations may be found. The author index makes it easy to trace quotations by a particular writer.

St Ambrose said that 'No duty is more urgent than that of returning thanks', and in the case of this book particular thanks are due to Ben Harris, former Commissioning Editor for Language Reference, for initiating this new edition and setting it on its way, and to Joanna Harris, Senior Editor, for advice and assistance in its later stages, to Jean Harker, Verity Mason, and Susanne Charlett for contributions to the Quotations Reading Programme, and to Penny Trumble for proofreading.

A special pleasure in working on this new edition has been the discovery of just how many interesting quotations it has been possible to add to increase the representation of a variety of ideas on so many subjects. I hope that the reader, like the editor, may frequently find themselves, in the words of the poet Robert Browning, 'Stung by the splendour of a sudden thought'.

SUSAN RATCLIFFE
Oxford, October 2009

List of themes

Ability

see also ACHIEVEMENT

1 Natural abilities are like natural
plants, that need pruning by study.
Francis Bacon 1561–1626 English
lawyer, courtier, philosopher, and
essayist: *Essays* (1625) 'Of Studies'

2 If a man write a better book, preach a
better sermon, or make a better
mouse-trap than his neighbour, tho'
he build his house in the woods, the
world will make a beaten path to his
door.
Ralph Waldo Emerson 1803–82
American philosopher and poet:
attributed

3 This very remarkable man
Commends a most practical plan:
You can do what you want
If you don't think you can't,
So don't think you can't think you
can.
Charles Inge 1868–1957: 'On Monsieur
Coué' (1928); see MEDICINE 5

4 Yes, we can.
Barack Obama 1961– American
Democratic statesman: presidential
campaign slogan, 2007–8

5 DUMBLEDORE: It is our choices, Harry,
that show what we truly are, far more
than our abilities.
J. K. Rowling 1965– English novelist:
Harry Potter and the Chamber of Secrets
(1998)

6 *Non omnia possumus omnes.*
We can't all do everything.
Virgil 70–19 BC Roman poet: *Eclogues*

Absence

see also MEETING, PARTING

1 When I came back to Dublin, I was
courtmartialled in my absence and
sentenced to death in my absence,
so I said they could shoot me in my
absence.
Brendan Behan 1923–64 Irish
dramatist: *Hostage* (1958)

2 The heart may think it knows better:
the senses know that absence blots
people out. We have really no absent
friends.
Elizabeth Bowen 1899–1973 Anglo-Irish
novelist: *Death of the Heart* (1938)

3 *Partir c'est mourir un peu.*
To go away is to die a little.
Edmond Haraucourt 1856–1941 French
poet: 'Rondel de l'Adieu' (1891)

4 Absence diminishes commonplace
passions and increases great ones, as
the wind extinguishes candles and
kindles fire.
Duc de la Rochefoucauld 1613–80
French moralist: *Maximes* (1678)

5 The more he looked inside the more
Piglet wasn't there.
A. A. Milne 1882–1956 English writer for
children: *The House at Pooh Corner*
(1928)

6 Omissions are not accidents.
Marianne Moore 1887–1972 American
poet: *Complete Poems* (1967) epigraph

7 Look for what's missing. Many
advisers can tell a president how to
improve what's proposed, or what's
gone amiss. Few are able to see what
isn't there.
Donald Rumsfeld 1932– American
Republican politician and
businessman: *Rumsfeld's Rules* (2001)

8 Most of what matters in your life
takes place in your absence.
Salman Rushdie 1947– Indian-born
British novelist: *Midnight's Children*
(1981)

9 I am reduced to a thing that wants Virginia.

Vita Sackville-West 1892–1962 English writer and gardener: letter to Virginia Woolf, 21 January 1926

Achievement

see also ABILITY, AMBITION, EFFORT, GREATNESS, SUCCESS

1 That's one small step for man, one giant leap for mankind.

stepping onto the moon

Neil Armstrong 1930– American astronaut: in *New York Times* 21 July 1969; interference in the transmission obliterated 'a' between 'for' and 'man'

2 We can lift ourselves out of ignorance, we can find ourselves as creatures of excellence and intelligence and skill.

Richard Bach 1936– American novelist: *Jonathan Livingston Seagull* (1970)

3 The desire accomplished is sweet to the soul.

Bible: Proverbs

4 That low man seeks a little thing to do,
Sees it and does it:
This high man, with a great thing to pursue,
Dies ere he knows it.
That low man goes on adding one to one,
His hundred's soon hit:
This high man, aiming at a million,
Misses an unit.

Robert Browning 1812–89 English poet: 'A Grammarian's Funeral' (1855)

5 To those of you who received honours, awards and distinctions, I say well done. And to the C students, I say you, too, can be president of the United States.

George W. Bush 1946– American

Republican statesman: in *Sunday Times* 27 May 2001

6 Here is the answer which I will give to President Roosevelt . . . Give us the tools and we will finish the job.

Winston Churchill 1874–1965 British Conservative statesman: radio broadcast, 9 February 1941

7 None climbs so high as he who knows not whither he is going.

Oliver Cromwell 1599–1658 English soldier and statesman: attributed

8 The distance is nothing; it is only the first step that is difficult.

commenting on the legend that St Denis, carrying his head in his hands, walked two leagues

Mme Du Deffand 1697–1780 French literary hostess: letter to Jean Le Rond d'Alembert, 7 July 1763

9 The reward of a thing well done, is to have done it.

Ralph Waldo Emerson 1803–82 American philosopher and poet: *Essays: Second Series* (1844) 'Nominalist and Realist'

10 Seriously, though, he's doing a grand job!

David Frost 1939– English broadcaster and writer: catch-phrase in 'That Was The Week That Was', on BBC Television, 1962–3

11 Those who believe that they are exclusively in the right are generally those who achieve something.

Aldous Huxley 1894–1963 English novelist: *Proper Studies* (1927) 'Note on Dogma'

12 He has, indeed, done it very well; but it is a foolish thing well done.

on Goldsmith's apology in the London Chronicle *for assaulting Thomas Evans*

Samuel Johnson 1709–84 English poet, critic, and lexicographer: James Boswell *Life of Johnson* (1791) 3 April 1773

13 It is sobering to consider that when Mozart was my age he had already been dead for a year.
> **Tom Lehrer** 1928– American humorist: attributed

14 He who does *something* at the head of one regiment, will eclipse him who does *nothing* at the head of a hundred.
> **Abraham Lincoln** 1809–65 American statesman: letter to Major-General David Hunter, 31 December 1861

15 Fame is an accident; merit a thing absolute.
> **Herman Melville** 1819–91 American novelist and poet: *Mardi* (1849)

16 Think nothing done while aught remains to do.
> **Samuel Rogers** 1763–1855 English poet: 'Human Life' (1819)

17 If you are not criticized, you may not be doing much.
> **Donald Rumsfeld** 1932– American Republican politician and businessman: 'Rumsfeld's Rules'; interview in *Wall Street Journal* 29 January 2001

18 There are two tragedies in life. One is not to get your heart's desire. The other is to get it.
> **George Bernard Shaw** 1856–1950 Irish dramatist: *Man and Superman* (1903)

19 We ourselves feel that what we are doing is just a drop in the ocean. But if that drop was not in the ocean, I think the ocean would be less because of that missing drop. I do not agree with the big way of doing things.
> **Mother Teresa** 1910–97 Roman Catholic nun and missionary: *A Gift for God* (1975)

Acting

see also ACTORS, CINEMA, FILMS, SHAKESPEARE, THEATRE

1 To grasp the full significance of life is the actor's duty, to interpret it is his problem, and to express it his dedication.
> **Marlon Brando** 1924–2004 American actor: David Shipman *Marlon Brando* (1974)

2 Just say the lines and don't trip over the furniture.
advice on acting
> **Noël Coward** 1899–1973 English dramatist, actor, and composer: D. Richards *The Wit of Noël Coward* (1968)

3 Acting is a masochistic form of exhibitionism. It is not quite the occupation of an adult.
> **Laurence Olivier** 1907–89 English actor and director: in *Time* 3 July 1978

4 Acting is merely the art of keeping a large group of people from coughing.
> **Ralph Richardson** 1902–83 English actor: in *New York Herald Tribune* 19 May 1946

5 Be not too tame neither, but let your own discretion be your tutor: suit the action to the word, the word to the action; with this special observance, that you o'erstep not the modesty of nature; for anything so overdone is from the purpose of playing, whose end, both at the first and now, was and is, to hold, as 'twere, the mirror up to nature.
> **William Shakespeare** 1564–1616 English dramatist: *Hamlet* (1601)

Action

see also IDLENESS, WORDS AND DEEDS

1 Better to light one candle than to curse the darkness.
> **Anonymous**: motto of the American Christopher Society, founded 1945

2 Under conditions of tyranny it is far easier to act than to think.
   Hannah Arendt 1906–75 American political philosopher: W. H. Auden *A Certain World* (1970)

3 But men must know, that in this theatre of man's life it is reserved only for God and angels to be lookers on.
   Francis Bacon 1561–1626 English lawyer, courtier, philosopher, and essayist: *The Advancement of Learning* (1605)

4 Vision without action is merely a dream. Action without vision just passes the time. Vision with action can change the world.
   Joel Arthur Barker American futurist: *The Power of Vision* (1991 video)

5 The world can only be grasped by action, not by contemplation . . . The hand is the cutting edge of the mind.
   Jacob Bronowski 1908–74 Polish-born mathematician and humanist: *The Ascent of Man* (1973)

6 It is vain to say that human beings ought to be satisfied with tranquillity: they must have action; and they will make it if they cannot find it.
   Charlotte Brontë 1816–55 English novelist: *Jane Eyre* (1847)

7 Action is consolatory. It is the enemy of thought and the friend of flattering illusions.
   Joseph Conrad 1857–1924 Polish-born English novelist: *Nostromo* (1904)

8 You have sat too long here for any good you have been doing. Depart, I say, and let us have done with you. In the name of God, go!
   addressing the Rump Parliament, 20 April 1653; quoted by Leo Amery to Neville Chamberlain in the House of Commons, 7 May 1940
   Oliver Cromwell 1599–1658 English soldier and statesman: oral tradition

9 Progression is going forwards. Going backwards is regression. Going sideways is just aggression.
   Noel Gallagher 1967– English pop singer: in *Observer* 18 February 2007

10 If it were done when 'tis done, then 'twere well
   It were done quickly.
   William Shakespeare 1564–1616 English dramatist: *Macbeth* (1606)

11 Let's go to work.
   Quentin Tarantino 1963– American film director and screenwriter: *Reservoir Dogs* (1992 film); spoken by Lawrence Tierney

Actors

see also ACTING, CINEMA, THEATRE

1 How different, how very different from the home life of our own dear Queen!
   comment overheard at a performance of Cleopatra by Sarah Bernhardt
   Anonymous: Irvin S. Cobb *A Laugh a Day* (1924); probably apocryphal

2 For an actress to be a success, she must have the face of a Venus, the brains of a Minerva, the grace of Terpsichore, the memory of a Macaulay, the figure of Juno, and the hide of a rhinoceros.
   Ethel Barrymore 1879–1959 American actress: George Jean Nathan *The Theatre in the Fifties* (1953)

3 The basic essential of a great actor is that he loves himself in acting.
   Charlie Chaplin 1889–1977 English film actor and director: *My Autobiography* (1964)

4 Theatre actors look down on film actors, who look down on TV actors. Thank God for reality shows or we wouldn't have anybody to look down on.

> **George Clooney** 1961– American actor and director: in *Observer* 10 February 2008

5 Don't put your daughter on the stage, Mrs Worthington.

> **Noël Coward** 1899–1973 English dramatist, actor, and composer: 'Mrs Worthington' (1935 song)

6 An actor is a kind of a guy who if you ain't talking about him ain't listening.

> **George Glass** 1910–84: Bob Thomas *Brando* (1973); often quoted by Marlon Brando, 1956 onwards

7 Actors are cattle.

> **Alfred Hitchcock** 1899–1980 British-born film director: in *Saturday Evening Post* 22 May 1943

8 When you do Shakespeare they think you must be intelligent because they *think* you understand what you're saying.

> **Helen Mirren** 1945– English actress: interviewed on *Ruby Wax Meets . . .* ; in *Mail on Sunday* 16 February 1997

9 She ran the whole gamut of the emotions from A to B.

> *of Katharine Hepburn at a Broadway first night, 1933*
>
> **Dorothy Parker** 1893–1967 American critic and humorist: attributed

10 Ladies, just a little more virginity, if you don't mind.

> *to a motley collection of women, assembled to play ladies-in-waiting to a queen*
>
> **Herbert Beerbohm Tree** 1852–1917 English actor-manager: Alexander Woollcott *Shouts and Murmurs* (1923)

Administration

see also BUREAUCRACY, CIVIL SERVICE, COMMITTEES

1 A memorandum is written not to inform the reader but to protect the writer.

> **Dean Acheson** 1893–1971 American politician: in *Wall Street Journal* 8 September 1977

2 Thank heavens we do not get all of the government that we are made to pay for.

> **Milton Friedman** 1912–2006 American economist: quoted in the House of Lords, 24 November 1994

3 *when his secretary suggested throwing away out-of-date files:*
A good idea, only be sure to make a copy of everything before getting rid of it.

> **Sam Goldwyn** 1882–1974 American film producer: Michael Freedland *The Goldwyn Touch* (1986)

4 Let's find out what everyone is doing, And then stop everyone from doing it.

> **A. P. Herbert** 1890–1971 English writer and humorist: 'Let's Stop Somebody from Doing Something!' (1930)

5 For forms of government let fools contest;
Whate'er is best administered is best.

> **Alexander Pope** 1688–1744 English poet: *An Essay on Man* Epistle 3 (1733)

6 If any man will draw up his case, and put his name at the foot of the first page, I will give him an immediate reply. Where he compels me to turn over the sheet, he must wait my leisure.

> *on appeals made by officers to the Navy Board*
>
> **Lord Sandwich** 1718–92 British politician and diplomat: N. W. Wraxall *Memoirs* (1884)

Adversity

see also MISFORTUNES, SUFFERING

1 What we learn in a time of pestilence: that there are more things to admire in men than to despise.
> **Albert Camus** 1913–60 French novelist, dramatist, and essayist: *The Plague* (1947)

2 Adversity is sometimes hard upon a man; but for one man who can stand prosperity, there are a hundred that will stand adversity.
> **Thomas Carlyle** 1795–1881 Scottish historian and political philosopher: *On Heroes, Hero-Worship, and the Heroic* (1841)

3 Life is not meant to be easy.
> **Malcolm Fraser** 1930– Australian Liberal statesman: 5th Alfred Deakin Lecture, 20 July 1971; see LIFE 34

4 Man needs difficulties; they are necessary for health.
> **Carl Gustav Jung** 1875–1961 Swiss psychologist: 'The Transcendent Function' (1916)

5 Into each life some rain must fall, Some days must be dark and dreary.
> **Henry Wadsworth Longfellow** 1807–82 American poet: 'The Rainy Day' (1842)

6 A woman is like a teabag—only in hot water do you realise how strong she is.
> **Nancy Reagan** 1923– American actress: in *Observer* 29 March 1981

7 Fire is the test of gold; adversity, of strong men.
> **Seneca ('the Younger')** *c.*4 BC–AD 65 Roman philosopher and poet: *Moral Essays* 'On Providence'

8 Sweet are the uses of adversity, Which like the toad, ugly and venomous,

Wears yet a precious jewel in his head.
> **William Shakespeare** 1564–1616 English dramatist: *As You Like It* (1599)

9 By trying we can easily learn to endure adversity. Another man's, I mean.
> **Mark Twain** 1835–1910 American writer: *Following the Equator* (1897)

10 The heart *prefers* to move against the grain of circumstance; perversity is the soul's very life.
> **John Updike** 1932–2009 American novelist and short-story writer: *Assorted Prose* (1965) 'More Love in the Western World'

Advertising

1 Word of mouth is the best medium of all.
> **Bill Bernbach** 1911–82 American advertising executive: *Bill Bernbach said* (1989)

2 A good poster is a visual telegram.
> **A. M. Cassandre** 1901–68 French illustrator: attributed

3 You can tell the ideals of a nation by its advertisements.
> **Norman Douglas** 1868–1952 Scottish-born novelist and essayist: *South Wind* (1917)

4 It is not necessary to advertise food to hungry people, fuel to cold people, or houses to the homeless.
> **J. K. Galbraith** 1908–2006 American economist: *American Capitalism* (1952)

5 It is far easier to write ten passably effective sonnets, good enough to take in the not too enquiring critic, than one effective advertisement that will take in a few thousand of the uncritical buying public.
> **Aldous Huxley** 1894–1963 English

novelist: *On the Margin* (1923)
'Advertisement'

6 Promise, large promise, is the soul of an advertisement.
Samuel Johnson 1709–84 English poet, critic, and lexicographer: in *The Idler* 20 January 1759

7 Society drives people crazy with lust and calls it advertising.
John Lahr 1941– American critic: in *Guardian* 2 August 1989

8 Advertising may be described as the science of arresting human intelligence long enough to get money from it.
Stephen Leacock 1869–1944 Canadian humorist: *Garden of Folly* (1924) 'The Perfect Salesman'

9 Half the money I spend on advertising is wasted, and the trouble is I don't know which half.
Lord Leverhulme 1851–1925 English industrialist and philanthropist: David Ogilvy *Confessions of an Advertising Man* (1963)

10 Advertising is the greatest art form of the twentieth century.
Marshall McLuhan 1911–80 Canadian communications scholar: in *Advertising Age* 3 September 1976

11 Good wine needs no bush,
And perhaps products that people really want need no hard-sell or soft-sell TV push.
Why not?
Look at pot.
Ogden Nash 1902–71 American humorist: 'Most Doctors Recommend or Yours For Fast, Fast, Fast Relief' (1972)

12 The consumer isn't a moron; she is your wife.
David Ogilvy 1911–99 British-born advertising executive: *Confessions of an Advertising Man* (1963)

13 Advertising is the rattling of a stick inside a swill bucket.
George Orwell 1903–50 English novelist: *Keep the Aspidistra Flying* (1936)

14 As advertising blather becomes the nation's normal idiom, language becomes printed noise.
George F. Will 1941– American columnist: *The Pursuit of Happiness and Other Sobering Thoughts* (1976)

Advice

1 Don't panic.
Douglas Adams 1952–2001 English science fiction writer: *Hitch Hiker's Guide to the Galaxy* (1979)

2 It was, perhaps, one of those cases in which advice is good or bad only as the event decides.
Jane Austen 1775–1817 English novelist: *Persuasion* (1818)

3 Books will speak plain when counsellors blanch.
Francis Bacon 1561–1626 English lawyer, courtier, philosopher, and essayist: *Essays* (1625) 'Of Counsel'

4 Well, if you knows of a better 'ole, go to it.
Bruce Bairnsfather 1888–1959 British cartoonist: *Fragments from France* (1915)

5 Of all the horrid, hideous notes of woe,
Sadder than owl-songs or the midnight blast,
Is that portentous phrase, 'I told you so.'
Lord Byron 1788–1824 English poet: *Don Juan* (1819–24)

6 In matters of religion and matrimony I never give any advice; because I will

not have anybody's torments in this world or the next laid to my charge.
Lord Chesterfield 1694–1773 English writer and politician: letter to Arthur Charles Stanhope, 12 October 1765

7 Fools need advice most, but wise men only are the better for it.
Benjamin Franklin 1706–90 American politician, inventor, and scientist: *Poor Richard's Almanac* (1758) January

8 Get the advice of everybody whose advice is worth having—they are very few—and then do what you think best yourself.
Charles Stewart Parnell 1846–91 Irish nationalist leader: Conor Cruise O'Brien *Parnell* (1957)

9 After all, when you seek advice from someone it's certainly not because you want them to give it. You just want them to be there while you talk to yourself.
Terry Pratchett 1948– English science fiction writer: *Jingo* (1997)

10 I always pass on good advice. It is the only thing to do with it. It is never of any use to oneself.
Oscar Wilde 1854–1900 Anglo-Irish dramatist and poet: *An Ideal Husband* (1895)

Africa

1 Your map of Africa is all very fine, but my map of Africa lies in Europe. Here is Russia and here is France, and we are in the middle; that is my map of Africa.
on colonial policy
Otto von Bismarck 1815–98 German statesman: to Eugen Wolf, 5 December 1888

2 The state of Africa is a scar on the conscience of the world.
Tony Blair 1953– British Labour statesman: speech to Labour Party Conference, 2 October 2001

3 We have Africa in our blood and Africa has our bones. We are all Africans.
Richard Dawkins 1941– English biologist: *A Devil's Chaplain* (2003)

4 I am a woman and a woman of Africa. I am a daughter of Nigeria and if she is in shame, I shall stay and mourn with her in shame.
Buchi Emecheta 1944– Nigerian writer: *Destination Biafra* (1982)

5 We are . . . a nation of dancers, singers and poets.
of the Ibo people
Olaudah Equiano c.1745–c.97 African writer and former slave: *Narrative of the Life of Olaudah Equiano* (1789)

6 The shape of Africa resembles a revolver, and the Congo is the trigger.
Frantz Fanon 1925–61 French West Indian psychoanalyst: attributed

7 Westerners have aggressive problem-solving minds; Africans experience people.
Kenneth Kaunda 1924– Zambian statesman: attributed, 1990

8 The wind of change is blowing through this continent.
Harold Macmillan 1894–1986 British Conservative statesman: speech at Cape Town, 3 February 1960

9 I have dedicated my life to this struggle of the African people. I have fought against white domination, and I have fought against black domination. I have cherished the ideal of a democratic and free society in which all persons live together in harmony with equal opportunities. It is an ideal which I hope to live for, and to see realized. But my lord, if

needs be, it is an ideal for which I am prepared to die.
> **Nelson Mandela** 1918– South African statesman: speech in Pretoria, 20 April 1964, which he quoted on his release in Cape Town, 11 February 1990

10 Blair, keep your England and let me keep my Zimbabwe.
> **Robert Mugabe** 1924– African statesman: at the Earth Summit in Johannesburg, 2 September 2002

11 *Semper aliquid novi Africam adferre.*
Africa always brings [us] something new.
> *often quoted as* 'Ex Africa semper aliquid novi [Always something new out of Africa]'
> **Pliny the Elder** AD 23–79 Roman statesman and scholar: *Historia Naturalis*

12 Democracy is an orphan in Zimbabwe.
> **Morgan Tsvangirai** 1952– Zimbabwean politician: in *Guardian* 7 April 2008

13 I who have cursed
The drunken officer of British rule,
  how choose
Between this Africa and the English tongue I love?
> **Derek Walcott** 1930– West Indian poet and dramatist: 'A Far Cry From Africa' (1962)

Ageing

see also OLD AGE

1 I recently turned sixty. Practically a third of my life is over.
> **Woody Allen** 1935– American film director, writer, and actor: in *Observer* 10 March 1996

2 The man who works and is not bored is never old.
> **Pablo Casals** 1876–1973 Spanish cellist, conductor, and composer: J. Lloyd Webber (ed.) *Song of the Birds* (1985)

3 Considering the alternative, it's not too bad at all.
> *when asked what he felt about the advancing years on his seventy-second birthday*
> **Maurice Chevalier** 1888–1972 French singer and actor: Michael Freedland *Maurice Chevalier* (1981)

4 Oh, to be seventy again!
> *on seeing a pretty girl on his eightieth birthday*
> **Georges Clemenceau** 1841–1929 French statesman: James Agate diary, 19 April 1938; also attributed to Oliver Wendell Holmes Jnr.

5 We turn not older with years, but newer every day.
> **Emily Dickinson** 1830–86 American poet: letter, 1874

6 You will recognize, my boy, the first sign of old age: it is when you go out into the streets of London and realize for the first time how young the policemen look.
> **Seymour Hicks** 1871–1949 English actor-manager and writer: C. R. D. Pulling *They Were Singing* (1952)

7 It's not the years, honey, it's the mileage.
> **George Lucas** 1944– American film director, producer, and screenwriter: *Raiders of the Lost Ark* (1981 film, with Philip Kaufman), spoken by Harrison Ford as Indiana Jones

8 The unending problem of growing old was not how he changed, but how things did.
> **Toni Morrison** 1931– American novelist: *Tar Baby* (1981)

9 Every man desires to live long; but no man would be old.
> **Jonathan Swift** 1667–1745 Anglo-Irish poet and satirist: *Thoughts on Various Subjects* (1727 ed.)

10 Do not go gentle into that good night,

Old age should burn and rave at
close of day;
Rage, rage against the dying of the
light.
Dylan Thomas 1914–53 Welsh poet: 'Do
Not Go Gentle into that Good Night'
(1952)

11 Hope I die before I get old.
Pete Townshend 1945– British rock
musician and songwriter: 'My
Generation' (1965 song)

12 The tragedy of old age is not that one
is old, but that one is young.
Oscar Wilde 1854–1900 Anglo-Irish
dramatist and poet: *The Picture of
Dorian Grey* (1891)

Aid and Development

see also FAMINE

1 Foreign aid is a system of taking
money from poor people in rich
countries and giving it to rich people
in poor countries.
Lord Bauer 1915–2002 British
economist: attributed

2 Feed the world
Let them know it's Christmas time
again.
Bob Geldof 1954– and **Midge Ure**
1953– Irish and Scottish rock
musicians: 'Do They Know it's
Christmas?' (1984 song)

3 No permanent elevation of a people
can be effected without commerce.
David Livingstone 1813–73 Scottish
missionary and explorer: in *Quarterly
Review* April 1861

4 Should we really let our people
starve so we can pay our debts?
Julius Nyerere 1922–99 Tanzanian
statesman: in *Guardian* 21 March 1985

5 It will be golden elephants next.
suggesting that the government of

*Montserrat was 'talking mad money' in
claiming assistance for evacuating the
island*
Clare Short 1946– British Labour
politician: in *Observer* 24 August 1997

Aids

1 and I swear sometimes
when I put my head to his chest
I can hear the virus humming
like a refrigerator.
Mark Doty 1953– American poet:
'Atlantis' (1996)

2 Sometimes I have a terrible feeling
that I am dying not from the virus,
but from being untouchable.
Amanda Heggs: in *Guardian* 12 June
1989

3 Societies need to have one illness
which becomes identified with evil,
and attaches blame to its 'victims'.
Susan Sontag 1933– American writer:
AIDS and its Metaphors (1989)

4 The Aids epidemic has rolled back a
big rotting log and revealed all the
squirming life underneath it, since it
involves, all at once, the main
themes of our existence: sex, death,
power, money, love, hate, disease
and panic. No American
phenomenon has been so
compelling since the Vietnam War.
Edmund White 1940– American writer
and critic: *States of Desire: Travels in Gay
America* (afterword to 1986 edition)

The Air Force

1 The bomber will always get through.
The only defence is in offence, which
means that you have to kill more
women and children more quickly
than the enemy if you want to save
yourselves.
Stanley Baldwin 1867–1947 British

Conservative statesman: speech, House of Commons, 10 November 1932

2 Never in the field of human conflict was so much owed by so many to so few.
on the skill and courage of British airmen
Winston Churchill 1874–1965 British Conservative statesman: speech, House of Commons, 20 August 1940

3 In bombers named for girls, we burned
The cities we had learned about in school—
Till our lives wore out; our bodies lay among
The people we had killed and never seen.
When we lasted long enough they gave us medals;
When we died they said, 'Our casualties were low.'
Randall Jarrell 1914–65 American poet: 'Losses' (1963)

4 Oh! I have slipped the surly bonds of earth
And danced the skies on laughter-silvered wings; . . .
And, while with silent lifting mind I've trod
The high, untrespassed sanctity of space,
Put out my hand and touched the face of God.
John Gillespie Magee 1922–41 American airman: 'High Flight' (1943)

5 Nor law, nor duty bade me fight,
Nor public men, nor cheering crowds,
A lonely impulse of delight
Drove to this tumult in the clouds;
I balanced all, brought all to mind,
The years to come seemed waste of breath,
A waste of breath the years behind
In balance with this life, this death.
W. B. Yeats 1865–1939 Irish poet: 'An Irish Airman Foresees his Death' (1919)

Air Travel

1 Every flyer who ventures across oceans to distant lands is a potential explorer; in his or her breast burns the same fire that urged the adventurers of old to set forth in their sailing-ships for foreign lands.
Jean Batten 1909–82 New Zealand aviator: *Alone in the Sky* (1979)

2 This flying is the most wonderful invention. A man ceases to be human up there. He feels that nothing is impossible.
Billy Bishop 1894–1956 Canadian fighter pilot: letter to his parents from Netheravon, England, 1 September 1915

3 The best mascot is a good mechanic.
Amelia Earhart 1898–1937 American aviator: Mary S. Lovell *The Sound of Wings* (1989)

4 Had I been a man I might have explored the Poles, or climbed Mount Everest, but as it was, my spirit found outlet in the air.
Amy Johnson 1903–41 English aviator: Margot Asquith (ed.) *Myself When Young* (1938)

5 I feel about airplanes the way I feel about diets. It seems to me that they are wonderful things for other people to go on.
Jean Kerr 1923–2003 American writer: *The Snake Has All the Lines* (1958)

6 I did not fully understand the dread term 'terminal illness' until I saw Heathrow for myself.
Dennis Potter 1935–94 English television dramatist: in *Sunday Times* 4 June 1978

7 The Devil himself had probably redesigned Hell in the light of information he had gained from observing airport layouts.
Anthony Price 1928– English writer and editor: *The Memory Trap* (1989)

8 Anything that is white is sweet.
Anything that is brown is meat.
Anything that is grey, don't eat.
on airline food
> **Stephen Sondheim** 1930– American
> songwriter: 'Do I Hear a Waltz?'
> (1965 song)

9 There are only two emotions in a
plane: boredom and terror.
> **Orson Welles** 1915–85 American actor
> and film director: interview in *Times*
> 6 May 1985

Alcohol

see also DRUNKENNESS, TEETOTALISM

1 A dusty thudding in his head made
the scene before him beat like a
pulse. His mouth had been used as a
latrine by some small creature of the
night, and then as its mausoleum.
> **Kingsley Amis** 1922–95 English novelist
> and poet: *Lucky Jim* (1954)

2 Let's get out of these wet clothes and
into a dry Martini.
> **Anonymous**: line coined in the 1920s by
> Robert Benchley's press agent and
> adopted by Mae West in *Every Day's a*
> *Holiday* (1937 film)

3 Your true amateur *sips* his wine; as
he lingers over each separate
mouthful, he obtains from each the
sum total of pleasure which he
would have experienced had he
emptied his glass at a single draught.
> **Anthelme Brillat-Savarin** 1755–1826
> French jurist and gourmet: *The*
> *Physiology of Taste* (1825) pt. 2

4 Freedom and Whisky gang thegither!
> **Robert Burns** 1759–96 Scottish poet:
> 'The Author's Earnest Cry and Prayer'
> (1786)

5 Alcohol is like love: the first kiss is
magic, the second is intimate, the
third is routine. After that you just
take the girl's clothes off.
> **Raymond Chandler** 1888–1959
> American writer of detective fiction: *The*
> *Long Good-Bye* (1953)

6 I have taken more out of alcohol
than alcohol has taken out of me.
> **Winston Churchill** 1874–1965 British
> Conservative statesman: Quentin
> Reynolds *By Quentin Reynolds* (1964)

7 A man shouldn't fool with booze
until he's fifty; then he's a damn fool
if he doesn't.
> **William Faulkner** 1897–1962 American
> novelist: James M. Webb and A. Wigfall
> Green *William Faulkner of Oxford*
> (1965)

8 Some weasel took the cork out of my
lunch.
> **W. C. Fields** 1880–1946 American
> humorist: *You Can't Cheat an Honest*
> *Man* (1939 film)

9 I often wonder what the Vintners buy
One half so precious as the Goods
they sell.
> **Edward Fitzgerald** 1809–83 English
> scholar and poet: *The Rubáiyát of Omar*
> *Khayyám* (1859)

10 A medium Vodka dry Martini—with
a slice of lemon peel. Shaken and not
stirred.
> **Ian Fleming** 1908–64 English thriller
> writer: *Dr No* (1958)

11 And malt does more than Milton can
To justify God's ways to man.
Ale, man, ale's the stuff to drink
For fellows whom it hurts to think.
> **A. E. Housman** 1859–1936 English poet:
> *A Shropshire Lad* (1896); see WRITING 25

12 We drink one another's healths, and
spoil our own.
> **Jerome K. Jerome** 1859–1927 English
> writer: *Idle Thoughts of an Idle Fellow*
> (1886)

13 Claret is the liquor for boys; port, for men; but he who aspires to be a hero (smiling) must drink brandy.

> **Samuel Johnson** 1709–84 English poet, critic, and lexicographer: James Boswell *Life of Johnson* (1791) 7 April 1779

14 O for a beaker full of the warm South, Full of the true, the blushful Hippocrene, With beaded bubbles winking at the brim, And purple-stainèd mouth.

> **John Keats** 1795–1821 English poet: 'Ode to a Nightingale' (1820)

15 Wine may well be considered the most healthful and most hygienic of beverages.

> **Louis Pasteur** 1822–95 French chemist and bacteriologist: *Études sur le vin* (1873)

16 A good general rule is to state that the bouquet is better than the taste, and vice versa.

on wine-tasting

> **Stephen Potter** 1900–69 British writer: *One-Upmanship* (1952)

17 Wine is bottled poetry.

> **Robert Louis Stevenson** 1850–94 Scottish novelist: *The Silverado Squatters* (1883)

18 Fifteen men on the dead man's chest Yo-ho-ho, and a bottle of rum! Drink and the devil had done for the rest— Yo-ho-ho, and a bottle of rum!

> **Robert Louis Stevenson** 1850–94 Scottish novelist: *Treasure Island* (1883)

19 It's a naïve domestic Burgundy without any breeding, but I think you'll be amused by its presumption.

> **James Thurber** 1894–1961 American humorist: cartoon caption in *New Yorker* 27 March 1937

Alzheimer's Disease

1 She is not sailing into the dark: the voyage is over, and under the dark escort of Alzheimer's she has arrived somewhere. So have I.

> **John Bayley** 1925– English academic: *Iris: A memoir of Iris Murdoch* (1998)

2 I can face death, but I cannot face watching myself disappear from within . . . I don't know who I am anymore.

from a conversation with the founder of The Right to Die Society about his Alzheimer's disease, a few months before his suicide

> **Claude Jutra** 1930–86 Canadian film director: in *Homemaker's Magazine* November–December 1991

3 An embuggerance.

announcing that he had been diagnosed with an early-onset form of Alzheimer's disease

> **Terry Pratchett** 1948– English science fiction writer: on the website www.paulkidby.com/news 11 December 2007

4 I now begin the journey that will lead me into the sunset of my life.

statement to the American people revealing that he had Alzheimer's disease, 1994

> **Ronald Reagan** 1911–2004 American Republican statesman: in *Daily Telegraph* 5 January 1995

5 I have gone from being her lover to her principal carer. When I hug her, it is almost a gesture she does not recognise. She doesn't know how to react.

on his wife who has Alzheimer's disease

> **John Suchet** 1944– Scottish broadcaster: in *Mail on Sunday* 22 February 2009

Ambition

see also ACHIEVEMENT, SUCCESS

1 No bird soars too high, if he soars
with his own wings.
   William Blake 1757–1827 English poet:
   The Marriage of Heaven and Hell
   (1790–3) 'Proverbs of Hell'

2 *Aut Caesar, aut nihil.*
   Caesar or nothing.
   Cesare Borgia 1476–1507 Italian
   statesman: motto inscribed on his
   sword

3 Ah, but a man's reach should exceed
his grasp,
   Or what's a heaven for?
   Robert Browning 1812–89 English poet:
   'Andrea del Sarto' (1855)

4 Well is it known that ambition can
creep as well as soar.
   Edmund Burke 1729–97 Irish-born
   Whig politician and man of letters:
   *Third Letter . . . on the Proposals for
   Peace with the Regicide Directory* (1797)

5 [I] had rather be first in a village than
second at Rome.
   Julius Caesar 100–44 BC Roman general
   and statesman: Plutarch *Parallel Lives*

6 All ambitions are lawful except those
which climb upwards on the
miseries or credulities of mankind.
   Joseph Conrad 1857–1924 Polish-born
   English novelist: *Some Reminiscences*
   (1912)

7 Do you sincerely want to be rich?
   stock question to salesmen
   Bernard Cornfeld 1927–95 American
   businessman: Charles Raw et al. *Do You
   Sincerely Want to be Rich?* (1971)

8 At the age of six I wanted to be a
cook. At seven I wanted to be
Napoleon. And my ambition has
been growing steadily ever since.
   Salvador Dali 1904–89 Spanish painter:
   The Secret Life of Salvador Dali (1948)

9 Remember that there is not one of
you who does not carry in his
cartridge-pouch the marshal's baton
of the duke of Reggio; it is up to you
to bring it forth.
   Louis XVIII 1755–1824 French
   monarch: speech to Saint-Cyr cadets,
   9 August 1819

10 Better to reign in hell, than serve in
heaven.
   John Milton 1608–74 English poet:
   Paradise Lost (1667)

11 Before this time to-morrow I shall
have gained a peerage, or
Westminster Abbey.
   Horatio, Lord Nelson 1758–1805 British
   admiral: before the battle of the Nile,
   1 August 1798

12 It is better to be a has-been than a
never-was.
   Cecil Parkinson 1932– British
   Conservative politician: in *Guardian*
   29 June 1990

13 Fain would I climb, yet fear I to fall.
   *line written on a window-pane; Queen
   Elizabeth I (1533–1603) replied 'If thy heart
   fails thee, climb not at all'*
   Walter Ralegh c.1552–1618 English
   explorer and courtier: Thomas Fuller
   Worthies of England (1662)

14 Yo I'll tell you what I want, what I
really really want
   so tell me what you want, what you
really really want.
   The Spice Girls English pop singers:
   'Wannabe' (1996 song, with Matthew
   Rowbottom and Richard Stannard)

15 Cromwell, I charge thee, fling away
ambition:
   By that sin fell the angels.
   William Shakespeare 1564–1616
   English dramatist: *Henry VIII* (1613)

16 There is always room at the top.
   Daniel Webster 1782–1852 American
   politician: attributed

American Cities and States

see also UNITED STATES

1 California is a fine place to live—if
you happen to be an orange.
   Fred Allen 1894–1956 American
   humorist: *American Magazine*
   December 1945

2 A Boston man is the east wind made
flesh.
   Thomas Gold Appleton 1812–84
   American epigrammatist: attributed

3 The state with the prettiest name,
the state that floats in brackish
   water,
held together by mangrove roots.
   Elizabeth Bishop 1911–79 American
   poet: 'Florida' (1946)

4 And this is good old Boston,
The home of the bean and the cod,
Where the Lowells talk to the Cabots
And the Cabots talk only to God.
   John Collins Bossidy 1860–1928
   American oculist: verse spoken at Holy
   Cross College alumni dinner in Boston,
   Massachusetts, 1910

5 I had forgotten just how flat and
empty it is. Stand on two phone
books almost anywhere in Iowa and
you get a view.
   of middle America
   Bill Bryson 1951– American travel
   writer: *The Lost Continent* (1989)

6 A big hard-boiled city with no more
personality than a paper cup.
   of Los Angeles
   Raymond Chandler 1888–1959
   American writer of detective fiction: *The
   Little Sister* (1949)

7 The present in New York is so
powerful that the past is lost.
   John Jay Chapman 1862–1933
   American essayist and poet: *Emerson
   and Other Essays* (rev. ed. 1909), preface

8 New York, New York,—a helluva
   town,
The Bronx is up but the Battery's
   down.
   Betty Comden 1917–2006 and **Adolph
   Green** 1915–2002: 'New York, New York'
   (1945 song)

9 I left my heart in San Francisco
High on a hill it calls to me.
To be where little cable cars climb
   half-way to the stars,
The morning fog may chill the air—
I don't care!
   Douglas Cross American songwriter: 'I
   Left My Heart in San Francisco'
   (1954 song)

10 Last week, I went to Philadelphia,
but it was closed.
   W. C. Fields 1880–1946 American
   humorist: Richard J. Anobile *Godfrey
   Daniels* (1975)

11 Washington is a city of southern
efficiency and northern charm.
   John F. Kennedy 1917–63 American
   Democratic statesman: Arthur M.
   Schlesinger Jr. *A Thousand Days* (1965)

12 A hundred times I have thought:
New York is a catastrophe, and fifty
times: it is a beautiful catastrophe.
   Le Corbusier 1887–1965 French
   architect: *When the Cathedrals were
   White* (1947) 'The Fairy Catastrophe'

13 This is Red Hook, not Sicily . . . This
is the gullet of New York swallowing
the tonnage of the world.
   Arthur Miller 1915–2005 American
   dramatist: *A View from the Bridge* (1955)

14 A trip through a sewer in a glass-
bottomed boat.
   of Hollywood
   Wilson Mizner 1876–1933 American
   dramatist: Alva Johnston *The Legendary
   Mizners* (1953)

15 Hog Butcher for the World,
Tool Maker, Stacker of Wheat,

Player with Railroads and the
Nation's Freight Handler;
Stormy, husky, brawling,
City of the Big Shoulders.
>   **Carl Sandburg** 1878–1967 American
>   poet: 'Chicago' (1916)

American Civil War

1   Give them the cold steel, boys!
>   **Lewis Addison Armistead** 1817–63
>   American army officer: attributed
>   during the American Civil War, 1863

2   There is Jackson with his Virginians,
standing like a stone wall. Let us
determine to die here, and we will
conquer.
*referring to General T. J. ('Stonewall')
Jackson*
>   **Barnard Elliott Bee** 1823–61 American
>   Confederate general: at the battle of
>   Bull Run, 21 July 1861

3   All quiet along the Potomac to-night,
No sound save the rush of the river,
While soft falls the dew on the face of
the dead—
The picket's off duty forever.
>   **Ethel Lynn Beers** 1827–79 American
>   poet: 'The Picket Guard' (1861); the first
>   line is also attributed to George B.
>   McClellan (1826–85)

4   Hold out. Relief is coming.
*usually quoted as 'Hold the fort! I am
coming!'*
>   **William Sherman** 1820–91 American
>   Union general: flag signal from
>   Kennesaw Mountain to General John
>   Murray Corse at Allatoona Pass,
>   5 October 1864

American War of Independence

1   What a glorious morning is this.
*traditionally quoted 'What a glorious
morning for America'*
>   **Samuel Adams** 1722–1803 American

revolutionary leader: on hearing gunfire
at Lexington, 19 April 1775

2   Here once the embattled farmers
stood,
And fired the shot heard round the
world.
>   **Ralph Waldo Emerson** 1803–82
>   American philosopher and poet: 'On the
>   Completion of the Monument at
>   Concord, April 1836'

3   Men, you are all marksmen—don't
one of you fire until you see the
white of their eyes.
>   **Israel Putnam** 1718–90 American
>   general: at Bunker Hill, 1775; also
>   attributed to William Prescott (1726–95)

4   We beat them to-day or Molly Stark's
a widow.
>   **John Stark** 1728–1822 American
>   Revolutionary officer: before the battle
>   of Bennington, 16 August 1777

Anger

1   A soft answer turneth away wrath.
>   **Bible**: Proverbs

2   The tygers of wrath are wiser than
the horses of instruction.
>   **William Blake** 1757–1827 English poet:
>   *The Marriage of Heaven and Hell*
>   (1790–3)

3   I'm mad as hell, and I'm not going to
take this anymore!
>   **Paddy Chayefsky** 1923–81 American
>   screenwriter: *Network* (1976 film),
>   spoken by Peter Finch as Howard Beale

4   We boil at different degrees.
>   **Ralph Waldo Emerson** 1803–82
>   American philosopher and poet: *Society
>   and Solitude* (1870)

5   Anger is never without an argument,
but seldom with a good one.
>   **Lord Halifax** 1633–95 English politician
>   and essayist: *Political, Moral, and*

Miscellaneous Thoughts and Reflections (1750)

6 Anger is a short madness.
   Horace 65–8 BC Roman poet: *Epistles*

7 When angry, count ten before you speak; if very angry a hundred.
   Thomas Jefferson 1743–1826 American Democratic Republican statesman: letter to Thomas Jefferson Smith, 21 February 1825; see ANGER 11

8 Anger in its time and place
   May assume a kind of grace.
   It must have some reason in it
   And not last beyond a minute.
   Charles Lamb 1775–1834 English writer: 'Anger'

9 It's my rule never to lose me temper till it would be dethrimental to keep it.
   Sean O'Casey 1880–1964 Irish dramatist: *The Plough and the Stars* (1926)

10 Anger always thinks it has power beyond its power.
   Publilius Syrus Roman freedman and writer of mimes of the 1st century BC: *Sententiae*

11 When angry, count four; when very angry, swear.
   Mark Twain 1835–1910 American writer: *Pudd'nhead Wilson* (1894); see ANGER 7

Animal Rights

1 It takes 40 dumb animals to make a fur coat, but only one to wear it.
   Anonymous: slogan of an anti-fur campaign poster, 1980s, sometimes attributed to David Bailey (1938–)

2 The question is not, Can they reason? nor, Can they talk? but, Can they suffer?
   Jeremy Bentham 1748–1832 English

philosopher: *Principles of Morals and Legislation* (1789)

3 A righteous man regardeth the life of his beast: but the tender mercies of the wicked are cruel.
   Bible: Proverbs

4 A robin red breast in a cage
   Puts all Heaven in a rage.
   William Blake 1757–1827 English poet: 'Auguries of Innocence' (*c*.1803)

5 Animals, whom we have made our slaves, we do not like to consider our equal.
   Charles Darwin 1809–82 English natural historian: Notebook B (1837–8)

6 'Twould ring the bells of Heaven
   The wildest peal for years,
   If Parson lost his senses
   And people came to theirs,
   And he and they together
   Knelt down with angry prayers
   For tamed and shabby tigers
   And dancing dogs and bears,
   And wretched, blind, pit ponies,
   And little hunted hares.
   Ralph Hodgson 1871–1962 English poet: 'Bells of Heaven' (1917)

7 Mankind's true moral test, its fundamental test (which lies deeply buried from view) consists of its attitudes towards those who are at its mercy: animals.
   Milan Kundera 1929– Czech novelist: *The Unbearable Lightness of Being* (1984)

Animals

see also ANIMAL RIGHTS, BIRDS, CATS, DOGS, HORSES

1 The rabbit has a charming face:
   Its private life is a disgrace.
   Anonymous: 'The Rabbit' (1925)

2 Old pond,
   leap-splash—

a frog.

> **Matsuo Basho** 1644–94 Japanese poet:
> translated by Lucien Stryk

3 When people call this beast to mind,
They marvel more and more
At such a little tail behind,
So large a trunk before.

> **Hilaire Belloc** 1870–1953 British poet,
> essayist, historian, novelist, and Liberal
> politician: 'The Elephant' (1896)

4 The Llama is a woolly sort of fleecy
hairy goat,
With an indolent expression and an
undulating throat
Like an unsuccessful literary man.

> **Hilaire Belloc** 1870–1953 British poet,
> essayist, historian, novelist, and Liberal
> politician: 'The Llama' (1897)

5 Tyger Tyger, burning bright,
In the forests of the night;
What immortal hand or eye,
Could frame thy fearful symmetry?

> **William Blake** 1757–1827 English poet:
> 'The Tiger' (1794)

6 A four-legged friend, a four-legged
friend,
He'll never let you down.

> *sung by Roy Rogers about his horse Trigger*
> **J. Brooks**: 'A Four Legged Friend'
> (1952 song)

7 To my mind, the only possible pet is
a cow. Cows love you . . . They will
listen to your problems and never
ask a thing in return. They will be
your friends for ever. And when you
get tired of them, you can kill and eat
them. Perfect.

> **Bill Bryson** 1951– American travel
> writer: *Neither Here Nor There* (1991)

8 All animals, except man, know that
the principal business of life is to
enjoy it—and they do enjoy it as
much as man and other
circumstances will allow.

> **Samuel Butler** 1835–1902 English
> novelist: *The Way of All Flesh* (1903)

9 With monstrous head and sickening
cry
And ears like errant wings,
The devil's walking parody
On all four-footed things.

> **G. K. Chesterton** 1874–1936 English
> essayist, novelist, and poet: 'The
> Donkey' (1900)

10 I am fond of pigs. Dogs look up to us.
Cats look down on us. Pigs treat us as
equals.

> **Winston Churchill** 1874–1965 British
> Conservative statesman: attributed

11 Worms have played a more
important part in the history of the
world than most persons would at
first suppose.

> **Charles Darwin** 1809–82 English
> natural historian: *The Formation of
> Vegetable Mould through the Action of
> Worms* (1881)

12 The giraffe, in their queer,
inimitable, vegetative
gracefulness . . . a family of rare,
long-stemmed, speckled gigantic
flowers slowly advancing.

> **Isak Dinesen** 1885–1962 Danish
> novelist and short-story writer: *Out of
> Africa* (1937)

13 Animals are such agreeable
friends—they ask no questions, they
pass no criticism.

> **George Eliot** 1819–80 English novelist:
> *Scenes of Clerical Life* (1858)

14 I hate a word like 'pets': it sounds so
much
Like something with no living of its
own.

> **Elizabeth Jennings** 1926–2001 English
> poet: 'My Animals' (1966)

15 The camel has a single hump;
The dromedary, two;
Or else the other way around,
I'm never sure. Are you?

> **Ogden Nash** 1902–71 American
> humorist: 'The Camel' (1936)

16 God in His wisdom made the fly
And then forgot to tell us why.
>   **Ogden Nash** 1902–71 American
>   humorist: 'The Fly' (1942)

17 Cats is 'dogs' and rabbits is 'dogs' and
so's Parrats, but this 'ere 'Tortis' is a
insect, and there ain't no charge for
it.
>   *railway porter to passenger*
>   **Punch** English humorous weekly
>   periodical: 6 March 1869

18 I think I could turn and live with
animals, they are so placid and
self-contained,
I stand and look at them long and
long.
They do not sweat and whine about
their condition,
They do not lie awake in the dark
and weep for their sins,
They do not make me sick discussing
their duty to God,
Not one is dissatisfied, not one is
demented with the mania of
owning things.
>   **Walt Whitman** 1819–92 American poet:
>   'Song of Myself' (written 1855)

19 But I freely admit that the best of my
fun
I owe it to horse and hound.
>   **George John Whyte-Melville** 1821–78
>   Scottish-born novelist: 'The Good Grey
>   Mare' (1933)

Apology and Excuses

1 Beware of too much explaining, lest
we end by too much excusing.
>   **Lord Acton** 1834–1902 British historian:
>   attributed by Acton to the Duc de
>   Broglie, *Lectures in Modern History*
>   (1906), lecture delivered Cambridge,
>   June 1895

2 Very sorry can't come. Lie follows by
post.
>   *telegraphed message to the Prince of Wales,*
>   *on being summoned to dine at the eleventh*
>   *hour*
>   **Lord Charles Beresford** 1846–1919
>   British politician: Ralph Nevill *The
>   World of Fashion 1837–1922* (1923)

3 Never make a defence or apology
before you be accused.
>   **Charles I** 1600–49 British monarch:
>   letter to Lord Wentworth, 3 September
>   1636

4 Never complain and never explain.
>   **Benjamin Disraeli** 1804–81 British Tory
>   statesman and novelist: J. Morley *Life of
>   William Ewart Gladstone* (1903)

5 To accuse requires less eloquence
(such is man's nature) than to
excuse.
>   **Thomas Hobbes** 1588–1679 English
>   philosopher: *Leviathan* (1651)

6 Never explain—your friends do not
need it and your enemies will not
believe you anyway.
>   **Elbert Hubbard** 1859–1915 American
>   writer: *The Motto Book* (1907)

7 Several excuses are always less
convincing than one.
>   **Aldous Huxley** 1894–1963 English
>   novelist: *Point Counter Point* (1928)

8 A man should never be ashamed to
own he has been in the wrong, which
is but saying, in other words, that he
is wiser to-day than he was
yesterday.
>   **Alexander Pope** 1688–1744 English
>   poet: *Miscellanies* (1727) vol. 2
>   'Thoughts on Various Subjects'

9 It is a good rule in life never to
apologize. The right sort of people do
not want apologies, and the wrong
sort take a mean advantage of them.
>   **P. G. Wodehouse** 1881–1975 English
>   writer: *The Man Upstairs* (1914)

Appearance

see also BODY, COSMETICS, FACE, FAT

1 A little of what you call frippery is very necessary towards looking like the rest of the world.
   Abigail Adams 1744–1818 American letter writer: letter to John Adams, 1 May 1780

2 Though I yield to no one in my admiration for Mr Coolidge, I do wish he did not look as if he had been weaned on a pickle.
   Anonymous: Alice Roosevelt Longworth *Crowded Hours* (1933)

3 It's as large as life, and twice as natural!
   Lewis Carroll 1832–98 English writer and logician: *Through the Looking-Glass* (1872)

4 Like the silver plate on a coffin.
   describing Robert Peel's smile
   John Philpot Curran 1750–1817 Irish judge: quoted by Daniel O'Connell, House of Commons, 26 February 1835

5 If everyone were cast in the same mould, there would be no such thing as beauty.
   Charles Darwin 1809–82 English natural historian: *The Descent of Man* (1871)

6 She may very well pass for forty-three
   In the dusk with a light behind her!
   W. S. Gilbert 1836–1911 English writer of comic and satirical verse: *Trial by Jury* (1875)

7 The most common error made in matters of appearance is the belief that one should disdain the superficial and let the true beauty of one's soul shine through. If there are places on one's body where this is a possibility, you are not attractive—you are leaking.
   Fran Lebowitz 1946– American writer: *Metropolitan Life* (1978)

8 The Lord prefers common-looking people. That is why he makes so many of them.
   Abraham Lincoln 1809–65 American Republican statesman: attributed; James Morgan *Our Presidents* (1928)

9 Sure, deck your lower limbs in pants;
   Yours are the limbs, my sweeting.
   You look divine as you advance—
   Have you seen yourself retreating?
   Ogden Nash 1902–71 American humorist: 'What's the Use?' (1940)

10 Men seldom make passes
   At girls who wear glasses.
   Dorothy Parker 1893–1967 American critic and humorist: 'News Item' (1937)

11 It costs a lot of money to look this cheap.
   Dolly Parton 1946– American singer and songwriter: attributed, perhaps apocryphal

12 An unforgiving eye, and a damned disinheriting countenance!
   Richard Brinsley Sheridan 1751–1816 Anglo-Irish dramatist: *The School for Scandal* (1777)

13 It is only shallow people who do not judge by appearances.
   Oscar Wilde 1854–1900 Irish dramatist and poet: *The Picture of Dorian Gray* (1891)

14 You can never be too rich or too thin.
   Duchess of Windsor 1896–1986 wife of the former Edward VIII: attributed

Archaeology

1 LORD CARNARVON: Can you see anything?

CARTER: Yes, wonderful things.
*on first looking into the tomb of
Tutankhamun, 26 November 1922*
> **Howard Carter** 1874–1939 English
> archaeologist: *The Tomb of Tut-ankh-
> Amen* (1923)

2 Every woman should marry an
archaeologist because she grows
increasingly attractive to him as she
grows increasingly to resemble a
ruin.
> **Agatha Christie** 1890–1976 English
> writer of detective fiction: Russell H.
> Fitzgibbon *The Agatha Christie
> Companion* (1980); attributed, perhaps
> apocryphal

3 A man who has once looked with the
archaeological eye will never see
quite normally. He will be wounded
by what other men call trifles. It is
possible to refine the sense of time
until an old shoe in the bunch grass
or a pile of nineteenth century beer
bottles in an abandoned mining
town tolls in one's head like a hall
clock.
> **Loren Eiseley** 1907–77 American
> anthropologist, educator, and writer:
> *The Night Country* (1971)

4 Every age has the Stonehenge it
deserves—or desires.
> **Jacquetta Hawkes** 1910–96 English
> archaeologist and writer: in *Antiquity*
> no. 41, 1967

5 I have gazed upon the face of
Agamemnon.
*on discovering a gold mask at Mycenae,
1876; traditional version of his telegram to
the minister at Athens: 'This one is very like
the picture which my imagination formed
of Agamemnon long ago'*
> **Heinrich Schliemann** 1822–90 German
> archaeologist: W. M. Calder and D. A.
> Traill *Myth, Scandal, and History* (1986)

6 Dead archaeology is the driest dust
that blows.
> **Mortimer Wheeler** 1890–1976 British

archaeologist: Glyn Daniel *A Short
History of Archaeology* (1981)

Architecture

see also BUILDINGS

1 In my experience, if you have to keep
the lavatory door shut by extending
your left leg, it's modern
architecture.
> **Nancy Banks-Smith**: in *Guardian*
> 20 February 1979

2 We shape our buildings, and
afterwards our buildings shape us.
> **Winston Churchill** 1874–1965 British
> Conservative statesman: in the House of
> Commons, 28 October 1943

3 He builded better than he knew;—
The conscious stone to beauty grew.
> **Ralph Waldo Emerson** 1803–82
> American philosopher and poet: 'The
> Problem' (1847)

4 Light (God's eldest daughter) is a
principal beauty in building.
> **Thomas Fuller** 1608–61 English
> preacher and historian: *The Holy State
> and the Profane State* (1642)

5 People ask me if I'm an artist or an
architect. But I think they're the
same.
> **Frank Gehry** 1929– Canadian-born
> American architect: in *Toronto Star*
> 4 September 1987

6 Architecture is the art of how to
waste space.
> **Philip Johnson** 1906–2005 American
> architect: in *New York Times*
> 27 December 1964

7 A house is a machine for living in.
> **Le Corbusier** 1887–1965 French
> architect: *Vers une architecture* (1923)

8 God is in the details.
> **Mies van der Rohe** 1886–1969 German-
> born architect and designer: in *New
> York Times* 19 August 1969

9 A bicycle shed is a building; Lincoln Cathedral is a piece of architecture. Nearly everything that encloses space on a scale sufficient for a human being to move in is a building; the term architecture applies only to buildings designed with a view to aesthetic appeal.

> **Nikolaus Pevsner** 1902–83 German-born architectural historian: *An Outline of European Architecture* (1943)

10 Little boxes on the hillside . . .
And they're all made out of ticky-tacky
And they all look just the same.
on the tract houses in the hills to the south of San Francisco

> **Malvina Reynolds** 1900–78 American songwriter: 'Little Boxes' (1962 song)

11 When we build, let us think that we build for ever.

> **John Ruskin** 1819–1900 English art and social critic: *Seven Lamps of Architecture* (1849)

12 Architecture in general is frozen music.

> **Friedrich von Schelling** 1775–1854 German philosopher: *Philosophie der Kunst* (1809)

13 Form follows function.

> **Louis Henri Sullivan** 1856–1924 American architect: *The Tall Office Building Artistically Considered* (1896)

14 Less is a bore.

> **Robert Venturi** 1925– American architect: *Complexity and Contradiction in Architecture* (1966); see SIMPLICITY 3

15 Now these should be so carried out that account is taken of strength, utility, grace.

> **Vitruvius** *fl.* 1st century BC Roman architect and military engineer: *On Architecture*

16 Well building hath three conditions. Commodity, firmness, and delight.

> **Henry Wotton** 1568–1639 English poet

and diplomat: *Elements of Architecture* (1624)

17 The physician can bury his mistakes, but the architect can only advise his client to plant vines—so they should go as far as possible from home to build their first buildings.

> **Frank Lloyd Wright** 1867–1959 American architect: in *New York Times* 4 October 1953

Argument

see also COMPROMISE, OPINION

1 Our disputants put me in mind of the skuttle fish, that when he is unable to extricate himself, blackens all the water about him, till he becomes invisible.

> **Joseph Addison** 1672–1719 English poet, dramatist, and essayist: in *The Spectator* 5 September 1712

2 Fear not those who argue but those who dodge.

> **Marie von Ebner-Eschenbach** 1830–1916 Austrian writer: *Aphorisms* (1905)

3 For your own good is a persuasive argument that will eventually make a man agree to his own destruction.

> **Janet Frame** 1924–2004 New Zealand writer: *Faces in the Water* (1961)

4 Persuasion is the resource of the feeble; and the feeble can seldom persuade.

> **Edward Gibbon** 1737–94 English historian: *The Decline and Fall of the Roman Empire* (1776–88)

5 Making noise is an effective means of opposition.

> **Joseph Goebbels** 1897–1945 German Nazi leader: Ernest K. Bramsted *Goebbels and National Socialist Propaganda 1925–45* (1965)

6 There is no arguing with Johnson; for when his pistol misses fire, he knocks you down with the butt end of it.

Oliver Goldsmith 1728–74 Anglo-Irish writer, poet, and dramatist: James Boswell *Life of Johnson* (1791) 26 October 1769

7 Any stigma, as the old saying is, will serve to beat a dogma.

Philip Guedalla 1889–1944 British historian and biographer: *Masters and Men* (1923)

8 It takes in reality only one to make a quarrel. It is useless for the sheep to pass resolutions in favour of vegetarianism, while the wolf remains of a different opinion.

William Ralph Inge 1860–1954 English writer; Dean of St. Paul's, 1911–34: *Outspoken Essays: First Series* (1919) 'Patriotism'

9 I hate a fellow whom pride, or cowardice, or laziness drives into a corner, and who does nothing when he is there but sit and *growl*; let him come out as I do, and *bark*.

Samuel Johnson 1709–84 English poet, critic, and lexicographer: James Boswell *Life of Johnson* 10 October 1782

10 There is no good in arguing with the inevitable. The only argument available with an east wind is to put on your overcoat.

James Russell Lowell 1819–91 American poet: *Democracy and other Addresses* (1887)

11 The Catholic and the Communist are alike in assuming that an opponent cannot be both honest and intelligent.

George Orwell 1903–50 English novelist: in *Polemic* January 1946

12 Who can refute a sneer?

William Paley 1743–1805 English theologian and philosopher: *Principles of Moral and Political Philosophy* (1785)

13 The argument of the broken window pane is the most valuable argument in modern politics.

Emmeline Pankhurst 1858–1928 English suffragette leader: George Dangerfield *The Strange Death of Liberal England* (1936)

14 'Yes, but not in the South', with slight adjustments, will do for any argument about any place, if not about any person.

Stephen Potter 1900–69 British writer: *Lifemanship* (1950)

15 I maintain that two and two would continue to make four, in spite of the whine of the amateur for three, or the cry of the critic for five.

James McNeill Whistler 1834–1903 American-born painter: *Whistler v. Ruskin. Art and Art Critics* (1878)

16 I am not arguing with you—I am telling you.

James McNeill Whistler 1834–1903 American-born painter: *The Gentle Art of Making Enemies* (1890)

17 Get your tanks off my lawn, Hughie.

to the trade union leader Hugh Scanlon, at Chequers in June 1969

Harold Wilson 1916–95 British Labour statesman: Peter Jenkins *The Battle of Downing Street* (1970)

Aristocracy

see also CLASS, TITLES

1 The rank is but the guinea's stamp, The man's the gowd for a' that!

Robert Burns 1759–96 Scottish poet: 'For a' that and a' that' (1790)

2 The Stately Homes of England, How beautiful they stand, To prove the upper classes Have still the upper hand.

Noël Coward 1899–1973 English dramatist, actor, and composer: 'The

Stately Homes of England' (1938 song);
see ARISTOCRACY 4

3 I can trace my ancestry back to a
protoplasmal primordial atomic
globule. Consequently, my family
pride is something in-conceivable. I
can't help it. I was born sneering.
   W. S. Gilbert 1836–1911 English writer
   of comic and satirical verse: *The Mikado*
   (1885)

4 The stately homes of England,
How beautiful they stand!
Amidst their tall ancestral trees,
O'er all the pleasant land.
   Felicia Hemans 1793–1835 English
   poet: 'The Homes of England' (1849);
   see ARISTOCRACY 2

5 As far as the fourteenth earl is
concerned, I suppose Mr Wilson,
when you come to think of it, is the
fourteenth Mr Wilson.
   replying to Harold Wilson's remark (on
   Home's becoming leader of the
   Conservative party) that 'the whole
   [democratic] *process has ground to a halt*
   with a fourteenth Earl'
   Lord Home 1903–95 British
   Conservative statesman: in *Daily*
   Telegraph 22 October 1963

6 I agree with you that there is a
natural aristocracy among men. The
grounds of this are virtue and talents.
   Thomas Jefferson 1743–1826 American
   Democratic Republican statesman:
   letter to John Adams, 28 October 1813

7 I am an ancestor.
   reply when taunted on his lack of ancestry
   having been made Duke of Abrantes, 1807
   Marshal Junot 1771–1813 French
   general: attributed

8 A fully-equipped duke costs as much
to keep up as two Dreadnoughts;
and dukes are just as great a terror
and they last longer.
   David Lloyd George 1863–1945 British
   Liberal statesman: speech at Newcastle,
   9 October 1909

9 An aristocracy in a republic is like a
chicken whose head has been cut
off: it may run about in a lively way,
but in fact it is dead.
   Nancy Mitford 1904–73 English writer:
   Noblesse Oblige (1956)

10 What can ennoble sots, or slaves, or
cowards?
Alas! Not all the blood of all the
Howards.
   Alexander Pope 1688–1744 English
   poet: *An Essay on Man* Epistle 4 (1734)

11 Kind hearts are more than coronets,
And simple faith than Norman
blood.
   Alfred, Lord Tennyson 1809–92 English
   poet: 'Lady Clara Vere de Vere' (1842)

The Army

see also AIR FORCE, NAVY, WAR

1 Lions led by donkeys.
   associated with British soldiers during the
   First World War
   Anonymous: attributed to Max
   Hoffman (1869–1927) in Alan Clark *The*
   Donkeys (1961); this attribution has not
   been traced elsewhere, and the phrase
   is of much earlier origin: 'You are lions
   led by packasses' was said in 1871 of
   French troops defeated by Prussians

2 O Death, where is thy sting-a-ling-
a-ling,
O grave, thy victory?
The bells of Hell go ting-a-ling-a-ling
For you but not for me.
   Anonymous: 'For You But Not For Me'
   (First World War song); see DEATH 3

3 There is no difference between the
Johnnies and the Mehmets to us
where they lie side by side in this
country of ours. You, the mothers,
who sent their sons from faraway
countries, wipe away your tears. Your
sons are now lying in our bosom and
are in peace. After having lost their

lives on this land, they have become our sons as well.

Kemal Atatürk 1881–1938 Turkish general and statesman: address to a group of visiting Australians at Anzac Cove, Gallipoli, 1934

4 To save your world you asked this man to die:
Would this man, could he see you now, ask why?

W. H. Auden 1907–73 English poet: 'Epitaph for the Unknown Soldier' (1955)

5 *C'est magnifique, mais ce n'est pas la guerre.*
It is magnificent, but it is not war.
on the charge of the Light Brigade

Pierre Bosquet 1810–61 French general: at Balaclava, 25 October 1854

6 For here the lover and killer are mingled
who had one body and one heart.
And death, who had the soldier singled
has done the lover mortal hurt.

Keith Douglas 1920–44 English poet: 'Vergissmeinnicht, 1943'

7 The sergeant is the army.

Dwight D. Eisenhower 1890–1969 American general and Republican statesman: attributed

8 Old soldiers never die,
They simply fade away.

J. Foley 1906–70 British songwriter: 'Old Soldiers Never Die' (1920 song); possibly a 'folk-song' from the First World War

9 Rascals, would you live for ever?
to hesitant Guards at Kolin, 18 June 1757

Frederick the Great 1712–86 Prussian monarch: attributed

10 The courage of a soldier is found to be the cheapest and most common quality of human nature.

Edward Gibbon 1737–94 English historian: *The Decline and Fall of the Roman Empire* (1776–1788)

11 I divide my officers into four classes as follows: the clever, the industrious, the lazy, and the stupid. Each officer always possesses two of these qualities. Those who are clever and industrious I appoint to the General Staff. Use can under certain circumstances be made of those who are stupid and lazy. The man who is clever and lazy qualifies for the highest leadership posts. He has the requisite and the mental clarity for difficult decisions. But whoever is stupid and industrious must be got rid of, for he is too dangerous.

Kurt von Hammerstein-Equord 1878–1943 German general: attributed, 1933; possibly apocryphal

12 Their shoulders held the sky suspended;
They stood, and earth's foundations stay;
What God abandoned, these defended,
And saved the sum of things for pay.

A. E. Housman 1859–1936 English poet: 'Epitaph on an Army of Mercenaries' (1922)

13 You'll get no promotion this side of the ocean,
So cheer up, my lads, Bless 'em all!
Bless 'em all! Bless 'em all! The long and the short and the tall.

Jimmy Hughes and **Frank Lake**: 'Bless 'Em All' (1940 song)

14 How do you ask a man to be the last man to die in Vietnam? How do you ask a man to be the last man to die for a mistake?

John Kerry 1943– American Democratic politician: speech to Senate Committee, 23 April 1971

15 For it's Tommy this, an' Tommy that, an' 'Chuck him out, the brute!'

But it's 'Saviour of 'is country' when
the guns begin to shoot.
Rudyard Kipling 1865–1936 English
writer and poet: 'Tommy' (1892)

16 An army marches on its stomach.
Napoleon I 1769–1821 French emperor:
attributed, 1816; also attributed to
Frederick the Great

17 What passing-bells for these who die
as cattle?
Only the monstrous anger of the
guns.
Only the stuttering rifles' rapid rattle
Can patter out their hasty orisons.
Wilfred Owen 1893–1918 English poet:
'Anthem for Doomed Youth' (written
1917)

18 I saw him stab
And stab again
A well-killed Boche.
This is the happy warrior,
This is he . . .
Herbert Read 1893–1968 English art
historian: 'The Happy Warrior' (1919)

19 Today we have naming of parts.
Yesterday,
We had daily cleaning. And
tomorrow morning,
We shall have what to do after firing.
But today,
Today we have naming of parts.
Henry Reed 1914–86 English poet and
dramatist: 'Lessons of the War: 1,
Naming of Parts' (1946)

20 If I were fierce, and bald, and short of
breath,
I'd live with scarlet Majors at the
Base,
And speed glum heroes up the line to
death.
Siegfried Sassoon 1886–1967 English
poet: 'Base Details' (1918)

21 Who will remember, passing through
this Gate,
The unheroic Dead who fed the
guns?

Who shall absolve the foulness of
their fate,—
Those doomed, conscripted,
unvictorious ones?
Siegfried Sassoon 1886–1967 English
poet: 'On Passing the New Menin Gate'
(1928)

22 I don't consider myself dovish and I
certainly don't consider myself
hawkish. Maybe I would describe
myself as owlish—that is, wise
enough to understand that you want
to do everything possible to avoid
war.
H. Norman Schwarzkopf III 1934–
American general: in *New York Times*
28 January 1991

23 You can always tell an old soldier by
the inside of his holsters and
cartridge boxes. The young ones
carry pistols and cartridges; the old
ones, grub.
George Bernard Shaw 1856–1950 Irish
dramatist: *Arms and the Man* (1898)

24 Theirs not to make reply,
Theirs not to reason why,
Theirs but to do and die:
Into the valley of Death
Rode the six hundred.
Alfred, Lord Tennyson 1809–92 English
poet: 'The Charge of the Light Brigade'
(1854)

25 I didn't fire him because he was a
dumb son of a bitch, although he
was, but that's not against the law for
generals. If it was, half to three-
quarters of them would be in jail.
of General MacArthur
Harry S. Truman 1884–1972 American
Democratic statesman: Merle Miller
Plain Speaking (1974)

26 Discipline is the soul of an army. It
makes small numbers formidable;
procures success to the weak and
esteem to all.
George Washington 1732–99 American

statesman: letter to the captains of the
Virginia Regiments, July 1759

27 As Lord Chesterfield said of the
generals of his day, 'I only hope that
when the enemy reads the list of
their names, he trembles as I do.'
*usually quoted as 'I don't know what effect
these men will have upon the enemy, but,
by God, they frighten me'*
Duke of Wellington 1769–1852 British
soldier and statesman: letter, 29 August
1810

28 Ours [our army] is composed of the
scum of the earth—the mere scum of
the earth.
Duke of Wellington 1769–1852 British
soldier and statesman: Philip Henry
Stanhope *Notes of Conversations with
the Duke of Wellington* (1888)
4 November 1831

Art

see also ACTING, ART AND SOCIETY, ARTS AND
SCIENCES, DESIGN, DRAWING, FAMOUS ARTISTS,
LITERATURE, MUSIC, PAINTING, PHOTOGRAPHY,
SCULPTURE, THEATRE

1 Art is born of humiliation.
W. H. Auden 1907–73 English poet:
Stephen Spender *World Within World*
(1951)

2 Do not imagine that Art is something
which is designed to give gentle
uplift and self-confidence. Art is not
a *brassière*. At least, not in the
English sense. But do not forget that
brassière is the French for life-jacket.
Julian Barnes 1946– English novelist:
Flaubert's Parrot (1984)

3 I suppose art is the only thing that
can go on mattering once it has
stopped hurting.
Elizabeth Bowen 1899–1973 Anglo-Irish
novelist: *Heat of the Day* (1949)

4 The history of art is the history of
revivals.
Samuel Butler 1835–1902 English
novelist: *Notebooks* (1912)

5 Art for art's sake, with no purpose,
for any purpose perverts art. But art
achieves a purpose which is not its
own.
Benjamin Constant 1767–1834 French
novelist, political philosopher, and
politician: diary 11 February 1804

6 Art is vice. You don't marry it
legitimately, you rape it.
Edgar Degas 1834–1917 French artist:
Paul Lafond *Degas* (1918)

7 I always said God was against art and
I still believe it.
Edward Elgar 1857–1934 English
composer: letter to A. J. Jaeger,
9 October 1900

8 Art is a jealous mistress.
Ralph Waldo Emerson 1803–82
American philosopher and poet: *The
Conduct of Life* (1860)

9 All art is autobiographical; the pearl
is the oyster's autobiography.
Federico Fellini 1920–93 Italian film
director: in *Atlantic Monthly* December
1965

10 The artist must be in his work as God
is in creation, invisible and all-
powerful; one must sense him
everywhere but never see him.
Gustave Flaubert 1821–80 French
novelist: letter to Mademoiselle Leroyer
de Chantepie, 18 March 1857

11 In art the best is good enough.
Johann Wolfgang von Goethe
1749–1832 German poet, novelist, and
dramatist: *Italienische Reise* (1816–17)
3 March 1787

12 The purpose of art is the lifelong
construction of a state of wonder.
Glenn Gould 1932–82 Canadian pianist
and composer: commencement

address, York University, Toronto,
6 November 1982

13 Art is not a mirror but a hammer.
  John Grierson 1888–1972 English
  documentary film-maker: H. Forsyth
  Hardy (ed.) *Grierson on Documentary*
  (1946, 1966)

14 We work in the dark—we do what we
can—we give what we have. Our
doubt is our passion and our passion
is our task. The rest is the madness of
art.
  Henry James 1843–1916 American
  novelist: 'The Middle Years' (short story,
  1893)

15 Life being all inclusion and
confusion, and art being all
discrimination and selection.
  Henry James 1843–1916 American
  novelist: *The Spoils of Poynton*
  (1909 ed.)

16 The artist, like the God of the
creation, remains within or behind
or beyond or above his handiwork,
invisible, refined out of existence,
indifferent, paring his fingernails.
  James Joyce 1882–1941 Irish novelist: *A
  Portrait of the Artist as a Young Man*
  (1916)

17 We know that the tail must wag the
  dog, for the horse is drawn by the
  cart;
But the Devil whoops, as he
  whooped of old: 'It's clever, but is it
  Art?'
  Rudyard Kipling 1865–1936 English
  writer and poet: 'The Conundrum of the
  Workshops' (1892)

18 Art is the objectification of feeling,
and the subjectification of nature.
  Susanne Langer 1895–1985 American
  philosopher: in *Mind* (1967)

19 Art is a revolt against fate.
  André Malraux 1901–76 French
  novelist, essayist, and art critic: *Les Voix
  du silence* (1951)

20 Filling a space in a beautiful way.
That's what art means to me.
  Georgia O'Keefe 1887–1986 American
  painter: in *Art News* December 1977

21 We all know that Art is not truth. Art
is a lie that makes us realize truth.
  Pablo Picasso 1881–1973 Spanish
  painter: Dore Ashton *Picasso on Art*
  (1972)

22 A work of art is good if it has grown
out of necessity.
  Rainer Maria Rilke 1875–1926 German
  poet: *Letters to a Young Poet* (1929)
  17 February 1903 (tr. R. Snell)

23 Art for art's sake is an empty phrase.
Art for the sake of the true, art for the
sake of the good and the beautiful,
that is the faith I am searching for.
  George Sand 1804–76 French novelist:
  letter to Alexandre Saint-Jean, 1872

24 Airing one's dirty linen never makes
for a masterpiece.
  François Truffaut 1932–84 French film
  director: *Bed and Board* (1972)

25 Another unsettling element in
modern art is that common
symptom of immaturity, the dread of
doing what has been done before.
  Edith Wharton 1862–1937 American
  novelist: *The Writing of Fiction* (1925)

26 All that I desire to point out is the
general principle that Life imitates
Art far more than Art imitates Life.
  Oscar Wilde 1854–1900 Anglo-Irish
  dramatist and poet: *Intentions* (1891)

Art and Society

1 I like honesty and sincerity; and I
maintain that an artist should not be
shabbily treated.
  *often quoted as 'No one should drive a hard
  bargain with an artist'*
  Ludwig van Beethoven 1770–1827

German composer: letter to C. F. Peters, 5 June 1822

2 The proletarian state must bring up thousands of excellent 'mechanics of culture', 'engineers of the soul'.
   Maxim Gorky 1868–1936 Russian writer and revolutionary: speech at the Writers' Congress 1934; see ART AND SOCIETY 4

3 If he [a composer] has a nice wife and some nice children, how can he let the children starve on his dissonances?
   Charles Ives 1874–1954 American composer: *Memos* (1972)

4 In free society art is not a weapon . . . Artists are not engineers of the soul.
   John F. Kennedy 1917–63 American Democratic statesman: speech at Amherst College, Mass., 26 October 1963; see ART AND SOCIETY 2

5 God help the Minister that meddles with art!
   Lord Melbourne 1779–1848 British Whig statesman: Lord David Cecil *Lord M* (1954)

6 Artists are the antennae of the race, but the bullet-headed many will never learn to trust their great artists.
   Ezra Pound 1885–1972 American poet: *Literary Essays* (1954)

7 The true artist will let his wife starve, his children go barefoot, his mother drudge for his living at seventy, sooner than work at anything but his art.
   George Bernard Shaw 1856–1950 Irish dramatist: *Man and Superman* (1903)

8 Politics in the middle of things that concern the imagination are like a pistol-shot in the middle of a concert.
   Stendhal 1783–1842 French novelist: *Scarlet and Black* (1830)

Arts and Sciences

1 The true men of action in our time, those who transform the world, are not the politicians and statesmen, but the scientists. Unfortunately poetry cannot celebrate them, because their deeds are concerned with things, not persons, and are, therefore, speechless. When I find myself in the company of scientists, I feel like a shabby curate who has strayed by mistake into a drawing room full of dukes.
   W. H. Auden 1907–73 English poet: *The Dyer's Hand* (1963) 'The Poet and the City'

2 A contemporary poet has characterized this sense of the personality of art and of the impersonality of science in these words—'Art is myself; science is ourselves'.
   Claude Bernard 1813–78 French physiologist: *Introduction à l'Étude de la Médecin Experiméntale* (1865)

3 Art is meant to disturb, science reassures.
   Georges Braque 1882–1963 French painter: *Le Jour et la nuit: Cahiers 1917–52*

4 In science, read, by preference, the newest works; in literature, the oldest.
   Edward Bulwer-Lytton 1803–73 British novelist and politician: *Caxtoniana* (1863) 'Hints on Mental Culture'

5 Poets do not go mad; but chess-players do. Mathematicians go mad, and cashiers; but creative artists very seldom. I am not, as will be seen, in any sense attacking logic: I only say that this danger does lie in logic, not in imagination.
   G. K. Chesterton 1874–1936 English essayist, novelist, and poet: *Orthodoxy* (1908)

6 Don't talk to me of your Archimedes'
lever. He was an absent-minded
person with a mathematical
imagination. Mathematics
commands all my respect, but I have
no use for engines. Give me the right
word and the right accent and I will
move the world.

> **Joseph Conrad** 1857–1924 Polish-born
> English novelist: *A Personal Record*
> (1919)

7 Scientists are explorers,
philosophers are tourists.

> **Richard Phillips Feynman** 1918–88
> American theoretical physicist:
> Christopher Sykes (ed.) *No Ordinary
> Genius* (1994)

8 Even if I could be Shakespeare, I
think I should still choose to be
Faraday.

> **Aldous Huxley** 1894–1963 English
> novelist: in 1925, attributed; Walter M.
> Elsasser *Memoirs of a Physicist in the
> Atomic Age* (1978)

9 If a scientist were to cut his ear off,
no one would take it as evidence of a
heightened sensibility.

> **Peter Medawar** 1915–87 English
> immunologist and writer: 'J. B. S.' (1968)

10 Science must begin with myths, and
with the criticism of myths.

> **Karl Popper** 1902–94 Austrian-born
> philosopher: 'The Philosophy of
> Science'; C. A. Mace (ed.) *British
> Philosophy in the Mid-Century* (1957)

11 Once or twice I have been provoked
and have asked the company how
many of them could describe the
Second Law of Thermodynamics.
The response was cold: it was also
negative. Yet I was asking something
which is about the scientific
equivalent of: *Have you read a work
of Shakespeare's?*

> **C. P. Snow** 1905–80 English novelist and
> scientist: *The Two Cultures* (1959)

12 If Watson and Crick had not
discovered the nature of DNA, one
can be virtually certain that other
scientists would eventually have
determined it. With art—whether
painting, music or literature — it is
quite different. If Shakespeare had
not written *Hamlet*, no other
playwright would have done so.

> **Lewis Wolpert** 1929– English biologist:
> *The Unnatural Nature of Science* (1993)

Asia

1 Nothing and no one can destroy the
Chinese people. They are relentless
survivors. They are the oldest
civilized people on earth. Their
civilization passes through phases
but its basic characteristics remain
the same. They yield, they bend to
the wind, but they do not break.

> **Pearl S. Buck** 1892–1973 American
> writer: *China, Past and Present* (1972)

2 Match me such marvel, save in
   Eastern clime,—
A rose-red city—half as old as Time!

> **John William Burgon** 1813–88 English
> clergyman: *Petra* (1845)

3 Nothing in India is identifiable, the
mere asking of a question causes it to
disappear or to merge in something
else.

> **E. M. Forster** 1879–1970 English
> novelist: *A Passage to India* (1924)

4 I cannot understand how anyone
can be an Indian and not be
proud—the richness and infinite
variety of our composite heritage,
the magnificence of the people's
spirit, equal to any disaster or
burden, firm in their faith . . . even in
poverty and hardship.

> **Indira Gandhi** 1917–84 Indian
> stateswoman: paper found after her
> death, *Remembered Moments* (1987)

5 If there is a paradise on earth, it is
this, it is this, it is this.
Amir Khusrau 1253–1325 Persian poet:
inscribed on the wall of the Diwan-
i-Khas [the hall of special audience] in
the Red Fort at Delhi

6 If one should ask you concerning the
spirit of a true Japanese, point to the
wild cherry blossom shining in the
sun.
Motoori Norinaga 1730–1801 Japanese
scholar and poet: attributed

7 The Japanese have perfected good
manners and made them
indistinguishable from rudeness.
Paul Theroux 1941– American novelist
and travel writer: *The Great Railway
Bazaar* (1975)

8 Nothing has been left undone, either
by man or Nature, to make India the
most extraordinary country that the
sun visits on his rounds.
Mark Twain 1835–1910 American
writer: *Following the Equator* (1897)

Assertiveness

see SELF-ESTEEM AND ASSERTIVENESS

Atheism

see also BELIEF

1 There's probably no God. Now stop
worrying and enjoy your life.
Advertising slogan: advertisement on
London buses (2008), supported by
English evolutionary biologist Richard
Dawkins (1941–)

2 An atheist is a man who has no
invisible means of support.
John Buchan 1875–1940 Scottish
novelist; Governor-General of Canada,
1935–40: H. E. Fosdick *On Being a Real
Person* (1943)

3 Thanks to God, I am still an atheist.
Luis Buñuel 1900–83 Spanish film
director: in *Le Monde* 16 December 1959

4 When men stop believing in God
they don't believe in nothing; they
believe in anything.
G. K. Chesterton 1874–1936 English
essayist, novelist, and poet: widely
attributed, although not traced in his
works

5 A young man who wishes to remain a
sound atheist cannot be too careful
of his reading.
C. S. Lewis 1898–1963 English literary
scholar: *Surprised by Joy* (1955)

6 He was an embittered atheist (the
sort of atheist who does not so much
disbelieve in God as personally
dislike Him), and took a sort of
pleasure in thinking that human
affairs would never improve.
George Orwell 1903–50 English
novelist: *Down and Out in Paris and
London* (1933)

7 I was told that the Chinese said they
would bury me by the Western Lake
and build a shrine to my memory. I
have some slight regret that this did
not happen as I might have become
a god, which would have been very
chic for an atheist.
Bertrand Russell 1872–1970 British
philosopher and mathematician:
Autobiography (1968)

Australia and New Zealand

1 Who knows but that England may
revive in New South Wales when it
has sunk in Europe.
Joseph Banks 1743–1820 English
botanist: letter to Governor Hunter,
30 March 1797

2 True patriots we; for be it
understood,

We left our country for our country's good.

Henry Carter 1806: prologue, written for, but not recited at, the opening of the Playhouse, Sydney, New South Wales, 16 January 1796, when the actors were principally convicts; previously attributed to George Barrington (b. 1755)

3 We have a great objective—the light on the hill—which we aim to reach by working for the betterment of mankind not only here but anywhere we may give a helping hand.

Joseph Benedict 'Ben' Chifley 1885–1951 Australian Labor statesman: speech to the Annual Conference of the New South Wales branch of the Australian Labor Party, 12 June 1949

4 From what I have said of the natives of New Holland, they may appear to some to be the most wretched people upon earth; but in reality they are far happier than we Europeans; being wholly unacquainted not only with the superfluous but the necessary conveniences so much sought after in Europe, they are happy in not knowing the use of them.

James Cook 1728–79 English explorer: diary, August 1770

5 The sailor lives, and stands beside us, paying
Out into time's wave
The stain of blood that writes an island story.

Allen Curnow 1911–2001 New Zealand poet and critic: 'Landfall in Unknown Seas' (1943)

6 I was so angry because they were denying they had done anything wrong, denying that a whole generation was stolen.

of official response to concerns about the 'stolen generation' of Aboriginal children forcibly removed from their families
Cathy Freeman 1973– Australian

athlete: interview in *Daily Telegraph* 16 July 2000

7 Australia is a huge rest home, where no unwelcome news is ever wafted on to the pages of the worst newspapers in the world.

Germaine Greer 1939– Australian feminist: in *Observer* 1 August 1982

8 And her five cities, like teeming sores,
Each drains her: a vast parasite robber-state
Where second-hand Europeans pullulate
Timidly on the edge of alien shores.

A. D. Hope 1907–2000 Australian poet: 'Australia' (1939)

9 Australia is a lucky country run mainly by second-rate people who share its luck.

Donald Richmond Horne 1921– : *The Lucky Country: Australia in the Sixties* (1964)

10 The idea of the 'convict stain', a moral blot soaked into our fabric, dominated all argument about Australian selfhood by the 1840s.

Robert Hughes 1938– Australian writer: *The Fatal Shore* (1987) introduction

11 Earth is here so kind, that just tickle her with a hoe and she laughs with a harvest.

Douglas Jerrold 1803–57 English dramatist and journalist: *The Wit and Opinions of Douglas Jerrold* (1859)

12 In joyful strains then let us sing Advance Australia fair.

the national anthem of Australia, from 1984
P. D. McCormick *c.*1834–1916 Australian musician: 'Advance Australia Fair' (1878 song)

13 Down under we send soldiers and wool abroad but keep poets and wine at home.

> **John Streeter Manifold** 1915–85 Australian poet: attributed, *Selected Verse* (1948)

14 What Great Britain calls the Far East is to us the near north.

> **Robert Gordon Menzies** 1894–1978 Australian Liberal statesman: in *Sydney Morning Herald* 27 April 1939

15 When New Zealanders emigrate to Australia, it raises the average IQ of both countries.

> **Robert Muldoon** 1921–92 New Zealand statesman: attributed

16 The scrubs are gone, the hunting and the laughter.
The eagle is gone, the emu and the kangaroo are gone from this place.
The bora ring is gone.
The corroboree is gone.
And we are going.

> **Oodgeroo Noonuccal** 1920–93 Australian poet: 'We are Going' (1964)

17 The crimson thread of kinship runs through us all.

> *on Australian federation*
> **Henry Parkes** 1815–95 English-born Australian statesman: speech at banquet in Melbourne, 6 February 1890

18 Once a jolly swagman camped by a billabong,
Under the shade of a coolibah tree;
And he sang as he watched and waited till his 'Billy' boiled:
'You'll come a-waltzing, Matilda, with me.'

> **'Banjo' Paterson** 1864–1941 Australian poet: 'Waltzing Matilda' (1903 song)

19 Above our writers—and other artists—looms the intimidating mass of Anglo-Saxon culture. Such a situation almost inevitably produces the characteristic Australian Cultural Cringe.

> **Arthur Angell Phillips** 1900–85 Australian critic and editor: *Meanjin* (1950) 'The Cultural Cringe'

20 In all directions stretched the great Australian Emptiness, in which the mind is the least of possessions.

> **Patrick White** 1912–90 Australian novelist: *The Vital Decade* (1968) 'The Prodigal Son'

21 By God what a site! By man what a mess!

> *of Sydney*
> **Clough Williams-Ellis** 1883–1978: *Architect Errant* (1971)

Autobiography

see also BIOGRAPHY

1 An autobiography is an obituary in serial form with the last instalment missing.

> **Quentin Crisp** 1908–99 English writer: *The Naked Civil Servant* (1968)

2 He made the books and he died.

> *his own 'sum and history of my life'*
> **William Faulkner** 1897–1962 American novelist: letter to Malcolm Cowley, 11 February 1949

3 Autobiography is now as common as adultery and hardly less reprehensible.

> **John Grigg** 1924– British writer and journalist: in *Sunday Times* 28 February 1962

4 I should be trading on the blood of my men.

> *refusing an offer to write his memoirs*
> **Robert E. Lee** 1807–70 American Confederate general: attributed, perhaps apocryphal

5 To write one's memoirs is to speak ill
of everybody except oneself.
> **Henri Philippe Pétain** 1856–1951
> French soldier and statesman: in
> *Observer* 26 May 1946

6 If you really want to hear about it,
the first thing you'll probably want to
know is where I was born, and what
my lousy childhood was like, and
how my parents were occupied and
all before they had me, and all that
David Copperfield kind of crap, but I
don't feel like going into it.
> **J. D. Salinger** 1919– American novelist
> and short-story writer: *Catcher in the
> Rye* (1951)

7 Only when one has lost all curiosity
about the future has one reached the
age to write an autobiography.
> **Evelyn Waugh** 1903–66 English novelist:
> *A Little Learning* (1964)

8 A man who publishes his letters
becomes a nudist—nothing shields
him from the world's gaze except his
bare skin.
> **E. B. White** 1899–1985 American
> humorist: letter to Corona Machemer,
> 11 June 1975

Autumn

1 But it's a long, long while
From May to December;
And the days grow short
When you reach September.
> **Maxwell Anderson** 1888–1959
> American dramatist: 'September Song'
> (1938 song)

2 Early autumn—
rice field, ocean,
one green.
> **Matsuo Basho** 1644–94 Japanese poet:
> translated by Lucien Stryk

3 Now is the time for the burning of
the leaves.
> **Laurence Binyon** 1869–1943 English
> poet: 'The Ruins' (1942)

4 'What is autumn?' 'A second spring,
where every leaf is a flower.'
> **Albert Camus** 1913–60 French novelist,
> dramatist, and essayist: *Théâtre, récits,
> nouvelles* (1967) 'Le Malentendu' (1944)

5 It was one of those perfect English
autumnal days which occur more
frequently in memory than in life.
> **P. D. James** 1920– English writer of
> detective stories: *A Taste For Death*
> (1986)

6 Season of mists and mellow
fruitfulness,
Close bosom-friend of the maturing
sun;
Conspiring with him how to load and
bless
With fruit the vines that round the
thatch-eaves run.
> **John Keats** 1795–1821 English poet: 'To
> Autumn' (1820)

7 I want to go south, where there is no
autumn, where the cold doesn't
crouch over one like a snow-leopard
waiting to pounce. The heart of the
North is dead, and the fingers of cold
are corpse fingers.
> **D. H. Lawrence** 1885–1930 English
> novelist and poet: letter to J. Middleton
> Murry, 3 October 1924

8 What of October, that ambiguous
month, the month of tension, the
unendurable month?
> **Doris Lessing** 1919– English writer:
> *Martha Quest* (1952)

9 For man, autumn is a time of
harvest, of gathering together. For
nature, it is a time of sowing, of
scattering abroad.
> **Edwin Way Teale** 1899–1980: *Autumn
> Across America* (1956)

10 In . . . the fall, the whole country goes to glory.
of North America
    Frances Trollope 1780–1863 English writer: *Domestic Manners of the Americans* (1832)

Awards

1 Members [of civil service orders] rise from CMG (known sometimes in Whitehall as 'Call Me God') to the KCMG ('Kindly Call Me God') to—for a select few governors and super-ambassadors—the GCMG ('God Calls Me God').
    Anonymous: Anthony Sampson *Anatomy of Britain* (1962)

2 Gongs and medals and ribbons really belong on a Christmas tree.
    J. G. Ballard 1930–2009 British writer: in *Independent* 14 July 2004

3 My career must be slipping. This is the first time I've been available to pick up an award.
    Michael Caine 1933– English film actor: at the Golden Globe awards, Beverly Hills, California, 24 January 1999

4 A medal glitters, but it also casts a shadow.
    a reference to the envy caused by the award of honours
    Winston Churchill 1874–1965 British Conservative statesman: in 1941; Kenneth Rose *King George V* (1983)

5 Awards are like piles. Sooner or later, every bum gets one.
    Maureen Lipman 1946– British actress: in *Independent* 31 July 1999

6 She says 'Men are monopolists of "stars, garters, buttons and other shining baubles."'
    Marianne Moore 1887–1972 American poet: 'Marriage' (1935)

7 The cross of the Legion of Honour has been conferred on me. However, few escape that distinction.
    Mark Twain 1835–1910 American writer: *A Tramp Abroad* (1880)

Babies

see also CHILDREN, PARENTS

1 There is no finer investment for any community than putting milk into babies.
    Winston Churchill 1874–1965 British Conservative statesman: radio broadcast, 21 March 1943

2 It is a pleasant thing to reflect upon, and furnishes a complete answer to those who contend for the general degeneration of the human species, that every baby born into the world is a finer one than the last.
    Charles Dickens 1812–70 English novelist: *Nicholas Nickleby* (1838–9)

3 There never was a child so lovely but his mother was glad to get asleep.
    Ralph Waldo Emerson 1803–82 American philosopher and poet: *Journal* 1836

4 Since you arrived, days have melted into night and back again and we are learning a new grammar, a long sentence whose punctuation marks are feeding and winding and nappy changing and these occasional moments of quiet.
    Fergal Keane 1961– Irish journalist: 'Letter to Daniel' (1996), in John Lewis-Stempel *Fatherhood: An Anthology* (2001)

5 A loud noise at one end and no sense of responsibility at the other.
    definition of a baby
    Ronald Knox 1888–1957 English writer and Roman Catholic priest: attributed

6 A baby is God's opinion that life should go on.

> **Carl Sandburg** 1878–1967 American poet: *Remembrance Rock* (1948)

Bachelors

see also MARRIAGE, MEN

1 It is a truth universally acknowledged, that a single man in possession of a good fortune, must be in want of a wife.

> **Jane Austen** 1775–1817 English novelist: *Pride and Prejudice* (1813)

2 A man in love is incomplete until he has married. Then he's finished.

> **Zsa Zsa Gabor** 1919– Hungarian-born film actress: in *Newsweek* 28 March 1960

3 Bachelors know more about women than married men. If they did not they would be married too.

> **H. L. Mencken** 1880–1956 American journalist and literary critic: *Chrestomathy* (1949)

4 Somehow a bachelor never quite gets over the idea that he is a thing of beauty and a boy forever.

> **Helen Rowland** 1875–1950 American writer: *A Guide to Men* (1922); see BEAUTY 17

The Balkans

1 Not worth the healthy bones of a single Pomeranian grenadier.
of possible German involvement in the Balkans

> **Otto von Bismarck** 1815–98 German statesman: George O. Kent *Bismarck and his Times* (1978)

2 If there is ever another war in Europe, it will come out of some damned silly thing in the Balkans.

> **Otto von Bismarck** 1815–98 German statesman: quoted in speech, House of Commons, 16 August 1945

3 No history much? Perhaps. Only this ominous
Dark beauty flowering under veils,
Trapped in the spectrum of a dying style:
A village like an instinct left to rust,
Composed around the echo of a pistol-shot.

> **Lawrence Durrell** 1912–90 English novelist, poet, and travel writer: 'Sarajevo' (1951)

4 Serbs out, Nato in, refugees back.

> **George Robertson** 1946– British Labour politician: summing up the Nato objective in Kosovo, 7 June 1999

Banking

see also MONEY

1 What is robbing a bank compared with founding a bank?

> **Bertolt Brecht** 1898–1956 German dramatist: *Die Dreigroschenoper* (1928)

2 We not only saved the world . . . Er, saved the banks.

> **Gordon Brown** 1951– British Labour statesman: speech, House of Commons, 10 December 2008

3 If these things were so large, how come everyone missed them?
asking why economists didn't see the credit crunch coming

> **Elizabeth II** 1926– British monarch: on a visit to the London School of Economics, in *Sunday Times* 9 November 2008

4 A bank is a place where they lend you an umbrella in fair weather and ask for it back when it begins to rain.

> **Robert Frost** 1874–1963 American poet: in *Muscatine Journal* 22 August 1961

5 What the chief accountant creates is a work of art.

describing financial reporting as less of a historical record and more of a forecast

Alan Greenspan 1926– American economist: speech, Boston, 9 November 2006

6 Put not your trust in money, but put your money in trust.

Oliver Wendell Holmes 1809–94 American physician, poet, and essayist: *The Autocrat of the Breakfast Table* (1858)

7 A bank is a place that will lend you money if you can prove that you don't need it.

Bob Hope 1903–2003 American comedian: Alan Harrington *Life in the Crystal Palace* (1959)

8 Banking establishments are more dangerous than standing armies.

Thomas Jefferson 1743–1826 American Democratic Republican statesman: letter to John Taylor, 28 May 1816

9 It's all just one big lie.

on his investment business after it collapsed

Bernard Madoff 1938– American businessman: in *Washington Post* 13 December 2008

Baseball

see also SPORTS

1 We live by the Golden Rule. Those who have the gold make the rules.

Buzzie Bavasi 1914–2008 American baseball manager: attributed; A. J. Maikovich and M. D. Brown (eds.) *Sports Quotations* (2000)

2 Think! How the hell are you gonna think and hit at the same time?

Yogi Berra 1925– American baseball player: *Nice Guys Finish Seventh* (1976)

3 If people don't want to come out to the ball park, nobody's going to stop 'em.

Yogi Berra 1925– American baseball player: attributed

4 A ball player's got to be kept hungry to become a big leaguer. That's why no boy from a rich family ever made the big leagues.

Joe DiMaggio 1914–99 American baseball player: in *New York Times* 30 April 1961

5 [Baseball] breaks your heart. It is designed to break your heart. The game begins in the spring, when everything else begins again, and it blossoms in the summer, filling the afternoons and evenings, and then as soon as the chill rains come, it stops and leaves you to face the fall alone.

A. Bartlett Giamatti 1938–89 American baseball player: *The Green Fields of the Mind* (1977)

6 Baseball is very big with my people. It figures. It's the only way we can get to shake a bat at a white man without starting a riot.

Dick Gregory 1932– American comedian and civil rights activist: D. H. Nathan (ed.) *Baseball Quotations* (1991)

7 Take me out to the ball game, Take me out with the crowd. Buy me some peanuts and cracker-jack—
I don't care if I never get back.

Jack Norworth 1879–1959 American songwriter: 'Take Me Out to the Ball Game' (1908 song)

8 All you have to do is keep the five players who hate your guts away from the five who are undecided.

Casey Stengel 1891–1975 American baseball player and manager: attributed

9 Baseball, it is said, is only a game. True. And the Grand Canyon is only a

hole in Arizona. Not all holes, or games, are created equal.
   George F. Will 1941– American columnist: *Men At Work: The Craft of Baseball* (1990)

10 Baseball gives every American boy a chance to excel. Not just to be as good as someone else, but to be better. This is the nature of man and the name of the game.
   Ted Williams 1918– American baseball player: *Baseball* (1994)

Beauty

see also BODY, COSMETICS

1 Beauty is power.
   Advertising slogan: Helena Rubinstein's Valaze Skin Food, 1904

2 There are as many kinds of beauty as there are habitual ways of seeking happiness.
   Charles Baudelaire 1821–67 French poet and critic: *The Salon of 1846* (1846) 'What is Romanticism?'

3 A pretty girl is like a melody That haunts you night and day.
   Irving Berlin 1888–1989 American songwriter: 'A Pretty Girl is like a Melody' (1919 song)

4 Being thought of as a beautiful woman has spared me nothing in life. No heartache, no trouble. Beauty is essentially meaningless.
   Halle Berry 1968– American actress: in *Observer* 8 August 2004

5 Consider the lilies of the field, how they grow; they toil not, neither do they spin:
   And yet I say unto you, That even Solomon in all his glory was not arrayed like one of these.
   Bible: St Matthew

6 She walks in beauty, like the night Of cloudless climes and starry skies;

And all that's best of dark and bright Meet in her aspect and her eyes.
   Lord Byron 1788–1824 English poet: 'She Walks in Beauty' (1815)

7 And she was fayr as is the rose in May.
   Geoffrey Chaucer c.1343–1400 English poet: *The Legend of Good Women* 'Cleopatra'

8 When a woman isn't beautiful, people always say, 'You have lovely eyes, you have lovely hair.'
   Anton Chekhov 1860–1904 Russian dramatist and short-story writer: *Uncle Vanya* (1897)

9 There is nothing ugly; *I never saw an ugly thing in my life*: for let the form of an object be what it may,—light, shade, and perspective will always make it beautiful.
   John Constable 1776–1837 English painter: C. R. Leslie *Memoirs of the Life of John Constable* (1843)

10 Love built on beauty, soon as beauty, dies.
   John Donne 1572–1631 English poet and divine: *Elegies* 'The Anagram' (c.1595)

11 The awful thing is that beauty is mysterious as well as terrible. God and devil are fighting there, and the battlefield is the heart of man.
   Fedor Dostoevsky 1821–81 Russian novelist: *The Brothers Karamazov* (1879–80)

12 Beauty will save the world.
   Fedor Dostoevsky 1821–81 Russian novelist: *The Idiot* (1868)

13 He was afflicted by the thought that where Beauty was, nothing ever ran quite straight, which, no doubt, was why so many people looked on it as immoral.
   John Galsworthy 1867–1933 English novelist: *In Chancery* (1920)

14 I have a left shoulder-blade that is a miracle of loveliness. People come miles to see it. My right elbow has a fascination that few can resist.

> **W. S. Gilbert** 1836–1911 English writer of comic and satirical verse: *The Mikado* (1885)

15 Is it too much to ask that women be spared the daily struggle for superhuman beauty in order to offer it to the caresses of a subhumanly ugly mate?

> **Germaine Greer** 1939– Australian feminist: *The Female Eunuch* (1970)

16 All things counter, original, spare, strange;
Whatever is fickle, freckled (who knows how?)
With swift, slow; sweet, sour; adazzle, dim;
He fathers-forth whose beauty is past change:
Praise him.

> **Gerard Manley Hopkins** 1844–89 English poet and priest: 'Pied Beauty' (written 1877)

17 Beauty is no quality in things themselves. It exists merely in the mind which contemplates them.

> **David Hume** 1711–76 Scottish philosopher: 'Of the Standard of Taste' (1757)

18 A thing of beauty is a joy for ever:
Its loveliness increases; it will never
Pass into nothingness.

> **John Keats** 1795–1821 English poet: *Endymion* (1818)

19 'Beauty is truth, truth beauty,'—that is all
Ye know on earth, and all ye need to know.

> **John Keats** 1795–1821 English poet: 'Ode on a Grecian Urn' (1820)

20 I'm tired of all this nonsense about beauty being only skin-deep. That's deep enough. What do you want—an adorable pancreas?

> **Jean Kerr** 1923–2003 American writer: *The Snake has all the Lines* (1958)

21 At some point in life the world's beauty becomes enough. You don't need to photograph, paint or even remember it. It is enough.

> **Toni Morrison** 1931– American novelist: *Tar Baby* (1981)

22 'Form follows profit' is the aesthetic principle of our times.

> **Richard Rogers** 1933– British architect: in *Times* 13 February 1991

23 Remember that the most beautiful things in the world are the most useless; peacocks and lilies for instance.

> **John Ruskin** 1819–1900 English art and social critic: *Stones of Venice* vol. 1 (1851)

24 Beauty is all very well at first sight; but who ever looks at it when it has been in the house three days?

> **George Bernard Shaw** 1856–1950 Irish dramatist: *Man and Superman* (1903)

25 Beauty is only a promise of happiness.

> **Stendhal** 1783–1842 French novelist: *L'Amour* (1822)

26 I do not know which to prefer,
The beauty of inflections
Or the beauty of innuendoes,
The blackbird whistling
Or just after.

> **Wallace Stevens** 1879–1955 American poet: 'Thirteen Ways of Looking at a Blackbird' (1923)

27 The beauty myth moves for men as a mirage; its power lies in its ever-receding nature. When the gap is closed, the lover embraces only his own disillusion.

> **Naomi Wolf** 1962– American writer: *The Beauty Myth* (1990)

Beginning

see also CHANGE, ENDING

1 In the beginning God created the heaven and the earth. And the earth was without form, and void; and darkness was upon the face of the deep. And the Spirit of God moved upon the face of the waters.
And God said, Let there be light: and there was light.
Bible: Genesis

2 'Where shall I begin, please your Majesty?' he asked. 'Begin at the beginning,' the King said, gravely, 'and go on till you come to the end: then stop.'
Lewis Carroll 1832–98 English writer and logician: *Alice's Adventures in Wonderland* (1865)

3 when god decided to invent
everything he took one
breath bigger than a circustent
and everything began
e. e. cummings 1894–1962 American poet: *1 x 1* (1944) no. 26

4 From so simple a beginning endless forms most beautiful and most wonderful have been, and are being, evolved.
Charles Darwin 1809–82 English natural historian: *On the Origin of Species* (1859)

5 In my beginning is my end.
T. S. Eliot 1888–1965 Anglo-American poet, critic, and dramatist: *Four Quartets* 'East Coker' (1940)

6 All this will not be finished in the first 100 days. Nor will it be finished in the first 1,000 days, nor in the life of this Administration, nor even perhaps in our lifetime on this planet. But let us begin.
John F. Kennedy 1917–63 American Democratic statesman: inaugural address, 20 January 1961

7 A tower of nine storeys begins with a heap of earth.
The journey of a thousand *li* starts from where one stands.
Lao Tzu *c.*604–*c.*531 BC Chinese philosopher: *Tao-te Ching*

8 A long time ago in a galaxy far, far away . . .
George Lucas 1944– American film director, producer, and screenwriter: *Star Wars* (1977 film)

9 I've started so I'll finish.
said when a contestant's time runs out while a question is being put
Magnus Magnusson 1929–2007 Scottish writer and broadcaster: *Mastermind*, BBC television (1972–97)

10 Ere time and place were, time and place were not;
Where primitive nothing something straight begot;
Then all proceeded from the great united what.
Lord Rochester 1647–80 English poet: 'Upon Nothing' (1680)

Behaviour

see also MANNERS, VULGARITY, WORDS AND DEEDS

1 When I go to Rome, I fast on Saturday, but here [Milan] I do not. Do you also follow the custom of whatever church you attend, if you do not want to give or receive scandal.
usually quoted as 'When in Rome, do as the Romans do'
St Ambrose *c.*339–397 French-born bishop of Milan: 'Letter 54 to Januarius' (AD *c.*400)

2 Private faces in public places
Are wiser and nicer
Than public faces in private places.
W. H. Auden 1907–73 English poet: *Orators* (1932)

3 He only does it to annoy,
Because he knows it teases.
> **Lewis Carroll** 1832–98 English writer
> and logician: *Alice's Adventures in*
> *Wonderland* (1865)

4 Take the tone of the company that
you are in.
> **Lord Chesterfield** 1694–1773 English
> writer and politician: *Letters to his Son*
> (1774) 16 October 1747

5 *O tempora, O mores!*
Oh, the times! Oh, the manners!
> **Cicero** 106–43 BC Roman orator and
> statesman: *In Catilinam*

6 Being tactful in audacity is knowing
how far one can go too far.
> **Jean Cocteau** 1889–1963 French
> dramatist and film director: *Le Rappel à*
> *l'ordre* (1926)

7 Careless she is with artful care,
Affecting to seem unaffected.
> **William Congreve** 1670–1729 English
> dramatist: 'Amoret'

8 I get too hungry for dinner at eight.
I like the theatre, but never come
late.
I never bother with people I hate.
That's why the lady is a tramp.
> **Lorenz Hart** 1895–1943 American
> songwriter: 'The Lady is a Tramp'
> (1937 song)

9 They teach the morals of a whore,
and the manners of a dancing
master.
> *of the* Letters *of Lord Chesterfield*
> **Samuel Johnson** 1709–84 English poet,
> critic, and lexicographer: James Boswell
> *Life of Samuel Johnson* (1791) 1754

10 Be a good animal, true to your
instincts.
> **D. H. Lawrence** 1885–1930 English
> novelist and poet: *The White Peacock*
> (1911)

11 There was a little girl
Who had a little curl

Right in the middle of her forehead,
When she was good
She was very, very good,
But when she was bad she was
horrid.
> *composed for, and sung to, his second*
> *daughter while a babe in arms, c.1850*
> **Henry Wadsworth Longfellow** 1807–82
> American poet: B. R. Tucker-Macchetta
> *The Home Life of Henry W. Longfellow*
> (1882)

12 Perfect behaviour is born of
complete indifference.
> **Cesare Pavese** 1908–50 Italian novelist,
> poet, and critic: diary 21 February 1940

13 Go directly—see what she's doing,
and tell her she mustn't.
> **Punch** English humorous weekly
> periodical: 16 November 1872

Belief

see also ATHEISM, DOUBT, FAITH

1 Of course, Behaviourism 'works'. So
does torture. Give me a no-
nonsense, down-to-earth
behaviourist, a few drugs, and
simple electrical appliances, and in
six months I will have him reciting
the Athanasian Creed in public.
> **W. H. Auden** 1907–73 English poet: *A*
> *Certain World* (1970)

2 For what a man would like to be true,
that he more readily believes.
> **Francis Bacon** 1561–1626 English
> lawyer, courtier, philosopher, and
> essayist: *Novum Organum* (1620)

3 Lord, I believe; help thou mine
unbelief.
> **Bible**: St Mark

4 Of course not, but I am told it works
even if you don't believe in it.
> *when asked whether he really believed a*
> *horseshoe hanging over his door would*
> *bring him luck, c.1930*
> **Niels Bohr** 1885–1962 Danish physicist:
> A. Pais *Inward Bound* (1986)

5 Just when we are safest, there's a
   sunset-touch,
   A fancy from a flower-bell, some
   one's death,
   A chorus-ending from Euripides,—
   And that's enough for fifty hopes and
   fears
   As old and new at once as nature's
   self . . .
   The grand Perhaps!
   > **Robert Browning** 1812–89 English poet:
   > 'Bishop Blougram's Apology' (1855)

6 Why, sometimes I've believed as
   many as six impossible things before
   breakfast.
   > **Lewis Carroll** 1832–98 English writer
   > and logician: *Through the Looking-
   > Glass* (1872)

7 plato told
   him: he couldn't
   believe it (jesus
   told him; he
   wouldn't believe
   it)
   > **e. e. cummings** 1894–1962 American
   > poet: *1 x 1* (1944) no. 13

8 I do not pretend to know where
   many ignorant men are sure—that is
   all that agnosticism means.
   > **Clarence Darrow** 1857–1938 American
   > lawyer: speech at the trial of John
   > Thomas Scopes, 15 July 1925

9 The deepest sin against the human
   mind is to believe things without
   evidence.
   > **T. H. Huxley** 1825–95 English biologist:
   > attributed

10 A believer is a songless bird in a cage,
   a freethinker is an eagle parting the
   clouds with tireless wings.
   > **Robert G. Ingersoll** 1833–99 American
   > agnostic: *An Arraignment of the Church,
   > and a Plea for Individuality* (1877)

11 I do not believe . . . I know.
   > **Carl Gustav Jung** 1875–1961 Swiss
   > psychologist: L. van der Post *Jung and
   > the Story of our Time* (1976)

12 Credulity is the man's weakness, but
   the child's strength.
   > **Charles Lamb** 1775–1834 English
   > writer: *Essays of Elia* (1823) 'Witches,
   > and Other Night-Fears'

13 There is a great deal of difference
   between *still* believing something,
   and *again* believing it.
   > **Georg Christoph Lichtenberg** 1742–99
   > German scientist and drama critic:
   > Notebook E no. 8 1775–6

14 Nothing is so firmly believed as that
   which we least know.
   > **Montaigne** 1533–92 French moralist
   > and essayist: *Essays* (1580)

15 *We can believe what we choose.* We
   are answerable for what we choose
   to believe.
   > **John Henry Newman** 1801–90 English
   > theologian and cardinal: letter to Mrs
   > William Froude, 27 June 1848

16 The sceptical are the most credulous.
   > **Blaise Pascal** 1623–62 French
   > mathematician, physicist, and moralist:
   > *Penseés* (1670)

17 Man is a credulous animal, and must
   believe *something*; in the absence of
   good grounds for belief, he will be
   satisfied with bad ones.
   > **Bertrand Russell** 1872–1970 British
   > philosopher and mathematician:
   > *Unpopular Essays* (1950) 'Outline of
   > Intellectual Rubbish'

18 I confused things with their names:
   that is belief.
   > **Jean-Paul Sartre** 1905–80 French
   > philosopher, novelist, dramatist, and
   > critic: *Les Mots* (1964)

19 *Certum est quia impossibile est.*
   It is certain because it is impossible.
   > *often quoted as* 'Credo quia impossibile [I
   > believe because it is impossible]'
   > **Tertullian** AD *c.*160–*c.*225 Roman
   > theologian: *De Carne Christi*

Bereavement

see also DEATH, SORROW

1 You can shed tears that she is gone or you can smile because she has lived.
    Anonymous: preface to the Order of Service at the funeral of Queen Elizabeth the Queen Mother, 2002

2 He was my North, my South, my East and West,
    My working week and my Sunday rest,
    My noon, my midnight, my talk, my song;
    I thought that love would last for ever: I was wrong.
    W. H. Auden 1907–73 English poet: 'Funeral Blues' (1936)

3 Blessed are they that mourn: for they shall be comforted.
    Bible: St Matthew

4 The Bustle in a House
    The Morning after Death
    Is solemnest of industries
    Enacted upon Earth—
    The Sweeping up the Heart
    And putting Love away
    We shall not want to use again
    Until Eternity.
    Emily Dickinson 1830–86 American poet: 'The Bustle in a House' (c.1866)

5 How small and selfish is sorrow. But it bangs one about until one is senseless.
    shortly after the death of George VI
    Queen Elizabeth, the Queen Mother 1900–2002 British Queen Consort: letter to Edith Sitwell, 1952; Victoria Glendinning *Edith Sitwell* (1983)

6 Do not stand at my grave and weep:
    I am not there. I do not sleep.
    I am a thousand winds that blow.
    I am the diamond glints on snow . . .
    Do not stand at my grave and cry;
    I am not there, I did not die.
    quoted in letter left by British soldier

Stephen Cummins when killed by the IRA, March 1989
    Mary E. Frye 1905–2004 American housewife and poet: originally circulated privately from 1932 on

7 Woman much missed, how you call to me, call to me.
    Thomas Hardy 1840–1928 English novelist and poet: 'The Voice' (1914)

8 All I have I would have given gladly not to be standing here today.
    following the assassination of John F. Kennedy
    Lyndon Baines Johnson 1908–73 American Democratic statesman: first speech to Congress as President, 27 November 1963

9 For a season there must be pain—
    For a little, little space
    I shall lose the sight of her face,
    Take back the old life again
    While She is at rest in her place.
    Rudyard Kipling 1865–1936 English writer and poet: 'The Widower'

10 Bereavement is a universal and integral part of our experience of love. It follows marriage as normally as marriage follows courtship or as autumn follows summer.
    C. S. Lewis 1898–1963 English literary scholar: *A Grief Observed* (1961)

11 A man's dying is more the survivors' affair than his own.
    Thomas Mann 1875–1955 German novelist: *The Magic Mountain* (1924)

12 Time does not bring relief; you all have lied
    Who told me time would ease me of my pain!
    I miss him in the weeping of the rain;
    I want him at the shrinking of the tide.
    Edna St Vincent Millay 1892–1950 American poet: 'Time does not bring relief'

13 I can't think of a more wonderful thanksgiving for the life I have had than that everyone should be jolly at my funeral.

> **Lord Mountbatten** 1900–79 British sailor, soldier, and statesman: Richard Hough *Mountbatten* (1980)

14 Forgive me.
If you are not living,
If you, beloved, my love,
If you have died
All the leaves will fall on my breast
It will rain on my soul, all night, all day
My feet will want to march to where you are sleeping
But I shall go on living.

> **Pablo Neruda** 1904–73 Chilean poet: 'The Dead Woman'

15 The pain of grief is just as much a part of life as the joy of love; it is, perhaps, the price we pay for love, the cost of commitment.

> *usually quoted as 'Grief is the price we pay for love'*
>
> **Colin Murray Parkes** 1928– English psychiatrist: *Bereavement: Studies of Grief in Adult Life* (1972)

16 Widow. The word consumes itself.

> **Sylvia Plath** 1932–63 American poet: 'Widow' (1971)

17 Moderate lamentation is the right of the dead, excessive grief the enemy to the living.

> **William Shakespeare** 1564–1616 English dramatist: *All's Well That Ends Well* (1601)

18 Honest plain words best pierce the ears of grief.

> **William Shakespeare** 1564–1616 English dramatist: *Love's Labour's Lost* (1595)

19 The bitterest tears shed over graves are for words left unsaid and deeds left undone.

> **Harriet Beecher Stowe** 1811–96 American novelist: *Little Foxes* (1871)

20 He first deceased; she for a little tried
To live without him: liked it not, and died.

> **Henry Wotton** 1568–1639 English poet and diplomat: 'Upon the Death of Sir Albertus Moreton's Wife' (1651)

Betrayal

see also SACRIFICE, TRUST

1 Just for a handful of silver he left us,
Just for a riband to stick in his coat.

> *of Wordsworth's apparent betrayal of his radical principles by accepting the position of poet laureate*
>
> **Robert Browning** 1812–89 English poet: 'The Lost Leader' (1845)

2 *Et tu, Brute?*
You too, Brutus?

> **Julius Caesar** 100–44 BC Roman general and statesman: traditional rendering of Suetonius *Lives of the Caesars* 'Divus Julius'

3 Anyone can rat, but it takes a certain amount of ingenuity to re-rat.

> *on rejoining the Conservatives twenty years after leaving them for the Liberals, c.1924*
>
> **Winston Churchill** 1874–1965 British Conservative statesman: Kay Halle *Irrepressible Churchill* (1966)

4 Anyone who hasn't experienced the ecstasy of betrayal knows nothing about ecstasy at all.

> **Jean Genet** 1910–86 French novelist, poet, and dramatist: *Prisoner of Love* (1986)

5 Treason doth never prosper, what's the reason?

For if it prosper, none dare call it
treason.

> **John Harington** 1561–1612 English
> writer and courtier: *Epigrams* (1618)

6 He who wields the knife never wears
the crown.

> **Michael Heseltine** 1933– British
> Conservative politician: in *New Society*
> 14 February 1986

7 The night of the long knives.

> **Adolf Hitler** 1889–1945 German
> dictator: phrase given to the massacre
> of Ernst Roehm and his associates by
> Hitler on 29–30 June 1934, taken from
> an early Nazi marching song;
> subsequently associated with Harold
> Macmillan's Cabinet dismissals of
> 13 July 1962

8 It is rather like sending your opening
batsmen to the crease only for them
to find the moment that the first
balls are bowled that their bats have
been broken before the game by the
team captain.

> **Geoffrey Howe** 1926– British
> Conservative politician: resignation
> speech as Deputy Prime Minister,
> House of Commons, 13 November 1990

9 To betray, you must first belong.

> **Kim Philby** 1912–88 British intelligence
> officer and Soviet spy: in *Sunday Times*
> 17 December 1967

10 *to the Emperor of Russia, who had spoken
bitterly of those who had betrayed the
cause of Europe:*
That, Sire, is a question of dates.
often quoted as 'treason is a matter of dates'

> **Charles-Maurice de Talleyrand**
> 1754–1838 French statesman: Duff
> Cooper *Talleyrand* (1932)

11 Greater love hath no man than this,
that he lay down his friends for his
life.
*on Harold Macmillan sacking seven of his
Cabinet on 13 July 1962*

> **Jeremy Thorpe** 1929– British Liberal
> politician: D. E. Butler and Anthony

King *The General Election of 1964*
(1965); see SACRIFICE 1

The Bible

1 The pencil of the Holy Ghost hath
laboured more in describing the
afflictions of Job than the felicities of
Solomon.

> **Francis Bacon** 1561–1626 English
> lawyer, courtier, philosopher, and
> essayist: *Essays* (1625) 'Of Adversity'

2 There's a great text in Galatians,
Once you trip on it, entails
Twenty-nine distinct damnations,
One sure, if another fails.

> **Robert Browning** 1812–89 English poet:
> 'Soliloquy of the Spanish Cloister'
> (1842)

3 An apology for the Devil: It must be
remembered that we have only
heard one side of the case. God has
written all the books.

> **Samuel Butler** 1835–1902 English
> novelist: *Notebooks* (1912)

4 It ain't necessarily so,
It ain't necessarily so,
De t'ings dat yo' li'ble
To read in de Bible
It ain't necessarily so.

> **Du Bose Heyward** 1885–1940 and **Ira
> Gershwin** 1896–1983 American
> songwriters: 'It ain't necessarily so'
> (1935)

5 The English Bible, a book which, if
everything else in our language
should perish, would alone suffice to
show the whole extent of its beauty
and power.

> **Lord Macaulay** 1800–59 English
> politician and historian: 'John Dryden'
> (1828)

6 I know of no book which has been a
source of brutality and sadistic

conduct, both public and private,
that can compare with the Bible.
Reginald Paget 1908–90 British Labour
politician: in *Observer* 28 June 1964

7 There's a Bible on that shelf there.
But I keep it next to Voltaire—poison
and antidote.
Bertrand Russell 1872–1970 British
philosopher and mathematician: in
Kenneth Harris Talking To (1971)
'Bertrand Russell'

8 The devil can cite Scripture for his
purpose.
William Shakespeare 1564–1616
English dramatist: *The Merchant of
Venice* (1596–8)

9 Saint Jerome also translated the
Bible into his mother tongue. Why
may not we also?
William Tyndale c.1494–1536 English
translator of the Bible and Protestant
martyr: *The Obedience of a Christian
Man* (1528)

10 LORD ILLINGWORTH: The Book of Life
begins with a man and a woman in
a garden.
MRS ALLONBY: It ends with
Revelations.
Oscar Wilde 1854–1900 Anglo-Irish
dramatist and poet: *A Woman of No
Importance* (1893)

Biography

see also AUTOBIOGRAPHY

1 And kept his heart a secret to the end
From all the picklocks of
biographers.
of Robert E. Lee
Stephen Vincent Benét 1898–1943
American poet and novelist: *John
Brown's Body* (1928)

2 The Art of Biography
Is different from Geography.
Geography is about Maps,

But Biography is about Chaps.
Edmund Clerihew Bentley 1875–1956
English writer: *Biography for Beginners*
(1905)

3 A well-written Life is almost as rare
as a well-spent one.
Thomas Carlyle 1795–1881 Scottish
historian and political philosopher:
Critical and Miscellaneous Essays (1838)
'Jean Paul Friedrich Richter'

4 Nobody can write the life of a man,
but those who have eat and drunk
and lived in social intercourse with
him.
Samuel Johnson 1709–84 English poet,
critic, and lexicographer: James Boswell
Life of Samuel Johnson (1791) 31 March
1772

5 Lives of great men all remind us
We can make our lives sublime,
And, departing, leave behind us
Footprints on the sands of time.
Henry Wadsworth Longfellow 1807–82
American poet: 'A Psalm of Life' (1838)

6 I have done my best to die before this
book is published. It now seems
possible that I may not succeed.
Robert Runcie 1921–99 English
Protestant clergyman; Archbishop of
Canterbury: letter to Humphrey
Carpenter, July 1996, in H. Carpenter
Robert Runcie (1996)

7 Discretion is not the better part of
biography.
Lytton Strachey 1880–1932 English
biographer: Michael Holroyd *Lytton
Strachey* vol. 1 (1967)

8 Then there is my noble and
biographical friend who has added a
new terror to death.
*on Lord Campbell's Lives of the Lord
Chancellors being written without the
consent of heirs or executors*
Charles Wetherell 1770–1846 English
lawyer and politician: Lord St Leonards
Misrepresentations in Campbell's Lives

of Lyndhurst and Brougham (1869); also
attributed to Lord Lyndhurst
(1772–1863)

9 Every great man nowadays has his
disciples, and it is always Judas who
writes the biography.
Oscar Wilde 1854–1900 Anglo-Irish
dramatist and poet: *Intentions* (1891)
'The Critic as Artist'

Biotechnology

see also LIFE SCIENCES, SCIENCE AND SOCIETY

1 Men will not be content to
manufacture life: they will want to
improve on it.
J. D. Bernal 1901–71 Irish-born
physicist: *The World, the Flesh and the
Devil* (1929)

2 Students accept astonishing things
happening in human genetics
without turning a hair but worry
about GM soya beans.
Steve Jones 1944– English geneticist:
in *Times Higher Education Supplement*
27 August 1999

3 We ought not to permit a cottage
industry in the God business.
*on hearing that British scientists had
successfully cloned a lamb*
John Marchi 1948–2009 American
Republican politician: in *Guardian*
28 February 1997

4 Genetic control will be the weapon
of the future.
Jeanette Winterson 1959– English
novelist and critic: *Art and Lies* (1994)

Birds

see also ANIMAL RIGHTS

1 That's the wise thrush; he sings each
song twice over,
Lest you should think he never could
recapture

The first fine careless rapture!
Robert Browning 1812–89 English poet:
'Home-Thoughts, from Abroad' (1845)

2 A nightingale . . . dies for shame if
another bird sings better.
Robert Burton 1577–1640 English
clergyman and scholar: *The Anatomy of
Melancholy* (1621–51)

3 It was the Rainbow gave thee birth,
And left thee all her lovely hues.
W. H. Davies 1871–1940 Welsh poet:
'Kingfisher' (1910)

4 At once a voice outburst among
The bleak twigs overhead
In a full-hearted evensong
Of joy illimited;
An aged thrush, frail, gaunt, and
small,
In blast-beruffled plume,
Had chosen thus to fling his soul
Upon the growing gloom.
Thomas Hardy 1840–1928 English
novelist and poet: 'The Darkling Thrush'
(1902)

5 I caught this morning morning's
minion, kingdom of daylight's
dauphin, dapple-dawn-drawn
Falcon.
Gerard Manley Hopkins 1844–89
English poet and priest: 'The
Windhover' (written 1877)

6 It took the whole of Creation
To produce my foot, my each
feather:
Now I hold Creation in my foot.
Ted Hughes 1930–98 English poet:
'Hawk Roosting' (1960)

7 Oh, a wondrous bird is the pelican!
His bill will hold more than his
belican.
He can take in his beak
Enough food for a week.
But I'm damned if I see how the
helican.
Dixon Lanier Merritt 1879–1972
American editor: adapted from the

original in *Nashville Banner* 22 April 1913

8 The Ostrich roams the great Sahara.
   Its mouth is wide, its neck is narra.
   It has such long and lofty legs,
   I'm glad it sits to lay its eggs.
   Ogden Nash 1902–71 American
   humorist: 'The Ostrich' (1957)

9 Hail to thee, blithe Spirit!
   Bird thou never wert,
   That from Heaven, or near it,
   Pourest thy full heart
   In profuse strains of unpremeditated
   art.
   Percy Bysshe Shelley 1792–1822
   English poet: 'To a Skylark' (1819)

10 Blackbirds are the cellos of the deep
   farms.
   Anne Stevenson 1933– English poet:
   'Green Mountain, Black Mountain'
   (1982)

11 Alone and warming his five wits,
   The white owl in the belfry sits.
   Alfred, Lord Tennyson 1809–92 English
   poet: 'Song—The Owl' (1830)

12 I once had a sparrow alight upon my
   shoulder for a moment while I was
   hoeing in a village garden, and I felt
   that I was more distinguished by that
   circumstance than I should have
   been by any epaulette I could have
   worn.
   Henry David Thoreau 1817–62
   American writer: *Walden* (1854) 'Winter
   Animals'

13 O blithe new-comer! I have heard,
   I hear thee and rejoice:
   O Cuckoo! Shall I call thee bird,
   Or but a wandering voice?
   William Wordsworth 1770–1850
   English poet: 'To the Cuckoo' (1807)

Birth

see also PREGNANCY

1 To be born is to be wrecked on an
   island.
   J. M. Barrie 1860–1937 Scottish writer
   and dramatist: preface to R. M.
   Ballantyne *The Coral Island* (1913 ed.)

2 Death and taxes and childbirth!
   There's never any convenient time
   for any of them.
   Margaret Mitchell 1900–49 American
   novelist: *Gone with the Wind* (1936)

3 Good work, Mary. We all knew you
   had it in you.
   *telegram to Mrs Sherwood on the arrival of
   her baby*
   Dorothy Parker 1893–1967 American
   critic and humorist: Alexander
   Woollcott *While Rome Burns* (1934)

4 Love set you going like a fat gold
   watch.
   The midwife slapped your footsoles,
   and your bald cry
   Took its place among the elements.
   Sylvia Plath 1932–63 American poet:
   'Morning Song' (1965)

5 The hour which gives us life begins
   to take it away.
   Seneca ('the Younger') *c*.4 BC–AD 65
   Roman philosopher and poet: *Hercules
   Furens*

6 I s'pect I growed. Don't think nobody
   never made me.
   said by Topsy
   Harriet Beecher Stowe 1811–96
   American novelist: *Uncle Tom's Cabin*
   (1852)

7 What you say of the pride of giving
   life to an immortal soul is very fine,
   dear, but I own I can not enter into
   that; I think much more of our being
   like a cow or a dog at such moments;
   when our poor nature becomes so
   very animal and unecstatic.
   Queen Victoria 1819–1901 British

monarch: letter to the Princess Royal,
15 June 1858

8 Our birth is but a sleep and a
   forgetting . . .
   Not in entire forgetfulness,
   And not in utter nakedness,
   But trailing clouds of glory do we
   come.
   William Wordsworth 1770–1850
   English poet: 'Ode. Intimations of
   Immortality' (1807)

Birth Control

see also PREGNANCY

1 A fast word about oral
   contraception. I asked a girl to go to
   bed with me and she said 'no'.
   Woody Allen 1935–   American film
   director, writer, and actor: at a nightclub
   in Washington, April 1965

2 It is now quite lawful for a Catholic
   woman to avoid pregnancy by a
   resort to mathematics, though she is
   still forbidden to resort to physics
   and chemistry.
   H. L. Mencken 1880–1956 American
   journalist and literary critic: *Notebooks*
   (1956)

3 Contraceptives should be used on all
   conceivable occasions.
   Spike Milligan 1918–2002 Irish
   comedian: *The Last Goon Show of All*
   (1972)

4 We want better reasons for having
   children than not knowing how to
   prevent them.
   Dora Russell 1894–1986 English
   feminist: *Hypatia* (1925)

5 Impotence and sodomy are socially
   O.K. but birth control is flagrantly
   middle-class.
   Evelyn Waugh 1903–66 English novelist:
   'An Open Letter' in Nancy Mitford (ed.)
   Noblesse Oblige (1956)

Birthdays

1 A diplomat is a man who always
   remembers a woman's birthday but
   never remembers her age.
   Robert Frost 1874–1963 American poet:
   attributed

2 Do you count your birthdays
   thankfully?
   Horace 65–8 BC Roman poet: *Epistles*

3 Presents and parties disappear,
   The cards grow fewer year by year.
   Till, when one reaches sixty-five,
   How many care we're still alive?
   Philip Larkin 1922–85 English poet:
   'Dear Charles, My Muse, alive or dead'
   (1982)

4 Believing, hear, what you deserve to
   hear:
   Your birthday as my own to me is
   dear . . .
   But yours gives most; for mine did
   only lend
   Me to the world; yours gave to me a
   friend.
   Martial AD *c.*40–*c.*104 Roman
   epigrammatist: *Epigrams*

5 EEYORE: But after all, what are
   birthdays? Here today and gone
   tomorrow.
   A. A. Milne 1882–1956 English writer for
   children: *The House at Pooh Corner*
   (1928) 'Tigger has Breakfast'

6 Our birthdays are feathers in the
   broad wing of time.
   Johann Paul Friedrich Richter
   1763–1825 German novelist: *Titan*
   (1803)

7 For every year of life we light
   A candle on your cake
   To mark the simple sort of progress
   Anyone can make,
   And then, to test your nerve or give
   A proper view of death,

You're asked to blow each light, each
  year,
Out with your own breath.
  James Simmons 1933–2001 British
  poet: 'A Birthday Poem' (1969)

Boats
see also SEA

1 Jolly boating weather,
  And a hay harvest breeze,
  Blade on the feather,
  Shade off the trees
  Swing, swing together
  With your body between your knees.
  William Cory 1823–92 English poet:
  'Eton Boating Song' in *Eton Scrap Book*
  (1865)

2 A wet sheet and a flowing sea,
  A wind that follows fast
  And fills the white and rustling sail
  And bends the gallant mast.
  Allan Cunningham 1784–1842 Scottish
  poet: 'A Wet Sheet and a Flowing Sea'
  (1825)

3 There is *nothing*—absolutely
  nothing—half so much worth doing
  as simply messing about in boats.
  Kenneth Grahame 1859–1932 Scottish-
  born writer: *The Wind in the Willows*
  (1908)

4 Ocean racing is like standing under a
  cold shower tearing up £5 notes.
  Edward Heath 1916–2005 British
  Conservative statesman: attributed

5 For soft is the song my paddle sings.
  Pauline Johnson (Tekahionwake)
  1861–1913 Canadian poet: 'The Song
  My Paddle Sings'

6 Quinquireme of Nineveh from
    distant Ophir
  Rowing home to haven in sunny
    Palestine,
  With a cargo of ivory,
  And apes and peacocks,

Sandalwood, cedarwood, and sweet
  white wine.
  John Masefield 1878–1967 English poet:
  'Cargoes' (1903)

7 Dirty British coaster with a salt-
    caked smoke stack,
  Butting through the Channel in the
    mad March days,
  With a cargo of Tyne coal,
  Road-rails, pig lead,
  Firewood, ironware, and cheap tin
    trays.
  John Masefield 1878–1967 English poet:
  'Cargoes' (1903)

The Body
see also APPEARANCE, FACE, FAT, HAIR, HEALTH,
SENSES

1 My brain? It's my second favourite
  organ.
  Woody Allen 1935–   American film
  director, writer, and actor: *Sleeper*
  (1973 film, with Marshall Brickman)

2 Shame on the soul, to falter on the
  road of life while the body still
  perseveres.
  Marcus Aurelius AD 121–180 Roman
  emperor: *Meditations*

3 Every tooth in a man's head is more
  valuable than a diamond.
  Cervantes 1547–1616 Spanish novelist:
  Don Quixote (1605)

4 A woman watches her body uneasily,
  as though it were an unreliable ally
  in the battle for love.
  Leonard Cohen 1934–   Canadian
  singer and writer: *The Favourite Game*
  (1963)

5 i like my body when it is with your
  body. It is so quite new a thing.
  Muscles better and nerves more.
  i like your body. i like what it does,
  i like its hows.
  e. e. cummings 1894–1962 American
  poet: 'Sonnets–Actualities' no. 8 (1925)

6 The leg, a source of much delight,
which carries weight and governs
height.
> **Ian Dury** 1942–2000 British rock singer
> and songwriter: 'The Body Song' (1981)

7 Anatomy is destiny.
> **Sigmund Freud** 1856–1939 Austrian
> psychiatrist: *Collected Writings* (1924)

8 I travel light; as light,
That is, as a man can travel who will
Still carry his body around because
Of its sentimental value.
> **Christopher Fry** 1907–2005 English
> dramatist: *The Lady's not for Burning*
> (1949)

9 I came in here in all good faith to
help my country. I don't mind giving
a reasonable amount [of blood], but
a pint . . . why that's very nearly an
armful.
> **Ray Galton** 1930– and **Alan Simpson**
> 1929– English scriptwriters: *The Blood
> Donor* (1961 BBC television
> programme) words spoken by Tony
> Hancock

10 The body says what words cannot.
> **Martha Graham** 1894–1991 American
> dancer, teacher, and choreographer:
> interview, *New York Times* 31 March
> 1985

11 When a young man came up to him
in Zurich and said, 'May I kiss the
hand that wrote *Ulysses*?' Joyce
replied, somewhat like King Lear,
'No, it did lots of other things too.'
> **James Joyce** 1882–1941 Irish novelist:
> Richard Ellmann *James Joyce* (1959)

12 Feet, why do I need them if I have
wings to fly?
> *after the amputation of her right leg due to
> gangrene*
> **Frida Kahlo** 1907–54 Mexican painter:
> diary entry, 1953; Martha Zamora *Frida
> Kahlo: the Brush of Anguish* (1990)

13 Modern body building is ritual,
religion, sport, art, and science,
awash in Western chemistry and
mathematics. Defying nature, it
surpasses it.
> **Camille Paglia** 1947– American writer
> and critic: *Sex, Art, and American
> Culture* (1992)

14 I don't really like knees.
> **Yves Saint Laurent** 1936–2008 French
> couturier: in *Observer* 3 August 1958

15 This Englishwoman is so refined
She has no bosom and no behind.
> **Stevie Smith** 1902–71 English poet and
> novelist: 'This Englishwoman' (1937)

16 An impersonal and scientific
knowledge of the structure of our
bodies is the surest safeguard against
prurient curiosity and lascivious
gloating.
> **Marie Stopes** 1880–1958 Scottish
> pioneer of birth-control clinics: *Married
> Love* (1918)

17 Every man is the builder of a temple,
called his body.
> **Henry David Thoreau** 1817–62
> American writer: *Walden* (1854)

18 Our body is a machine for living. It is
organized for that, it is its nature. Let
life go on in it unhindered and let it
defend itself, it will do more than if
you paralyse it by encumbering it
with remedies.
> **Leo Tolstoy** 1828–1910 Russian novelist:
> *War and Peace* (1865–9)

19 I sing the body electric.
> **Walt Whitman** 1819–92 American poet:
> title of poem (1855)

20 The human body is the best picture
of the human soul.
> **Ludwig Wittgenstein** 1889–1951
> Austrian-born philosopher:
> *Philosophical Investigations* (1953)

Books

see also CRIME FICTION, DICTIONARIES, FANTASY, FICTION, LIBRARIES, LITERATURE, PUBLISHING, READING, REVIEWS, SCIENCE FICTION, WRITING

1 Some books are undeservedly forgotten; none are undeservedly remembered.

> **W. H. Auden** 1907–73 English poet: *The Dyer's Hand* (1963) 'Reading'

2 Some books are to be tasted, others to be swallowed, and some few to be chewed and digested.

> **Francis Bacon** 1561–1626 English lawyer, courtier, philosopher, and essayist: *Essays* (1625) 'Of Studies'

3 Books say: she did this because. Life says: she did this. Books are where things are explained to you; life is where things aren't . . . Books make sense of life. The only problem is that the lives they make sense of are other people's lives, never your own.

> **Julian Barnes** 1946– English novelist: *Flaubert's Parrot* (1984)

4 Of making many books there is no end; and much study is a weariness of the flesh.

> **Bible**: Ecclesiastes

5 The possession of a book becomes a substitute for reading it.

> **Anthony Burgess** 1917–93 English novelist and critic: in *New York Times Book Review* 4 December 1966

6 'What is the use of a book', thought Alice, 'without pictures or conversations?'

> **Lewis Carroll** 1832–98 English writer and logician: *Alice's Adventures in Wonderland* (1865)

7 I don't trust books. They're all fact, no heart.

> **Stephen Colbert** 1964– American satirist: *The Colbert Report* 17 October 2005

8 The good of a book lies in its being read.

> **Umberto Eco** 1932– Italian novelist and semiotician: *The Name of the Rose* (1981)

9 Books are made not like children but like pyramids . . . and they're just as useless! and they stay in the desert! . . . Jackals piss at their foot and the bourgeois climb up on them.

> **Gustave Flaubert** 1821–80 French novelist: letter to Ernest Feydeau, November/December 1857

10 I suggest that the only books that influence us are those for which we are ready, and which have gone a little farther down our particular path than we have yet got ourselves.

> **E. M. Forster** 1879–1970 English novelist: *Two Cheers for Democracy* (1951)

11 Long books, when read, are usually overpraised, because the reader wishes to convince others and himself that he has not wasted his time.

> **E. M. Forster** 1879–1970 English novelist: note from commonplace book; O. Stallybrass (ed.) *Aspects of the Novel and Related Writings* (1974)

12 A bad book is as much of a labour to write as a good one; it comes as sincerely from the author's soul.

> **Aldous Huxley** 1894–1963 English novelist: *Point Counter Point* (1928)

13 A book must be the axe for the frozen sea within us.

> **Franz Kafka** 1883–1924 Czech novelist: letter, 27 January 1904

14 Your *borrowers of books*—those mutilators of collections, spoilers of the symmetry of shelves, and creators of odd volumes.

> **Charles Lamb** 1775–1834 English writer: *Essays of Elia* (1823) 'The Two Races of Men'

15 All books are either dreams or
swords,
You can cut, or you can drug, with
words.
   Amy Lowell 1874–1925 American poet:
   'Sword Blades and Poppy Seed' (1914)

16 The book is the greatest interactive
medium of all time. You can
underline it, write in the margins,
fold down a page, skip ahead. And
you can take it anywhere.
on taking over as head of Penguin Books
   Michael Lynton English publisher: in
   Daily Telegraph 19 August 1996

17 A good book is the precious life-
blood of a master spirit, embalmed
and treasured up on purpose to a life
beyond life.
   John Milton 1608–74 English poet:
   Areopagitica (1644)

18 This is not a novel to be tossed aside
lightly. It should be thrown with
great force.
   Dorothy Parker 1893–1967 American
   critic and humorist: R. E. Drennan *Wit's
   End* (1973)

19 There is no book so bad that some
good cannot be got out of it.
   Pliny the Elder AD 23–79 Roman
   statesman and scholar: Pliny the
   Younger *Letters*

20 The principle of procrastinated rape
is said to be the ruling one in all the
great best-sellers.
   V. S. Pritchett 1900–97 English writer
   and critic: *The Living Novel* (1946)
   'Clarissa'

21 Books can not be killed by fire.
People die, but books never die. No
man and no force can abolish
memory . . . In this war, we know,
books are weapons. And it is a part of
your dedication always to make
them weapons for man's freedom.
   Franklin D. Roosevelt 1882–1945
   American Democratic statesman:
   'Message to the Booksellers of America'
   6 May 1942

22 A best-seller is the gilded tomb of a
mediocre talent.
   Logan Pearsall Smith 1865–1946
   American-born man of letters:
   Afterthoughts (1931)

23 No furniture so charming as books.
   Sydney Smith 1771–1845 English
   clergyman and essayist: Lady Holland
   Memoir (1855)

24 I kept always two books in my
pocket, one to read, one to write in.
   Robert Louis Stevenson 1850–94
   Scottish novelist: *Memories and
   Portraits* (1887)

25 Books that told me everything about
the wasp, except why.
   Dylan Thomas 1914–53 Welsh poet: *A
   Child's Christmas in Wales* (1954)

26 A good book is the best of friends,
the same to-day and for ever.
   Martin Tupper 1810–89 English writer:
   Proverbial Philosophy Series I (1838) 'Of
   Reading'

27 '*Classic*'. A book which people praise
and don't read.
   Mark Twain 1835–1910 American
   writer: *Following the Equator* (1897)

28 There is no such thing as a moral or
an immoral book. Books are well
written, or badly written.
   Oscar Wilde 1854–1900 Anglo-Irish
   dramatist and poet: *The Picture of
   Dorian Gray* (1891)

Boredom

1 Nothing happens, nobody comes,
nobody goes, it's awful!
   Samuel Beckett 1906–89 Irish
   dramatist, novelist, and poet: *Waiting
   for Godot* (1955)

2 Life, friends, is boring. We must not
    say so . . .
    And moreover my mother taught me
      as a boy
    (repeatedly) 'Ever to confess you're
      bored
    means you have no
    Inner Resources.' I conclude now I
      have no
    inner resources, because I am heavy
      bored.
    John Berryman 1914–72 American
    poet: *77 Dream Songs* (1964) no. 14

3 What's wrong with being a boring
    kind of guy?
    *during the campaign for the Republican
    nomination*
    George Bush 1924– American
    Republican statesman: in *Daily
    Telegraph* 28 April 1988

4 Someone has somewhere
    commented on the fact that millions
    long for immortality who don't know
    what to do with themselves on a
    rainy Sunday afternoon.
    Susan Ertz 1894–1985 American writer:
    Anger in the Sky (1943)

5 Nothing, like something, happens
    anywhere.
    Philip Larkin 1922–85 English poet: 'I
    Remember, I Remember' (1955)

6 We often forgive those who bore us,
    but we cannot forgive those whom
    we bore.
    Duc de la Rochefoucauld 1613–80
    French moralist: *Maxims* (1678)

7 Boredom is . . . a vital problem for
    the moralist, since half the sins of
    mankind are caused by the fear of it.
    Bertrand Russell 1872–1970 British
    philosopher and mathematician: *The
    Conquest of Happiness* (1930)

8 A desire for desires—boredom.
    Leo Tolstoy 1828–1910 Russian novelist:
    Anna Karenina (1873–6)

9 He is an old bore. Even the grave
    yawns for him.
    of Israel Zangwill
    Herbert Beerbohm Tree 1852–1917
    English actor-manager: Max Beerbohm
    Herbert Beerbohm Tree (1920)

10 A healthy male adult bore consumes
    each year one and a half times his
    own weight in other people's
    patience.
    John Updike 1932–2009 American
    novelist and short-story writer: *Assorted
    Prose* (1965) 'Confessions of a Wild Bore'

11 The secret of being a bore . . . is to
    tell everything.
    Voltaire 1694–1778 French writer and
    philosopher: *Discours en vers sur
    l'homme* (1737)

Boxing

see also SPORTS

1 Float like a butterfly, sting like a bee.
    summary of his boxing strategy
    Muhammad Ali 1942– American
    boxer: G. Sullivan *Cassius Clay Story*
    (1964); probably originated by Drew
    'Bundini' Brown

2 Boxing's just show business with
    blood.
    Frank Bruno 1961– English boxer: in
    Guardian 20 November 1991; also
    attributed to David Belasco in 1915

3 Honey, I just forgot to duck.
    on losing the World Heavyweight title
    Jack Dempsey 1895–1983 American
    boxer: to his wife, 23 September 1926;
    after a failed attempt on his life in 1981,
    Ronald Reagan quipped to his wife
    'Honey, I forgot to duck'

4 We was robbed!
    *after Jack Sharkey beat Max Schmeling (of
    whom Jacobs was manager) in the
    heavyweight title fight, 21 June 1932*
    Joe Jacobs 1896–1940 American boxing
    manager: Peter Heller *In This Corner*
    (1975)

5 We're all endowed with God-given talents. Mine happens to be hitting people in the head.

> **Sugar Ray Leonard** 1956– American boxer: Thomas Hauser *The Black Lights* (1986)

6 He can run. But he can't hide.

of Billy Conn, his opponent

> **Joe Louis** 1914–81 American boxer: before a heavyweight title fight, 19 June 1946; *Louis: My Life Story* (1947)

7 *when asked by the coroner if he had intended to 'get Doyle in trouble':*

Mister, it's my *business* to get him in trouble.

following the death of Jimmy Doyle from his injuries after fighting Robinson, 24 June 1947

> **Sugar Ray Robinson** 1920–89 American boxer: *Sugar Ray* (1970, with Dave Anderson)

Britain

see also BRITISH CITIES, ENGLAND, SCOTLAND, WALES

1 Great Britain has lost an empire and has not yet found a role.

> **Dean Acheson** 1893–1971 American politician: speech at the Military Academy, West Point, 5 December 1962

2 You cannot trust people who have such bad cuisine. It is the country with the worst food after Finland.

on the British

> **Jacques Chirac** 1932– French statesman: in *Times* 5 July 2005

3 The British nation is unique in this respect. They are the only people who like to be told how bad things are, who like to be told the worst.

> **Winston Churchill** 1874–1965 British Conservative statesman: speech in the House of Commons, 10 June 1941

4 Britain will be honoured by historians more for the way she

disposed of an empire than for the way in which she acquired it.

> **Lord Harlech** 1918–85 British diplomat: in *New York Times* 28 October 1962

5 Fifty years on from now, Britain will still be the country of long shadows on county [cricket] grounds, warm beer, invincible green suburbs, dog lovers, and—as George Orwell said—old maids bicycling to Holy Communion through the morning mist.

> **John Major** 1943– British Conservative statesman: speech to the Conservative Group for Europe, 22 April 1993; see ENGLAND 14

6 He [the Briton] is a barbarian, and thinks that the customs of his tribe and island are the laws of nature.

> **George Bernard Shaw** 1856–1950 Irish dramatist: *Caesar and Cleopatra* (1901)

7 Rule, Britannia, rule the waves; Britons never will be slaves.

> **James Thomson** 1700–48 Scottish poet: *Alfred: a Masque* (1740)

8 A soggy little island huffing and puffing to keep up with Western Europe.

> **John Updike** 1932–2009 American novelist and short-story writer: 'London Life' (written 1969)

9 Other nations use 'force'; we Britons alone use 'Might'.

> **Evelyn Waugh** 1903–66 English novelist: *Scoop* (1938)

British Cities and Towns

see also LONDON, OXFORD

1 Oh! who can ever be tired of Bath?

> **Jane Austen** 1775–1817 English novelist: *Northanger Abbey* (1818)

2 One has no great hopes from
Birmingham. I always say there is
something direful in the sound.
   Jane Austen 1775–1817 English novelist:
   Emma (1816)

3 Come, friendly bombs, and fall on
   Slough!
It isn't fit for humans now,
There isn't grass to graze a cow.
Swarm over, Death!
   John Betjeman 1906–84 English poet:
   'Slough' (1937)

4 O the bricks they will bleed and the
   rain it will weep
And the damp Lagan fog lull the city
   to sleep;
It's to hell with the future and live on
   the past:
May the Lord in His mercy be kind to
   Belfast.
*based on the traditional refrain 'May God
in His mercy look down on Belfast'*
   Maurice James Craig 1919– : 'Ballad to
   a Traditional Refrain' (1974)

5 Bugger Bognor.
*comment made either in 1929, when it was
proposed that the town be renamed Bognor
Regis following the king's convalescence
there; or on his deathbed when someone
said 'Cheer up, your Majesty, you will soon
be at Bognor again.'*
   George V 1865–1936 British monarch:
   Kenneth Rose *King George V* (1983)

6 City of perspiring dreams.
of Cambridge
   Frederic Raphael 1931– British
   novelist and screenwriter: *The Glittering
   Prizes* (1976); see OXFORD 2

7 It is from the midst of this putrid
sewer that the greatest river of
human industry springs up and
carries fertility to the whole world.
From this foul drain pure gold flows
forth.
of Manchester
   Alexis de Tocqueville 1805–59 French
   historian and politician: *Voyage en*

Angleterre et en Irlande de 1835 2 July
1835

Buildings

see also ARCHITECTURE

1 The existence of St Sophia is
atmospheric; that of St Peter's,
overpoweringly, imminently
substantial. One is a church to God:
the other a salon for his agents. One
is consecrated to reality, the other, to
illusion. St Sophia in fact is large, and
St Peter's is vilely, tragically small.
   Robert Byron 1905–41 English traveller,
   art critic, and historian: *The Road to
   Oxiana* (1937)

2 A monstrous carbuncle on the face
of a much-loved and elegant friend.
*on the proposed extension to the National
Gallery, London*
   Charles, Prince of Wales 1948– British
   prince: speech to the Royal Institute of
   British Architects, 30 May 1984

3 It looks like a portable typewriter full
of oyster shells, and to the
contention that it echoes the sails of
yachts on the harbour I can only
point out that the yachts on the
harbour don't waste any time
echoing opera houses.
of the Sydney Opera House
   Clive James 1939– Australian critic and
   writer: *Flying Visits* (1984)

4 That temple of silence and
reconciliation where the enmities of
twenty generations lie buried.
of Westminster Abbey
   Lord Macaulay 1800–59 English
   politician and historian: *Essays
   Contributed to the Edinburgh Review*
   (1843) 'Warren Hastings'

5 Brighton Pavilion looks as if St Paul's
had slipped down to Brighton and
pupped.
   Sydney Smith 1771–1845 English

clergyman and essayist: attributed; Alan Bell (ed.) *The Sayings of Sydney Smith* (1993)

Bureaucracy

see also ADMINISTRATION, COMMITTEES

1 It is an inevitable defect, that bureaucrats will care more for routine than for results.
   Walter Bagehot 1826–77 English economist and essayist: *The English Constitution* (1867)

2 Guidelines for bureaucrats: (1) When in charge, ponder. (2) When in trouble, delegate. (3) When in doubt, mumble.
   James H. Boren 1925– American bureaucrat: in *New York Times* 8 November 1970

3 Whatever was required to be done, the Circumlocution Office was beforehand with all the public departments in the art of perceiving—HOW NOT TO DO IT.
   Charles Dickens 1812–70 English novelist: *Little Dorrit* (1857)

4 Where there is officialism every human relationship suffers.
   E. M. Forster 1879–1970 English novelist: *A Passage to India* (1924)

5 What is official
   Is incontestable. It undercuts
   The problematical world and sells us life
   At a discount.
   Christopher Fry 1907–2005 English dramatist: *The Lady's not for Burning* (1949)

6 Official dignity tends to increase in inverse ratio to the importance of the country in which the office is held.
   Aldous Huxley 1894–1963 English novelist: *Beyond the Mexique Bay* (1934)

7 A desk is a dangerous place from which to watch the world.
   John le Carré 1931– English thriller writer: *The Honourable Schoolboy* (1977)

8 The truth in these matters may be stated as a scientific law: 'The persistence of public officials varies inversely with the importance of the matter on which they are persisting.'
   Bernard Levin 1928–2004 British journalist: *In These Times* (1986)

9 Bureaucracy, the rule of no one, has become the modern form of despotism.
   Mary McCarthy 1912–89 American novelist: *On the Contrary* (1961)

10 The man who is denied the opportunity of taking decisions of importance begins to regard as important the decisions he is allowed to take.
   C. Northcote Parkinson 1909–93 English writer: *Parkinson's Law* (1958)

11 Back in the East you can't do much without the right papers, but *with* the right papers you can do *anything*. They *believe* in papers. Papers are power.
   Tom Stoppard 1937– British dramatist: *Neutral Ground* (1983)

12 The concept of the 'official secret' is its [bureaucracy's] specific invention.
   Max Weber 1864–1920 German sociologist: 'Politik als Beruf' (1919)

Business

see also ECONOMICS, SHOPPING

1 There is nothing more requisite in business than dispatch.
   Joseph Addison 1672–1719 English poet, dramatist, and essayist: *The Drummer* (1716)

2 I liked it so much, I bought the
company!
> **Advertising slogan**: Remington
> Shavers, 1980; spoken by the company's
> new owner Victor Kiam (1926–2001)

3 A merchant shall hardly keep himself
from doing wrong.
> **Bible**: Ecclesiasticus

4 NINOTCHKA: Why should you carry
other people's bags?
PORTER: Well, that's my business,
Madame.
NINOTCHKA: That's no business. That's
social injustice.
PORTER: That depends on the tip.
> **Charles Brackett** 1892–1969 and **Billy
> Wilder** 1906–2002 American
> screenwriters: *Ninotchka* (1939 film,
> with Walter Reisch)

5 Here's the rule for bargains: 'Do other
men, for they would do you.' That's
the true business precept.
> **Charles Dickens** 1812–70 English
> novelist: *Martin Chuzzlewit* (1844)

6 *Knowledge is the only meaningful
resource today.* The traditional
'factors of production'—land (i.e.
natural resources), labour and
capital—have not disappeared. But
they have become secondary.
> **Peter F. Drucker** 1909– Austrian-born
> American management consultant,
> educator, and writer: *Post-Capitalist
> Society* (1993)

7 Making money from money should
be replaced with making money
from making.
> **James Dyson** 1947– English inventor
> and businessman: in *Observer*
> 8 February 2009

8 The salary of the chief executive of
the large corporation is not a market
reward for achievement. It is
frequently in the nature of a warm

personal gesture by the individual to
himself.
> **J. K. Galbraith** 1908–2006 American
> economist: *Annals of an Abiding Liberal*
> (1979)

9 Only the paranoid survive.
*dictum on which he has long run his
company, the Intel Corporation*
> **Andrew Grove** 1936– American
> businessman: in *New York Times*
> 18 December 1994

10 Accountants are the witch-doctors of
the modern world and willing to turn
their hands to any kind of magic.
> **Charles Eustace Harman** 1894–1970
> British judge: speech, February 1964

11 The green shoots of economic spring
are appearing once again.
*often quoted as 'the green shoots of
recovery'*
> **Norman Lamont** 1942– British
> Conservative politician: speech at
> Conservative Party Conference,
> 9 October 1991

12 Doing well by doing good.
later the slogan of Monsanto
> **Tom Lehrer** 1928– American humorist:
> 'The Old Dope Peddler' (1953 song)

13 How to succeed in business without
really trying.
> **Shepherd Mead** 1914–94 American
> advertising executive: title of book
> (1952)

14 For a salesman, there is no rock
bottom to the life . . . A salesman is
got to dream, boy. It comes with the
territory.
> **Arthur Miller** 1915–2005 American
> dramatist: *Death of a Salesman* (1949)

15 After a certain point money is
meaningless. It ceases to be the goal.
The game is what counts.
> **Aristotle Onassis** 1906–75 Greek
> shipping magnate and international
> businessman: attributed, perhaps
> apocryphal

16 We even sell a pair of earrings for under £1, which is cheaper than a prawn sandwich from Marks & Spencers. But I have to say the earrings probably won't last as long.
  Gerald Ratner 1949– English businessman: speech to the Institute of Directors, Albert Hall, 23 April 1991

17 The customer is never wrong.
  César Ritz 1850–1918 Swiss hotel proprietor: R. Nevill and C. E. Jerningham *Piccadilly to Pall Mall* (1908)

18 The most striking thing about modern industry is that it requires so much and accomplishes so little. Modern industry seems to be inefficient to a degree that surpasses one's ordinary powers of imagination. Its inefficiency therefore remains unnoticed.
  E. F. Schumacher 1911–77 German-born economist: *Small is Beautiful* (1973)

19 People of the same trade seldom meet together, even for merriment and diversion, but the conversation ends in a conspiracy against the public, or in some contrivance to raise prices.
  Adam Smith 1723–90 Scottish philosopher and economist: *Wealth of Nations* (1776)

20 To found a great empire for the sole purpose of raising up a people of customers, may at first sight appear a project fit only for a nation of shopkeepers. It is, however, a project altogether unfit for a nation of shopkeepers; but extremely fit for a nation whose government is influenced by shopkeepers.
  Adam Smith 1723–90 Scottish philosopher and economist: *Wealth of Nations* (1776)

21 I love the smell of commerce in the morning.
  Kevin Smith 1970– American screenwriter and director: *Mallrats* (1995 film), spoken by Jason Lee

22 Corporations have neither bodies to be punished, nor souls to be condemned, they therefore do as they like.
  often quoted as 'Did you ever expect a corporation to have a conscience, when it has no soul to be damned, and no body to be kicked?'
  Lord Thurlow 1731–1806 English jurist: John Poynder *Literary Extracts* (1844)

23 Deals are my art form. Other people paint beautifully on canvas or write wonderful poetry. I like making deals, preferably big deals. That's how I get my kicks.
  Donald Trump 1946– American businessman: Donald Trump and Tony Schwartz *The Art of the Deal* (1987)

24 The public be damned! I'm working for my stockholders.
  William H. Vanderbilt 1821–85 American railway magnate: comment to a news reporter, 2 October 1882

25 There is only one boss. The customer. And he can fire everybody in the company from the chairman on down, simply by spending his money somewhere else.
  Sam Walton 1919–92 American businessman: *Sam Walton: Made in America, My Story*, with J. Huey (1990)

26 Being good in business is the most fascinating kind of art.
  Andy Warhol 1927–87 American artist: *Philosophy of Andy Warhol (From A to B and Back Again)* (1975)

27 You cannot be a success in any business without believing that it is the greatest business in the world . . . You have to put your heart

in the business and the business in
your heart.

> **Thomas Watson Snr.** 1874–1956
> American businessman: Robert Sobel
> *IBM: Colossus in Transition* (1981)

28 For years I thought what was good
for our country was good for General
Motors and vice versa.

> **Charles E. Wilson** 1890–1961 American
> industrialist: testimony to the Senate
> Armed Services Committee on his
> proposed nomination for Secretary of
> Defence, 15 January 1953

29 Nothing is illegal if one hundred
well-placed business men decide to
do it.

> **Andrew Young** 1932– American
> clergyman and diplomat: Morris K.
> Udall *Too Funny to be President* (1988)

Canada

1 North of the 49th parallel we value
equality; south of it, they treasure
freedom.

> **Michael Adams** Canadian market
> researcher and writer: *Sex in the Snow*
> (1997)

2 People put down Canadian literature
and ask us why there isn't a *Moby
Dick*. The reason there isn't a
Moby Dick is that if a Canadian did
a *Moby Dick*, it would be done from
the point of view of the whale.

> **Margaret Atwood** 1939– Canadian
> novelist: in *Saturday Night* November
> 1972

3 A Canadian is somebody who knows
how to make love in a canoe.

> **Pierre Berton** 1920–2004 Canadian
> writer: in *The Canadian* 22 December
> 1973

4 We French, we English, never lost
our civil war,
endure it still, a bloodless civil bore;

no wounded lying about, no
Whitman wanted.
It's only by our lack of ghosts we're
haunted.

> **Earle Birney** 1904–95 Canadian poet:
> 'Can.Lit.' (1962)

5 I bow to no man for I am considered
a prince among my own people. But
I will gladly shake your hand.

on being presented to George III

> **Joseph Brant (Thayendanegea)**
> 1742–1807 American-born Canadian
> Mohawk leader: attributed

6 Dusty, cobweb-covered, maimed,
and set at naught,
Beauty crieth in an attic, and no man
regardeth.
O God! O Montreal!

> **Samuel Butler** 1835–1902 English
> novelist: 'Psalm of Montreal' (1878)

7 Some say that no one ever leaves
Montreal, for that city, like Canada
itself, is designed to preserve the
past, a past that happened
somewhere else.

> **Leonard Cohen** 1934– Canadian
> singer and writer: *The Favourite Game*
> (1963)

8 Canada could have enjoyed:
English government,
French culture,
and American know-how.

Instead it ended up with:
English know-how,
French government,
and American culture.

*a similar (prose) summary has been
attributed to Lester Pearson (1897–1972)*

> **John Robert Colombo** 1936– Canadian
> writer: 'O Canada' (1965)

9 I don't have a moral plan. I'm a
Canadian.

> **David Cronenberg** 1943– Canadian
> film director: attributed

10 I see Canada as a country torn
between a very northern, rather

extraordinary, mystical spirit which it fears and its desire to present itself to the world as a Scotch banker.

Robertson Davies 1913–95 Canadian novelist: *The Enthusiasms of Robertson Davies* (1990)

11 *Vive Le Québec Libre.*

Long Live Free Quebec.

Charles de Gaulle 1890–1970 French soldier and statesman: speech in Montreal, 24 July 1967

12 When the white man came we had the land and they had the bibles; now they have the land and we have the bibles.

Dan George 1899–1981 Canadian native chief and actor: Gerald Walsh *Indians in Transition: An Inquiry Approach* (1971)

13 If some countries have too much history, we have too much geography.

William Lyon Mackenzie King 1874–1950 Canadian Liberal statesman: speech on Canada as an international power, 18 June 1936

14 The nineteenth century was the century of the United States. I think we can claim that it is Canada that shall fill the twentieth century.

usually quoted as 'The twentieth century belongs to Canada'

Wilfrid Laurier 1841–1919 Canadian politician: speech in Ottawa, 18 January 1904

15 Canadians are Americans with no Disneyland.

Margaret Mahy 1936– New Zealand writer for children: *The Changeover* (1984)

16 This is the flag of the future, but it does not dishonour the past.

on Canada obtaining a flag of its own, a project Pearson successfully achieved

Lester Pearson 1897–1972 Canadian diplomat and Liberal statesman: speech in the House of Commons, Ottawa, 15 December 1964

17 The Americans are our best friends whether we like it or not.

Robert Norman Thompson 1914–97 American-born Canadian mission worker, politician and academic: Peter C. Newman *Home Country: People, Places, and Power Politics* (1973)

18 Ours is a sovereign nation
Bows to no foreign will
But whenever they cough in Washington
They spit on Parliament Hill.

Joe Wallace 1890–1975 Canadian poet: attributed

19 *O Canada! Terre de nos aïeux,*
Ton front est ceint de fleurons glorieux!
Car ton bras sait porter l'épée,
Il sait porter la croix!

O Canada! Our home and native land!
True patriot love in all thy sons command.
With glowing hearts we see thee rise,
The True North strong and free!

Robert Stanley Weir 1856–1926 Canadian lawyer: 'O Canada' (1908 song); French words written in 1880 by Adolphe-Basile Routhier (1839–1920)

20 Canadians do not like heroes, and so they do not have them.

George Woodcock 1912–95 Canadian writer: *Canada and the Canadians* (1970)

Cancer

see also SICKNESS

1 The best sentence in the English language is not 'I love you' but 'It's benign'.

Woody Allen 1935– American film director, writer, and actor: *Deconstructing Harry* (1998 film)

2 My final word, before I'm done,
Is 'Cancer can be rather fun'.

Thanks to the nurses and Nye Bevan
The NHS is quite like heaven
Provided one confronts the tumour
With a sufficient sense of humour.
J. B. S. Haldane 1892–1964 Scottish
mathematical biologist: 'Cancer's a
Funny Thing' (1968)

3 Human nature seldom walks up to
the word 'cancer'.
Rudyard Kipling 1865–1936 English
writer and poet: *Debits and Credits*
(1926)

Capitalism

see also CLASS, COMMUNISM

1 There is a good deal of solemn cant
about the common interests of
capital and labour. As matters stand,
their only common interest is that of
cutting each other's throat.
Brooks Atkinson 1894–1984 American
journalist and critic: *Once Around the
Sun* (1951)

2 The worker is the slave of capitalist
society, the female worker is the
slave of that slave.
James Connolly 1868–1916 Irish labour
leader and nationalist: *The Re-conquest
of Ireland* (1915)

3 History suggests that capitalism is a
necessary condition for political
freedom. Clearly it is not a sufficient
condition for it.
Milton Friedman 1912–2006 American
economist: *Capitalism and Freedom*
(1962)

4 Capital as such is not evil, it is its
wrong use that is evil. Capital in
some form or other will always be
needed.
Mahatma Gandhi 1869–1948 Indian
statesman: in *Harijan* 28 July 1940

5 The unpleasant and unacceptable
face of capitalism.
on the Lonrho affair
Edward Heath 1916–2005 British
Conservative statesman: speech, House
of Commons, 15 May 1973

6 Yes to the market economy, No to the
market society.
Lionel Jospin 1937– French statesman:
in *Independent* 16 September 1998

7 Whether you like it or not, history is
on our side. We will bury you.
Nikita Khrushchev 1894–1971 Soviet
statesman: speech to Western
diplomats in Moscow, 18 November
1956

8 Imperialism is the monopoly stage of
capitalism.
Lenin 1870–1924 Russian revolutionary:
*Imperialism as the Last Stage of
Capitalism* (1916) 'Briefest possible
definition of imperialism'

9 Normally speaking, it may be said
that the forces of a capitalist society,
if left unchecked, tend to make the
rich richer and the poor poorer and
thus increase the gap between them.
Jawaharlal Nehru 1889–1964 Indian
statesman: 'Basic Approach' in Vincent
Shean *Nehru . . .* (1960)

10 In the first stone which he [the
savage] flings at the wild animals he
pursues, in the first stick that he
seizes to strike down the fruit which
hangs above his reach, we see the
appropriation of one article for the
purpose of aiding in the acquisition
of another, and thus discover the
origin of capital.
Robert Torrens 1780–1864 British
economist: *An Essay on the Production
of Wealth* (1821)

11 You have riches and freedom here
but I feel no sense of faith or
direction. You have so many

computers, why don't you use them in the search for love?

Lech Wałęsa 1943– Polish trade unionist and statesman: in Paris, on his first journey outside the Soviet area, in *Daily Telegraph* 14 December 1988

Careers

see also AMBITION, WORK

1 For promotion cometh neither from the east, nor from the west: nor yet from the south.
   Bible: Psalm 75

2 McJob: A low-pay, low-prestige, low-dignity, low benefit, no-future job in the service sector.
   Douglas Coupland 1961– Canadian writer: *Generation X* (1991)

3 To do nothing and get something, formed a boy's ideal of a manly career.
   Benjamin Disraeli 1804–81 British Tory statesman and novelist: *Sybil* (1845)

4 Don't worry me—I am an 8 ulcer man on 4 ulcer pay.
   Stephen T. Early 1889–1951: letter to Harry S. Truman; William Hillman *Mr President* (1952)

5 If I would be a young man again and had to decide how to make my living, I would not try to become a scientist or scholar or teacher. I would rather choose to be a plumber or a peddler in the hope to find that modest degree of independence still available under present circumstances.
   Albert Einstein 1879–1955 German-born theoretical physicist: in *Reporter* 18 November 1954

6 By working faithfully eight hours a day, you may eventually get to be a boss and work twelve hours a day.
   Robert Frost 1874–1963 American poet: attributed

7 I didn't get where I am today without . . . .
   catch-phrase used by the manager C. J.
   David Nobbs 1935– British comedy writer: *The Death of Reginald Perrin* (1975); and subsequently the BBC TV series *The Fall and Rise of Reginald Perrin* (1976–80)

8 Thou art not for the fashion of these times,
   Where none will sweat but for promotion.
   William Shakespeare 1564–1616 English dramatist: *As You Like It* (1599)

9 All professions are conspiracies against the laity.
   George Bernard Shaw 1856–1950 Irish dramatist: *The Doctor's Dilemma* (1911)

10 It is difficult to get a man to understand something when his salary depends on his not understanding it.
   Upton Sinclair 1878–1968 American novelist and social reformer: *I, Candidate for Governor* (1935)

11 The test of a vocation is the love of the drudgery it involves.
   Logan Pearsall Smith 1865–1946 American-born man of letters: *Afterthoughts* (1931) 'Art and Letters'

Cars

see also SPEED

1 A car crash harnesses elements of eroticism, aggression, desire, speed, drama, kinaesthetic factors, the stylizing of motion, consumer goods, status—all these in one event. I myself see the car crash as a tremendous sexual event really: a liberation of human and machine libido (if there is such a thing).
   J. G. Ballard 1930–2009 British writer: interview in *Penthouse* September 1970

2 I think that cars today are almost the exact equivalent of the great Gothic cathedrals: I mean the supreme creation of an era, conceived with passion by unknown artists, and consumed in image if not in usage by a whole population which appropriates them as a purely magical object.

   Roland Barthes 1915–80 French writer and critic: *Mythologies* (1957) 'La nouvelle Citroën'

3 Take it easy driving—the life you save may be mine.

   James Dean 1931–55 American actor: 29 July 1955, Val Holley *James Dean* (1995)

4 [There are] only two classes of pedestrians in these days of reckless motor traffic—the quick, and the dead.

   Lord Dewar 1864–1930 British industrialist: George Robey *Looking Back on Life* (1933)

5 The poetry of motion! The *real* way to travel! The *only* way to travel! Here today—in next week tomorrow! Villages skipped, towns and cities jumped—always somebody else's horizon! O bliss! O poop-poop! O my! O my!
on the car

   Kenneth Grahame 1859–1932 Scottish-born writer: *The Wind in the Willows* (1908)

6 The automobile changed our dress, manners, social customs, vacation habits, the shape of our cities, consumer purchasing patterns, common tastes and positions in intercourse.

   John Keats 1920– : *The Insolent Chariots* (1958)

7 To George F. Babbitt, as to most prosperous citizens of Zenith, his motor car was poetry and tragedy, love and heroism. The office was his pirate ship but the car his perilous excursion ashore.

   Sinclair Lewis 1885–1951 American novelist: *Babbitt* (1922)

8 The car has become an article of dress without which we feel uncertain, unclad and incomplete in the urban compound.

   Marshall McLuhan 1911–80 Canadian communications scholar: *Understanding Media* (1964)

9 Beneath this slab
John Brown is stowed.
He watched the ads,
And not the road.

   Ogden Nash 1902–71 American humorist: 'Lather as You Go' (1942)

10 At 60 miles an hour the loudest noise in this new Rolls-Royce comes from the electric clock.

   David Ogilvy 1911–99 British-born advertising executive: advertising slogan for the Silver Cloud, 1959

11 When a man opens the car door for his wife, it's either a new car or a new wife.

   Prince Philip, Duke of Edinburgh 1921– husband of Elizabeth II: in *Today* 2 March 1988

Cats

see also ANIMALS

1 Macavity, Macavity, there's no one like Macavity,
There never was a Cat of such deceitfulness and suavity.
He always has an alibi, and one or two to spare:
At whatever time the deed took place—MACAVITY WASN'T THERE!

   T. S. Eliot 1888–1965 Anglo-American poet, critic, and dramatist: 'Macavity: the Mystery Cat' (1939)

2 The Naming of Cats is a difficult
matter,
It isn't just one of your holiday
games;
You may think at first I'm as mad as a
hatter
when I tell you, a cat must have
THREE DIFFERENT NAMES.
T. S. Eliot 1888–1965 Anglo-American
poet, critic, and dramatist: 'The Naming
of Cats' (1939)

3 Daylong this tomcat lies stretched
flat
As an old rough mat, no mouth and
no eyes,
Continual wars and wives are what
Have tattered his ears and battered
his head.
Ted Hughes 1930–98 English poet:
'Esther's Tomcat' (1960)

4 He walked by himself, and all places
were alike to him.
Rudyard Kipling 1865–1936 English
writer and poet: *Just So Stories* (1902)
'The Cat that Walked by Himself'

5 Cats seem to go on the principle that
it never does any harm to ask for
what you want.
Joseph Wood Krutch 1893–1970
American critic and naturalist: *Twelve
Seasons* (1949)

6 If a fish is the movement of water
embodied, given shape, then cat is a
diagram and pattern of subtle air.
Doris Lessing 1919– English writer:
Particularly Cats (1967)

7 When I play with my cat, who knows
whether she isn't amusing herself
with me more than I am with her?
Montaigne 1533–92 French moralist
and essayist: *Essays* (1580)

8 The trouble with a kitten is
THAT
Eventually it becomes a

CAT.
Ogden Nash 1902–71 American
humorist: 'The Kitten' (1940)

9 The greater cats with golden eyes
Stare out between the bars.
Deserts are there, and different skies,
And night with different stars.
Vita Sackville-West 1892–1962 English
writer and gardener: *The King's
Daughter* (1929)

10 For I will consider my Cat
Jeoffrey. . . .
For he counteracts the powers of
darkness by his electrical skin and
glaring eyes.
For he counteracts the Devil, who is
death, by his brisking about the life.
Christopher Smart 1722–71 English
poet: *Jubilate Agno* (c.1758–63)

11 Cats, no less liquid than their
shadows,
Offer no angles to the wind.
They slip, diminished, neat, through
loopholes
Less than themselves.
A. S. J. Tessimond 1902–62: *Cats* (1934)

Causes and Consequences

1 Whenever anything which has
several parts is such that the whole is
something over and above its parts,
and not just the sum of them all, like
a heap, then it always has some
cause.
*probably the origin of the saying 'The
whole is more than the sum of the parts'*
Aristotle 384–322 BC Greek
philosopher: *Metaphysics*

2 The present contains nothing more
than the past, and what is found in
the effect was already in the cause.
Henri Bergson 1859–1941 French
philosopher: *L'Évolution créatrice*
(1907)

3 Whatsoever a man soweth, that shall he also reap.
  Bible: Galatians

4 One leak will sink a ship, and one sin will destroy a sinner.
  John Bunyan 1628–88 English writer and Nonconformist preacher: *The Pilgrim's Progress* (1684)

5 You have broader considerations that might follow what you might call the 'falling domino' principle. You have a row of dominoes set up. You knock over the first one, and what will happen to the last one is that it will go over very quickly. So you have the beginning of a disintegration that would have the most profound influences.
  Dwight D. Eisenhower 1890–1969 American general and Republican statesman: speech at press conference, 7 April 1954

6 Whoever wills the end, wills also (so far as reason decides his conduct) the means in his power which are indispensably necessary thereto.
  Immanuel Kant 1724–1804 German philosopher: *Fundamental Principles of the Metaphysics of Ethics* (1785)

7 As it will be in the future, it was at the birth of Man —
  There are only four things certain since Social Progress began:
  That the Dog returns to his Vomit and the Sow returns to her Mire,
  And the burnt Fool's bandaged finger goes wabbling back to the Fire;
  And that after this is accomplished, and the brave new world begins
  When all men are paid for existing and no man must pay for his sins,
  As surely as Water will wet us, as surely as Fire will burn,
  The Gods of the Copybook Headings with terror and slaughter return!
  Rudyard Kipling 1865–1936 English writer and poet: 'The Gods of the Copybook Headings' (1919)

8 The structure of a play is always the story of how the birds came home to roost.
  Arthur Miller 1915–2005 American dramatist: in *Harper's Magazine* August 1958

9 Every positive value has its price in negative terms . . . The genius of Einstein leads to Hiroshima.
  Pablo Picasso 1881–1973 Spanish painter: F. Gilot and C. Lake *Life With Picasso* (1964)

10 Sow an act, and you reap a habit. Sow a habit and you reap a character. Sow a character, and you reap a destiny.
  Charles Reade 1814–84 English novelist and dramatist: attributed

11 If you wish to make an apple pie from scratch, you must first invent the universe.
  Carl Sagan 1934–96 American scientist and writer: *Cosmos* (1980)

12 There are more consequences to a shipwreck than the underwriters notice.
  Henry David Thoreau 1817–62 American writer: *Cape Cod* (1865)

Caution

see also DANGER, RISK

1 Happy is that city which in time of peace thinks of war.
  inscription found in the armoury of Venice
  Anonymous: Robert Burton *The Anatomy of Melancholy* (1621–51)

2 And always keep a-hold of Nurse
  For fear of finding something worse.
  Hilaire Belloc 1870–1953 British poet, essayist, historian, novelist, and Liberal politician: *Cautionary Tales* (1907) 'Jim'

3 Prudence is a rich, ugly, old maid
courted by Incapacity.
    William Blake 1757–1827 English poet:
    The Marriage of Heaven and Hell
    (1790–3)

4 Beware of desperate steps. The
darkest day
(Live till tomorrow) will have passed
away.
    William Cowper 1731–1800 English
    poet: 'The Needless Alarm' (written
    c.1790)

5 I'm basically a cautious person . . . I
believe that it is better to light one
candle than promise a million light
bulbs.
    announcing his party's full platform on
    13 January 2006
    Stephen Harper 1959– Canadian
    Conservative statesman: in *New York*
    Times 24 January 2006

6 Tar-baby ain't sayin' nuthin', en Brer
Fox, he lay low.
    Joel Chandler Harris 1848–1908
    American writer: *Uncle Remus and His*
    Legends of the Old Plantation (1881)

7 Them that asks no questions isn't
told a lie.
Watch the wall, my darling, while the
Gentlemen go by!
    Rudyard Kipling 1865–1936 English
    writer and poet: 'A Smuggler's Song'
    (1906)

8 All the security around the American
president is just to make sure the
man who shoots him gets caught.
    Norman Mailer 1923–2007 American
    novelist and essayist: in *Sunday*
    Telegraph 4 March 1990

9 Of all forms of caution, caution in
love is perhaps the most fatal to true
happiness.
    Bertrand Russell 1872–1970 British
    philosopher and mathematician: *The*
    Conquest of Happiness (1930)

10 Put all your eggs in the one basket,
and—WATCH THAT BASKET.
    Mark Twain 1835–1910 American
    writer: *Pudd'nhead Wilson* (1894)

Celebrations

see also CHRISTMAS

1 Hogmanay, like all festivals, being
but a bank from which we can only
draw what we put in.
    J. M. Barrie 1860–1937 Scottish writer
    and dramatist: *Sentimental Tommy*
    (1896)

2 Hurrah for the fun!
Is the pudding done?
Hurrah for the pumpkin pie!
    Lydia Maria Child 1802–80 American
    abolitionist and suffragist:
    'Thanksgiving Day'

3 The holiest of all holidays are those
Kept by ourselves in silence and
apart;
The secret anniversaries of the heart.
    Henry Wadsworth Longfellow 1807–82
    American poet: 'Holidays' (1877)

4 Time has no divisions to mark its
passage, there is never a
thunderstorm or blare of trumpets to
announce the beginning of a new
month or year. Even when a new
century begins it is only we mortals
who ring bells and fire off pistols.
    Thomas Mann 1875–1955 German
    novelist: *The Magic Mountain* (1924)

5 Tonight's December thirty-first,
Something is about to burst . . .
Hark, it's midnight, children dear.
Duck! Here comes another year!
    Ogden Nash 1902–71 American
    humorist: 'Good Riddance. But Now
    What?' (1949)

6 Ring out the old, ring in the new,
Ring, happy bells, across the snow:
The year is going, let him go;

Ring out the false, ring in the true.
Alfred, Lord Tennyson 1809–92 English poet: *In Memoriam A. H. H.* (1850)

7 *April 1.* This is the day upon which we are reminded of what we are on the other three hundred and sixty-four.
Mark Twain 1835–1910 American writer: *Pudd'nhead Wilson* (1894) 'Pudd'nhead Wilson's Calendar'

Celibacy

1 Nobody dies from lack of sex. It's lack of love we die from.
Margaret Atwood 1939– Canadian novelist: *The Handmaid's Tale* (1986)

2 Being an old maid is like death by drowning, a really delightful sensation after you cease to struggle.
Edna Ferber 1887–1968 American writer: R. E. Drennan *Wit's End* (1973)

3 Chastity—the most unnatural of all the sexual perversions.
Aldous Huxley 1894–1963 English novelist: *Eyeless in Gaza* (1936)

4 Marriage has many pains, but celibacy has no pleasures.
Samuel Johnson 1709–84 English poet, critic, and lexicographer: *Rasselas* (1759)

Censorship

see also PORNOGRAPHY

1 So cryptic as to be almost meaningless. If there is a meaning, it is doubtless objectionable.
banning the film The Seashell and the Clergyman
Anonymous: British Board of Film Censors, 1929

2 As to the evil which results from a censorship, it is impossible to measure it, because it is impossible to tell where it ends.
Jeremy Bentham 1748–1832 English philosopher: *Theory of Legislation* (1864) 'Principles of the Penal Code'

3 Everybody favours free speech in the slack moments when no axes are being ground.
Heywood Broun 1888–1939 American journalist: in *New York World* 23 October 1926

4 The reading or non-reading a book—will never keep down a single petticoat.
Lord Byron 1788–1824 English poet: letter to Richard Hoppner, 29 October 1819

5 In a free state, tongues too should be free.
Erasmus *c.*1469–1536 Dutch Christian humanist: *The Education of a Christian Prince* (1516)

6 It's red hot, mate. I hate to think of this sort of book getting into the wrong hands. As soon as I've finished this, I shall recommend they ban it.
Ray Galton 1930– and **Alan Simpson** 1929– English scriptwriters: *The Missing Page* (1960 BBC television programme) words spoken by Tony Hancock

7 Censorship is never over for those who have experienced it.
Nadine Gordimer 1923– South African novelist and short-story writer: 'Censorship and its Aftermath', keynote address to International Writers' Day, P.E.N. International, 2 June 1990

8 Is it a book you would even wish your wife or your servants to read?
of D. H. Lawrence's Lady Chatterley's Lover
Mervyn Griffith-Jones 1909–79 British lawyer: speech for the prosecution at the Central Criminal Court, Old Bailey, 20 October 1960

9 Wherever books will be burned, men also, in the end, are burned.

Heinrich Heine 1797–1856 German poet: *Almansor* (1823)

10 The most stringent protection of free speech would not protect a man falsely shouting fire in a theatre and causing a panic . . . The question in every case is whether the words used are used in such circumstances and are of such a nature as to create a clear and present danger that they will bring about the substantive evils that Congress has a right to prevent.

sometimes quoted as, 'shouting fire in a crowded theatre'

Oliver Wendell Holmes Jr. 1841–1935 American lawyer: in *Schenck v. United States* (1919)

11 Our censor's rule condemns the doves while acquitting the ravens.

Juvenal AD *c.*60–*c.*130 Roman satirist: *Satires* no. 2 (tr. N. Rudd)

12 One has to multiply thoughts to the point where there aren't enough policemen to control them.

Stanislaw Lec 1909–66 Polish writer: *Unkempt Thoughts* (1962)

13 We have long passed the Victorian Era when asterisks were followed after a certain interval by a baby.

W. Somerset Maugham 1874–1965 English novelist: *The Constant Wife* (1926)

14 Those whom books will hurt will not be proof against events. Events, not books, should be forbid.

Herman Melville 1819–91 American novelist and poet: *The Piazza Tales* (1856) 'The Encantadas'

15 You have not converted a man, because you have silenced him.

Lord Morley 1838–1923 British Liberal politician: *On Compromise* (1874)

16 If these writings of the Greeks agree with the book of God, they are useless and need not be preserved; if they disagree, they are pernicious and ought to be destroyed.

on burning the library of Alexandria, AD *c.641*

Caliph Omar *c.*581–644 Muslim caliph: Edward Gibbon *The Decline and Fall of the Roman Empire* (1776–88)

17 Don't you see that the whole aim of Newspeak is to narrow the range of thought? In the end we shall make thoughtcrime literally impossible, because there will be no words in which to express it.

George Orwell 1903–50 English novelist: *Nineteen Eighty-Four* (1949)

18 What is freedom of expression? Without the freedom to offend, it ceases to exist.

Salman Rushdie 1947– Indian-born British novelist: in *Weekend Guardian* 10 February 1990

19 Assassination is the extreme form of censorship.

George Bernard Shaw 1856–1950 Irish dramatist: *The Showing-Up of Blanco Posnet* (1911)

20 If decade after decade the truth cannot be told, each person's mind begins to roam irretrievably. One's fellow countrymen become harder to understand than Martians.

Alexander Solzhenitsyn 1918–2008 Russian novelist: *Cancer Ward* (1968)

21 The state has no place in the nation's bedrooms.

Pierre Trudeau 1919–2000 Canadian Liberal statesman: interview, Ottawa, 22 December 1967

22 Those who want the Government to regulate matters of the mind and spirit are like men who are so afraid of being murdered that they commit suicide to avoid assassination.

Harry S. Truman 1884–1972 American Democratic statesman: address at the

National Archives, Washington, D.C., 15 December 1952

23 I disapprove of what you say, but I will defend to the death your right to say it.
his attitude towards Helvétius following the burning of the latter's De l'esprit *in 1759*
> **Voltaire** 1694–1778 French writer and philosopher: attributed to Voltaire, the words are in fact S. G. Tallentyre's summary; *The Friends of Voltaire* (1907)

24 God forbid that any book should be banned. The practice is as indefensible as infanticide.
> **Rebecca West** 1892–1983 English novelist and journalist: *The Strange Necessity* (1928)

Certainty

see also DOUBT, FANATICISM

1 My mind is not a bed to be made and re-made.
> **James Agate** 1877–1947 British drama critic and novelist: *Ego 6* (1944) 9 June 1943

2 We often call a certainty a hope, to bring it luck.
> **Elizabeth Bibesco** 1897–1945 British writer: *Haven* (1951)

3 I beseech you, in the bowels of Christ, think it possible you may be mistaken.
> **Oliver Cromwell** 1599–1658 English soldier and statesman: letter to the General Assembly of the Kirk of Scotland, 3 August 1650

4 What, never?
No, never!
What, *never?*
Hardly ever!
> **W. S. Gilbert** 1836–1911 English writer of comic and satirical verse: *HMS Pinafore* (1878)

5 I wish I was as cocksure of anything as Tom Macaulay is of everything.
> **Lord Melbourne** 1779–1848 British Whig statesman: Lord Cowper's preface to *Lord Melbourne's Papers* (1889)

6 Ah, what a dusty answer gets the soul When hot for certainties in this our life!
> **George Meredith** 1828–1909 English novelist and poet: *Modern Love* (1862)

7 The only certainty is that nothing is certain.
> **Pliny the Elder** AD 23–79 Roman statesman and scholar: *Historia Naturalis*

8 Human beings are perhaps never more frightening than when they are convinced beyond doubt that they are right.
> **Laurens van der Post** 1906–96 South African explorer and writer: *The Lost World of the Kalahari* (1958)

9 Doubt is not a pleasant condition. But certainty is an absurd one.
> **Voltaire** 1694–1778 French writer and philosopher: letter to Frederick the Great, 28 November 1770

Chance

see also LUCK

1 The chapter of knowledge is a very short, but the chapter of accidents is a very long one.
> **Lord Chesterfield** 1694–1773 English writer and politician: letter to Solomon Dayrolles, 16 February 1753

2 If an army of monkeys were strumming on typewriters they *might* write all the books in the British Museum.
> **Arthur Eddington** 1882–1944 British astrophysicist: *The Nature of the Physical World* (1928)

3 At any rate, I am convinced that *He*
[God] does not play dice.
often quoted as 'God does not play dice'
  Albert Einstein 1879–1955 German-
  born theoretical physicist: letter to Max
  Born, 4 December 1926

4 The ball no question makes of Ayes
and Noes,
But here or there as strikes the player
goes.
  Edward Fitzgerald 1809–83 English
  scholar and poet: *The Rubáiyát of Omar
  Khayyám* (4th ed., 1879)

5 Mr Bond, they have a saying in
Chicago: 'Once is happenstance.
Twice is coincidence. The third time
it's enemy action.'
  Ian Fleming 1908–64 English thriller
  writer: *Goldfinger* (1959)

6 A million million spermatozoa,
All of them alive:
Out of their cataclysm but one poor
Noah
Dare hope to survive.
And among that billion minus one
Might have chanced to be
Shakespeare, another Newton, a new
Donne—
But the One was Me.
  Aldous Huxley 1894–1963 English
  novelist: 'Fifth Philosopher's Song'
  (1920)

7 Predictability: Does the flap of a
butterfly's wings in Brazil set off a
tornado in Texas?
  Edward N. Lorenz 1917–2008 American
  meteorologist: title of paper given to the
  American Association for the
  Advancement of Science, Washington,
  29 December 1979

8 A throw of the dice will never
eliminate chance.
  Stéphane Mallarmé 1842–98 French
  poet: title of poem (1897)

9 O! many a shaft, at random sent,
Finds mark the archer little meant!

And many a word, at random
spoken,
May soothe or wound a heart that's
broken.
  Sir Walter Scott 1771–1832 Scottish
  novelist and poet: *The Lord of the Isles*
  (1813)

Change

see also PROGRESS

1 The unripe grape, the ripe, and the
dried. All things are changes, not into
nothing, but into that which is not at
present.
  Marcus Aurelius AD 121–180 Roman
  emperor: *Meditations*

2 He that will not apply new remedies
must expect new evils; for time is the
greatest innovator.
  Francis Bacon 1561–1626 English
  lawyer, courtier, philosopher, and
  essayist: *Essays* (1625) 'Of Innovations'

3 Can the Ethiopian change his skin,
or the leopard his spots?
  Bible: Jeremiah

4 'Yes,' I answered you last night;
'No,' this morning, sir, I say.
Colours seen by candle-light
Will not look the same by day.
  Elizabeth Barrett Browning 1806–61
  English poet: 'The Lady's Yes' (1844)

5 And now for something completely
different.
  Graham Chapman 1941–89 and **John
  Cleese** 1939– British comedy writers
  and actors: *Monty Python's Flying Circus*
  (BBC TV programme, 1970, with Terry
  Gilliam, Eric Idle, Terry Jones, and
  Michael Palin)

6 All conservatism is based upon the
idea that if you leave things alone
you leave them as they are. But you

do not. If you leave a thing alone you
leave it to a torrent of change.

> **G. K. Chesterton** 1874–1936 English
> essayist, novelist, and poet: *Orthodoxy*
> (1908)

7 Variety's the very spice of life,
That gives it all its flavour.

> **William Cowper** 1731–1800 English
> poet: *The Task* (1785)

8 Change is inevitable in a progressive
country. Change is constant.

> **Benjamin Disraeli** 1804–81 British Tory
> statesman and novelist: speech at
> Edinburgh, 29 October 1867

9 When it is not necessary to change, it
is necessary not to change.

> **Lucius Cary, Lord Falkland** 1610–43
> English royalist politician: speech, 1641

10 Most of the change we think we see
in life
Is due to truths being in and out of
favour.

> **Robert Frost** 1874–1963 American poet:
> 'The Black Cottage' (1914)

11 We must be the change we wish to
see in the world.

> **Mahatma Gandhi** 1869–1948 Indian
> statesman: not traced in Gandhi's
> writings, but said to be a favourite
> saying; attributed

12 Everything flows and nothing
stays . . . You can't step twice into the
same river.

> **Heraclitus** *c.*540–*c.*480 BC Greek
> philosopher: Plato *Cratylus*

13 There are three things which the
public will always clamour for,
sooner or later: namely, novelty,
novelty, novelty.

> **Thomas Hood** 1799–1845 English poet
> and humorist: *Announcement of Comic
> Annual for 1836*, in *'Quote . . . Unquote'*
> newsletter January 2001

14 There is a certain relief in change,
even though it be from bad to

worse . . . it is often a comfort to shift
one's position and be bruised in a
new place.

> **Washington Irving** 1783–1859
> American writer: *Tales of a Traveller*
> (1824)

15 Change is not made without
inconvenience, even from worse to
better.

> **Samuel Johnson** 1709–84 English poet,
> critic, and lexicographer: *A Dictionary
> of the English Language* (1755)

16 *Plus ça change, plus c'est la même
chose.*
The more things change, the more
they are the same.

> **Alphonse Karr** 1808–90 French novelist
> and journalist: *Les Guêpes* January 1849

17 There is nothing stable in the
world—uproar's your only music.

> **John Keats** 1795–1821 English poet:
> letter to George and Thomas Keats,
> 13 January 1818

18 If we want things to stay as they are,
things will have to change.

> **Giuseppe di Lampedusa** 1896–1957
> Italian writer: *The Leopard* (1957)

19 Toto, I've a feeling we're not in
Kansas any more.

> **Noel Langley** 1911–80, **Florence
> Ryerson**, and **Edgar Allan Wolfe**
> American screenwriters: *The Wizard of
> Oz* (1939 film); spoken by Judy Garland

20 Change and decay in all around I see;
O Thou, who changest not, abide
with me.

> **Henry Francis Lyte** 1793–1847 British
> hymn-writer: 'Abide with Me' (*c.*1847)

21 At last he rose, and twitched his
mantle blue:
Tomorrow to fresh woods, and
pastures new.

> **John Milton** 1608–74 English poet:
> 'Lycidas' (1638)

22 Growth [is] the only evidence of life.
*Newman's summary of a doctrine of the
biblical scholar Thomas Scott (1747–1821)*
John Henry Newman 1801–90 English
theologian and cardinal: *Apologia pro
Vita Sua* (1864)

23 God, give us the serenity to accept
what cannot be changed;
Give us the courage to change what
should be changed;
Give us the wisdom to distinguish
one from the other.
Reinhold Niebuhr 1892–1971 American
theologian: prayer said to have been
first published in 1951; Richard
Wightman Fox *Reinhold Niebuhr* (1985)

24   Forward, forward let us range,
Let the great world spin for ever
down the ringing grooves of
change.
Alfred, Lord Tennyson 1809–92 English
poet: 'Locksley Hall' (1842)

25 The old order changeth, yielding
place to new,
And God fulfils himself in many
ways,
Lest one good custom should
corrupt the world.
Alfred, Lord Tennyson 1809–92 English
poet: *Idylls of the King* 'The Passing of
Arthur' (1869)

26 If we do not find anything pleasant,
at least we shall find something new.
Voltaire 1694–1778 French writer and
philosopher: *Candide* (1759)

Chaos

1 Chaos often breeds life, when order
breeds habit.
Henry Brooks Adams 1838–1918
American man of letters: *The Education
of Henry Adams* (1907)

2 With ruin upon ruin, rout on rout,
Confusion worse confounded.
John Milton 1608–74 English poet:
Paradise Lost (1667)

3 One must have a chaos inside
oneself to give birth to a dancing
star.
Friedrich Nietzsche 1844–1900 German
philosopher and writer: *Thus Spake
Zarathustra* (1883)

4 The whole worl's in a state o' chassis!
Sean O'Casey 1880–1964 Irish
dramatist: *Juno and the Paycock* (1925)

5 Things fall apart; the centre cannot
hold;
Mere anarchy is loosed upon the
world,
The blood-dimmed tide is loosed,
and everywhere
The ceremony of innocence is
drowned.
W. B. Yeats 1865–1939 Irish poet: 'The
Second Coming' (1921)

Character

see also HUMAN NATURE

1 It is not in the still calm of life, or the
repose of a pacific station, that great
characters are formed . . . Great
necessities call out great virtues.
Abigail Adams 1744–1818 American
letter writer: letter to John Quincy
Adams, 19 January 1780

2 A thick skin is a gift from God.
Konrad Adenauer 1876–1967 German
statesman: in *New York Times*
30 December 1959

3 There exists a great chasm between
those, on one side, who relate
everything to a single central
vision . . . and, on the other side,
those who pursue many ends, often
unrelated and even
contradictory . . . The first kind of

intellectual and artistic personality belongs to the hedgehogs, the second to the foxes.

Isaiah Berlin 1909–97 British philosopher: *The Hedgehog and the Fox* (1953); see KNOWLEDGE 2

4 I am not at all the sort of person you and I took me for.

Jane Carlyle 1801–66 wife of Thomas Carlyle: letter to Thomas Carlyle, 7 May 1822

5 Qualities too elevated often unfit a man for society. We don't take ingots with us to market; we take silver or small change.

Nicolas-Sébastien Chamfort 1741–94 French writer: *Maximes et Pensées* (1796)

6 We are all worms. But I do believe that I am a glow-worm.

Winston Churchill 1874–1965 British Conservative statesman: Violet Bonham-Carter *Winston Churchill as I Knew Him* (1965)

7 Talent develops in quiet places, character in the full current of human life.

Johann Wolfgang von Goethe 1749–1832 German poet, novelist, and dramatist: *Torquato Tasso* (1790)

8 Those who stand for nothing fall for anything.

Alex Hamilton 1936– British writer and broadcaster: 'Born Old' (radio broadcast), in *Listener* 9 November 1978

9 A man's character is his fate.

Heraclitus c.540–c.480 BC Greek philosopher: *On the Universe*

10 A propensity to hope and joy is real riches: One to fear and sorrow, real poverty.

David Hume 1711–76 Scottish philosopher: *Essays Moral, Political, and Literary* (ed. T. H. Green and T. H. Grose, 1875) 'The Sceptic' (1741–2)

11 Nothing gives one person so great advantage over another, as to remain always cool and unruffled under all circumstances.

Thomas Jefferson 1743–1826 American Democratic Republican statesman: letter to Francis Wayles Eppes, 21 May 1816

12 Though I've belted you and flayed you,
By the livin' Gawd that made you,
You're a better man than I am, Gunga Din!

Rudyard Kipling 1865–1936 English writer and poet: 'Gunga Din' (1892)

13 If you can trust yourself when all men doubt you,
But make allowance for their doubting too;
If you can wait and not be tired by waiting,
Or being lied about, don't deal in lies,
Or being hated, don't give way to hating,
And yet don't look too good, nor talk too wise.

Rudyard Kipling 1865–1936 English writer and poet: 'If—' (1910)

14 Underneath this flabby exterior is an enormous lack of character.

Oscar Levant 1906–72 American pianist: *Memoirs of an Amnesiac* (1965)

15 You can tell a lot about a fellow's character by his way of eating jellybeans.

Ronald Reagan 1911–2004 American Republican statesman: in *New York Times* 15 January 1981

16   My nature is subdued
To what it works in, like the dyer's hand.

William Shakespeare 1564–1616 English dramatist: sonnet 111

17 A man of great common sense and good taste, meaning thereby a man without originality or moral courage.
George Bernard Shaw 1856–1950 Irish dramatist: *Notes to Caesar and Cleopatra* (1901) 'Julius Caesar'

18 We are what we pretend to be.
Kurt Vonnegut 1922–2007 American novelist and short-story writer: *Mother Night* (1961)

19 The two kinds of people on earth I mean
Are the people who lift, and the people who lean.
Ella Wheeler Wilcox 1855–1919 American poet: 'Which Are You?' (1904)

20 Slice him where you like, a hellhound is always a hellhound.
P. G. Wodehouse 1881–1975 English writer: *The Code of the Woosters* (1938)

21 The Child is father of the Man.
William Wordsworth 1770–1850 English poet: 'My heart leaps up when I behold' (1807)

Charity

see also GIFTS, GOODNESS

1 The living need charity more than the dead.
George Arnold 1834–65 American humorist: 'The Jolly Old Pedagogue' (1866)

2 Without trampling down twelve others
You cannot help one poor man.
Bertolt Brecht 1898–1956 German dramatist: *The Good Woman of Setzuan* (1938)

3 CHAIRMAN: What is service?
CANDIDATE: The rent we pay for our room on earth.
admission ceremony of Toc H
Tubby Clayton 1885–1972 Australian-born British clergyman: Tresham Lever *Clayton of Toc H* (1971)

4 The best form of charity I know is the art of meeting a payroll.
J. Paul Getty 1892–1976 American industrialist: Russell Miller *The House of Getty* (1985)

5 Let humble Allen, with an awkward shame,
Do good by stealth, and blush to find it fame.
Alexander Pope 1688–1744 English poet: *Imitations of Horace* (1738)

6 'Tis not enough to help the feeble up, But to support him after.
William Shakespeare 1564–1616 English dramatist: *Timon of Athens* (c.1607)

7 Thy necessity is yet greater than mine.
on giving his water-bottle to a dying soldier on the battle-field of Zutphen, 1586; commonly quoted as 'thy need is greater than mine'
Philip Sidney 1554–86 English soldier, poet, and courtier: Fulke Greville *Life of Sir Philip Sidney* (1652)

8 Oh I am a cat that likes to
Gallop about doing good.
Stevie Smith 1902–71 English poet and novelist: 'The Galloping Cat' (1972)

9 Charity begins today. Today somebody is suffering, today somebody is in the street, today somebody is hungry. Our work is for today, yesterday has gone, tomorrow has not yet come. We have only today.
Mother Teresa 1910–97 Roman Catholic nun and missionary: in *Osservatore Romano* 8 April 1991

10 No one would remember the Good Samaritan if he'd only had good intentions. He had money as well.
Margaret Thatcher 1925– British Conservative stateswoman: television interview, 6 January 1980

11 Friends, I have lost a day.
*on reflecting that he had done nothing to
help anybody all day*
> **Titus** AD 39–81 Roman emperor:
> Suetonius *Lives of the Caesars* 'Titus'

12 I have always depended on the
kindness of strangers.
> **Tennessee Williams** 1911–83 American
> dramatist: *A Streetcar Named Desire*
> (1947)

Charm

1 Charm . . . it's a sort of bloom on a
woman. If you have it, you don't
need to have anything else; and if
you don't have it, it doesn't much
matter what else you have.
> **J. M. Barrie** 1860–1937 Scottish writer
> and dramatist: *What Every Woman
> Knows* (1918)

2 You know what charm is: a way of
getting the answer yes without
having asked any clear question.
> **Albert Camus** 1913–60 French novelist,
> dramatist, and essayist: *The Fall* (1957)

3 Oozing charm from every pore,
He oiled his way around the floor.
> **Alan Jay Lerner** 1918–86 American
> songwriter: 'You Did It' (1956 song)
> from *My Fair Lady*

4 Charm is the great English blight. It
does not exist outside these damp
islands. It spots and kills anything it
touches. It kills love, it kills art.
> **Evelyn Waugh** 1903–66 English novelist:
> *Brideshead Revisited* (1945)

Chemistry

see also SCIENCE

1 Wherever we look, the work of the
chemist has raised the level of our
civilisation and has increased the
productive capacity of the nation.
> **Calvin Coolidge** 1872–1933 American

statesman: White House lawn speech to
American Chemical Society, April 1924

2 Chemistry: that most excellent child
of intellect and art
> **Cyril Hinshelwood** 1897–1967 British
> chemist: C. A. Coulson *Science and
> Christian Belief* (1956)

3 I was captured for life by chemistry
and by crystals.
> **Dorothy Hodgkin** 1910–94 British
> chemist: Georgina Ferry *Dorothy
> Hodgkin* (1998)

4 I love crystals, the beauty of their
forms and formation; liquids,
dormant, distilling, sloshing! The
fumes, the odors—good or bad, the
rainbow of colours; the gleaming
vessels of every size, shape and
purpose.
> **Robert Burns Woodward** 1917–79
> American chemist: Arthur Clay Cope
> Address, Chicago, 28 August 1973

Childhood

see also CHILDREN

1 Childhood is measured out by
sounds and smells
And sights before the dark of reason
grows.
> **John Betjeman** 1906–84 English poet:
> *Summoned by Bells* (1960)

2 Alas, regardless of their doom,
The little victims play!
No sense have they of ills to come,
Nor care beyond to-day.
> **Thomas Gray** 1716–71 English poet:
> *Ode on a Distant Prospect of Eton
> College* (1747)

3 There is always one moment in
childhood when the door opens and
lets the future in.
> **Graham Greene** 1904–91 English
> novelist: *The Power and the Glory* (1940)

4 When I look back on my childhood I
wonder how I managed to survive at

all. It was, of course, a miserable childhood: the happy childhood is hardly worth your while. Worse than the ordinary miserable childhood is the miserable Irish childhood, and worse yet is the miserable Irish Catholic childhood.

Frank McCourt 1930–2009 Irish-born American writer: *Angela's Ashes* (1996)

5 Childhood is the kingdom where nobody dies.
Nobody that matters, that is.

Edna St Vincent Millay 1892–1950 American poet: 'Childhood is the Kingdom where Nobody dies' (1934)

6 The summer that I was ten—
Can it be there was only one summer that I was ten? It must have been a long one then.

May Swenson 1919–89 American poet: 'The Centaur' (1958)

Children

see also BABIES, CHILDHOOD, FAMILY, PARENTS, SCHOOLS, YOUTH

1 Children sweeten labours, but they make misfortunes more bitter.

Francis Bacon 1561–1626 English lawyer, courtier, philosopher, and essayist: *Essays* (1625) 'Of Parents and Children'

2 Quality time? There's always another load of washing.

Julian Barnes 1946– English novelist: *Love, Etc.* (2000)

3 There is no end to the violations committed by children on children, quietly talking alone.

Elizabeth Bowen 1899–1973 Anglo-Irish novelist: *The House in Paris* (1935)

4 The place is very well and quiet and the children only scream in a low voice.

Lord Byron 1788–1824 English poet:

letter to Lady Melbourne, 21 September 1813

5 There is no such thing as other people's children.

Hillary Rodham Clinton 1947– American lawyer and Republican politician: in *Newsweek* 15 January 1996

6 We don't need any more kids—we have plenty of people on this planet.

Cameron Diaz 1972– American actress: in *Daily Mail* 11 June 2009

7 Our greatest natural resource is the minds of our children.

Walt Disney 1901–66 American animator and film producer: on wall of American Adventure, Epcot Centre, Walt Disney World

8 HOMER SIMPSON: Kids are the best, Apu. You can teach them to hate the things you hate. And they practically raise themselves, what with the internet and all.

Matt Groening 1954– American humorist and satirist: *The Simpsons* 'Eight Misbehavin'' (1999) written by Matt Selman

9 Allow them [children] to be happy their own way, for what better way will they ever find?

Samuel Johnson 1709–84 English poet, critic, and lexicographer: letter to Mrs Thrale, 4 July 1780

10 If there is anything that we wish to change in the child, we should first examine it and see whether it is not something that could better be changed in ourselves.

Carl Gustav Jung 1875–1961 Swiss psychologist: 'Vom Werden der Persönlichkeit' (1932)

11 A child is owed the greatest respect; if you ever have something disgraceful in mind, don't ignore your son's tender years.

Juvenal AD c.60–c.130 Roman satirist: *Satires*

12 Literature is mostly about having sex and not much about having children. Life is the other way round.

> **David Lodge** 1935– English novelist: *The British Museum is Falling Down* (1965)

13 With the birth of each child, you lose two novels.

> **Candia McWilliam** 1955– English novelist: in *Guardian* 5 May 1993

14 It should be noted that children at play are not playing about; their games should be seen as their most serious-minded activity.

> **Montaigne** 1533–92 French moralist and essayist: *Essays* (1580)

15 But all children matures,
Maybe even yours.

> **Ogden Nash** 1902–71 American humorist: 'Soliloquy in Circles' (1949)

16 If you have a great passion it seems that the logical thing is to see the fruit of it, and the fruit are children.

> **Roman Polanski** 1933– French film director, of Polish descent: in *Independent on Sunday* 12 May 1991

17 Behold the child, by Nature's kindly law
Pleased with a rattle, tickled with a straw.

> **Alexander Pope** 1688–1744 English poet: *An Essay on Man* Epistle 2 (1733)

18 A child is not a vase to be filled, but a fire to be lit.

> **François Rabelais** *c.*1494–*c.*1553 French humanist, satirist, and physician: attributed; see EDUCATION 17

19 Children are given us to discourage our better emotions.

> **Saki** 1870–1916 Scottish writer: *Reginald* (1904)

20 A child becomes an adult when he realizes that he has a right not only to be right but also to be wrong.

> **Thomas Szasz** 1920– Hungarian-born psychiatrist: *The Second Sin* (1973)

Choice

see also COMPROMISE, INDECISION

1 In a word, everything that we choose we choose for the sake of something else—except happiness, which is an end.

> **Aristotle** 384–322 BC Greek philosopher: *Nicomachean Ethics*

2 From this day you must be a stranger to one of your parents.—Your mother will never see you again if you do *not* marry Mr Collins, and I will never see you again if you *do*.

> **Jane Austen** 1775–1817 English novelist: *Pride and Prejudice* (1813)

3 For many are called, but few are chosen.

> **Bible**: St Matthew

4 White shall not neutralize the black, nor good
Compensate bad in man, absolve him so:
Life's business being just the terrible choice.

> **Robert Browning** 1812–89 English poet: *The Ring and the Book* (1868–9)

5 If it has to choose who is to be crucified, the crowd will always save Barabbas.

> **Jean Cocteau** 1889–1963 French dramatist and film director: *Le Rappel à l'ordre* (1926)

6 Was there ever in anyone's life span a point free in time, devoid of memory, a night when choice was any more than the sum of all the choices gone before?

> **Joan Didion** 1934– American writer: *Run River* (1963)

7 A woman can hardly ever choose . . .
she is dependent on what happens
to her. She must take meaner things,
because only meaner things are
within her reach.
   George Eliot 1819–80 English novelist:
   Felix Holt (1866)

8 Any customer can have a car painted
any colour that he wants so long as it
is black.
on the Model T Ford, 1909
   Henry Ford 1863–1947 American car
   manufacturer: *My Life and Work* (with
   Samuel Crowther, 1922)

9 Two roads diverged in a wood, and
I—
I took the one less travelled by,
And that has made all the difference.
   Robert Frost 1874–1963 American poet:
   'The Road Not Taken' (1916)

10 How happy could I be with either,
Were t'other dear charmer away!
   John Gay 1685–1732 English poet and
   dramatist: *The Beggar's Opera* (1728)

11 Many men would take the death-
sentence without a whimper to
escape the life-sentence which fate
carries in her other hand.
   T. E. Lawrence 1888–1935 English
   soldier and writer: *The Mint* (1955)

12 I'll make him an offer he can't refuse.
   Mario Puzo 1920–99 American novelist:
   The Godfather (1969)

13 To be, or not to be: that is the
question.
   William Shakespeare 1564–1616
   English dramatist: *Hamlet* (1601)

14 There is no real alternative.
popularly encapsulated in the acronym
TINA
   Margaret Thatcher 1925– British
   Conservative stateswoman: speech at
   Conservative Women's Conference,
   21 May 1980

15 Chips with everything.
   Arnold Wesker 1932– English
   dramatist: title of play (1962)

16 Between two evils, I always pick the
one I never tried before.
   Mae West 1892–1980 American film
   actress: *Klondike Annie* (1936 film)

Christianity

see also CHURCH, CLERGY, GOD, RELIGION

1 Christians have burnt each other,
   quite persuaded
That all the Apostles would have
   done as they did.
   Lord Byron 1788–1824 English poet:
   Don Juan (1819–24)

2 The Christian ideal has not been
tried and found wanting. It has been
found difficult; and left untried.
   G. K. Chesterton 1874–1936 English
   essayist, novelist, and poet: *What's
   Wrong with the World* (1910)

3 He who begins by loving Christianity
better than Truth will proceed by
loving his own sect or church better
than Christianity, and end by loving
himself better than all.
   Samuel Taylor Coleridge 1772–1834
   English poet, critic, and philosopher:
   Aids to Reflection (1825)

4 His Christianity was muscular.
   Benjamin Disraeli 1804–81 British Tory
   statesman and novelist: *Endymion*
   (1880)

5 The Christian religion not only was
at first attended with miracles, but
even at this day cannot be believed
by any reasonable person without
one.
   David Hume 1711–76 Scottish
   philosopher: *An Enquiry Concerning
   Human Understanding* (1748)

6 We are an Easter people and Alleluia is our song.

> **Pope John Paul II** 1920–2005 Polish cleric: speech in Harlem, New York, 2 October 1979

7 The chief contribution of Protestantism to human thought is its massive proof that God is a bore.

> **H. L. Mencken** 1880–1956 American journalist and literary critic: *Minority Report* (1956)

8 Perhaps it is no wonder that the women were first at the Cradle and last at the Cross. They had never known a man like this Man—there never has been such another . . . who never made arch jokes about them, never treated them either as 'The women, God help us', or 'The ladies, God bless them!'

> **Dorothy L. Sayers** 1893–1957 English writer of detective fiction: *Unpopular Opinions* (1946)

9 If you're going to do a thing, you should do it thoroughly. If you're going to be a Christian, you may as well be a Catholic.

> **Muriel Spark** 1918–2006 British novelist: in *Independent* 2 August 1989

10 Christianity is the most materialistic of all great religions.

> **William Temple** 1881–1944 English theologian: *Readings in St John's Gospel* vol. 1 (1939)

11 See how these Christians love one another.

> **Tertullian** AD *c*.160–*c*.225 Roman theologian: *Apologeticus*

12 You have no idea how much nastier I would be if I was not a Catholic. Without supernatural aid I would hardly be a human being.

> **Evelyn Waugh** 1903–66 English novelist: Noel Annan *Our Age* (1990)

13 The Gospel of Christ knows of no religion but social; no holiness but social holiness.

> **John Wesley** 1703–91 English preacher: *Hymns and Sacred Poems* (1739) preface

14 Scratch the Christian and you find the pagan—spoiled.

> **Israel Zangwill** 1864–1926 Jewish spokesman and writer: *Children of the Ghetto* (1892)

Christmas

1 I'm dreaming of a white Christmas, Just like the ones I used to know.

> **Irving Berlin** 1888–1989 American songwriter: 'White Christmas' (1942 song)

2 And girls in slacks remember Dad, And oafish louts remember Mum, And sleepless children's hearts are glad, And Christmas-morning bells say 'Come!'

> **John Betjeman** 1906–84 English poet: 'Christmas' (1954)

3 She brought forth her firstborn son, and wrapped him in swaddling clothes, and laid him in a manger; because there was no room for them in the inn.

> **Bible**: St Luke

4 Yes, Virginia, there is a Santa Claus.

> *replying to a letter from eight-year-old Virginia O'Hanlon*
> **Francis Pharcellus Church** 1839–1906 American journalist: editorial in New York *Sun*, 21 September 1897

5 Christmas is the Disneyfication of Christianity.

> **Don Cupitt** 1934– British theologian: in *Independent* 19 December 1996

6 'Bah,' said Scrooge. 'Humbug!'

> **Charles Dickens** 1812–70 English novelist: *A Christmas Carol* (1843)

7 A lovely thing about Christmas is
that it's compulsory, like a
thunderstorm, and we all go through
it together.

> **Garrison Keillor** 1942– American
> humorous writer and broadcaster:
> *Leaving Home* (1987)

8 But, oh! Father Christmas, if you love
me at all,
Bring me a big, red India-rubber ball!

> **A. A. Milne** 1882–1956 English writer for
> children: 'King John's Christmas' (1927)

9 'Twas the night before Christmas,
when all through the house
Not a creature was stirring, not even
a mouse;
The stockings were hung by the
chimney with care,
In hopes that St Nicholas soon would
be there.

> **Clement C. Moore** 1779–1863 American
> writer: 'A Visit from St Nicholas'
> (December 1823)

10 Christmas begins about the first of
December with an office party and
ends when you finally realize what
you spent, around April fifteenth of
the next year.

> **P. J. O'Rourke** 1947– American
> humorous writer: *Modern Manners*
> (1984)

11 Still xmas is a good time with all
those presents and good food and i
hope it will never die out or at any
rate not until i am grown up and hav
to pay for it all.

> **Geoffrey Willans** 1911–58 and **Ronald
> Searle** 1920– English humorous
> writers: *How To Be Topp* (1954)

12 Be nice to yu turkeys dis Christmas
Cos' turkeys just wanna hav fun.

> **Benjamin Zephaniah** 1958– British
> poet: 'Talking Turkeys!!' (1994)

The Church
see also CHRISTIANITY, CLERGY

1 It is the peculiarity of the Church of
God . . . to endure blows, not to give
them; but yet you will be pleased to
remember, that it is an anvil on
which many a hammer has been
broken.
*reply to the King of Navarre after the
massacre of the Huguenots at Vassey in
March 1562*

> **Theodore Beza** 1519–1605 French
> Calvinist theologian: G. de Félice
> *Histoire des protestants de France* (1851)

2 I see it as an elderly lady, who
mutters away to herself in a corner,
ignored most of the time.
on the Church of England

> **Archbishop George Carey** 1935–
> English cleric: in *Readers Digest* (British
> ed.) March 1991

3 He cannot have God for his father
who has not the church for his
mother.

> **St Cyprian** AD *c.*200–258 Latin Christian
> writer and martyr: *De Ecclesiae
> Catholicae Unitate*

4 I want to throw open the windows of
the Church so that we can see out
and the people can see in.

> **Pope John XXIII** 1881–1963 Italian
> cleric: attributed

5 A serious house on serious earth it is,
In whose blent air all our
compulsions meet,
Are recognised, and robed as
destinies.

> **Philip Larkin** 1922–85 English poet:
> 'Church Going' (1955)

6 The Church should go forward along
the path of progress and be no

longer satisfied only to represent the
Conservative Party at prayer.

> **Maude Royden** 1876–1956 English
> religious writer: address at Queen's Hall,
> London, 16 July 1917

7 As often as we are mown down by
you, the more we grow in numbers;
the blood of Christians is the seed.
*traditionally 'The blood of the martyrs is
the seed of the Church'*

> **Tertullian** AD c.160–c.225 Roman
> theologian: *Apologeticus*

The Cinema

see also ACTORS, FILMS

1 JOE GILLIS: You used to be in pictures.
You used to be big.
NORMA DESMOND: I am big. It's the
pictures that got small.

> **Charles Brackett** 1892–1969 and **Billy
> Wilder** 1906–2002 American
> screenwriters: *Sunset Boulevard*
> (1950 film, with D. M. Marshman Jr.)

2 There are no rules in filmmaking.
Only sins. And the cardinal sin is
dullness.

> **Frank Capra** 1897–1991 Italian-born
> American film director: in *People*
> 16 September 1991

3 If my books had been any worse, I
should not have been invited to
Hollywood, and if they had been any
better, I should not have come.

> **Raymond Chandler** 1888–1959
> American writer of detective fiction:
> letter to Charles W. Morton,
> 12 December 1945

4 Words are cheap. The biggest thing
you can say is 'elephant'.
on the universality of silent films

> **Charlie Chaplin** 1889–1977 English film
> actor and director: B. Norman *The
> Movie Greats* (1981)

5 Directing is really exciting. In the
end, it is more fun to be the painter
than the paint.

> **George Clooney** 1961– American actor
> and director: in *Independent*
> 27 December 2003

6 Never judge a book by its movie.

> **J. W. Eagan**: attributed; Michael Lent
> *Breakfast with Sharks* (2004)

7 Photography is truth. The cinema is
truth 24 times per second.

> **Jean-Luc Godard** 1930– French film
> director: *Le Petit Soldat* (1960 film)

8 *Ce n'est pas une image juste, c'est
juste une image.*
This is not a just image, it is just an
image.

> **Jean-Luc Godard** 1930– French film
> director: Colin MacCabe *Godard:
> Images, Sounds, Politics* (1980)

9 GEORGES FRANJU: Movies should have
a beginning, a middle and an end.
JEAN-LUC GODARD: Certainly. But not
necessarily in that order.

> **Jean-Luc Godard** 1930– French film
> director: in *Time* 14 September 1981

10 Nobody knows anything.
on the film industry

> **William Goldman** 1931– American
> novelist, dramatist, and screenwriter:
> *Adventures in the Screen Trade* (1984)

11 Why should people go out and pay to
see bad movies when they can stay at
home and see bad television for
nothing?

> **Sam Goldwyn** 1882–1974 American film
> producer: in *Observer* 9 September 1956

12 Pictures are for entertainment,
messages should be delivered by
Western Union.

> **Sam Goldwyn** 1882–1974 American film
> producer: Arthur Marx *Goldwyn* (1976)

13 What we need is a story that starts with an earthquake and works its way up to a climax.
> **Sam Goldwyn** 1882–1974 American film producer: attributed, perhaps apocryphal

14 If I made Cinderella, the audience would immediately be looking for a body in the coach.
> **Alfred Hitchcock** 1899–1980 British-born film director: in *Newsweek* 11 June 1956

15 The words 'Kiss Kiss Bang Bang' which I saw on an Italian movie poster, are perhaps the briefest statement imaginable of the basic appeal of movies.
> **Pauline Kael** 1919–2001 American film critic: *Kiss Kiss Bang Bang* (1968)

16 Hollywood money isn't money. It's congealed snow, melts in your hand, and there you are.
> **Dorothy Parker** 1893–1967 American critic and humorist: Malcolm Cowley *Writers at Work* 1st Series (1958)

17 There is only one thing that can kill the movies, and that is education.
> **Will Rogers** 1879–1935 American actor and humorist: *Autobiography of Will Rogers* (1949)

18 Once a month the sky falls on my head, I come to, and I see another movie I want to make.
> **Steven Spielberg** 1947– American film director and producer: in *Time* 8 June 1998

19 This is the biggest electric train a boy ever had!
> *of the RKO studios*
> **Orson Welles** 1915–85 American actor and film director: Roy Fowler *Orson Welles* (1946)

20 I wouldn't say when you've seen one Western you've seen the lot; but when you've seen the lot you get the feeling you've seen one.
> **Katharine Whitehorn** 1928– English journalist: *Sunday Best* (1976) 'Decoding the West'

Circumstance and Situation

see also FATE

1 To every thing there is a season, and a time to every purpose under the heaven:
A time to be born, and a time to die . . .
A time to weep, and a time to laugh; a time to mourn, and a time to dance.
> **Bible**: Ecclesiastes

2 But for the grace of God there goes John Bradford.
> *on seeing a group of criminals being led to their execution; usually quoted as, 'There but for the grace of God go I'*
> **John Bradford** *c.*1510–55 English Protestant martyr: in *Dictionary of National Biography* (1917–)

3 People should be taught what is, not what should be. All my humour is based on destruction and despair. If the whole world were tranquil, without disease and violence, I'd be standing in the breadline.
> **Lenny Bruce** 1925–66 American comedian: *The Essential Lenny Bruce* (1967)

4 We are so made, that we can only derive intense enjoyment from a contrast, and only very little from a state of things.
> **Sigmund Freud** 1856–1939 Austrian psychiatrist: *Civilization and its Discontents* (1930)

5 *No se puede mirar.*
One cannot look at this.
> **Goya** 1746–1828 Spanish painter: *The Disasters of War* (1863) title of etching

6 If, of all words of tongue and pen,
The saddest are, 'It might have been,'
More sad are these we daily see:
'It is, but hadn't ought to be!'
> **Bret Harte** 1836–1902 American poet: 'Mrs Judge Jenkins' (1867); see CIRCUMSTANCE 15 below

7 Isn't it pretty to think so?
> **Ernest Hemingway** 1899–1961 American novelist: *The Sun Also Rises* (1926)

8 It would not be better if things happened to men just as they wish.
> **Heraclitus** *c.*540–*c.*480 BC Greek philosopher: *On the Universe* fragment 104

9 There is a Chinese curse which says 'May he live in interesting times.' Like it or not we live in interesting times. They are times of danger and uncertainty; but they are also more open to the creative energy of men than any other time in history.
> **Robert Kennedy** 1925–68 American Democratic politician: speech, Cape Town, 6 June 1966

10 Anyone who isn't confused doesn't really understand the situation.
on the Vietnam War
> **Ed Murrow** 1908–65 American broadcaster and journalist: Walter Bryan *The Improbable Irish* (1969)

11 And, spite of Pride, in erring Reason's spite,
One truth is clear, 'Whatever IS, is RIGHT.'
> **Alexander Pope** 1688–1744 English poet: *An Essay on Man* Epistle 1 (1733)

12 These things never happened, but are always.
> **Sallustius** *fl. c.*AD 363 Roman writer: *On the Gods and the World*

13 The time is out of joint; O cursèd spite,
That ever I was born to set it right!
> **William Shakespeare** 1564–1616 English dramatist: *Hamlet* (1601)

14 We shall generally find that the triangular person has got into the square hole, the oblong into the triangular, and a square person has squeezed himself into the round hole. The officer and the office, the doer and the thing done, seldom fit so exactly that we can say they were almost made for each other.
> **Sydney Smith** 1771–1845 English clergyman and essayist: *Sketches of Moral Philosophy* (1849)

15 For of all sad words of tongue or pen,
The saddest are these: 'It might have been!'
> **John Greenleaf Whittier** 1807–92 American poet: 'Maud Muller' (1854)

Cities

see also AMERICAN CITIES, BRITISH CITIES, COUNTRY

1 Woe unto them that join house to house, that lay field to field, till there be no place.
> **Bible**: Isaiah

2 Slums may well be breeding-grounds of crime, but middle-class suburbs are incubators of apathy and delirium.
> **Cyril Connolly** 1903–74 English writer: *The Unquiet Grave* (1944)

3 God made the country, and man made the town.
> **William Cowper** 1731–1800 English poet: *The Task* (1785)

4 It is not what they built. It is what they knocked down.
It is not the houses. It is the spaces between the houses.

It is not the streets that exist. It is the streets that no longer exist.
James Fenton 1949– English poet: *German Requiem* (1981)

5 The materials of city planning are sky, space, trees, steel and cement in that order and in that hierarchy.
Le Corbusier 1887–1965 French architect: in *Times* 1965

6 A city is a place where there is no need to wait for next week to get the answer to a question, to taste the food of any country, to find new voices to listen to and familiar ones to listen to again.
Margaret Mead 1901–78 American anthropologist: *World Enough* (1975)

7 The city is not a concrete jungle, it is a human zoo.
Desmond Morris 1928– English anthropologist: *The Human Zoo* (1969)

8 The country places and the trees won't teach me anything, and the people in the city do.
Plato 429–347 BC Greek philosopher: *Phaedrus*

9 I come from suburbia . . . and I don't ever want to go back. It's the one place in the world that's further away than anywhere else.
Frederic Raphael 1931– British novelist and screenwriter: *The Glittering Prizes* (1976)

10 What is the city but the people?
William Shakespeare 1564–1616 English dramatist: *Coriolanus* (1608)

11 The modern city is a place for banking and prostitution and very little else.
Frank Lloyd Wright 1867–1959 American architect: Robert C. Twombly *Frank Lloyd Wright* (1973)

Civilization

see also CULTURE

1 You think that a wall as solid as the earth separates civilization from barbarism. I tell you the division is a thread, a sheet of glass.
John Buchan 1875–1940 Scottish novelist: *The Power House* (1916)

2 The three great elements of modern civilization, Gunpowder, Printing, and the Protestant Religion.
Thomas Carlyle 1795–1881 Scottish historian and political philosopher: *Critical and Miscellaneous Essays* (1838) 'The State of German Literature'

3 The world's civilization started from the day on which everyone received reward for labour.
Andrew Carnegie 1835–1919 American industrialist and philanthropist: *Autobiography* (1920)

4 All civilization has from time to time become a thin crust over a volcano of revolution.
Havelock Ellis 1859–1939 English sexologist: *Little Essays of Love and Virtue* (1922)

5 JOURNALIST: Mr Gandhi, what do you think of modern civilization?
GANDHI: That would be a good idea.
on arriving in England in 1930
Mahatma Gandhi 1869–1948 Indian statesman: E. F. Schumacher *Good Work* (1979)

6 If a nation expects to be ignorant and free, in a state of civilization, it expects what never was and never will be.
Thomas Jefferson 1743–1826 American Democratic Republican statesman: letter to Colonel Charles Yancey, 6 January 1816

7 If civilization had been left in female hands, we would still be living in grass huts.

> **Camille Paglia** 1947–   American writer and critic: *Sexual Personae* (1990)

8 Civilization advances by extending the number of important operations which we can perform without thinking about them.

> **Alfred North Whitehead** 1861–1947 English philosopher and mathematician: *Introduction to Mathematics* (1911)

The Civil Service

1 The Civil Service is profoundly deferential — 'Yes, Minister! No, Minister! If you wish it, Minister!'

> **Richard Crossman** 1907–74 British Labour politician: diary, 22 October 1964

2 Sack the lot!

on overmanning and overspending within government departments

> **John Arbuthnot Fisher** 1841–1920 British admiral: letter to *Times*, 2 September 1919

3 This high official, all allow, Is grossly overpaid; There wasn't any Board, and now There isn't any Trade.

> **A. P. Herbert** 1890–1971 English writer and humorist: 'The President of the Board of Trade' (1922)

4 A civil servant doesn't make jokes.

> **Eugène Ionesco** 1912–94 French dramatist: *The Killer* (1958)

5 In the case of nutrition and health, just as in the case of education, the gentleman in Whitehall really does know better what is good for people than the people know themselves.

> **Douglas Jay** 1907–96 British Labour politician: *The Socialist Case* (1939)

6 I think it will be a clash between the political will and the administrative won't.

> **Jonathan Lynn** 1943–   and **Antony Jay** 1930–   English writers: *Yes Prime Minister* (1987) vol. 2

Class

see also COMMUNISM

1 The rich man in his castle, The poor man at his gate, God made them, high or lowly, And ordered their estate.

> **Cecil Frances Alexander** 1818–95 Irish poet and hymn writer: 'All Things Bright and Beautiful' (1848)

2 *Il faut épater le bourgeois.*
One must astonish the bourgeois.

> **Charles Baudelaire** 1821–67 French poet and critic: attributed

3 Dear me, I never knew that the lower classes had such white skins.
supposedly said when watching troops bathing during the First World War

> **Lord Curzon** 1859–1925 British Conservative politician: K. Rose *Superior Person* (1969)

4 O let us love our occupations, Bless the squire and his relations, Live upon our daily rations, And always know our proper stations.

> **Charles Dickens** 1812–70 English novelist: *The Chimes* (1844) 'The Second Quarter'

5 All the world over, I will back the masses against the classes.

> **W. E. Gladstone** 1809–98 British Liberal statesman: speech in Liverpool, 28 June 1886

6 The bourgeois prefers comfort to pleasure, convenience to liberty, and a pleasant temperature to the deathly inner consuming fire.

> **Hermann Hesse** 1877–1962 German

novelist and poet: *Der Steppenwolf*
(1927)

7 How beastly the bourgeois is
Especially the male of the species.
D. H. Lawrence 1885–1930 English
novelist and poet: 'How Beastly the
Bourgeois Is' (1929)

8 The proletarians have nothing to
lose but their chains. They have a
world to win. WORKING MEN OF ALL
COUNTRIES, UNITE!
*commonly rendered as 'Workers of the
world, unite!'*
Karl Marx 1818–83 and **Friedrich
Engels** 1820–95 Co-founders of modern
Communism: *The Communist
Manifesto* (1848)

9 We of the sinking middle class . . .
may sink without further struggles
into the working class where we
belong, and probably when we get
there it will not be so dreadful as we
feared, for, after all, we have nothing
to lose but our aitches.
George Orwell 1903–50 English
novelist: *The Road to Wigan Pier* (1937)

10 You can be in the Horseguards and
still be common, dear.
Terence Rattigan 1911–77 English
dramatist: *Separate Tables* (1954)

11 Ladies were ladies in those days; they
did not do things themselves.
Gwen Raverat 1885–1957 English
wood-engraver: *Period Piece* (1952)

12 The bourgeois are other people.
Jules Renard 1864–1910 French novelist
and dramatist: diary, 28 January 1890

13 When Adam dalfe and Eve spane
Go spire if thou may spede,
Where was than the pride of man
That now merres his mede?
*traditionally taken by John Ball as the text
of his revolutionary sermon on the
outbreak of the Peasants' Revolt, 1381, in*

*the form 'When Adam delved and Eve
span, who was then the gentleman?'*
Richard Rolle de Hampole *c.*1290–1349
English mystic: G. G. Perry *Religious
Pieces* (1914)

14 Civilization has made the peasantry
its pack animal. The bourgeoisie in
the long run only changed the form
of the pack.
Leon Trotsky 1879–1940 Russian
revolutionary: *History of the Russian
Revolution* (1933)

15 Any who have heard that sound will
shrink at the recollection of it; it is
the sound of English county families
baying for broken glass.
Evelyn Waugh 1903–66 English novelist:
Decline and Fall (1928)

Clergy

see also CHRISTIANITY, CHURCH

1 Pray remember, Mr Dean, no dogma,
no Dean.
Benjamin Disraeli 1804–81 British Tory
statesman and novelist: W. Monypenny
and G. Buckle *Life of Benjamin Disraeli*
vol. 4 (1916)

2 In all ages of the world, priests have
been enemies of liberty.
David Hume 1711–70 Scottish
philosopher: 'Of the Parties of Great
Britain' (1741–2)

3 Anybody can be pope; the proof of
this is that I have become one.
Pope John XXIII 1881–1963 Italian
cleric: Henri Fesquet *Wit and Wisdom of
Good Pope John* (1964)

4 As the French say, there are three
sexes—men, women, and
clergymen.
Sydney Smith 1771–1845 English
clergyman and essayist: Lady Holland
Memoir (1855)

5 How can a bishop marry? How can
   he flirt? The most he can say is, 'I will
   see you in the vestry after service.'
   Sydney Smith 1771–1845 English
   clergyman and essayist: Lady Holland
   Memoir (1855)

6 I never saw, heard, nor read, that the
   clergy were beloved in any nation
   where Christianity was the religion
   of the country. Nothing can render
   them popular, but some degree of
   persecution.
   Jonathan Swift 1667–1745 Anglo-Irish
   poet and satirist: *Thoughts on Religion*
   (1765)

7 There is a species of person called a
   'Modern Churchman' who draws the
   full salary of a beneficed clergyman
   and need not commit himself to any
   religious belief.
   Evelyn Waugh 1903–66 English novelist:
   Decline and Fall (1928)

8 I asked why he was a priest, and he
   said if you have to work for anybody
   an absentee boss is best.
   Jeanette Winterson 1959–   English
   novelist and critic: *The Passion* (1987)

Clothes

see also FASHION

1 It is totally impossible to be well
   dressed in cheap shoes.
   Hardy Amies 1909–2003 English
   couturier: *The Englishman's Suit* (1994)

2 The trick of wearing mink is to look
   as though you were wearing a cloth
   coat. The trick of wearing a cloth
   coat is to look as though you are
   wearing mink.
   Pierre Balmain 1914–82 French
   couturier: in *Observer* 25 December
   1955

3 From the cradle to the grave,
   underwear first, last and all the time.
   Bertolt Brecht 1898–1956 German
   dramatist: *The Threepenny Opera* (1928)

4 Look for the woman in the dress. If
   there is no woman, there is no dress.
   Coco Chanel 1883–1971 French
   couturière: in *New York Times* 23 August
   1964

5 A good uniform must work its way
   with the women, sooner or later.
   Charles Dickens 1812–70 English
   novelist: *Pickwick Papers* (1837)

6 When I was young, I found out that
   the big toe always ends up making a
   hole in a sock. So I stopped wearing
   socks.
   Albert Einstein 1879–1955 German-
   born theoretical physicist: to Philippe
   Halsman; A. P. French *Einstein: A
   Centenary Volume* (1979)

7 The sense of being well-dressed
   gives a feeling of inward tranquillity
   which religion is powerless to
   bestow.
   Miss C. F. Forbes 1817–1911 English
   writer: R. W. Emerson *Letters and Social
   Aims* (1876)

8 The origins of clothing are not
   practical. They are mystical and
   erotic. The primitive man in the
   wolf-pelt was not keeping dry; he
   was saying: 'Look what I killed. Aren't
   I the best?'
   Katharine Hamnett 1947–   British
   fashion designer: in *Independent on
   Sunday* 10 March 1991

9 Dress cute wherever you go. Life is
   too short to blend in.
   Paris Hilton 1981–   American heiress:
   Confessions of an Heiress (2004)

10 You should never have your best
   trousers on when you go out to fight
   for freedom and truth.
   Henrik Ibsen 1828–1906 Norwegian

dramatist: *An Enemy of the People* (1882)

11 If people don't want to listen to *you*, what makes you think they want to hear from your sweater?
on slogans on clothing
Fran Lebowitz 1946– American writer: *Metropolitan Life* (1978)

12 A tie is a noose, and inverted though it is, it will hang a man nonetheless if he's not careful.
Yann Martel 1963– Canadian writer: *Life of Pi* (2001)

13 *on being asked what she wore in bed:*
Chanel No. 5.
Marilyn Monroe 1926–62 American actress: Pete Martin *Marilyn Monroe* (1956)

14 The clothes in themselves do not make a statement. The woman makes the statement and the dress helps.
Jean Muir 1928–95 English fashion designer: in *Vogue* August 1995

15 Where's the man could ease a heart like a satin gown?
Dorothy Parker 1893–1967 American critic and humorist: 'The Satin Dress' (1937)

16 I wish I had invented blue jeans.
Yves Saint Laurent 1936–2008 French couturier: in *Ritz* no. 85 (1984)

17 His socks compelled one's attention without losing one's respect.
Saki 1870–1916 Scottish writer: *Chronicles of Clovis* (1911)

18 Costly thy habit as thy purse can buy,
But not expressed in fancy; rich, not gaudy;
For the apparel oft proclaims the man.
William Shakespeare 1564–1616 English dramatist: *Hamlet* (1601)

19 Beware of all enterprises that require new clothes.
Henry David Thoreau 1817–62 American writer: *Walden* (1854) 'Economy'

20 Clothes don't make the man . . . but they go a long way toward making a businessman.
Thomas Watson Snr. 1874–1956 American businessman: Robert Sobel *IBM: Colossus in Transition* (1981)

21 Does my bum look big in this?
Arabella Weir British actress: title of book (1997)

22 When you're all dressed up and have no place to go.
George Whiting American songwriter: title of song (1912)

Colours

1 I cannot pretend to feel impartial about the colours. I rejoice with the brilliant ones, and am genuinely sorry for the poor browns.
Winston Churchill 1874–1965 British Conservative statesman: *Thoughts and Adventures* (1932)

2 Women today want continual change, they will have colour and plenty of it. Colour seems to radiate happiness and the spirit of modern life and movement, and I cannot put too much of it into my designs to please women.
Clarice Cliff 1899–1972 English ceramic artist: in 1930; Leonard Griffin *Clarice Cliff: the Art of the Bizarre* (1999)

3 Green how I love you green.
Green wind.
Green boughs.
The ship on the sea
and the horse on the mountain.
Federico García Lorca 1899–1936 Spanish poet and dramatist: *Romance sonámbulo* (1924–7)

4 If artists do see fields blue they are deranged and should go to an asylum. If they only pretend to see them blue, they are criminals and should go to prison.

Adolf Hitler 1889–1945 German dictator: speech in Munich, July 1937

5 Colour has taken hold of me; no longer do I have to chase after it. I know that it has hold of me for ever. That is the significance of this blessed moment.

on a visit to Tunis in 1914

Paul Klee 1879–1940 Swiss painter: Herbert Read *A Concise History of Modern Painting* (1968)

6 I own I like definite form in what my eyes are to rest upon; and if landscapes were sold, like the sheets of characters of my boyhood, one penny plain and twopence coloured, I should go the length of twopence every day of my life.

Robert Louis Stevenson 1850–94 Scottish novelist: *Travels with a Donkey* (1879)

7 If I could find anything blacker than black, I'd use it.

J. M. W. Turner 1775–1851 English landscape painter: remark, 1844

8 If there be green in paradise, it cannot but be of this shade, which most surely is the true green of hope!

Jules Verne 1828–1905 French novelist: *The Green Ray* (1882)

9 Pink is the navy blue of India.

Diana Vreeland 1903–89: attributed, 1977

10 I think it pisses God off if you walk by the colour purple in a field somewhere and don't notice it.

Alice Walker 1944– American poet: *The Colour Purple* (1982)

Comedy

see also HUMOUR

1 Comedy is tragedy that happens to *other* people.

Angela Carter 1940–92 English novelist: *Wise Children* (1991)

2 All I need to make a comedy is a park, a policeman and a pretty girl.

Charlie Chaplin 1889–1977 English film actor and director: *My Autobiography* (1964)

3 The funniest thing about comedy is that you never know why people laugh. I know *what* makes them laugh but trying to get your hands on the *why* of it is like trying to pick an eel out of a tub of water.

W. C. Fields 1880–1946 American humorist: R. J. Anobile *A Flask of Fields* (1972)

4 It is intriguing to win the prize for best comedy, as I thought I was writing a tragedy.

on winning the Evening Standard Award for her play Art

Yasmina Reza 1969– Iranian-born French dramatist: comment, 1996

Commitment

see also DETERMINATION, FAITHFULNESS

1 To say yes, you have to sweat and roll up your sleeves and plunge both hands into life up to the elbows.

Jean Anouilh 1910–87 French dramatist: *Antigone* (1942) tr. L. Galantière

2 Wherever you go, go with all your heart.

Confucius 551–479 BC Chinese philosopher: *Shu Jing*

3 Nothing great was ever achieved without enthusiasm.

> **Ralph Waldo Emerson** 1803–82 American philosopher and poet: *Essays* (1841) 'Circles'

4 My tongue swore, but my mind's unsworn.

on the breaking of an oath

> **Euripides** *c*.485–*c*.406 BC Greek dramatist: *Hippolytus*

5 With malice toward none; with charity for all; with firmness in the right, as God gives us to see the right, let us strive on to finish the work we are in.

> **Abraham Lincoln** 1809–65 American Republican statesman: Second Inaugural Address, 4 March 1865

Committees

see also ADMINISTRATION, MANAGEMENT

1 Committee—a group of men who individually can do nothing but as a group decide that nothing can be done.

> **Fred Allen** 1894–1956 American humorist: attributed

2 No academic person is ever voted into the chair until he has reached an age at which he has forgotten the meaning of the word 'irrelevant'.

> **Francis M. Cornford** 1874–1943 English academic: *Microcosmographia Academica* (1908)

3 No grand idea was ever born in a conference, but a lot of foolish ideas have died there.

> **F. Scott Fitzgerald** 1896–1940 American novelist: Edmund Wilson (ed.) *The Crack-Up* (1945) 'Note-Books E'

4 A camel is a horse designed by a committee.

> **Alec Issigonis** 1906–88 British engineer: attributed

5 Time spent on any item of the agenda will be in inverse proportion to the sum involved.

> **C. Northcote Parkinson** 1909–93 English writer: *Parkinson's Law* (1958)

6 The length of a meeting rises with the square of the number of people present.

> **Eileen Shanahan**: in *New York Times Magazine* 17 March 1968

Communism

see also CAPITALISM, CLASS, RUSSIA

1 Are you now, or have you ever been, a member of the Communist Party?

> **Anonymous**: from 1947, the question habitually put by the House Un-American Activities Committee (HUAC) to those appearing before it, now particularly associated with the McCarthy period of the 1950s

2 Capitalism, it is said, is a system wherein man exploits man. And communism—is vice versa.

quoting 'a Polish intellectual'

> **Daniel Bell** 1919– American journalist and sociologist: *The End of Ideology* (1960)

3 It is as wholly wrong to blame Marx for what was done in his name, as it is to blame Jesus for what was done in his.

> **Tony Benn** 1925– British Labour politician: Alan Freeman *The Benn Heresy* (1982)

4 Capitalism is using its money; we socialists throw it away.

> **Fidel Castro** 1927– Cuban statesman: in *Observer* 8 November 1964

5 From Stettin in the Baltic to Trieste in the Adriatic an iron curtain has descended across the Continent.
the expression 'iron curtain' previously had been applied by others to the Soviet Union or her sphere of influence
Winston Churchill 1874–1965 British Conservative statesman: speech at Westminster College, Fulton, Missouri, 5 March 1946

6 In the service of the people we followed such a policy that socialism would not lose its human face.
Alexander Dubček 1921–92 Czechoslovak statesman: in *Rudé Právo* 19 July 1968

7 The tree was already rotten. I just gave it a good shake and the rotten apples fell.
of the Soviet Union
Pope John Paul II 1920–2005 Polish cleric: Carl Bernstein and Marco Politi *His Holiness: John Paul II and the Hidden History of our Time* (1996)

8 Communism is Soviet power plus the electrification of the whole country.
Lenin 1870–1924 Russian revolutionary: Report to 8th Congress, 1920

9 All I know is that I am not a Marxist.
Karl Marx 1818–83 German political philosopher: attributed in a letter from Friedrich Engels to Conrad Schmidt, 5 August 1890

10 A spectre is haunting Europe—the spectre of Communism.
Karl Marx 1818–83 and **Friedrich Engels** 1820–95 Co-founders of modern Communism: *The Communist Manifesto* (1848)

11 Communism is like prohibition, it's a good idea but it won't work.
Will Rogers 1879–1935 American actor and humorist: in 1927; *Weekly Articles* (1981)

12 The clock of communism has stopped striking. But its concrete building has not yet come crashing down. For that reason, instead of freeing ourselves, we must try to save ourselves being crushed by the rubble.
Alexander Solzhenitsyn 1918–2008 Russian novelist: in *Komsomolskaya Pravda* 18 September 1990

13 The State is an instrument in the hands of the ruling class, used to break the resistance of the adversaries of that class.
Joseph Stalin 1879–1953 Soviet dictator: *Foundations of Leninism* (1924)

14 I have seen the future; and it works.
following a visit to the Soviet Union in 1919
Lincoln Steffens 1866–1936 American journalist: *Letters* (1938)

Compassion

see also SORROW, SUFFERING

1 Nobody can tell what I suffer! But it is always so. Those who do not complain are never pitied.
Jane Austen 1775–1817 English novelist: *Pride and Prejudice* (1813)

2 Hatred is a tonic, it makes one live, it inspires vengeance; but pity kills, it makes our weakness weaker.
Honoré de Balzac 1799–1850 French novelist: *La Peau de Chagrin* (1831)

3 Then cherish pity, lest you drive an angel from your door.
William Blake 1757–1827 English poet: 'Holy Thursday' (1789)

4 If you want others to be happy, practise compassion. If you want to be happy, practise compassion.
Dalai Lama 1935– the spiritual head of Tibetan Buddhism: attributed

5 O divine Master, grant that I may not so much seek

To be consoled as to console;
To be understood as to understand.

St Francis of Assisi 1181–1226 Italian
monk: 'Prayer of St Francis'; attributed

6 Our sympathy is cold to the relation
of distant misery.

Edward Gibbon 1737–94 English
historian: *The Decline and Fall of the
Roman Empire* (1776–88)

7 Any victim demands allegiance.

Graham Greene 1904–91 English
novelist: *The Heart of the Matter* (1948)

8 If a madman were to come into this
room with a stick in his hand, no
doubt we should pity the state of his
mind; but our primary consideration
would be to take care of ourselves.
We should knock him down first, and
pity him afterwards.

Samuel Johnson 1709–84 English poet,
critic, and lexicographer: House of
Commons, 3 April 1776

9 We are all strong enough to bear the
misfortunes of others.

Duc de la Rochefoucauld 1613–80
French moralist: *Maximes* (1678)

10 The fact that I have no remedy for
the sorrows of the world is no reason
for my accepting yours. It simply
supports the strong probability that
yours is a fake.

H. L. Mencken 1880–1956 American
journalist and literary critic: *Minority
Report* (1956)

11 Pity was always a waste of one's time.
Existence is terrible, pity won't
change that.
It's better to keep quiet, jaws
clenched.

Cesare Pavese 1908–50 Italian novelist,
poet, and critic: 'Fallen Women' (1950)
tr. Geoffrey Buck

12 Only the hopeless are starkly sincere
and . . . only the unhappy can either
give or take sympathy.

Jean Rhys c.1890–1979 British novelist

and short-story writer: *The Left Bank*
(1927)

13 But yet the pity of it, Iago! O! Iago, the
pity of it, Iago!

William Shakespeare 1564–1616
English dramatist: *Othello* (1602–4)

14 If you see anybody fallen by the
wayside and lying in the ditch, it isn't
much good climbing into the ditch
and lying by his side.

Dick Sheppard 1880–1937 British
clergyman: Carolyn Scott *Dick
Sheppard* (1977)

15 When times get rough,
And friends just can't be found
Like a bridge over troubled water
I will lay me down.

Paul Simon 1942– American singer
and songwriter: 'Bridge over Troubled
Water' (1970 song)

Compromise

see also ARGUMENT, CHOICE, TOLERANCE

1 Every human benefit, every virtue
and every prudent act, is founded on
compromise.

Edmund Burke 1729–97 Irish-born
Whig politician and man of letters: *On
Conciliation with America* (1775)

2 An agreement between two men to
do what both agree is wrong.

Lord Edward Cecil 1867–1918 British
soldier and civil servant: letter,
3 September 1911

3 He never wants anything but what's
right and fair; only when you come
to settle what's right and fair, it's
everything that he wants and
nothing that you want. And that's his
idea of a compromise. Give me the
Brown compromise when I'm on his
side.

Thomas Hughes 1822–96 English
lawyer, politician, and writer: *Tom
Brown's Schooldays* (1857)

4 If one cannot catch the bird of
paradise, better take a wet hen.
  Nikita Khrushchev 1894–1971 Soviet
  statesman: in *Time* 6 January 1958

5 A compromise in the sense that
being bitten in half by a shark is a
compromise with being swallowed
whole.
  P. J. O'Rourke 1947– American
  humorous writer: *Parliament of Whores*
  (1991)

Computers

see also INTERNET

1 To err is human but to really foul
things up requires a computer.
  Anonymous: *Farmers' Almanac for 1978*
  'Capsules of Wisdom'

2 Computers are composed of nothing
more than logic gates stretched out
to the horizon in a vast numerical
irrigation system.
  Stan Augarten: *State of the Art: A
  Photographic History of the Integrated
  Circuit* (1983)

3 A modern computer hovers between
the obsolescent and the nonexistent.
  Sydney Brenner 1927– British
  scientist: attributed in *Science* 5 January
  1990

4 Silicon Valley is the Florence of the
late 20th century.
  Francis Fukuyama 1952– American
  historian: in *Independent* 19 June 1999

5 I think computer viruses should
count as life. Maybe it says
something about human nature, that
the only form of life we have created
so far is purely destructive.
  Stephen Hawking 1942– English
  theoretical physicist: 'Life in the
  Universe', undated lecture on
  www.hawking.org (September 2008)

6 The PC is the LSD of the '90s.
  Timothy Leary 1920–96 American

psychologist: remark made in the early
1990s; in *Guardian* 1 June 1996

7 The Analytical Engine weaves
algebraic patterns just as the
Jacquard loom weaves flowers and
leaves.
  of Babbage's mechanical computer
  Ada Lovelace 1815–52 English
  mathematican: Luigi Menabrea *Sketch
  of the Analytical Engine invented by
  Charles Babbage* (1843), translated and
  annotated by Ada Lovelace, Note A

8 Computer says No.
  Matt Lucas as 'Carol'
  Matt Lucas 1974– and **David Walliams**
  1971– British comedians: catchphrase
  in *Little Britain* (BBC television
  programme 2004–)

9 You have zero privacy anyway. Get
over it.
  Scott McNealy 1954– American
  businessman: the co-founder of Sun
  Microsystems on the introduction of
  Jini networking technology; quoted in
  Wired News (online edition), 26 January
  1999

10 Like the anthropologist returning
home from a foreign culture, the
voyager in virtuality can return home
to a real world better equipped to
understand its artifices.
  Sherry Turkle 1948– American
  sociologist: *Life on the Screen: Identity
  in the Age of the Internet* (1995)

11 I think there is a world market for
maybe five computers.
  Thomas Watson Snr. 1874–1956
  American businessman: commonly
  attributed to the chairman of IBM, but
  not traced; stated by IBM to derive from
  a misunderstanding of an occasion on
  28 April 1953 when Thomas Watson Jnr.
  informed a meeting of IBM
  stockholders that 'we expected to get
  orders for five machines, we came
  home with orders for 18'

Conformity

see also INDIVIDUALITY

1 You cannot make a man by standing a sheep on its hind-legs. But by standing a flock of sheep in that position you can make a crowd of men.

> **Max Beerbohm** 1872–1956 English critic, essayist, and caricaturist: *Zuleika Dobson* (1911)

2 'It's always best on these occasions to do what the mob do.' 'But suppose there are two mobs?' suggested Mr Snodgrass. 'Shout with the largest,' replied Mr Pickwick.

> **Charles Dickens** 1812–70 English novelist: *Pickwick Papers* (1837)

3 The Party line is that there is no Party line.

> **Milovan Djilas** 1911– Yugoslav politician and writer: comment on reforms of the Yugoslavian Communist Party, November 1952; Fitzroy Maclean *Disputed Barricade* (1957)

4 Whoso would be a man must be a nonconformist.

> **Ralph Waldo Emerson** 1803–82 American philosopher and poet: *Essays* (1841) 'Self-Reliance'

5 Imitation lies at the root of most human actions. A respectable person is one who conforms to custom. People are called good when they do as others do.

> **Anatole France** 1844–1924 French novelist and man of letters: *Crainquebille* (1923)

6 These are the days when men of all social disciplines and all political faiths seek the comfortable and the accepted; when the man of controversy is looked upon as a disturbing influence; when originality is taken to be a mark of instability; and when, in minor

modification of the scriptural parable, the bland lead the bland.

> **J. K. Galbraith** 1908–2006 American economist: *The Affluent Society* (1958)

7 Never forget that only dead fish swim with the stream.

> **Malcolm Muggeridge** 1903–90 British journalist: quoting a supporter; in *Radio Times* 9 July 1964

8 Her exotic daydreams do not prevent her from being small-town bourgeois at heart, clinging to conventional ideas or committing this or that conventional violation of the conventional, adultery being a most conventional way to rise above the conventional.

> **Vladimir Nabokov** 1899–1977 Russian novelist: *Lectures on Literature* (1980) 'Madame Bovary'

9 While we were talking came by several poor creatures carried by, by constables, for being at a conventicle . . . I would to God they would either conform, or be more wise, and not be catched!

> **Samuel Pepys** 1633–1703 English diarist: diary 7 August 1664

10 The Normal is the good smile in a child's eyes—all right. It is also the dead stare in a million adults. It both sustains and kills—like a God. It is the Ordinary made beautiful; it is also the Average made lethal.

> **Peter Shaffer** 1926– English dramatist: *Equus* (1983 ed.)

11 Teach him to think for himself? Oh, my God, teach him rather to think like other people!
on her son's education

> **Mary Shelley** 1797–1851 English novelist: Matthew Arnold *Essays in Criticism* Second Series (1888) 'Shelley'

12 If a man does not keep pace with his companions, perhaps it is because he hears a different drummer. Let him step to the music which he hears, however measured or far away.

Henry David Thoreau 1817–62 American writer: *Walden* (1854)

Conscience

see also FORGIVENESS, SIN

1 Conscience is thoroughly well-bred and soon leaves off talking to those who do not wish to hear it.

Samuel Butler 1835–1902 English novelist: *Further Extracts from Notebooks* (1934)

2 In many walks of life, a conscience is a more expensive encumbrance than a wife or a carriage.

Thomas De Quincey 1785–1859 English essayist and critic: *Confessions of an English Opium-Eater* (1822)

3 A good conscience is a continual Christmas.

Benjamin Franklin 1706–90 American politician, inventor, and scientist: *Poor Richard's Almanac* (1733)

4 I cannot and will not cut my conscience to fit this year's fashions.

Lillian Hellman 1905–84 American dramatist: letter to John S. Wood, 19 May 1952

5 A man's conscience and his judgement is the same thing; and as the judgement, so also the conscience, may be erroneous.

Thomas Hobbes 1588–1679 English philosopher: *Leviathan* (1651)

6 Sufficient conscience to bother him, but not sufficient to keep him straight.

of Ramsay MacDonald

David Lloyd George 1863–1945 British Liberal statesman: A. J. Sylvester *Life with Lloyd George* (1975)

7 Conscience: the inner voice which warns us that someone may be looking.

H. L. Mencken 1880–1956 American journalist and literary critic: *A Little Book in C major* (1916)

8 If I am obliged to bring religion into after-dinner toasts (which indeed does not seem quite the thing) I shall drink—to the Pope, if you please—still, to Conscience first, and to the Pope afterwards.

John Henry Newman 1801–90 English theologian and cardinal: *A Letter Addressed to the Duke of Norfolk . . .* (1875)

9 Thus conscience doth make cowards of us all.

William Shakespeare 1564–1616 English dramatist: *Hamlet* (1601)

10 Most people sell their souls, and live with a good conscience on the proceeds.

Logan Pearsall Smith 1865–1946 American-born man of letters: *Afterthoughts* (1931)

Consequences

see CAUSES AND CONSEQUENCES

Consistency

1 A foolish consistency is the hobgoblin of little minds, adored by little statesmen and philosophers and divines. With consistency a great soul has simply nothing to do.

Ralph Waldo Emerson 1803–82 American philosopher and poet: *Essays* (1841) 'Self-Reliance'

2 Consistency is contrary to nature, contrary to life. The only completely consistent people are the dead.

Aldous Huxley 1894–1963 English novelist: *Do What You Will* (1929)

3 Do I contradict myself?
Very well then I contradict myself,
(I am large, I contain multitudes.)
  Walt Whitman 1819–92 American poet:
  'Song of Myself' (written 1855)

Consumer Society

see also BUSINESS, POSSESSIONS, SHOPPING

1 Consumer wants can have bizarre,
frivolous, or even immoral origins,
and an admirable case can still be
made for a society that seeks to
satisfy them. But the case cannot
stand if it is the process of satisfying
wants that creates the wants.
  J. K. Galbraith 1908–2006 American
  economist: *The Affluent Society* (1958)

2 In a consumer society there are
inevitably two kinds of slaves: the
prisoners of addiction and the
prisoners of envy.
  Ivan Illich 1926–2002 American
  sociologist: *Tools for Conviviality* (1973)

3 The consumer, so it is said, is the
king . . . each is a voter who uses his
money as votes to get the things
done that he wants done.
  Paul A. Samuelson 1915– American
  economist: *Economics* (8th ed., 1970)

Conversation

see also GOSSIP, SPEECH

1 On every formal visit a child ought to
be of the party, by way of provision
for discourse.
  Jane Austen 1775–1817 English novelist:
  Sense and Sensibility (1811)

2 JOHNSON: Well, we had a good talk.
BOSWELL: Yes, Sir; you tossed and
gored several persons.
  James Boswell 1740–95 Scottish lawyer
  and biographer: *Life of Samuel Johnson*
  (1791) Summer 1768

3 Although there exist many thousand
subjects for elegant conversation,
there are persons who cannot meet a
cripple without talking about feet.
  Ernest Bramah 1868–1942 English
  writer: *The Wallet of Kai Lung* (1900)

4 'The time has come,' the Walrus said,
'To talk of many things:
Of shoes—and ships—and sealing
wax—
Of cabbages—and kings—
And why the sea is boiling hot—
And whether pigs have wings.'
  Lewis Carroll 1832–98 English writer
  and logician: *Through the Looking-
  Glass* (1872)

5 Religion is by no means a proper
subject of conversation in a mixed
company.
  Lord Chesterfield 1694–1773 English
  writer and politician: *Letters . . . to his
  Godson and Successor* (1890)

6 Too much agreement kills a chat.
  Eldridge Cleaver 1935–98 American
  political activist: *Soul on Ice* (1968)
  'Letters from Prison'

7 Two may talk and one may hear, but
three cannot take part in a
conversation of the most sincere and
searching sort.
  Ralph Waldo Emerson 1803–82
  American philosopher and poet: *Essays*
  (1841) 'Friendship'

8 How time flies when you're doin' all
the talking.
  Harvey Fierstein 1954– American
  dramatist and actor: *Torch Song Trilogy*
  (1979)

9 Someone to tell it to is one of the
fundamental needs of human
beings.
  Miles Franklin 1879–1954 Australian
  writer: *Childhood at Brindabella* (1963)

10 It is the province of knowledge to speak and it is the privilege of wisdom to listen.
   Oliver Wendell Holmes 1809–94 American physician, poet, and essayist: *The Poet at the Breakfast-Table* (1872)

11 And, when you stick on conversation's burrs,
   Don't strew your pathway with those dreadful *urs*.
   Oliver Wendell Holmes 1809–94 American physician, poet, and essayist: 'A Rhymed Lesson' (1848)

12 If you are ever at a loss to support a flagging conversation, introduce the subject of eating.
   Leigh Hunt 1784–1859 English poet and essayist: attributed

13 Questioning is not the mode of conversation among gentlemen. It is assuming a superiority.
   Samuel Johnson 1709–84 English poet, critic, and lexicographer: James Boswell *Life of Samuel Johnson* (1791) 25 March 1776

14 Must I always be a mere listener?
   Juvenal AD *c*.60–*c*.130 Roman satirist: *Satires* no. 1

15 The opposite of talking isn't listening. The opposite of talking is waiting.
   Fran Lebowitz 1946– American writer: *Social Studies* (1981)

16 With thee conversing I forget all time.
   John Milton 1608–74 English poet: *Paradise Lost* (1667)

17 For what should a man live, if not for the pleasures of discourse?
   Plato 429–347 BC Greek philosopher: *Phaedrus*

18 The feast of reason and the flow of soul.
   Alexander Pope 1688–1744 English poet: *Imitations of Horace*

19 He never knew what to say. If life was a party, he wasn't even in the kitchen.
   Terry Pratchett 1948– English science fiction writer: *Thief of Time* (2001)

20 I am not bound to please thee with my answer.
   William Shakespeare 1564–1616 English dramatist: *The Merchant of Venice* (1596–8)

21 There is no such thing as conversation. It is an illusion. There are intersecting monologues, that is all.
   Rebecca West 1892–1983 English novelist and journalist: *There is No Conversation* (1935)

Cooking

see also EATING, FOOD

1 Anyone who tells a lie has not a pure heart, and cannot make a good soup.
   Ludwig van Beethoven 1770–1827 German composer: Ludwig Nohl *Beethoven Depicted by his Contemporaries* (1880)

2 Be content to remember that those who can make omelettes properly can do nothing else.
   Hilaire Belloc 1870–1953 British poet, essayist, historian, novelist, and Liberal politician: *A Conversation with a Cat* (1931)

3 Cooking is the most ancient of the arts, for Adam was born hungry.
   Anthelme Brillat-Savarin 1755–1826 French jurist and gourmet: *Physiologie du Goût* (1825)

4 Good food is always a trouble and its preparation should be regarded as a labour of love.
   Elizabeth David 1913–92 British cook and writer: *French Country Cooking* (1951) introduction

5 Hot on Sunday,
   Cold on Monday,

Hashed on Tuesday,
Minced on Wednesday,
Curried Thursday,
Broth on Friday,
Cottage pie Saturday.
> **Dorothy Hartley** 1893–1985 English writer: *Food in England* (1954) 'Vicarage Mutton'

6 Home-made dishes that drive one from home.
> **Thomas Hood** 1799–1845 English poet and humorist: *Miss Kilmansegg and her Precious Leg* (1841–3)

7 Kissing don't last: cookery do!
> **George Meredith** 1828–1909 English novelist and poet: *The Ordeal of Richard Feverel* (1859)

8 On the Continent people have good food; in England people have good table manners.
> **George Mikes** 1912–87 Hungarian-born writer: *How to be an Alien* (1946)

9 I never see any home cooking. All I get is fancy stuff.
> **Prince Philip, Duke of Edinburgh** 1921– husband of Elizabeth II: in *Observer* 28 October 1962

10 The cook was a good cook, as cooks go; and as cooks go, she went.
> **Saki** 1870–1916 Scottish writer: *Reginald* (1904)

11 You won't be surprised that diseases are innumerable—count the cooks.
> **Seneca ('the Younger')** *c.*4 BC–AD 65 Roman philosopher and poet: *Epistles*

12 I want to focus on my salad.
> *when questioned about insider trading during her cookery spot*
> **Martha Stewart** 1941– American businesswoman: on CBS *The Early Show* 25 June 2002

13 I discovered that dinners follow the order of creation — fish first, then

entrées, then joints, lastly the apple as dessert. The soup is chaos.
> **Sylvia Townsend Warner** 1893–1978 English writer: diary, 26 May 1929

Cooperation

1 The lion and the calf shall lie down together but the calf won't get much sleep.
> **Woody Allen** 1935– American film director, writer, and actor: in *New Republic* 31 August 1974

2 If a house be divided against itself, that house cannot stand.
> **Bible**: St Mark

3 Bear ye one another's burdens.
> **Bible**: Galatians

4 When bad men combine, the good must associate; else they will fall, one by one, an unpitied sacrifice in a contemptible struggle.
> **Edmund Burke** 1729–97 Irish-born Whig politician and man of letters: *Thoughts on the Cause of the Present Discontents* (1770); see EVIL 3

5 Then join hand in hand, brave Americans all,—
By uniting we stand, by dividing we fall.
> **John Dickinson** 1732–1808 American politician: 'The Liberty Song' (1768)

6 All for one, one for all.
> *motto of the Three Musketeers*
> **Alexandre Dumas** 1802–70 French novelist and dramatist: *The Three Musketeers* (1844)

7 We must indeed all hang together, or, most assuredly, we shall all hang separately.
> **Benjamin Franklin** 1706–90 American politician, inventor, and scientist: at the signing of the Declaration of Independence, 4 July 1776; possibly not original

8 If someone claps his hand a sound
arises. Listen to the sound of the
single hand!

> **Hakuin** 1686–1769 Japanese monk,
> writer and artist: attributed

9 We must learn to live together as
brothers or perish together as fools.

> **Martin Luther King** 1929–68 American
> civil rights leader: speech at St Louis,
> 22 March 1964

10 Why don't you do something to *help*
me?

> **Stan Laurel** 1890–1965 American film
> comedian, born in Britain: *Drivers'
> Licence Sketch* (1947 film); words
> spoken by Oliver Hardy

11 In a place where 'please' is
pronounced 'I s'pose you couldn't'
it is rare to meet with any belief in
help.

> **Les A. Murray** 1938– Australian poet:
> *The Boys Who Stole the Funeral* (1989)

12 You may call it combination, you
may call it the accidental and
fortuitous concurrence of atoms.

> *on a projected Palmerston–Disraeli
> coalition*
> **Lord Palmerston** 1784–1865 British
> statesman: speech, House of Commons,
> 5 March 1857

13 Government and co-operation are in
all things the laws of life; anarchy
and competition the laws of death.

> **John Ruskin** 1819–1900 English art and
> social critic: *Unto this Last* (1862)

14 To my daughter Leonora without
whose never-failing sympathy and
encouragement this book would
have been finished in half the time.

> **P. G. Wodehouse** 1881–1975 English
> writer: *The Heart of a Goof* (1926)
> dedication

Corruption

1 When their lordships asked Bacon
How many bribes he had taken
He had at least the grace
To get very red in the face.

> **Edmund Clerihew Bentley** 1875–1956
> English writer: 'Bacon' (1939)

2 I stuffed their mouths with gold.

> *on his handling of the consultants during
> the establishment of the National Health
> Service*
> **Aneurin Bevan** 1897–1960 British
> Labour politician: Brian Abel-Smith *The
> Hospitals 1800–1948* (1964)

3 Nothing to be done without a bribe I
find, in love as well as law.

> **Susannah Centlivre** c.1669–1723
> English actress and dramatist: *The
> Perjured Husband* (1700)

4 Follow the money.

> **William Goldman** 1931– American
> novelist, dramatist, and screenwriter:
> *All the President's Men* (1976 film);
> spoken by Hal Holbrook as Deep Throat
> to Bob Woodward

5 Men are more often bribed by their
loyalties and ambitions than money.

> **Robert H. Jackson** 1892–1954 American
> lawyer and judge: dissenting opinion in
> *United States v. Wunderlich* 1951

6 . . . *Omnia Romae
Cum pretio.*
Everything in Rome—at a price.

> **Juvenal** AD c.60–c.130 Roman satirist:
> *Satires*

7 To accept a favour is to sell your
freedom.

> **Publilius Syrus** Roman freedman and
> writer of mimes of the 1st century BC:
> *Sententiae*

8 I am not worth purchasing, but such
as I am, the King of Great Britain is
not rich enough to do it.

> *replying to an offer from Governor George*

Johnstone of £10,000, and any office in the
Colonies in the King's gift, if he were able
successfully to promote a Union between
Britain and America
Joseph Reed 1741–85 American
Revolutionary politician: W. B. Read *Life
and Correspondence of Joseph Reed*
(1847)

9 I note with considerable satisfaction
that I am whiter than white.
*of the inquiry into fraud at the European
Commission*
Jacques Santer 1937– Luxembourgeois
politician: at a news conference,
16 March 1999

10 But the jingling of the guinea helps
the hurt that Honour feels.
Alfred, Lord Tennyson 1809–92 English
poet: 'Locksley Hall' (1842)

11 All those men have their price.
of fellow parliamentarians
Robert Walpole 1676–1745 English
Whig statesman: W. Coxe *Memoirs of Sir
Robert Walpole* (1798)

12 The flood of money that gushes into
politics today is a pollution of
democracy.
Theodore H. White 1915–86 American
writer and journalist: in *Time*
19 November 1984

Cosmetics

1 Women have been trained to speak
softly and carry lipstick. Those days
are over.
Bella Abzug 1920–98 American
politician: attributed; in *Times* 2 April
1998

2 Most women are not so young as
they are painted.
Max Beerbohm 1872–1956 English
critic, essayist, and caricaturist: *The
Yellow Book* (1894)

3 A girl whose cheeks are covered with
paint

Has an advantage with me over one
whose ain't.
Ogden Nash 1902–71 American
humorist: 'Biological Reflection' (1931)

4 What's the difference between a
hockey mom and a pitbull? Lipstick.
Sarah Palin 1964– American
Republican politician: speech to
Republican Party convention,
3 September 2008

5 In the factory we make cosmetics; in
the store we sell hope.
Charles Revson 1906–75 American
businessman: A. Tobias *Fire and Ice*
(1976)

6 Anything which says it can magically
take away your wrinkles is a
scandalous lie.
Anita Roddick 1942–2007 English
businesswoman: in *Daily Telegraph*
19 October 2000

7 There are no ugly women, only lazy
ones.
Helena Rubinstein 1882–1965
American beautician: *My Life for Beauty*
(1966)

Counselling

see also ADVICE, MIND

1 Therapy has become what I think of
as the tenth American muse.
Jacob Bronowski 1908–74 Polish-born
mathematician and humanist:
attributed

2 Before I went into analysis I told
everyone lies—but when you spend
all that money, you tell the truth.
Jane Fonda 1937– American actress:
Thomas Kiernan *Jane: An Intimate
Biography of Jane Fonda* (1973)

3 Why waste money on psychotherapy when you can listen to the B Minor Mass?

Michael Torke 1961– American composer: in *Observer* 23 September 1990

The Country

see also CITIES, FARMING

1 'Tis distance lends enchantment to the view,
And robes the mountain in its azure hue.

Thomas Campbell 1777–1844 Scottish poet: *Pleasures of Hope* (1799)

2 It is my belief, Watson, founded upon my experience, that the lowest and vilest alleys in London do not present a more dreadful record of sin than does the smiling and beautiful countryside.

Arthur Conan Doyle 1859–1930 Scottish-born writer of detective fiction: *The Adventures of Sherlock Holmes* (1892) 'The Copper Beeches'

3 Green belts should be the start of the countryside, not a ditch between Subtopias.

Hugh Gaitskell 1906–63 British Labour politician: in *Observer* 1 January 1961

4 There is nothing good to be had in the country, or if there is, they will not let you have it.

William Hazlitt 1778–1830 English essayist: *The Round Table* (1817)

5 It will be said of this generation that it found England a land of beauty and left it a land of 'beauty spots'.

C. E. M. Joad 1891–1953 English philosopher: *The Horrors of the Countryside* (1931)

6 So *that's* what hay looks like.
said at Badminton House, where she was evacuated during the Second World War
Queen Mary 1867–1953 British Queen Consort: James Pope-Hennessy *Life of Queen Mary* (1959)

7 Oh, give me land, lots of land under starry skies above,
Don't fence me in.
Let me ride through the wide open country that I love,
Don't fence me in.

Cole Porter 1891–1964 American songwriter: 'Don't Fence Me In' (1944 song)

8 I have no relish for the country; it is a kind of healthy grave.

Sydney Smith 1771–1845 English clergyman and essayist: letter to Miss G. Harcourt, 1838

9 Anybody can be good in the country.

Oscar Wilde 1854–1900 Anglo-Irish dramatist and poet: *The Picture of Dorian Gray* (1891)

Courage

see also COWARDICE, FEAR

1 Courage is the thing. All goes if courage goes!

J. M. Barrie 1860–1937 Scottish writer and dramatist: Rectorial Address at St Andrews, 3 May 1922

2 No coward soul is mine,
No trembler in the world's storm-troubled sphere:
I see Heaven's glories shine,
And faith shines equal, arming me from fear.

Emily Brontë 1818–48 English novelist and poet: 'No coward soul is mine' (1846)

3 Courage is rightly esteemed the first of human qualities because as has been said, it is the quality which guarantees all others.

Winston Churchill 1874–1965 British Conservative statesman: *Great Contemporaries* (1937)

4 Boldness, and again boldness, and
always boldness!
Georges Jacques Danton 1759–94
French revolutionary: speech to the
Legislative Committee of General
Defence, 2 September 1792

5 None but the brave deserves the fair.
John Dryden 1631–1700 English poet,
critic, and dramatist: *Alexander's Feast*
(1697)

6 Courage is the price that Life exacts
for granting peace.
Amelia Earhart 1898–1937 American
aviator: 'Courage' (1927)

7 Grace under pressure.
*when asked what he meant by 'guts', in an
interview with Dorothy Parker*
Ernest Hemingway 1899–1961
American novelist: in *New Yorker*
30 November 1929

8 In the fell clutch of circumstance,
I have not winced nor cried aloud:
Under the bludgeonings of chance
My head is bloody, but unbowed.
W. E. Henley 1849–1903 English poet
and dramatist: 'Invictus. In Memoriam
R.T.H.B.' (1888)

9 Tender-handed stroke a nettle,
And it stings you for your pains;
Grasp it like a man of mettle,
And it soft as silk remains.
Aaron Hill 1685–1750 English poet and
dramatist: 'Verses Written on a Window
in Scotland'

10 Courage is not simply *one* of the
virtues but the form of every virtue at
the testing point.
C. S. Lewis 1898–1963 English literary
scholar: Cyril Connolly *The Unquiet
Grave* (1944)

11 As to moral courage, I have very
rarely met with two o'clock in the
morning courage: I mean
instantaneous courage.
Napoleon I 1769–1821 French emperor:
E. A. de Las Cases *Mémorial de Ste-
Hélène* (1823) 4–5 December 1815

12 Courage is the knowledge of what is
and is not to be feared.
literally 'what is to be dreaded or dared'
Nicias *c.*470–413 BC Greek politician
and Athenian general: Plato *Laches*

13 Had we lived, I should have had a
tale to tell of the hardihood,
endurance, and courage of my
companions which would have
stirred the heart of every
Englishman. These rough notes and
our dead bodies must tell the tale.
Robert Falcon Scott 1868–1912 English
polar explorer: 'Message to the Public'
in late editions of *Times* 11 February
1913

14 Boldness be my friend!
Arm me, audacity.
William Shakespeare 1564–1616
English dramatist: *Cymbeline* (1609–10)

15 My valour is certainly going!—it is
sneaking off!—I feel it oozing out as
it were at the palms of my hands!
Richard Brinsley Sheridan 1751–1816
Anglo-Irish dramatist: *The Rivals* (1775)

16 Perhaps those, who, trembling most,
maintain a dignity in their fate, are
the bravest: resolution on reflection
is real courage.
Horace Walpole 1717–97 English writer
and connoisseur: *Memoirs of the Reign
of King George II* (1757)

Courtship

see also LOVE, LOVERS

1 A man chases a girl (until she catches
him).
Irving Berlin 1888–1989 American
songwriter: title of song (1949)

2 Courtship to marriage, as a very
witty prologue to a very dull play.
William Congreve 1670–1729 English
dramatist: *The Old Bachelor* (1693)

3 Everyone knows that dating in your thirties is not the happy-go-lucky free-for-all it was when you were twenty-two.

> **Helen Fielding** 1958– British writer: *Bridget Jones's Diary* (1996)

4 Holding hands at midnight
'Neath a starry sky,
Nice work if you can get it,
And you can get it if you try.

> **Ira Gershwin** 1896–1983 American songwriter: 'Nice Work If You Can Get It' (1937 song)

5 Had we but world enough, and time,
This coyness, lady, were no crime.

> **Andrew Marvell** 1621–78 English poet: 'To His coy Mistress' (1681)

6 Wooing, so tiring.

> **Nancy Mitford** 1904–73 English writer: *The Pursuit of Love* (1945)

7 I court others in verse: but I love thee in prose:
And they have my whimsies, but thou hast my heart.

> **Matthew Prior** 1664–1721 English poet: 'A Better Answer' (1718)

8 She is a woman, therefore may be wooed;
She is a woman, therefore may be won.

> **William Shakespeare** 1564–1616 English dramatist: *Titus Andronicus* (1590)

9 You think that you are Ann's suitor; that you are the pursuer and she the pursued . . . Fool: it is you who are the pursued, the marked down quarry, the destined prey.

> **George Bernard Shaw** 1856–1950 Irish dramatist: *Man and Superman* (1903)

10 She knew how to allure by denying, and to make the gift rich by delaying it.

> **Anthony Trollope** 1815–82 English novelist: *Phineas Finn* (1869)

11 We've got to have
We plot to have
For it's so dreary not to have
That certain thing called the Boy Friend.

> **Sandy Wilson** 1924– English songwriter: 'The Boyfriend' (1954 song)

Cowardice

see also COURAGE, FEAR

1 Cowardice, as distinguished from panic, is almost always simply a lack of ability to suspend the functioning of the imagination.

> **Ernest Hemingway** 1899–1961 American novelist: *Men at War* (1942)

2 It is thus that mutual cowardice keeps us in peace. Were one half of mankind brave and one half cowards, the brave would be always beating the cowards. Were all brave, they would lead a very uneasy life; all would be continually fighting: but being all cowards, we go on very well.

> **Samuel Johnson** 1709–84 English poet, critic, and lexicographer: James Boswell *Life of Samuel Johnson* (1791) 28 April 1778

3 For all men would be cowards if they durst.

> **Lord Rochester** 1647–80 English poet: 'A Satire against Mankind' (1679)

4 Cowards die many times before their deaths;
The valiant never taste of death but once.

> **William Shakespeare** 1564–1616 English dramatist: *Julius Caesar* (1599)

5 As an old soldier I admit the cowardice: it's as universal as sea sickness, and matters just as little.

> **George Bernard Shaw** 1856–1950 Irish dramatist: *Man and Superman* (1903)

Creativity

1 The urge for destruction is also a creative urge!

> **Michael Bakunin** 1814–76 Russian revolutionary and anarchist: *Jahrbuch für Wissenschaft und Kunst* (1842) 'Die Reaktion in Deutschland' (under the pseudonym 'Jules Elysard')

2 The more you reason, the less you create

> **Raymond Chandler** 1888–1959 American writer of detective fiction: letter, 28 October 1947

3 If the devil doesn't exist, but man has created him, he has created him in his own image and likeness.

> **Fedor Dostoevsky** 1821–81 Russian novelist: *The Brothers Karamazov* (1879–80)

4 Think before you speak is criticism's motto; speak before you think creation's.

> **E. M. Forster** 1879–1970 English novelist: *Two Cheers for Democracy* (1951)

5 Like a piece of ice on a hot stove the poem must ride on its own melting. A poem may be worked over once it is in being, but may not be worried into being.

> **Robert Frost** 1874–1963 American poet: *Collected Poems* (1939) 'The Figure a Poem Makes'

6 Birds build—but not I build; no, but strain,
Time's eunuch, and not breed one work that wakes.

> **Gerard Manley Hopkins** 1844–89 English poet and priest: 'Thou art indeed just, Lord' (written 1889)

7 That which is creative must create itself.

> **John Keats** 1795–1821 English poet: letter to Hessey, 8 October 1818

8 Poems are made by fools like me,
But only God can make a tree.

> **Joyce Kilmer** 1886–1918 American poet: 'Trees' (1914)

9 Nothing can be created out of nothing.

> **Lucretius** *c.*94–55 BC Roman poet: *De Rerum Natura*

10 An artist has no need to express his thought directly in his work for the latter to reflect its quality; it has even been said that the highest praise of God consists in the denial of Him by the atheist who finds creation so perfect that it can dispense with a creator.

> **Marcel Proust** 1871–1922 French novelist: *Guermantes Way* (1921)

11 Why does my Muse only speak when she is unhappy?
She does not, I only listen when I am unhappy
When I am happy I live and despise writing
For my Muse this cannot but be dispiriting.

> **Stevie Smith** 1902–71 English poet and novelist: 'My Muse' (1964)

12 Our current obsession with creativity is the result of our continued striving for immortality in an era when most people no longer believe in an after-life.

> **Arianna Stassinopoulos** 1950– Greek-born American writer: *The Female Woman* (1973)

13 The worst crime is to leave a man's hands empty.
Men are born makers, with that primal simplicity
In every maker since Adam.

> **Derek Walcott** 1930– West Indian poet and dramatist: *Omeros* (1990)

14 Urge and urge and urge,
Always the procreant urge of the
world.
Walt Whitman 1819–92 American poet:
'Song of Myself' (written 1855)

Cricket

1 In Affectionate Remembrance
of
ENGLISH CRICKET,
Which Died at The Oval
on
29th August, 1882.
Deeply lamented by a large circle of
sorrowing friends and
acquaintances.
R. I. P.
N. B.—The body will be cremated
and
the ashes taken to Australia.
*following England's defeat by the
Australians*
Anonymous: in *Sporting Times*
September 1882

2 They have paid to see Dr Grace bat,
not to see you bowl.
*said to the bowler when the umpire had
called 'not out' after W. G. Grace was
unexpectedly bowled first ball*
Anonymous: Harry Furniss *A Century of
Grace* (1985); perhaps apocryphal

3 Never read print, it spoils one's eye
for the ball.
habitual advice to his players
W. G. Grace 1848–1915 English
cricketer: Harry Furniss *A Century of
Grace* (1985)

4 It's more than a game. It's an
institution.
of cricket
Thomas Hughes 1822–96 English
lawyer, politician, and writer: *Tom
Brown's Schooldays* (1857)

5 Cricket—a game which the English,
not being a spiritual people, have

invented in order to give themselves
some conception of eternity.
Lord Mancroft 1914–87 British
Conservative politician: *Bees in Some
Bonnets* (1979)

6 There's a breathless hush in the
Close to-night—
Ten to make and the match to win—
A bumping pitch and a blinding
light,
An hour to play and the last man in.
Henry Newbolt 1862–1938 English
lawyer, poet, and man of letters: 'Vitaï
Lampada' (1897)

7 I don't think I can be expected to take
seriously any game which takes less
than three days to reach its
conclusion.
a cricket enthusiast on baseball
Tom Stoppard 1937– British dramatist:
in *Guardian* 24 December 1984

8 Personally, I have always looked on
cricket as organized loafing.
William Temple 1881–1944 English
theologian: attributed

9 It's a well-known fact that, when I'm
on 99, I'm the best judge of a run in
all the bloody world.
Alan Wharton 1923–93 English
cricketer: Freddie Trueman *You Nearly
Had Me That Time* (1978)

Crime

see also LAWS, MURDER, POLICE, PUNISHMENT

1 Labour is the party of law and order
in Britain today. Tough on crime and
tough on the causes of crime.
Tony Blair 1953– British Labour
statesman: speech at the Labour Party
Conference, 30 September 1993

2 The fear of burglars is not only the
fear of being robbed, but also the
fear of a sudden and unexpected
clutch out of the darkness.
Elias Canetti 1905–94 Bulgarian-born

writer and novelist: *Crowds and Power*
(1960)

3 Once in the racket you're always in it.
Al Capone 1899–1947 Italian-born
American gangster: in *Philadelphia
Public Ledger* 18 May 1929

4 Crime isn't a disease, it's a symptom.
Cops are like a doctor that gives you
aspirin for a brain tumour.
Raymond Chandler 1888–1959
American writer of detective fiction: *The
Long Good-Bye* (1953)

5 Thieves respect property. They
merely wish the property to become
their property that they may more
perfectly respect it.
G. K. Chesterton 1874–1936 English
essayist, novelist, and poet: *The Man
who was Thursday* (1908)

6 Thou shalt not steal; an empty feat,
When it's so lucrative to cheat.
Arthur Hugh Clough 1819–61 English
poet: 'The Latest Decalogue' (1862)

7 Singularity is almost invariably a
clue. The more featureless and
commonplace a crime is, the more
difficult is it to bring it home.
Arthur Conan Doyle 1859–1930
Scottish-born writer of detective fiction:
The Adventures of Sherlock Holmes
(1892) 'The Boscombe Valley Mystery'

8 Major Strasser has been shot. Round
up the usual suspects.
Julius J. Epstein 1909–2001: *Casablanca*
(1942 film, with Philip G. Epstein and
Howard Koch)

9 A clever theft was praiseworthy
amongst the Spartans; and it is
equally so amongst Christians,
provided it be on a sufficiently large
scale.
Herbert Spencer 1820–1903 English
philosopher: *Social Statics* (1850)

Crime Fiction

1 Sapper, Buchan, Dornford Yates,
practitioners in that school of
Snobbery with Violence that runs
like a thread of good-class tweed
through twentieth-century
literature.
Alan Bennett 1934– English actor and
dramatist: *Forty Years On* (1969)

2 When in doubt have a man come
through the door with a gun in his
hand.
Raymond Chandler 1888–1959
American writer of detective fiction:
attributed

3 Detection is, or ought to be, an exact
science, and should be treated in the
same cold and unemotional manner.
You have attempted to tinge it with
romanticism, which produces much
the same effect as if you worked a
love-story or an elopement into the
fifth proposition of Euclid.
Arthur Conan Doyle 1859–1930
Scottish-born writer of detective fiction:
The Sign of Four (1890)

4 What the detective story is about is
not murder but the restoration of
order.
P. D. James 1920– English writer of
detective stories: in *Face* December
1986

5 The detective novel is the art-for-
art's-sake of our yawning
Philistinism, the classic example of a
specialized form of art removed from
contact with the life it pretends to
build on.
V. S. Pritchett 1900–97 English writer
and critic: in *New Statesman* 16 June
1951

Crises

see also DISASTERS

1 Comin' in on a wing and a pray'r.
the contemporary comment of a war pilot,
speaking from a disabled plane to ground
control
 Harold Adamson 1906–80 American
 songwriter: title of song (1943)

2 We won't make a drama out of a
 crisis.
 Advertising slogan: Commercial Union
 insurance

3 Crisis? What Crisis?
headline summarizing James Callaghan's
remark of 10 January 1979: 'I don't think
other people in the world would share the
view there is mounting chaos'
 Anonymous: in *Sun* 11 January 1979

4 Keep calm and carry on.
 Anonymous: poster designed by the
 Ministry of Information in 1939 but not
 used in World War II; re-discovered and
 popularized in the early 21st century

5 The die is cast.
at the crossing of the Rubicon
 Julius Caesar 100–44 BC Roman general
 and statesman: Suetonius *Lives of the*
 Caesars 'Divus Julius'; Plutarch *Parallel*
 Lives 'Pompey'

6 Moments of crisis produce in man a
 redoubling of life.
 François-René Chateaubriand
 1768–1848 French writer and diplomat:
 Mémoires d'outre-tombe (1849–50)

7 I felt as if I was walking with destiny,
 and that all my past life had been but
 a preparation for this hour and this
 trial.
 Winston Churchill 1874–1965 British
 Conservative statesman: on becoming
 Prime Minister, 10 May 1940

8 We do not experience and thus we
 have no measure of the disasters we
 prevent.
 J. K. Galbraith 1908–2006 American
 economist: *A Life in our Times* (1981)

9 Swimming for his life, a man does
 not see much of the country through
 which the river winds.
 W. E. Gladstone 1809–98 British Liberal
 statesman: diary, 31 December 1868

10 The illustrious bishop of Cambrai
 was of more worth than his
 chambermaid, and there are few of
 us that would hesitate to pronounce,
 if his palace were in flames, and the
 life of only one of them could be
 preserved, which of the two ought to
 be preferred.
 William Godwin 1756–1836 English
 philosopher and novelist: *An Enquiry*
 concerning the Principles of Political
 Justice (1793)

11 In bygone days, commanders were
 taught that when in doubt, they
 should march their troops towards
 the sound of gunfire. I intend to
 march my troops towards the sound
 of gunfire.
 Jo Grimond 1913–93 British Liberal
 politician: speech at Liberal Party
 Annual Assembly, 14 September 1963

12 For it is your business, when the wall
 next door catches fire.
 Horace 65–8 BC Roman poet: *Epistles*

13 We have the wolf by the ears; and we
 can neither hold him, nor safely let
 him go. Justice is in one scale, and
 self-preservation in the other.
on slavery
 Thomas Jefferson 1743–1826 American
 Democratic Republican statesman:
 letter to John Holmes, 22 April 1820

14 As someone pointed out recently, if
 you can keep your head when all
 about you are losing theirs, it's just

possible you haven't grasped the situation.

Jean Kerr 1923–2003 American writer: *Please Don't Eat the Daisies* (1957)

15 If you can keep your head when all about you
Are losing theirs and blaming it on you . . .

Rudyard Kipling 1865–1936 English writer and poet: 'If—' (1910)

16 There cannot be a crisis next week. My schedule is already full.

Henry Kissinger 1923– American politician: in *New York Times Magazine* 1 June 1969

17 A trifle consoles us because a trifle upsets us.

Blaise Pascal 1623–62 French mathematician, physicist, and moralist: *Pensées* (1670)

18 We're eyeball to eyeball, and I think the other fellow just blinked.
on the Cuban missile crisis

Dean Rusk 1909– American politician: comment, 24 October 1962

19 It is exciting to have a real crisis on your hands, when you have spent half your political life dealing with humdrum issues like the environment.
on the Falklands campaign, 1982

Margaret Thatcher 1925– British Conservative stateswoman: speech to Scottish Conservative Party conference, 14 May 1982

20 I myself have always deprecated . . . in crisis after crisis, appeals to the Dunkirk spirit as an answer to our problems.

Harold Wilson 1916–95 British Labour statesman: in the House of Commons, 26 July 1961

21 I'm at my best in a messy, middle-of-the-road muddle.

Harold Wilson 1916–95 British Labour

statesman: remark in Cabinet, 21 January 1975

Critics

see also LIKES, REVIEWS, TASTE

1 A critic is a bundle of biases held loosely together by a sense of taste.

Whitney Balliett 1926–2007 American writer: *Dinosaurs in the Morning* (1962)

2 She was one of the people who say 'I don't know anything about music really, but I know what I like.'

Max Beerbohm 1872–1956 English critic, essayist, and caricaturist: *Zuleika Dobson* (1911)

3 A man must serve his time to every trade
Save censure—critics all are ready made.

Lord Byron 1788–1824 English poet: *English Bards and Scotch Reviewers* (1809)

4 Whom the gods wish to destroy they first call promising.

Cyril Connolly 1903–74 English writer: *Enemies of Promise* (1938)

5 *Il n'y a pas de hors-texte.*
There is nothing outside of the text.

Jacques Derrida 1930–2004 French philosopher and critic: *Of Grammatology* (1967)

6 You know who the critics are? The men who have failed in literature and art.

Benjamin Disraeli 1804–81 British Tory statesman and novelist: *Lothair* (1870)

7 Long experience has taught me that to be criticized is not always to be wrong.
speech at Lord Mayor's Guildhall banquet during the Suez crisis

Anthony Eden 1897–1977 British Conservative statesman: in *Daily Herald* 10 November 1956

8 When I read something saying I've not done anything as good as *Catch-22* I'm tempted to reply, 'Who has?'
Joseph Heller 1923–99 American novelist: in *Times* 9 June 1993

9 Parodies and caricatures are the most penetrating of criticisms.
Aldous Huxley 1894–1963 English novelist: *Point Counter Point* (1928)

10 We must grant the artist his subject, his idea, his *donnée*: our criticism is applied only to what he makes of it.
Henry James 1843–1916 American novelist: *Partial Portraits* (1888) 'Art of Fiction'

11 You *may* abuse a tragedy, though you cannot write one. You may scold a carpenter who has made you a bad table, though you cannot make a table. It is not your trade to make tables.
on literary criticism
Samuel Johnson 1709–84 English poet, critic, and lexicographer: James Boswell *Life of Samuel Johnson* (1791) 25 June 1763

12 I have always suspected that the reading is right, which requires many words to prove it wrong; and the emendation wrong, that cannot without so much labour appear to be right.
Samuel Johnson 1709–84 English poet, critic, and lexicographer: *Plays of William Shakespeare . . .* (1765)

13 Never trust the artist. Trust the tale. The proper function of a critic is to save the tale from the artist who created it.
D. H. Lawrence 1885–1930 English novelist and poet: *Studies in Classic American Literature* (1923)

14 People ask you for criticism, but they only want praise.
W. Somerset Maugham 1874–1965

English novelist: *Of Human Bondage* (1915)

15 One should look long and carefully at oneself before one considers judging others.
Molière 1622–73 French comic dramatist: *Le Misanthrope* (1666)

16 There is more business in interpreting interpretations than in interpreting things, and more books on books than on any other subject: all we do is gloss each other. All is a-swarm with commentaries: of authors there is a dearth.
Montaigne 1533–92 French moralist and essayist: *Essays* (1580)

17 Insects sting, not out of malice, but because they too want to live: likewise our critics; they want, not to hurt us, but to take our blood.
Friedrich Nietzsche 1844–1900 German philosopher and writer: *Human All Too Human* (1879)

18 You don't expect me to know what to say about a play when I don't know who the author is, do you?
George Bernard Shaw 1856–1950 Irish dramatist: *Fanny's First Play* (1914)

19 Remember, a statue has never been set up in honour of a critic!
Jean Sibelius 1865–1957 Finnish composer: Bengt de Törne *Sibelius: A Close-Up* (1937)

20 Interpretation is the revenge of the intellect upon art.
Susan Sontag 1933– American writer: in *Evergreen Review* December 1964

21 Yet malice never was his aim;
He lashed the vice, but spared the name;
No individual could resent,
Where thousands equally were meant.
Jonathan Swift 1667–1745 Anglo-Irish poet and satirist: 'Verses on the Death of Dr Swift' (1731)

22 He *sees* more in my pictures than I ever painted!
of John Ruskin
> **J. M. W. Turner** 1775–1851 English landscape painter: Mary Lloyd *Sunny Memories* (1879)

23 A critic is a man who knows the way but can't drive the car.
> **Kenneth Tynan** 1927–80 English theatre critic: in *New York Times Magazine* 9 January 1966

24 Literature is strewn with the wreckage of men who have minded beyond reason the opinions of others.
> **Virginia Woolf** 1882–1941 English novelist: *A Room of One's Own* (1929)

25 You who scribble, yet hate all who write . . .
And with faint praises one another damn.
of theatre critics
> **William Wycherley** *c.*1640–1716 English dramatist: *The Plain Dealer* (1677)

Cruelty

1 Boys throw stones at frogs for fun, but the frogs don't die for 'fun', but in sober earnest.
> **Bion** *c.*325–*c.*255 BC Greek popular philosopher: Plutarch *Moralia*

2 The wish to hurt, the momentary intoxication with pain, is the loophole through which the pervert climbs into the minds of ordinary men.
> **Jacob Bronowski** 1908–74 Polish-born mathematician and humanist: *The Face of Violence* (1954)

3 Man's inhumanity to man
Makes countless thousands mourn!
> **Robert Burns** 1759–96 Scottish poet: 'Man was made to Mourn' (1786)

4 *There* were his young barbarians all at play,
There was their Dacian mother—he, their sire,
Butchered to make a Roman holiday.
> **Lord Byron** 1788–1824 English poet: *Childe Harold's Pilgrimage* (1812–18)

5 Strike him so that he can feel that he is dying.
> **Caligula** AD 12–41 Roman emperor: Suetonius *Lives of the Caesars* 'Gaius Caligula'

6 Being cruel to be kind is just ordinary cruelty with an excuse made for it . . . And it is right that it should be more resented, as it is.
> **Ivy Compton-Burnett** 1884–1969 English novelist: *Daughters and Sons* (1937)

7 Cruelty, like every other vice, requires no motive outside itself—it only requires opportunity.
> **George Eliot** 1819–80 English novelist: *Scenes of Clerical Life* (1858)

8 The healthy man does not torture others—generally it is the tortured who turn into torturers.
> **Carl Gustav Jung** 1875–1961 Swiss psychologist: in *Du* May 1941

9 The infliction of cruelty with a good conscience is a delight to moralists. That is why they invented Hell.
> **Bertrand Russell** 1872–1970 British philosopher and mathematician: *Sceptical Essays* (1928) 'On the Value of Scepticism'

10 I must be cruel only to be kind.
> **William Shakespeare** 1564–1616 English dramatist: *Hamlet* (1601)

Culture

see also CIVILIZATION, MUSEUMS

1 I must study politics and war that my sons may have liberty to study

mathematics and philosophy. My sons ought to study mathematics and philosophy, geography, natural history, naval architecture, navigation, commerce, and agriculture, in order to give their children a right to study painting, poetry, music, architecture, statuary, tapestry, and porcelain.
John Adams 1735–1826 American statesman: letter to Abigail Adams, 12 May 1780

2 Some refer to it as a cultural Chernobyl. I think of it as a cultural Stalingrad.
of Euro Disney
J. G. Ballard 1930–2009 British writer: in *Daily Telegraph* 2 July 1994; see CULTURE 8

3 Sooner or later we must absorb Islam if our own culture is not to die of anaemia.
Basil Bunting 1900–85 English poet: Omar Pound *Arabic and Persian Poems* (1970) foreword

4 What are we waiting for, gathered in the market-place?
The barbarians are to arrive today.
Constantine Cavafy 1863–1933 Greek poet: 'Waiting for the Barbarians' (1904)

5 Cultured people are merely the glittering scum which floats upon the deep river of production.
on hearing his son Randolph criticize the lack of culture of the Calgary oil magnates, probably c.1929
Winston Churchill 1874–1965 British Conservative statesman: Martin Gilbert *In Search of Churchill* (1994)

6 Culture may even be described simply as that which makes life worth living.
T. S. Eliot 1888–1965 Anglo-American poet, critic, and dramatist: *Notes Towards a Definition of Culture* (1948)

7 Whenever I hear the word culture . . . I release the safety-catch of my Browning!
often quoted as: 'Whenever I hear the word culture, I reach for my pistol!'
Hanns Johst 1890–1978 German dramatist: *Schlageter* (1933); often attributed to Hermann Goering

8 A cultural Chernobyl.
of Euro Disney
Ariane Mnouchkine 1934– French theatre director: in *Harper's Magazine* July 1992

9 All my wife has ever taken from the Mediterranean—from that whole vast intuitive culture—are four bottles of Chianti to make into lamps.
Peter Shaffer 1926– English dramatist: *Equus* (1973)

10 In Italy for thirty years under the Borgias they had warfare, terror, murder, bloodshed—they produced Michelangelo, Leonardo da Vinci and the Renaissance. In Switzerland they had brotherly love, five hundred years of democracy and peace and what did that produce . . . ? The cuckoo clock.
Orson Welles 1915–85 American actor and film director: *The Third Man* (1949 film); words added by Welles to Graham Greene's script

11 Mrs Ballinger is one of the ladies who pursue Culture in bands, as though it were dangerous to meet it alone.
Edith Wharton 1862–1937 American novelist: *Xingu and Other Stories* (1916)

Custom

see also HABIT

1 Custom reconciles us to everything.
Edmund Burke 1729–97 Irish-born Whig politician and man of letters: *On the Sublime and Beautiful* (1757)

2 If one were to order all mankind to choose the best set of rules in the world, each group would, after due consideration, choose its own customs; each group regards its own as being by far the best.

Herodotus c.485–c.425 BC Greek historian: *Histories*

3 Custom, then, is the great guide of human life.

David Hume 1711–76 Scottish philosopher, economist, and historian: *An Enquiry Concerning Human Understanding* (1748)

4 The Lord says in the gospel; 'I am the Truth'. He does not say 'I am custom'. Therefore, when the truth is made manifest, custom must give way to truth.

Libosus of Vaga *fl.* AD 256 Roman bishop: St Augustine of Hippo *On Baptism*

5 Everyone calls barbarism what is not customary to him.

Montaigne 1533–92 French moralist and essayist: *Essays* (1580)

6 Laws are sand, customs are rock. Laws can be evaded and punishment escaped, but an openly transgressed custom brings sure punishment.

Mark Twain 1835–1910 American writer: *The Gorky Incident* (1906)

Cynicism

see also DISILLUSION

1 Kill them all; God will recognize his own.

when asked how the true Catholics could be distinguished from the heretics at the massacre of Béziers, 1209

Arnald-Amaury d. 1225 French abbot: Jonathan Sumption *The Albigensian Crusade* (1978)

2 Nothing matters very much and very few things matter at all.

Arthur James Balfour 1848–1930 British Conservative statesman: Clodagh Anson *Book: discreet memoirs* (1931)

3 CYNIC, *n.* A blackguard whose faulty vision sees things as they are, not as they ought to be.

Ambrose Bierce 1842–c.1914 American writer: *Cynic's Word Book* (1906)

4 What makes all doctrines plain and clear?
About two hundred pounds a year.
And that which was proved true before,
Prove false again? Two hundred more.

Samuel Butler 1612–80 English poet: *Hudibras* pt. 3 (1680)

5 *when asked why he was begging for alms from a statue:*
To get practice in being refused.

Diogenes c.400–c.325 BC Greek Cynic philosopher: Diogenes Laertius *Lives of the Philosophers*

6 Cynicism is an unpleasant way of saying the truth.

Lillian Hellman 1905–84 American dramatist: *The Little Foxes* (1939)

7 Paris is well worth a mass.
a Huguenot view on becoming King of France

Henri IV 1553–1610 French monarch: attributed; alternatively attributed to his minister Sully, in conversation with Henri

8 Cynicism is our shared common language, the Esperanto that actually caught on.

Nick Hornby 1957– British novelist and journalist: *How to be Good* (2001)

9 If someone tells you he is going to make a 'realistic decision', you immediately understand that he has resolved to do something bad.

Mary McCarthy 1912–89 American novelist: *On the Contrary* (1961) 'American Realist Playwrights'

10 'Blessed is the man who expects nothing, for he shall never be disappointed' was the ninth beatitude.

Alexander Pope 1688–1744 English poet: letter to Fortescue, 23 September 1725

11 A man who knows the price of everything and the value of nothing.
definition of a cynic

Oscar Wilde 1854–1900 Anglo-Irish dramatist and poet: *Lady Windermere's Fan* (1892)

Dance

1 There may be trouble ahead,
But while there's moonlight and music and love and romance,
Let's face the music and dance.

Irving Berlin 1888–1989 American songwriter: 'Let's Face the Music and Dance' (1936 song)

2 Heaven—I'm in Heaven—And my heart beats so that I can hardly speak;
And I seem to find the happiness I seek
When we're out together dancing cheek-to-cheek.

Irving Berlin 1888–1989 American songwriter: 'Cheek-to-Cheek' (1935 song)

3 On with the dance! let joy be unconfined;
No sleep till morn, when Youth and Pleasure meet
To chase the glowing Hours with flying feet.

Lord Byron 1788–1824 English poet: *Childe Harold's Pilgrimage* (1812–18)

4 Will you, won't you, will you, won't you, will you join the dance?

Lewis Carroll 1832–98 English writer and logician: *Alice's Adventures in Wonderland* (1865)

5 The truest expression of a people is in its dances and its music. Bodies never lie.

Agnes de Mille 1908–93 American dancer and choreographer: in *New York Times Magazine* 11 May 1975

6 Dance is the hidden language of the soul.

Martha Graham 1894–1991 American dancer, teacher, and choreographer: *Blood Memory* (1991)

7 Dancing appears glamorous, easy, delightful. But the path to the paradise of achievement is not easier than any other. There is fatigue so great that the body cries, even in its sleep.

Martha Graham 1894–1991 American dancer, teacher, and choreographer: *Blood Memory* (1991)

8 Come, and trip it as ye go
On the light fantastic toe.

John Milton 1608–74 English poet: 'L'Allegro' (1645)

9 I wish I could shimmy like my sister Kate,
She shivers like the jelly on a plate.

Armand J. Piron: 'Shimmy like Kate' (1919 song)

10 [Dancing is] a perpendicular expression of a horizontal desire.

George Bernard Shaw 1856–1950 Irish dramatist: in *New Statesman* 23 March 1962

11 O body swayed to music, O brightening glance,
How can we know the dancer from the dance?

W. B. Yeats 1865–1939 Irish poet: 'Among School Children' (1928)

Danger

see also RISK, SECURITY

1 Dangers by being despised grow great.
   Edmund Burke 1729–97 Irish-born Whig politician and man of letters: speech on the Petition of the Unitarians, 11 May 1792

2 When there is no peril in the fight, there is no glory in the triumph.
   Pierre Corneille 1606–84 French dramatist: *Le Cid* (1637)

3 In skating over thin ice, our safety is in our speed.
   Ralph Waldo Emerson 1803–82 American philosopher and poet: *Essays* (1841) 'Prudence'

4 Danger is a good teacher, and makes apt scholars.
   William Hazlitt 1778–1830 English essayist: *Table Talk* vol. 1 (1821)

5 Fasten your seat-belts, it's going to be a bumpy night.
   Joseph L. Mankiewicz 1909–93 American screenwriter, producer, and director: *All About Eve* (1950 film); spoken by Bette Davis

6 Out of this nettle, danger, we pluck this flower, safety.
   William Shakespeare 1564–1616 English dramatist: *Henry IV, Part 1* (1597)

7 Considering how dangerous everything is, nothing is really very frightening!
   Gertrude Stein 1874–1946 American writer: *Everybody's Autobiography* (1937)

Day

see also EVENING, NIGHT

1 Morning has broken
Like the first morning,
Blackbird has spoken
Like the first bird.
   Eleanor Farjeon 1881–1965 English writer for children: 'A Morning Song (for the First Day of Spring)' (1957)

2 Awake! for Morning in the bowl of night
Has flung the stone that puts the stars to flight:
And Lo! the Hunter of the East has caught
The Sultan's turret in a noose of light.
   Edward Fitzgerald 1809–83 English scholar and poet: *The Rubáiyát of Omar Khayyám* (1859)

3 What are days for?
Days are where we live.
They come, they wake us
Time and time over.
They are to be happy in:
Where can we live but days?
   Philip Larkin 1922–85 English poet: 'Days' (1964)

4 Night's candles are burnt out, and jocund day
Stands tiptoe on the misty mountain tops.
   William Shakespeare 1564–1616 English dramatist: *Romeo and Juliet* (1595)

5 And ghastly through the drizzling rain
On the bald street breaks the blank day.
   Alfred, Lord Tennyson 1809–92 English poet: *In Memoriam A. H. H.* (1850)

Death

see also BEREAVEMENT, DYING, EPITAPHS, LAST WORDS, MURDER, SUICIDE

1 Death has got something to be said for it:
There's no need to get out of bed for it;
Wherever you may be,

They bring it to you, free.

Kingsley Amis 1922–95 English novelist and poet: 'Delivery Guaranteed' (1979)

2 Even death is unreliable: instead of zero it may be some ghastly hallucination, such as the square root of minus one.

Samuel Beckett 1906–89 Irish dramatist, novelist, and poet: attributed

3 O death, where is thy sting? O grave, where is thy victory?

Bible: I Corinthians

4 In the midst of life we are in death.

The Book of Common Prayer 1662: *The Burial of the Dead*

5 Forasmuch as it hath pleased Almighty God of his great mercy to take unto himself the soul of our dear brother here departed, we therefore commit his body to the ground; earth to earth, ashes to ashes, dust to dust; in sure and certain hope of the Resurrection to eternal life.

The Book of Common Prayer 1662: *The Burial of the Dead* Interment

6 Don't be afraid of death so much as an inadequate life.

Bertolt Brecht 1898–1956 German dramatist: *The Mother* (1957)

7 He shouts play death more sweetly this Death is a master from Deutschland

he shouts scrape your strings darker you'll rise then as smoke to the sky you'll have a grave then in the clouds there you won't lie too cramped.

Paul Celan 1920–70 German poet: 'Deathfugue' (written 1944)

8 This parrot is no more! It has ceased to be! It's expired and gone to meet its maker! This is a late parrot! It's a stiff! Bereft of life it rests in peace — if you hadn't nailed it to the perch it would be pushing up the daisies! It's rung down the curtain and joined the choir invisible! THIS IS AN EX-PARROT!

Graham Chapman 1941–89 and **John Cleese** 1939–   British comedy writers and actors: *Monty Python's Flying Circus* (BBC TV programme, 1969, with Terry Gilliam, Eric Idle, Terry Jones, and Michael Palin)

9 Death be not proud, though some have called thee
Mighty and dreadful, for thou art not so.

John Donne 1572–1631 English poet and divine: *Holy Sonnets* (1609)

10 Any man's death diminishes me, because I am involved in Mankind; And therefore never send to know for whom the bell tolls; it tolls for thee.

John Donne 1572–1631 English poet and divine: *Devotions upon Emergent Occasions* (1624)

11 The bodies of those that made such a noise and tumult when alive, when dead, lie as quietly among the graves of their neighbours as any others.

Jonathan Edwards 1703–58 American theologian: *Miscellaneous Discourses* sermon on procrastination

12 Webster was much possessed by death
And saw the skull beneath the skin; And breastless creatures underground
Leaned backward with a lipless grin.

T. S. Eliot 1888–1965 Anglo-American poet, critic, and dramatist: 'Whispers of Immortality' (1919)

13 My thoughts are crowded with death and it draws so oddly on the sexual that I am confused
confused to be attracted
by, in effect, my own annihilation.

Thom Gunn 1929–2004 English poet: 'In Time of Plague' (1992)

14 Death is nothing at all; it does not count. I have only slipped away into the next room.

> **Henry Scott Holland** 1847–1918 English theologian and preacher: sermon preached on Whitsunday 1910

15 *Non omnis moriar.*

I shall not altogether die.

> **Horace** 65–8 BC Roman poet: *Odes*

16 So here it is at last, the distinguished thing!

on experiencing his first stroke

> **Henry James** 1843–1916 American novelist: Edith Wharton *A Backward Glance* (1934)

17 Darkling I listen; and, for many a time

I have been half in love with easeful Death,

Called him soft names in many a musèd rhyme,

To take into the air my quiet breath;

Now more than ever seems it rich to die,

To cease upon the midnight with no pain.

> **John Keats** 1795–1821 English poet: 'Ode to a Nightingale' (1820)

18 The dead don't die. They look on and help.

> **D. H. Lawrence** 1885–1930 English novelist and poet: letter to J. Middleton Murry, 2 February 1923

19   This is death.

To die and know it. This is the Black Widow, death.

> **Robert Lowell** 1917–77 American poet: 'Mr Edwards and the Spider' (1950)

20 There are no dead.

> **Maurice Maeterlinck** 1862–1949 Belgian poet, dramatist, and essayist: *L'Oiseau bleu* (1909)

21 Let me die a youngman's death

Not a clean & in-between-

The-sheets, holy-water death,

Not a famous-last-words

Peaceful out-of-breath death.

> **Roger McGough** 1937– English poet: 'Let Me Die a Youngman's Death' (1967)

22 Life is a great surprise. I do not see why death should not be an even greater one.

> **Vladimir Nabokov** 1899–1977 Russian novelist: *Pale Fire* (1962)

23 And all our calm is in that balm—

Not lost but gone before.

> **Caroline Norton** 1808–77 English poet and songwriter: 'Not Lost but Gone Before'

24 We die containing a richness of lovers and tribes, tastes we have swallowed, bodies we have plunged into and swum up as if rivers of wisdom, characters we have climbed into as if trees, fears we have hidden as if in caves.

> **Michael Ondaatje** 1943– Canadian writer: *The English Patient* (1992)

25 We shall die alone.

> **Blaise Pascal** 1623–62 French mathematician, physicist, and moralist: *Pensées* (1670)

26 Only we die in earnest, that's no jest.

> **Walter Ralegh** c.1552–1618 English explorer and courtier: 'On the Life of Man'

27 Anyone can stop a man's life, but no one his death; a thousand doors open on to it.

> **Seneca ('the Younger')** c.4 BC–AD 65 Roman philosopher and poet: *Phoenissae*

28 I care not; a man can die but once; we owe God a death.

> **William Shakespeare** 1564–1616 English dramatist: *Henry IV, Part 2* (1597)

29   To die, to sleep;

To sleep: perchance to dream: ay, there's the rub;

For in that sleep of death what
  dreams may come
When we have shuffled off this
  mortal coil,
Must give us pause.
> **William Shakespeare** 1564–1616
> English dramatist: *Hamlet* (1601)

30 In the arts of life man invents
nothing; but in the arts of death he
outdoes Nature herself, and
produces by chemistry and
machinery all the slaughter of
plague, pestilence and famine.
> **George Bernard Shaw** 1856–1950 Irish
> dramatist: *Man and Superman* (1903)

31 The cemetery is an open space
among the ruins, covered in winter
with violets and daisies. It might
make one in love with death, to think
that one should be buried in so
sweet a place.
> **Percy Bysshe Shelley** 1792–1822
> English poet: *Adonais* (1821)

32 If there wasn't death, I think you
couldn't go on.
> **Stevie Smith** 1902–71 English poet and
> novelist: in *Observer* 9 November 1969

33 Death must be distinguished from
dying, with which it is often
confused.
> **Sydney Smith** 1771–1845 English
> clergyman and essayist: H. Pearson *The
> Smith of Smiths* (1934)

34 To fear death, my friends, is only to
think ourselves wise, without being
wise: for it is to think that we know
what we do not know.
> **Socrates** 469–399 BC Greek philosopher:
> Plato *Apology*

35 One death is a tragedy, a million
deaths a statistic.
> **Joseph Stalin** 1879–1953 Soviet dictator:
> attributed

36 For though from out our bourne of
time and place

The flood may bear me far,
I hope to see my pilot face to face
When I have crossed the bar.
> **Alfred, Lord Tennyson** 1809–92 English
> poet: 'Crossing the Bar' (1889)

37 Though lovers be lost love shall not;
And death shall have no dominion.
> **Dylan Thomas** 1914–53 Welsh poet:
> 'And death shall have no dominion'
> (1936)

38 Just try and set death aside. It sets
you aside, and that's the end of it!
> **Ivan Turgenev** 1818–83 Russian
> novelist: *Fathers and Sons* (1862)

39 All say, 'How hard it is to die'—a
strange complaint to come from the
mouths of people who have had to
live.
> **Mark Twain** 1835–1910 American
> writer: *Pudd'nhead Wilson* (1894)

40 So it goes.
> **Kurt Vonnegut** 1922–2007 American
> novelist and short-story writer:
> *Slaughterhouse Five* (1969)

41 Death is not an event in life: we do
not live to experience death.
> **Ludwig Wittgenstein** 1889–1951
> Austrian-born philosopher: *Tractatus
> Logico-Philosophicus* (1922)

42 He knows death to the bone—
Man has created death.
> **W. B. Yeats** 1865–1939 Irish poet: 'Death'
> (1933)

Debt

see also LENDING, MONEY

1 Dreading that climax of all human
ills,
The inflammation of his weekly bills.
> **Lord Byron** 1788–1824 English poet:
> *Don Juan* (1819–24)

2 They hired the money, didn't they?
on the subject of war debts incurred by England and others
> **Calvin Coolidge** 1872–1933 American Republican statesman: John H. McKee *Coolidge: Wit and Wisdom* (1933)

3 Annual income twenty pounds, annual expenditure nineteen nineteen six, result happiness. Annual income twenty pounds, annual expenditure twenty pounds nought and six, result misery.
> **Charles Dickens** 1812–70 English novelist: *David Copperfield* (1850)

4 Rather go to bed supperless than rise in debt.
> **Benjamin Franklin** 1706–90 American politician, inventor, and scientist: *The Way to Wealth* (1758)

5 You can't put your VISA bill on your American Express card.
> **P. J. O'Rourke** 1947– American humorous writer: *The Bachelor Home Companion* (1987)

6 All decent people live beyond their incomes nowadays, and those who aren't respectable live beyond other peoples'.
> **Saki** 1870–1916 Scottish writer: *Chronicles of Clovis* (1911)

7 The National Debt is a very Good Thing and it would be dangerous to pay it off, for fear of Political Economy.
> **W. C. Sellar** 1898–1951 and **R. J. Yeatman** 1898–1968 British writers: *1066 and All That* (1930)

8 A small debt makes a man your debtor; a large one, an enemy.
> **Seneca ('the Younger')** c.4 BC–AD 65 Roman philosopher and poet: *Epistulae ad Lucilium*

9 Sixteen tons, what do you get? Another day older and deeper in debt.

Say brother, don't you call me 'cause I can't go
I owe my soul to the company store.
> **Merle Travis** 1917–83 American country singer: 'Sixteen Tons' (1947 song)

10 One must have some sort of occupation nowadays. If I hadn't my debts I shouldn't have anything to think about.
> **Oscar Wilde** 1854–1900 Anglo-Irish dramatist and poet: *A Woman of No Importance* (1893)

Deception

see also HYPOCRISY, LIES

1 I count false words the foulest plague of all.
> **Aeschylus** c.525–456 BC Greek tragedian: *Prometheus Bound*

2 Doubtless the pleasure is as great Of being cheated, as to cheat. As lookers-on feel most delight, That least perceive a juggler's sleight.
> **Samuel Butler** 1612–80 English poet: *Hudibras* pt. 2 (1664)

3 It was the men I deceived the most that I loved the most.
> **Marguerite Duras** 1914–96 French writer: *Practicalities* (1990)

4 An open foe may prove a curse, But a pretended friend is worse.
> **John Gay** 1685–1732 English poet and dramatist: *Fables* (1727) 'The Shepherd's Dog and the Wolf'

5 It was beautiful and simple as all truly great swindles are.
> **O. Henry** 1862–1910 American short-story writer: *Gentle Grafter* (1908)

6 You may fool all the people some of the time; you can even fool some of the people all the time; but you can't fool all of the people all the time.
> **Abraham Lincoln** 1809–65 American Republican statesman: Alexander K.

McClure *Lincoln's Yarns and Stories* (1904); also attributed to Phineas Barnum

7 And if, to be sure, sometimes you need to conceal a fact with words, do it in such a way that it does not become known, or, if it does become known, that you have a ready and quick defence.
> **Niccolò Machiavelli** 1469–1527 Florentine statesman and political philosopher: 'Advice to Raffaello Girolami when he went as Ambassador to the Emperor' (October 1522)

8 To break a treaty is contempt for the gods. But to outwit an enemy is not only just and glorious—but profitable and sweet.
> *often quoted in the form 'To deceive a friend is impious. But . . . '*
> **Plutarch** *c.*AD 46–*c.*120 Greek philosopher and biographer: *Parallel Lives* 'Agesilaus'

9 A deception that elevates us is dearer than a host of low truths.
> **Alexander Pushkin** 1799–1837 Russian poet: 'Hero' (1830)

10 O what a tangled web we weave, When first we practise to deceive!
> **Sir Walter Scott** 1771–1832 Scottish novelist and poet: *Marmion* (1808)

Deeds

see WORDS AND DEEDS

Defeat

see also FAILURE, WINNING

1 History to the defeated
May say Alas but cannot help or pardon.
> **W. H. Auden** 1907–73 English poet: 'Spain 1937' (1937)

2 You do well to weep as a woman over what you could not defend as a man.
> *reproach to her son Boabdil (Muhammad*

XI), who had surrendered Granada to Ferdinand and Isabella
> **Ayesha** *fl.* 1492 Moorish princess: traditional attribution; Washington Irving *The Alhambra* (1832; rev. ed. 1851) ch. 18

3 Victory has a hundred fathers, but no-one wants to recognise defeat as his own.
> **Count Galeazzo Ciano** 1903–44 Italian fascist politician: diary, 9 September 1942

4 'The game,' said he, 'is never lost till won.'
> **George Crabbe** 1754–1832 English poet: *Tales of the Hall* (1819) 'Gretna Green'

5 Once I moved about like the wind. Now I surrender to you and that is all.
> **Geronimo** *c.*1829–1909 American Apache chief: surrendering to General Crook, 25 March 1886

6 Man is not made for defeat. A man can be destroyed but not defeated.
> **Ernest Hemingway** 1899–1961 American novelist: *The Old Man and the Sea* (1952)

7 The war situation has developed not necessarily to Japan's advantage.
> **Emperor Hirohito** 1901–89 Japanese emperor: announcing Japan's surrender on 15 August 1945

8 A man able to think isn't defeated—even when he is defeated.
> **Milan Kundera** 1929– Czech novelist: in *Sunday Times* 20 May 1984

9 Show me a good loser and I'll show you a loser.
> **Vince Lombardi** 1913–70 American football coach: attributed

10 *Vae victis.*
Down with the defeated!
> *cry (already proverbial) of the Gallic King, Brennus, on capturing Rome (390* BC*)*
> **Livy** 59 BC–AD 17 Roman historian: *Ab Urbe Condita*

11 There are some defeats more
triumphant than victories.
Montaigne 1533–92 French moralist
and essayist: *Essays* (1580)

12 Defeat doesn't finish a man—quit
does. A man is not finished when he's
defeated. He's finished when he
quits.
Richard Nixon 1913–94 American
Republican statesman: William Safire
Before the Fall (1975)

13 We are not interested in the
possibilities of defeat; they do not
exist.
on the Boer War during 'Black Week',
December 1899
Queen Victoria 1819–1901 British
monarch: Lady Gwendolen Cecil *Life of*
Robert, Marquis of Salisbury (1931)

14 The only safe course for the defeated
is to expect no safety.
Virgil 70–19 BC Roman poet: *Aeneid*

Defiance

see also DETERMINATION

1 You may shoot me with your words,
You may cut me with your eyes,
You may kill me with your
hatefulness,
But still, like air, I'll rise.
Maya Angelou 1928– American writer:
'Still I Rise' (1978)

2 No surrender!
the defenders of the besieged city of Derry
to the army of James II, April 1689
Anonymous: adopted as a slogan of
Protestant Ulster

3 I was ever a fighter, so—one fight
more,
The best and the last!
I would hate that death bandaged
my eyes, and forbore,

And bade me creep past.
Robert Browning 1812–89 English poet:
'Prospice' (1864)

4 She won't go quietly, that's the
problem. I'll fight to the end.
Diana, Princess of Wales 1961–97
former wife of Charles, Prince of Wales:
interview on *Panorama*, BBC1 TV,
20 November 1995

5 He will give him seven feet of English
ground, or as much more as he may
be taller than other men.
his offer to the invader Harald Hardrada,
before the battle of Stamford Bridge, 1066
Harold II *c*.1019–66 English monarch:
Snorri Sturluson *Heimskringla* (c.1260)
'King Harald's Saga'

6 *No pasarán.*
They shall not pass.
Dolores Ibarruri 1895–1989 Spanish
Communist leader: radio broadcast,
Madrid, 19 July 1936

7 Nuts!
Anthony McAuliffe 1898–1975
American general: replying to the
German demand for surrender at
Bastogne, Belgium, 22 December 1944

8 Get up, stand up
Stand up for your rights
Get up, stand up
Never give up the fight.
Bob Marley 1945–81 Jamaican reggae
musician and songwriter: 'Get up, Stand
up' (1973 song)

9 . . . What though the field be lost?
All is not lost; the unconquerable
will,
And study of revenge, immortal hate,
And courage never to submit or
yield:
And what is else not to be overcome?
John Milton 1608–74 English poet:
Paradise Lost (1667)

10 I grow, I prosper;
Now, gods, stand up for bastards!
William Shakespeare 1564–1616
English dramatist: *King Lear* (1605–6)

Delay

see also IDLENESS, PUNCTUALITY, WAITING

1 Hesitating doesn't matter if only you win out.
Bertolt Brecht 1898–1956 German dramatist: *The Good Woman of Setzuan* (1938)

2 No admittance till the week after next!
Lewis Carroll 1832–98 English writer and logician: *Through the Looking-Glass* (1872)

3 A wrong decision isn't forever; it can always be reversed. The losses from a delayed decision *are* forever; they can never be retrieved.
J. K. Galbraith 1908–2006 American economist: *A Life in our Times* (1981)

4 He gave her a bright fake smile; so much of life was a putting-off of unhappiness for another time. Nothing was ever lost by delay.
Graham Greene 1904–91 English novelist: *The Heart of the Matter* (1948)

5 procrastination is the
art of keeping
up with yesterday.
Don Marquis 1878–1937 American poet and journalist: *archy and mehitabel* (1927)

6 Never do to-day what you can put off till to-morrow.
Punch English humorous weekly periodical: 22 December 1849

7 He who hesitates is sometimes saved.
James Thurber 1894–1961 American humorist: *The Thurber Carnival* (1945)

Democracy

see also ELECTIONS, MINORITIES, POLITICS

1 The cure for the ills of Democracy is more Democracy.
Jane Addams 1860–1935 American social worker: *Democracy and Social Ethics* (1902)

2 The basis of a democratic state is liberty.
Aristotle 384–322 BC Greek philosopher: *Politics*

3 After each war there is a little less democracy to save.
Brooks Atkinson 1894–1984 American journalist and critic: *Once Around the Sun* (1951)

4 Democracy means government by discussion, but it is only effective if you can stop people talking.
Clement Attlee 1883–1967 British Labour statesman: speech at Oxford, 14 June 1957

5 No one pretends that democracy is perfect or all-wise. Indeed, it has been said that democracy is the worst form of Government except all those other forms that have been tried from time to time.
Winston Churchill 1874–1965 British Conservative statesman: speech, House of Commons, 11 November 1947

6 So Two cheers for Democracy: one because it admits variety and two because it permits criticism. Two cheers are quite enough: there is no occasion to give three. Only Love the Beloved Republic deserves that.
E. M. Forster 1879–1970 English novelist: *Two Cheers for Democracy* (1951)

7 No, Democracy is *not* identical with majority rule. Democracy is a *State* which recognizes the subjection of the minority to the majority, that is, an organization for the systematic use of *force* by one class against the other, by one part of the population against another.

> **Lenin** 1870–1924 Russian revolutionary: *State and Revolution* (1919)

8 Fourscore and seven years ago our fathers brought forth upon this continent a new nation, conceived in liberty, and dedicated to the proposition that all men are created equal . . . we here highly resolve that the dead shall not have died in vain, that this nation, under God, shall have a new birth of freedom; and that government of the people, by the people, and for the people, shall not perish from the earth.
the Lincoln Memorial inscription reads 'by the people, for the people'

> **Abraham Lincoln** 1809–65 American Republican statesman: address at the Dedication of the National Cemetery at Gettysburg, 19 November 1863, as reported the following day

9 Democracy is the theory that the common people know what they want, and deserve to get it good and hard.

> **H. L. Mencken** 1880–1956 American journalist and literary critic: *A Little Book in C major* (1916)

10 Man's capacity for justice makes democracy possible, but man's inclination to injustice makes democracy necessary.

> **Reinhold Niebuhr** 1892–1971 American theologian: *Children of Light and Children of Darkness* (1944)

11 Democracy substitutes election by the incompetent many for appointment by the corrupt few.

> **George Bernard Shaw** 1856–1950 Irish dramatist: *Man and Superman* (1903) 'Maxims: Democracy'

12 It's not the voting that's democracy, it's the counting.

> **Tom Stoppard** 1937– British dramatist: *Jumpers* (1972)

13 The world must be made safe for democracy.

> **Woodrow Wilson** 1856–1924 American Democratic statesman: speech to Congress, 2 April 1917

Depression

see also DESPAIR, UNHAPPINESS

1 Frozen anger.
his definition of depression

> **Sigmund Freud** 1856–1939 Austrian psychiatrist: attributed

2 When you're depressed, there *are* no molehills.

> **Randall Jarrell** 1914–65 American poet: William H. Pritchard *Randall Jarrell: A Literary Life* (1990)

3 The black dog I hope always to resist, and in time to drive, though I am deprived of almost all those that used to help me . . . When I rise my breakfast is solitary, the black dog waits to share it, from breakfast to dinner he continues barking, except that Dr Brocklesby for a little keeps him at a distance . . . Night comes at last, and some hours of restlessness and confusion bring me again to a day of solitude. What shall exclude the black dog from a habitation like this?
on his attacks of melancholia; more recently associated with Winston Churchill, who used the phrase 'black dog' when alluding to his own periodic bouts of depression

> **Samuel Johnson** 1709–84 English poet, critic, and lexicographer: letter to Mrs Thrale, 28 June 1783

4 I am in that temper that if I were under water I would scarcely kick to come to the top.

   John Keats 1795–1821 English poet: letter to Benjamin Bailey, 25 May 1818

5 I was aware of a little grey shadow, as it might have been a snowflake seen against the light, floating at an immense distance in the background of my brain.

   Rudyard Kipling 1865–1936 English writer and poet: *Actions and Reactions* (1909) 'The House Surgeon'

6 Noble deeds and hot baths are the best cures for depression.

   Dodie Smith 1896–1990 English novelist and dramatist: *I Capture the Castle* (1949)

Design

see also ART

1 The space you leave behind is as important as the space you fill.

   Susie Cooper 1902–95 English ceramic designer and manufacturer: Ann Eatwell and Andrew Casey (eds.) *Susie Cooper: a Pioneer of Modern Design* (2002)

2 Art has to move you and design does not, unless it's a good design for a bus.

   David Hockney 1937– British artist: in *Guardian* 26 October 1988

3 Design, in art, is a recognition of the relation between various things, various elements in the creative flux. You can't *invent* a design. You recognize it, in the fourth dimension. That is, with your blood and your bones, as well as with your eyes.

   D. H. Lawrence 1885–1930 English novelist and poet: *Phoenix* (1936) 'Art and Morality'

4 Design is not for philosophy—it's for life.

   Issey Miyake 1935– Japanese fashion designer: in *International Herald Tribune* 23 March 1992

5 Good design is intelligence made visible.

   Frank Pick 1878–1941 British transport administrator, responsible for the design aspects of London Transport: attributed

6 The two great rules for design are these: *1st, that there should be no features about a building which are not necessary for convenience, construction or propriety; 2nd, that all ornament should consist of the essential construction of the building.* The neglect of these two rules is the cause of all the bad architecture of the present time.

   Augustus Welby Pugin 1812–52 English architect and designer: *True Principles* (1841)

7 A hen's egg is, quite simply, a work of art, a masterpiece of design and construction with, it has to be said, brilliant packaging.

   Delia Smith English cookery expert: *How To Cook* (1998)

Despair

see also HOPE, PESSIMISM, SORROW

1 Despair, in short, seeks its own environment as surely as water finds its own level.

   Alfred Alvarez 1929– English critic, poet, and novelist: *The Savage God* (1971)

2 My God, my God, look upon me; why hast thou forsaken me?

   Bible: Psalm 22

3 I give the fight up: let there be an end,

A privacy, an obscure nook for me.
I want to be forgotten even by God.

Robert Browning 1812–89 English poet:
Paracelsus (1835)

4 In despair there are the most intense
enjoyments, especially when one is
very acutely conscious of the
hopelessness of one's position.

Fedor Dostoevsky 1821–81 Russian
novelist: *Notes from Underground*
(1864)

5 There is no despair so absolute as
that which comes with the first
moments of our first great sorrow,
when we have not yet known what it
is to have suffered and be healed, to
have despaired and have recovered
hope.

George Eliot 1819–80 English novelist:
Adam Bede (1859)

6 In a real dark night of the soul it is
always three o'clock in the morning.

F. Scott Fitzgerald 1896–1940 American
novelist: 'Handle with Care' in *Esquire*
March 1936

7 Despair is the price one pays for
setting oneself an impossible aim.

Graham Greene 1904–91 English
novelist: *Heart of the Matter* (1948)

8 Not, I'll not, carrion comfort,
Despair, not feast on thee;
Not untwist—slack they may
be—these last strands of man
In me or, most weary, cry *I can no
more*. I can;
Can something, hope, wish day
come, not choose not to be.

Gerard Manley Hopkins 1844–89
English poet and priest: 'Carrion
Comfort' (written 1885)

9 Don't despair, not even over the fact
that you don't despair.

Franz Kafka 1883–1924 Czech novelist:
diary, 21 July 1913

10 Human life begins on the far side of
despair.

Jean-Paul Sartre 1905–80 French
philosopher, novelist, dramatist, and
critic: *Les Mouches* (1943)

11 Everywhere I see bliss, from which I
alone am irrevocably excluded.

Mary Shelley 1797–1851 English
novelist: *Frankenstein* (1818)

Determination

see also COMMITMENT, DEFIANCE, PERSISTENCE,
STRENGTH

1 Thought shall be the harder, heart
the keener, courage the greater, as
our might lessens.

Anonymous: *The Battle of Maldon*
(c.1000)

2 I can only go one way. I've not got a
reverse gear.

Tony Blair 1953– British Labour
statesman: speech, Labour Party
Conference, Bournemouth,
30 September 2003

3 It's a great life if you don't weaken.

John Buchan 1875–1940 Scottish
novelist; Governor-General of Canada,
1935–40: *Mr Standfast* (1919)

4 I will fight for what I believe in until I
drop dead. And that's what keeps
you alive.

Barbara Castle 1910–2002 British
Labour politician: in *Guardian*
14 January 1998

5 Never give in. Never give in, *never,
never, never, never*—in nothing, great
or small, large or petty—never give
in, except to convictions of honour
and good sense. Never yield to force:
never yield to the apparently
overwhelming might of the enemy.

Winston Churchill 1874–1965 British
Conservative statesman: speech to boys
at Harrow School, 29 October 1941

6 The best way out is always through.
> **Robert Frost** 1874–1963 American poet:
> 'A Servant to Servants' (1914)

7 Climb ev'ry mountain, ford ev'ry stream
Follow ev'ry rainbow, till you find your dream!
> **Oscar Hammerstein II** 1895–1960
> American songwriter: *Climb Ev'ry Mountain* (1959 song)

8 I have not yet begun to fight.
as his ship was sinking, 23 September 1779, having been asked whether he had lowered his flag
> **John Paul Jones** 1747–92 American
> admiral: Mrs Reginald De Koven *Life and Letters of John Paul Jones* (1914)

9 Here stand I. I can do no other. God help me. Amen.
> **Martin Luther** 1483–1546 German
> Protestant theologian: speech at the
> Diet of Worms, 18 April 1521; attributed

10 There comes a time in a man's life when to get where he has to go—if there are no doors or windows—he walks through a wall.
> **Bernard Malamud** 1914–86 American
> novelist and short-story writer:
> *Rembrandt's Hat* (1972)

11 One man that has a mind and knows it can always beat ten men who haven't and don't.
> **George Bernard Shaw** 1856–1950 Irish
> dramatist: *The Apple Cart* (1930)

12 She's as headstrong as an allegory on the banks of the Nile.
> **Richard Brinsley Sheridan** 1751–1816
> Anglo-Irish dramatist: *The Rivals* (1775)

13 Do not underestimate the determination of a quiet man.
> **Iain Duncan Smith** 1954– British
> Conservative politician: speech to the
> Conservative Party Conference,
> 10 October 2002

14 That which we are, we are;
One equal temper of heroic hearts,
Made weak by time and fate, but strong in will
To strive, to seek, to find, and not to yield.
> **Alfred, Lord Tennyson** 1809–92 English
> poet: 'Ulysses' (1842)

15 We shall not be diverted from our course. To those waiting with bated breath for that favourite media catch-phrase, the U-turn, I have only this to say. 'You turn if you want; the lady's not for turning.'
final line from alteration of the title of Christopher Fry's 1949 play The Lady's Not For Burning
> **Margaret Thatcher** 1925– British
> Conservative stateswoman: speech at
> Conservative Party Conference in
> Brighton, 10 October 1980

16 Children, if you are tired, keep going; if you are scared, keep going; if you are hungry, keep going; if you want to taste freedom, keep going.
> **Harriet Tubman** c.1820–1913 American
> abolitionist: attributed, but apparently
> a modern paraphrase of her views

Development

see AID AND DEVELOPMENT

Diaries

1 What is more dull than a discreet diary? One might just as well have a discreet soul.
> **Henry ('Chips') Channon** 1897–1958
> American-born British Conservative
> politician and diarist: diary, 26 July 1935

2 Ten years after your death
I meet on a page of your journal, as never before,
The shock of your joy.
> **Ted Hughes** 1930–98 English poet:
> *Birthday Letters* (1998) 'Visit'

3 To write a diary every day is like returning to one's own vomit.

Enoch Powell 1912–98 British Conservative politician: interview in *Sunday Times* 6 November 1977

4 I have decided to keep a full journal, in the hope that my life will perhaps seem more interesting when it is written down.

Sue Townsend 1946– English writer: *Adrian Mole: The Wilderness Years* (1993)

5 One need not write in a diary what one is to remember for ever.

Sylvia Townsend Warner 1893–1978 English writer: diary, 22 October 1930

6 I always say, keep a diary and some day it'll keep you.

Mae West 1892–1980 American film actress: *Every Day's a Holiday* (1937 film)

7 I never travel without my diary. One should always have something sensational to read in the train.

Oscar Wilde 1854–1900 Anglo-Irish dramatist and poet: *The Importance of Being Earnest* (1895)

8 What sort of diary should I like mine to be? . . . I should like it to resemble some deep old desk, or capacious hold-all, in which one flings a mass of odds and ends without looking them through.

Virginia Woolf 1882–1941 English novelist: diary, 20 April 1919

Dictionaries

1 The greatest masterpiece in literature is only a dictionary out of order.

Jean Cocteau 1889–1963 French dramatist and film director: attributed

2 *Lexicographer.* A writer of dictionaries, a harmless drudge.

Samuel Johnson 1709–84 English poet, critic, and lexicographer: *A Dictionary of the English Language* (1755)

3 Dictionaries are like watches, the worst is better than none, and the best cannot be expected to go quite true.

Samuel Johnson 1709–84 English poet, critic, and lexicographer: letter to Francesco Sastres, 21 August 1784

4 [The] collective unconscious of the race is the OED.

James Merrill 1926– American poet: in *American Poetry Review* September/ October 1979

5 I suppose that so long as there are people in the world, they will publish dictionaries defining what is unknown in terms of something equally unknown.

Flann O'Brien 1911–66 Irish novelist and journalist: *Myles Away from Dublin* (1990)

6 I've been in *Who's Who*, and I know what's what, but it'll be the first time I ever made the dictionary.
on having an inflatable life jacket named after her

Mae West 1892–1980 American film actress: letter to the RAF, early 1940s; Fergus Cashin *Mae West* (1981)

Diets

see also EATING, FAT

1 I repent of my diets, the delicious dishes rejected out of vanity, as much as I lament the opportunities for making love that I let go by because of pressing tasks or puritanical virtue.

Isabel Allende 1942– Chilean novelist: in *Times* 25 April 1998

2 The first law of dietetics seems to be: if it tastes good, it's bad for you.

Isaac Asimov 1920–92 Russian-born biochemist and science fiction writer: attributed

3 The right diet directs sexual energy into the parts that matter.
> **Barbara Cartland** 1901–2000 English writer: in *Observer* 11 January 1981

4 It was brilliant. You die of a heart attack but so what? You die thin.
on the Atkins diet
> **Bob Geldof** 1954– Irish rock musician: in *Independent* 23 August 2003

5 Diets are like boyfriends—it never works to go back to them.
> **Nigella Lawson** 1960– British journalist and cookery writer: in *Sunday Times* 5 March 2006

6 Food is an important part of a balanced Diet.
> **Fran Lebowitz** 1946– American writer: *Metropolitan Life* (1978)

Difference

see SIMILARITY AND DIFFERENCE

Diplomacy

see also INTERNATIONAL RELATIONS

1 I do not regard the procuring of peace as a matter in which we should play the role of arbiter between different opinions . . . more that of an honest broker who really wants to press the business forward.
> **Otto von Bismarck** 1815–98 German statesman: speech to the Reichstag, 19 February 1878

2 An appeaser is one who feeds a crocodile hoping it will eat him last.
> **Winston Churchill** 1874–1965 British Conservative statesman: in the House of Commons, January 1940

3 To jaw-jaw is always better than to war-war.
> **Winston Churchill** 1874–1965 British Conservative statesman: speech at White House, 26 June 1954

4 The gentleman can not have forgotten his own sentiment, uttered even on the floor of this House, 'peaceably if we can, forcibly if we must'.
> **Henry Clay** 1777–1852 American politician: speech in Congress, 8 January 1813

5 One of the things I learnt when I was negotiating was that until I changed myself I could not change others.
> **Nelson Mandela** 1918– South African statesman: in *Sunday Times* 16 April 2000

6 Personally I feel happier now that we have no allies to be polite to and to pamper.
> **George VI** 1895–1952 British monarch: to Queen Mary, 27 June 1940; John Wheeler-Bennett *King George VI* (1958)

7 Let us never negotiate out of fear. But let us never fear to negotiate.
> **John F. Kennedy** 1917–63 American Democratic statesman: inaugural address, 20 January 1961

8 Negotiating with de Valera . . . is like trying to pick up mercury with a fork.
to which de Valera replied, 'Why doesn't he use a spoon?'
> **David Lloyd George** 1863–1945 British Liberal statesman: M. J. MacManus *Eamon de Valera* (1944)

9 We are prepared to go to the gates of Hell—but no further.
attempting to reach an agreement with Napoleon, c.1800–1
> **Pope Pius VII** 1742–1823 Italian cleric: J. M. Robinson *Cardinal Consalvi* (1987)

10 There is a homely old adage which runs: 'Speak softly and carry a big stick; you will go far.' If the American nation will speak softly, and yet build and keep at a pitch of the highest training a thoroughly efficient navy, the Monroe Doctrine will go far.
> **Theodore Roosevelt** 1858–1919

American Republican statesman:
speech in Chicago, 3 April 1903

11 You can no more make an agreement
with those leaders of Colombia than
you can nail currant jelly to the wall.
And the failure to nail currant jelly to
the wall is not due to the nail. It's due
to the currant jelly.
at the time of the Panama revolution, 1903
   Theodore Roosevelt 1858–1919
American statesman:
attributed by Edmund Morris, John F.
Kennedy Presidential Historians Forum,
5 March 2002

12 A diplomat . . . is a person who can
tell you to go to hell in such a way
that you actually look forward to the
trip.
   Caskie Stinnett 1911– American
writer: *Out of the Red* (1960)

13 A diplomat these days is nothing but
a head-waiter who's allowed to sit
down occasionally.
   Peter Ustinov 1921–2004 British actor,
director, and writer: *Romanoff and
Juliet* (1956)

14 An ambassador is an honest man
sent to lie abroad for the good of his
country.
   Henry Wotton 1568–1639 English poet
and diplomat: written in the album of
Christopher Fleckmore in 1604

Disability

1 Does he take sugar?
   Anonymous: title of programme, BBC
Radio 4

2 When we were first told the extent of
Ivan's disability I thought that we
would suffer having to care for him
but at least he would benefit from
our care. Now as I look back I see that
it was all the other way round. It was
only him that ever really suffered and

it was us—Sam, me, Nancy and
Elwen—who gained more than I ever
believed possible from having and
loving such a wonderfully special
and beautiful boy.
   David Cameron 1966– British
Conservative politician: email sent to
Conservative party members,
28 February 2009, after the death of his
son Ivan

3 And now she is like everyone else.
*on the death of his daughter, who had been
born with Down's Syndrome*
   Charles de Gaulle 1890–1970 French
soldier and statesman: attributed

4 My disability is that I cannot use my
legs. My handicap is your negative
perception of that disability, and
thus of me.
   Rick Hansen 1957– Canadian
wheelchair athlete: *Rick Hansen: Man
in Motion* (1987, with Jim Taylor)

5 You and I have been physically given
two hands and two legs and half-
decent brains. Some people have not
been born like that for a reason. The
karma is working from another
lifetime.
   Glenn Hoddle 1957– English
footballer: in *Times* 30 January 1999

6 When I consider how my light is
   spent,
E're half my days, in this dark world
   and wide,
And that one talent which is death to
   hide
Lodged with me useless.
on his blindness
   John Milton 1608–74 English poet:
'When I consider how my light is spent'
(1673)

7 And so I betake myself to that course,
which is almost as much as to see
myself go into my grave—for which,
and all the discomforts that will

accompany my being blind, the good God prepare me!

> **Samuel Pepys** 1633–1703 English diarist: diary 31 May 1669, closing words

8 To be able to feel the lightest touch is really a gift.

> *regaining some movement after being paralysed in a riding accident seven years before*
> **Christopher Reeve** 1952–2004 American actor: in *Sunday Times* 15 September 2002

9 Does it matter?—losing your
>   sight? . . .
> There's such splendid work for the blind;
> And people will always be kind,
> As you sit on the terrace
>   remembering
> And turning your face to the light.

> **Siegfried Sassoon** 1886–1967 English poet: 'Does it Matter?' (1918)

Disasters

see also NINE-ELEVEN

1 We are putting passengers off in small boats . . . Engine room getting flooded . . . CQ.

> *CQD was the original SOS call for shipping*
> **Anonymous**: last signals sent from the *Titanic*, 15 April 1912

2 They have everything they need, they have medical care, hot food . . . Of course, their current lodgings are a bit temporary. But they should see it like a weekend of camping.

> *on the thousands of people left homeless by the L'Aquila earthquake*
> **Silvio Berlusconi** 1936– Italian media entrepreneur and statesman: in *Telegraph* 8 April 2009 (online ed.)

3 Does any one know where the love of God goes

When the waves turn the minutes to hours?

> **Gordon Lightfoot** 1938– Canadian singer and songwriter: 'The Wreck of the Edmund Fitzgerald' (1976 song)

4 It's bursting into flames . . . Oh, the humanity, and all the passengers!

> *eyewitness account of the Hindenburg airship bursting into flames*
> **Herbert 'Herb' Morrison** d. 1989 American radio announcer: recorded broadcast, 6 May 1937

5 I noticed the sea was all frothy like the top of a beer. It was bubbling.

> *collecting an award from the Marine Society for helping to save 100 tourists from the tsunami of December 2004 by remembering her geography lesson*
> **Tilly Smith** 1994– British schoolgirl: in *Sunday Times* 11 September 2005

Discontent

1 You never know what is enough unless you know what is more than enough.

> **William Blake** 1757–1827 English poet: *The Marriage of Heaven and Hell* (1790–3) 'Proverbs of Hell'

2 When you don't have any money, the problem is food. When you have money, it's sex. When you have both it's health.

> **J. P. Donleavy** 1926– Irish-American novelist: *The Ginger Man* (1955)

3 It is an uneasy lot at best, to be what we call highly taught and yet not to enjoy: to be present at this great spectacle of life and never to be liberated from a small hungry shivering self.

> **George Eliot** 1819–80 English novelist: *Middlemarch* (1871–2)

4 Modern man lives under the illusion that he knows what he wants, while

he actually wants what he is
supposed to want.

Erich Fromm 1900–80 American
philosopher and psychologist: *The Fear
of Freedom* (1942)

5   It is a flaw
In happiness, to see beyond our
    bourn—
It forces us in summer skies to
    mourn:
It spoils the singing of the
    nightingale.

John Keats 1795–1821 English poet: 'To
J. H. Reynolds, Esq.' (written 1818)

6 It is better to be a human being
dissatisfied than a pig satisfied;
better to be Socrates dissatisfied
than a fool satisfied.

John Stuart Mill 1806–73 English
philosopher and economist:
Utilitarianism (1863)

7 Whoever is dissatisfied with himself
is continually ready for revenge, and
we others will be his victims.

Friedrich Nietzsche 1844–1900 German
philosopher and writer: *The Gay Science*
(1882)

8 The heart is a small thing, but
desireth great matters. It is not
sufficient for a kite's dinner, yet the
whole world is not sufficient for it.

Francis Quarles 1592–1644 English
poet: *Emblems* (1635)

9 As long as I have a want, I have a
reason for living. Satisfaction is
death.

George Bernard Shaw 1856–1950 Irish
dramatist: *Overruled* (1916)

10 The stoical scheme of supplying our
wants, by lopping off our desires, is
like cutting off our feet when we
want shoes.

Jonathan Swift 1667–1745 Anglo-Irish
poet and satirist: *Thoughts on Various
Subjects* (1711)

11 'Tis just like a summer birdcage in a
garden; the birds that are without
despair to get in, and the birds that
are within despair, and are in a
consumption, for fear they shall
never get out.

John Webster *c.*1580–*c.*1625 English
dramatist: *The White Devil* (1612)

12 He spoke with a certain what-is-it in
his voice, and I could see that, if not
actually disgruntled, he was far from
being gruntled.

P. G. Wodehouse 1881–1975 English
writer: *The Code of the Woosters* (1938)

13 Content is disillusioning to behold:
what is there to be content about?

Virginia Woolf 1882–1941 English
novelist: diary 5 May 1920

Discoveries

see INVENTIONS AND DISCOVERIES

Disillusion

see also CYNICISM

1 Never glad confident morning again!

Robert Browning 1812–89 English poet:
'The Lost Leader' (1845)

2 I never nursed a dear Gazelle, to glad
me with its soft black eye, but when
it came to know me well, and love
me, it was sure to marry a market-
gardener.

Charles Dickens 1812–70 English
novelist: *The Old Curiosity Shop* (1841);
see TRANSIENCE 12

3 And nothing to look backward to
    with pride,
And nothing to look forward to with
    hope.

Robert Frost 1874–1963 American poet:
'The Death of the Hired Man' (1914)

4 Take the life-lie away from the average man and straight away you take away his happiness.
Henrik Ibsen 1828–1906 Norwegian dramatist: *The Wild Duck* (1884)

5 Man hands on misery to man.
It deepens like a coastal shelf.
Get out as early as you can,
And don't have any kids yourself.
Philip Larkin 1922–85 English poet: 'This Be The Verse' (1974)

6 The flesh, alas, is wearied; and I have read all the books there are.
Stéphane Mallarmé 1842–98 French poet: 'Brise Marin' (1887)

7 Reason and Progress, the old firm, is selling out! Everyone get out while the going's good. Those forgotten shares you had in the old traditions, the old beliefs are going up—up and up and up.
John Osborne 1929–94 English dramatist: *Look Back in Anger* (1956)

8 Oh, life is a glorious cycle of song,
A medley of extemporanea;
And love is a thing that can never go wrong;
And I am Marie of Roumania.
Dorothy Parker 1893–1967 American critic and humorist: 'Comment' (1937)

9 Like all dreamers, I mistook disenchantment for truth.
Jean-Paul Sartre 1905–80 French philosopher, novelist, dramatist, and critic: *Les Mots* (1964) 'Écrire'

10 Disillusionment in living is the finding out nobody agrees with you not those that are and were fighting with you. Disillusionment in living is the finding out nobody agrees with you not those that are fighting for you. Complete disillusionment is when you realise that no one can for they can't change.
Gertrude Stein 1874–1946 American writer: *Making of Americans* (1934)

11 If he paid for each day's comfort with the small change of his illusions, he grew daily to value the comfort more and set less store upon the coin.
Edith Wharton 1862–1937 American novelist: *The Descent of Man* (1904)

Dislikes

see LIKES AND DISLIKES

Divorce

1 A divorce is like an amputation; you survive, but there's less of you.
Margaret Atwood 1939– Canadian novelist: in *Time*, 1973

2 He taught me housekeeping; when I divorce I keep the house.
of her fifth husband
Zsa Zsa Gabor 1919– Hungarian-born film actress: Ned Sherrin *Cutting Edge* (1984)

3 A TV host asked my wife, 'Have you ever considered divorce?' She replied: 'Divorce never, murder often.'
Charlton Heston 1924–2008 American actor: in *Independent* 21 July 1999

4 There is a rhythm to the ending of a marriage just like the rhythm of a courtship—only backward. You try to start again but get into blaming over and over. Finally you are both worn out, exhausted, hopeless. Then the lawyers are called in to pick clean the corpses. The death has occurred much earlier.
Erica Jong 1942– American novelist: *How To Save Your Own Life* (1977)

5 There are four stages to a marriage. First there's the affair, then the marriage, then children and finally the fourth stage, without which you cannot know a woman, the divorce.
Norman Mailer 1923–2007 American novelist and essayist: in *Nova*, 1969

6 Staying married may have long-term benefits. You can elicit much more sympathy from friends over a bad marriage than you ever can from a good divorce.

    P. J. O'Rourke 1947– American humorous writer: *Modern Manners* (1984)

7 However often marriage is dissolved, it remains indissoluble. Real divorce, the divorce of heart and nerve and fibre, does not exist, since there is no divorce from memory.

    Virgilia Peterson 1904–66: *A Matter of Life and Death* (1961)

8 Love the quest; marriage the conquest; divorce the inquest.

    Helen Rowland 1875–1950 American writer: *Reflections of a Bachelor Girl* (1903)

Dogs

see also ANIMALS

1 There is no good flock without a good shepherd, and no good shepherd without a good dog.

    Anonymous: motto of the International Sheep Dog Society, said to derive from a Scottish proverb

2 The great pleasure of a dog is that you may make a fool of yourself with him and not only will he not scold you, but he will make a fool of himself too.

    Samuel Butler 1835–1902 English novelist: *Notebooks* (1912)

3 Near this spot are deposited the remains of one who possessed beauty without vanity, strength without insolence, courage without ferocity, and all the virtues of Man, without his vices.

    Lord Byron 1788–1824 English poet: 'Inscription on the Monument of a Newfoundland Dog' (1808)

4 Brothers and Sisters, I bid you beware
Of giving your heart to a dog to tear.

    Rudyard Kipling 1865–1936 English writer and poet: 'The Power of the Dog' (1909)

5 I'm a lean dog, a keen dog, a wild dog, and lone;
I'm a rough dog, a tough dog, hunting on my own.

    Irene Rutherford McLeod 1891–1964: 'Lone Dog' (1915)

6 A door is what a dog is perpetually on the wrong side of.

    Ogden Nash 1902–71 American humorist: 'A Dog's Best Friend is his Illiteracy' (1953)

7 Any man who hates dogs and babies can't be all bad.

    of W. C. Fields, and often attributed to him

    Leo Rosten 1908–97 American writer and social scientist: speech at Masquers' Club dinner, 16 February 1939

8 That indefatigable and unsavoury engine of pollution, the dog.

    John Sparrow 1906–92 English academic: letter to *Times* 30 September 1975

9 I detest dogs, those protectors of cowards who have not the courage to bite the assailant themselves.

    popularly quoted as 'People who keep dogs are cowards who haven't got the guts to bite people themselves

    August Strindberg 1849–1912 Swedish dramatist and novelist: *A Madman's Manifesto* (1895)

10 The more one gets to know of men, the more one values dogs.

    also attributed to Mme Roland in the form 'The more I see of men, the more I like dogs'

    A. Toussenel 1803–85 French writer: *L'Esprit des bêtes* (1847)

11 The dog is a gentleman; I hope to go to his heaven, not man's.
> **Mark Twain** 1835–1910 American writer: letter to W. D. Howells, 2 April 1899

Doubt

see also BELIEF, CERTAINTY, FAITH, INDECISION

1 If a man will begin with certainties, he shall end in doubts; but if he will be content to begin with doubts, he shall end in certainties.
> **Francis Bacon** 1561–1626 English lawyer, courtier, philosopher, and essayist: *The Advancement of Learning* (1605)

2 Oh! let us never, never doubt
What nobody is sure about!
> **Hilaire Belloc** 1870–1953 British poet, essayist, historian, novelist, and Liberal politician: 'The Microbe' (1897)

3 How long halt ye between two opinions?
> **Bible**: I Kings

4 I'm a man of no convictions. At least, I think I am.
> **Christopher Hampton** 1946– English dramatist: *The Philanthropist* (1970)

5 I am too much of a sceptic to deny the possibility of anything.
> **T. H. Huxley** 1825–95 English biologist: letter to Herbert Spencer, 22 March 1886

6 I respect faith but doubt is what gets you an education.
> **Wilson Mizner** 1876–1933 American dramatist: H. L. Mencken *A New Dictionary of Quotations* (1942)

7 Ten thousand difficulties do not make one doubt.
> **John Henry Newman** 1801–90 English theologian and cardinal: *Apologia pro Vita Sua* (1864)

8 It was not the power of the Spaniards that destroyed the Aztec Empire but the disbelief of the Aztecs in themselves.
> **E. F. Schumacher** 1911–77 German-born economist: *Roots of Economic Growth* (1962)

9 There lives more faith in honest doubt,
Believe me, than in half the creeds.
> **Alfred, Lord Tennyson** 1809–92 English poet: *In Memoriam A. H. H.* (1850)

10 Life is doubt,
And faith without doubt is nothing but death.
> **Miguel de Unamuno** 1864–1937 Spanish philosopher and writer: 'Salmo II' (1907)

Drawing

see also FAMOUS ARTISTS, ART, PAINTING

1 I rarely draw what I see—I draw what I feel in my body.
> **Barbara Hepworth** 1903–75 English sculptor: Alan Bowness *Barbara Hepworth—Drawings from a Sculptor's Landscape* (1966)

2 *Le dessin est la probité de l'art.*
Drawing is the true test of art.
> **J. A. D. Ingres** 1780–1867 French painter: *Pensées d'Ingres* (1922)

3 An active line on a walk, moving freely without a goal. A walk for walk's sake.
> **Paul Klee** 1879–1940 Swiss painter: *Pedagogical Sketchbook* (1925)

4 As in the fourteen lines of a sonnet, a few strokes of the pencil can hold immensity.
> **Laura Knight** 1877–1970 English painter: *The Magic of a Line* (1965)

5 When I was the age of these children I could draw like Raphael: it took me many years to learn how to draw like these children.

to Herbert Read, when visiting an exhibition of childen's drawings

> **Pablo Picasso** 1881–1973 Spanish painter: quoted in letter from Read to *Times* 27 October 1956

6 I find a particular delight in taking the caricature as far as I can. It satisfies me to stretch the human frame about and recreate it and yet keep a likeness.

> **Gerald Scarfe** 1936– English caricaturist: *Scarfe by Scarfe* (1986)

Dreams

see also SLEEP

1 Have you noticed . . . there is never any third act in a nightmare? They bring you to a climax of terror and then leave you there. They are the work of poor dramatists.

> **Max Beerbohm** 1872–1956 English critic, essayist, and caricaturist: S. N. Behrman *Conversations with Max* (1960)

2 The armoured cars of dreams, contrived to let us do so many a dangerous thing.

> **Elizabeth Bishop** 1911–79 American poet: 'Sleeping Standing Up' (1946)

3 All the things one has forgotten scream for help in dreams.

> **Elias Canetti** 1905–94 Bulgarian-born writer and novelist: *Die Provinz der Menschen* (1973)

4 When we dream that we are dreaming, the moment of awakening is at hand.

> **J. M. Coetzee** 1940– South African novelist: *In the Heart of the Country* (1977)

5 The interpretation of dreams is the royal road to a knowledge of the unconscious activities of the mind.

often quoted as, 'Dreams are the royal road to the unconscious'

> **Sigmund Freud** 1856–1939 Austrian psychiatrist: *The Interpretation of Dreams* (2nd ed., 1909)

6 The dream of reason produces monsters.

> **Goya** 1746–1828 Spanish painter: *Los Caprichos* (1799)

7 Was it a vision, or a waking dream? Fled is that music:—do I wake or sleep?

> **John Keats** 1795–1821 English poet: 'Ode to a Nightingale' (1820)

8 Those who dream by day are cognizant of many things which escape those who dream only by night.

> **Edgar Allan Poe** 1809–49 American writer: *Eleonora* (1842)

9 O God! I could be bounded in a nut-shell, and count myself a king of infinite space, were it not that I have bad dreams.

> **William Shakespeare** 1564–1616 English dramatist: *Hamlet* (1601)

10 How many of our daydreams would darken into nightmares if there seemed any danger of their coming true!

> **Logan Pearsall Smith** 1865–1946 American-born man of letters: *Afterthoughts* (1931)

11 I have spread my dreams under your feet;
Tread softly because you tread on my dreams.

> **W. B. Yeats** 1865–1939 Irish poet: 'He Wishes for the Cloths of Heaven' (1899)

Drink

see FOOD AND DRINK

Drugs

1 Just say no.
   Anonymous: slogan of the Nancy
   Reagan Drug Abuse Fund, founded 1985

2 LSD? Nothing much happened, but I
   did get the distinct impression that
   some birds were trying to
   communicate with me.
   W. H. Auden 1907–73 English poet:
   George Plimpton (ed.) *The Writer's
   Chapbook* (1989)

3 Cocaine habit-forming? Of course
   not. I ought to know. I've been using
   it for years.
   Tallulah Bankhead 1903–68 American
   actress: *Tallulah* (1952)

4 I'll die young, but it's like kissing
   God.
   on his drug addiction
   Lenny Bruce 1925–66 American
   comedian: attributed

5 Junk is the ideal product . . . the
   ultimate merchandise. No sales talk
   necessary. The client will crawl
   through a sewer and beg to buy.
   William S. Burroughs 1914–97
   American novelist: *The Naked Lunch*
   (1959)

6 I experimented with marijuana a
   time or two. And I didn't like it, and I
   didn't inhale.
   Bill Clinton 1946– American
   Democratic statesman: in *Washington
   Post* 30 March 1992

7 Thou hast the keys of Paradise, oh
   just, subtle, and mighty opium!
   Thomas De Quincey 1785–1859 English
   essayist and critic: *Confessions of an
   English Opium Eater* (1822)

8 Drugs is like getting up and having a
   cup of tea in the morning.
   Noel Gallagher 1967– English pop
   singer: radio interview, 28 January 1997

9 I saw the best minds of my
   generation destroyed by madness,
   starving hysterical naked,
   dragging themselves through the
   negro streets at dawn looking for
   an angry fix,
   angelheaded hipsters burning for
   the ancient heavenly connection to
   the starry dynamo in the
   machinery of the night.
   Allen Ginsberg 1926–97 American poet
   and novelist: *Howl* (1956)

10 In this country, don't forget, a habit is
   no damn private hell. There's no
   solitary confinement outside of jail.
   A habit is hell for those you love.
   Billie Holiday 1915–59 American
   singer: *Lady Sings the Blues* (1956, with
   William F. Duffy)

11 Every form of addiction is bad, no
   matter whether the narcotic be
   alcohol or morphine or idealism.
   Carl Gustav Jung 1875–1961 Swiss
   psychologist: *Erinnerungen, Träume,
   Gedanken* (1962)

12 Sure thing, man. I used to be a
   laboratory myself once.
   *on being asked to autograph a fan's school
   chemistry book*
   Keith Richards 1943– English rock
   musician: in *Independent on Sunday*
   7 August 1994

13 A drug is neither moral or
   immoral—it's a chemical
   compound. The compound itself is
   not a menace to society until a
   human being treats it as if
   consumption bestowed a temporary
   licence to act like an asshole.
   Frank Zappa 1940–93 American rock
   musician and songwriter: *The Real
   Frank Zappa Book* (1989)

Drunkenness

see also ALCOHOL

1 BESSIE BRADDOCK: Winston, you're drunk.
CHURCHILL: Bessie, you're ugly. But tomorrow I shall be sober.
>   **Winston Churchill** 1874–1965 British Conservative statesman: J. L. Lane (ed.) *Sayings of Churchill* (1992)

2 After a man has had his coffee it's tomorrow: it has to be! . . . And tomorrow it's just a hangover; you ain't still drunk tomorrow.
>   **William Faulkner** 1897–1962 American novelist: *Pylon* (1935)

3 Licker talks mighty loud w'en it git loose fum de jug.
>   **Joel Chandler Harris** 1848–1908 American writer: *Uncle Remus: His Songs and His Sayings* (1880)

4 Drink not the third glass.
>   **George Herbert** 1593–1633 English poet and clergyman: 'Perirrhanterium'

5 A man who exposes himself when he is intoxicated, has not the art of getting drunk.
>   **Samuel Johnson** 1709–84 English poet, critic, and lexicographer: James Boswell *Life of Samuel Johnson* (1791) 24 April 1779

6 You're not drunk if you can lie on the floor without holding on.
>   **Dean Martin** 1917– American singer and actor: Paul Dickson *Official Rules* (1978)

7 One more drink and I'd have been under the host.
>   **Dorothy Parker** 1893–1967 American critic and humorist: Howard Teichmann *George S. Kaufman* (1972)

8 Drink, sir, is a great provoker of three things . . . nose-painting, sleep, and urine. Lechery, sir, it provokes, and unprovokes; it provokes the desire, but it takes away the performance.
>   **William Shakespeare** 1564–1616 English dramatist: *Macbeth* (1606)

9 But I'm not so think as you drunk I am.
>   **J. C. Squire** 1884–1958 English man of letters: 'Ballade of Soporific Absorption' (1931)

10 A man you don't like who drinks as much as you do.
definition of an alcoholic
>   **Dylan Thomas** 1914–53 Welsh poet: Constantine Fitzgibbon *Life of Dylan Thomas* (1965)

Duty

see also RESPONSIBILITY

1 Do your duty, and leave the outcome to the Gods.
>   **Pierre Corneille** 1606–84 French dramatist: *Horace* (1640)

2 Duty is what no-one else will do at the moment.
>   **Penelope Fitzgerald** 1916–2000 English novelist and biographer: *Offshore* (1979)

3 Let no guilty man escape, if it can be avoided . . . No personal consideration should stand in the way of performing a public duty.
on the implication of his private secretary in a tax fraud
>   **Ulysses S. Grant** 1822–85 American Unionist general and statesman: endorsement of a letter relating to the Whiskey Ring received 29 July 1875

4 My duty is to obey orders.
>   **Thomas Jonathan 'Stonewall' Jackson** 1824–63 American Confederate general: attributed

5 Do the work that's nearest,
Though it's dull at whiles,
Helping, when we meet them,

Lame dogs over stiles.
  Charles Kingsley 1819–75 English
  writer and clergyman: 'The Invitation.
  To Tom Hughes' (1856)

6 I could not love thee, Dear, so much,
  Loved I not honour more.
  Richard Lovelace 1618–58 English poet:
  'To Lucasta, Going to the Wars' (1649)

7 If we believe a thing to be bad, and if
  we have a right to prevent it, it is our
  duty to try to prevent it and to damn
  the consequences.
  Lord Milner 1854–1925 British colonial
  administrator: speech in Glasgow,
  26 November 1909

8 England expects that every man will
  do his duty.
  Horatio, Lord Nelson 1758–1805 British
  admiral: at the battle of Trafalgar,
  21 October 1805

9 A sense of duty is useful in work, but
  offensive in personal relations.
  People wish to be liked, not to be
  endured with patient resignation.
  Bertrand Russell 1872–1970 British
  philosopher and mathematician: *The
  Conquest of Happiness* (1930)

10 When a stupid man is doing
   something he is ashamed of, he
   always declares that it is his duty.
   George Bernard Shaw 1856–1950 Irish
   dramatist: *Caesar and Cleopatra* (1901)

11 I know this—a man got to do what he
   got to do.
   John Steinbeck 1902–68 American
   novelist: *Grapes of Wrath* (1939)

12 The path of duty was the way to
   glory.
   Alfred, Lord Tennyson 1809–92 English
   poet: 'Ode on the Death of the Duke of
   Wellington' (1852)

13 On an occasion of this kind it
   becomes more than a moral duty to
   speak one's mind. It becomes a
   pleasure.
   Oscar Wilde 1854–1900 Anglo-Irish
   dramatist and poet: *The Importance of
   Being Earnest* (1895)

Dying

see also DEATH

1 It's not that I'm afraid to die. I just
  don't want to be there when it
  happens.
  Woody Allen 1935– American film
  director, writer, and actor: *Death* (1975)

2 To die will be an awfully big
  adventure.
  J. M. Barrie 1860–1937 Scottish writer
  and dramatist: *Peter Pan* (1928)

3 Death is nothing if one can approach
  it as such. I am just a tiny night-
  light, suffocated in its own wax, and
  on the point of expiring.
  E. M. Forster 1879–1970 English
  novelist: Philip Gardner (ed.) *E. M.
  Forster: Commonplace Book* (1985)

4 I have received two wonderful
  graces. First, I have been given time
  to prepare for a new future.
  Secondly, I find
  myself—uncharacteristically—calm
  and at peace.
  *breaking the news of his imminent death
  from cancer*
  Basil Hume 1923–99 English cardinal:
  letter to priests of Westminster diocese,
  16 April 1999

5 It matters not how a man dies, but
  how he lives. The act of dying is not
  of importance, it lasts so short a
  time.
  Samuel Johnson 1709–84 English poet,
  critic, and lexicographer: James Boswell
  Life of Samuel Johnson (1791)
  26 October 1769

6 Dying is a very dull, dreary affair.
And my advice to you is to have
nothing whatever to do with it.
W. Somerset Maugham 1874–1965
English novelist: Robin Maugham
Conversations with Willie (1978)

7 How long does a man spend dying?
Pablo Neruda 1904–73 Chilean poet:
'And How Long?' (1958)

8 Dying,
Is an art, like everything else.
Sylvia Plath 1932–63 American poet:
'Lady Lazarus' (1963)

9 Deception is not as creative as truth.
We do best in life if we look at it with
clear eyes, and I think that applies to
coming up to death as well.
of the Hospice movement
Cicely Saunders 1916–2005 English
founder of St Christopher's Hospice,
London: in *Time* 5 September 1988

10 Nothing in his life
Became him like the leaving it.
William Shakespeare 1564–1616
English dramatist: *Macbeth* (1606)

11 Nor dread nor hope attend
A dying animal;
A man awaits his end
Dreading and hoping all.
W. B. Yeats 1865–1939 Irish poet: 'Death'
(1933)

The Earth

see also ENVIRONMENT, MAPS, NATURE,
POLLUTION, UNIVERSE

1 The earth is what we all have in
common.
Wendell Berry 1934– American poet
and novelist: *The Unsettling of America*
(1977)

2 How inappropriate to call this planet
Earth when it is clearly Ocean.
Arthur C. Clarke 1917–2008 English
science fiction writer: in *Nature* 1990;
attributed

3 Now there is one outstandingly
important fact regarding Spaceship
Earth, and that is that no instruction
book came with it.
R. Buckminster Fuller 1895–1983
American designer and architect:
Operating Manual for Spaceship Earth
(1969)

4 Let me enjoy the earth no less
Because the all-enacting Might
That fashioned forth its loveliness
Had other aims than my delight.
Thomas Hardy 1840–1928 English
novelist and poet: 'Let me Enjoy' (1909)

5 The new electronic interdependence
recreates the world in the image of a
global village.
Marshall McLuhan 1911–80 Canadian
communications scholar: *The
Gutenberg Galaxy* (1962)

6 Gaia is a tough bitch. People think
the earth is going to die and they
have to save it, that's ridiculous . . .
There's no doubt that Gaia can
compensate for our output of
greenhouse gases, but the
environment that's left will not be
happy for any people.
Lynn Margulis 1938– American
biologist: in *New York Times
Biographical Service* January 1996

7 To me, it underscores our
responsibility to deal more kindly
with one another, and to preserve
and cherish the pale blue dot, the
only home we've ever known.
of Earth as photographed by Voyager 1
Carl Sagan 1934–96 American scientist
and writer: *Pale Blue Dot* (1995)

8 God owns heaven
but He craves the earth.
Anne Sexton 1928–74 American poet:
'The Earth' (1975)

9 We have a beautiful
mother
Her green lap
immense
Her brown embrace
eternal
Her blue body
everything
we know.

> **Alice Walker** 1944– American poet: 'We
> Have a Beautiful Mother' (1991)

10 The earth does not argue,
Is not pathetic, has no arrangements,
Does not scream, haste, persuade,
   threaten, promise,
Makes no discriminations, has no
   conceivable failures,
Closes nothing, refuses nothing,
   shuts none out.

> **Walt Whitman** 1819–92 American poet:
> 'A Song of the Rolling Earth' (1881)

11 Need for a knowledge of geography
is greater than the need of gardens
for water after the stars have failed to
fulfil their promise of rain.

> **Yāqūt** d. 1229 Arab geographer

Eating

see also COOKING, DIETS, FOOD

1 Tell me what you eat and I will tell
you what you are.

> **Anthelme Brillat-Savarin** 1755–1826
> French jurist and gourmet: *Physiologie
> du Goût* (1825)

2 Some have meat and cannot eat,
Some cannot eat that want it:
But we have meat and we can eat,
Sae let the Lord be thankit.

> **Robert Burns** 1759–96 Scottish poet:
> 'The Kirkudbright Grace' (1790), also
> known as 'The Selkirk Grace'

3 The healthy stomach is nothing if
not conservative. Few radicals have
good digestions.

> **Samuel Butler** 1835–1902 English
> novelist: *Notebooks* (1912)

4 It's a very odd thing—
As odd as can be—
That whatever Miss T eats
Turns into Miss T.

> **Walter de la Mare** 1873–1956 English
> poet and novelist: 'Miss T' (1913)

5 Gluttony is an emotional escape, a
sign something is eating us.

> **Peter De Vries** 1910–93 American
> novelist and humorist: *Comfort Me With
> Apples* (1956)

6 It [bingeing] gives you a feeling of
comfort. It's like having a pair of
arms around you, but it's temporary.
Then you're disgusted at the
bloatedness of your stomach, and
then you bring it all up again.

> **Diana, Princess of Wales** 1961–97
> former wife of Charles, Prince of Wales:
> interview on *Panorama*, BBC1 TV,
> 20 November 1995

7 I do wish we could chat longer, but
I'm having an old friend for dinner.

> **Thomas Harris** 1940– and **Ted Tally**
> 1952– American writer; American
> screenwriter: *The Silence of the Lambs*
> (1991 film); spoken by Anthony Hopkins
> as Hannibal Lecter

8 A hungry stomach has no ears.

> **Jean de la Fontaine** 1621–95 French
> poet: *Fables* bk. 9 (1678–9) 'The Kite and
> the Nightingale'

9 I don't eat anything with a face.

> **Linda McCartney** 1941–98 American
> photographer, wife of Paul McCartney:
> quoted in *BBC News* (online edition)
> 19 April 1998; obituary

10 Time for a little something.

> **A. A. Milne** 1882–1956 English writer for
> children: *Winnie-the-Pooh* (1926)

11 Hunger is insolent, and will be fed.

> **Alexander Pope** 1688–1744 English
> poet: translation of *The Odyssey* (1725)

12 Now good digestion wait on
appetite,

And health on both!
William Shakespeare 1564–1616
English dramatist: *Macbeth* (1606)

13 We each day dig our graves with our teeth.
Samuel Smiles 1812–1904 English writer: *Duty* (1880)

14 He sows hurry and reaps indigestion.
Robert Louis Stevenson 1850–94 Scottish novelist: *Virginibus Puerisque* (1881) 'An Apology for Idlers'

15 I'll fill hup the chinks wi' cheese.
R. S. Surtees 1805–64 English sporting journalist and novelist: *Handley Cross* (1843)

16 Lunch? You gotta be kidding. Lunch is for wimps.
Stanley Weiser and **Oliver Stone** 1946– : *Wall Street* (1987 film); spoken by Michael Douglas as Gordon Gecko

17 One cannot think well, love well, sleep well, if one has not dined well.
Virginia Woolf 1882–1941 English novelist: *A Room of One's Own* (1929)

Economics

see also BANKING, BUSINESS, DEBT, MONEY

1 There's no such thing as a free lunch.
Anonymous: colloquial axiom in US economics from the 1960s, much associated with Milton Friedman; recorded from 1938

2 Everyone is always in favour of general economy and particular expenditure.
Anthony Eden 1897–1977 British Conservative statesman: in *Observer* 17 June 1956

3 Inflation is the one form of taxation that can be imposed without legislation.
Milton Friedman 1912–2006 American economist: in *Observer* 22 September 1974

4 Trickle-down theory—the less than elegant metaphor that if one feeds the horse enough oats, some will pass through to the road for the sparrows.
J. K. Galbraith 1908–2006 American economist: *The Culture of Contentment* (1992)

5 In a community where public services have failed to keep abreast of private consumption things are very different. Here, in an atmosphere of private opulence and public squalor, the private goods have full sway.
J. K. Galbraith 1908–2006 American economist: *The Affluent Society* (1958)

6 The labour of women in the house, certainly enables men to produce more wealth than they otherwise could; and in this way women are economic factors in society. But so are horses.
Charlotte Perkins Gilman 1860–1935 American writer and feminist: *Women and Economics* (1898)

7 Balancing the budget is like going to heaven. Everybody wants to do it, but nobody wants to do what you have to do to get there.
Phil Gramm 1942– American Republican politician: in a television interview, 16 September 1990

8 Having a little inflation is like being a little pregnant.
Leon Henderson 1895–1956 American economist: J. K. Galbraith *A Life in Our Times* (1981)

9 The best of all monopoly profits is a quiet life.
J. R. Hicks 1904–89 British economist: *Econometrica* (1935)

10 Lenin was right. There is no subtler, no surer means of overturning the existing basis of society than to debauch the currency.

John Maynard Keynes 1883–1946 English economist: *The Economic Consequences of the Peace* (1919)

11 First of all the Georgian silver goes, and then all that nice furniture that used to be in the saloon. Then the Canalettos go.

on privatization; often quoted as 'selling the family silver'

Harold Macmillan 1894–1986 British Conservative statesman: speech to the Tory Reform Group, 8 November 1985

12 If the policy isn't hurting, it isn't working.

on controlling inflation

John Major 1943– British Conservative statesman: speech in Northampton, 27 October 1989

13 Demand for commodities is not demand for labour.

John Stuart Mill 1806–73 English philosopher and economist: *Principles of Political Economy* (1848)

14 Expenditure rises to meet income.

C. Northcote Parkinson 1909–93 English writer: *The Law and the Profits* (1960)

15 We have always known that heedless self-interest was bad morals; we know now that it is bad economics.

Franklin D. Roosevelt 1882–1945 American Democratic statesman: second inaugural address, 20 January 1937

16 Small is beautiful. A study of economics as if people mattered.

E. F. Schumacher 1911–77 German-born economist: title of book (1973)

17 Call a thing immoral or ugly, soul-destroying or a degradation of man, a peril to the peace of the world or to the well-being of future generations: as long as you have not shown it to be 'uneconomic' you have not really questioned its right to exist, grow, and prosper.

E. F. Schumacher 1911–77 German-born economist: *Small is Beautiful* (1973)

18 The cold metal of economic theory is in Marx's pages immersed in such a wealth of steaming phrases as to acquire a temperature not naturally its own.

Joseph Alois Schumpeter 1883–1950 American economist: *Capitalism, Socialism and Democracy* (1942)

19 A continually 'growing economy' is no longer healthy but a cancer.

Gary Snyder 1930– American poet: *A Place in Space* (1995)

20 What a country calls its vital economic interests are not the things which enable its citizens to live, but the things which enable it to make war.

Simone Weil 1909–43 French essayist and philosopher: W. H. Auden *A Certain World* (1971)

Education

see also EXAMINATIONS, SCHOOLS, TEACHING, UNIVERSITIES

1 What sculpture is to a block of marble, education is to a human soul.

Joseph Addison 1672–1719 English poet, dramatist, and essayist: *The Spectator* no. 215 (6 November 1711)

2 The roots of education are bitter, but the fruit is sweet.

Aristotle 384–322 BC Greek philosopher: Diogenes Laertius *Lives of Philosophers*

3 I read Shakespeare and the Bible and I can shoot dice. That's what I call a liberal education.

Tallulah Bankhead 1903–68 American actress: attributed

4 Go to the pine if you want to learn about the pine.

> **Matsuo Basho** 1644–94 Japanese poet: Nobuyuki Yuasa (ed.) *Basho. The Narrow Road to the Deep North* (1966) introduction

5 Ask me my three main priorities for Government, and I tell you: education, education and education.

> **Tony Blair** 1953– British Labour statesman: speech at the Labour Party Conference, 1 October 1996

6 The liberally educated person is one who is able to resist the easy and preferred answers, not because he is obstinate but because he knows others worthy of consideration.

> **Allan Bloom** 1930–92 American writer and educator: *The Closing of the American Mind* (1987)

7 Education makes a people easy to lead, but difficult to drive; easy to govern, but impossible to enslave.

> **Lord Brougham** 1778–1868 Scottish lawyer and politician: attributed

8 To live for a time close to great minds is the best kind of education.

> **John Buchan** 1875–1940 Scottish novelist: *Memory Hold-the-Door* (1940)

9 Gie me ae spark o' Nature's fire, That's a' the learning I desire.

> **Robert Burns** 1759–96 Scottish poet: 'Epistle to J. L[aprai]k' (1786)

10 The empires of the future are the empires of the mind.

> **Winston Churchill** 1874–1965 British Conservative statesman: speech at Harvard, 6 September 1943

11 In education there should be no class distinction.

> **Confucius** 551–479 BC Chinese philosopher: *Analects*

12 Education is the ability to listen to almost anything without losing your temper or your self-confidence.

> **Robert Frost** 1874–1963 American poet: in *Reader's Digest* April 1960

13 The aim of education is the knowledge not of facts but of values.

> **William Ralph Inge** 1860–1954 English writer; Dean of St Paul's, 1911–34: 'The Training of the Reason' in A. C. Benson (ed.) *Cambridge Essays on Education* (1917)

14 If you are truly serious about preparing your child for the future, don't teach him to subtract—teach him to deduct.

> **Fran Lebowitz** 1946– American writer: *Social Studies* (1981)

15 If you educate a man you educate one person, but if you educate a woman you educate a family.

> **Ruby Manikan** Indian church leader: in *Observer* 30 March 1947

16 If you want to know the reason why I'm standing here, it's because of education. I never cut class.

> **Michelle Obama** 1964– American First Lady: to schoolgirls at Elizabeth Garrett Anderson School, London, 2 April 2009

17 For the mind does not require filling like a bottle, but rather, like wood, it only requires kindling to create in it an impulse to think independently and an ardent desire for the truth.

> **Plutarch** c.AD 46–c.120 Greek philosopher and biographer: *Moralia* sect. 48c 'On Listening to Lectures'; see CHILDREN 18

18 Education is what survives when what has been learned has been forgotten.

> **B. F. Skinner** 1904–90 American psychologist: in *New Scientist* 21 May 1964

19 What does education often do? It makes a straight-cut ditch of a free, meandering brook.

> **Henry David Thoreau** 1817–62 American writer: *Journal* November 1850

20 It [education] has produced a vast population able to read but unable to distinguish what is worth reading, an easy prey to sensations and cheap appeals.

> **G. M. Trevelyan** 1876–1962 English historian: *English Social History* (1942)

21 Soap and education are not as sudden as a massacre, but they are more deadly in the long run.

> **Mark Twain** 1835–1910 American writer: *A Curious Dream* (1872) 'Facts concerning the Recent Resignation'

22 Education ent only books and music—it's asking questions, all the time. There are millions of us, all over the country, and no one, not one of us, is asking questions, we're all taking the easiest way out.

> **Arnold Wesker** 1932– English dramatist: *Roots* (1959)

23 The best thing for being sad . . . is to learn something.

> **T. H. White** 1906–64 English novelist: *The Sword in the Stone* (1938)

24 Education is an admirable thing, but it is well to remember from time to time that nothing that is worth knowing can be taught.

> **Oscar Wilde** 1854–1900 Anglo-Irish dramatist and poet: *Intentions* (1891)

25 When you educate a girl you begin to change the face of a nation.

opening her school for poor South African girls near Johannesburg

> **Oprah Winfrey** 1954– American talk show hostess: in *Independent on Sunday* 7 January 2007

Effort

1 For twenty years he has held a season-ticket on the line of least resistance and has gone wherever the train of events has carried him, lucidly justifying his position at whatever point he has happened to find himself.

of Herbert Asquith

> **Leo Amery** 1873–1955 British Conservative politician: in *Quarterly Review* July 1914

2 Now, *here*, you see, it takes all the running *you* can do, to keep in the same place. If you want to get somewhere else, you must run at least twice as fast as that!

> **Lewis Carroll** 1832–98 English writer and logician: *Through the Looking-Glass* (1872)

3 Say not the struggle naught availeth
The labour and the wounds are vain,
The enemy faints not, nor faileth,
And as things have been, things remain.

> **Arthur Hugh Clough** 1819–61 English poet: 'Say not the struggle naught availeth' (1855)

4 Also say to them, that they suffre hym this day to wynne his spurres, for if god be pleased, I woll this journey be his, and the honoure therof.

commonly quoted as 'Let the boy win his spurs'

> **Edward III** 1312–77 English monarch: speaking of the Black Prince at the battle of Crécy, 1346; *The Chronicle of Froissart* (translated by John Bourchier 1523–5)

5 Oh, how I am tired of the struggle!
> **Johann Wolfgang von Goethe** 1749–1832 German poet, novelist, and dramatist: *Wandrers Nachtlied* (1821)

6 HOMER SIMPSON: Kids, you tried your best, and you failed miserably. The lesson is, never try.

Matt Groening 1954– American humorist and satirist: *The Simpsons* 'Burns' Heir' (1994) written by Jack Richdale

7 Between us and excellence, the gods have placed the sweat of our brows.

Hesiod *fl. c.*700 BC Greek poet: *Works and Days*

8 *Parturient montes, nascetur ridiculus mus.*

Mountains will go into labour, and a silly little mouse will be born.

Horace 65–8 BC Roman poet: *Ars Poetica*

9 I had done all that I could; and no man is well pleased to have his all neglected, be it ever so little.

Samuel Johnson 1709–84 English poet, critic, and lexicographer: letter to Lord Chesterfield, 7 February 1755

10 The world is an oyster, but you don't crack it open on a mattress.

Arthur Miller 1915–2005 American dramatist: *Death of a Salesman* (1949)

11 But the fruit that can fall without shaking,
Indeed is too mellow for me.

Lady Mary Wortley Montagu 1689–1762 English writer: 'Answered, for Lord William Hamilton' (1758)

12 The world is divided into people who do things and people who get the credit. Try, if you can, to belong to the first class. There's far less competition.

Dwight Morrow 1873–1931 American lawyer, banker, and diplomat: letter to his son; Harold Nicolson *Dwight Morrow* (1935)

13 Superhuman effort isn't worth a damn unless it achieves results.

Ernest Shackleton 1874–1922 British explorer: to his navigator Frank Worsley, 1916; F. P. Worsley *Endurance* (1931)

14 Things won are done; joy's soul lies in the doing.

William Shakespeare 1564–1616 English dramatist: *Troilus and Cressida* (1602)

15 It is a folly to expect men to do all that they may reasonably be expected to do.

Richard Whately 1787–1863 English philosopher and theologian: *Apophthegms* (1854)

Elections

see also DEMOCRACY

1 It's The Sun Wot Won It.

following the 1992 general election

Anonymous: headline in *Sun* 11 April 1992

2 Vote for the man who promises least; he'll be the least disappointing.

Bernard Baruch 1870–1965 American financier: Meyer Berger *New York* (1960)

3 The accursed power which stands on Privilege
(And goes with Women, and Champagne, and Bridge)
Broke—and Democracy resumed her reign:
(Which goes with Bridge, and Women and Champagne).

Hilaire Belloc 1870–1953 British poet, essayist, historian, novelist, and Liberal politician: 'On a Great Election' (1923)

4 The American people have spoken—but it's going to take a little while to determine exactly what they said.

on the US presidential election of 2000

Bill Clinton 1946– American Democratic statesman: in *Mail on Sunday* 12 November 2000; see ELECTIONS 13

5 You campaign in poetry. You govern in prose.

> **Mario Cuomo** 1932– American Democratic politician: in *New Republic*, Washington, DC, 8 April 1985

6 An election is coming. Universal peace is declared, and the foxes have a sincere interest in prolonging the lives of the poultry.

> **George Eliot** 1819–80 English novelist: *Felix Holt* (1866)

7 Hell, I never vote *for* anybody. I always vote *against*.

> **W. C. Fields** 1880–1946 American humorist: Robert Lewis Taylor *W. C. Fields* (1950)

8 Don't buy a single vote more than necessary. I'll be damned if I'm going to pay for a landslide.

> *telegraphed message from his father, read at a Gridiron dinner in Washington, 15 March 1958, and almost certainly JFK's invention*
> **John F. Kennedy** 1917–63 American Democratic statesman: J. F. Cutler *Honey Fitz* (1962)

9 To give victory to the right, not bloody bullets, but peaceful ballots only, are necessary.

> *usually quoted 'The ballot is stronger than the bullet'*
> **Abraham Lincoln** 1809–65 American Republican statesman: speech, 18 May 1858

10 If voting changed anything, they'd abolish it.

> **Ken Livingstone** 1945– British Labour politician: title of book, 1987

11 If there had been any formidable body of cannibals in the country he would have promised to provide them with free missionaries fattened at the taxpayer's expense.

> *of Harry Truman's success in the 1948 presidential campaign*
> **H. L. Mencken** 1880–1956 American journalist and literary critic: in *Baltimore Sun* 7 November 1948

12 The English people believes itself to be free; it is gravely mistaken; it is free only during the election of Members of Parliament; as soon as the Members are elected, the people is enslaved; it is nothing.

> **Jean-Jacques Rousseau** 1712–78 French philosopher and novelist: *Du Contrat social* (1762)

13 One of the nuisances of the ballot is that when the oracle has spoken you never know what it means.

> **Lord Salisbury** 1830–1903 British Conservative statesman: after the Renfrew by-election of October 1877; Andrew Roberts *Salisbury: Victorian Titan* (1999); see ELECTIONS 4

14 You won the elections, but I won the count.

> *replying to an accusation of ballot-rigging*
> **Anastasio Somoza** 1925–80 Nicaraguan dictator: in *Guardian* 17 June 1977

Emotions

1 The desires of the heart are as crooked as corkscrews.

> **W. H. Auden** 1907–73 English poet: 'Death's Echo' (1937)

2 There is a road from the eye to the heart that does not go through the intellect.

> **G. K. Chesterton** 1874–1936 English essayist, novelist, and poet: *The Defendant* (1901)

3 The world of the emotions that are so lightly called physical.

> **Colette** 1873–1954 French novelist: *Le Blé en herbe* (1923)

4 The human heart likes a little disorder in its geometry.

> **Louis de Bernières** 1954– British

novelist and short-story writer: *Captain Corelli's Mandolin* (1994)

5 In the realm of the emotions, the real is indistinguishable from the imaginary.
André Gide 1869–1951 French novelist and critic: *The Counterfeiters* (1925)

6 As you pass from the tender years of youth into harsh and embittered manhood, make sure you take with you on your journey all the human emotions! Don't leave them on the road, for you will not pick them up afterwards!
Nikolai Gogol 1809–52 Russian writer: *Dead Souls* (1842)

7 They had been corrupted by money, and he had been corrupted by sentiment. Sentiment was the more dangerous, because you couldn't name its price. A man open to bribes was to be relied upon below a certain figure, but sentiment might uncoil in the heart at a name, a photograph, even a smell remembered.
Graham Greene 1904–91 English novelist: *The Heart of the Matter* (1948)

8 A man who has not passed through the inferno of his passions has never overcome them.
Carl Gustav Jung 1875–1961 Swiss psychologist: *Erinnerungen, Träume, Gedanken* (1962)

9 There is no such thing as inner peace. There is only nervousness or death.
Fran Lebowitz 1946– American writer: *Metropolitan Life* (1978)

10 Sentimentality is the emotional promiscuity of those who have no sentiment.
Norman Mailer 1923–2007 American novelist and essayist: *Cannibals and Christians* (1966)

11 Calm of mind, all passion spent.
John Milton 1608–74 English poet: *Samson Agonistes* (1671)

12 The heart is an organ of fire.
Michael Ondaatje 1943– Canadian writer: *The English Patient* (1992)

13 Oh heavens, how I long for a little ordinary human enthusiasm. Just enthusiasm—that's all. I want to hear a warm, thrilling voice cry out Hallelujah! Hallelujah! I'm alive!
John Osborne 1929–94 English dramatist: *Look Back in Anger* (1956)

14 *on being told there was no English word equivalent to* sensibilité:
Yes we have. Humbug.
Lord Palmerston 1784–1865 British statesman: attributed

15 The heart has its reasons which reason knows nothing of.
Blaise Pascal 1623–62 French mathematician, physicist, and moralist: *Pensées* (1670)

16 The ruling passion, be it what it will,
The ruling passion conquers reason still.
Alexander Pope 1688–1744 English poet: *Epistles to Several Persons* 'To Lord Bathurst' (1733)

17 Our passions are most like to floods and streams;
The shallow murmur, but the deep are dumb.
Walter Ralegh c.1552–1618 English explorer and courtier: 'Sir Walter Ralegh to the Queen' (1655)

18 The heart of another is a dark forest.
Ivan Turgenev 1818–83 Russian novelist: *A Month in the Country* (1850)

19 One must have a heart of stone to read the death of Little Nell without laughing.
Oscar Wilde 1854–1900 Anglo-Irish dramatist and poet: Ada Leverson *Letters to the Sphinx* (1930)

20 Now that my ladder's gone
I must lie down where all the ladders start
In the foul rag-and-bone shop of the heart.
W. B. Yeats 1865–1939 Irish poet: 'The Circus Animals' Desertion' (1939)

Employment

see also CAREERS, MANAGEMENT, RETIREMENT, TRADE UNIONS, UNEMPLOYMENT, WORK

1 A professional is a man who can do his job when he doesn't feel like it. An amateur is a man who can't do his job when he does feel like it.
James Agate 1877–1947 British drama critic and novelist: diary, 19 July 1945

2 Lord Finchley tried to mend the Electric Light
Himself. It struck him dead: And serve him right!
It is the business of the wealthy man
To give employment to the artisan.
Hilaire Belloc 1870–1953 British poet, essayist, historian, novelist, and Liberal politician: 'Lord Finchley' (1911)

3 Dr — well remembered that he had a salary to receive, and only forgot that he had a duty to perform.
Edward Gibbon 1737–94 English historian: *Memoirs of My Life* (1796)

4 That state is a state of slavery in which a man does what he likes to do in his spare time and in his working time that which is required of him.
Eric Gill 1882–1940 English sculptor, engraver, and typographer: *Art-nonsense and Other Essays* (1929)

5 It is wonderful, when a calculation is made, how little the mind is actually employed in the discharge of any profession.
Samuel Johnson 1709–84 English poet, critic, and lexicographer: James Boswell *Life of Samuel Johnson* (1791) 6 April 1775

6 Professional men, they have no cares;
Whatever happens, they get theirs.
Ogden Nash 1902–71 American humorist: 'I Yield to My Learned Brother' (1935)

7 Which of us . . . is to do the hard and dirty work for the rest—and for what pay? Who is to do the pleasant and clean work, and for what pay?
John Ruskin 1819–1900 English art and social critic: *Sesame and Lilies* (1865)

8 Work is of two kinds: first, altering the position of matter at or near the earth's surface relatively to other such matter; second, telling other people to do so. The first kind is unpleasant and ill paid; the second is pleasant and highly paid.
Bertrand Russell 1872–1970 British philosopher and mathematician: *In Praise of Idleness and Other Essays* (1986) title essay (1932)

9 When domestic servants are treated as human beings it is not worth while to keep them.
George Bernard Shaw 1856–1950 Irish dramatist: *Man and Superman* (1903)

Ending

1 It ain't over till it's over.
Yogi Berra 1925– American baseball player: comment on National League pennant race, 1973, quoted in many versions

2 Better is the end of a thing than the beginning thereof.
Bible: Ecclesiastes

3 All tragedies are finished by a death,
All comedies are ended by a marriage;
The future states of both are left to faith.
Lord Byron 1788–1824 English poet: *Don Juan* (1819–24)

4 Now this is not the end. It is not even
the beginning of the end. But it is,
perhaps, the end of the beginning.
on the Battle of Egypt
> **Winston Churchill** 1874–1965 British
> Conservative statesman: speech at the
> Mansion House, London, 10 November
> 1942

5 The party's over, it's time to call it a
day.
> **Betty Comden** 1917–2006 and **Adolph
> Green** 1915–2002: 'The Party's Over'
> (1956 song)

6 What if this present were the world's
last night?
> **John Donne** 1572–1631 English poet
> and divine: *Holy Sonnets* (after 1609)

7 This is the way the world ends
Not with a bang but a whimper.
> **T. S. Eliot** 1888–1965 Anglo-American
> poet, critic, and dramatist: 'The Hollow
> Men' (1925)

8 Some say the world will end in fire,
Some say in ice.
From what I've tasted of desire
I hold with those who favour fire.
> **Robert Frost** 1874–1963 American poet:
> 'Fire and Ice' (1923)

9 You cannot reheat a soufflé.
discounting rumours of a Beatles reunion
> **Paul McCartney** 1942– English pop
> singer and songwriter: attributed; L.
> Botts *Loose Talk* (1980)

10 In my end is my beginning.
> **Mary, Queen of Scots** 1542–87 Scottish
> monarch: motto; letter from William
> Drummond of Hawthornden to Ben
> Jonson in 1619

11 *Dies irae, dies illa,*
Solvet saeclum in favilla,
Teste David cum Sibylla.
That day, the day of wrath, will turn
the universe to ashes, as David
foretells (and the Sibyl too).
> **The Missal**: *Order of Mass for the Dead*

'Sequentia' (commonly known as *Dies
Irae*); attributed to Thomas of Celano,
c.1190–1260

12 The rest is silence.
> **William Shakespeare** 1564–1616
> English dramatist: *Hamlet* (1601)

13 This is the beginning of the end.
*on the announcement of Napoleon's
Pyrrhic victory at Borodino, 1812*
> **Charles-Maurice de Talleyrand**
> 1754–1838 French statesman:
> attributed; Sainte-Beuve *M. de
> Talleyrand* (1870)

14 They think it's all over—it is now.
> **Kenneth Wolstenholme** 1920–2002
> English sports commentator: television
> commentary in closing moments of the
> World Cup Final, 30 July 1966

Enemies

see also HATRED

1 *on someone observing that Nye Bevan was
sometimes his own worst enemy:*
Not while I'm alive 'e ain't!
> **Ernest Bevin** 1881–1951 British Labour
> politician and trade unionist: Roderick
> Barclay *Ernest Bevin and the Foreign
> Office* (1975)

2 He that is not with me is against me.
> **Bible**: St Matthew

3 Love your enemies, do good to them
which hate you.
> **Bible**: St Luke

4 He that wrestles with us strengthens
our nerves, and sharpens our skill.
Our antagonist is our helper.
> **Edmund Burke** 1729–97 Irish-born
> Whig politician and man of letters:
> *Reflections on the Revolution in France*
> (1790)

5 You shall judge of a man by his foes
as well as by his friends.
> **Joseph Conrad** 1857–1924 Polish-born
> English novelist: *Lord Jim* (1900)

6 Better to have him inside the tent
pissing out, than outside pissing in.
of J. Edgar Hoover
> **Lyndon Baines Johnson** 1908–73
> American Democratic statesman: David
> Halberstam *The Best and the Brightest*
> (1972)

7 People wish their enemies
dead—but I do not; I say give them
the gout, give them the stone!
> **Lady Mary Wortley Montagu** 1689–1762
> English writer: letter from Horace
> Walpole to George Harcourt,
> 17 September 1778

8 I am the enemy you killed, my friend.
I knew you in this dark: for you so
frowned
Yesterday through me as you jabbed
and killed . . .
Let us sleep now.
> **Wilfred Owen** 1893–1918 English poet:
> 'Strange Meeting' (written 1918)

9 Scratch a lover, and find a foe.
> **Dorothy Parker** 1893–1967 American
> critic and humorist: 'Ballade of a Great
> Weariness' (1937)

10 There is nothing in the whole world
so painful as feeling that one is not
liked. It always seems to me that
people who hate me must be
suffering from some strange form of
lunacy.
> **Sei Shōnagon** *c.*966–*c.*1013 Japanese
> diarist and writer: *The Pillow Book of Sei
> Shōnagon*

11 Heat not a furnace for your foe so hot
That it do singe yourself.
> **William Shakespeare** 1564–1616
> English dramatist: *Henry VIII* (1613)

12 The worst kind of enemies, those
who praise you.
> **Tacitus** AD *c.*56–after 117 Roman
> senator and historian: *Agricola*

13 He makes no friend who never made
a foe.
> **Alfred, Lord Tennyson** 1809–92 English

poet: *Idylls of the King* 'Lancelot and
Elaine' (1859)

14 A man cannot be too careful in the
choice of his enemies.
> **Oscar Wilde** 1854–1900 Anglo-Irish
> dramatist and poet: *The Picture of
> Dorian Gray* (1891)

England

see also BRITAIN, BRITISH CITIES

1 Think of what our Nation stands for,
Books from Boots' and country
lanes,
Free speech, free passes, class
distinction,
Democracy and proper drains.
> **John Betjeman** 1906–84 English poet:
> 'In Westminster Abbey' (1940)

2 I will not cease from mental fight,
Nor shall my sword sleep in my
hand,
Till we have built Jerusalem,
In England's green and pleasant
land.
> **William Blake** 1757–1827 English poet:
> *Milton* (1804–10) 'And did those feet in
> ancient time'

3 God! I will pack, and take a train,
And get me to England once again!
For England's the one land, I know,
Where men with Splendid Hearts
may go.
> **Rupert Brooke** 1887–1915 English poet:
> 'The Old Vicarage, Grantchester' (1915)

4 In England there are sixty different
religions, and only one sauce.
> **Francesco Caracciolo** 1752–99
> Neapolitan diplomat: attributed

5 Mad dogs and Englishmen
Go out in the midday sun.
> **Noël Coward** 1899–1973 English

dramatist, actor, and composer: 'Mad Dogs and Englishmen' (1931 song)

6 England's not a bad country . . . It's just a mean, cold, ugly, divided, tired, clapped-out, post-imperial, post-industrial slag-heap covered in polystyrene hamburger cartons.

Margaret Drabble 1939– English novelist: *A Natural Curiosity* (1989)

7 It is not that the Englishman can't feel—it is that he is afraid to feel. He has been taught at his public school that feeling is bad form.

E. M. Forster 1879–1970 English novelist: *Abinger Harvest* (1936) 'Notes on English Character'

8 An Englishman, even if he is alone, forms an orderly queue of one.

George Mikes 1912–87 Hungarian-born writer: *How to be an Alien* (1946)

9 I am American bred,
I have seen much to hate here—much to forgive,
But in a world where England is finished and dead,
I do not wish to live.

Alice Duer Miller 1874–1942 American writer: *The White Cliffs* (1940)

10 The English are busy; they don't have time to be polite.

Montesquieu 1689–1755 French political philosopher: *Pensées et fragments inédits* . . . vol. 2 (1901)

11 England is a nation of shopkeepers.
the phrase 'nation of shopkeepers' had been used earlier by Samuel Adams and Adam Smith

Napoleon I 1769–1821 French emperor: Barry E. O'Meara *Napoleon in Exile* (1822)

12 Let us pause to consider the English,
Who when they pause to consider themselves they get all reticently thrilled and tinglish,
Because every Englishman is convinced of one thing, viz.:

That to be an Englishman is to belong to the most exclusive club there is.

Ogden Nash 1902–71 American humorist: 'England Expects' (1938)

13 Down here it was still the England I had known in my childhood: the railway cuttings smothered in wild flowers . . . the red buses, the blue policemen—all sleeping the deep, deep sleep of England, from which I sometimes fear that we shall never wake till we are jerked out of it by the roar of bombs.

George Orwell 1903–50 English novelist: *Homage to Catalonia* (1938)

14 Old maids biking to Holy Communion through the mists of the autumn mornings . . . these are not only fragments, but *characteristic* fragments, of the English scene.

George Orwell 1903–50 English novelist: *The Lion and the Unicorn* (1941) 'England Your England'; see BRITAIN 5

15 There'll always be an England
While there's a country lane,
Wherever there's a cottage small
Beside a field of grain.

Ross Parker 1914–74 and **Hugh Charles** 1907–95 British songwriters: 'There'll always be an England' (1939 song)

16 Ask any man what nationality he would prefer to be, and ninety-nine out of a hundred will tell you that they would prefer to be Englishmen.

Cecil Rhodes 1853–1902 South African statesman: Gordon Le Sueur *Cecil Rhodes* (1913)

17 This royal throne of kings, this sceptred isle,
This earth of majesty, this seat of Mars . . .

This blessèd plot, this earth, this
  realm, this England.
  William Shakespeare 1564–1616
  English dramatist: *Richard II* (1595)

18 Englishmen never will be slaves: they
  are free to do whatever the
  Government and public opinion
  allow them to do.
  George Bernard Shaw 1856–1950 Irish
  dramatist: *Man and Superman* (1903)

19 America is a land whose centre is
  nowhere; England one whose centre
  is everywhere.
  John Updike 1932–2009 American
  novelist and short-story writer: *Picked
  Up Pieces* (1976) 'London Life' (written
  1969)

20 You never find an Englishman
  among the under-dogs—except in
  England, of course.
  Evelyn Waugh 1903–66 English novelist:
  The Loved One (1948)

21 We must be free or die, who speak
  the tongue
  That Shakespeare spake; the faith
  and morals hold
  Which Milton held.
  William Wordsworth 1770–1850
  English poet: 'It is not to be thought of
  that the Flood' (1807)

The Environment

see also CITIES, EARTH, POLLUTION

1 Think globally, act locally.
  Anonymous: Friends of the Earth
  slogan, *c.*1985

2 The desert shall rejoice, and blossom
  as the rose.
  Bible: Isaiah

3 I do not know of any environmental
  group in any country that does not
  view its government as an adversary.
  Gro Harlem Brundtland 1939–

Norwegian stateswoman: in *Time*
25 September 1989

4 Man has been endowed with reason,
  with the power to create, so that he
  can add to what he's been given. But
  up to now he hasn't been a creator,
  only a destroyer. Forests keep
  disappearing, rivers dry up, wild life's
  become extinct, the climate's ruined
  and the land grows poorer and uglier
  every day.
  Anton Chekhov 1860–1904 Russian
  dramatist and short-story writer: *Uncle
  Vanya* (1897)

5 Mankind has probably done more
  damage to the earth in the 20th
  century than in all of previous
  human history.
  Jacques Cousteau 1910–97 French
  underwater explorer: 'Consumer
  Society is the Enemy' in *New
  Perspectives Quarterly* Summer 1996

6 Make it a *green* peace.
  *at a meeting of the Don't Make a Wave
  Committee, which preceded the formation
  of Greenpeace*
  Bill Darnell Canadian
  environmentalist: in Vancouver, 1970;
  Robert Hunter *The Greenpeace
  Chronicle* (1979)

7 The poor tread lightest upon the
  earth. The higher our income, the
  more resources we control and the
  more havoc we wreak.
  Paul Harrison 1936– American
  dramatist and director: in *Guardian*
  1 May 1992

8 What would the world be, once
  bereft
  Of wet and wildness? Let them be
  left,
  O let them be left, wildness and wet;
  Long live the weeds and the
  wilderness yet.
  Gerard Manley Hopkins 1844–89
  English poet and priest: 'Inversnaid'
  (written 1881)

9 In my view, climate change is the most severe problem we are facing today—more serious even than the threat of terrorism.

view of the British Government's chief scientific adviser

David King 1939– British scientist: in *Science* 9 January 2004

10   All that remains
For us will be concrete and tyres.

Philip Larkin 1922–85 English poet: 'Going, Going' (1974)

11 They paved paradise
And put up a parking lot,
With a pink hotel,
A boutique, and a swinging hot spot.

Joni Mitchell 1945– Canadian singer and songwriter: 'Big Yellow Taxi' (1970 song)

12 What have they done to the earth?
What have they done to our fair sister?
Ravaged and plundered and ripped her and did her,
Stuck her with knives in the side of the dawn,
And tied her with fences and dragged her down.

Jim Morrison 1943–71 American rock singer and songwriter: 'When the Music's Over' (1967 song)

13 I think that I shall never see
A billboard lovely as a tree.
Perhaps, unless the billboards fall,
I'll never see a tree at all.

Ogden Nash 1902–71 American humorist: 'Song of the Open Road' (1933); see TREES 10

14 It's not that easy being green.

sung by Kermit the frog

Joe Raposo 1937–89 American songwriter: 'Bein' Green', song from Jim Henson's *Sesame Street* (TV show, 1969–)

15 If I were a Brazilian without land or money or the means to feed my children, I would be burning the rain forest too.

Sting 1951– English rock singer, songwriter, and actor: in *International Herald Tribune* 14 April 1989

16 In wildness is the preservation of the world.

Henry David Thoreau 1817–62 American writer: *Walking* (1862)

17 We cannot cheat on DNA. We cannot get round photosynthesis. We cannot say I am not going to give a damn about phytoplankton. All these tiny mechanisms provide the preconditions of our planetary life. To say we do not care is to say in the most literal sense that 'we choose death'.

Barbara Ward 1914–81 British writer and educator: *Only One Earth* (1972)

Envy

1 May good confront the man on top and the man below. But let him who is jealous of another's position choke with his envy.

Chinua Achebe 1930– Nigerian novelist: *Arrow of God* (1988)

2 Thou shalt not covet; but tradition
Approves all forms of competition.

Arthur Hugh Clough 1819–61 English poet: 'The Latest Decalogue' (1862)

3 Fools out of favour grudge at knaves in place.

Daniel Defoe 1660–1731 English novelist and journalist: *The True-Born Englishman* (1701)

4 Do we want laurels for ourselves most,
Or most that no one else shall have any?

Amy Lowell 1874–1925 American poet: 'La Ronde du Diable' (1925)

5 The envious may die, but envy,
never.
> **Molière** 1622–73 French comic
> dramatist: *Le Tartuffe* (1669)

6 If something pleasant happens to
you, don't forget to tell it to your
friends, to make them feel bad.
> **Casimir, Comte de Montrond**
> 1768–1843 French diplomat: attributed;
> Comte J. d'Estourmel *Derniers
> Souvenirs* (1860)

7 Envy can scarcely hold back her
tears, when she sees nothing to cry
about.
> **Ovid** 43 BC–c.AD 17 Roman poet:
> *Metamorphoses*

Epitaphs

see also DEATH

1 What thou art now, wayfarer, world-
renowned,
I was: what I am now, so shall thou
be.
epitaph written for himself
> **Alcuin** *c.*735–804 English scholar and
> theologian: translation by Helen
> Waddell *Mediaeval Latin Lyrics* (1929)

2 Commander Jacques-Yves Cousteau
has rejoined the world of silence.
Cousteau (1910–97) published The Silent
World *in 1953*
> **Anonymous**: announcement by the
> Cousteau Foundation, Paris, 25 June
> 1997

3 Free at last, free at last
Thank God almighty
We are free at last.
*epitaph of Martin Luther King (1929–68),
Atlanta, Georgia*
> **Anonymous**: spiritual, with which he
> ended his 'I have a dream' speech

4 I will return. And I will be millions.
> **Anonymous**: inscription on the tomb of
> Eva Perón (1919–52), Buenos Aires

5 Rest in peace. The mistake shall not
be repeated.
> **Anonymous**: inscription on the
> cenotaph at Hiroshima, Japan

6 A soldier of the Great War known
unto God.
*standard epitaph for the unidentified dead
of World War One*
> **Anonymous**: adopted by the War
> Graves Commission

7 Timothy has passed . . .
*announcing the death of Timothy Leary
(1920–96)*
> **Anonymous**: message on his Internet
> home page, 31 May 1996

8 Hereabouts died a very gallant
gentleman, Captain L. E. G. Oates of
the Inniskilling Dragoons. In March
1912, returning from the Pole, he
walked willingly to his death in a
blizzard to try and save his
comrades, beset by hardships.
> **E. L. Atkinson** 1882–1929 and **Apsley
> Cherry-Garrard** 1882–1959 British
> polar explorers: epitaph on cairn
> erected in the Antarctic, 15 November
> 1912

9 When I am dead, I hope it may be
said:
'His sins were scarlet, but his books
were read.'
> **Hilaire Belloc** 1870–1953 British poet,
> essayist, historian, novelist, and Liberal
> politician: 'On His Books' (1923)

10 Their bodies are buried in peace; but
their name liveth for evermore.
> **Bible**: Ecclesiasticus

11 They shall grow not old, as we that
are left grow old.
Age shall not weary them, nor the
years condemn.
At the going down of the sun and in
the morning

We will remember them.
particularly associated with Remembrance Day services
> **Laurence Binyon** 1869–1943 English poet: 'For the Fallen' (1914)

12 When you go home, tell them of us and say,
'For your tomorrows these gave their today.'
particularly associated with the dead of the Burma campaign of the Second World War, in the form 'For your tomorrow we gave our today.'
> **John Maxwell Edmonds** 1875–1958 English classicist: *Inscriptions Suggested for War Memorials* (1919)

13 Here lies W. C. Fields. I would rather be living in Philadelphia.
suggested epitaph for himself
> **W. C. Fields** 1880–1946 American humorist: in *Vanity Fair* June 1925

14 Life is a jest; and all things show it. I thought so once; but now I know it.
> **John Gay** 1685–1732 English poet and dramatist: 'My Own Epitaph' (1720)

15 His foe was folly and his weapon wit.
> **Anthony Hope** 1863–1933 English novelist: inscription on W. S. Gilbert's memorial on the Victoria Embankment, London, 1915

16 Here lies one whose name was writ in water.
epitaph for himself
> **John Keats** 1795–1821 English poet: Richard Monckton Milnes *Life, Letters and Literary Remains of John Keats* (1848)

17 Here lie I, Martin Elginbrodde:
Hae mercy o' my soul, Lord God;
As I wad do, were I Lord God,
And ye were Martin Elginbrodde.
> **George MacDonald** 1824–1905 Scottish writer and poet: *David Elginbrod* (1863)

18 *Duirt me leat go raibh me breoite.*
I told you I was ill.
> **Spike Milligan** 1918–2002 Irish comedian: inscription on his gravestone

19 Excuse My Dust.
suggested epitaph for herself (1925)
> **Dorothy Parker** 1893–1967 American critic and humorist: Alexander Woollcott *While Rome Burns* (1934)

20 Good friend, for Jesu's sake forbear
To dig the dust enclosed here.
Blest be the man that spares these stones,
And curst be he that moves my bones.
> **William Shakespeare** 1564–1616 English dramatist: epitaph on his tomb, probably composed by himself

21 Go, tell the Spartans, thou who passest by,
That here obedient to their laws we lie.
epitaph for the Spartans who died at Thermopylae
> **Simonides** c.556–468 BC Greek poet: attributed; Herodotus *Histories*

22 Without you, Heaven would be too dull to bear,
And Hell would not be Hell if you are there.
epitaph for Maurice Bowra (1898–1971)
> **John Sparrow** 1906–92 English academic: in *Times Literary Supplement* 30 May 1975

23 This be the verse you grave for me:
'Here he lies where he longed to be;
Home is the sailor, home from sea,
And the hunter home from the hill.'
> **Robert Louis Stevenson** 1850–94 Scottish novelist: 'Requiem' (1887)

24 Where fierce indignation can no longer tear his heart.
Swift's epitaph
> **Jonathan Swift** 1667–1745 Anglo-Irish poet and satirist: S. Leslie *The Skull of Swift* (1928)

25 I always thought I'd like my tombstone to be blank. No epitaph, and no name. Well, actually I'd like it to say 'figment'.

Andy Warhol 1927–87 American artist: *America* (1985)

Equality

see also HUMAN RIGHTS

1 There is no method by which men can be both free and equal.

Walter Bagehot 1826–77 English economist and essayist: in *The Economist* 5 September 1863

2 Equality may perhaps be a right, but no power on earth can ever turn it into a fact.

Honoré de Balzac 1799–1850 French novelist: *La Duchesse de Langeais* (1834)

3 What makes equality such a difficult business is that we only want it with our superiors.

Henry Becque 1837–99 French dramatist and critic: *Querelles littéraires* (1890)

4 He maketh his sun to rise on the evil and on the good, and sendeth rain on the just and on the unjust.

Bible: St Matthew

5 A man's a man for a' that.

Robert Burns 1759–96 Scottish poet: 'For a' that and a' that' (1790)

6 While there is a lower class, I am in it; while there is a criminal element, I am of it; while there is a soul in prison, I am not free.

Eugene Victor Debs 1855–1926 founder of the Socialist party of America: speech at his trial for sedition in Cleveland, Ohio, 14 September 1918

7 When every one is somebodee, Then no one's anybody.

W. S. Gilbert 1836–1911 English writer of comic and satirical verse: *The Gondoliers* (1889)

8 Sir, there is no settling the point of precedency between a louse and a flea.

on the relative merits of two minor poets

Samuel Johnson 1709–84 English poet, critic, and lexicographer: James Boswell *Life of Samuel Johnson* (1791) 1783

9 I have a dream that one day on the red hills of Georgia the sons of former slaves and the sons of former slave owners will be able to sit down together at the table of brotherhood.

Martin Luther King 1929–68 American civil rights leader: speech at Civil Rights March in Washington, 28 August 1963

10 Oh, East is East, and West is West, and never the twain shall meet, Till Earth and Sky stand presently at God's great Judgement Seat; But there is neither East nor West, Border, nor Breed, nor Birth, When two strong men stand face to face, tho' they come from the ends of earth!

Rudyard Kipling 1865–1936 English writer and poet: 'The Ballad of East and West' (1892)

11 All animals are equal but some animals are more equal than others.

George Orwell 1903–50 English novelist: *Animal Farm* (1945)

12 Hath not a Jew eyes? hath not a Jew hands, organs, dimensions, senses, affections, passions? fed with the same food, hurt with the same weapons, subject to the same diseases, healed by the same means, warmed and cooled by the same winter and summer, as a Christian is? If you prick us, do we not bleed? if you tickle us, do we not laugh? if you poison us, do we not die? and if you wrong us, shall we not revenge?

William Shakespeare 1564–1616 English dramatist: *The Merchant of Venice* (1596–8)

13 Those who dread a dead-level of
income or wealth . . . do not dread, it
seems, a dead-level of law and order,
and of security for life and property.
   R. H. Tawney 1880–1962 British
   economic historian: *Equality* (4th ed.,
   1931)

14 Make all men equal today, and God
has so created them that they shall
all be unequal tomorrow.
   Anthony Trollope 1815–82 English
   novelist: *Autobiography* (1883)

15 The constitution does not provide
for first and second class citizens.
   Wendell Willkie 1892–1944 American
   lawyer and politician: *An American
   Programme* (1944)

Europe

see also EUROPEAN UNION, FRANCE, GREECE,
INTERNATIONAL RELATIONS, ITALY

1 It's where they commit suicide and
the king rides a bicycle, Sweden.
   Alan Bennett 1934– English actor and
   dramatist: *Enjoy* (1980)

2 If you open that Pandora's Box, you
never know what Trojan 'orses will
jump out.
   on the Council of Europe
   Ernest Bevin 1881–1951 British Labour
   politician and trade unionist: Roderick
   Barclay *Ernest Bevin and the Foreign
   Office* (1975)

3 Whoever speaks of Europe is wrong,
[it is] a geographical concept.
   Otto von Bismarck 1815–98 German
   statesman: marginal note on a letter
   from the Russian Chancellor
   Gorchakov, November 1876

4 Fog in Channel—Continent isolated.
   Russell Brockbank 1913–79 British
   cartoonist: newspaper placard in

cartoon, *Round the Bend with
Brockbank* (1948)

5 They're Germans. Don't mention the
war.
   John Cleese 1939– and **Connie Booth**:
   Fawlty Towers 'The Germans' (BBC TV
   programme, 1975)

6 Yes, it is Europe, from the Atlantic to
the Urals, it is Europe, it is the whole
of Europe, that will decide the fate of
the world.
   Charles de Gaulle 1890–1970 French
   soldier and statesman: speech to the
   people of Strasbourg, 23 November
   1959

7 Without Britain Europe would
remain only a torso.
   Ludwig Erhard 1897–1977 German
   statesman: remark on West German
   television, 27 May 1962

8 Leave this Europe where they are
never done talking of Man, yet
murder men everywhere they find
them.
   Frantz Fanon 1925–61 French West
   Indian psychoanalyst: *The Wretched of
   the Earth* (1961)

9 Purity of race does not exist. Europe
is a continent of energetic mongrels.
   H. A. L. Fisher 1856–1940 English
   historian: *A History of Europe* (1935)

10 What cleanliness everywhere! You
dare not throw your cigarette into
the lake. No graffiti in the urinals.
Switzerland is proud of this; but I
believe this is just what she lacks:
manure.
   André Gide 1869–1951 French novelist
   and critic: diary, Lucerne, 10 August
   1917

11 In the eighteenth and nineteenth
centuries you weren't considered

cultured unless you made the
European tour, and so it should be.

> **Edward Heath** 1916–2005 British
> Conservative statesman: in *Observer*
> 18 November 1990

12 The European view of a poet is not of
much importance unless the poet
writes in Esperanto.

> **A. E. Housman** 1859–1936 English poet:
> in *Cambridge Review* 1915

13 I grew up in Europe, where the
history comes from.

> **Eddie Izzard** 1962– British comedian:
> *Dressed to Kill* (stageshow, San
> Francisco, 1998)

14 We Americans used to say that the
American Dream is worth dying for.
The new European Dream is worth
living for.

> **Jeremy Rifkin** 1945– American social
> thinker: *The European Dream: How
> Europe's vision of the Future is Quietly
> Eclipsing the American Dream* (2004)

15 You're thinking of Europe as
Germany and France. I don't. I think
that's old Europe. If you look at the
entire Nato Europe today, the centre
of gravity is shifting to the east.

> *to journalists who asked him about
> European hostility to a possible war,
> 22 January 2003*
> **Donald Rumsfeld** 1932– American
> Republican politician and
> businessman: in *Independent*
> 21 February 2003

16 We are part of the community of
Europe and we must do our duty as
such.

> **Lord Salisbury** 1830–1903 British
> Conservative statesman: speech at
> Caernarvon, 10 April 1888

17 Europe is in danger of plunging into
a cold peace.

> **Boris Yeltsin** 1931–2007 Russian
> statesman: at the summit meeting of
> the Conference on Security and Co-
> operation in Europe, December 1994

The European Union

1 It means the end of a thousand years
of history.

> *on a European federation*
> **Hugh Gaitskell** 1906–63 British Labour
> politician: speech at Labour Party
> Conference, 3 October 1962

2 The policy of European integration is
in reality a question of war and peace
in the 21st century.

> **Helmut Kohl** 1930– German
> statesman: speech at Louvain
> University, 2 February 1996

3 'We went in ,' he said, 'to screw the
French by splitting them off from the
Germans. The French went in to
protect their inefficient farmers from
commercial competition. The
Germans went in to cleanse
themselves of genocide and apply
for readmission to the human race.'

> **Jonathan Lynn** 1943– and **Antony Jay**
> 1930– English writers: *Yes, Minister*
> (1982) vol. 2

4 Whereas in England all is permitted
that is not expressly prohibited, it
has been said that in Germany all is
prohibited unless expressly
permitted and in France all is
permitted that is expressly
prohibited. In the European
Common Market (as it then was) no-
one knows what is permitted and it
all costs more.

> **Robert Megarry** 1910–2006 British
> judge: lecture, London, 22 March 1972

5 We have not successfully rolled back
the frontiers of the State in Britain
only to see them reimposed at
European level, with a European
super-State exercising a new
dominance from Brussels.

> **Margaret Thatcher** 1925– British
> Conservative stateswoman: speech in
> Bruges, 20 September 1988

Evening

see also DAY, NIGHT

1 Let us go then, you and I,
When the evening is spread out
   against the sky
Like a patient etherized upon a table.
   T. S. Eliot 1888–1965 Anglo-American
   poet, critic, and dramatist: 'The Love
   Song of J. Alfred Prufrock' (1917)

2 The curfew tolls the knell of parting
   day,
The lowing herd wind slowly o'er the
   lea,
The ploughman homeward plods his
   weary way,
And leaves the world to darkness and
   to me.
   Thomas Gray 1716–71 English poet:
   Elegy Written in a Country Churchyard
   (1751)

3 I have a horror of sunsets, they're so
   romantic, so operatic.
   Marcel Proust 1871–1922 French
   novelist: *Cities of the Plain* (1922)

4 It is a beauteous evening, calm and
   free;
The holy time is quiet as a nun
Breathless with adoration.
   William Wordsworth 1770–1850
   English poet: 'It is a beauteous evening,
   calm and free' (1807)

Evil

see also GOODNESS, SIN

1 It was as though in those last
   minutes he [Eichmann] was
   summing up the lessons that this
   long course in human wickedness
   had taught us—the lesson of the
   fearsome, word-and-thought-
   defying *banality of evil.*
   Hannah Arendt 1906–75 American
   political philosopher: *Eichmann in
   Jerusalem* (1963)

2 I and the public know
What all schoolchildren learn,
Those to whom evil is done
Do evil in return.
   W. H. Auden 1907–73 English poet:
   'September 1, 1939' (1940)

3 It is necessary only for the good man
   to do nothing for evil to triumph.
   Edmund Burke 1729–97 Irish-born
   Whig politician and man of letters:
   attributed (in a number of forms) to
   Burke, but not found in his writings; see
   COOPERATION 4

4 The face of 'evil' is always the face of
   total need.
   William S. Burroughs 1914–97
   American novelist: *The Naked Lunch*
   (1959)

5 As soon as men decide that all means
   are permitted to fight an evil, then
   their good becomes
   indistinguishable from the evil that
   they set out to destroy.
   Christopher Dawson 1889–1970
   English historian: *The Judgement of the
   Nations* (1942)

6 Imagine that you are creating a
   fabric of human destiny with the
   object of making men happy in the
   end, giving them peace and rest at
   last, but that it was essential and
   inevitable to torture to death only
   one tiny creature . . . and to found
   that edifice on its unavenged tears,
   would you consent to be the
   architect on those conditions?
   Fedor Dostoevsky 1821–81 Russian
   novelist: *The Brothers Karamazov*
   (1879–80)

7 What we call evil is simply ignorance
   bumping its head in the dark.
   Henry Ford 1863–1947 American car
   manufacturer: in *Observer* 16 March
   1930

8 In my humble opinion, non-cooperation with evil is as much a duty as is cooperation with good.
Mahatma Gandhi 1869–1948 Indian statesman: speech in Ahmadabad, 23 March 1922

9 Anyone who moved through those years without understanding that man produces evil as a bee produces honey, must have been blind or wrong in the head.
of the Second World War
William Golding 1911–93 English novelist: *The Hot Gates* (1965) 'Fable'

10 To respond to evil by committing another evil does not eliminate evil but allows it to go on forever.
Václav Havel 1936– Czech dramatist and statesman: letter, 5 November 1989

11 Farewell remorse! All good to me is lost;
Evil, be thou my good.
John Milton 1608–74 English poet: *Paradise Lost* (1667)

12 We never do evil so fully and cheerfully as when we do it out of conscience.
Blaise Pascal 1623–62 French mathematician, physicist, and moralist: *Pensées* (1670)

13 There is nothing either good or bad, but thinking makes it so.
William Shakespeare 1564–1616 English dramatist: *Hamlet* (1601)

14 The line dividing good and evil cuts through the heart of every human being. And who is willing to destroy a piece of his own heart?
Alexander Solzhenitsyn 1918–2008 Russian novelist: *The Gulag Archipelago* (1973–5)

15 There are a thousand hacking at the branches of evil to one who is striking at the root.
Henry David Thoreau 1817–62

American writer: *Walden* (1854) 'Economy'

Examinations

1 I wrote my name at the top of the page. I wrote down the number of the question '1'. After much reflection I put a bracket round it thus '(1)'. But thereafter I could not think of anything connected with it that was either relevant or true. . . . It was from these slender indications of scholarship that Mr Welldon drew the conclusion that I was worthy to pass into Harrow. It is very much to his credit.
Winston Churchill 1874–1965 British Conservative statesman: *My Early Life* (1930)

2 Examinations are formidable even to the best prepared, for the greatest fool may ask more than the wisest man can answer.
Charles Caleb Colton *c.*1780–1832 English clergyman and writer: *Lacon* (1820)

3 I evidently knew more about economics than my examiners.
explaining why he performed badly in the Civil Service examinations
John Maynard Keynes 1883–1946 English economist: Roy Harrod *Life of John Maynard Keynes* (1951)

4 Four times, under our educational rules, the human pack is shuffled and cut—at eleven-plus, sixteen-plus, eighteen-plus and twenty-plus—and happy is he who comes top of the deck on each occasion, but especially the last. This is called Finals, the very name of which implies that nothing of importance can happen after it.
David Lodge 1935– English novelist: *Changing Places* (1975)

5 These are not statistics, these are people's futures.
on queries over A-level grades
Estelle Morris 1952– British Labour politician: in *Independent* 21 September 2002

6 In examinations those who do not wish to know ask questions of those who cannot tell.
Walter Raleigh 1861–1922 English lecturer and critic: *Laughter from a Cloud* (1923)

7 Do not on any account attempt to write on both sides of the paper at once.
W. C. Sellar 1898–1951 and **R. J. Yeatman** 1898–1968 British writers: *1066 and All That* (1930) 'Test Paper 5'

8 Had silicon been a gas, I would have been a major-general by now.
having been found 'deficient in chemistry' in a West Point examination
James McNeill Whistler 1834–1903 American-born painter: E. R. and J. Pennell *The Life of James McNeill Whistler* (1908)

Excellence

see also PERFECTION

1 The dullard's envy of brilliant men is always assuaged by the suspicion that they will come to a bad end.
Max Beerbohm 1872–1956 English critic, essayist, and caricaturist: *Zuleika Dobson* (1911)

2 The danger chiefly lies in acting well;
No crime's so great as daring to excel.
Charles Churchill 1731–64 English poet: *An Epistle to William Hogarth* (1763)

3 The pretension is nothing; the performance every thing. A good apple is better than an insipid peach.
Leigh Hunt 1784–1859 English poet and essayist: *The Story of Rimini* (1832 ed.)

4 The best is the best, though a hundred judges have declared it so.
Arthur Quiller-Couch 1863–1944 English writer and critic: *Oxford Book of English Verse* (1900) preface

5 The best is the enemy of the good.
Voltaire 1694–1778 French writer and philosopher: *Contes* (1772) 'La Begueule'; derived from an Italian proverb

6 The best lack all conviction, while the worst
Are full of passionate intensity.
W. B. Yeats 1865–1939 Irish poet: 'The Second Coming' (1921)

Excuses

see APOLOGY AND EXCUSES

Executions

1 Let's do it!
to the firing squad at his execution; after his conviction for murder, Gilmore had refused to appeal, and petitioned the Supreme Court that the execution should be carried out
Gary Gilmore 1941–77 American murderer: Norman Mailer *The Executioner's Song* (1979)

2 Depend upon it, Sir, when a man knows he is to be hanged in a fortnight, it concentrates his mind wonderfully.
on the execution of Dr Dodd
Samuel Johnson 1709–84 English poet, critic, and lexicographer: James Boswell *Life of Samuel Johnson* (1791) 19 September 1777

3 *He* nothing common did or mean
Upon that memorable scene:
But with his keener eye
The axe's edge did try.
on the execution of Charles I
Andrew Marvell 1621–78 English metaphysical poet and politician: 'An

Horatian Ode upon Cromwell's Return
from Ireland' (written 1650)

4 I went out to Charing Cross, to see
Major-general Harrison hanged,
drawn, and quartered; which was
done there, he looking as cheerful as
any man could do in that condition.
Samuel Pepys 1633–1703 English
diarist: diary 13 October 1660

5 'Tis a sharp remedy, but a sure one
for all ills.
*on feeling the edge of the axe prior to his
execution*
Walter Ralegh *c.*1552–1618 English
explorer and courtier: D. Hume *History
of Great Britain* (1754)

6 I hate victims who respect their
executioners.
Jean-Paul Sartre 1905–80 French
philosopher, novelist, dramatist, and
critic: *Les Séquestrés d'Altona* (1960)

7 It is a bad cause which cannot bear
the words of a dying man.
*as drums and trumpets were ordered to
sound at his execution to drown anything
he might say*
Henry Vane 1613–62 English politician
and writer: Charles Dickens *A Child's
History of England* (1853)

Exercise

see also HEALTH

1 I'd love to go to the gym, but I just
can't get my head around the
footwear.
Victoria Beckham 1974– British pop
singer: interview, GMTV, in *Daily Mail*
15 May 2008

2 If you walk hard enough, you
probably don't need any other God.
Bruce Chatwin 1940–89 English writer
and traveller: *In Patagonia* (1977)

3 Exercise is the yuppie version of
bulimia.
Barbara Ehrenreich 1941– American

sociologist and writer: *The Worst Years of
Our Lives* (1991) 'Food Worship'

4 Exercise is bunk. If you are healthy,
you don't need it: if you are sick you
shouldn't take it.
Henry Ford 1863–1947 American car
manufacturer: attributed

5 The sovereign invigorator of the
body is exercise, and of all the
exercises, walking is best.
Thomas Jefferson 1743–1826 American
Democratic Republican statesman:
letter to Thomas Mann Randolph Jr.,
27 August 1786

6 A bear, however hard he tries,
Grows tubby without exercise.
A. A. Milne 1882–1956 English writer for
children: 'Teddy Bear' (1924)

7 The only exercise I take is walking
behind the coffins of friends who
took exercise.
Peter O'Toole 1932– British actor: in
Mail on Sunday 27 December 1998

8 Avoid running at all times.
Leroy ('Satchel') Paige 1906–82
American baseball player: *How To Stay
Young* (1953)

9 There's no easy way out. If there
were, I would have bought it. And
believe me, it would be one of my
favourite things!
of exercise
Oprah Winfrey 1954– American talk
show hostess: in *O: the Oprah Magazine*
February 2005

Exile

1 Once we had a country and we
thought it fair,
Look in the atlas and you'll find it
there:
We cannot go there now, my dear, we
cannot go there now.
W. H. Auden 1907–73 English poet:
'Refugee Blues' (1940)

2 No longer shall our children, like our cattle, be brought up for export.

> **Eamon de Valera** 1882–1975 American-born Irish statesman: speech in Dáil Éireann, 1934

3 Fair these broad meads, these hoary woods are grand;
But we are exiles from our fathers' land.

> **John Galt** 1779–1839 Scottish writer: 'Canadian Boat Song' (1829); translated from the Gaelic; attributed

4 For an exile, there are no continuities, merely succession.

> **Candia McWilliam** 1955– English novelist: *Debatable Land* (1994)

5 What captivity was to the Jews, exile has been to the Irish. America and American influence has educated them.

> **Oscar Wilde** 1854–1900 Anglo-Irish dramatist and poet: in *Pall Mall Gazette* 13 April 1889

Experience

see also MATURITY

1 All experience is an arch to build upon.

> **Henry Brooks Adams** 1838–1918 American man of letters: *The Education of Henry Adams* (1907)

2 You should make a point of trying every experience once, excepting incest and folk-dancing.

> **Anonymous**: Arnold Bax (1883–1953), quoting 'a sympathetic Scot'; *Farewell My Youth* (1943)

3 Experience isn't interesting till it begins to repeat itself—in fact, till it does that, it hardly *is* experience.

> **Elizabeth Bowen** 1899–1973 Anglo-Irish novelist: *Death of the Heart* (1938)

4 Experience is the best of schoolmasters, only the school fees are heavy.

> **Thomas Carlyle** 1795–1881 Scottish historian and political philosopher: *Miscellaneous Essays* (1838) 'Goethe's Helena'

5 I learned . . . that one can never go back, that one should not ever try to go back—that the essence of life is going forward. Life is really a One Way Street.

> **Agatha Christie** 1890–1976 English writer of detective fiction: *At Bertram's Hotel* (1965)

6 The light which experience gives is a lantern on the stern, which shines only on the waves behind us!

> **Samuel Taylor Coleridge** 1772–1834 English poet, critic, and philosopher: *Table Talk* (1835) 18 December 1831

7 The courtiers who surround him have forgotten nothing and learnt nothing.

of Louis XVIII

> **Charles François du Périer Dumouriez** 1739–1823 French general: at the time of the Declaration of Verona, September 1795; quoted by Napoleon in his Declaration to the French on his return from Elba; a similar saying is attributed to Talleyrand

8 We had the experience but missed the meaning.

> **T. S. Eliot** 1888–1965 Anglo-American poet, critic, and dramatist: *Four Quartets* 'The Dry Salvages' (1941)

9 The years teach much which the days never know.

> **Ralph Waldo Emerson** 1803–82 American philosopher and poet: *Essays. Second Series* (1844) 'Experience'

10 Damaged people are dangerous. They know they can survive.

> **Josephine Hart**: *Damage* (1991)

11 Experience is not what happens to a man; it is what a man does with what happens to him.

> **Aldous Huxley** 1894–1963 English novelist: *Texts and Pretexts* (1932)

12 I've looked at life from both sides now,
From win and lose and still somehow
It's life's illusions I recall;
I really don't know life at all.

> **Joni Mitchell** 1945– Canadian singer and songwriter: 'Both Sides Now' (1967 song)

13 Education is when you read the fine print; experience is what you get when you don't.

> **Pete Seeger** 1919– American folk singer and songwriter: L. Botts *Loose Talk* (1980)

14 *Experto credite.*
Trust one who has gone through it.

> **Virgil** 70–19 BC Roman poet: *Aeneid*

15 I've been things and seen places.

> **Mae West** 1892–1980 American film actress: *I'm No Angel* (1933 film)

16 *replying to the question: 'For two days' labour, you ask two hundred guineas?':*
No, I ask it for the knowledge of a lifetime.

> **James McNeill Whistler** 1834–1903 American-born painter: in his case against Ruskin; D. C. Seitz *Whistler Stories* (1913)

17 Experience is the name every one gives to their mistakes.

> **Oscar Wilde** 1854–1900 Anglo-Irish dramatist and poet: *Lady Windermere's Fan* (1892)

Experiment

see also FACTS, SCIENCE, THEORY

1 Observation is a passive science, experimentation an active science.

> **Claude Bernard** 1813–78 French physiologist: *An Introduction to the Study of Experimental Medicine* (1865)

2 Nothing is too wonderful to be true, if it be consistent with the laws of nature, and in such things as these, experiment is the best test of such consistency.

> **Michael Faraday** 1791–1867 English physicist and chemist: diary, 19 March 1849

3 The best scale for an experiment is 12 inches to a foot.

> **John Arbuthnot Fisher** 1841–1920 British admiral: *Memories* (1919)

4 If anyone wishes to observe the works of nature, he should put his trust not in books of anatomy but in his own eyes.

> **Galen** AD 129–199 Greek physician: *On the Usefulness of the Parts of the Body*

5 It may be so, there is no arguing against facts and experiments.
when told of an experiment which appeared to destroy his theory

> **Isaac Newton** 1642–1727 English mathematician and physicist: reported by John Conduit, 1726

6 Where observation is concerned, chance favours only the prepared mind.

> **Louis Pasteur** 1822–95 French chemist and bacteriologist: address given on the inauguration of the Faculty of Science, University of Lille, 7 December 1854

7 Aristotle maintained that women have fewer teeth than men; although he was twice married, it never occurred to him to verify this statement by examining his wives' mouths.

> **Bertrand Russell** 1872–1970 British philosopher and mathematician: *The Impact of Science on Society* (1952)

8 It is much easier to make measurements than to know exactly what you are measuring.

J. W. N. Sullivan 1886–1937 English journalist and science writer: comment, 1928

9 An experiment is a device to make Nature speak intelligibly. After that one has only to listen.

George Wald 1904–97 American biochemist: in *Science* vol. 162 (1968)

Experts

see also KNOWLEDGE

1 Too bad that all the people who know how to run the country are busy driving taxicabs and cutting hair.

George Burns 1896–1996 American comedian: in *Life* December 1979

2 An expert is one who knows more and more about less and less.

Nicholas Murray Butler 1862–1947 President of Columbia University: commencement address at Columbia University; attributed

3 Experts have
their expert fun
ex-cathedra
telling one
just how nothing
can be done.

Piet Hein 1905–96 Danish poet and cartoonist: 'Experts' (1966)

4 An expert is someone who knows some of the worst mistakes that can be made in his subject and who manages to avoid them.

Werner Heisenberg 1901–76 German mathematical physicist: *Der Teil und das Ganze* (1969)

5 No lesson seems to be so deeply inculcated by the experience of life as that you never should trust experts. If you believe the doctors, nothing is wholesome: if you believe the theologians, nothing is innocent: if you believe the soldiers, nothing is safe. They all require to have their strong wine diluted by a very large admixture of insipid common sense.

Lord Salisbury 1830–1903 British Conservative statesman: letter to Lord Lytton, 15 June 1877

Exploration

see also MAPS, TRAVEL

1 Why do people so love to wander? I think the civilized parts of the world will suffice for me in the future.

Mary Cassatt 1844–1926 American artist: letter to Louisine Havemeyer, 11 February 1911

2 Polar exploration is at once the cleanest and most isolated way of having a bad time which has been devised.

Apsley Cherry-Garrard 1882–1959 British polar explorer: *The Worst Journey in the World* (1922)

3 To speak, in conclusion, only of what has been done during this hurried voyage, their Highnesses will see that I can give them as much gold as they desire, if they will give me a little assistance.

Christopher Columbus 1451–1506 Italian-born Spanish explorer: letter to Luis De Sant' Angel, 15 February 1493

4 Ambition leads me not only farther than any other man has been before me, but as far as I think it possible for man to go.

James Cook 1728–79 English explorer: diary, 30 January 1774

5 It was a melancholy day for human nature when that stupid Lord Anson, after beating about for three years, found himself again at Greenwich.

The circumnavigation of our globe was accomplished, but the illimitable was annihilated and a fatal blow [dealt] to all imagination.

Benjamin Disraeli 1804–81 British Tory statesman and novelist: written 1860, in *Reminiscences* (ed. H. and M. Swartz, 1975)

6 We shall not cease from exploration
And the end of all our exploring
Will be to arrive where we started
And know the place for the first time.

T. S. Eliot 1888–1965 Anglo-American poet, critic, and dramatist: *Four Quartets* 'Little Gidding' (1942)

7 One doesn't discover new lands without consenting to lose sight of the shore for a very long time.

André Gide 1869–1951 French novelist and critic: *The Counterfeiters* (1925)

8 We have an unknown distance yet to run, an unknown river to explore. What falls there are, we know not; what rocks beset the channel, we know not; what walls rise over the river, we know not.

John Wesley Powell 1834–1902 American explorer and geologist: *Exploration of the Colorado River of the West and Its Tributaries* (1875)

9 These are the voyages of the starship *Enterprise*. Its five-year mission . . . to boldly go where no man has gone before.

Gene Roddenberry 1921–91 American film producer: *Star Trek* (television series, from 1966)

10 Great God! this is an awful place.
of the South Pole

Robert Falcon Scott 1868–1912 English polar explorer: diary, 17 January 1912

11 Ship and stores have gone—so now we'll go home.
to his men on the loss of the Endurance, *27 October 1915*

Ernest Shackleton 1874–1922 British explorer: *South* (1991 ed.)

12 Go West, young man, go West!

John L. B. Soule 1815–91 American journalist: in *Terre Haute* [Indiana] *Express* (1851)

13   I am become a name;
For always roaming with a hungry heart

Alfred, Lord Tennyson 1809–92 English poet: 'Ulysses' (1842)

14 There is no land unhabitable nor sea innavigable.

Robert Thorne 1527 English merchant and geographical writer: Richard Hakluyt *The Principal Navigations, Voyages, and Discoveries of the English Nation* (1589)

The Face

see also COSMETICS

1 My face looks like a wedding-cake left out in the rain.

W. H. Auden 1907–73 English poet: Humphrey Carpenter *W. H. Auden* (1981)

2 I think your whole life shows in your face and you should be proud of that.

Lauren Bacall 1924– American actress: in *Daily Telegraph* 2 March 1988

3 A merry heart maketh a cheerful countenance.

Bible: Proverbs

4 Was this the face that launched a thousand ships,
And burnt the topless towers of Ilium?
Sweet Helen, make me immortal with a kiss!

Christopher Marlowe 1564–93 English dramatist and poet: *Doctor Faustus* (1604)

5 At 50, everyone has the face he deserves.

George Orwell 1903–50 English

novelist: last words in his notebook,
17 April 1949

6 Had Cleopatra's nose been shorter,
the whole face of the world would
have changed.
   Blaise Pascal 1623–62 French
   mathematician, physicist, and moralist:
   Pensées (1670)

7 Her face, at first . . . just ghostly
Turned a whiter shade of pale.
   Keith Reid 1946– English pop singer
   and songwriter: 'A Whiter Shade of Pale'
   (1967 song)

8 A large nose is in fact the sign of an
affable man, good, courteous, witty,
liberal, courageous, such as I am.
   Edmond Rostand 1868–1918 French
   dramatist: *Cyrano de Bergerac* (1897)

9 There's no art
To find the mind's construction in
the face.
   William Shakespeare 1564–1616
   English dramatist: *Macbeth* (1606)

10 Bah! the thing is not a nose at all, but
a bit of primordial chaos clapped on
to my face.
   H. G. Wells 1866–1946 English novelist:
   Select Conversations with an Uncle
   (1895) 'The Man with a Nose'

Facts

see also THEORY

1 When someone walks like a duck,
swims like a duck, and quacks like a
duck, he's a duck.
   *of Communist affiliations during the
   McCarthy era*
   James B. Carey 1911–73 American
   labour leader: in *New York Times*
   3 September 1948

2 In fact the *a priori* reasoning is so
entirely satisfactory to me that if the

facts won't fit in, why so much the
worse for the facts is my feeling.
   after reading The Origin of Species
   Erasmus Darwin 1804–81 English
   physician: letter to Charles Darwin,
   23 November 1859

3 Now, what I want is, Facts . . . Facts
alone are wanted in life.
   Charles Dickens 1812–70 English
   novelist: *Hard Times* (1854)

4 Facts do not cease to exist because
they are ignored.
   Aldous Huxley 1894–1963 English
   novelist: *Proper Studies* (1927)

5 Roundabout the accredited and
orderly fact of every science there
ever floats a sort of dust cloud of
exceptional observations, of
occurences minute and irregular and
seldom met with, which it always
proves more easy to ignore than to
attend to.
   William James 1842–1910 American
   philosopher: attributed

6 Extraordinary claims require
extraordinary evidence.
   Carl Sagan 1934–96 American scientist
   and writer: *Billions and Billions:
   Thoughts on Life and Death at the Brink
   of the Millennium* (1997)

7 Some circumstantial evidence is very
strong, as when you find a trout in
the milk.
   Henry David Thoreau 1817–62
   American writer: diary, 11 November
   1850

8 Get your facts first, and then you can
distort 'em as much as you please.
   Mark Twain 1835–1910 American
   writer: Rudyard Kipling *From Sea to Sea*
   (1899) letter 37

Failure

see also DEFEAT, SUCCESS

1 Ever tried. Ever failed. No matter. Try
again. Fail again. Fail better.
   Samuel Beckett 1906–89 Irish
   dramatist, novelist, and poet:
   Worstward Ho (1983)

2 The world is made of people who
never quite get into the first team
and who just miss the prizes at the
flower show.
   Jacob Bronowski 1908–74 Polish-born
   mathematician and humanist: *Face of
   Violence* (1954)

3 The conduct of a losing party never
appears right: at least it never can
possess the only infallible criterion
of wisdom to vulgar
judgements—success.
   Edmund Burke 1729–97 Irish-born
   Whig politician and man of letters:
   *Letter to a Member of the National
   Assembly* (1791)

4 'Tis better to have fought and lost,
Than never to have fought at all.
   Arthur Hugh Clough 1819–61 English
   poet: 'Peschiera' (1854)

5 Amid the fluctuating waves of our
social life, somebody is always at the
drowning-point.
   Nathaniel Hawthorne 1804–64
   American novelist: *The House of the
   Seven Gables* (1851)

6 Failure is not an option.
   *summarized version of announcement to
   ground crew in Houston, 14 April 1970, as
   Apollo 13 approached the critical earth-to-
   moon decision loop*
   Gene Kranz 1933– American space
   flight director: title of autobiography,
   2000

7 There is only one step from the
sublime to the ridiculous.
   *to De Pradt, Polish ambassador, after the
   retreat from Moscow in 1812*
   Napoleon I 1769–1821 French emperor:
   D. G. De Pradt *Histoire de l'Ambassade
   dans le grand-duché de Varsovie en 1812*
   (1815)

8 MACBETH: If we should fail,—
   LADY MACBETH: We fail!
   But screw your courage to the
   sticking-place,
   And we'll not fail.
   William Shakespeare 1564–1616
   English dramatist: *Macbeth* (1606)

9 You [the Mensheviks] are pitiful
isolated individuals; you are
bankrupts; your role is played out.
Go where you belong from now on —
into the dustbin of history!
   Leon Trotsky 1879–1940 Russian
   revolutionary: *History of the Russian
   Revolution* (1933)

10 Anybody seen in a bus over the age
of 30 has been a failure in life.
   Loelia, Duchess of Westminster
   1902–93 English aristocrat: in *The Times*
   4 November 1993; habitual remark

Faith

see also BELIEF

1 The Sea of Faith
Was once, too, at the full, and round
   earth's shore
Lay like the folds of a bright girdle
   furled.
But now I only hear
Its melancholy, long, withdrawing
   roar.
   Matthew Arnold 1822–88 English poet
   and essayist: 'Dover Beach' (1867)

2 A faith is something you die for; a
doctrine is something you kill for:

there is all the difference in the world.

> **Tony Benn** 1925– British Labour politician: in *Observer* 16 April 1989

3 Yes, I believe in God.
reply to gunman

> **Cassie Bernall** 1981–99 American student: attributed last words, Columbine High School, Littleton, Colorado, 20 April 1999; the words have also been attributed to a survivor

4 Faith without works is dead.

> **Bible**: James

5 You can do very little with faith, but you can do nothing without it.

> **Samuel Butler** 1835–1902 English novelist: *Notebooks* (1912)

6 The faith that stands on authority is not faith.

> **Ralph Waldo Emerson** 1803–82 American philosopher and poet: *Essays* (1841) 'The Over-Soul'

7 And I said to the man who stood at the gate of the year: 'Give me a light that I may tread safely into the unknown.'
And he replied:
'Go out into the darkness and put your hand into the Hand of God. That shall be to you better than light and safer than a known way.'
quoted by King George VI in his Christmas broadcast, 25 December 1939

> **Minnie Louise Haskins** 1875–1957 English teacher and writer: *Desert* (1908) 'God Knows'

8 The great act of faith is when a man decides he is not God.

> **Oliver Wendell Holmes Jr.** 1841–1935 American lawyer: letter to William James, 24 March 1907

9 A man with God is always in the majority.

> **John Knox** *c.*1505–72 Scottish Protestant reformer: inscription on the Reformation Monument, Geneva

10 Faith may be defined briefly as an illogical belief in the occurrence of the improbable.

> **H. L. Mencken** 1880–1956 American journalist and literary critic: *Prejudices* (1922)

11 A miracle, my friend, is an event which creates faith. That is the purpose and nature of miracles . . . Frauds deceive. An event which creates faith does not deceive: therefore it is not a fraud, but a miracle.

> **George Bernard Shaw** 1856–1950 Irish dramatist: *Saint Joan* (1924)

12 'Tis not the dying for a faith that's so hard, Master Harry—every man of every nation has done that—'tis the living up to it that is difficult.

> **William Makepeace Thackeray** 1811–63 English novelist: *The History of Henry Esmond* (1852)

13 In the darkness . . . the sound of a man
Breathing, testing his faith
On emptiness, nailing his questions
One by one to an untenanted cross.

> **R. S. Thomas** 1913–2000 Welsh poet and clergyman: 'Pietà' (1966)

Faithfulness

see also COMMITMENT, LOYALTY

1 I'll love you, dear, I'll love you
Till China and Africa meet
And the river jumps over the mountain
And the salmon sing in the street,

I'll love you till the ocean
Is folded and hung up to dry
And the seven stars go squawking
Like geese about the sky.

> **W. H. Auden** 1907–73 English poet: 'As I Walked Out One Evening' (1940)

2 There is no infidelity when there has been no love.

> **Honoré de Balzac** 1799–1850 French novelist: letter to Mme Hanska, August 1833

3 It is better to be unfaithful than faithful without wanting to be.

> **Brigitte Bardot** 1934– French actress: in *Observer* 18 February 1968

4 The highest level of sexual excitement is in a monogamous relationship.

> **Warren Beatty** 1937– American actor, film director, and screenwriter: in *Observer* 27 October 1991

5 You're . . . turning into a kind of serial monogamist.

> **Richard Curtis** 1956– New Zealand-born writer: *Four Weddings and a Funeral* (1994 film)

6 But I was desolate and sick of an old passion,
Yea, all the time, because the dance was long:
I have been faithful to thee, Cynara! in my fashion.

> **Ernest Dowson** 1867–1900 English poet: 'Non Sum Qualis Eram' (1896); also known as 'Cynara'

7 Bright star, would I were steadfast as thou art—.

> **John Keats** 1795–1821 English poet: 'Bright star, would I were steadfast as thou art' (written 1819)

8 No, the heart that has truly loved never forgets,
But as truly loves on to the close,
As the sun-flower turns on her god, when he sets,
The same look which she turned when he rose.

> **Thomas Moore** 1779–1852 Irish musician and songwriter: 'Believe me, if all those endearing young charms' (1807)

9 Why fool around with hamburger when you have steak at home?
when asked if he had difficulty staying faithful to his wife Joanne Woodward

> **Paul Newman** 1925–2008 American actor and film director: attributed

10 But I'm always true to you, darlin', in my fashion.
Yes I'm always true to you, darlin', in my way.

> **Cole Porter** 1891–1964 American songwriter: 'Always True to You in my Fashion' (1949 song)

11 But true love is a durable fire,
In the mind ever burning,
Never sick, never old, never dead,
From itself never turning.

> **Walter Ralegh** c.1552–1618 English explorer and courtier: 'Walsinghame'

12 Your idea of fidelity is not having more than one man in bed at the same time.

> **Frederic Raphael** 1931– British novelist and screenwriter: *Darling* (1965)

13 If I could pray to move, prayers would move me;
But I am constant as the northern star.

> **William Shakespeare** 1564–1616 English dramatist: *Julius Caesar* (1599)

14 My true love hath my heart and I have his,
By just exchange one for the other giv'n.

> **Philip Sidney** 1554–86 English soldier, poet, and courtier: *Arcadia* (1581)

15 His honour rooted in dishonour stood,
And faith unfaithful kept him falsely true.

> **Alfred, Lord Tennyson** 1809–92 English poet: *Idylls of the King* 'Lancelot and Elaine' (1859)

Falklands War

1 GOTCHA!
Anonymous: headline on the sinking of the *General Belgrano*, in *Sun* 4 May 1982

2 The Falklands thing was a fight between two bald men over a comb.
Jorge Luis Borges 1899–1986 Argentinian writer: in *Time* 14 February 1983

3 I counted them all out and I counted them all back.
on the number of British aeroplanes (which he was not permitted to disclose) joining the raid on Port Stanley in the Falkland Islands
Brian Hanrahan 1949– British journalist: BBC broadcast report, 1 May 1982

4 Just rejoice at that news and congratulate our forces and the Marines . . . Rejoice!
on the recapture of South Georgia; usually quoted as 'Rejoice, rejoice'
Margaret Thatcher 1925– British Conservative stateswoman: to newsmen outside Downing Street, 25 April 1982

5 We have to see that the spirit of the South Atlantic—the real spirit of Britain—is kindled not only by war but can now be fired by peace. We have the first prerequisite. We know that we can do it—we haven't lost the ability. That is the Falklands Factor.
Margaret Thatcher 1925– British Conservative stateswoman: speech in Cheltenham, 3 July 1982

Fame

see also REPUTATION

1 What price glory?
Maxwell Anderson 1888–1959 American dramatist: title of play (1924, with Lawrence Stallings)

2 Now who is responsible for this work of development on which so much depends? To whom must the praise be given? To the boys in the back rooms. They do not sit in the limelight. But they are the men who do the work.
Lord Beaverbrook 1879–1964 Canadian-born British newspaper proprietor and Conservative politician: in *Listener* 27 March 1941

3 There's no such thing as bad publicity except your own obituary.
Brendan Behan 1923–64 Irish dramatist: Dominic Behan *My Brother Brendan* (1965)

4 He's always backing into the limelight.
of T. E. Lawrence
Lord Berners 1883–1950 English composer, artist, and writer: oral tradition

5 The celebrity is a person who is known for his well-knownness.
Daniel J. Boorstin 1914–2004 American historian: *The Image* (1961)

6 I awoke one morning and found myself famous.
on the instantaneous success of Childe Harold
Lord Byron 1788–1824 English poet: Thomas Moore *Letters and Journals of Lord Byron* (1830)

7 I don't care what you say about me, as long as you say *something* about me, and as long as you spell my name right.
said to a newspaperman in 1912
George M. Cohan 1878–1942 American songwriter, dramatist, and producer: John McCabe *George M. Cohan* (1973)

8 Fancy being remembered around the world for the invention of a mouse!
Walt Disney 1901–66 American animator and film producer: during his last illness; Leonard Mosley *Disney's World* (1985)

9 The deed is all, the glory nothing.
> **Johann Wolfgang von Goethe**
> 1749–1832 German poet, novelist, and
> dramatist: *Faust* pt. 2 (1832)

10 Full many a flower is born to blush
unseen,
And waste its sweetness on the
desert air.
> **Thomas Gray** 1716–71 English poet:
> *Elegy Written in a Country Churchyard*
> (1751)

11 Popularity? It is glory's small change.
> **Victor Hugo** 1802–85 French poet,
> novelist, and dramatist: *Ruy Blas* (1838)

12 Every man has a lurking wish to
appear considerable in his native
place.
> **Samuel Johnson** 1709–84 English poet,
> critic, and lexicographer: letter to
> Joshua Reynolds, 17 July 1771

13 Kids want to be famous. They don't
want to be good at anything any
more.
> **Ronan Keating** 1977– Irish pop singer:
> in *The Times* 5 April 2003

14 No path of flowers leads to glory.
> **Jean de la Fontaine** 1621–95 French
> poet: *Fables* (1694) 'The Two
> Adventurers and the Talisman'

15 The best fame is a writer's fame: it's
enough to get a table at a good
restaurant, but not enough that you
get interrupted when you eat.
> **Fran Lebowitz** 1946– American writer:
> in *Observer* 30 May 1993

16 We're more popular than Jesus now; I
don't know which will go first—rock
'n' roll or Christianity.
> *of The Beatles*
> **John Lennon** 1940–80 English pop
> singer and songwriter: interview in
> *Evening Standard* 4 March 1966

17 Fame is the spur that the clear spirit
doth raise

(That last infirmity of noble mind)
To scorn delights, and live laborious
days.
> **John Milton** 1608–74 English poet:
> 'Lycidas' (1638)

18 So long as men can breathe, or eyes
can see,
So long lives this, and this gives life
to thee.
> **William Shakespeare** 1564–1616
> English dramatist: sonnet 18

19 Martyrdom . . . the only way in
which a man can become famous
without ability.
> **George Bernard Shaw** 1856–1950 Irish
> dramatist: *The Devil's Disciple* (1901)

20 Celebrity is a mask that eats into the
face.
> **John Updike** 1932–2009 American
> novelist and short-story writer: *Self-
> Consciousness: Memoirs* (1989)

21 In the future everybody will be world
famous for fifteen minutes.
> **Andy Warhol** 1927–87 American artist:
> *Andy Warhol* (1968)

22 It's better to be looked over than
overlooked.
> **Mae West** 1892–1980 American film
> actress: *Belle of the Nineties* (1934 film)

Familiarity

1 A prophet is not without honour,
save in his own country, and in his
own house.
> **Bible**: St Matthew

2 Think you, if Laura had been
Petrarch's wife,
He would have written sonnets all
his life?
> **Lord Byron** 1788–1824 English poet:
> *Don Juan* (1819–24)

3 There is nothing that God hath
established in a constant course of

nature, and which therefore is done every day, but would seem a Miracle, and exercise our admiration, if it were done but once.

John Donne 1572–1631 English poet and divine: *LXXX Sermons* (1640) Easter Day, 25 March 1627

4 A maggot must be born i' the rotten cheese to like it.

George Eliot 1819–80 English novelist: *Adam Bede* (1859)

5 I've grown accustomed to the trace
Of something in the air;
Accustomed to her face.

Alan Jay Lerner 1918–86 American songwriter: 'I've Grown Accustomed to her Face' (1956 song)

6 The mind loves the unknown. It loves images whose meaning is unknown, since the meaning of the mind itself is unknown.

René Magritte 1898–1967 Belgian surrealist painter : Suzy Gablik *Magritte* (1970)

7 Only the unknown frightens men. But once a man has faced the unknown, that terror becomes known.

Antoine de Saint-Exupéry 1900–44 French novelist: *Wind, Sand and Stars* (1939)

8 Old friends are best. King James used to call for his old shoes; they were easiest for his feet.

John Selden 1584–1654 English historian and antiquary: *Table Talk* (1689) 'Friends'

9 There are no conditions of life to which a man cannot get accustomed, especially if he sees them accepted by everyone about him.

Leo Tolstoy 1828–1910 Russian novelist: *Anna Karenina* (1875–7)

10 Familiarity breeds contempt—and children.

Mark Twain 1835–1910 American writer: *Notebooks* (1935)

The Family

see also CHILDREN, IN-LAWS, PARENTS

1 He that hath wife and children hath given hostages to fortune; for they are impediments to great enterprises, either of virtue or mischief.

Francis Bacon 1561–1626 English lawyer, courtier, philosopher, and essayist: *Essays* (1625) 'Of Marriage and the Single Life'

2 The worst families are those in which the members never really speak their minds to one another; they maintain an atmosphere of unreality, and everyone always lives in an atmosphere of suppressed ill-feeling.

Walter Bagehot 1826–77 English economist and essayist: *The English Constitution* (ed. 2, 1872) introduction

3 I have never understood this liking for war. It panders to instincts already catered for within the scope of any respectable domestic establishment.

Alan Bennett 1934– English actor and dramatist: *Forty Years On* (1969)

4 We begin our public affections in our families. No cold relation is a zealous citizen.

Edmund Burke 1729–97 Irish-born Whig politician and man of letters: *Reflections on the Revolution in France* (1790)

5 [It is] time to turn our attention to pressing challenges like . . . how to

make American families more like
the Waltons and a little bit less like
the Simpsons.

> **George Bush** 1924– American
> Republican statesman: speech, Neenah,
> Wisconsin, 27 July 1992

6   The truth is that it is not the sins of
the fathers that descend unto the
third generation, but the sorrows of
the mothers.

> **Marilyn French** 1929–2009 American
> writer: *Her Mother's Daughter* (1987)

7   I am the family face;
Flesh perishes, I live on,
Projecting trait and trace
Through time to times anon,
And leaping from place to place
Over oblivion.

> **Thomas Hardy** 1840–1928 English
> novelist and poet: 'Heredity' (1917)

8   Far from being the basis of the good
society, the family, with its narrow
privacy and tawdry secrets, is the
source of all our discontents.

> **Edmund Leach** 1910–89 English
> anthropologist: BBC Reith Lectures,
> 1967

9   One would be in less danger
From the wiles of the stranger
If one's own kin and kith
Were more fun to be with.

> **Ogden Nash** 1902–71 American
> humorist: 'Family Court' (1931)

10   Family history, of course, has its
proper dietary laws. One is supposed
to swallow and digest only the
permitted parts of it, the halal
portions of the past, drained of their
redness, their blood.

> **Salman Rushdie** 1947– Indian-born
> British novelist: *Midnight's Children*
> (1981)

11   I detest collaterals. Blood may be
thicker than water, but it is also a
great deal nastier.

> **Edith Œ Somerville** 1858–1949 and
> **Martin Ross** 1862–1915 Irish writers:
> *Some Experiences of an Irish R.M.* (1899)

12   Family! . . . the home of all social
evil, a charitable institution for
comfortable women, an anchorage
for house-fathers, and a hell for
children.

> **August Strindberg** 1849–1912 Swedish
> dramatist and novelist: *The Son of a
> Servant* (1886)

13   If a man's character is to be abused,
say what you will, there's nobody like
a relation to do the business.

> **William Makepeace Thackeray**
> 1811–63 English novelist: *Vanity Fair*
> (1847–8)

14   All happy families resemble one
another, but each unhappy family is
unhappy in its own way.

> **Leo Tolstoy** 1828–1910 Russian novelist:
> *Anna Karenina* (1875–7)

15   Relations are simply a tedious pack
of people, who haven't got the
remotest knowledge of how to live,
nor the smallest instinct about when
to die.

> **Oscar Wilde** 1854–1900 Anglo-Irish
> dramatist and poet: *The Importance of
> Being Earnest* (1899)

16   No test tube can breed love and
affection. No frozen packet of semen
ever read a story to a sleepy child.

> **Shirley Williams** 1930– British
> politician: in *Daily Mirror* 2 March 1978

17   It is no use telling me that there are
bad aunts and good aunts. At the
core, they are all alike. Sooner or
later, out pops the cloven hoof.

> **P. G. Wodehouse** 1881–1975 English
> writer: *The Code of the Woosters* (1938)

Famine

see also AID

1 Where mass hunger reigns, we
cannot speak of peace.
> **Willy Brandt** 1913–92 German
> statesman: *World Armament and World
> Hunger* (1986)

2 They that die by famine die by
inches.
> **Matthew Henry** 1662–1714 English
> divine: *An Exposition on the Old and
> New Testament* (1710)

3 Clay is the word and clay is the flesh
Where the potato-gatherers like
mechanized scarecrows move
Along the side-fall of the
hill—Maguire and his men.
> **Patrick Kavanagh** 1904–67 Irish poet:
> 'The Great Hunger' (1947)

4 There's famine in the land, its grip is
tightening still!
There's trouble, black and bitter, on
every side I glance.
> **Emily Lawless** 1845–1913 Irish poet: 'An
> Exile's Mother'

5 How can you frighten a man whose
hunger is not only in his own
cramped stomach but in the
wretched bellies of his children? You
can't scare him—he has known a fear
beyond every other.
> **John Steinbeck** 1902–68 American
> novelist: *The Grapes of Wrath* (1939)

6 Famine sighs like scythe
across the field of statistics and the
desert
is a moving mouth.
> **Derek Walcott** 1930– West Indian poet
> and dramatist: 'The Fortunate Traveller'
> (1981)

Famous Artists

see also ART, DRAWING, PAINTING

1 Monet is only an eye, but what an
eye!
> **Paul Cézanne** 1839–1906 French
> painter: attributed

2 In Claude's landscape all is
lovely—all amiable—all is amenity
and repose;—the calm sunshine of
the heart.
> **John Constable** 1776–1837 English
> painter: lecture, 2 June 1836

3 Picasso is Spanish, I am too. Picasso
is a genius. I am too. Picasso will be
seventy-two and I about forty-eight.
Picasso is known in every country of
the world; so am I. Picasso is a
Communist; I am not.
> **Salvador Dali** 1904–89 Spanish painter:
> lecture in Madrid, 12 October 1951

4 It's amazing what you can do with an
E in A-level art, twisted imagination
and a chainsaw.
after winning the 1995 Turner Prize
> **Damien Hirst** 1965– English artist: in
> *Observer* 3 December 1995

5 If Botticelli were alive today he'd be
working for *Vogue*.
> **Peter Ustinov** 1921–2004 British actor,
> director, and writer: in *Observer*
> 21 October 1962

6 A genius with the IQ of a moron.
of Andy Warhol
> **Gore Vidal** 1925– American novelist
> and critic: in *Observer* 18 June 1989

Famous Musicians

1 Everything will pass, and the world
will perish but the Ninth Symphony
will remain.
of Beethoven's Ninth Symphony
> **Michael Bakunin** 1814–76 Russian
> revolutionary and anarchist: Edmund
> Wilson *To The Finland Station* (1940)

2 It may be that when the angels go about their task of praising God, they play only Bach. I am sure, however, that when they are together *en famille*, they play Mozart.

Karl Barth 1886–1968 Swiss Protestant theologian: *Wolfgang Amadeus Mozart* (1956)

3 Too much counterpoint; what is worse, Protestant counterpoint.

of Johann Sebastian Bach
Thomas Beecham 1879–1961 English conductor: in *Guardian* 8 March 1971

4 The immortal god of harmony.

of Johann Sebastian Bach
Ludwig van Beethoven 1770–1827 German composer: letter to the publishers Breitkopf und Härtel, 22 April 1801

5 It will be generally admitted that Beethoven's Fifth Symphony is the most sublime noise that has ever penetrated into the ear of man.

E. M. Forster 1879–1970 English novelist: *Howards End* (1910)

6 Too beautiful for our ears, and much too many notes, dear Mozart.

of The Abduction from the Seraglio *(1782)*
Joseph II 1741–90 Holy Roman Emperor: attributed; Franz Xaver Niemetschek *Life of Mozart* (1798)

7 Something touched me deep inside The day the music died.

on the death of Buddy Holly
Don McLean 1945– American songwriter: 'American Pie' (1972 song)

8 If anyone has conducted a Beethoven performance, and then doesn't have to go to an osteopath, then there's something wrong.

Simon Rattle 1955– English conductor: in *Guardian* 31 May 1990

9 Wagner has lovely moments but awful quarters of an hour.

Gioacchino Rossini 1792–1868 Italian composer: said to Emile Naumann, April 1867; E. Naumann *Italienische Tondichter* (1883)

10 Ravel refuses the Legion of Honour, but all his music accepts it.

Erik Satie 1866–1925 French composer: Jean Cocteau *Le Discours d'Oxford* (1956)

11 Children are given Mozart because of the small *quantity* of the notes; grown-ups avoid Mozart because of the great *quality* of the notes.

Artur Schnabel 1882–1951 Austrian-born pianist: *My Life and Music* (1961)

Famous People

see also FAMOUS ARTISTS, FAMOUS MUSICIANS, FAMOUS POETS, FAMOUS POLITICIANS, FAMOUS WRITERS

1 Egghead weds hourglass.

on the marriage of Arthur Miller and Marilyn Monroe
Anonymous: headline in *Variety* 1956; attributed

2 To us he is no more a person now but a whole climate of opinion.

W. H. Auden 1907–73 English poet: 'In Memory of Sigmund Freud' (1940)

3 In defeat unbeatable: in victory unbearable.

of Lord Montgomery
Winston Churchill 1874–1965 British Conservative statesman: Edward Marsh *Ambrosia and Small Beer* (1964)

4 Goodbye Norma Jean . . .
And it seems to me you lived your life
Like a candle in the wind.
Never knowing who to cling to
When the rain set in . . .

of Marilyn Monroe
Elton John 1947– and **Bernie Taupin** 1950– English pop singer and songwriter; songwriter: 'Candle in the Wind' (song, 1973); see ROYAL FAMILY 8, SINGING 10

5 A man who so much resembled a Baked Alaska—sweet, warm and gungy on the outside, hard and cold within.

of C. P. Snow

    Francis King 1923– British writer: *Yesterday Came Suddenly* (1993)

6 Every word she writes is a lie, including 'and' and 'the'.

of Lillian Hellman

    Mary McCarthy 1912–89 American novelist: in *New York Times* 16 February 1980

7 So we think of Marilyn who was every man's love affair with America, Marilyn Monroe who was blonde and beautiful and had a sweet little rinky-dink of a voice and all the cleanliness of all the clean American backyards.

    Norman Mailer 1923–2007 American novelist and essayist: *Marilyn* (1973)

8 The thinking man's crumpet.

of Joan Bakewell

    Frank Muir 1920–98 English writer and broadcaster: attributed

9 If only Bapu knew the cost of setting him up in poverty!

of Mahatma Gandhi

    Sarojini Naidu 1879–1949 Indian politician: A. Campbell-Johnson *Mission with Mountbatten* (1951)

10 A doormat in a world of boots.

of herself

    Jean Rhys *c.*1890–1979 British novelist and short-story writer: in *Guardian* 6 December 1990

11 She would rather light a candle than curse the darkness, and her glow has warmed the world.

on learning of Eleanor Roosevelt's death

    Adlai Stevenson 1900–65 American Democratic politician: in *New York Times* 8 November 1962

12 He snatched the lightning shaft from heaven, and the sceptre from tyrants.

of Benjamin Franklin, inventor of the lightning conductor and American statesman

    A. R. J. Turgot 1727–81 French economist and statesman: inscription for a bust

13 What, when drunk, one sees in other women, one sees in Garbo sober.

of Greta Garbo

    Kenneth Tynan 1927–80 English theatre critic: *Curtains* (1961)

14 As time requireth, a man of marvellous mirth and pastimes, and sometime of as sad gravity, as who say: a man for all seasons.

of Sir Thomas More

    Robert Whittington *c.*1480–*c.*1553 English grammarian: *Vulgaria* (1521)

Famous Poets

1 He spoke, and loosed our heart in tears.
He laid us as we lay at birth
On the cool flowery lap of earth.

of Wordsworth

    Matthew Arnold 1822–88 English poet and essayist: 'Memorial Verses, April 1850' (1852)

2 In poetry, no less than in life, he is 'a beautiful and ineffectual angel, beating in the void his luminous wings in vain'.

    Matthew Arnold 1822–88 English poet and essayist: *Essays in Criticism* Second Series (1888) 'Shelley'

3 You were silly like us; your gift survived it all:
The parish of rich women, physical decay,
Yourself. Mad Ireland hurt you into poetry.

    W. H. Auden 1907–73 English poet: 'In Memory of W. B. Yeats' (1940)

4 The reason Milton wrote in fetters
when he wrote of Angels and God,
and at liberty when of Devils and
Hell, is because he was a true Poet,
and of the Devil's party without
knowing it.

> **William Blake** 1757–1827 English poet:
> *The Marriage of Heaven and Hell*
> (1790–3)

5 How thankful we ought to be that
Wordsworth was only a poet and not
a musician. Fancy a symphony by
Wordsworth! Fancy having to sit it
out! And fancy what it would have
been if he had written fugues!

> **Samuel Butler** 1835–1902 English
> novelist: *Notebooks* (1912)

6 He could not think up to the height
of his own towering style.

> *of Tennyson*
> **G. K. Chesterton** 1874–1936 English
> essayist, novelist, and poet: *The
> Victorian Age in Literature* (1912)

7 With Donne, whose muse on
dromedary trots,
Wreathe iron pokers into true-love
knots.

> **Samuel Taylor Coleridge** 1772–1834
> English poet, critic, and philosopher:
> 'On Donne's Poetry' (1818)

8 You who desired so much—in vain to
ask—
Yet fed your hunger like an endless
task,
Dared dignify the labor, bless the
quest—
Achieved that stillness ultimately
best,
Being, of all, least sought for: Emily,
hear!

> **Hart Crane** 1899–1932 American poet:
> 'To Emily Dickinson' (1927)

9 'Tis sufficient to say, according to the
proverb, that here is God's plenty.

> *of Chaucer*
> **John Dryden** 1631–1700 English poet,

critic, and dramatist: *Fables Ancient and
Modern* (1700)

10 How unpleasant to meet Mr Eliot!
With his features of clerical cut,
And his brow so grim
And his mouth so prim
And his conversation, so nicely
Restricted to What Precisely
And If and Perhaps and But.

> **T. S. Eliot** 1888–1965 Anglo-American
> poet, critic, and dramatist: 'Five-Finger
> Exercises' (1936)

11 *Hugo—hélas!*
Hugo—alas!

> *when asked who was the greatest 19th-
> century poet*
> **André Gide** 1869–1951 French novelist
> and critic: Claude Martin *La Maturité
> d'André Gide* (1977)

12 Dr Donne's verses are like the peace
of God; they pass all understanding.

> **James I** 1566–1625 (James VI of
> Scotland): remark recorded by
> Archdeacon Plume (1630–1704)

13 Milton, Madam, was a genius that
could cut a Colossus from a rock; but
could not carve heads upon cherry-
stones.

> *to Hannah More, who had expressed a
> wonder that the poet who had written
> Paradise Lost should write such poor
> sonnets*
> **Samuel Johnson** 1709–84 English poet,
> critic, and lexicographer: James Boswell
> *Life of Samuel Johnson* (1791) 13 June
> 1784

14 Mad, bad, and dangerous to know.

> *of Byron, after their first meeting*
> **Lady Caroline Lamb** 1785–1828 wife of
> Lord Melbourne: diary, March 1812

15 An Archangel a little damaged.

> *of Coleridge*
> **Charles Lamb** 1775–1834 English
> writer: letter to Wordsworth, 26 April
> 1816

16 Self-contempt, well-grounded.
on the foundation of T. S. Eliot's work
F. R. Leavis 1895–1978 English literary
critic: in *Times Literary Supplement*
21 October 1988

17 The high-water mark, so to speak, of
Socialist literature is W. H. Auden, a
sort of gutless Kipling.
George Orwell 1903–50 English
novelist: *The Road to Wigan Pier* (1937)

18 A cloud-encircled meteor of the air,
A hooded eagle among blinking
owls.
of Coleridge
Percy Bysshe Shelley 1792–1822
English poet: 'Letter to Maria Gisborne'
(1820)

19 Life's a curse, love's a blight, God's a
blaggard, cherry blossom is quite
nice.
on A. E. Housman
Tom Stoppard 1937– British dramatist:
The Invention of Love (1997)

20 To see him fumbling with our rich
and delicate language is to
experience all the horror of seeing a
Sèvres vase in the hands of a
chimpanzee.
of Stephen Spender
Evelyn Waugh 1903–66 English novelist:
in *The Tablet* 5 May 1951

21 Chaos, illumined by flashes of
lightning.
on Robert Browning's 'style'
Oscar Wilde 1854–1900 Anglo-Irish
dramatist and poet: Ada Leverson
Letters to the Sphinx (1930)

22 I thought of Chatterton, the
marvellous boy,
The sleepless soul that perished in its
pride.
William Wordsworth 1770–1850
English poet: 'Resolution and
Independence' (1807)

Famous Politicians

1 Richard Nixon impeached himself.
He gave us Gerald Ford as his
revenge.
Bella Abzug 1920–98 American
politician: in *Rolling Stone*; Linda Botts
Loose Talk (1980)

2 Winston is back.
*on Churchill's reappointment as First Sea
Lord*
Anonymous: Board of Admiralty signal
to the Fleet, 3 September 1939

3 The iron lady.
*of Margaret Thatcher, in Soviet defence
ministry newspaper* Red Star, *which
accused her of trying to revive the cold war*
Anonymous: in *Sunday Times*
25 January 1976

4 He can't see a belt without hitting
below it.
of David Lloyd George
Margot Asquith 1864–1945 British
political hostess: in *Listener* 11 June
1953

5 Few thought he was even a starter
There were many who thought
themselves smarter
But he ended PM
CH and OM
An earl and a knight of the garter.
of himself
Clement Attlee 1883–1967 British
Labour statesman: letter to Tom Attlee,
8 April 1956

6 I thought he was a young man of
promise, but it appears he is a young
man of promises.
of Winston Churchill
Arthur James Balfour 1848–1930
British Conservative statesman:
Winston Churchill *My Early Life* (1930)

7 [Lloyd George] did not seem to care which way he travelled providing he was in the driver's seat.

> **Lord Beaverbrook** 1879–1964 Canadian-born British newspaper proprietor and Conservative politician: *The Decline and Fall of Lloyd George* (1963)

8 A lath of wood painted to look like iron.

of Lord Salisbury

> **Otto von Bismarck** 1815–98 German statesman: attributed, but vigorously denied by Sidney Whitman in *Personal Reminiscences of Prince Bismarck* (1902)

9 A monster of wickedness, insatiable in his lust for blood and plunder . . . this bloodthirsty guttersnipe.

of Adolf Hitler

> **Winston Churchill** 1874–1965 British Conservative statesman: radio broadcast, 26 June 1941

10 A modest man who has a good deal to be modest about.

of Clement Attlee

> **Winston Churchill** 1874–1965 British Conservative statesman: in *Chicago Sunday Tribune Magazine of Books* 27 June 1954

11 She cannot see an institution without hitting it with her handbag.

of Margaret Thatcher

> **Julian Critchley** 1930–2000 British Conservative politician and journalist: in *The Times* 21 June 1982

12 It is not necessary that every time he rises he should give his famous imitation of a semi-house-trained polecat.

of Norman Tebbit

> **Michael Foot** 1913– British Labour politician: speech, House of Commons, 2 March 1978

13 Comrades, this man has a nice smile, but he's got iron teeth.

of Mikhail Gorbachev

> **Andrei Gromyko** 1909–89 Soviet

statesman: speech to Soviet Communist Party Central Committee, 11 March 1985

14 She has no hinterland; in particular she has no sense of history.

of Margaret Thatcher

> **Edna Healey** 1918– British writer: Denis Healey *The Time of My Life* (1989)

15 This extraordinary figure of our time, this syren, this goat-footed bard, this half-human visitor to our age from the hag-ridden magic and enchanted woods of Celtic antiquity.

of David Lloyd George

> **John Maynard Keynes** 1883–1946 English economist: *Essays in Biography* (1933) 'Mr Lloyd George'

16 The first time you meet Winston you see all his faults and the rest of your life you spend in discovering his virtues.

of Winston Churchill

> **Lady Lytton** 1874–1971: letter to Sir Edward Marsh, December 1905

17 She has the eyes of Caligula, but the mouth of Marilyn Monroe.

of Margaret Thatcher

> **François Mitterrand** 1916–96 French statesman: comment to his new European Minister Roland Dumas; in *Observer* 25 November 1990

18 He mobilized the English language and sent it into battle to steady his fellow countrymen and hearten those Europeans upon whom the long dark night of tyranny had descended.

of Winston Churchill

> **Ed Murrow** 1908–65 American broadcaster and journalist: broadcast, 30 November 1954

19 If I saw Mr Haughey buried at midnight at a crossroads, with a stake driven through his heart—politically speaking—I should continue to wear a clove of garlic round my neck, just in case.

Conor Cruise O'Brien 1917–2008 Irish politician, writer, and journalist: in *Observer* 10 October 1982

20 Too clever by half.
of Iain Macleod

Lord Salisbury 1893–1972 British Conservative politician: speech, House of Lords, 7 March 1961

21 Ronald Reagan . . . is attempting a great breakthrough in political technology—he has been perfecting the Teflon-coated Presidency. He sees to it that nothing sticks to him.

Patricia Schroeder 1940– American Democratic politician: speech in the US House of Representatives, 2 August 1983

22 A racing tipster who only reached Hitler's level of accuracy would not do well for his clients.

A. J. P. Taylor 1906–90 British historian: *The Origins of the Second World War* (1961)

23 A triumph of the embalmer's art.
of Ronald Reagan

Gore Vidal 1925– American novelist and critic: in *Observer* 26 April 1981

24 No, *no. Jimmy Stewart* for governor—Reagan for his best friend.
on hearing that Reagan was seeking nomination as Governor of California, 1966

Jack Warner 1892–1978 Canadian-born American film producer: Max Wilk *The Wit and Wisdom of Hollywood* (1972)

25 He mastered the art of walking backward into the future. He would say 'After me'. And some people went ahead, and some went behind, and he would go backward.
of Mikhail Gorbachev

Mikhail Zhvanetsky 1934– Russian writer: in *Time* 12 September 1994; attributed

Famous Writers

see also FAMOUS POETS, SHAKESPEARE

1 Shaw's plays are the price we pay for Shaw's prefaces.

James Agate 1877–1947 British drama critic and novelist: diary, 10 March 1933

2 Sophocles said that he drew men as they ought to be, whereas Euripides drew them as they are.

Aristotle 384–322 BC Greek philosopher: *Poetics*

3 What should I do with your strong, manly, spirited sketches, full of variety and glow?—How could I possibly join them on to the little bit (two inches wide) of ivory on which I work with so fine a brush, as produces little effect after much labour?

Jane Austen 1775–1817 English novelist: letter to J. Edward Austen, 16 December 1816

4 He describes London like a special correspondent for posterity.

Walter Bagehot 1826–77 English economist and essayist: *National Review* 7 October 1858 'Charles Dickens'

5 We were put to Dickens as children but it never quite took. That unremitting humanity soon had me cheesed off.

Alan Bennett 1934– English actor and dramatist: *The Old Country* (1978)

6 Thou large-brained woman and large-hearted man.

Elizabeth Barrett Browning 1806–61 English poet: 'To George Sand—A Desire' (1844)

7 Coleridge was a drug addict. Poe was an alcoholic. Marlowe was stabbed by a man whom he was treacherously trying to stab. Pope took money to keep a woman's name out of a satire; then wrote a piece so

that she could still be recognized anyhow. Chatterton killed himself. Byron was accused of incest. *Do you still want to be a writer—and if so, why?*

> **Bennett Cerf** 1898–1971 American humorist: *Shake Well Before Using* (1948)

8 Hardy went down to botanize in the swamp, while Meredith climbed towards the sun. Meredith became, at his best, a sort of daintily dressed Walt Whitman: Hardy became a sort of village atheist brooding and blaspheming over the village idiot.

> **G. K. Chesterton** 1874–1936 English essayist, novelist, and poet: *The Victorian Age in Literature* (1912)

9 He could not blow his nose without moralising on the state of the handkerchief industry.
of George Orwell

> **Cyril Connolly** 1903–74 English writer: in *Sunday Times* 29 September 1968

10 The mama of dada.
of Gertrude Stein

> **Clifton Fadiman** 1904–99 American critic: *Party of One* (1955)

11 A dogged attempt to cover the universe with mud, an inverted Victorianism, an attempt to make crossness and dirt succeed where sweetness and light failed.
of James Joyce's Ulysses

> **E. M. Forster** 1879–1970 English novelist: *Aspects of the Novel* (1927)

12 The work of Henry James has always seemed divisible by a simple dynastic arrangement into three reigns: James I, James II, and the Old Pretender.

> **Philip Guedalla** 1889–1944 British historian and biographer: *Supers and Supermen* (1920)

13 A good man fallen among Fabians.
of George Bernard Shaw

> **Lenin** 1870–1924 Russian revolutionary: Arthur Ransome *Six Weeks in Russia in 1919* (1919) 'Notes of Conversations with Lenin'

14 He seemed at ease and to have the look of the last gentleman in Europe.
of Oscar Wilde

> **Ada Leverson** 1865–1936 English novelist: *Letters to the Sphinx* (1930)

15 E. M. Forster never gets any further than warming the teapot. He's a rare fine hand at that. Feel this teapot. Is it not beautifully warm? Yes, but there ain't going to be no tea.

> **Katherine Mansfield** 1888–1923 New Zealand-born short-story writer: diary, May 1917

16 English literature's performing flea.
of P. G. Wodehouse

> **Sean O'Casey** 1880–1964 Irish dramatist: P. G. Wodehouse *Performing Flea* (1953)

17 For years a secret shame destroyed my peace—
I'd not read Eliot, Auden or MacNeice.
But then I had a thought that brought me hope—
Neither had Chaucer, Shakespeare, Milton, Pope.

> **Justin Richardson** 1900–75 British poet: 'Take Heart, Illiterates' (1966)

18 The Big Bow-Wow strain I can do myself like any now going; but the exquisite touch, which renders ordinary commonplace things and characters interesting, from the truth of the description and the sentiment, is denied to me.
on Jane Austen

> **Sir Walter Scott** 1771–1832 Scottish novelist and poet: diary, 14 March 1826

19 I enjoyed talking to her, but thought *nothing* of her writing. I considered her 'a beautiful little knitter'.

of Virginia Woolf

    Edith Sitwell 1887–1964 English poet and critic: letter to Geoffrey Singleton, 11 July 1955

20 It is leviathan retrieving pebbles. It is a magnificent but painful hippopotamus resolved at any cost, even at the cost of its dignity, upon picking up a pea which has got into a corner of its den.

of Henry James

    H. G. Wells 1866–1946 English novelist: *Boon* (1915)

21 Meredith's a prose Browning, and so is Browning.

    Oscar Wilde 1854–1900 Anglo-Irish dramatist and poet: *Intentions* (1891) 'The Critic as Artist'

22 The scratching of pimples on the body of the bootboy at Claridges.

of James Joyce's Ulysses

    Virginia Woolf 1882–1941 English novelist: letter to Lytton Strachey, 24 April 1922

23 She is so odd a blend of Little Nell and Lady Macbeth. It is not so much the familiar phenomenon of a hand of steel in a velvet glove as a lacy sleeve with a bottle of vitriol concealed in its folds.

of Dorothy Parker

    Alexander Woollcott 1887–1943 American writer: *While Rome Burns* (1934)

Fanaticism

see also CERTAINTY, IDEAS

1 Just as every conviction begins as a whim so does every emancipator serve his apprenticeship as a crank. A fanatic is a great leader who is just entering the room.

    Heywood Broun 1888–1939 American journalist: in *New York World* 6 February 1928

2 A fanatic is one who can't change his mind and won't change the subject.

    Winston Churchill 1874–1965 British Conservative statesman: attributed

3 I would remind you that extremism in the defence of liberty is no vice! And let me remind you also that moderation in the pursuit of justice is no virtue!

    Barry Goldwater 1909–98 American Republican politician: accepting the presidential nomination, 16 July 1964

4 What is objectionable, what is dangerous about extremists is not that they are extreme but that they are intolerant.

    Robert Kennedy 1925–68 American Democratic politician: *The Pursuit of Justice* (1964)

5 Fanaticism consists in redoubling your effort when you have forgotten your aim.

    George Santayana 1863–1952 Spanish-born philosopher and critic: *The Life of Reason* (1905)

Fantasy

see also FICTION, IMAGINATION

1 All fantasy should have a solid base in reality.

    Max Beerbohm 1872–1956 English critic, essayist, and caricaturist: *Zuleika Dobson* (1946 ed.) note

2 Fantasy deals with things that are not and cannot be. Science fiction deals with things that can be, that some day may be.

    Frederic Brown 1906–72 American science fiction writer: *Angels and Spaceships* (1955)

3 Fantasy is like jam: you have to
spread it on a solid piece of bread.
> **Italo Calvino** 1923–85 Italian novelist
> and short-story writer: attributed; in
> *New York Review of Books* 21 November
> 1985

4 We need metaphors of magic and
monsters in order to understand the
human condition.
> **Stephen Donaldson** 1947– American
> writer: Stan Nicholls (ed.) *Wordsmiths of
> Wonder* (1993)

5 Most modern fantasy just rearranges
the furniture in Tolkien's attic.
> **Terry Pratchett** 1948– English science
> fiction writer: Stan Nicholls (ed.)
> *Wordsmiths of Wonder* (1993)

Farming

see also COUNTRY

1 We plough the fields, and scatter
The good seed on the land,
But it is fed and watered
By God's almighty hand.
> **Jane Montgomery Campbell** 1817–78
> English hymn-writer: 'We plough the
> fields, and scatter' (1861 hymn)

2 For of all gainful professions,
nothing is better, nothing more
pleasing, nothing more delightful,
nothing better becomes a well-bred
man than agriculture.
> **Cicero** 106–43 BC Roman orator and
> statesman: *De Officiis*

3 Farming looks mighty easy when
your plough is a pencil, and you're a
thousand miles from the corn field.
> **Dwight D. Eisenhower** 1890–1969
> American general and Republican
> statesman: speech, Peoria,
> 25 September 1956

4 Agriculture is the foundation of
manufactures; since the productions
of nature are the materials of art.
> **Edward Gibbon** 1737–94 English

historian: *The Decline and Fall of the
Roman Empire* (1776–88)

5 The Farmer will never be happy
again;
He carries his heart in his boots;
For either the rain is destroying his
grain
Or the drought is destroying his
roots.
> **A. P. Herbert** 1890–1971 English writer
> and humorist: 'The Farmer' (1922)

6 Cultivators of the earth are the most
valuable citizens. They are the most
vigorous, the most independent, the
most virtuous, and they are tied to
their country and wedded to its
liberty and interests by the most
lasting bands.
> **Thomas Jefferson** 1743–1826 American
> Democratic Republican statesman:
> letter to John Jay, 23 August 1785

7 A farm is an irregular patch of nettles
bounded by short-term notes,
containing a fool and his wife who
didn't know enough to stay in the
city.
> **S. J. Perelman** 1904–79 American
> humorist: *The Most of S. J. Perelman*
> (1959) 'Acres and Pains'

8 O farmers excessively fortunate if
only they recognized their blessings!
> **Virgil** 70–19 BC Roman poet: *Georgics*

Fashion

see also CLOTHES

1 I never cared for fashion much.
Amusing little seams and witty little
pleats. It was the girls I liked.
> **David Bailey** 1938– English
> photographer: in *Independent*
> 5 November 1990

2 Uncool people never hurt
anybody—all they do is collect
stamps, read science-fiction books

and stand on the end of railway platforms staring at trains.
> **Ben Elton** 1959– British writer and performer: in *Radio Times* 18/24 April 1998

3 Haute Couture should be fun, foolish and almost unwearable.
> **Christian Lacroix** 1951– French couturier: attributed, 1987

4 Hip is the sophistication of the wise primitive in a giant jungle.
> **Norman Mailer** 1923–2007 American novelist and essayist: *Voices of Dissent* (1959)

5 Fashion is more usually a gentle progression of revisited ideas.
> **Bruce Oldfield** 1950– English fashion designer: in *Independent* 9 September 1989

6 Fashion is something barbarous, for it produces innovation without reason and imitation without benefit.
> **George Santayana** 1863–1952 Spanish-born philosopher and critic: *The Life of Reason* (1905)

7 You cannot be both fashionable and first-rate.
> **Logan Pearsall Smith** 1865–1946 American-born man of letters: *Afterthoughts* (1931)

8 Every generation laughs at the old fashions, but follows religiously the new.
> **Henry David Thoreau** 1817–62 American writer: *Walden* (1854)

9 It is charming to totter into vogue.
> **Horace Walpole** 1717–97 English writer and connoisseur: letter to George Selwyn, 2 December 1765

10 Radical Chic . . . is only radical in Style; in its heart it is part of Society

and its tradition—Politics, like Rock, Pop, and Camp, has its uses.
> **Tom Wolfe** 1931– American writer: in *New York* 8 June 1970

Fat

see also APPEARANCE, DIETS

1 Outside every fat man there was an even fatter man trying to close in.
> **Kingsley Amis** 1922–95 English novelist and poet: *One Fat Englishman* (1963)

2 Imprisoned in every fat man a thin one is wildly signalling to be let out.
> **Cyril Connolly** 1903–74 English writer: *The Unquiet Grave* (1944)

3 it's a sex object if you're pretty and no love
or love and no sex if you're fat
> **Nikki Giovanni** 1943– American poet: 'Woman Poem' (1970)

4 Fat is a feminist issue.
> **Susie Orbach** 1946– American psychotherapist: title of book (1978)

5 CARRIER: Try zideways, Mrs Jones, try zideways!
MRS JONES: Lar' bless 'ee John, I ain't got no zideways!
cartoon of a stout lady trying to enter a doorway
> **Punch** English humorous weekly periodical: 17 October 1900

6 To ask women to become unnaturally thin is to ask them to relinquish their sexuality.
> **Naomi Wolf** 1962– American writer: *The Beauty Myth* (1990)

Fate

see also CIRCUMSTANCE, NECESSITY

1 The spring is wound up tight. It will uncoil of itself. That is what is so convenient in tragedy. The least little

turn of the wrist will do the job.
Anything will set it going.

> **Jean Anouilh** 1910–87 French
> dramatist: *Antigone* (1944)

2 Must it be? It must be.

> **Ludwig van Beethoven** 1770–1827
> German composer: String Quartet in F
> Major, Opus 135, epigraph

3 Canst thou bind the sweet influences
of Pleiades, or loose the bands of
Orion?

> **Bible**: Job

4 Fate is not an eagle, it creeps like a
rat.

> **Elizabeth Bowen** 1899–1973 Anglo-Irish
> novelist: *The House in Paris* (1935)

5 There once was a man who said,
'Damn!
It is borne in upon me I am
An engine that moves
In predestinate grooves,
I'm not even a bus, I'm a tram.'

> **Maurice Evan Hare** 1886–1967 English
> limerick writer: 'Limerick' (1905)

6 I go the way that Providence dictates
with the assurance of a sleepwalker.

> **Adolf Hitler** 1889–1945 German
> dictator: speech in Munich, 15 March
> 1936

7 It's no go my honey love, it's no go
my poppet;
Work your hands from day to day,
the winds will blow the profit.
The glass is falling hour by hour, the
glass will fall for ever,
But if you break the bloody glass you
won't hold up the weather.

> **Louis MacNeice** 1907–63 British poet,
> born in Belfast: 'Bagpipe Music' (1938)

8 I [Death] was astonished to see him
in Baghdad, for I had an
appointment with him tonight in
Samarra.

> **W. Somerset Maugham** 1874–1965
> English novelist: *Sheppey* (1933)

9 What we call fate does not come into
us from the outside, but emerges
from us.

> **Rainer Maria Rilke** 1875–1926 German
> poet: *Letters to a Young Poet* (1929)
> 12 August 1904 (tr. S. Mitchell)

10 There's a divinity that shapes our
ends,
Rough-hew them how we will.

> **William Shakespeare** 1564–1616
> English dramatist: *Hamlet* (1601)

11 We are merely the stars' tennis-balls,
struck and bandied
Which way please them.

> **John Webster** *c.*1580–*c.*1625 English
> dramatist: *The Duchess of Malfi* (1623)

12 Every bullet has its billet.

> **William III** 1650–1702 British monarch:
> John Wesley's diary, 6 June 1765

Fathers

see also PARENTS

1 I'm a father, that's what matters
most. Nothing matters more.
on the birth of his son John

> **Gordon Brown** 1951– British Labour
> statesman: in *Observer* 19 October 2003

2 You can't understand it until you
experience the simple joy of the first
time your son points at a seagull and
says 'duck'.
on fatherhood

> **Russell Crowe** 1964– New Zealand
> actor: in *Observer* 29 May 2005

3 There must be many fathers around
the country who have experienced
the cruellest, most crushing
rejection of all: their children have
ended up supporting the wrong
team.

> **Nick Hornby** 1957– British novelist
> and journalist: *Fever Pitch* (1992)

4 Being a father
Is quite a bother,

But I like it, rather.

> **Ogden Nash** 1902–71 American
> humorist: 'Soliloquy in Circles' (1949)

5 What makes a man a man is not the ability to have a child but to raise one.

> **Barack Obama** 1961– American
> Democratic statesman: speech,
> Cincinnnati, 15 July 2008

6 I can do one of two things. I can be president of the United States or I can control Alice. I cannot possibly do both.

> **Theodore Roosevelt** 1858–1919
> American Republican statesman:
> Marcus Connelly *Voices Offstage* (1965)

7 The fundamental defect of fathers, in our competitive society, is that they want their children to be a credit to them.

> **Bertrand Russell** 1872–1970 British
> philosopher and mathematician:
> *Sceptical Essays* (1928) 'Freedom versus
> Authority in Education'

8 There is no good father, that's the rule. Don't lay the blame on men but on the bond of paternity, which is rotten. To beget children, nothing better; to *have* them, what iniquity!

> **Jean-Paul Sartre** 1905–80 French
> philosopher, novelist, dramatist, and
> critic: *Les Mots* (1964)

9 It doesn't matter who my father was; it matters who I remember he was.

> **Anne Sexton** 1928–74 American poet:
> diary, 1 January 1972

10 Fatherhood is a mirror in which we catch glimpses of ourselves as we really are.

> **Hugo Williams** 1942– British writer
> and poet: Sean French (ed.) *Fatherhood*
> (1992)

Fear

see also COURAGE, COWARDICE

1 In space no one can hear you scream.

> **Anonymous**: advertising slogan for
> *Alien* (1979 film)

2 Most people go through life dreading they'll have a traumatic experience. Freaks are born with their trauma. They've already passed it. They're aristocrats.

> **Diane Arbus** 1923–71 American
> photographer: *Diane Arbus* (1972)

3 Real freedom is freedom from fear, and unless you can live free from fear you cannot live a dignified human life.

> **Aung San Suu Kyi** 1945– Burmese
> political leader: undated interview with
> the BBC; transcript on BBC World
> Service website

4 Now a man talks frankly only with his wife, at night, with the blanket over his head.

> **Isaac Babel** 1894–1940 Russian short-
> story writer: remark *c.*1937; Solomon
> Volkov *St Petersburg* (1996)

5 We must travel in the direction of our fear.

> **John Berryman** 1914–72 American
> poet: 'A Point of Age' (1942)

6 No passion so effectually robs the mind of all its powers of acting and reasoning as fear.

> **Edmund Burke** 1729–97 Irish-born
> Whig politician and man of letters: *On
> the Sublime and Beautiful* (1757)

7 Wee, sleekit, cow'rin', tim'rous beastie,
O what a panic's in thy breastie!

> **Robert Burns** 1759–96 Scottish poet:
> 'To a Mouse' (1786)

8 The horror! The horror!
Joseph Conrad 1857–1924 Polish-born English novelist: *Heart of Darkness* (1902)

9 Be afraid. Be very afraid.
David Cronenberg 1943– Canadian film director: advertising slogan for *The Fly* (1986 film)

10 Nothing in life is to be feared, it is only to be understood.
Marie Curie 1867–1934 Polish-born French physicist: attributed

11 I will show you fear in a handful of dust.
T. S. Eliot 1888–1965 Anglo-American poet, critic, and dramatist: *The Waste Land* (1922)

12 They cannot scare me with their empty spaces
Between stars—on stars where no human race is.
I have it in me so much nearer home
To scare myself with my own desert places.
Robert Frost 1874–1963 American poet: 'Desert Places' (1936)

13 There is no terror in a bang, only in the anticipation of it.
Alfred Hitchcock 1899–1980 British-born film director: attributed

14 Terror . . . often arises from a pervasive sense of disestablishment; that things are in the unmaking.
Stephen King 1947– American writer: *Danse Macabre* (1981)

15 The thing I fear most is fear.
Montaigne 1533–92 French moralist and essayist: *Essays* (1580); see FEAR 17

16 Anxiety is love's greatest killer. It makes others feel as you might when a drowning man holds on to you. You want to save him, but you know he will strangle you with his panic.
Anais Nin 1903–77 French-born

American writer: *The Diary of Anais Nin* vol. 4 (1944–7)

17 The only thing we have to fear is fear itself.
Franklin D. Roosevelt 1882–1945 American Democratic statesman: inaugural address, 4 March 1933; see FEAR 15

18 To fear love is to fear life, and those who fear life are already three parts dead.
Bertrand Russell 1872–1970 British philosopher and mathematician: *Marriage and Morals* (1929)

19 Present fears
Are less than horrible imaginings.
William Shakespeare 1564–1616 English dramatist: *Macbeth* (1606)

20 Better be killed than frightened to death.
R. S. Surtees 1805–64 English sporting journalist and novelist: *Mr Facey Romford's Hounds* (1865)

21 Every drop of ink in my pen ran cold.
Horace Walpole 1717–97 English writer and connoisseur: letter to George Montagu, 30 July 1752

Fiction

see also CRIME FICTION, FAMOUS WRITERS, FANTASY, LITERATURE, SCIENCE FICTION, WRITING

1 I hate things all *fiction* . . . there should always be some foundation of fact for the most airy fabric and pure invention is but the talent of a liar.
Lord Byron 1788–1824 English poet: letter to John Murray, 2 April 1817

2 Literature is a luxury; fiction is a necessity.
G. K. Chesterton 1874–1936 English essayist, novelist, and poet: *The Defendant* (1901) 'A Defence of Penny Dreadfuls'

3 The central function of imaginative literature is to make you realize that other people act on moral convictions different from your own.
   William Empson 1906–84 English poet and literary critic: *Milton's God* (1981)

4 Yes—oh dear yes—the novel tells a story.
   E. M. Forster 1879–1970 English novelist: *Aspects of the Novel* (1927)

5 Merely corroborative detail, intended to give artistic verisimilitude to an otherwise bald and unconvincing narrative.
   W. S. Gilbert 1836–1911 English writer of comic and satirical verse: *The Mikado* (1885)

6 The Story is just the spoiled child of art.
   Henry James 1843–1916 American novelist: *The Ambassadors* (1909 ed.) preface

7 What is character but the determination of incident? What is incident but the illustration of character?
   Henry James 1843–1916 American novelist: *Partial Portraits* (1888) 'The Art of Fiction'

8 A beginning, a muddle, and an end.
   on the 'classic formula' for a novel
   Philip Larkin 1922–85 English poet: in *New Fiction* January 1978

9 If you try to nail anything down in the novel, either it kills the novel, or the novel gets up and walks away with the nail.
   D. H. Lawrence 1885–1930 English novelist and poet: *Phoenix* (1936) 'Morality and the Novel'

10 The things I like to find in a story are punch and poetry.
   Sean O'Faolain 1900–91 Irish writer: *The Short Story* (1948) foreword

11 As artists they're rot, but as providers they're oil wells; they gush.
   on lady novelists
   Dorothy Parker 1893–1967 American critic and humorist: Malcolm Cowley *Writers at Work* 1st Series (1958)

12 'Thou shalt not' might reach the head, but it takes 'Once upon a time' to reach the heart.
   Philip Pullman 1946– English writer: in *Independent* 18 July 1996

13 A novel is a mirror which passes over a highway. Sometimes it reflects to your eyes the blue of the skies, at others the churned-up mud of the road.
   Stendhal 1783–1842 French novelist: *Le Rouge et le noir* (1830)

14 Sex is more exciting on the screen and between the pages than between the sheets.
   Andy Warhol 1927–87 American artist: *Philosophy of Andy Warhol (From A to B and Back Again)* (1975)

15 The good ended happily, and the bad unhappily. That is what fiction means.
   Oscar Wilde 1854–1900 Anglo-Irish dramatist and poet: *The Importance of Being Earnest* (1895)

Field Sports

see also FISHING, HUNTING

1 A sportsman is a man who, every now and then, simply has to get out and kill something. Not that he's cruel. He wouldn't hurt a fly. It's not big enough.
   Stephen Leacock 1869–1944 Canadian humorist: *My Remarkable Uncle* (1942)

2 I don't think doing it [killing animals] for money makes it any more moral. I don't think a prostitute is more moral than a wife, but they are doing the same thing.

comparing participation in blood sports to selling slaughtered meat

> **Prince Philip, Duke of Edinburgh** 1921– husband of Elizabeth II: speech in London, 6 December 1988

3 When a man wants to murder a tiger he calls it sport; when a tiger wants to murder him, he calls it ferocity.

> **George Bernard Shaw** 1856–1950 Irish dramatist: *Man and Superman* (1903)

4 The fascination of shooting as a sport depends almost wholly on whether you are at the right or wrong end of the gun.

> **P. G. Wodehouse** 1881–1975 English writer: *Mr Mulliner Speaking* (1929)

Films

see also CINEMA

1 Just when you thought it was safe to go back in the water.

> **Advertising slogan**: publicity for *Jaws 2* (1978 film)

2 It would have been cheaper to lower the Atlantic!

of the disaster movie Raise the Titanic

> **Lew Grade** 1906–98 British television producer and executive: *Still Dancing: My Story* (1987)

3 I just couldn't go on speaking those bloody awful, banal lines. I'd had enough of the mumbo-jumbo.

of his refusal to play Obi-Wan Kenobi in Star Wars *sequels*

> **Alec Guinness** 1914–2000 English actor: attributed, September 1998

4 If we'd had as many soldiers as that, we'd have won the war!

on seeing the number of Confederate troops in Gone with the Wind *at the 1939 premiere*

> **Margaret Mitchell** 1900–49 American

novelist: W. G. Harris *Gable and Lombard* (1976)

5 Fiction is the great virus waiting to do away with fact—that is one of the most ominous meanings of the film.

of Citizen Kane

> **David Thomson** 1941– British film critic: *Rosebud: the Story of Orson Welles* (1996)

6 It is like writing history with lightning. And my only regret is that it is all so terribly true.

on seeing D. W. Griffith's film The Birth of a Nation

> **Woodrow Wilson** 1856–1924 American Democratic statesman: at the White House, 18 February 1915

Fishing

see also FIELD SPORTS

1 If fishing is a religion, fly fishing is high church.

> **Tom Brokaw** 1940– American journalist: in *International Herald Tribune* 10 September 1991

2 I love fishing. It's like transcendental meditation with a punch-line.

> **Billy Connolly** 1942– Scottish comedian: *Gullible's Travels* (1982)

3 All men are equal before fish.

> **Herbert Hoover** 1874–1964 American Republican statesman: *Addresses Upon The American Road* (1955)

4 Fishing is unquestionably a form of madness but, happily, for the once-bitten there is no cure.

> **Lord Home** 1903–95 British Conservative statesman: *The Way the Wind Blows* (1976)

5 Fly fishing may be a very pleasant amusement; but angling or float fishing I can only compare to a stick and a string, with a worm at one end and a fool at the other.

> **Samuel Johnson** 1709–84 English poet,

critic, and lexicographer: attributed;
Hawker *Instructions to Young Sportsmen*
(1859); also attributed to Jonathan
Swift, in *The Indicator* 27 October 1819

6 As no man is born an artist, so no
man is born an angler.
Izaak Walton 1593–1683 English writer:
The Compleat Angler (1653)

Flattery

see also PRAISE

1 If you are flattering a woman, it pays
to be a little more subtle. You don't
have to bother with men, they
believe any compliment
automatically.
Alan Ayckbourn 1939– English
dramatist: *Round and Round the
Garden* (1975)

2 Everyone likes flattery; and when
you come to Royalty you should lay it
on with a trowel.
Benjamin Disraeli 1804–81 British Tory
statesman and novelist: to Matthew
Arnold; G. W. E. Russell *Collections and
Recollections* (1898); see PRIME MINISTERS 2

3 Madam, before you flatter a man so
grossly to his face, you should
consider whether or not your flattery
is worth his having.
Samuel Johnson 1709–84 English poet,
critic, and lexicographer: Fanny
Burney's diary, August 1778

4 Everybody is himself his own
foremost and greatest flatterer.
Plutarch c.AD 46–c.120 Greek
philosopher and biographer: *Moralia*

5 But when I tell him he hates
flatterers,
He says he does, being then most
flattered.
William Shakespeare 1564–1616
English dramatist: *Julius Caesar* (1599)

6 I suppose flattery hurts no one, that
is, if he doesn't inhale.
Adlai Stevenson 1900–65 American
Democratic politician: television
broadcast, 30 March 1952

Flowers

see also GARDENS

1 Unkempt about those hedges blows
An English unofficial rose.
Rupert Brooke 1887–1915 English poet:
'The Old Vicarage, Grantchester' (1915)

2 Oh, no man knows
Through what wild centuries
Roves back the rose.
Walter de la Mare 1873–1956 English
poet and novelist: 'All That's Past' (1912)

3 Flowers . . . are a proud assertion
that a ray of beauty outvalues all the
utilities of the world.
Ralph Waldo Emerson 1803–82
American philosopher and poet: *Essays*
(Second Series, 1844) 'Gifts'

4 Here are sweet peas, on tip-toe for a
flight.
John Keats 1795–1821 English poet: 'I
stood tip-toe upon a little hill' (1817)

5 Hey, buds below, up is where to grow,
Up with which below can't compare
with.
Hurry! It's lovely up here! *Hurry!*
Alan Jay Lerner 1918–86 American
songwriter: 'It's Lovely Up Here' (1965)

6 The rose of all the world is not for
me.
I want for my part
Only the little white rose of Scotland
That smells sharp and sweet—and
breaks the heart.
Hugh MacDiarmid 1892–1978 Scottish
poet and nationalist: 'The Little White
Rose' (1934)

7 Flowers. Those free gifts laid out
on Mother Nature's perfume counter.
> **Roger McGough** 1937– English poet:
> 'Perfume' (1999)

8 People from a planet without flowers
would think we must be mad with
joy the whole time to have such
things about us.
> **Iris Murdoch** 1919–99 English novelist:
> *A Fairly Honourable Defeat* (1970)

9 I know a bank whereon the wild
thyme blows,
Where oxlips and the nodding violet
grows
Quite over-canopied with luscious
woodbine,
With sweet musk-roses, and with
eglantine:
> **William Shakespeare** 1564–1616
> English dramatist: *A Midsummer Night's
> Dream* (1595–6)

10   Daffodils,
That come before the swallow dares,
and take
The winds of March with beauty;
violets dim,
But sweeter than the lids of Juno's
eyes.
> **William Shakespeare** 1564–1616
> English dramatist: *The Winter's Tale*
> (1610–11)

11 From my experience of life I believe
my personal motto should be
'Beware of men bearing flowers.'
> **Muriel Spark** 1918–2006 British
> novelist: *Curriculum Vitae* (1992)

12 As well as any bloom upon a flower
I like the dust on the nettles, never
lost
Except to prove the sweetness of a
shower.
> **Edward Thomas** 1878–1917 English
> poet: 'Tall Nettles' (1917)

13 Summer set lip to earth's bosom
bare,
And left the flushed print in a poppy
there.
> **Francis Thompson** 1859–1907 English
> poet: 'The Poppy' (1913)

14 I wandered lonely as a cloud
That floats on high o'er vales and
hills,
When all at once I saw a crowd,
A host, of golden daffodils;
Beside the lake, beneath the trees,
Fluttering and dancing in the breeze.
> **William Wordsworth** 1770–1850
> English poet: 'I wandered lonely as a
> cloud' (1815 ed.)

15 I never see a flower that pleases me,
but I wish for you.
> **William Wordsworth** 1770–1850
> English poet: letter to his wife Mary,
> 1810

Fog

see also WEATHER

1 This is a London particular . . . A fog,
miss.
> **Charles Dickens** 1812–70 English
> novelist: *Bleak House* (1853)

2 The yellow fog that rubs its back
upon the window-panes.
> **T. S. Eliot** 1888–1965 Anglo-American
> poet, critic, and dramatist: 'The Love
> Song of J. Alfred Prufrock' (1917)

3 The fog comes
on little cat feet.
It sits looking
over harbour and city
on silent haunches
and then moves on.
> **Carl Sandburg** 1878–1967 American
> poet: 'Fog' (1916)

Food and Drink

see also ALCOHOL, COOKING, DIETS, EATING

1 Shake and shake
The catsup bottle.

None will come,
And then a lot'll.
> **Richard Armour** 1906–89: 'Going to
> Extremes' (1949)

2 An egg boiled very soft is not
unwholesome.
> **Jane Austen** 1775–1817 English novelist:
> *Emma* (1816)

3 Fair fa' your honest, sonsie face,
Great chieftain o' the puddin'-race!
> **Robert Burns** 1759–96 Scottish poet:
> 'To a Haggis' (1787)

4 I'm President of the United States,
and I'm not going to eat any more
broccoli!
> **George Bush** 1924– American
> Republican statesman: in *New York
> Times* 23 March 1990

5 Doubtless God could have made a
better berry, but doubtless God
never did.
on the strawberry
> **William Butler** 1535–1618 English
> physician: Izaak Walton *The Compleat
> Angler* (3rd ed., 1661)

6 Tea, although an Oriental,
Is a gentleman at least;
Cocoa is a cad and coward,
Cocoa is a vulgar beast.
> **G. K. Chesterton** 1874–1936 English
> essayist, novelist, and poet: 'Song of
> Right and Wrong' (1914)

7 Take away that pudding—it has no
theme.
> **Winston Churchill** 1874–1965 British
> Conservative statesman: Lord Home
> *The Way the Wind Blows* (1976)

8 Milk's leap toward immortality.
of cheese
> **Clifton Fadiman** 1904–99 American
> critic: *Any Number Can Play* (1957)

9 Roast Beef, Medium, is not only a
food. It is a philosophy.
> **Edna Ferber** 1887–1968 American
> writer: *Roast Beef, Medium* (1911)

10 I ate his liver with some fava beans
and a nice chianti.
> **Thomas Harris** 1940– and **Ted Tally**
> 1952– American writer; American
> screenwriter: *The Silence of the Lambs*
> (1991 film); spoken by Anthony Hopkins
> as Hannibal Lecter

11 A cucumber should be well sliced,
and dressed with pepper and
vinegar, and then thrown out, as
good for nothing.
> **Samuel Johnson** 1709–84 English poet,
> critic, and lexicographer: James Boswell
> *Journal of a Tour to the Hebrides* (1785)
> 5 October 1773

12 *What* is the matter with Mary Jane?
She's perfectly well and she hasn't a
pain,
*And it's lovely rice pudding for dinner
again!*
What *is* the matter with Mary Jane?
> **A. A. Milne** 1882–1956 English writer for
> children: 'Rice Pudding' (1924)

13 I had ants in Africa recently: they
were rather nice and crispy.
> **Desmond Morris** 1928– English
> anthropologist: in *Mail on Sunday*
> 20 July 2008

14 Parsley
Is gharsley.
> **Ogden Nash** 1902–71 American
> humorist: 'Further Reflections on
> Parsley' (1942)

15 A fruit is a vegetable with looks and
money. Plus, if you let fruit rot, it
turns into wine, something Brussels
sprouts never do.
> **P. J. O'Rourke** 1947– American
> humorous writer: *The Bachelor Home
> Companion* (1987)

16 The ordinary human being would
sooner starve than live on brown
bread and raw carrots. And the
peculiar evil is this, that the less
money you have, the less inclined
you feel to spend it on wholesome

food. A millionaire may enjoy breakfasting off orange juice and ryvita biscuits; [but] . . . When you are underfed, harassed, bored and miserable, you don't *want* to eat dull wholesome food. You want something a little bit 'tasty.'
  George Orwell 1903–50 English novelist: *The Road to Wigan Pier* (1937)

17 Coffee, (which makes the politician wise,
And see thro' all things with his half-shut eyes).
  Alexander Pope 1688–1744 English poet: *The Rape of the Lock* (1714)

18 It is said that the effect of eating too much lettuce is 'soporific'.
  Beatrix Potter 1866–1943 English writer for children: *The Tale of the Flopsy Bunnies* (1909)

19 Look here, Steward, if this is coffee, I want tea; but if this is tea, then I wish for coffee.
  Punch English humorous weekly periodical: 23 July 1902

20 Methinks sometimes I have no more wit than a Christian or an ordinary man has; but I am a great eater of beef, and I believe that does harm to my wit.
  William Shakespeare 1564–1616 English dramatist: *Twelfth Night* (1601)

21 There is no love sincerer than the love of food.
  George Bernard Shaw 1856–1950 Irish dramatist: *Man and Superman* (1903)

22 Let onion atoms lurk within the bowl,
And, scarce-suspected, animate the whole.
  Sydney Smith 1771–1845 English clergyman and essayist: Lady Holland *Memoir* (1855) 'Receipt for a Salad'

23 Many's the long night I've dreamed of cheese—toasted, mostly.
  Robert Louis Stevenson 1850–94 Scottish novelist: *Treasure Island* (1883)

24 Cauliflower is nothing but cabbage with a college education.
  Mark Twain 1835–1910 American writer: *Pudd'nhead Wilson* (1894)

25 MOTHER: It's broccoli, dear.
CHILD: I say it's spinach, and I say the hell with it.
  E. B. White 1899–1985 American humorist: *New Yorker* 8 December 1928 (cartoon caption)

26 *to a waiter:*
When I ask for a watercress sandwich, I do not mean a loaf with a field in the middle of it.
  Oscar Wilde 1854–1900 Anglo-Irish dramatist and poet: Max Beerbohm, letter to Reggie Turner, 15 April 1893

Fools

see also INTELLIGENCE

1 The world is full of fools, and he who would not see it should live alone and smash his mirror.
  Anonymous: adaptation from an original form attributed to Claude Le Petit (1640–65)

2 There's a sucker born every minute.
  Phineas T. Barnum 1810–91 American showman: attributed

3 A fool sees not the same tree that a wise man sees.
  William Blake 1757–1827 English poet: *The Marriage of Heaven and Hell* (1790–3)

4 A fool can always find a greater fool to admire him.
  Nicolas Boileau 1636–1711 French critic and poet: *L'Art poétique* (1674)

5 'Tis hard if all is false that I advance
A fool must now and then be right,
by chance.
   William Cowper 1731–1800 English
   poet: 'Conversation' (1782)

6 Never give a sucker an even break.
   W. C. Fields 1880–1946 American
   humorist: title of a W. C. Fields film
   (1941); the catch-phrase (Fields's own)
   is said to have originated in the musical
   comedy *Poppy* (1923)

7 I won't say she was silly, but I think
one of us was silly, and it wasn't me.
   Elizabeth Gaskell 1810–65 English
   novelist: *Wives and Daughters* (1866)

8 So dumb he can't fart and chew gum
at the same time.
   of Gerald Ford
   Lyndon Baines Johnson 1908–73
   American Democratic statesman:
   Richard Reeves *A Ford, not a Lincoln*
   (1975)

9 As we journey through life,
discarding baggage along the way,
we should keep an iron grip, to the
very end, on the capacity for
silliness. It preserves the soul from
desiccation.
   Humphrey Lyttelton 1922–2008 English
   jazz musician and broadcaster: *It Just
   Occurred to Me* (2006)

10 A knowledgeable fool is a greater fool
than an ignorant fool.
   Molière 1622–73 French comic
   dramatist: *Les Femmes savantes* (1672)

11 For fools rush in where angels fear to
tread.
   Alexander Pope 1688–1744 English
   poet: *An Essay on Criticism* (1711)

12 The follies which a man regrets most,
in his life, are those which he didn't
commit when he had the
opportunity.
   Helen Rowland 1875–1950 American
   writer: *A Guide to Men* (1922)

13 With stupidity the gods themselves
struggle in vain.
   Friedrich von Schiller 1759–1805
   German dramatist and poet: *Die
   Jungfrau von Orleans* (1801)

14 The ae half of the warld thinks the
tither daft.
   Sir Walter Scott 1771–1832 Scottish
   novelist and poet: *Redgauntlet* (1824)

15 The ultimate result of shielding men
from the effects of folly, is to fill the
world with fools.
   Herbert Spencer 1820–1903 English
   philosopher: *Essays* (1891) vol. 3 'State
   Tamperings with Money and Banks'

16 Better to keep your mouth shut and
appear stupid than to open it and
remove all doubt.
   Mark Twain 1835–1910 American
   writer: attributed, perhaps apocryphal

17   Be wise with speed;
A fool at forty is a fool indeed.
   Edward Young 1683–1765 English poet
   and dramatist: *The Love of Fame*
   (1725–8)

Football

see also SPORTS

1 The great fallacy is that the game is
first and last about winning. It is
nothing of the kind. The game is
about glory, it is about doing things
in style and with a flourish, about
going out and beating the lot, not
waiting for them to die of boredom.
   Danny Blanchflower 1926–93 English
   footballer: attributed, 1972

2 Football, wherein is nothing but
beastly fury, and extreme violence,
whereof proceedeth hurt, and
consequently rancour and malice do
remain with them that be wounded.
   Thomas Elyot 1499–1546 English
   diplomatist and writer: *Book of the
   Governor* (1531)

3 Football is an art more central to our culture than anything the Arts Council deigns to recognize.
> **Germaine Greer** 1939– Australian feminist: in *Independent* 28 June 1996

4 The natural state of the football fan is bitter disappointment, no matter what the score.
> **Nick Hornby** 1957– British novelist and journalist: *Fever Pitch* (1992)

5 Football is a simple game; 22 men chase a ball for 90 minutes and at the end, the Germans win.
> **Gary Lineker** 1960– English footballer: attributed

6 Oh, he's football crazy, he's football mad
And the football it has robbed him o' the wee bit sense he had.
And it would take a dozen skivvies, his clothes to wash and scrub,
Since our Jock became a member of that terrible football club.
> **Jimmie McGregor** 1932– Scottish singer and songwriter: 'Football Crazy' (1960 song)

7 The goal was scored a little bit by the hand of God, another bit by head of Maradona.
> *on his controversial goal against England in the 1986 World Cup*
> **Diego Maradona** 1960– Argentine football player: in *Guardian* 1 July 1986

8 When you've done it all, what do you do for an encore?
> *of Arsenal's League and FA cup double in 1971*
> **Bertie Mee** 1918–2001 English football player and manager: in *Times* 23 October 2001, obituary

9 Football? It's the beautiful game.
> **Pelé** 1940– Brazilian footballer: attributed; his autobiography (1977) was *My Life and the Beautiful Game*

10 To say that these men paid their shillings to watch twenty-two hirelings kick a ball is merely to say that a violin is wood and catgut, that *Hamlet* is so much paper and ink. For a shilling the Bruddersford United AFC offered you Conflict and Art.
> **J. B. Priestley** 1894–1984 English novelist, dramatist, and critic: *Good Companions* (1929)

11 For when the One Great Scorer comes to mark against your name, He writes—not that you won or lost—but how you played the Game.
> **Grantland Rice** 1880–1954 American sports writer: 'Alumnus Football' (1941)

12 Some people think football is a matter of life and death . . . I can assure them it is much more serious than that.
> **Bill Shankly** 1913–81 Scottish footballer: in *Guardian* 24 December 1973

13 Football and cookery are the two most important subjects in the country.
> **Delia Smith** English cookery expert: in *Observer* 23 February 1997

Foresight

see also FUTURE

1 Science fiction writers foresee the inevitable, and although problems and catastrophes may be inevitable, solutions are not.
> **Isaac Asimov** 1920–92 Russian-born biochemist and science fiction writer: in *Natural History* April 1975

2 Some of the jam we thought was for tomorrow, we've already eaten.
> **Tony Benn** 1925– British Labour politician: attributed, 1969

3 It was déjà vu all over again.
> **Yogi Berra** 1925– American baseball player: attributed

4 Predictions can be very difficult—especially about the future.
> **Niels Bohr** 1885–1962 Danish physicist: H. Rosovsky *The University: An Owners Manual* (1991)

5 You can never plan the future by the past.
> **Edmund Burke** 1729–97 Irish-born Whig politician and man of letters: *Letter to a Member of the National Assembly* (1791)

6 The best laid schemes o' mice an' men
Gang aft a-gley.
> **Robert Burns** 1759–96 Scottish poet: 'To a Mouse' (1786)

7 She felt that those who prepared for all the emergencies of life beforehand may equip themselves at the expense of joy.
> **E. M. Forster** 1879–1970 English novelist: *Howards End* (1910)

8 The best way to suppose what may come, is to remember what is past.
> **Lord Halifax** 1633–95 English politician and essayist: *Political, Moral, and Miscellaneous Thoughts and Reflections* (1750) 'Miscellaneous: Experience'

9 What all the wise men promised has not happened, and what all the d—d fools said would happen has come to pass.
> *of the Catholic Emancipation Act (1829)*
> **Lord Melbourne** 1779–1848 British Whig statesman: H. Dunckley *Lord Melbourne* (1890)

10 The man who has fed the chicken every day throughout its life at last wrings its neck instead, showing that a more refined view as to the uniformity of nature would have been useful to the chicken.
> **Bertrand Russell** 1872–1970 British philosopher and mathematician: *The Problems of Philosophy* (1912)

11 Prognostics do not always prove prophecies,—at least the wisest prophets make sure of the event first.
> **Horace Walpole** 1717–97 English writer and connoisseur: letter to Thomas Walpole, 19 February 1785

12 God damn you all: I told you so.
> *suggestion for his own epitaph, 1939*
> **H. G. Wells** 1866–1946 English novelist: Ernest Barker *Age and Youth* (1953)

Forgiveness

1 You ought certainly to forgive them as a Christian, but never to admit them in your sight, or allow their names to be mentioned in your hearing.
> **Jane Austen** 1775–1817 English novelist: *Pride and Prejudice* (1813)

2 I never forgive but I always forget.
> **Arthur James Balfour** 1848–1930 British Conservative statesman: R. Blake *Conservative Party* (1970)

3 It is easier to forgive an enemy than to forgive a friend.
> **William Blake** 1757–1827 English poet: *Jerusalem* (1815) 'Chapter 4' (plate 91, l. 1)

4 I believe any person who asks for forgiveness has to be prepared to give it.
> **Bill Clinton** 1946– American Democratic statesman: statement after being acquitted by the Senate, 12 February 1999

5 I ain't sayin' you treated me unkind
You could have done better but I don't mind
You just kinda wasted my precious time
But don't think twice, it's all right.
> **Bob Dylan** 1941– American singer and songwriter: 'Don't Think Twice, It's All Right' (1963 song)

6 After such knowledge, what
forgiveness?
> **T. S. Eliot** 1888–1965 Anglo-American
> poet, critic, and dramatist: 'Gerontion'
> (1920)

7 God will pardon me, it is His trade.
on his deathbed
> **Heinrich Heine** 1797–1856 German
> poet: Alfred Meissner *Heinrich Heine.*
> *Erinnerungen* (1856)

8 Every one says forgiveness is a lovely
idea, until they have something to
forgive.
> **C. S. Lewis** 1898–1963 English literary
> scholar: *Mere Christianity* (1952)

9 True reconciliation does not consist
in merely forgetting the past.
> **Nelson Mandela** 1918– South African
> statesman: speech, 7 January 1996

10 We read that we ought to forgive our
enemies; but we do not read that we
ought to forgive our friends.
> **Cosimo de' Medici** 1389–1464 Italian
> statesman and patron of the arts:
> Francis Bacon *Apophthegms* (1625)

11 When a deep injury is done to us, we
never recover until we forgive.
> **Alan Paton** 1903–88 South African
> writer: *Too Late the Phalarope* (1953)

12 To err is human; to forgive, divine.
> **Alexander Pope** 1688–1744 English
> poet: *An Essay on Criticism* (1711)

13 The stupid neither forgive nor forget;
the naïve forgive and forget; the wise
forgive but do not forget.
> **Thomas Szasz** 1920– Hungarian-born
> psychiatrist: *The Second Sin* (1973)

14 And blessings on the falling out
That all the more endears,
When we fall out with those we love
And kiss again with tears!
> **Alfred, Lord Tennyson** 1809–92 English
> poet: *The Princess* (1847), song (added
> 1850)

15 God of forgiveness, do not forgive
those murderers of Jewish children
here.
> **Elie Wiesel** 1928– Romanian-born
> American writer: at an unofficial
> ceremony at Auschwitz, 26 January 1995

France

see also INTERNATIONAL RELATIONS

1 Everything ends this way in France.
Weddings, christenings, duels,
burials, swindlings, affairs of
state—everything is a pretext for a
good dinner.
> **Jean Anouilh** 1910–87 French
> dramatist: *Cécile* (1951)

2 France was long a despotism
tempered by epigrams.
> **Thomas Carlyle** 1795–1881 Scottish
> historian and political philosopher:
> *History of the French Revolution* (1837)

3 France is the only place where you
can make love in the afternoon
without people hammering on your
door.
> **Barbara Cartland** 1901–2000 English
> writer: in *Guardian* 24 December 1984

4 How can you govern a country which
has 246 varieties of cheese?
> **Charles de Gaulle** 1890–1970 French
> soldier and statesman: Ernest Mignon
> *Les Mots du Général* (1962)

5 *Vive la différence, mais vive l'entente
cordiale.*
Long live the difference, but long live
the Entente Cordiale.
> **Elizabeth II** 1926– British monarch:
> speech, Paris, 5 April 2004 in *Times*
> 6 April 2004

6 The last time I saw Paris
Her heart was warm and gay,
I heard the laughter of her heart in
ev'ry street café.
> **Oscar Hammerstein II** 1895–1960

American songwriter: 'The Last Time I saw Paris' (1941 song)

7 Paris is a movable feast.
   Ernest Hemingway 1899–1961 American novelist: *A Movable Feast* (1964)

8 Yet, who can help loving the land that has taught us
   Six hundred and eighty-five ways to dress eggs?
   Thomas Moore 1779–1852 Irish musician and songwriter: *The Fudge Family in Paris* (1818)

9 The French are a logical people, which is one reason the English dislike them so intensely. The other is that they own France, a country which we have always judged to be much too good for them.
   Robert Morley 1908–92 English actor, director, and dramatist: *A Musing Morley* (1974)

10 France has more need of me than I have need of France.
   Napoleon I 1769–1821 French emperor: speech to the Corps Législatif, Paris, 31 December 1813

11 They order, said I, this matter better in France.
   Laurence Sterne 1713–68 English novelist: *A Sentimental Journey* (1768)

12 If the French noblesse had been capable of playing cricket with their peasants, their chateaux would never have been burnt.
   G. M. Trevelyan 1876–1962 English historian: *English Social History* (1942)

Friendship

see also RELATIONSHIPS

1 One friend in a lifetime is much; two are many; three are hardly possible. Friendship needs a certain

parallelism of life, a community of thought, a rivalry of aim.
   Henry Brooks Adams 1838–1918 American man of letters: *The Education of Henry Adams* (1907)

2 Oh, the comfort—the inexpressible comfort of feeling safe with a person, having neither to weigh thoughts, nor measure words, but pouring them all out, just as they are, chaff and grain together; knowing that a faithful hand will take and sift them—keep what is worth keeping—and with the breath of kindness blow the rest away.
   Anonymous: 'Friendship'; often attributed to George Eliot (1819–80) or Dinah Mulock Craik (1826–87)

3 *when asked 'What is a friend?':*
   One soul inhabiting two bodies.
   Aristotle 384–322 BC Greek philosopher: Diogenes Laertius *Lives of Philosophers*

4 Champagne for my real friends, real pain for my sham friends.
   Francis Bacon 1909–92 Irish painter: in the 1950s; Michael Peppiatt *Francis Bacon* (1996)

5 There is a friend that sticketh closer than a brother.
   Bible: Proverbs

6 The bird a nest, the spider a web, man friendship.
   William Blake 1757–1827 English poet: *The Marriage of Heaven and Hell* (1790–3)

7 We must take our friends as they are.
   James Boswell 1740–95 Scottish lawyer and biographer: diary, 25 February 1791

8 Friendship is one of the most tangible things in a world which offers fewer and fewer supports.
   Kenneth Branagh 1960– Northern Irish actor: in *Daily Telegraph* 4 November 1992

9 Should auld acquaintance be forgot
And never brought to mind?
   Robert Burns 1759–96 Scottish poet:
   'Auld Lang Syne' (1796)

10 Friendship is like money, easier
made than kept.
   Samuel Butler 1835–1902 English
   novelist: *Notebooks* (1912)

11 Friendship is Love without his wings!
   Lord Byron 1788–1824 English poet:
   'L'Amitié est l'amour sans ailes' (written
   1806)

12 Give me the avowed, erect and
   manly foe;
Firm I can meet, perhaps return the
   blow;
But of all plagues, good Heaven, thy
   wrath can send,
Save me, oh, save me, from the
   candid friend.
   George Canning 1770–1827 British Tory
   statesman: 'New Morality' (1821)

13 A woman can become a man's friend
only in the following stages—first an
acquaintance, next a mistress, and
only then a friend.
   Anton Chekhov 1860–1904 Russian
   dramatist and short-story writer: *Uncle
   Vanya* (1897)

14 The man that hails you Tom or Jack,
And proves by thumps upon your
   back
How he esteems your merit,
Is such a friend, that one had need
Be very much his friend indeed
To pardon or to bear it.
   William Cowper 1731–1800 English
   poet: 'Friendship' (1782)

15 To find a friend one must close one
eye. To keep him—two.
   Norman Douglas 1868–1952 Scottish-
   born novelist and essayist: *South Wind*
   (1917)

16 Friendships begin with liking or
gratitude—roots that can be pulled
up.
   George Eliot 1819–80 English novelist:
   Daniel Deronda (1876)

17 No man can be friends with a
woman he finds attractive. He always
wants to have sex with her. Sex is
always out there. Friendship is
ultimately doomed and that is the
end of the story.
   Nora Ephron 1941– American writer
   and journalist: *When Harry Met Sally*
   (1989 film)

18 Of all the means which wisdom
acquires to ensure happiness
throughout the whole of life, by far
the most important is friendship.
   Epicurus 341–271 BC Greek
   philosopher: Diogenes Laertius *Lives of
   Eminent Philosophers* bk. 10, sect. 148

19 Louis, I think this is the beginning of
a beautiful friendship.
   Julius J. Epstein 1909–2001: *Casablanca*
   (1942 film, with Philip G. Epstein and
   Howard Koch), spoken by Humphrey
   Bogart

20 We have fewer friends than we
imagine, but more than we know.
   Hugo von Hofmannsthal 1874–1929
   Austrian poet and writer: *Book of
   Friends* (1922)

21 My father always used to say that
when you die, if you've got five real
friends, you've had a great life.
   Lee Iacocca 1924– American
   businessman: *Iacocca: An
   Autobiography* (1984)

22 My life is spent in a perpetual
alternation between two rhythms,
the rhythm of attracting people for
fear I may be lonely, and the rhythm
of trying to get rid of them because I
know that I am bored.
   C. E. M. Joad 1891–1953 English

philosopher: in *Observer* 12 December 1948

23 If a man does not make new acquaintance as he advances through life, he will soon find himself left alone. A man, Sir, should keep his friendship in constant repair.
Samuel Johnson 1709–84 English poet, critic, and lexicographer: James Boswell *Life of Samuel Johnson* (1791) 1755

24 God's apology for relations.
on friends
Hugh Kingsmill 1889–1949 English man of letters: Michael Holroyd *The Best of Hugh Kingsmill* (1970)

25 However rare true love may be, true friendship is rarer.
Duc de la Rochefoucauld 1613–80 French moralist: *Maxims*

26 Oh I get by with a little help from my friends.
John Lennon 1940–80 and **Paul McCartney** 1942– English pop singers and songwriters: 'With a Little Help From My Friends' (1967 song)

27 Levin wanted friendship and got friendliness; he wanted steak and they offered spam.
Bernard Malamud 1914–86 American novelist and short-story writer: *A New Life* (1961)

28 I count myself in nothing else so happy
As in a soul remembering my good friends.
William Shakespeare 1564–1616 English dramatist: *Richard II* (1595)

29 I do not believe that friends are necessarily the people you like best, they are merely the people who got there first.
Peter Ustinov 1921–2004 British actor, director, and writer: *Dear Me* (1977)

30 I have lost friends, some by death . . . others through sheer inability to cross the street.
Virginia Woolf 1882–1941 English novelist: *The Waves* (1931)

31 Think where man's glory most begins and ends,
And say my glory was I had such friends.
W. B. Yeats 1865–1939 Irish poet: 'The Municipal Gallery Re-visited' (1939)

Futility

1 You will never make a crab walk straight.
Aristophanes *c.*450–*c.*385 BC Greek comic dramatist: *Peace*

2 O plunge your hands in water,
Plunge them in up to the wrist;
Stare, stare in the basin
And wonder what you've missed.
The glacier knocks in the cupboard,
The desert sighs in the bed,
And the crack in the tea-cup opens
A lane to the land of the dead.
W. H. Auden 1907–73 English poet: 'As I Walked Out One Evening' (1940)

3 Nothing to be done.
Samuel Beckett 1906–89 Irish dramatist, novelist, and poet: *Waiting for Godot* (1955)

4 Vanity of vanities, saith the Preacher, vanity of vanities; all is vanity.
Bible: Ecclesiastes

5 We are the hollow men
We are the stuffed men
Leaning together
Headpiece filled with straw. Alas!
T. S. Eliot 1888–1965 Anglo-American poet, critic, and dramatist: 'The Hollow Men' (1925)

6 Pathos, piety, courage—they exist,
but are identical, and so is filth.
Everything exists, nothing has value.

> **E. M. Forster** 1879–1970 English
> novelist: *A Passage to India* (1924)

7 He's a real nowhere man
Sitting in his nowhere land
Making all his nowhere plans for
nobody.

> **John Lennon** 1940–80 and **Paul
> McCartney** 1942– English pop singers
> and songwriters: 'Nowhere Man'
> (1966 song)

8 I'm not going to rearrange the
furniture on the deck of the Titanic.

> *having lost five of the last six primaries as
> President Ford's campaign manager*
> **Rogers Morton** 1914–79 American
> public relations officer: *Washington Post*
> 16 May 1976

9 There aren't any good, brave causes
left. If the big bang does come, and
we all get killed off, it won't be in aid
of the old-fashioned, grand design.
It'll just be for the Brave New-
nothing-very-much-thank-you.
About as pointless and inglorious as
stepping in front of a bus.

> **John Osborne** 1929–94 English
> dramatist: *Look Back in Anger* (1956)

10 'Strange friend,' I said, 'here is no
cause to mourn.'
'None,' said that other, 'save the
undone years,
The hopelessness. Whatever hope is
yours,
Was my life also.'

> **Wilfred Owen** 1893–1918 English poet:
> 'Strange Meeting' (written 1918)

11 Who breaks a butterfly upon a
wheel?

> **Alexander Pope** 1688–1744 English
> poet: 'An Epistle to Dr Arbuthnot' (1735)

12 Nothingness haunts being.

> **Jean-Paul Sartre** 1905–80 French

philosopher, novelist, dramatist, and
critic: *Being and Nothingness* (1956)

13 How weary, stale, flat, and
unprofitable
Seem to me all the uses of this world.

> **William Shakespeare** 1564–1616
> English dramatist: *Hamlet* (1601)

14 'My name is Ozymandias, king of
kings:
Look on my works, ye Mighty, and
despair!'
Nothing beside remains. Round the
decay
Of that colossal wreck, boundless
and bare
The lone and level sands stretch far
away.

> **Percy Bysshe Shelley** 1792–1822
> English poet: 'Ozymandias' (1819)

The Future

see also FORESIGHT

1 'We are always doing', says he,
'something for Posterity, but I would
fain see Posterity do something for
us.'

> **Joseph Addison** 1672–1719 English
> poet, dramatist, and essayist: in *The
> Spectator* 20 August 1714

2 The future's bright, the future's
Orange.

> **Advertising slogan**: Orange telecom
> company, mid 1990s

3 More than any other time in history,
mankind faces a crossroads. One
path leads to despair and utter
hopelessness. The other, to total
extinction. Let us pray we have the
wisdom to choose correctly.

> **Woody Allen** 1935– American film
> director, writer, and actor: *Side Effects*
> (1980) 'My Speech to the Graduates'

4 The future ain't what it used to be.

> **Yogi Berra** 1925– American baseball
> player: attributed

5 People will not look forward to
posterity, who never look backward
to their ancestors.
> **Edmund Burke** 1729–97 Irish-born
> Whig politician and man of letters:
> *Reflections on the Revolution in France*
> (1790)

6 And now, we can see a new world
coming into view. A world in which
there is the very real prospect of a
new world order.
> **George Bush** 1924– American
> Republican statesman: speech, in *New
> York Times* 7 March 1991

7 He seems to think that posterity is a
pack-horse, always ready to be
loaded.
> **Benjamin Disraeli** 1804–81 British Tory
> statesman and novelist: speech, 3 June
> 1862; attributed

8 I never think of the future. It comes
soon enough.
> **Albert Einstein** 1879–1955 German-
> born theoretical physicist: in an
> interview given on the *Belgenland*,
> December 1930

9 You cannot fight against the future.
Time is on our side.
> **W. E. Gladstone** 1809–98 British Liberal
> statesman: speech on the Reform Bill,
> House of Commons, 27 April 1866

10 You will eat, bye and bye,
In that glorious land above the sky;
Work and pray, live on hay,
You'll get pie in the sky when you die.
> **Joe Hill** 1879–1915 Swedish-born
> American labour leader: 'Preacher and
> the Slave' (1911 song)

11 The best way to predict the future is
to invent it.
> **Alan Kay** 1940– American computer
> scientist: in 1971, at the Palo Alto
> Research Center

12 *In the long run* we are all dead.
> **John Maynard Keynes** 1883–1946

English economist: *A Tract on Monetary
Reform* (1923)

13 We have trained them [men] to think
of the Future as a promised land
which favoured heroes attain—not
as something which everyone
reaches at the rate of sixty minutes
an hour, whatever he does, whoever
he is.
> **C. S. Lewis** 1898–1963 English literary
> scholar: *The Screwtape Letters* (1942)

14 If you want a picture of the future,
imagine a boot stamping on a
human face—for ever.
> **George Orwell** 1903–50 English
> novelist: *Nineteen Eighty-Four* (1949)

15 They spend their time mostly
looking forward to the past.
> **John Osborne** 1929–94 English
> dramatist: *Look Back in Anger* (1956)

16 If there must be trouble, let it be in
my day, that my child may have
peace.
> **Thomas Paine** 1737–1809 English
> political theorist: *The Crisis* (December
> 1776)

17 The visions we offer our children
shape the future. It *matters* what
those visions are. Often they become
self-fulfilling prophecies. Dreams are
maps.
> **Carl Sagan** 1934–96 American scientist
> and writer: *Pale Blue Dot* (1995)

18 Lord! we know what we are, but
know not what we may be.
> **William Shakespeare** 1564–1616
> English dramatist: *Hamlet* (1601)

19 So many worlds, so much to do,
So little done, such things to be.
> **Alfred, Lord Tennyson** 1809–92 English
> poet: *In Memoriam A. H. H.* (1850)

Games

see SPORTS AND GAMES

Gardens

see also FLOWERS

1 God Almighty first planted a garden; and, indeed, it is the purest of human pleasures.
Francis Bacon 1561–1626 English lawyer, courtier, philosopher, and essayist: *Essays* (1625) 'Of Gardens'

2 Nothing is more pleasant to the eye than green grass kept finely shorn.
Francis Bacon 1561–1626 English lawyer, courtier, philosopher, and essayist: *Essays* (1625) 'Of Gardens'

3 As long as one has a garden, one has a future; and as long as one has a future one is alive.
Frances Hodgson Burnett 1849–1924 British-born American novelist: *In the Garden* (1925)

4 I just come and talk to the plants, really—very important to talk to them, they respond I find.
Charles, Prince of Wales 1948– British prince: television interview, 21 September 1986

5 What is a weed? A plant whose virtues have not been discovered.
Ralph Waldo Emerson 1803–82 American philosopher and poet: *Fortune of the Republic* (1878)

6 The kiss of the sun for pardon, The song of the birds for mirth, One is nearer God's Heart in a garden Than anywhere else on earth.
Dorothy Frances Gurney 1858–1932 English poet: 'God's Garden' (1913)

7 But though an old man, I am but a young gardener.
Thomas Jefferson 1743–1826 American Democratic Republican statesman: letter to Charles Willson Peale, 20 August 1811

8 The Glory of the Garden lies in more than meets the eye.
Rudyard Kipling 1865–1936 English writer and poet: 'The Glory of the Garden' (1911)

9 A garden was the primitive prison till man with Promethean felicity and boldness luckily sinned himself out of it.
Charles Lamb 1775–1834 English writer: letter to William Wordsworth, 22 January 1830

10 Weeds are not supposed to grow, But by degrees Some achieve a flower, although No one sees.
Philip Larkin 1922–85 English poet: 'Modesties' (1951)

11 Annihilating all that's made To a green thought in a green shade.
Andrew Marvell 1621–78 English poet: 'The Garden' (1681)

12 All gardening is landscape-painting.
Alexander Pope 1688–1744 English poet: Joseph Spence *Anecdotes* (1966)

13 Perennials are the ones that grow like weeds, biennials are the ones that die this year instead of next and hardy annuals are the ones that never come up at all.
Katharine Whitehorn 1928– English journalist: *Observations* (1970)

The Generation Gap

see also OLD AGE, YOUTH

1 What's the point in growing old if you can't hound and persecute the young?
Kenneth Clarke 1940– British Conservative politician: in *Observer* 27 May 2007

2 It is the one war in which everyone changes sides.

> **Cyril Connolly** 1903–74 English writer: Tom Driberg, speech in House of Commons, 30 October 1959

3 Come mothers and fathers,
Throughout the land
And don't criticize
What you can't understand . . .
For the times they are a-changin'!

> **Bob Dylan** 1941– American singer and songwriter: 'The Times They Are A-Changing' (1964 song)

4 *Si jeunesse savait; si vieillesse pouvait.*
If youth knew; if age could.

> **Henri Estienne** 1531–98 French printer and publisher: *Les Prémices* (1594)

5 Every generation revolts against its fathers and makes friends with its grandfathers.

> **Lewis Mumford** 1895–1990 American sociologist: *The Brown Decades* (1931)

6 Grown-ups never understand anything for themselves, and it is tiresome for children to be always and forever explaining things to them.

> **Antoine de Saint-Exupéry** 1900–44 French novelist: *Le Petit Prince* (1943)

7 The young have aspirations that never come to pass, the old have reminiscences of what never happened.

> **Saki** 1870–1916 Scottish writer: *Reginald* (1904)

8 The young man who has not wept is a savage, and the old man who will not laugh is a fool.

> **George Santayana** 1863–1952 Spanish-born philosopher and critic: *Dialogues in Limbo* (1925)

9 Crabbed age and youth cannot live together:

Youth is full of pleasance, age is full of care.

> **William Shakespeare** 1564–1616 English dramatist: *The Passionate Pilgrim* (1599)

10 Youth, which is forgiven everything, forgives itself nothing: age, which forgives itself everything, is forgiven nothing.

> **George Bernard Shaw** 1856–1950 Irish dramatist: *Man and Superman* (1903)

11 Nothing so dates a man as to decry the younger generation.

> **Adlai Stevenson** 1900–65 American Democratic politician: speech, 8 October 1952

12 When I was a boy of 14, my father was so ignorant I could hardly stand to have the old man around. But when I got to be 21, I was astonished at how much the old man had learned in seven years.

> **Mark Twain** 1835–1910 American writer: attributed in *Reader's Digest* September 1939, but not traced in his works

13 O Man! that from thy fair and shining youth
Age might but take the things Youth needed not!

> **William Wordsworth** 1770–1850 English poet: 'The Small Celandine' (1807)

Genius

see also GREATNESS

1 There is more beauty in the works of a great genius who is ignorant of all the rules of art, than in the works of a little genius, who not only knows but scrupulously observes them.

> **Joseph Addison** 1672–1719 English poet, dramatist, and essayist: in *The Spectator* 10 September 1714

2 Geniuses are the luckiest of mortals because what they must do is the same as what they most want to do.
> **W. H. Auden** 1907–73 English poet: Dag Hammarskjöld *Markings* (1964)

3 Since when was genius found respectable?
> **Elizabeth Barrett Browning** 1806–61 English poet: *Aurora Leigh* (1857)

4 Great wits are sure to madness near allied,
And thin partitions do their bounds divide.
> **John Dryden** 1631–1700 English poet, critic, and dramatist: *Absalom and Achitophel* (1681)

5 Genius is one per cent inspiration, ninety-nine per cent perspiration.
> **Thomas Alva Edison** 1847–1931 American inventor: said *c*.1903, in *Harper's Monthly Magazine* September 1932

6 Little minds are interested in the extraordinary; great minds in the commonplace.
> **Elbert Hubbard** 1859–1915 American writer: *Thousand and One Epigrams* (1911)

7 The true genius is a mind of large general powers, accidentally determined to some particular direction.
> **Samuel Johnson** 1709–84 English poet, critic, and lexicographer: *Lives of the English Poets* (1779–81) 'Cowley'

8 A man of genius makes no mistakes. His errors are volitional and are the portals of discovery.
> **James Joyce** 1882–1941 Irish novelist: *Ulysses* (1922)

9 It's not fun being a genius. It's torture.
> **John Lennon** 1940–80 English pop singer and songwriter: interview for *Rolling Stone* magazine in December

1970, broadcast for the first time in the UK on 3 December 2005

10 Genius does what it must, and Talent does what it can.
> **Owen Meredith** 1831–91 English poet and statesman: 'Last Words of a Sensitive Second-Rate Poet' (1868)

11 Genius is always allowed some leeway, once the hammer has been pried from its hands and the blood has been cleaned up.
> **Terry Pratchett** 1948– English science fiction writer: *Thief of Time* (2001)

12 When a true genius appears in the world, you may know him by this sign, that the dunces are all in confederacy against him.
> **Jonathan Swift** 1667–1745 Anglo-Irish poet and satirist: *Thoughts on Various Subjects* (1711)

13 I know of no genius but the genius of hard work.
> **J. M. W. Turner** 1775–1851 English landscape painter: John Ruskin *Notes by Mr Ruskin on His Collection of Drawings by the late J. M. W. Turner* (1878)

14 I have nothing to declare except my genius.
at the New York Custom House
> **Oscar Wilde** 1854–1900 Anglo-Irish dramatist and poet: Frank Harris *Oscar Wilde* (1918)

Genocide

15 This happened near the core
Of a world's culture. This
Occurred among higher things.
This was a philosophical conclusion.
Everybody gets what he deserves.

The bare drab rubble of the place.
The dull damp stone. The rain.
The emptiness. The human lack.
> **Alan Bold** 1943– Scottish poet: 'June 1967 at Buchenwald' (1969); see JUSTICE 2

2 After September 30 you won't need the UN. You will simply need men with shovels and bleached white linen and headstones.

on the situation in Darfur, urging the deployment of a UN peacekeeping force

> **George Clooney** 1961– American actor and director: addressing the United Nations Security Council, 14 September 2006

3 I herewith commission you to carry out all preparations with regard to . . . a *total solution* of the Jewish question in those territories of Europe which are under German influence.

> **Hermann Goering** 1893–1946 German Nazi leader: instructions to Heydrich, 31 July 1941; W. L. Shirer *The Rise and Fall of the Third Reich* (1962)

4 After all, who remembers today the extermination of the Armenians?

> **Adolf Hitler** 1889–1945 German dictator: comment, 22 August 1939

5 Our language lacks words to express this offence, the demolition of a man.

of a year spent in Auschwitz

> **Primo Levi** 1919–87 Italian novelist and poet: *If This is a Man* (1958)

6 We wish to inform you that we have heard that tomorrow we will be killed with our families.

letter from seven Adventist pastors in Rwanda to their religious leader, 15 April 1994; the massacre of Tutsi refugees at Mugonero took place the following day

> **Ezekiel Semugeshi and six others**: Philip Gourevitch *We Wish to Inform You that Tomorrow We Will Be Killed with our Families* (1998)

7 We know that a man can read Goethe or Rilke in the evening, that he can play Bach and Schubert, and go to his day's work at Auschwitz in the morning.

> **George Steiner** 1926– American

French-born critic and writer: *Language and Silence* (1967)

8 600,000 to 800,00 human beings were murdered. We know now, as we knew then, they could have been saved, and they were not.

recalling the genocide in Rwanda

> **Elie Wiesel** 1928– Romanian-born American writer: addressing the United Nations Security Council, 14 September 2006, on the situation in Darfur

Gifts

see also CHARITY

1 It is more blessed to give than to receive.

> **Bible**: Acts of the Apostles

2 They gave it me,—for an un-birthday present.

> **Lewis Carroll** 1832–98 English writer and logician: *Through the Looking-Glass* (1872)

3 One must be poor to know the luxury of giving.

> **George Eliot** 1819–80 English novelist: *Middlemarch* (1871–2)

4 A gift though small is welcome.

> **Homer** *fl. c.*750 BC Greek poet: *Odyssey*

5 Teach us, good Lord, to serve Thee as Thou deservest:
To give and not to count the cost;
To fight and not to heed the wounds;
To toil and not to seek for rest;
To labour and not to ask for any reward
Save that of knowing that we do Thy will.

> **St Ignatius Loyola** 1491–1556 Spanish theologian: 'Prayer for Generosity' (1548)

6 I know it's not much, but it's the best I can do,

My gift is my song and this one's for you.

Elton John 1947– and **Bernie Taupin** 1950– English pop singer and songwriter; songwriter: 'Your Song' (1970 song)

7 Presents, I often say, endear Absents.

Charles Lamb 1775–1834 English writer: *Essays of Elia* (1823) 'A Dissertation upon Roast Pig'

8 Why is it no one ever sent me yet
One perfect limousine, do you suppose?
Ah no, it's always just my luck to get
One perfect rose.

Dorothy Parker 1893–1967 American critic and humorist: 'One Perfect Rose' (1937)

9 The key to a woman's heart is an unexpected gift at an unexpected time.

Mike Rich 1959– American screenwriter: *Finding Forrester* (2000 film); spoken by Sean Connery

10 *Equo ne credite, Teucri.*
Quidquid id est, timeo Danaos et dona ferentes.

Do not trust the horse, Trojans.
Whatever it is, I fear the Greeks even when they bring gifts.

Virgil 70–19 BC Roman poet: *Aeneid*

11 Behold, I do not give lectures or a little charity,
When I give I give myself.

Walt Whitman 1819–92 American poet: 'Song of Myself' (written 1855)

God

see also ATHEISM, BELIEF, BIBLE, CHRISTIANITY, RELIGION

1 If only God would give me some clear sign! Like making a large deposit in my name at a Swiss bank.

Woody Allen 1935– American film director, writer, and actor: in *New Yorker* 5 November 1973

2 The nature of God is a circle of which the centre is everywhere and the circumference is nowhere.

Anonymous: said to have been traced to a lost treatise of Empedocles; quoted in the *Roman de la Rose*, and by St Bonaventura in *Itinerarius Mentis in Deum*

3 God has been replaced, as he has all over the West, with respectability and air-conditioning.

Imamu Amiri Baraka 1934– American poet and dramatist: *Midstream* (1963)

4 If I were Her what would really piss me off the worst is that they cannot even get My gender right for Christsakes.

Roseanne Barr 1953– American comedian: *Roseanne* (1990)

5 With men this is impossible; but with God all things are possible.

Bible: St Matthew

6 He that loveth not knoweth not God; for God is love.

Bible: I John

7 I'm sorry, we don't do God.

when Tony Blair was asked about his Christian faith in an interview for Vanity Fair *magazine*

Alastair Campbell 1957– British journalist: in *Daily Telegraph* 5 May 2003

8 And almost every one when age, Disease, or sorrows strike him, Inclines to think there is a God, Or something very like Him.

Arthur Hugh Clough 1819–61 English poet: *Dipsychus* (1865)

9 God moves in a mysterious way His wonders to perform.

William Cowper 1731–1800 English poet: 'Light Shining out of Darkness' (1779 hymn)

10 It is the final proof of God's omnipotence that he need not exist in order to save us.

> **Peter De Vries** 1910–93 American novelist and humorist: *The Mackerel Plaza* (1958)

11 But I can't think for you
You'll have to decide,
Whether Judas Iscariot
Had God on his side.

> **Bob Dylan** 1941– American singer and songwriter: 'With God on our Side' (1963 song)

12 God is subtle but he is not malicious.

> **Albert Einstein** 1879–1955 German-born theoretical physicist: remark made at Princeton University, May 1921

13 'I didn't exist at Creation
I didn't exist at the Flood,
And I won't be around for Salvation
To sort out the sheep from the cud—
'Or whatever the phrase is. The fact is
In soteriological terms
I'm a crude existential malpractice
And you are a diet of worms.'

> **James Fenton** 1949– English poet: 'God, A Poem' (1983)

14 Forgive, O Lord, my little jokes on Thee
And I'll forgive Thy great big one on me.

> **Robert Frost** 1874–1963 American poet: 'Cluster of Faith' (1962)

15 God, to me, it seems,
is a verb
not a noun,
proper or improper.

> **R. Buckminster Fuller** 1895–1983 American designer and architect: *No More Secondhand God* (1963)

16 Mine eyes have seen the glory of the coming of the Lord:
He is trampling out the vintage where the grapes of wrath are stored;

He hath loosed the fateful lightning of his terrible swift sword:
His truth is marching on.

> **Julia Ward Howe** 1819–1910 American Unitarian lay preacher: 'Battle Hymn of the Republic' (1862)

17 Operationally, God is beginning to resemble not a ruler but the last fading smile of a cosmic Cheshire cat.

> **Julian Huxley** 1887–1975 English biologist: *Religion without Revelation* (1957 ed.)

18 I am not clear that God manoeuvres physical things . . . After all, a conjuring trick with bones only proves that it is as clever as a conjuring trick with bones.
of the Resurrection

> **David Jenkins** 1925– English theologian: 'Poles Apart' (BBC radio, 4 October 1984)

19 God seems to have left the receiver off the hook, and time is running out.

> **Arthur Koestler** 1905–83 Hungarian-born writer: *The Ghost in the Machine* (1967)

20 God is love, but get it in writing.

> **Gypsy Rose Lee** 1914–70 American striptease artiste: attributed

21 Though the mills of God grind slowly, yet they grind exceeding small;
Though with patience He stands waiting, with exactness grinds He all.

> **Henry Wadsworth Longfellow** 1807–82 American poet: translation of *Sinnegedichte* (1654) by Friedrich von Logau (1604–55), of classical origin

22 Better authentic mammon than a bogus god.

> **Louis MacNeice** 1907–63 British poet, born in Belfast: *Autumn Journal* (1939)

23 If the triangles were to make a God they would give him three sides.

Montesquieu 1689–1755 French political philosopher: *Lettres Persanes* (1721)

24 God is dead: but considering the state the species Man is in, there will perhaps be caves, for ages yet, in which his shadow will be shown.

Friedrich Nietzsche 1844–1900 German philosopher and writer: *Die fröhliche Wissenschaft* (1882)

25 'God is or he is not.' But to which side shall we incline? . . . Let us weigh the gain and the loss in wagering that God is. Let us estimate the two chances. If you gain, you gain all; if you lose, you lose nothing. Wager then without hesitation that he is.

known as Pascal's wager

Blaise Pascal 1623–62 French mathematician, physicist, and moralist: *Pensées* (1670)

26 God is really only another artist. He invented the giraffe, the elephant, and the cat. He has no real style. He just goes on trying other things.

Pablo Picasso 1881–1973 Spanish painter: F. Gilot and C. Lake *Life With Picasso* (1964)

27 God is always doing geometry.

Plato 429–347 BC Greek philosopher: Plutarch *Moralia*

28 God heard the embattled nations sing and shout
'Gott strafe England!' and 'God save the King!'
God this, God that, and God the other thing—
'Good God!' said God, 'I've got my work cut out.'

J. C. Squire 1884–1958 English man of letters: 'The Dilemma' (1916)

29 It is a mistake to suppose that God is only, or even chiefly, concerned with religion.

William Temple 1881–1944 English theologian: R. V. C. Bodley *In Search of Serenity* (1955)

30 Prayer carries us half way to God, fasting brings us to the door of his palace, and alms procure us admission.

Umar ibn Abd al-Aziz c.682–720 Arabcaliph: George Sale *The Koran* (1734) 'Preliminary Discourse'

31 If God did not exist, it would be necessary to invent him.

Voltaire 1694–1778 French writer and philosopher: *Épîtres* no. 96 'A l'Auteur du livre des trois imposteurs'

32 Any God I ever felt in church I brought in with me. And I think all the other folks did too. They come to church to *share* God not find God.

Alice Walker 1944– American poet: *The Colour Purple* (1982)

33 If God is your emotional role model, very few human relationships will match up to it.

Jeanette Winterson 1959– English novelist and critic: *Oranges are Not the Only Fruit* (1985)

Golf

1 If you watch a game, it's fun. If you play it, it's recreation. If you work at it, it's golf.

Bob Hope 1903–2003 American comedian: in *Reader's Digest* October 1958

2 A decision of the courts decided that the game of golf may be played on Sunday, not being a game within the view of the law, but being a form of moral effort.

Stephen Leacock 1869–1944 Canadian humorist: *Over the Footlights* (1923)

3 Golf is so popular simply because it is the best game in the world at which to be bad.

A. A. Milne 1882–1956 English writer for children: *Not That It Matters* (1919)

4 Golf is a good walk spoiled.

Mark Twain 1835–1910 American writer: attributed

5 The least thing upset him on the links. He missed short putts because of the uproar of the butterflies in the adjoining meadows.

P. G. Wodehouse 1881–1975 English writer: *The Clicking of Cuthbert* (1922)

6 Golf . . . is the infallible test. The man who can go into a patch of rough alone, with the knowledge that only God is watching him, and play his ball where it lies, is the man who will serve you faithfully and well.

P. G. Wodehouse 1881–1975 English writer: *The Clicking of Cuthbert* (1922)

Goodness

see also CHARITY, EVIL, SIN

1 Waste no more time arguing what a good man should be. Be one.

Marcus Aurelius AD 121–180 Roman emperor: *Meditations*

2 I'm as pure as the driven slush.

Tallulah Bankhead 1903–68 American actress: in *Saturday Evening Post* 12 April 1947

3 Terrible is the temptation to be good.

Bertolt Brecht 1898–1956 German dramatist: *The Caucasian Chalk Circle* (1948)

4 No one can be good for long when goodness is not in demand.

Bertolt Brecht 1898–1956 German

dramatist: *The Good Woman of Setzuan* (1938)

5 No people do so much harm as those who go about doing good.

Mandell Creighton 1843–1901 English prelate: *The Life and Letters of Mandell Creighton* by his wife (1904)

6   What after all
Is a halo? It's only one more thing to keep clean.

Christopher Fry 1907–2005 English dramatist: *The Lady's not for Burning* (1949)

7 The virtue which requires to be ever guarded is scarce worth the sentinel.

Oliver Goldsmith 1728–74 Anglo-Irish writer, poet, and dramatist: *The Vicar of Wakefield* (1766)

8 I expect to pass through this world but once; any good thing therefore that I can do, or any kindness that I can show to any fellow-creature, let me do it now; let me not defer or neglect it, for I shall not pass this way again.

Stephen Grellet 1773–1855 French missionary: attributed; there are many other claimants to authorship

9 Good, but not religious-good.

Thomas Hardy 1840–1928 English novelist and poet: *Under the Greenwood Tree* (1872)

10 If some great Power would agree to make me always think what is true and do what is right, on condition of being turned into a sort of clock and wound up every morning before I got out of bed, I should instantly close with the offer.

T. H. Huxley 1825–95 English biologist: 'On Descartes' *Discourse on Method*' (written 1870)

11 Be good, sweet maid, and let who
will be clever.
Charles Kingsley 1819–75 English
writer and clergyman: 'A Farewell'
(1858)

12 Good and evil shall not be held
equal. Turn away evil with that which
is better; and behold the man
between whom and thyself there was
enmity, shall become, as it were, thy
warmest friend.
The Koran: sura 41

13 Mostly, we are good when it makes
sense. A good society is one that
makes sense of being good.
Ian McEwan 1948– English novelist:
Enduring Love (1998)

14 When men grow virtuous in their old
age, they only make a sacrifice to
God of the devil's leavings.
Alexander Pope 1688–1744 English
poet: *Miscellanies* (1727) 'Thoughts on
Various Subjects'

15 How far that little candle throws his
beams!
So shines a good deed in a naughty
world.
William Shakespeare 1564–1616
English dramatist: *The Merchant of
Venice* (1596–8)

16 More people are flattered into virtue
than bullied out of vice.
R. S. Surtees 1805–64 English sporting
journalist and novelist: *The Analysis of
the Hunting Field* (1846)

17 My strength is as the strength of ten,
Because my heart is pure.
Alfred, Lord Tennyson 1809–92 English
poet: 'Sir Galahad' (1842)

18 Would that we had spent one whole
day well in this world!
Thomas à Kempis c.1380–1471 German
ascetical writer: *The Imitation of Christ*

19 Few things are harder to put up with
than the annoyance of a good
example.
Mark Twain 1835–1910 American
writer: *Pudd'nhead Wilson* (1894)

20 Virtue knows to a farthing what it has
lost by not having been vice.
Horace Walpole 1717–97 English writer
and connoisseur: L. Kronenberger *The
Extraordinary Mr Wilkes* (1974)

21 'Goodness, what beautiful
diamonds!'
'Goodness had nothing to do with it.'
Mae West 1892–1980 American film
actress: *Night After Night* (1932 film)

22 I used to be Snow White . . . but I
drifted.
Mae West 1892–1980 American film
actress: Joseph Weintraub *Peel Me a
Grape* (1975)

23 It is better to be beautiful than to be
good. But . . . it is better to be good
than to be ugly.
Oscar Wilde 1854–1900 Anglo-Irish
dramatist and poet: *The Picture of
Dorian Gray* (1891)

24 If all the good people were clever,
And all clever people were good,
The world would be nicer than ever
We thought that it possibly could.
But somehow, 'tis seldom or never
The two hit it off as they should;
The good are so harsh to the clever,
The clever so rude to the good!
Elizabeth Wordsworth 1840–1932
English educationist: 'Good and Clever'

25 That best portion of a good man's
life,
His little, nameless, unremembered,
acts
Of kindness and of love.
William Wordsworth 1770–1850
English poet: 'Lines composed a few
miles above Tintern Abbey' (1798)

Gossip

see also REPUTATION

1 Every man is surrounded by a neighbourhood of voluntary spies.

    Jane Austen 1775–1817 English novelist: *Northanger Abbey* (1818)

2 Gossip is a sort of smoke that comes from the dirty tobacco-pipes of those who diffuse it: it proves nothing but the bad taste of the smoker.

    George Eliot 1819–80 English novelist: *Daniel Deronda* (1876)

3 Love and scandal are the best sweeteners of tea.

    Henry Fielding 1707–54 English novelist and dramatist: *Love in Several Masques* (1728)

4 Like all gossip—it's merely one of those half-alive things that try to crowd out real life.

    E. M. Forster 1879–1970 English novelist: *A Passage to India* (1924)

5 Blood sport is brought to its ultimate refinement in the gossip columns.

    Bernard Ingham 1932– British journalist: speech, 5 February 1986

6 Men have always detested women's gossip because they suspect the truth: their measurements are being taken and compared.

    Erica Jong 1942– American novelist: *Fear of Flying* (1973)

7 Anyone who has obeyed nature by transmitting a piece of gossip experiences the explosive relief that accompanies the satisfying of a primary need.

    Primo Levi 1919–87 Italian novelist and poet: in *La Stampa* 24 June 1986

8 I hope there's a tinge of disgrace about me. Hopefully, there's one good scandal left in me yet.

    Diana Rigg 1938– British actress: in *The Times* 3 May 1999

9 No one gossips about other people's secret virtues.

    Bertrand Russell 1872–1970 British philosopher and mathematician: *On Education Especially in Early Childhood* (1926)

10 Be thou as chaste as ice, as pure as snow, thou shalt not escape calumny.

    William Shakespeare 1564–1616 English dramatist: *Hamlet* (1601)

11 It takes your enemy and your friend, working together, to hurt you to the heart: the one to slander you and the other to get the news to you.

    Mark Twain 1835–1910 American writer: *Following the Equator* (1897)

12 There is only one thing in the world worse than being talked about, and that is not being talked about.

    Oscar Wilde 1854–1900 Anglo-Irish dramatist and poet: *The Picture of Dorian Gray* (1891)

Government

see also CIVIL SERVICE, INTERNATIONAL RELATIONS, PARLIAMENT, POLITICS, SOCIETY

1 Let them hate, so long as they fear.

    Accius 170–*c*.86 BC Latin poet and dramatist: from *Atreus*; Seneca *Dialogues*

2 A government of laws, and not of men.

    John Adams 1735–1826 American statesman: *Boston Gazette* (1774) 'Novanglus' papers; later incorporated in the Massachusetts Constitution (1780)

3 The happiness of society is the end of government.
> **John Adams** 1735–1826 American statesman: *Thoughts on Government* (1776)

4 The poor have sometimes objected to being governed badly; the rich have always objected to being governed at all.
> **G. K. Chesterton** 1874–1936 English essayist, novelist, and poet: *The Man who was Thursday* (1908) ch. 11

5 My faith in the people governing is, on the whole, infinitesimal; my faith in The People governed is, on the whole, illimitable.
> **Charles Dickens** 1812–70 English novelist: speech at Birmingham and Midland Institute, 27 September 1869

6 A billion here and a billion there, and pretty soon you're talking real money.
> *on federal spending*
> **Everett Dirksen** 1896–1969 American Republican politician: attributed, perhaps apocryphal

7 No Government can be long secure without a formidable Opposition.
> **Benjamin Disraeli** 1804–81 British Tory statesman and novelist: *Coningsby* (1844)

8 Though God hath raised me high, yet this I count the glory of my crown: that I have reigned with your loves.
> **Elizabeth I** 1533–1603 English monarch: The Golden Speech, 1601

9 The State is not 'abolished', *it withers away*.
> **Friedrich Engels** 1820–95 German socialist: *Anti-Dühring* (1878)

10 If the Government is big enough to give you everything you want, it is big enough to take away everything you have.
> **Gerald Ford** 1909–2006 American Republican statesman: John F. Parker *If Elected* (1960)

11 The state is like the human body. Not all of its functions are dignified.
> **Anatole France** 1844–1924 French novelist and man of letters: *Les Opinions de M. Jerome Coignard* (1893)

12 The English and, more latterly, the British, have the habit of acquiring their institutions by chance or inadvertence, and shedding them in a fit of absent-mindedness.
> **Lord Hailsham** 1907–2001 British Conservative politician: 'The Granada Guildhall Lecture' 10 November 1987

13 Many journalists have fallen for the conspiracy theory of government. I do assure you that they would produce more accurate work if they adhered to the cock-up theory.
> **Bernard Ingham** 1932– British journalist: in *Observer* 17 March 1985

14 I would not give half a guinea to live under one form of government rather than another. It is of no moment to the happiness of an individual.
> **Samuel Johnson** 1709–84 English poet, critic, and lexicographer: James Boswell *Life of Samuel Johnson* (1791) 31 March 1772

15 I work for a Government I despise for ends I think criminal.
> **John Maynard Keynes** 1883–1946 English economist: letter to Duncan Grant, 15 December 1917

16 How is the world ruled and how do wars start? Diplomats tell lies to journalists and then believe what they read.
> **Karl Kraus** 1874–1936 Austrian satirist: *Aphorisms and More Aphorisms* (1909)

17 We give the impression of being in office but not in power.
> **Norman Lamont** 1942– British

Conservative politician: speech, House
of Commons, 9 June 1993

18 While the State exists, there can be
no freedom. When there is freedom
there will be no State.
Lenin 1870–1924 Russian revolutionary:
State and Revolution (1919)

19 To govern is to choose.
Duc de Lévis 1764–1830 French soldier
and writer: *Maximes et Réflexions*
(1812 ed.)

20 The reluctant obedience of distant
provinces generally costs more than
it [the territory] is worth.
Lord Macaulay 1800–59 English
politician and historian: *Essays
Contributed to the Edinburgh Review*
(1843) 'The War of Succession in Spain'

21 Because it is difficult to join them
together, it is much safer for a prince
to be feared than loved, if he is to fail
in one of the two.
Niccolò Machiavelli 1469–1527
Florentine statesman and political
philosopher: *The Prince* (written 1513)

22 If men were
angels, no
government
would be
necessary.
James Madison 1751–1836 American
Democratic Republican statesman: *The
Federalist* (1788)

23 I don't want to abolish government. I
simply want to reduce it to the size
where I can drag it into the
bathroom and drown it in the
bathtub.
Grover Norquist 1956– American
lobbyist: interview on National Public
Radio, Morning Edition, 25 May 2001

24 BIG BROTHER IS WATCHING YOU.
George Orwell 1903–50 English
novelist: *Nineteen Eighty-Four* (1949)

25 Government, even in its best state, is
but a necessary evil . . . Government,

like dress, is the badge of lost
innocence; the palaces of kings are
built upon the ruins of the bowers of
paradise.
Thomas Paine 1737–1809 English
political theorist: *Common Sense* (1776)

26 When, in countries that are called
civilized, we see age going to the
workhouse and youth to the gallows,
something must be wrong in the
system of government.
Thomas Paine 1737–1809 English
political theorist: *The Rights of Man* pt.
2 (1792)

27 Government of the busy by the bossy
for the bully.
on over-government
Arthur Seldon 1916–2005 British
economist: *Capitalism* (1990)

28 A government which robs Peter to
pay Paul can always depend on the
support of Paul.
George Bernard Shaw 1856–1950 Irish
dramatist: *Everybody's Political What's
What?* (1944)

29 A fainéant government is not the
worst government that England can
have. It has been the great fault of
our politicians that they have all
wanted to do something.
Anthony Trollope 1815–82 English
novelist: *Phineas Finn* (1869)

30 Governments need both shepherds
and butchers.
Voltaire 1694–1778 French writer and
philosopher: 'The Piccini Notebooks'
(*c*.1735–50)

Grammar

1 Would you convey my compliments
to the purist who reads your proofs
and tell him or her that I write in a
sort of broken-down patois which is
something like the way a Swiss
waiter talks, and that when I split an

infinitive, God damn it, I split it so it will stay split.

Raymond Chandler 1888–1959 American writer of detective fiction: letter to Edward Weeks, 18 January 1947

2 Colourless green ideas sleep furiously.

illustrating that grammatical structure is independent of meaning

Noam Chomsky 1928– American linguistics scholar: *Syntactic Structures* (1957)

3 This is the sort of English up with which I will not put.

Winston Churchill 1874–1965 British Conservative statesman: Ernest Gowers *Plain Words* (1948)

4 I will not go down to posterity talking bad grammar.

while correcting proofs of his last Parliamentary speech, 31 March 1881

Benjamin Disraeli 1804–81 British Tory statesman and novelist: Robert Blake *Disraeli* (1966)

5 The English-speaking world may be divided into (1) those who neither know nor care what a split infinitive is; (2) those who do not know, but care very much; (3) those who know and condemn; (4) those who know and distinguish. Those who neither know nor care are the vast majority, and are a happy folk, to be envied by most of the minority classes.

H. W. Fowler 1858–1933 English lexicographer and grammarian: *Modern English Usage* (1926)

6 The only person entitled to use the imperial 'we' in speaking of himself is a king, an editor, and a man with a tapeworm.

Robert G. Ingersoll 1833–99 American agnostic: in *Los Angeles Times* 6 October 1914

7 Every sentence he manages to utter scatters its component parts like pond water from a verb chasing its own tail.

of George Bush

Clive James 1939– Australian critic and writer: *The Dreaming Swimmer* (1992)

8 The subjunctive mood is in its death throes, and the best thing to do is to put it out of its misery as soon as possible.

W. Somerset Maugham 1874–1965 English novelist: *A Writer's Notebook* (1949) written in 1941

9 I don't want to talk grammar, I want to talk like a lady.

George Bernard Shaw 1856–1950 Irish dramatist: *Pygmalion* (1916)

10 Save the gerund and screw the whale.

Tom Stoppard 1937– British dramatist: *The Real Thing* (1988 rev. ed.)

Gratitude

see also INGRATITUDE, THANKS

1 He's coming to hate the gratitude of women. It's like being fawned on by rabbits, or being covered with syrup: you can't get it off.

Margaret Atwood 1939– Canadian novelist: *Alias Grace* (1996)

2 Maybe the only thing worse than having to give gratitude constantly all the time, is having to accept it.

William Faulkner 1897–1962 American novelist: *Requiem for a Nun* (1951)

3 The obligation of gratitude may easily become a trap, and the young are often caught and maimed in it.

Eric Gill 1882–1940 English sculptor, engraver, and typographer: *Autobiography* (1940)

4 There are minds so impatient of inferiority, that their gratitude is a species of revenge, and they return

benefits, not because recompense is a pleasure, but because obligation is a pain.

Samuel Johnson 1709–84 English poet, critic, and lexicographer: in *The Rambler* 15 January 1751

5 In most of mankind gratitude is merely a secret hope for greater favours.

Duc de la Rochefoucauld 1613–80 French moralist: *Maximes* (1678)

6 [Gratitude] is a sickness suffered by dogs.

Joseph Stalin 1879–1953 Soviet dictator: Nikolai Tolstoy *Stalin's Secret War* (1981)

Greatness

see also ACHIEVEMENT, GENIUS

1 I'm looking for a dare-to-be-great situation.

Cameron Crowe 1957– American film director: *Say Anything* (1989 film); spoken by John Cusack as Lloyd Dobler

2 A man is seldom ashamed of feeling that he cannot love a woman so well when he sees a certain greatness in her: nature having intended greatness for men.

George Eliot 1819–80 English novelist: *Middlemarch* (1871–2)

3 Is it so bad, then, to be misunderstood? Pythagoras was misunderstood, and Socrates, and Jesus, and Luther, and Copernicus, and Galileo, and Newton, and every pure and wise spirit that ever took flesh. To be great is to be misunderstood.

Ralph Waldo Emerson 1803–82 American philosopher and poet: *Essays* (1841) 'Self-Reliance'

4 A man does not attain the status of Galileo merely because he is persecuted; he must also be right.

Stephen Jay Gould 1941–2002

American palaeontologist: *Ever since Darwin* (1977)

5 The glory of great men should always be measured against the means they used to acquire it.

Duc de la Rochefoucauld 1613–80 French moralist: *Maxims* (1678)

6 If I am a great man, then all great men are frauds.

Andrew Bonar Law 1858–1923 Canadian-born British Conservative statesman: Lord Beaverbrook *Politicians and the War* (1932)

7 Everything we think of as great has come to us from neurotics. It is they and they alone who found religions and create great works of art. The world will never realise how much it owes to them and what they have suffered in order to bestow their gifts on it.

Marcel Proust 1871–1922 French novelist: *Guermantes Way* (1921)

8 The first test of a truly great man is his humility.

John Ruskin 1819–1900 English art and social critic: *Modern Painters* (1856)

9 But be not afraid of greatness: some men are born great, some achieve greatness, and some have greatness thrust upon them.

William Shakespeare 1564–1616 English dramatist: *Twelfth Night* (1601)

10 All the world's great have been little boys who wanted the moon.

John Steinbeck 1902–68 American novelist: *Cup of Gold* (1953)

11   In me there dwells
No greatness, save it be some far-off touch
Of greatness to know well I am not great.

Alfred, Lord Tennyson 1809–92 English poet: *Idylls of the King* 'Lancelot and Elaine' (1859)

Greece

1 The isles of Greece, the isles of
   Greece!
   Where burning Sappho loved and
   sung,
   Where grew the arts of war and
   peace,
   Where Delos rose, and Phoebus
   sprung!
   Eternal summer gilds them yet,
   But all, except their sun, is set!
   Lord Byron 1788–1824 English poet:
   Don Juan (1819–24)

2 If you take Greece apart, in the end
   you will see remaining to you an
   olive tree, a vineyard and a ship.
   Which means: with just so much you
   can put her back together.
   Odysseus Elytis 1911– Greek poet:
   'The Little Seafarer' (1988)

3 Except the blind forces of Nature,
   nothing moves in this world which is
   not Greek in its origin.
   Henry Maine 1822–88 English jurist:
   Village Communities (3rd ed., 1876)

4 Taking everything together then, I
   declare that our city is an education
   to Greece.
   of Athens
   Pericles *c.*495–429 BC Greek statesman
   and Athenian general: Thucydides
   History of the Peloponnesian War

5 Let there be light! said Liberty,
   And like sunrise from the sea,
   Athens arose!
   Percy Bysshe Shelley 1792–1822
   English poet: *Hellas* (1822)

Greed

see also MONEY

1 Greed is all right . . . Greed is healthy.
   You can be greedy and still feel good
   about yourself.
   Ivan F. Boesky 1937– American

businessman: commencement address,
Berkeley, California, 18 May 1986

2 You shall not crucify mankind upon
   a cross of gold.
   William Jennings Bryan 1860–1925
   American Democratic politician:
   speech at the Democratic National
   Convention, Chicago, 1896

3 There is enough in the world for
   everyone's need, but not enough for
   everyone's greed.
   Frank Buchman 1878–1961 American
   evangelist: *Remaking the World* (1947)

4 Please, sir, I want some more.
   Charles Dickens 1812–70 English
   novelist: *Oliver Twist* (1838)

5 But the music that excels is the
   sound of oil wells
   As they slurp, slurp, slurp into the
   barrels . . .
   I want an old-fashioned house
   With an old-fashioned fence
   And an old-fashioned millionaire.
   Marve Fisher American songwriter: 'An
   Old-Fashioned Girl' (1954 song)

6 *in reply to his mother's warning 'You'll be
   sick tomorrow', when stuffing himself with
   cakes at tea:*
   I'll be sick tonight.
   Jack Llewelyn-Davies 1894–1959:
   Andrew Birkin *J. M. Barrie and the Lost
   Boys* (1979); Barrie used the line in Little
   Mary (1903)

7 If all the rich people in the world
   divided up their money among
   themselves there wouldn't be
   enough to go round.
   Christina Stead 1902–83 Australian
   novelist: *House of All Nations* (1938)

8 To what do you not drive human
   hearts, cursed craving for gold!
   Virgil 70–19 BC Roman poet: *Aeneid*

9 Greed—for lack of a better word—is
   good. Greed is right. Greed works.
   Stanley Weiser and **Oliver Stone**
   1946– : *Wall Street* (1987 film)

Guests

see HOSTS AND GUESTS

Guilt

see also INNOCENCE

1 He that is without sin among you, let him first cast a stone at her.
   Bible: St John

2 Good women always think it is their fault when someone else is being offensive. Bad women never take the blame for anything.
   Anita Brookner 1928– British novelist and art historian: *Hotel du Lac* (1984)

3 In former days, everyone found the assumption of innocence so easy; today we find fatally easy the assumption of guilt.
   Amanda Cross 1926–2003 American crime writer and academic: *Poetic Justice* (1970)

4 Of all means to regeneration Remorse is surely the most wasteful. It cuts away healthy tissue with the poisoned. It is a knife that probes far deeper than the evil.
   E. M. Forster 1879–1970 English novelist: *Howards End* (1910)

5 To be absolutely honest, what I feel really bad about is that I don't feel worse. That's the ineffectual liberal's problem in a nutshell.
   Michael Frayn 1933– English writer: in *Observer* 8 August 1965

6 True guilt is guilt at the obligation one owes to oneself to be oneself. False guilt is guilt felt at not being what other people feel one ought to be or assume that one is.
   R. D. Laing 1927–89 Scottish psychiatrist: *Self and Others* (1961)

7 Guilt feelings so often arise from accusations rather than from crimes.
   Iris Murdoch 1919–99 English novelist: *The Sea, The Sea* (1978)

8 I brought myself down. I gave them a sword. And they stuck it in.
   Richard Nixon 1913–94 American Republican statesman: television interview, 19 May 1977

9 Here's the smell of the blood still: all the perfumes of Arabia will not sweeten this little hand.
   William Shakespeare 1564–1616 English dramatist: *Macbeth* (1606)

10 What hangs people . . . is the unfortunate circumstance of guilt.
   Robert Louis Stevenson 1850–94 Scottish novelist: *The Wrong Box* (with Lloyd Osbourne, 1889)

11 *Non! rien de rien,*
   Non! je ne regrette rien.
   No, no regrets,
   No, we will have no regrets.
   Michel Vaucaire: 'Non, je ne regrette rien' (1960 song); sung by Edith Piaf

Gulf War 1991

1 The mother of battles.
   popular interpretation of his description of the approaching Gulf War
   Saddam Hussein 1937–2006 Iraqi statesman: speech in Baghdad, 6 January 1991; *The Times*, 7 January 1991, reported that Saddam had no intention of relinquishing Kuwait and was ready for the 'mother of all wars'

2 If Kuwait grew carrots we wouldn't give a damn.
   Lawrence Korb 1939– American government official: in *International Herald Tribune* 21 August 1990

3 First, we are going to cut it off, and then, we are going to kill it.

strategy for dealing with the Iraqi Army in the Gulf War

Colin Powell 1937– American general: at a press conference, 23 January 1991

Habit

see also CUSTOM

1 The less of routine, the more of life.
Amos Bronson Alcott 1799–1888
American reformer: *Table Talk* (1877)

2 Neither by nature, then, nor contrary to nature do the virtues arise in us; nature gives us the capacity to receive them, and this capacity is brought to maturity by habit.
often quoted in the form 'We are what we repeatedly do'
Aristotle 384–322 BC Greek philosopher: *Nicomachean Ethics*

3 Routine, in an intelligent man, is a sign of ambition.
W. H. Auden 1907–73 English poet: 'The Life of That-There Poet' (1958)

4 The air is full of our cries. (*He listens*) But habit is a great deadener.
Samuel Beckett 1906–89 Irish dramatist, novelist, and poet: *Waiting for Godot* (1955)

5 A leopard does not change his spots, or change his feeling that spots are rather a credit.
Ivy Compton-Burnett 1884–1969 English novelist: *More Women than Men* (1933)

6 Habit with him was all the test of truth,
'It must be right: I've done it from my youth.'
George Crabbe 1754–1832 English poet: *The Borough* (1810)

7 People wish to be settled: only as far as they are unsettled is there any hope for them.
Ralph Waldo Emerson 1803–82 American philosopher and poet: *Essays* (1841) 'Circles'

8 *Good* habits: they are never good, because they are habits.
Jean-Paul Sartre 1905–80 French philosopher, novelist, dramatist, and critic: attributed

Hair

1 It was a blonde. A blonde to make a bishop kick a hole in a stained glass window.
Raymond Chandler 1888–1959 American writer of detective fiction: *Farewell, My Lovely* (1940)

2 Being blonde is definitely a different state of mind. I can't really put my finger on it, but the artifice of being blonde has some incredible sort of sexual connotation.
Madonna 1958– American pop singer and actress: in *Rolling Stone* 23 March 1989

3 When I had curls
I knew more girls.
I do more reading
Now my hair is receding.
James Simmons 1933–2001 British poet: 'Epigrams'

4 There is more felicity on the far side of baldness than young men can possibly imagine.
Logan Pearsall Smith 1865–1946 American-born man of letters: *Afterthoughts* (1931)

5 In England and America a beard usually means that its owner would rather be considered venerable than virile; on the continent of Europe it often means that its owner makes a special claim to virility.

Rebecca West 1892–1983 English novelist and journalist: *The Thinking Reed* (1936)

6 Only God, my dear,
Could love you for yourself alone
And not your yellow hair.

W. B. Yeats 1865–1939 Irish poet: 'Anne Gregory' (1932)

Happiness

see also PLEASURE, UNHAPPINESS

1 A large income is the best recipe for happiness I ever heard of. It certainly may secure all the myrtle and turkey part of it.

Jane Austen 1775–1817 English novelist: *Mansfield Park* (1814)

2 There may be Peace without Joy, and Joy without Peace, but the two combined make Happiness.

John Buchan 1875–1940 Scottish novelist: *Memory-Hold-the-Door* (1940)

3 Happiness is . . . finding two olives in your martini when you're hungry.

Johnny Carson 1925–2005 American broadcaster and comedian: *Happiness is—a Dry Martini* (1966)

4 Happiness is a mystery like religion, and should never be rationalized.

G. K. Chesterton 1874–1936 English essayist, novelist, and poet: *Heretics* (1905)

5 Bring me sunshine in your smile
Bring me laughter all the while.

Sylvia Dee 1914–67 American songwriter: 'Bring Me Sunshine' (1966 song, music by Arthur Kent), theme song of Eric Morecambe and Ernie Wise

6 For all the happiness mankind can gain

Is not in pleasure, but in rest from pain.

John Dryden 1631–1700 English poet, critic, and dramatist: *The Indian Emperor* (1665)

7 The happiest women, like the happiest nations, have no history.

George Eliot 1819–80 English novelist: *The Mill on the Floss* (1860)

8 Happiness makes up in height for what it lacks in length.

Robert Frost 1874–1963 American poet: title of poem (1942)

9 Ah, this, that we call happiness, how intimate a part of the soul it is, and of what little importance are the outside elements which seem to go to its making!

André Gide 1869–1951 French novelist and critic: *Strait is the Gate* (1909) tr. D. Bussy

10 Point me out the happy man and I will point you out either egotism, selfishness, evil—or else an absolute ignorance.

Graham Greene 1904–91 English novelist: *The Heart of the Matter* (1948)

11 Happiness is a how, not a what; a talent, not an object.

Hermann Hesse 1877–1962 German novelist and poet: attributed

12 Happiness is not an ideal of reason but of imagination.

Immanuel Kant 1724–1804 German philosopher: *Fundamental Principles of the Metaphysics of Ethics* (1785)

13 A man enjoys the happiness he feels, a woman the happiness she gives.

Pierre Choderlos de Laclos 1741–1803 French soldier and writer: *Les Liaisons dangereuses* (1782)

14 Happiness is a warm gun.

John Lennon 1940–80 English pop singer and songwriter: title of song (1968); see HAPPINESS 20

15 Ask yourself whether you are happy, and you cease to be so.
John Stuart Mill 1806–73 English philosopher and economist: *Autobiography* (1873)

16 But headlong joy is ever on the wing.
John Milton 1608–74 English poet: 'The Passion' (1645)

17 Not to admire, is all the art I know, To make men happy, and to keep them so.
Alexander Pope 1688–1744 English poet: *Imitations of Horace*

18 For if unhappiness develops the forces of the mind, happiness alone is salutary to the body.
Marcel Proust 1871–1922 French novelist: *Time Regained* (1926)

19 To be without some of the things you want is an indispensable part of happiness.
Bertrand Russell 1872–1970 British philosopher and mathematician: *The Conquest of Happiness* (1930)

20 Happiness is a warm puppy.
Charles Monroe Schulz 1922–2000 American cartoonist: title of book (1962); see HAPPINESS 14

21 We have no more right to consume happiness without producing it than to consume wealth without producing it.
George Bernard Shaw 1856–1950 Irish dramatist: *Candida* (1898)

22 But a lifetime of happiness! No man alive could bear it: it would be hell on earth.
George Bernard Shaw 1856–1950 Irish dramatist: *Man and Superman* (1903)

23 Happiness is an imaginary condition, formerly often attributed by the living to the dead, now usually attributed by adults to children, and by children to adults.
Thomas Szasz 1920– Hungarian-born psychiatrist: *The Second Sin* (1973)

24 There's only one way of being comfortable, and that is to stop running round after happiness. If you make up your mind not to be happy there's no reason why you shouldn't have a fairly good time.
often quoted as 'If only we'd stop trying to be happy we could have a pretty good time'
Edith Wharton 1862–1937 American novelist: *The Hermit and the Wild Woman and Other Stories* (1908) 'The Last Asset'

25 For sudden joys, like griefs, confound at first.
Robert Wild 1615–79 English nonconformist minister and poet: 'Dr Wild's Humble Thanks for His Majesty's Gracious Declaration' (1672)

Hatred

see also ENEMIES

1 Now hatred is by far the longest pleasure;
Men love in haste, but they detest at leisure.
Lord Byron 1788–1824 English poet: *Don Juan* (1819–24)

2 I tell you there is such a thing as creative hate!
Willa Cather 1873–1947 American novelist: *The Song of the Lark* (1915)

3 I never hated a man enough to give him diamonds back.
Zsa Zsa Gabor 1919– Hungarian-born film actress: in *Observer* 25 August 1957

4 We can scarcely hate any one that we know.
William Hazlitt 1778–1830 English essayist: *Table Talk* (1822) 'On Criticism'

5 If you hate a person, you hate something in him that is part of yourself. What isn't part of ourselves doesn't disturb us.

> **Hermann Hesse** 1877–1962 German novelist and poet: *Demian* (1919)

6 No one is born hating another person because of the colour of his skin, or his background, or his religion. People must learn to hate, and if they can learn to hate, they can be taught to love, for love comes more naturally to the human heart than its opposite.

> **Nelson Mandela** 1918– South African statesman: *Long Walk to Freedom* (1994)

7 Any kiddie in school can love like a fool,
But hating, my boy, is an art.

> **Ogden Nash** 1902–71 American humorist: 'Plea for Less Malice Toward None' (1933)

8 Always give your best, never get discouraged, never be petty; always remember, others may hate you. Those who hate you don't win unless you hate them. And then you destroy yourself.

> **Richard Nixon** 1913–94 American Republican statesman: address to staff, 9 August 1974

9 Hatred is a feeling which leads to the extinction of values.

> **José Ortega y Gasset** 1883–1955 Spanish writer and philosopher: *Meditations on Quixote* (1914)

10 I have loved him too much not to feel any hatred for him.

> **Jean Racine** 1639–99 French tragedian: *Andromaque* (1667)

Health

see also BODY, EXERCISE, MEDICINE, SICKNESS

1 In the face of such overwhelming statistical possibilities, hypochondria has always seemed to me to be the only rational position to take on life.

> **John Diamond**: *C: Because Cowards Get Cancer Too* (1998)

2 The first wealth is health.

> **Ralph Waldo Emerson** 1803–82 American philosopher and poet: *The Conduct of Life* (1860)

3 Health is worth more than learning.

> **Thomas Jefferson** 1743–1826 American Democratic Republican statesman: letter to John Garland Jefferson, 11 June 1790

4 *Orandum est ut sit mens sana in corpore sano.*
You should pray to have a sound mind in a sound body.

> **Juvenal** AD *c.*60–*c.*130 Roman satirist: *Satires*

5 Life's not just being alive, but being well.

> **Martial** AD *c.*40–*c.*104 Roman epigrammatist: *Epigrammata*

6 A man dies and is buried, and all his words and actions are forgotten, but the food he has eaten lives after him in the sound or rotten bones of his children.

> **George Orwell** 1903–50 English novelist: *The Road to Wigan Pier* (1937)

7 Look to your health; and if you have it, praise God, and value it next to a good conscience; for health is the second blessing that we mortals are capable of; a blessing that money cannot buy.

> **Izaak Walton** 1593–1683 English writer: *The Compleat Angler* (1653)

8 To get back my youth I would do anything in the world, except take exercise, get up early, or be respectable.

> **Oscar Wilde** 1854–1900 Anglo-Irish dramatist and poet: *The Picture of Dorian Grey* (1891)

Heaven

1 Whose love is given over-well
Shall look on Helen's face in hell
Whilst they whose love is thin and wise
Shall see John Knox in Paradise.
Dorothy Parker 1893–1967 American critic and humorist: 'Partial Comfort' (1937)

2 The true paradises are the paradises that we have lost.
Marcel Proust 1871–1922 French novelist: *Time Regained* (1926)

3 My idea of heaven is, eating *pâté de foie gras* to the sound of trumpets.
the view of Smith's friend Henry Luttrell
Sydney Smith 1771–1845 English clergyman and essayist: H. Pearson *The Smith of Smiths* (1934)

4 I will spend my heaven doing good on earth.
St Teresa 1873–97 French Carmelite nun: T. N. Taylor (ed.) *Soeur Thérèse of Lisieux* (1912)

5 There is no expeditious road
To pack and label men for God,
And save them by the barrel-load.
Some may perchance, with strange surprise,
Have blundered into Paradise.
Francis Thompson 1859–1907 English poet: 'A Judgement in Heaven' (1913)

6 We may be surprised at the people we find in heaven. God has a soft spot for sinners. His standards are quite low.
Desmond Tutu 1931– South African Anglican clergyman: in *Sunday Times* 15 April 2001

Hell

1 Hell, madam, is to love no more.
Georges Bernanos 1888–1948 French novelist and essayist: *Journal d'un curé de campagne* (1936)

2 Then I saw that there was a way to Hell, even from the gates of heaven.
John Bunyan 1628–88 English writer and Nonconformist preacher: *The Pilgrim's Progress* (1678)

3 LASCIATE OGNI SPERANZA VOI CH'ENTRATE!
Abandon all hope, you who enter!
inscription at the entrance to Hell; now often quoted as 'Abandon hope, all ye who enter here'
Dante Alighieri 1265–1321 Italian poet: *Divina Commedia* 'Inferno'

4 What is hell?
Hell is oneself,
Hell is alone, the other figures in it
Merely projections.
T. S. Eliot 1888–1965 Anglo-American poet, critic, and dramatist: *The Cocktail Party* (1950)

5 Hell is other people.
Jean-Paul Sartre 1905–80 French philosopher, novelist, dramatist, and critic: *Huis Clos* (1944)

6 Heaven for climate, and hell for society.
Mark Twain 1835–1910 American writer: *Speeches* (1910)

Heroes

1 In such a regime, I say, you died a good death if your life had inspired someone to come forward and shoot your murderer in the chest—without asking to be paid.
Chinua Achebe 1930– Nigerian novelist: *A Man of the People* (1966)

2 Faster than a speeding bullet! . . . Look! Up in the sky! It's a bird! It's a plane! It's Superman! Yes, it's Superman! Strange visitor from

another planet . . . Who can change the course of mighty rivers, bend steel with his bare hands, and who—disguised as Clark Kent, mild-mannered reporter for a great metropolitan newspaper—fights a never ending battle for truth, justice and the American way!

Anonymous: *Superman* (US radio show, 1940 onwards)

3 We can be heroes
Just for one day.
David Bowie 1947– English rock musician: 'Heroes' (1977 song)

4 ANDREA: Unhappy the land that has no heroes! . . .
GALILEO: No. Unhappy the land that needs heroes.
Bertolt Brecht 1898–1956 German dramatist: *The Life of Galileo* (1939)

5 Down these mean streets a man must go who is not himself mean, who is neither tarnished nor afraid.
Raymond Chandler 1888–1959 American writer of detective fiction: in *Atlantic Monthly* December 1944 'The Simple Art of Murder'

6 No man is a hero to his valet.
Mme Cornuel 1605–94 French society hostess: *Lettres de Mlle Aïssé à Madame C* (1787) Letter 13 'De Paris, 1728'

7 Men reject their prophets and slay them, but they love their martyrs and honour those whom they have slain.
Fedor Dostoevsky 1821–81 Russian novelist: *The Brothers Karamazov* (1879–80)

8 Every hero becomes a bore at last.
Ralph Waldo Emerson 1803–82 American philosopher and poet: *Representative Men* (1850)

9 Show me a hero and I will write you a tragedy.
F. Scott Fitzgerald 1896–1940 American novelist: Edmund Wilson (ed.) *The Crack-Up* (1945) 'Note-Books E'

10 If the myth gets bigger than the man, print the myth.
Dorothy Johnson 1905–84: *Indian Country* (1953) 'The Man Who Shot Liberty Valance'; see also JOURNALISM 4

11 It was involuntary. They sank my boat.
on being asked how he became a war hero
John F. Kennedy 1917–63 American Democratic statesman: Arthur M. Schlesinger Jr. *A Thousand Days* (1965)

12 Ultimately a hero is a man who would argue with the Gods, and so awakens devils to contest his vision.
Norman Mailer 1923–2007 American novelist and essayist: *The Presidential Papers* (1976)

13 Go to Spain and get killed. The movement needs a Byron.
on being asked by Stephen Spender in the 1930s how best a poet could serve the Communist cause
Harry Pollitt 1890–1960 British Communist politician: Frank Johnson *Out of Order* (1982); attributed, perhaps apocryphal

14 Heroing is one of the shortest-lived professions there is.
Will Rogers 1879–1935 American actor and humorist: newspaper article, 15 February 1925

15 A hero is the one who does what he can. The others don't.
Romain Rolland 1866–1944 French writer: *Jean-Christophe* (1904–12)

16 Hero-worship is strongest where there is least regard for human freedom.
Herbert Spencer 1820–1903 English philosopher: *Social Statics* (1850)

17 In this world I would rather live two days like a tiger, than two hundred years like a sheep.
Tipu Sultan *c.*1750–99: Alexander Beatson *A View of the Origin and*

Conduct of the War with Tippoo Sultaun (1800)

History

see also ARCHAEOLOGY, PAST

1 Does history repeat itself, the first time as tragedy, the second time as farce? No, that's too grand, too considered a process. History just burps, and we taste again that raw-onion sandwich it swallowed centuries ago.
> **Julian Barnes** 1946– English novelist: *A History of the World in 10½ Chapters* (1989); see HISTORY 10

2 That great dust-heap called 'history'.
> **Augustine Birrell** 1850–1933 British essayist: *Obiter Dicta* (1884)

3 History repeats itself; historians repeat one another.
> **Rupert Brooke** 1887–1915 English poet: letter to Geoffrey Keynes, 4 June 1906; see HISTORY 10

4 It has been said that though God cannot alter the past, historians can; it is perhaps because they can be useful to Him in this respect that He tolerates their existence.
> **Samuel Butler** 1835–1902 English novelist: *Erewhon Revisited* (1901); see PAST 1

5 To be ignorant of what occurred before you were born is to remain forever a child.
> **Cicero** 106–43 BC Roman orator and statesman: *De Oratore*

6 A people without history
Is not redeemed from time, for history is a pattern
Of timeless moments. So, while the light fails
On a winter's afternoon, in a secluded chapel
History is now and England.
> **T. S. Eliot** 1888–1965 Anglo-American

poet, critic, and dramatist: *Four Quartets* 'Little Gidding' (1942)

7 History is more or less bunk.
> **Henry Ford** 1863–1947 American car manufacturer: interview with Charles N. Wheeler in *Chicago Tribune* 25 May 1916

8 History is past politics, and politics is present history.
> **E. A. Freeman** 1823–92 English historian: *Methods of Historical Study* (1886)

9 What experience and history teach is this—that nations and governments have never learned anything from history, or acted upon any lessons they might have drawn from it.
> **G. W. F. Hegel** 1770–1831 German idealist philosopher: *Lectures on the Philosophy of World History: Introduction* (1830)

10 Hegel says somewhere that all great events and personalities in world history reappear in one fashion or another. He forgot to add: the first time as tragedy, the second as farce.
> **Karl Marx** 1818–83 German political philosopher: *The Eighteenth Brumaire of Louis Bonaparte* (1852)

11 Happy the people whose annals are blank in history-books!
> **Montesquieu** 1689–1755 French political philosopher: attributed; in Thomas Carlyle *History of Frederick the Great*

12 And even I can remember
A day when the historians left blanks in their writings,
I mean for things they didn't know.
> **Ezra Pound** 1885–1972 American poet: *Draft of XXX Cantos* (1930)

13 History is not what you thought. *It is what you can remember.*
> **W. C. Sellar** 1898–1951 and **R. J. Yeatman** 1898–1968 British writers: *1066 and All That* (1930)

14 History gets thicker as it approaches recent times.

A. J. P. Taylor 1906–90 British historian: *English History 1914–45* (1965) bibliography

15 I have written my work, not as an essay which is to win the applause of the moment, but as a possession for all time.

Thucydides *c.*455–*c.*400 BC Greek historian: *History of the Peloponnesian War*

16 Human history becomes more and more a race between education and catastrophe.

H. G. Wells 1866–1946 English novelist: *The Outline of History* (1920)

Holidays

see also LEISURE, TRAVEL

1 May I ask what you were hoping to see out of a Torquay bedroom window? Sydney Opera House, perhaps? The Hanging Gardens of Babylon? Herds of wildebeeste sweeping majestically . . .

John Cleese 1939– and **Connie Booth**: *Fawlty Towers* 'Communication Problems' (BBC TV programme, 1979)

2 There's sand in the porridge and sand in the bed,
And if this is pleasure we'd rather be dead.

Noël Coward 1899–1973 English dramatist, actor, and composer: 'The English Lido' (1928)

3 How pleasant to sit on the beach,
On the beach, on the sand, in the sun,
With ocean galore within reach,
And nothing at all to be done!

Ogden Nash 1902–71 American humorist: 'Pretty Halcyon Days' (1935)

4 A perpetual holiday is a good working definition of hell.

George Bernard Shaw 1856–1950 Irish dramatist: *Parents and Children* (1914)

5 We're all going on a summer holiday,
No more worries for a week or two.

Bruce Welch and **Brian Bennett**: 'Summer Holiday' (1963 song)

Home

see also HOUSES

1 It is a most miserable thing to feel ashamed of home.

Charles Dickens 1812–70 English novelist: *Great Expectations* (1861)

2 'Home is the place where, when you have to go there,
They have to take you in.'
'I should have called it
Something you somehow haven't to deserve.'

Robert Frost 1874–1963 American poet: 'The Death of the Hired Man' (1914)

3   The best
Thing we can do is to make wherever we're lost in
Look as much like home as we can.

Christopher Fry 1907–2005 English dramatist: *The Lady's not for Burning* (1949)

4 What's the good of a home if you are never in it?

George Grossmith 1847–1912 and **Weedon Grossmith** 1854–1919 English writers: *The Diary of a Nobody* (1894)

5 One never reaches home, but wherever friendly paths intersect the whole world looks like home for a time.

Hermann Hesse 1877–1962 German novelist and poet: *Demian* (1919)

6 Any old place I can hang my hat is home sweet home to me.

William Jerome 1865–1932 American songwriter: title of song (1901)

7 The accent of one's birthplace lingers in the mind and in the heart as it does in one's speech.
  Duc de la Rochefoucauld 1613–80 French moralist: *Maximes* (1678)

8 Mid pleasures and palaces though we may roam,
  Be it ever so humble, there's no place like home.
  J. H. Payne 1791–1852 American actor, dramatist, and songwriter: 'Home, Sweet Home' (1823 song)

9 Home is the girl's prison and the woman's workhouse.
  George Bernard Shaw 1856–1950 Irish dramatist: *Man and Superman* (1903) 'Maxims: Women in the Home'

10 Show me a man who cares no more for one place than another, and I will show you in that same person one who loves nothing but himself. Beware of those who are homeless by choice.
  Robert Southey 1774–1843 English poet and writer: *The Doctor* (1812)

11 Home is where you come to when you have nothing better to do.
  Margaret Thatcher 1925– British Conservative stateswoman: in *Vanity Fair* May 1991

12 I'm not living with you. We occupy the same cage.
  Tennessee Williams 1911–83 American dramatist: *Cat on a Hot Tin Roof* (1955)

Homosexuality

see also LESBIANISM, SEX

1 My dear fellow, buggers can't be choosers.
  on being told he should not marry anyone as plain as his fiancée
  Maurice Bowra 1898–1971 English scholar and literary critic: Hugh Lloyd-Jones *Maurice Bowra: a Celebration* (1974); possibly apocryphal

2 If homosexuality were the normal way, God would have made Adam and Bruce.
  Anita Bryant 1940– : in *New York Times* 5 June 1977

3 In homosexual sex you know exactly what the other person is feeling, so you are identifying with the other person completely. In heterosexual sex you have no idea what the other person is feeling.
  William S. Burroughs 1914–97 American novelist: Victor Bockris *With William Burroughs: A Report from the Bunker* (1981)

4 The worst part of being gay in the twentieth century is all that damn disco music to which one has to listen.
  Quentin Crisp 1908–99 English writer: *Manners From Heaven* (1984)

5 I am the Love that dare not speak its name.
  Lord Alfred Douglas 1870–1945 English poet: 'Two Loves' (1896)

6 In homosexual love the passion is homosexuality itself. What a homosexual loves, as if it were his lover, his country, his art, his land, is homosexuality.
  Marguerite Duras 1914–96 French writer: *Practicalities* (1990)

7 There is probably no sensitive heterosexual alive who is not preoccupied with his latent homosexuality.
  Norman Mailer 1923–2007 American novelist and essayist: *Advertisement for Myself* (1959)

8 When I was in the military, they gave me a medal for killing two men and a discharge for loving one.
  Leonard Matlovich 1943–88 American Air Force Sergeant: attributed

9 I have heard some say . . .
[homosexual] practices are allowed
in France and in other NATO
countries. We are not French, and we
are not other nationals. We are
British, thank God!
*on the 2nd reading of the Sexual Offences
Bill*
Lord Montgomery 1887–1976 British
field marshal: speech, House of Lords,
24 May 1965

10 Don't ask, don't tell.
*summary of the Clinton administration's
compromise policy on homosexuals
serving in the armed forces*
Sam Nunn 1938– American
Democratic politician: in *New York
Times* 12 May 1993

Honesty

see also DECEPTION, LIES, TRUTH

1 This is hard to answer, so I'll tell the
truth.
David Ben-Gurion 1886–1973 Israeli
statesman: at the Zionist Actions
Committee session, London, 14 August
1945

2 Integrity has no need of rules.
Albert Camus 1913–60 French novelist,
dramatist, and essayist: *The Myth of
Sisyphus* (1942)

3 Remark all these roughnesses,
pimples, warts, and everything as
you see me; otherwise I will never
pay a farthing for it.
to Lely, commonly quoted as 'warts and all'
Oliver Cromwell 1599–1658 English
soldier and statesman: Horace Walpole
Anecdotes of Painting in England vol. 3
(1763)

4 The louder he talked of his honour,
the faster we counted our spoons.
Ralph Waldo Emerson 1803–82
American philosopher and poet: *The
Conduct of Life* (1860)

5 Being totally honest with oneself is a
good exercise.
Sigmund Freud 1856–1939 Austrian
psychiatrist: letter to Wilhelm Fliess,
15 October 1897

6 In all life one should comfort the
afflicted but verily, also, one should
afflict the comfortable, especially
when they are comfortably,
contentedly, even happily wrong.
J. K. Galbraith 1908–2006 American
economist: in *Observer* 30 July 1989

7 It is always the best policy to speak
the truth—unless, of course, you are
an exceptionally good liar.
Jerome K. Jerome 1859–1927 English
writer: in *The Idler* February 1892

8 Honesty is praised and left to shiver.
Juvenal AD *c.*60–*c.*130 Roman satirist:
Satires

9 honesty is a good
thing but
it is not profitable to
its possessor
unless it is
kept under control.
Don Marquis 1878–1937 American poet
and journalist: *archys life of mehitabel*
(1933)

10 An honest man's the noblest work of
God.
Alexander Pope 1688–1744 English
poet: *An Essay on Man* Epistle 4 (1734)

11 Always be sincere, even if you don't
mean it.
Harry S. Truman 1884–1972 American
Democratic statesman: attributed

12 Honesty is the best policy; but he
who is governed by that maxim is not
an honest man.
Richard Whately 1787–1863 English
philosopher and theologian:
Apophthegms (1854)

13 A little sincerity is a dangerous thing, and a great deal of it is absolutely fatal.

> **Oscar Wilde** 1854–1900 Anglo-Irish dramatist and poet: *Intentions* (1891)

Hope

see also DESPAIR, OPTIMISM, PESSIMISM

1 Providence has given human wisdom the choice between two fates: either hope and agitation, or hopelessness and calm.

> **Yevgeny Baratynsky** 1800–44 Russian poet: 'Two Fates' (1823)

2 What is hope? nothing but the paint on the face of Existence; the least touch of truth rubs it off, and then we see what a hollow-cheeked harlot we have got hold of.

> **Lord Byron** 1788–1824 English poet: letter to Thomas Moore, 28 October 1815

3 If hopes were dupes, fears may be liars.

> **Arthur Hugh Clough** 1819–61 English poet: 'Say not the struggle naught availeth' (1855)

4 Hope raises no dust.

> **Paul Éluard** 1895–1952 French poet: 'Ailleurs, ici, partout' (1946)

5 I'm not a dreamer . . . but I believe in miracles. I have to.

> *planning a fund-raising run across Canada; he completed two thirds of his 'Marathon of Hope'*
>
> **Terry Fox** 1958–81 Canadian runner, whose right leg was amputated because of cancer: letter to the Canadian Cancer Society, 15 October 1979

6 He that lives upon hope will die fasting.

> **Benjamin Franklin** 1706–90 American politician, inventor, and scientist: *Poor Richard's Almanac* (1758)

7 Walk on, walk on, with hope in your heart,
And you'll never walk alone.

> **Oscar Hammerstein II** 1895–1960 American songwriter: 'You'll never walk alone' (1945 song)

8 Hope is definitely not the same thing as optimism. It is not the conviction that something will turn out well, but the certainty that something makes sense, regardless of how it turns out.

> **Václav Havel** 1936– Czech dramatist and statesman: *Disturbing the Peace* (1986)

9 *Nil desperandum.*
Never despair.

> **Horace** 65–8 BC Roman poet: *Odes*

10 After all, tomorrow is another day.

> **Margaret Mitchell** 1900–49 American novelist: *Gone with the Wind* (1936)

11 The hope of a skinny kid with a funny name who believes that America has a place for him, too. The audacity of hope!

> **Barack Obama** 1961– American Democratic statesman: Democratic National Convention keynote address, 27 July 2004

12 Hope springs eternal in the human breast:
Man never Is, but always To be blest.

> **Alexander Pope** 1688–1744 English poet: *An Essay on Man* Epistle 1 (1733)

13 He who has never hoped can never despair.

> **George Bernard Shaw** 1856–1950 Irish dramatist: *Caesar and Cleopatra* (1901)

Horses

1 Where in this wide world can man find nobility without pride,

Friendship without envy, or beauty without vanity?
Ronald Duncan 1914–82 English dramatist: 'In Praise of the Horse' (1962)

2   I saw the horses:
Huge in the dense grey—ten together—
Megalith-still. They breathed, making no move,
With draped manes and tilted hind-hooves,
Making no sound.
I passed: not one snorted or jerked its head.
Grey silent fragments
Of a grey silent world.
Ted Hughes 1930–98 English poet: 'The Horses' (1957)

3 I know two things about the horse
And one of them is rather coarse.
Naomi Royde-Smith c.1875–1964 English novelist and dramatist: *Weekend Book* (1928)

Hosts and Guests

1 The guest will judge better of a feast than the cook.
Aristotle 384–322 BC Greek philosopher: *Politics*

2 It was a delightful visit;——perfect, in being much too short.
Jane Austen 1775–1817 English novelist: *Emma* (1816)

3 Mankind is divisible into two great classes: hosts and guests.
Max Beerbohm 1872–1956 English critic, essayist, and caricaturist: *And Even Now* (1920)

4 Guests can be, and often are, delightful, but they should never be allowed to get the upper hand.
Elizabeth, Countess von Arnim 1866–1941 Australian-born British writer: *All the Dogs in My Life* (1936)

5 Hospitality consists in a little fire, a little food, and an immense quiet.
Ralph Waldo Emerson 1803–82 American philosopher and poet: Journal 1856

6 A host is like a general: misfortunes often reveal his genius.
Horace 65–8 BC Roman poet: *Satires*

7 Some people can stay longer in an hour than others can in a week.
William Dean Howells 1837–1920 American novelist and critic: attributed

8 My father used to say,
'Superior people never make long visits,
have to be shown Longfellow's grave or the glass flowers at Harvard.'
Marianne Moore 1887–1972 American poet: 'Silence' (1935)

9 For I, who hold sage Homer's rule the best,
Welcome the coming, speed the going guest.
Alexander Pope 1688–1744 English poet: *Imitations of Horace* (1734); 'speed the parting guest' in Pope's translation of The Odyssey (1725–6)

10   Unbidden guests
Are often welcomest when they are gone.
William Shakespeare 1564–1616 English dramatist: *Henry VI, Part 1* (1592)

11 This door will open at a touch to welcome every friend.
Henry Van Dyke 1852–1933 American Presbyterian minister and writer: 'Inscription for a Friend's House'

Houses

see also HOME

1 It takes a heap o' livin' in a house t' make it home.
Edgar A. Guest 1881–1959 American writer, journalist, and poet: 'Home'

2 There is no such thing as a perfect house. (What one thinks of as perfection is merely what other people are living in.)

Phyllis McGinley 1905–78 American poet: *Sixpence in her Shoe* (1964)

3 Does anybody mind if I don't live in a house that is quaint?
Because, for one thing, quaint houses are generally houses where plumbing ain't.

Ogden Nash 1902–71 American humorist: 'No Wonder Our Fathers Died' (1938)

4 A comfortable house is a great source of happiness. It ranks immediately after health and a good conscience.

Sydney Smith 1771–1845 English clergyman and essayist: letter to Lord Murray, 29 September 1843

5 But every house where Love abides
And Friendship is a guest,
Is surely home, and home, sweet home,
For there the heart can rest.

Henry Van Dyke 1852–1933 American Presbyterian minister and writer: 'Home Song'

Housework

see also HOME

1 Cleanliness, punctuality, order, and method, are essentials in the character of a housekeeper.

Isabella Beeton 1836–65 English writer on cookery: *Book of Cookery and Household Management* (1861)

2 Conran's Law of Housework—it expands to fill the time available plus half an hour.

Shirley Conran 1932– English writer: *Superwoman 2* (1977)

3 There was no need to do any housework at all. After the first four years the dirt doesn't get any worse.

Quentin Crisp 1908–99 English writer: *The Naked Civil Servant* (1968)

4 Few tasks are more like the torture of Sisyphus than housework, with its endless repetition . . . The housewife wears herself out marking time: she makes nothing, simply perpetuates the present.

Simone de Beauvoir 1908–86 French novelist and feminist: *The Second Sex* (1949)

5 'I hate discussions of feminism that end up with who does the dishes,' she said. So do I. But at the end, there are always the damned dishes.

Marilyn French 1929–2009 American writer: *The Women's Room* (1977)

6 At the worst, a house unkempt cannot be so distressing as a life unlived.

Rose Macaulay 1881–1958 English novelist: *Problems of a Woman's Life* (1926)

7 The dust comes secretly day after day,
Lies on my ledge and dulls my shining things.
But O this dust that I shall drive away
Is flowers and Kings,
Is Solomon's temple, poets, Nineveh.

Viola Meynell 1886–1956 English poet: 'Dusting' (1919)

8 There is scarcely any less bother in the running of a family than in that of an entire state. And domestic business is no less importunate for being less important.

Montaigne 1533–92 French moralist and essayist: *Essays* (1580)

9 How often does a house need to be cleaned, anyway? As a general rule, once every girlfriend.

P. J. O'Rourke 1947– American

humorous writer: *The Bachelor Home Companion* (1987)

10 God walks among the pots and pans.
St Teresa of Ávila 1512–82 Spanish Carmelite nun and mystic: *Book of the Foundations* (1610)

11 MR PRITCHARD: I must dust the blinds and then I must raise them.
MRS OGMORE-PRITCHARD: And before you let the sun in, mind it wipes its shoes.
Dylan Thomas 1914–53 Welsh poet: *Under Milk Wood* (1954)

12 Hatred of domestic work is a natural and admirable result of civilization.
Rebecca West 1892–1983 English novelist and journalist: in *The Freewoman* 6 June 1912

Human Nature

see also BEHAVIOUR, CHARACTER, HUMAN RACE

1 Civilized ages inherit the human nature which was victorious in barbarous ages, and that nature is, in many respects, not at all suited to civilized circumstances.
Walter Bagehot 1826–77 English economist and essayist: *Physics and Politics* (1872)

2 That is ever the way. 'Tis all jealousy to the bride and good wishes to the corpse.
J. M. Barrie 1860–1937 Scottish writer and dramatist: *Quality Street* (1913)

3 There's a man all over for you, blaming on his boots the faults of his feet.
Samuel Beckett 1906–89 Irish dramatist, novelist, and poet: *Waiting for Godot* (1955)

4 By nature men are alike. Through practice they have become far apart.
Confucius 551–479 BC Chinese philosopher: *Analects*

5 The terrorist and the policeman both come from the same basket.
Joseph Conrad 1857–1924 Polish-born English novelist: *The Secret Agent* (1907)

6 Subdue your appetites my dears, and you've conquered human natur.
Charles Dickens 1812–70 English novelist: *Nicholas Nickleby* (1839)

7 I still believe that people are really good at heart.
Anne Frank 1929–45 German-born Jewish diarist: diary, 15 July 1944

8 Goodness has only once found a perfect incarnation in a human body and never will again, but evil can always find a home there. Human nature is not black and white but black and grey.
Graham Greene 1904–91 English novelist: 'The Lost Childhood' (1951)

9 Most human beings have an almost infinite capacity for taking things for granted.
Aldous Huxley 1894–1963 English novelist: *Themes and Variations* (1950)

10 But good God, people don't do such things!
Henrik Ibsen 1828–1906 Norwegian dramatist: *Hedda Gabler* (1890)

11 The natural man has only two primal passions, to get and beget.
William Osler 1849–1919 Canadian-born physician: *Science and Immortality* (1904)

12 It is part of human nature to hate the man you have hurt.
Tacitus AD *c.*56–after 117 Roman senator and historian: *Agricola*

13 Adam was but human—this explains it all. He did not want the apple for the apple's sake; he wanted it only because it was forbidden.
Mark Twain 1835–1910 American writer: *Pudd'nhead Wilson* (1894)

The Human Race

see also HUMAN NATURE, LIFE SCIENCES

1 Men are more like the times they live in than they are like their fathers.
   Ali ibn-Abi-Talib *c.*602–661 Arab ruler: attributed

2 In all my work what I try to say is that as human beings we are more alike than we are unalike.
   Maya Angelou 1928– American writer: interview in *New York Times* 20 January 1993

3 We are born of risen apes, not fallen angels, and the apes were armed killers beside.
   Robert Ardrey 1908–80 American dramatist and evolutionist: *African Genesis* (1961)

4 Drinking when we are not thirsty and making love all year round, madam; that is all there is to distinguish us from other animals.
   Pierre-Augustin Caron de Beaumarchais 1732–99 French dramatist: *Le Mariage de Figaro* (1785)

5 We carry within us the wonders we seek without us: there is all Africa and her prodigies in us.
   Sir Thomas Browne 1605–82 English writer and physician: *Religio Medici* (1643)

6 I hate 'Humanity' and all such abstracts: but I love *people*. Lovers of 'Humanity' generally hate *people and children*, and keep parrots or puppy dogs.
   Roy Campbell 1901–57 South African poet: *Light on a Dark Horse* (1951)

7 Disinterested love for all living creatures, the most noble attribute of man.
   Charles Darwin 1809–82 English natural historian: *The Descent of Man* (1871)

8 The animal needing something knows how much it needs, the man does not.
   Democritus *c.*460–*c.*370 BC Greek philosopher: fragment 198

9 What is man, when you come to think upon him, but a minutely set, ingenious machine for turning, with infinite artfulness, the red wine of Shiraz into urine?
   Isak Dinesen 1885–1962 Danish novelist and short-story writer: *Seven Gothic Tales* (1934) 'The Dreamers'

10 This is Plato's man.
   presenting Plato's disciples with a plucked chicken after Plato defined Man as 'a two-footed, featherless animal'; Plato subsequently added 'with broad flat nails'
   Diogenes *c.*400–*c.*325 BC Greek Cynic philosopher: Diogenes Laertius *Lives of the Philosophers*

11 Is man an ape or an angel? Now I am on the side of the angels.
   Benjamin Disraeli 1804–81 British Tory statesman and novelist: speech at Oxford, 25 November 1864; see LIFE SCIENCES 20

12   Human kind
   Cannot bear very much reality.
   T. S. Eliot 1888–1965 Anglo-American poet, critic, and dramatist: *Four Quartets* 'Burnt Norton' (1936)

13 Man is a tool-making animal.
   Benjamin Franklin 1706–90 American politician, inventor, and scientist: James Boswell *Life of Samuel Johnson* (1791) 7 April 1778

14 I am all at once what Christ is, since he was what I am, and
   This Jack, joke, poor potsherd, patch, matchwood, immortal diamond,
   Is immortal diamond.
   Gerard Manley Hopkins 1844–89 English poet and priest: 'That Nature is a Heraclitean Fire' (written 1888)

15 The life of man is of no greater importance to the universe than that of an oyster.
>   **David Hume** 1711–76 Scottish philosopher: 'On Suicide' (1783)

16 Many people believe that they are attracted by God, or by Nature, when they are only repelled by man.
>   **William Ralph Inge** 1860–1954 English writer; Dean of St. Paul's, 1911–34: *More Lay Thoughts of a Dean* (1931)

17 Man, biologically considered, and whatever else he may be into the bargain, is simply the most formidable of all the beasts of prey, and, indeed, the only one that preys systematically on its own species.
>   **William James** 1842–1910 American philosopher: in *Atlantic Monthly* December 1904

18 Taking a very gloomy view of the future of the human race, let us suppose that it can only expect to survive for two thousand million years longer, a period about equal to the past age of the earth. Then, regarded as a being destined to live for three-score years and ten, humanity, although it has been born in a house seventy years old, is itself only three days old.
>   **James Jeans** 1877–1946 English astronomer, physicist, and mathematician: *Eos* (1928)

19 Out of the crooked timber of humanity no straight thing can ever be made.
>   **Immanuel Kant** 1724–1804 German philosopher: *Idee zu einer allgemeinen Geschichte in weltbürgerlicher Absicht* (1784)

20 O mankind, We have created you male and female, and appointed you races and tribes, that you may know one another.
>   **The Koran**: sura 49

21 Limited in his nature, infinite in his desires, man is a fallen god who remembers heaven.
>   **Alphonse de Lamartine** 1790–1869 French poet: 'L'Homme' (1820)

22 Every man carries the entire form of human condition.
>   **Montaigne** 1533–92 French moralist and essayist: *Essays* (1580)

23 To say, for example, that a man is made up of certain chemical elements is a satisfactory description only for those who intend to use him as a fertilizer.
>   **H. J. Muller** 1890–1967 American geneticist: *Science and Criticism* (1943)

24 I teach you the superman. Man is something to be surpassed.
>   **Friedrich Nietzsche** 1844–1900 German philosopher and writer: *Also Sprach Zarathustra* (1883)

25 Man is only a reed, the weakest thing in nature; but he is a thinking reed.
>   **Blaise Pascal** 1623–62 French mathematician, physicist, and moralist: *Pensées* (1670)

26 Know then thyself, presume not God to scan;
The proper study of mankind is man.
>   **Alexander Pope** 1688–1744 English poet: *An Essay on Man* Epistle 2 (1733)

27 Man is the measure of all things.
>   **Protagoras** *c.*485 BC Greek sophist: Plato *Theaetetus*

28 I wish I loved the Human Race;
I wish I loved its silly face;
I wish I liked the way it walks;
I wish I liked the way it talks;
And when I'm introduced to one
I wish I thought *What Jolly Fun!*
>   **Walter Raleigh** 1861–1922 English lecturer and critic: 'Wishes of an Elderly Man' (1923)

29 What a piece of work is a man! How noble in reason! how infinite in faculty! in form, in moving, how express and admirable! in action how like an angel! in apprehension how like a god! the beauty of the world! the paragon of animals! And yet, to me, what is this quintessence of dust?

William Shakespeare 1564–1616 English dramatist: *Hamlet* (1601)

30 There are many wonderful things, and nothing is more wonderful than man.

Sophocles *c.*496–406 BC Greek dramatist: *Antigone*

31 Man, unlike any other thing organic or inorganic in the universe, grows beyond his work, walks up the stairs of his concepts, emerges ahead of his accomplishments.

John Steinbeck 1902–68 American novelist: *The Grapes of Wrath* (1939)

32 Notwithstanding, if he could be reincarnated and placed in a New York subway—provided that he were bathed, shaved, and dressed in modern clothing—it is doubtful whether he would attract any more attention than some of its other denizens.
of Neanderthal man

William L. Strauss and **A. J. E. Cave**: in *Quarterly Review of Biology* Winter 1957

33 Principally I hate and detest that animal called man; although I heartily love John, Peter, Thomas, and so forth.

Jonathan Swift 1667–1745 Anglo-Irish poet and satirist: letter to Pope, 29 September 1725

34 I am a man, I count nothing human foreign to me.

Terence *c.*190–159 BC Roman comic dramatist: *Heauton Timorumenos*

35 Man is the Only Animal that Blushes. Or needs to.

Mark Twain 1835–1910 American writer: *Following the Equator* (1897)

36 I can stand any society. All that I care to know is that a man is a human being—that is enough for me; he can't be any worse.

Mark Twain 1835–1910 American writer: *How To Tell a Story and other essays* (1900) 'Concerning the Jews'

37 We're all of us guinea pigs in the laboratory of God. Humanity is just a work in progress.

Tennessee Williams 1911–83 American dramatist: *Camino Real* (1953)

Human Rights

see also EQUALITY, JUSTICE

1 We hold these truths to be self-evident, that all men are created equal, that they are endowed by their Creator with certain unalienable rights, that among these are life, liberty and the pursuit of happiness.

Anonymous: The American Declaration of Independence, 4 July 1776; from a draft by Thomas Jefferson (1743–1826)

2 *Liberté! Égalité! Fraternité!*
Freedom! Equality! Brotherhood!

Anonymous: motto of the French Revolution, but of earlier origin

3 All human beings are born free and equal in dignity and rights.

Anonymous: *Universal Declaration of Human Rights* (1948) article 1

4 Men, their rights, and nothing more; women, their rights, and nothing less.

Susan Brownell Anthony 1820–1906 American feminist and political activist: motto of the newspaper *The Revolution*, 8 January 1868

5 Natural rights is simple nonsense: natural and imprescriptible rights,

rhetorical nonsense—nonsense
upon stilts.

> **Jeremy Bentham** 1748–1832 English
> philosopher: *Anarchical Fallacies* (1843)

6 I would like to see a time when man
loves his fellow man and forgets his
colour or his creed. We will never be
civilized until that time comes. I
know the Negro race has a long road
to go. I believe that the life of the
Negro race has been a life of tragedy,
of injustice, of oppression. The law
has made him equal, but man has
not.

> **Clarence Darrow** 1857–1938 American
> lawyer: speech in Detroit, 19 May 1926

7 No man can put a chain about the
ankle of his fellow man without at
last finding the other end fastened
about his own neck.

> **Frederick Douglass** *c.*1818–95
> American former slave and civil rights
> campaigner: speech at Civil Rights Mass
> Meeting, Washington, DC, 22 October
> 1883

8 That the slave trade is contrary to the
laws of God and to the rights of men.
*proposing its abolition in the House of
Commons in 1776*

> **David Hartley** 1731–1813 English Whig
> politician: Charles Stuart *A Memoir of
> Granville Sharp* (1836)

9 We have talked long enough in this
country about equal rights. We have
talked for a hundred years or more. It
is time now to write the next chapter,
and to write it in the books of law.

> **Lyndon Baines Johnson** 1908–73
> American Democratic statesman:
> speech to Congress, 27 November 1963

10 No free man shall be taken or
imprisoned or dispossessed, or
outlawed or exiled, or in any way
destroyed, nor will we go upon him,
nor will we send against him except

by the lawful judgement of his peers
or by the law of the land.

> **Magna Carta** 1215 Political charter
> signed by King John: clause 39

11 Hearts starve as well as bodies: Give
us Bread, but give us Roses.

> **James Oppenheim** 1882–1932
> American poet and novelist: 'Bread and
> Roses' (1911)

12 The price of championing human
rights is a little inconsistency at
times.

> **David Owen** 1938– British Social
> Democratic politician: speech, House of
> Commons, 30 March 1977

13 Any law which violates the
inalienable rights of man is
essentially unjust and tyrannical; it is
not a law at all.

> **Maximilien Robespierre** 1758–94
> French revolutionary: *Déclaration des
> droits de l'homme* 24 April 1793

14 We look forward to a world founded
upon four essential human
freedoms. The first is freedom of
speech and expression—everywhere
in the world. The second is freedom
of every person to worship God in
his own way—everywhere in the
world. The third is freedom from
want . . . everywhere in the world.
The fourth is freedom from fear . . .
anywhere in the world.

> **Franklin D. Roosevelt** 1882–1945
> American Democratic statesman:
> message to Congress, 6 January 1941

15 A right is not effectual by itself, but
only in relation to the obligation to
which it corresponds . . . An
obligation which goes unrecognized
by anybody loses none of the full
force of its existence. A right which
goes unrecognized by anybody is not
worth very much.

> **Simone Weil** 1909–43 French essayist
> and philosopher: *L'Enracinement* (1949)

16 It is justice, not charity, that is wanting in the world.
   Mary Wollstonecraft 1759–97 English feminist: *A Vindication of the Rights of Woman* (1792)

Humility

see also PRIDE, SELF-ESTEEM

1 Blessed are the meek: for they shall inherit the earth.
   Bible: St Matthew

2 He that is down needs fear no fall,
He that is low no pride.
He that is humble ever shall
Have God to be his guide.
   John Bunyan 1628–88 English writer and Nonconformist preacher: *The Pilgrim's Progress* (1684) 'Shepherd Boy's Song'

3 We are so very 'umble.
   Charles Dickens 1812–70 English novelist: *David Copperfield* (1850)

4 The tumult and the shouting dies—
The captains and the kings depart—
Still stands Thine ancient Sacrifice,
An humble and a contrite heart.
Lord God of Hosts, be with us yet,
Lest we forget—lest we forget!
   Rudyard Kipling 1865–1936 English writer and poet: 'Recessional' (1897)

5 In 1969 I published a small book on Humility. It was a pioneering work which has not, to my knowledge, been superseded.
   Lord Longford 1905–2001 British Labour politician and philanthropist: in *Tablet* 22 January 1994

Humour

see also COMEDY, WIT

1 Among all kinds of writing, there is none in which authors are more apt to miscarry than in works of humour, as there is none in which they are more ambitious to excel.
   Joseph Addison 1672–1719 English poet, dramatist, and essayist: in *The Spectator* 10 April 1711

2 The marvellous thing about a joke with a double meaning is that it can only mean one thing.
   Ronnie Barker 1929–2005 English comedian: *Sauce* (1977)

3 I make myself laugh at everything, for fear of having to weep at it.
   Pierre-Augustin Caron de Beaumarchais 1732–99 French dramatist: *Le Barbier de Séville* (1775)

4 Mark my words, when a society has to resort to the lavatory for its humour, the writing is on the wall.
   Alan Bennett 1934– English actor and dramatist: *Forty Years On* (1969)

5 Of all days, the one most surely wasted is the one on which one has not laughed.
   Nicolas-Sébastien Chamfort 1741–94 French writer: *Maximes et Pensées* (1796)

6 Freud's theory was that when a joke opens a window and all those bats and bogeymen fly out, you get a marvellous feeling of relief and elation. The trouble with Freud is that he never had to play the old Glasgow Empire on a Saturday night after Rangers and Celtic had both lost.
   Ken Dodd 1927– British comedian: in *Guardian* 30 April 1991; quoted in many, usually much contracted, forms since the mid-1960s

7 Nothing is so impenetrable as laughter in a language you don't understand.
   William Golding 1911–93 English novelist: *An Egyptian Journal* (1985)

8 What do you mean, funny? Funny-peculiar or funny ha-ha?
Ian Hay 1876–1952 Scottish novelist and dramatist: *The Housemaster* (1938)

9 Laughter is nothing else but sudden glory arising from some sudden conception of some eminency in ourselves, by comparison with the infirmity of others, or with our own formerly.
Thomas Hobbes 1588–1679 English philosopher: *Human Nature* (1650)

10 Humour very often cuts the knot of serious questions more trenchantly and successfully than severity.
Horace 65–8 BC Roman poet: *Satires*

11 We must laugh before we are happy, for fear of dying without having laughed at all.
Jean de la Bruyère 1645–96 French satiric moralist: *Les Caractères ou les moeurs de ce siècle* (1688)

12 Fun is fun but no girl wants to laugh all of the time.
Anita Loos 1893–1981 American writer: *Gentlemen Prefer Blondes* (1925)

13 Good taste and humour . . . are a contradiction in terms, like a chaste whore.
Malcolm Muggeridge 1903–90 British journalist: in *Time* 14 September 1953

14 Whatever is funny is subversive, every joke is ultimately a custard pie . . . A dirty joke is a sort of mental rebellion.
George Orwell 1903–50 English novelist: in *Horizon* September 1941 'The Art of Donald McGill'

15 Everything is funny as long as it is happening to Somebody Else.
Will Rogers 1879–1935 American actor and humorist: *The Illiterate Digest* (1924)

16 People sometimes divide others into those you laugh at and those you laugh with. The young Auden was someone you could laugh-at-with.
Stephen Spender 1909–95 English poet: *W. H. Auden* (1973)

17 Humour is emotional chaos remembered in tranquillity.
James Thurber 1894–1961 American humorist: in *New York Post* 29 February 1960; see POETRY 29

18 Laughter would be bereaved if snobbery died.
Peter Ustinov 1921–2004 British actor, director, and writer: in *Observer* 13 March 1955

19 We are not amused.
Queen Victoria 1819–1901 British monarch: attributed; Caroline Holland *Notebooks of a Spinster Lady* (1919) 2 January 1900

20 I love such mirth as does not make friends ashamed to look upon one another next morning.
Izaak Walton 1593–1683 English writer: *The Compleat Angler* (1653)

21 It's hard to be funny when you have to be clean.
Mae West 1892–1980 American film actress: Joseph Weintraub *The Wit and Wisdom of Mae West* (1967)

Hunting

see also ANIMAL RIGHTS, FIELD SPORTS

1 I do not see why I should break my neck because a dog chooses to run after a nasty smell.
on being asked why he did not hunt
Arthur James Balfour 1848–1930 British Conservative statesman: Ian Malcolm *Lord Balfour: A Memory* (1930)

2 Yes, I ken John Peel and Ruby too, Ranter and Ringwood, Bellman and True;
From a find to a check, from a check to a view,

From a view to a death in the
morning.
John Woodcock Graves 1795–1886
British huntsman and songwriter: 'John
Peel' (1820)

3 It is very strange, and very
melancholy, that the paucity of
human pleasures should persuade
us ever to call hunting one of them.
Samuel Johnson 1709–84 English poet,
critic, and lexicographer: Hester Lynch
Piozzi *Anecdotes of . . . Johnson* (1786)

4 They do you a decent death on the
hunting-field.
John Mortimer 1923–2009 English
novelist, barrister, and dramatist:
Paradise Postponed (1985)

5 Most of their discourse was about
hunting, in a dialect I understand
very little.
Samuel Pepys 1633–1703 English
diarist: diary, 22 November 1663

6 It is my belief that six out of every
dozen people who go out hunting
are disagreeably conscious of a
nervous system, and two out of six
are in what is brutally called 'a blue
funk'.
Edith Œ Somerville 1858–1949 and
Martin Ross 1862–1915 Irish writers:
Some Experiences of an Irish R.M. (1899)

7 It ar'n't that I loves the fox less, but
that I loves the 'ound more.
R. S. Surtees 1805–64 English sporting
journalist and novelist: *Handley Cross*
(1843)

8 'Unting is all that's worth living
for—all time is lost wot is not spent
in 'unting—it is like the hair we
breathe—if we have it not we
die—it's the sport of kings, the image
of war without its guilt, and only five-
and-twenty per cent of its danger.
R. S. Surtees 1805–64 English sporting
journalist and novelist: *Handley Cross*
(1843)

9 The English country gentleman
galloping after a fox—the
unspeakable in full pursuit of the
uneatable.
Oscar Wilde 1854–1900 Anglo-Irish
dramatist and poet: *A Woman of No
Importance* (1893)

Husbands

see also MARRIAGE, MEN

1 You may marry the man of your
dreams, ladies, but 14 years later
you're married to a couch that burps.
Roseanne Barr 1953– American
comedian: *Roseanne* (American TV
series, 1988–)

2 Being a husband is a whole-time job.
That is why so many husbands fail.
They cannot give their entire
attention to it.
Arnold Bennett 1867–1931 English
novelist: *The Title* (1918)

3 Never marry a man who hates his
mother, because he'll end up hating
you.
Jill Bennett 1931–90 English actress: in
Observer 12 September 1982

4 Why should marriage bring only
tears?
All I wanted was a man
With a single heart,
And we would stay together
As our hair turned white,
Not somebody always after wriggling
fish
With his big bamboo rod.
Chuo Wen-chun *c.*179–117 BC Chinese
poet: 'A Song of White Hair'

5 I've never yet met a man who could
look after me. I don't need a
husband. What I need is a wife.
Joan Collins 1933– British actress: in
Sunday Times 27 December 1987

6 I never married because there was
no need. I have three pets at home

which answer the same purpose as a husband. I have a dog which growls every morning, a parrot which swears all the afternoon, and a cat that comes home late at night.

    Marie Corelli 1855–1924 English writer of romantic fiction: attributed

7 Husbands are like fires. They go out when unattended.

    Zsa Zsa Gabor 1919– Hungarian-born film actress: in *Newsweek* 28 March 1960

8 The men that women marry,
And why they marry them, will always be
A marvel and a mystery to the world.

    Henry Wadsworth Longfellow 1807–82 American poet: *Michael Angelo* (1883)

9 He tells you when you've got on too much lipstick,
And helps you with your girdle when your hips stick.

    Ogden Nash 1902–71 American humorist: 'The Perfect Husband' (1949)

10 A husband is what is left of a lover, after the nerve has been extracted.

    Helen Rowland 1875–1950 American writer: *A Guide to Men* (1922)

11 If you cannot have your dear husband for a comfort and a delight, for a breadwinner and a crosspatch, for a sofa, chair or a hot-water bottle, one can use him as a Cross to be Borne.

    Stevie Smith 1902–71 English poet and novelist: *Novel on Yellow Paper* (1936)

12 Chumps always make the best husbands. When you marry, Sally, grab a chump. Tap his forehead first, and if it rings solid, don't hesitate. All the unhappy marriages come from the husbands having brains.

    P. G. Wodehouse 1881–1975 English writer: *The Adventures of Sally* (1920)

Hypocrisy

see also DECEPTION

1 Conventionality is not morality. Self-righteousness is not religion. To attack the first is not to assail the last. To pluck the mask from the face of the Pharisee, is not to lift an impious hand to the Crown of Thorns.

    Charlotte Brontë 1816–55 English novelist: *Jane Eyre* (2nd ed., 1848)

2 Keep up appearances; there lies the test;
The world will give thee credit for the rest.
Outward be fair, however foul within;
Sin if thou wilt, but then in secret sin.

    Charles Churchill 1731–64 English poet: *Night* (1761)

3 Hypocrisy is a tribute which vice pays to virtue.

    Duc de la Rochefoucauld 1613–80 French moralist: *Maximes* (1678)

4 In the mouths of many men soft words are like roses that soldiers put into the muzzles of their muskets on holidays.

    Henry Wadsworth Longfellow 1807–82 American poet: *Table-Talk* (1857) 'Driftwood'

5 Hypocrisy is the most difficult and nerve-racking vice that any man can pursue; it needs an unceasing vigilance and a rare detachment of spirit. It cannot, like adultery or gluttony, be practised at spare moments; it is a whole-time job.

    W. Somerset Maugham 1874–1965 English novelist: *Cakes and Ale* (1930)

6   I want that glib and oily art
To speak and purpose not.

    William Shakespeare 1564–1616 English dramatist: *King Lear* (1605–6)

7 All Reformers, however strict their social conscience, live in houses just as big as they can pay for.
   Logan Pearsall Smith 1865–1946 American-born man of letters: *Afterthoughts* (1931) 'Other People'

8 I sit on a man's back, choking him and making him carry me, and yet assure myself and others that I am very sorry for him and wish to ease his lot by all possible means—except by getting off his back.
   Leo Tolstoy 1828–1910 Russian novelist: *What Then Must We Do?* (1886)

9 I hope you have not been leading a double life, pretending to be wicked and being really good all the time. That would be hypocrisy.
   Oscar Wilde 1854–1900 Anglo-Irish dramatist and poet: *The Importance of Being Earnest* (1895)

Idealism

1 A cause may be inconvenient, but it's magnificent. It's like champagne or high heels, and one must be prepared to suffer for it.
   Arnold Bennett 1867–1931 English novelist: *The Title* (1918)

2 Where there is no vision, the people perish.
   Bible: Proverbs

3 Oh, the vision thing.
   responding to the suggestion that he turn his attention from short-term campaign objectives and look to the longer term
   George Bush 1924– American Republican statesman: in *Time* 26 January 1987

4 You never reach the promised land. You can march towards it.
   James Callaghan 1912–2005 British Labour statesman: television interview, 20 July 1978

5 To dream the impossible dream, To reach the unreachable star!
   Joe Darion 1917–2001 American songwriter: 'The Impossible Dream' (1965 song)

6 Hitch your wagon to a star.
   Ralph Waldo Emerson 1803–82 American philosopher and poet: *Society and Solitude* (1870)

7 Each time a man stands up for an ideal, or acts to improve the lot of others, or strikes out against injustice, he sends forth a tiny ripple of hope, and crossing each other from a million different centres of energy and daring those ripples build a current which can sweep down the mightiest walls of oppression and resistance.
   Robert Kennedy 1925–68 American Democratic politician: speech, Cape Town, 6 June 1966

8 I submit to you that if a man hasn't discovered something he will die for, he isn't fit to live.
   Martin Luther King 1929–68 American civil rights leader: speech in Detroit, 23 June 1963

9 I am an idealist. I don't know where I'm going but I'm on the way.
   Carl Sandburg 1878–1967 American poet: *Incidentals* (1907)

10 The first thing a man will do for his ideals is lie.
   J. A. Schumpeter 1883–1950 Austrian-born American economist: *History of Economic Analysis* (1954)

11 When they come downstairs from their Ivory Towers, Idealists are very apt to walk straight into the gutter.
   Logan Pearsall Smith 1865–1946 American-born man of letters: *Afterthoughts* (1931) 'Other People'

12 We are all in the gutter, but some of us are looking at the stars.
   Oscar Wilde 1854–1900 Anglo-Irish

dramatist and poet: *Lady Windermere's Fan* (1892)

13 Plain living and high thinking are no more:
The homely beauty of the good old cause
Is gone.
William Wordsworth 1770–1850 English poet: 'O friend! I know not which way I must look' (1807)

14 We were the last romantics — chose for theme
Traditional sanctity and loveliness.
W. B. Yeats 1865–1939 Irish poet: 'Coole and Ballylee, 1931' (1933)

Ideas

see also FACTS, MIND, PROBLEMS, THEORY, THINKING

1 Nothing is more dangerous than an idea, when you have only one idea.
Alain 1868–1951 French poet and philosopher: *Propos sur la religion* (1938)

2 Our ideas are only intellectual instruments which we use to break into phenomena; we must change them when they have served their purpose, as we change a blunt lancet that we have used long enough.
Claude Bernard 1813–78 French physiologist: *An Introduction to the Study of Experimental Medicine* (1865)

3 A man is not necessarily intelligent because he has plenty of ideas, any more than he is a good general because he has plenty of soldiers.
Nicolas-Sébastien Chamfort 1741–94 French writer: *Maximes et Pensées* (1796)

4 What we need is hatred. From it our ideas are born.
Jean Genet 1910–86 French novelist, poet, and dramatist: *The Blacks* (1959); epigraph

5 Every now and then a man's mind is stretched by a new idea or sensation, and never shrinks back to its former dimensions.
Oliver Wendell Holmes 1809–94 American physician, poet, and essayist: *Autocrat of the Breakfast Table* (1891)

6 A stand can be made against invasion by an army; no stand can be made against invasion by an idea.
Victor Hugo 1802–85 French poet, novelist, and dramatist: *Histoire d'un Crime* (1877)

7 It is better to entertain an idea than to take it home to live with you for the rest of your life.
Randall Jarrell 1914–65 American poet: *Pictures from an Institution* (1954)

8 Madmen in authority, who hear voices in the air, are distilling their frenzy from some academic scribbler of a few years back.
John Maynard Keynes 1883–1946 English economist: *General Theory* (1947 ed.)

9 New opinions are always suspected, and usually opposed, without any other reason but because they are not already common.
John Locke 1632–1704 English philosopher: *An Essay concerning Human Understanding* (1690)

10 General notions are generally wrong.
Lady Mary Wortley Montagu 1689–1762 English writer: letter to her husband Edward Wortley Montagu, 28 March 1710

11 The English approach to ideas is not to kill them, but to let them die of neglect.
Jeremy Paxman 1950– British journalist and broadcaster: *The English: a portrait of a people* (1998)

12 For an idea ever to be fashionable is ominous, since it must afterwards be always old-fashioned.
   George Santayana 1863–1952 Spanish-born philosopher and critic: *Winds of Doctrine* (1913)

13 You see things; and you say 'Why?' But I dream things that never were; and I say 'Why not?'
   George Bernard Shaw 1856–1950 Irish dramatist: *Back to Methuselah* (1921)

14 I share no one's ideas. I have my own.
   Ivan Turgenev 1818–83 Russian novelist: *Fathers and Sons* (1862)

15 *Ideas won't keep.* Something must be done about them.
   Alfred North Whitehead 1861–1947 English philosopher and mathematician: *Dialogues* (1954) 28 April 1938

16 No ideas but in things.
   William Carlos Williams 1883–1963 American poet: *Autobiography* (1967)

Idleness

see also DELAY, WORDS AND DEEDS

1 A man who has nothing to do with his own time has no conscience in his intrusion on that of others.
   Jane Austen 1775–1817 English novelist: *Sense and Sensibility* (1811)

2 Oh! how I hate to get up in the morning,
   Oh! how I'd love to remain in bed.
   Irving Berlin 1888–1989 American songwriter: *Oh! How I Hate to Get Up in the Morning* (1918 song)

3 The foul sluggard's comfort: 'It will last my time.'
   Thomas Carlyle 1795–1881 Scottish historian and political philosopher: *Critical and Miscellaneous Essays* (1838)

4 Idleness is only the refuge of weak minds.
   Lord Chesterfield 1694–1773 English writer and politician: *Letters to his Son* (1774) 20 July 1749

5 I do nothing, granted. But I see the hours pass—which is better than trying to fill them.
   E. M. Cioran 1911–95 Romanian-born French philosopher: in *Guardian* 11 May 1993

6 Inertia can develop its own momentum.
   Douglas Hurd 1930– British Conservative politician: in *Mail on Sunday* 27 May 2001

7 It is impossible to enjoy idling thoroughly unless one has plenty of work to do.
   Jerome K. Jerome 1859–1927 English writer: *Idle Thoughts of an Idle Fellow* (1886)

8 If you are idle, be not solitary; if you are solitary, be not idle.
   Samuel Johnson 1709–84 English poet, critic, and lexicographer: letter to Boswell, 27 October 1779

9 I was raised to feel that doing nothing was a sin. I had to learn to do nothing.
   Jenny Joseph 1932– English poet: in *Observer* 19 April 1998

10 Far from idleness being the root of evil, rather it is the true good.
   Sören Kierkegaard 1813–55 Danish philosopher: *Either/Or* (1843) pt. 1, ch. 6 'Crop Rotation'

11 The time you enjoy wasting is not wasted time.
   commenting on a remark by Bertrand Russell; frequently attributed to Russell
   Laurence J. Peter 1919–90 Canadian writer: *Quotations for Our Time* (1977)

12 How dull it is to pause, to make an end,

To rust unburnished, not to shine in use!
As though to breathe were life.

Alfred, Lord Tennyson 1809–92 English poet: 'Ulysses' (1842)

Ignorance

see also KNOWLEDGE

1 Happy the hare at morning, for she cannot read
The Hunter's waking thoughts.

W. H. Auden 1907–73 English poet: *Dog beneath the Skin* (with Christopher Isherwood, 1935)

2 Where people wish to attach, they should always be ignorant. To come with a well-informed mind, is to come with an inability of administering to the vanity of others, which a sensible person would always wish to avoid. A woman especially, if she have the misfortune of knowing any thing, should conceal it as well as she can.

Jane Austen 1775–1817 English novelist: *Northanger Abbey* (1818)

3 Ignorance is an evil weed, which dictators may cultivate among their dupes, but which no democracy can afford among its citizens.

William Henry Beveridge 1879–1963 British economist: *Full Employment in a Free Society* (1944)

4 Ignorance is not innocence but sin.

Robert Browning 1812–89 English poet: *The Inn Album* (1875)

5 I know nothing—nobody tells me anything.

John Galsworthy 1867–1933 English novelist: *Man of Property* (1906)

6 Where ignorance is bliss,
'Tis folly to be wise.

Thomas Gray 1716–71 English poet: *Ode on a Distant Prospect of Eton College* (1747)

7 Ignorance, madam, pure ignorance.
on being asked why he had defined pastern *as the 'knee' of a horse*

Samuel Johnson 1709–84 English poet, critic, and lexicographer: James Boswell *Life of Samuel Johnson* (1791) 1755

8 Nothing in all the world is more dangerous than sincere ignorance and conscientious stupidity.

Martin Luther King 1929–68 American civil rights leader: *Strength to Love* (1963)

9 A bishop wrote gravely to the *Times* inviting all nations to destroy 'the formula' of the atomic bomb. There is no simple remedy for ignorance so abysmal.

Peter Medawar 1915–87 English immunologist and writer: *The Hope of Progress* (1972)

10 You know everybody is ignorant, only on different subjects.

Will Rogers 1879–1935 American actor and humorist: in *New York Times* 31 August 1924

11 Learn to say, 'I don't know.' If used when appropriate, it will be often.

Donald Rumsfeld 1932– American Republican politician and businessman: 'Rumsfeld's Rules'; interview in *Wall Street Journal* 29 January 2001

12 For most men, an ignorant enjoyment is better than an informed one; it is better to conceive the sky as a blue dome than a dark cavity; and the cloud as a golden throne than a sleety mist.

John Ruskin 1819–1900 English art and social critic: *Modern Painters* (1856)

13 If one does not know to which port one is sailing, no wind is favourable.

Seneca ('the Younger') c.4 BC–AD 65 Roman philosopher and poet: *Epistulae Morales*

14 *Only* ignorance! How can you talk
about only *ignorance*! Don't you
know that it is the worst thing in the
world next to wickedness.

> **Anna Sewell** 1820–78 English writer:
> *Black Beauty* (1877)

15 It was absolutely marvellous working
for Pauli. You could ask him
anything. There was no worry that he
would think a particular question
was stupid, since he thought *all*
questions were stupid.

> **Victor Weisskopf** 1908–2002 American
> physicist: in *American Journal of Physics*
> 1977

16 Ignorance is like a delicate exotic
fruit; touch it and the bloom is gone.
The whole theory of modern
education is radically unsound.
Fortunately, in England, at any rate,
education produces no effect
whatsoever.

> **Oscar Wilde** 1854–1900 Anglo-Irish
> dramatist and poet: *The Importance of
> Being Earnest* (1895)

17 As any fule kno.

> **Geoffrey Willans** 1911–58 and **Ronald
> Searle** 1920– English humorous
> writers: *Down with Skool!* (1953)

Imagination

see also FANTASY

1 To see a world in a grain of sand
And a heaven in a wild flower
Hold infinity in the palm of your
hand
And eternity in an hour.

> **William Blake** 1757–1827 English poet:
> 'Auguries of Innocence' (*c*.1803)

2 When the imagination sleeps, words
are emptied of their meaning.

> **Albert Camus** 1913–60 French novelist,
> dramatist, and essayist: *Resistance,
> Rebellion and Death* (1961)

3 An adventure is only an
inconvenience rightly considered.
An inconvenience is only an
adventure wrongly considered.

> **G. K. Chesterton** 1874–1936 English
> essayist, novelist, and poet: *All Things
> Considered* (1908) 'On Running after
> one's Hat'

4 Where there is no imagination there
is no horror.

> **Arthur Conan Doyle** 1859–1930
> Scottish-born writer of detective fiction:
> *A Study in Scarlet* (1888)

5 Imagination is more important than
knowledge.

> **Albert Einstein** 1879–1955 German-
> born theoretical physicist: in *Saturday
> Evening Post* 26 October 1929

6 He said he should prefer not to know
the sources of the Nile, and that
there should be some unknown
regions preserved as hunting-
grounds for the poetic imagination.

> **George Eliot** 1819–80 English novelist:
> *Middlemarch* (1871–2)

7 Imagination isn't merely a surplus
mental department meant for
entertainment, but the most
essential piece of machinery we have
if we are going to live the lives of
human beings.

> **Ted Hughes** 1930–98 English poet: in
> *Children's Literature in Education*
> March 1970

8 Were it not for imagination, Sir, a
man would be as happy in the arms
of a chambermaid as of a Duchess.

> **Samuel Johnson** 1709–84 English poet,
> critic, and lexicographer: James Boswell
> *Life of Samuel Johnson* (1791) 9 May
> 1778

9 The same that oft-times hath
Charmed magic casements, opening
on the foam

Of perilous seas, in faery lands
forlorn.
> **John Keats** 1795–1821 English poet:
> 'Ode to a Nightingale' (1820)

10 Almost any man may, like the spider,
spin from his own inwards his own
airy citadel.
> **John Keats** 1795–1821 English poet:
> letter to J. H. Reynolds, 19 February
> 1818

11 His imagination resembled the
wings of an ostrich. It enabled him to
run, though not to soar.
> **Lord Macaulay** 1800–59 English
> politician and historian: T. F. Ellis (ed.)
> *Miscellaneous Writings of Lord
> Macaulay* (1860) 'John Dryden' (1828)

12 Must then a Christ perish in torment
in every age to save those that have
no imagination?
> **George Bernard Shaw** 1856–1950 Irish
> dramatist: *Saint Joan* (1924)

13 Though our brother is on the rack, as
long as we ourselves are at our ease,
our senses will never inform us of
what he suffers . . . It is by
imagination that we can form any
conception of what are his
sensations.
> **Adam Smith** 1723–90 Scottish
> philosopher and economist: *Theory of
> Moral Sentiments* (2nd ed., 1762)

14 The imagination is man's power over
nature.
> **Wallace Stevens** 1879–1955 American
> poet: 'Adagia' (1959)

15 Whither is fled the visionary gleam?
Where is it now, the glory and the
dream?
> **William Wordsworth** 1770–1850
> English poet: 'Ode. Intimations of
> Immortality' (1807)

Impartiality

see also INDIFFERENCE

1 I decline utterly to be impartial as
between the fire brigade and the fire.
> *replying to complaints of his bias in editing
> the* British Gazette *during the General
> Strike*
> **Winston Churchill** 1874–1965 British
> Conservative statesman: speech, House
> of Commons, 7 July 1926

2 When people feel deeply,
impartiality is bias.
> **Lord Reith** 1889–1971 British
> administrator and politician: *Into the
> Wind* (1945)

3 Take sides. Neutrality helps the
oppressor, never the victim. Silence
encourages the tormentor, never the
tormented.
> *accepting the Nobel Peace Prize*
> **Elie Wiesel** 1928– Romanian-born
> American writer: in *New York Times*
> 11 December 1986

Impulsiveness

1 May I ask whether these pleasing
attentions proceed from the impulse
of the moment, or are the result of
previous study?
> **Jane Austen** 1775–1817 English novelist:
> *Pride and Prejudice* (1813)

2 A first impulse was never a crime.
> **Pierre Corneille** 1606–84 French
> dramatist: *Horace* (1640)

3 Have no truck with first impulses for
they are always generous ones.
> **Casimir, Comte de Montrond**
> 1768–1843 French diplomat: attributed;
> Comte J. d'Estourmel *Derniers
> Souvenirs* (1860)

4 Impulse has more effect than conscious purpose in moulding men's lives.

> **Bertrand Russell** 1872–1970 British philosopher and mathematician: *Autobiography* (1967)

Indecision

see also CERTAINTY, DOUBT

1 Often undecided whether to desert a sinking ship for one that might not float, he would make up his mind to sit on the wharf for a day.

of Lord Curzon

> **Lord Beaverbrook** 1879–1964 Canadian-born British newspaper proprietor and Conservative politician: *Men and Power* (1956)

2 The archbishop is usually to be found nailing his colours to the fence.

of Archbishop Runcie

> **Frank Field** 1942– British Labour politician: attributed in *Crockfords 1987/88* (1987)

3 I'll give you a definite maybe.

> **Sam Goldwyn** 1882–1974 American film producer: attributed

4 A very weak-minded fellow I am afraid, and, like the feather pillow, bears the marks of the last person who has sat on him!

of Lord Derby

> **Earl Haig** 1861–1928 British Field Marshall: letter to Lady Haig, 14 January 1918

5 There is no more miserable human being than one in whom nothing is habitual but indecision.

> **William James** 1842–1910 American philosopher: *The Principles of Psychology* (1890)

6 The tragedy of a man who could not make up his mind.

> **Laurence Olivier** 1907–89 English actor

and director: introduction to his 1948 screen adaptation of *Hamlet*

7 She floats, she hesitates; in a word, she's a woman.

> **Jean Racine** 1639–99 French tragedian: *Athalie* (1691)

8 I must have a prodigious quantity of mind; it takes me as much as a week, sometimes, to make it up.

> **Mark Twain** 1835–1910 American writer: *The Innocents Abroad* (1869)

Indifference

see also IMPARTIALITY

1 All colours will agree in the dark.

> **Francis Bacon** 1561–1626 English lawyer, courtier, philosopher, and essayist: *Essays* (1625) 'Of Unity in Religion'

2 I come from a people who gave the ten commandments to the world. Time has come to strengthen them by three additional ones, which we ought to adopt and commit ourselves to: thou shalt not be a perpetrator; thou shalt not be a victim; and thou shalt never, but never, be a bystander.

> **Yehuda Bauer** 1926– Czech-born Israeli historian: speech to the German Bundestag, 1998, quoted in his own speech to the Stockholm International Forum on the Holocaust, 26 July 2000

3 There is nothing upon the face of the earth so insipid as a medium. Give me love or hate! a friend that will go to jail for me, or an enemy that will run me through the body!

> **Fanny Burney** 1752–1840 English novelist and diarist: *Camilla* (1796)

4 Catholics and Communists have committed great crimes, but at least they have not stood aside, like an established society, and been

indifferent. I would rather have blood on my hands than water like Pilate.

Graham Greene 1904–91 English novelist: *The Comedians* (1966)

5 Science may have found a cure for most evils; but it has found no remedy for the worst of them all—the apathy of human beings.

Helen Keller 1880–1968 American writer and social reformer: *My Religion* (1927)

6 I wish I could care what you do or where you go but I can't . . . My dear, I don't give a damn.

'Frankly, my dear, I don't give a damn!' in the 1939 screen version by Sidney Howard

Margaret Mitchell 1900–49 American novelist: *Gone with the Wind* (1936)

7 When Hitler attacked the Jews I was not a Jew, therefore, I was not concerned. And when Hitler attacked the Catholics, I was not a Catholic, and therefore, I was not concerned. And when Hitler attacked the unions and the industrialists, I was not a member of the unions and I was not concerned. Then, Hitler attacked me and the Protestant church—and there was nobody left to be concerned.

often quoted in the form 'In Germany they came first for the Communists, and I didn't speak up because I wasn't a Communist . . . ' and so on

Martin Niemöller 1892–1984 German theologian: in *Congressional Record* 14 October 1968

8 Vacant heart and hand, and eye,— Easy live and quiet die.

Sir Walter Scott 1771–1832 Scottish novelist and poet: *The Bride of Lammermoor* (1819)

9 The worst sin towards our fellow creatures is not to hate them, but to be indifferent to them: that's the essence of inhumanity.

George Bernard Shaw 1856–1950 Irish dramatist: *The Devil's Disciple* (1901)

10 Am I bovvered?

Catherine Tate 1968– English actress and comedienne: teenager Lauren, in *The Catherine Tate Show* (BBC TV, 2004–)

11 The opposite of love is not hate, it's indifference. The opposite of art is not ugliness, it's indifference. The opposite of faith is not heresy, it's indifference. And the opposite of life is not death, it's indifference.

Elie Wiesel 1928– Romanian-born American writer: in *U.S. News and World Report* 27 October 1986

12 Cast a cold eye On life, on death. Horseman, pass by!

W. B. Yeats 1865–1939 Irish poet: 'Under Ben Bulben' (1939)

Individuality

see also CONFORMITY, SELF

1 PERSONALITY TITHE: A price paid for becoming a couple.

Douglas Coupland 1961– Canadian writer: *Generation X* (1991)

2 It is easier to live through someone else than to become complete yourself.

Betty Friedan 1921–2006 American feminist: *The Feminine Mystique* (1963)

3 No human relation gives one possession in another—every two souls are absolutely different. In friendship or in love, the two side by side raise hands together to find what one cannot reach alone.

Kahlil Gibran 1883–1931 Lebanese-born American writer and painter: *Beloved Prophet: the love letters of Kahlil Gibran and Mary Haskell and her private journal* (1972)

4 Human beings have an inalienable right to invent themselves; when that right is pre-empted it is called brainwashing.

> **Germaine Greer** 1939– Australian feminist: in *The Times* 1 February 1986

5 Whatever you may be sure of, be sure at least of this, that you are dreadfully like other people.

> **James Russell Lowell** 1819–91 American poet: *My Study Windows* (1871)

6 Most people are other people. Their thoughts are someone else's opinions, their lives a mimicry, their passions a quotation.

> **Oscar Wilde** 1854–1900 Irish dramatist and poet: *De Profundis* (1905)

Information

see also KNOWLEDGE

1 Information can tell us everything. It has all the answers. But they are answers to questions we have not asked, and which doubtless don't even arise.

> **Jean Baudrillard** 1929–2007 French sociologist and cultural critic: *Cool Memories* (1987)

2 Not many people know that.

> **Michael Caine** 1933– English film actor: title of book (1984)

3 Now that I do know it, I shall do my best to forget it.

> **Arthur Conan Doyle** 1859–1930 Scottish-born writer of detective fiction: *A Study in Scarlet* (1887)

4 The motto of all the mongoose family is, 'Run and find out.'

> **Rudyard Kipling** 1865–1936 English writer and poet: *The Jungle Book* (1897)

5 You will find it a very good practice always to verify your references, sir!

> **Martin Joseph Routh** 1755–1854 English classicist: John William Burgon *Lives of Twelve Good Men* (1888 ed.)

6 What is wanted is not the will to believe, but the wish to find out, which is its exact opposite.

> **Bertrand Russell** 1872–1970 British philosopher and mathematician: *Free Thought and Official Propaganda* (1922)

7 Everybody gets so much information all day long that they lose their common sense.

> **Gertrude Stein** 1874–1946 American writer: *Reflection on the Atomic Bomb* (1946)

8 That was a little bit more information than I needed to know.

> **Quentin Tarantino** 1963– American film director and screenwriter: *Pulp Fiction* (1994 film); spoken by Uma Thurman

Ingratitude

see also GRATITUDE

1 That's the way with these directors, they're always biting the hand that lays the golden egg.

> **Sam Goldwyn** 1882–1974 American film producer: Alva Johnston *The Great Goldwyn* (1937)

2 How sharper than a serpent's tooth it is
To have a thankless child!

> **William Shakespeare** 1564–1616 English dramatist: *King Lear* (1605–6)

3 There's plenty of boys that will come hankering and grovelling around you when you've got an apple, and beg the core off of you; but when they've got one, and you beg for the core and remind them how you give them a core one time, they say thank you 'most to death, but there ain't-a-going to be no core.

> **Mark Twain** 1835–1910 American writer: *Tom Sawyer Abroad* (1894)

4 My children are ungrateful: they don't care. That is my great reward. They are free.

> **Fay Weldon** 1931– British novelist and scriptwriter: *Praxis* (1978)

In-Laws

see also FAMILY, MARRIAGE

1 I should, many a good day, have blown my brains out, but for the recollection that it would have given pleasure to my mother-in-law; and, even *then*, if I could have been certain to haunt her . . .

> **Lord Byron** 1788–1824 English poet: letter, 28 January 1817

2 The ideal is to marry an orphan.

> **Jilly Cooper** 1937– British writer: *How to Stay Married* (1977)

3 The awe and dread with which the untutored savage contemplates his mother-in-law are amongst the most familiar facts of anthropology.

> **James George Frazer** 1854–1941 Scottish anthropologist: *The Golden Bough* (2nd ed., 1900)

4 I was a post-war, utility son-in-law! Not quite the Frog-Prince. Maybe the Swineherd.

> **Ted Hughes** 1930–98 English poet: *Birthday Letters* (1998) 'A Pink Wool Knitted Dress'

Innocence

see also GUILT

1 *Honi soit qui mal y pense.*

Evil be to him who evil thinks.

> **Anonymous**: motto of the Order of the Garter, originated by Edward III, probably on 23 April of 1348 or 1349

2 Unto the pure all things are pure.

> **Bible**: Titus

3 It is not only our fate but our business to lose innocence, and once we have lost that, it is futile to attempt a picnic in Eden.

> **Elizabeth Bowen** 1899–1973 Anglo-Irish novelist: 'Out of a Book' in *Orion III* (1946)

4 Innocence always calls mutely for protection, when we would be so much wiser to guard ourselves against it: innocence is like a dumb leper who has lost his bell, wandering the world meaning no harm.

> **Graham Greene** 1904–91 English novelist: *The Quiet American* (1955)

5 All things truly wicked start from an innocence.

> **Ernest Hemingway** 1899–1961 American novelist: *A Moveable Feast* (1964)

6 I love my work and my children. God Is distant, difficult. Things happen. Too near the ancient troughs of blood
Innocence is no earthly weapon.

> **Geoffrey Hill** 1932– English poet: 'Ovid in the Third Reich' (1968)

7 Never such innocence,
Never before or since,
As changed itself to past
Without a word—the men
Leaving the gardens tidy,
The thousands of marriages
Lasting a little while longer:
Never such innocence again.

> **Philip Larkin** 1922–85 English poet: 'MCMXIV' (1964)

8 To the Puritan all things are impure, as somebody says.

> **D. H. Lawrence** 1885–1930 English novelist and poet: *Etruscan Places* (1932)

9 We are stardust,
We are golden,
And we got to get ourselves

Back to the garden.
Joni Mitchell 1945– Canadian singer
and songwriter: 'Woodstock'
(1969 song)

10 I'd the upbringing a nun would
envy . . . Until I was fifteen I was
more familiar with Africa than my
own body.
Joe Orton 1933–67 English dramatist:
Entertaining Mr Sloane (1964)

11 The innocent and the beautiful
Have no enemy but time.
W. B. Yeats 1865–1939 Irish poet: 'In
Memory of Eva Gore Booth and Con
Markiewicz' (1933)

Insight

see also SELF-KNOWLEDGE

1 The world is like a Mask dancing. If
you want to see it well you do not
stand in one place.
Chinua Achebe 1930– Nigerian
novelist: *Arrow of God* (1988)

2 If the doors of perception were
cleansed everything would appear to
man as it is, infinite.
William Blake 1757–1827 English poet:
The Marriage of Heaven and Hell
(1790–3)

3 Know what I mean, Harry?
Frank Bruno 1961– English boxer:
supposed to have been said in interview
with sports commentator Harry
Carpenter, possibly apocryphal

4 One sees great things from the valley;
only small things from the peak.
G. K. Chesterton 1874–1936 English
essayist, novelist, and poet: *The
Innocence of Father Brown* (1911)

5 If we had a keen vision and feeling of
all ordinary human life, it would be
like hearing the grass grow and the
squirrel's heart beat, and we should

die of that roar which lies on the
other side of silence.
George Eliot 1819–80 English novelist:
Middlemarch (1871–2)

6 The crown of life is neither
happiness nor annihilation; it is
understanding.
Winifred Holtby 1898–1935 British
novelist and journalist: Vera Brittain
Testament of Friendship (1940)

7 Deprivation is for me what daffodils
were for Wordsworth.
Philip Larkin 1922–85 English poet:
Required Writing (1983)

8 Come to the edge.
We might fall.
Come to the edge.
It's too high!
COME TO THE EDGE!
And they came
and he pushed
and they flew . . .
on Apollinaire
Christopher Logue 1926– English
poet: 'Come to the edge' (1969)

9 The fact that for a long time Cubism
has not been understood and that
even today there are people who
cannot see anything in it, means
nothing. I do not read English, an
English book is a blank book to me.
This does not mean that the English
language does not exist.
Pablo Picasso 1881–1973 Spanish
painter: interview with Marius de Zayas,
1923

10 He—in whose nature, is the ugly
disposition
Sees not the peacock,—only his ugly
foot.
Sadi *c.*1213–91 Persian poet: *The Bustan*
(1257)

11 It is only with the heart that one can
see rightly; what is essential is
invisible to the eye.
> **Antoine de Saint-Exupéry** 1900–44
> French novelist: *Le Petit Prince* (1943)

12 Each had but known one part, and
no man all;
Hence into deadly error each did fall.
No way to know the All man's heart
can find:
Can knowledge e'er accompany the
blind?
> *on blind men's conclusions on touching*
> *different parts of an elephant*
> **Sana'i** d. *c.*1131 Persian poet: 'The Blind
> Men and the Elephant'

13 I have striven not to laugh at human
actions, not to weep at them, nor to
hate them, but to understand them.
> **Baruch Spinoza** 1632–77 Dutch
> philosopher: *Tractatus Politicus* (1677)

14 *Tout comprendre rend très indulgent.*
To be totally understanding makes
one very indulgent.
> **Mme de Staël** 1766–1817 French writer:
> *Corinne* (1807)

15 Everything I have written seems like
straw by comparison with what I
have seen and what has been
revealed to me.
> *following a mystical experience, after*
> *which he did no more teaching or writing*
> **St Thomas Aquinas** 1225–74 Italian
> Dominican theologian: on 6 December
> 1273

16 The only people who remain
misunderstood are those who either
do not know what they want or are
not worth understanding.
> **Ivan Turgenev** 1818–83 Russian
> novelist: *Rudin* (1856)

Insults

1 I think I detect sarcasm. I can't be
doing with sarcasm. You know what
they say? Sarcasm is the greatest
weapon of the smallest mind.
> **Alan Ayckbourn** 1939– English
> dramatist: *Woman in Mind* (1986)

2 An injury is much sooner forgotten
than an insult.
> **Lord Chesterfield** 1694–1773 English
> writer and politician: *Letters to his Son*
> (1774) 9 October 1746

3 How easy it is to call rogue and
villain, and that wittily! But how hard
to make a man appear a fool, a
blockhead, or a knave, without using
any of those opprobrious terms! To
spare the grossness of the names,
and to do the thing yet more
severely, is to draw a full face, and to
make the nose and cheeks stand out,
and yet not to employ any depth of
shadowing.
> **John Dryden** 1631–1700 English poet,
> critic, and dramatist: *Of Satire* (1693)

4 Like being savaged by a dead sheep.
> *on being criticized by Geoffrey Howe*
> **Denis Healey** 1917– British Labour
> politician: speech in the House of
> Commons, 14 June 1978

5 I decided the worst thing you can call
Paul Keating, quite frankly, is Paul
Keating.
> **John Hewson** 1946– Australian Liberal
> politician: Michael Gordon *A Question*
> *of Leadership* (1993)

6 This little flower, this delicate little
beauty, this cream puff, is supposed
to be beyond personal criticism . . .
He is simply a shiver looking for a
spine to run up.
> *of John Hewson*
> **Paul Keating** 1944– Australian Labor
> statesman: attributed

7 Curse the blasted, jelly-boned
swines, the slimy, the belly-wriggling
invertebrates, the miserable sodding
rotters, the flaming sods, the

snivelling, dribbling, dithering, palsied, pulse-less lot that make up England today. They've got white of egg in their veins, and their spunk is that watery it's a marvel they can breed. They *can* nothing but frog-spawn—the gibberers! God, how I hate them!

D. H. Lawrence 1885–1930 English novelist and poet: letter to Edward Garnett, 3 July 1912

8 The devil damn thee black, thou cream-faced loon!
Where gott'st thou that goose look?

William Shakespeare 1564–1616 English dramatist: *Macbeth* (1606)

9 Silence is the most perfect expression of scorn.

George Bernard Shaw 1856–1950 Irish dramatist: *Back to Methuselah* (1921)

10 JUDGE: You are extremely offensive, young man.
SMITH: As a matter of fact, we both are, and the only difference between us is that I am trying to be, and you can't help it.

F. E. Smith 1872–1930 British Conservative politician and lawyer: 2nd Earl of Birkenhead *Earl of Birkenhead* (1933)

11 Okie use' ta mean you was from Oklahoma. Now it means you're a dirty son-of-a-bitch. Okie means you're scum. Don't mean nothing itself, it's the way they say it.

John Steinbeck 1902–68 American novelist: *The Grapes of Wrath* (1939)

Intellectuals

1 To the man-in-the-street, who, I'm sorry to say,
Is a keen observer of life,
The word 'Intellectual' suggests straight away

A man who's untrue to his wife.

W. H. Auden 1907–73 English poet: *New Year Letter* (1941)

2 *La trahison des clercs.*

The treachery of the intellectuals.

Julien Benda 1867–1956 French philosopher and novelist: title of book (1927)

3 An intellectual is someone whose mind watches itself.

Albert Camus 1913–60 French novelist, dramatist, and essayist: *Carnets, 1935–42* (1962)

4 'Hullo! friend,' I call out, 'Won't you lend us a hand?' 'I am an intellectual and don't drag wood about,' came the answer. 'You're lucky,' I reply. 'I too wanted to become an intellectual, but I didn't succeed.'

Albert Schweitzer 1875–1965 Franco-German missionary: *Mitteilungen aus Lambarene* (1928)

5 What is a highbrow? He is a man who has found something more interesting than women.

Edgar Wallace 1875–1932 English thriller writer: in *New York Times* 24 January 1932

6 I know I've got a degree. Why does that mean I have to spend my life with intellectuals? I've got a life-saving certificate but I don't spend my evenings diving for a rubber brick with my pyjamas on.

Victoria Wood 1953– British writer and comedienne: *Mens Sana in Thingummy Doodah* (1990)

Intelligence

1 It takes little talent to see clearly what lies under one's nose, a good deal of it to know in which direction to point that organ.

W. H. Auden 1907–73 English poet: *The Dyer's Hand* (1963)

2 He [Hercule Poirot] tapped his forehead. 'These little grey cells. It is "up to them".'

> **Agatha Christie** 1890–1976 English writer of detective fiction: *The Mysterious Affair at Styles* (1920)

3 'Excellent,' I cried. 'Elementary,' said he.

> **Arthur Conan Doyle** 1859–1930 Scottish-born writer of detective fiction: *The Memoirs of Sherlock Holmes* (1894); 'Elementary, my dear Watson' is not found in any book by Conan Doyle, but is first found in P. G. Wodehouse *Psmith Journalist* (1915)

4 As a human being, one has been endowed with just enough intelligence to be able to see clearly how utterly inadequate that intelligence is when confronted with what exists.

> **Albert Einstein** 1879–1955 German-born theoretical physicist: letter to Queen Elisabeth of Belgium, 19 September 1932

5 The test of a first-rate intelligence is the ability to hold two opposed ideas in the mind at the same time, and still retain the ability to function.

> **F. Scott Fitzgerald** 1896–1940 American novelist: in *Esquire* February 1936, 'The Crack-Up'

6 The clever men at Oxford
Know all that there is to be knowed.
But they none of them know one half as much
As intelligent Mr Toad!

> **Kenneth Grahame** 1859–1932 Scottish-born writer: *Wind in the Willows* (1908)

7 Sir, I have found you an argument; but I am not obliged to find you an understanding.

> **Samuel Johnson** 1709–84 English poet, critic, and lexicographer: James Boswell *Life of Samuel Johnson* (1791) June 1784

8 No one in this world, so far as I know—and I have searched the records for years, and employed agents to help me—has ever lost money by underestimating the intelligence of the great masses of the plain people.

> **H. L. Mencken** 1880–1956 American journalist and literary critic: in *Chicago Tribune* 19 September 1926

9 You beat your pate, and fancy wit will come:
Knock as you please, there's nobody at home.

> **Alexander Pope** 1688–1744 English poet: 'Epigram: You beat your pate' (1732)

10 Intelligence is quickness to apprehend as distinct from ability, which is capacity to act wisely on the thing apprehended.

> **Alfred North Whitehead** 1861–1947 English philosopher and mathematician: *Dialogues* (1954) 15 December 1939

International Relations

see also DIPLOMACY, GOVERNMENT, POLITICS

1 Palestine is the cement that holds the Arab world together, or it is the explosive that blows it apart.

> **Yasser Arafat** 1929–2004 Palestinian statesman: in *Time* 11 November 1974

2 Nations touch at their summits.

> **Walter Bagehot** 1826–77 English economist and essayist: *The English Constitution* (1867)

3 Since the day of the air, the old frontiers are gone. When you think of the defence of England you no longer think of the chalk cliffs of Dover; you think of the Rhine. That is where our frontier lies.

> **Stanley Baldwin** 1867–1947 British Conservative statesman: speech, House of Commons, 30 July 1934

4 Alliance is not allegiance.
on Europe's relations with America
　Michel Barnier 1951– French
　politician: in *Independent* 29 October
　2004

5 [Winston Churchill] does not talk the
language of the 20th century but that
of the 18th. He is still fighting
Blenheim all over again. His only
answer to a difficult situation is send
a gun-boat.
　Aneurin Bevan 1897–1960 British
　Labour politician: speech at Labour
　Party Conference, Scarborough,
　2 October 1951

6 If you carry this resolution you will
send Britain's Foreign Secretary
naked into the conference chamber.
*on a motion proposing unilateral nuclear
disarmament by the UK*
　Aneurin Bevan 1897–1960 British
　Labour politician: speech at Labour
　Party Conference in Brighton, 3 October
　1957

7 My [foreign] policy is to be able to
take a ticket at Victoria Station and
go anywhere I damn well please.
　Ernest Bevin 1881–1951 British Labour
　politician and trade unionist: in
　Spectator 20 April 1951

8 This policy cannot succeed through
speeches, and shooting-matches,
and songs; it can only be carried out
through blood and iron.
　Otto von Bismarck 1815–98 German
　statesman: speech in the Prussian
　House of Deputies, 28 January 1886

9 Red China is not the powerful nation
seeking to dominate the world.
Frankly, in the opinion of the Joint
Chiefs of Staff, this strategy would
involve us in the wrong war, at the
wrong place, at the wrong time, and
with the wrong enemy.
　Omar Bradley 1893–1981 American
　general: *US Cong. Senate Comm. on
　Armed Services* (1951)

10 States like these . . . constitute an
axis of evil, arming to threaten the
peace of this world.
of Iraq, Iran, and North Korea
　George W. Bush 1946– American
　Republican statesman: State of the
　Union address, in *Newsweek*
　11 February 2002

11 The day of small nations has long
passed away. The day of Empires has
come.
　Joseph Chamberlain 1836–1914 British
　Liberal politician: speech at
　Birmingham, 12 May 1904

12 If Hitler invaded hell I would make at
least a favourable reference to the
devil in the House of Commons.
　Winston Churchill 1874–1965 British
　Conservative statesman: *The Second
　World War* (1950) vol. 3

13 Excessive dealings with tyrants are
not good for the security of free
states.
　Demosthenes *c.*384–*c.*322 BC Greek
　orator and Athenian statesman: *Second
　Philippic*

14 We do not tilt on either side . . . we
walk upright.
*when asked by a reporter why India
'always tilted towards the Soviet Union'*
　Indira Gandhi 1917–84 Indian
　stateswoman: in Washington, 1982;
　Inder Malhotra *Indira Gandhi* (1989)

15 The clash of civilizations and the
remaking of world order.
　Samuel Huntington 1927–2008
　American political scientist: title of
　book, 1996, expanding a theory
　originally introduced in an article 'The
　Clash of Civilizations?' in *Foreign Affairs*
　Summer 1993

16 Peace, commerce, and honest
friendship with all
nations—entangling alliances with
none.
　Thomas Jefferson 1743–1826 American

Democratic Republican statesman:
inaugural address, 4 March 1801

17 We hope that the world will not
narrow into a neighbourhood before
it has broadened into a brotherhood.
Lyndon Baines Johnson 1908–73
American Democratic statesman:
speech at the lighting of the Nation's
Christmas Tree, 22 December 1963

18 *Ich bin ein Berliner.*
I am a Berliner.
*expressing US commitment to the support
and defence of West Berlin*
John F. Kennedy 1917–63 American
Democratic statesman: speech in West
Berlin, 26 June 1963

19 The great nations have always acted
like gangsters, and the small nations
like prostitutes.
Stanley Kubrick 1928–99 American film
director: in *Guardian* 5 June 1963

20 [The Commonwealth] is a largely
meaningless relic of Empire—like
the smile on the face of the Cheshire
Cat which remains when the cat has
disappeared.
Nigel Lawson 1932– British
Conservative politician: attributed,
1993

21 We face neither East nor West: we
face forward.
Kwame Nkrumah 1900–72 Ghanaian
statesman: conference speech, Accra,
7 April 1960

22 Whatever it is that the government
does, sensible Americans would
prefer that the government does it to
somebody else. This is the idea
behind foreign policy.
P. J. O'Rourke 1947– American
humorous writer: *Parliament of Whores*
(1991)

23 We have no eternal allies and we
have no perpetual enemies. Our
interests are eternal and perpetual,
and those interests it is our duty to
follow.
Lord Palmerston 1784–1865 British
statesman: speech, House of Commons,
1 March 1848

24 In the field of world policy I would
dedicate this Nation to the policy of
the good neighbour.
Franklin D. Roosevelt 1882–1945
American Democratic statesman:
inaugural address, 4 March 1933

25 Living next to you is in some ways
like sleeping with an elephant. No
matter how friendly and even-
tempered the beast, one is affected
by every twitch and grunt.
on relations between Canada and the US
Pierre Trudeau 1919–2000 Canadian
Liberal statesman: speech at National
Press Club, Washington DC, 25 March
1969

26 Armed neutrality is ineffectual
enough at best.
Woodrow Wilson 1856–1924 American
Democratic statesman: speech to
Congress, 2 April 1917

The Internet

see also COMPUTERS

1 There is a great danger that it
becomes a place where untruths
start to spread more than truths.
*on the future of the Internet if left to
develop unchecked*
Tim Berners-Lee 1955– English
computer scientist: in *Guardian*
3 November 2006

2 Google is white bread for the mind.
Tara Brabazon 1969– Australian
academic: title of inaugural lecture at
the University of Brighton, 16 January
2008

3 The Internet is an elite organisation; most of the population of the world has never even made a phone call.

> **Noam Chomsky** 1928– American linguistics scholar: in *Observer* 18 February 1996

4 The email of the species is deadlier than the mail.

> **Stephen Fry** 1957– English comedian, actor, and writer: in *Sunday Telegraph* 23 December 2001

5 On the Internet, nobody knows you're a dog.

> **Peter Steiner** 1940– American cartoonist: cartoon caption in *New Yorker* 5 July 1993

6 We've all heard that a million monkeys banging on a million typewriters will eventually reproduce the entire works of Shakespeare. Now, thanks to the Internet, we know this is not true.

> **Robert Wilensky** 1951– American academic: in *Mail on Sunday* 16 February 1997 'Quotes of the Week'; see CHANCE 2

Inventions and Discoveries

see also SCIENCE, TECHNOLOGY

1 When man wanted to make a machine that would walk he created the wheel, which does not resemble a leg.

> **Guillaume Apollinaire** 1880–1918 French poet: *Les Mamelles de Tirésias* (1918)

2 *Eureka!*
I've got it!

> **Archimedes** *c.*287–212 BC Greek mathematician and inventor: Vitruvius Pollio *De Architectura*

3 The discovery of a new dish does more for human happiness than the discovery of a star.

> **Anthelme Brillat-Savarin** 1755–1826 French jurist and gourmet: *Physiologie du Goût* (1826)

4 Thus first necessity invented stools,
Convenience next suggested elbow-chairs,
And luxury the accomplished sofa last.

> **William Cowper** 1731–1800 English poet: *The Task* (1785) 'The Sofa'

5 It's true that by blundering about, we stumbled on gold, but the fact remains that we were looking for gold.

> *of the discovery of the structure of DNA*
> **Francis Crick** 1916–2004 English biophysicist: *What Mad Pursuit* (1988)

6 After the idea, there is plenty of time to learn the technology.

> **James Dyson** 1947– English inventor and businessman: *Against the Odds* (1997)

7 For most of my life I refused to work at any problem unless its solution seemed to be capable of being put to commercial use.

> **Thomas Alva Edison** 1847–1931 American inventor: interview, in *New York Sun* February 1917

8 The unleashed power of the atom has changed everything save our modes of thinking and we thus drift toward unparalleled catastrophe.

> **Albert Einstein** 1879–1955 German-born theoretical physicist: telegram to prominent Americans, 24 May 1946

9 Why sir, there is every possibility that you will soon be able to tax it!

> *to Gladstone, when asked about the usefulness of electricity*
> **Michael Faraday** 1791–1867 English physicist and chemist: W. E. H. Lecky *Democracy and Liberty* (1899 ed.)

10 Whatever Nature has in store for mankind, unpleasant as it may be, men must accept, for ignorance is never better than knowledge.

> **Enrico Fermi** 1901–54 Italian-born American atomic physicist: Laura Fermi *Atoms in the Family* (1955)

11 What is the use of a new-born child?

when asked what was the use of a new invention

> **Benjamin Franklin** 1706–90 American politician, inventor, and scientist: J. Parton *Life and Times of Benjamin Franklin* (1864)

12 SALVIATI: Now you see how easy it is to understand.

SAGREDO: So are all truths, once they are discovered.

often quoted as 'All truths are easy to understand, once they are discovered; the point is, to discover them'

> **Galileo Galilei** 1564–1642 Italian astronomer and physicist: *Dialogue Concerning the two Chief World Systems* (1632)

13 My reflection, when I first made myself master of the central idea of the 'Origin', was, How extremely stupid not to have thought of that!

> **T. H. Huxley** 1825–95 English biologist: 'On the Reception of the "Origin of Species"' in F. Darwin *Life and Letters of Charles Darwin* vol. 2 (1888)

14 Nothing is more contrary to the organization of the mind, of the memory, and of the imagination . . . It's just tormenting the people with trivia!!!

on the introduction of the metric system

> **Napoleon I** 1769–1821 French emperor: *Mémoires . . . écrits à Ste-Hélène* (1823–5)

15 praise without end the go-ahead zeal of whoever it was invented the wheel;
but never a word for the poor soul's sake

that thought ahead, and invented the brake.

> **Howard Nemerov** 1920–91 American poet and novelist: 'To the Congress of the United States, Entering Its Third Century' 26 February 1989

16 I don't know what I may seem to the world, but as to myself, I seem to have been only like a boy playing on the sea-shore and diverting myself in now and then finding a smoother pebble or a prettier shell than ordinary, whilst the great ocean of truth lay all undiscovered before me.

> **Isaac Newton** 1642–1727 English mathematician and physicist: Joseph Spence *Anecdotes* (ed. J. Osborn, 1966)

17 The Patent Office is the gatekeeper to the new age.

> **Tom Stoppard** 1937– British dramatist: *The Invention of Love* (1997)

18 Discovery consists of seeing what everybody has seen and thinking what nobody has thought.

> **Albert von Szent-Györgyi** 1893–1986 Hungarian-born biochemist: Irving Good (ed.) *The Scientist Speculates* (1962)

19 Name the greatest of all the inventors. Accident.

> **Mark Twain** 1835–1910 American writer: *Notebook* (1935)

Iraq War

1 If this is not civil war, then God knows what civil war is.

> **Iyad Allawi** 1945– Iraqi statesman: interview on BBC Television *Sunday AM*, 19 March 2006

2 Downing Street's dodgy dossier of 'intelligence' about Iraq.

referring to a briefing document on Iraqi weaponry which was later withdrawn

> **Anonymous**: leading article, in *Observer* 9 February 2003

3 This is not the time to falter.
> **Tony Blair** 1953– British Labour statesman: speech in the House of Commons, 18 March 2003

4 We have not found any smoking guns.
> *of weapons inspections in Iraq*
> **Hans Blix** 1928– Swedish diplomat: in *Newsweek* 20 January 2003

5 I expect you to rock their world. Wipe them out if that is what they choose. But if you are ferocious in battle remember to be magnanimous in victory.
> **Tim Collins** 1960– British soldier: speech to the men under his command on arrival in Iraq, 20 March 2003

6 They found more dangerous chemicals in Coca-Cola's Dasani mineral water than they did in the whole of Iraq.
> **Robin Cook** 1946–2005 British Labour politician: speaking at the Edinburgh Book Festival, in *Observer* 29 August 2004

7 This will be a campaign unlike any other in history. A campaign characterized by shock, by surprise, by flexibility, by the employment of precise munitions on a scale never before seen, and by the application of overwhelming force.
> *encapsulated in the phrase 'shock and awe', originally deriving from a Pentagon briefing document of 1996 by Harlan Ullman and James P. Wade*
> **Tommy Franks** 1945– American general: briefing in Qatar, 22 March 2003

8 My son was just a piece of meat to them, just a number.
> *on the politicians who sent her son to his death in Iraq*
> **Rose Gentle** Scottish mother: in *Mail on Sunday* 4 July 2004

9 I have spoken to a British official who was involved in the preparation of the dossier, and he told me that until the week before it was published, the draft dossier produced by the intelligence services added little to what was already publicly known. He said: [Voiceover]: 'It was transformed in the week before it was published, to make it sexier'.
> **Andrew Gilligan** 1968– British journalist: BBC Radio 4 *Today* programme, 29 May 2003; in *Guardian* 27 June 2003

10 Baghdad is determined to force the Mongols of our age to commit suicide at its gates.
> **Saddam Hussein** 1937–2006 Iraqi statesman: in *Independent* 18 January 2003

11 I hope in my heart that one day the Prime Minister will be able to say sorry, that one day he will say sorry to the families of the bereaved.
> *the father of a soldier killed in Iraq, in a speech after losing to Tony Blair in the 2005 general election*
> **Reg Keys** 1952– British father: in *Mail on Sunday* 8 May 2005

12 The enemy we're fighting is a bit different than the one we war-gamed against.
> *of the campaign in Iraq*
> **William Wallace** American general: in *New York Times* 28 March 2003

Ireland

see also NORTHERN IRELAND

1 Do you not feel that this island is moored only lightly to the sea-bed, and might be off for the Americas at any moment?
> **Sebastian Barry** 1955– Irish writer and dramatist: *Prayers of Sherkin* (1991)

2 I could wish that the English kept history in mind more, that the Irish kept it in mind less.

> **Elizabeth Bowen** 1899–1973 Anglo-Irish novelist: 'Notes on Eire' 9 November 1949

3 For the great Gaels of Ireland
Are the men that God made mad,
For all their wars are merry,
And all their songs are sad.

> **G. K. Chesterton** 1874–1936 English essayist, novelist, and poet: *The Ballad of the White Horse* (1911)

4 Don't be surprised
If I demur, for, be advised
My passport's green.
No glass of ours was ever raised
To toast *The Queen*.
rebuking the editors of The Penguin Book of Contemporary British Poetry *for including him among its authors*

> **Seamus Heaney** 1939– Irish poet: *Open Letter* (1983)

5 Ireland is the old sow that eats her farrow.

> **James Joyce** 1882–1941 Irish novelist: *A Portrait of the Artist as a Young Man* (1916)

6 Ireland was contented when
All could use the sword and pen,
And when Tara rose so high
That her turrets split the sky.

> **Walter Savage Landor** 1775–1864 English poet: 'Ireland never was contented' (1853)

7 In Ireland the inevitable never happens and the unexpected constantly occurs.

> **John Pentland Mahaffy** 1839–1919 Irish writer: W. B. Stanford and R. B. McDowell *Mahaffy* (1971)

8 I'm Irish. We think sideways.

> **Spike Milligan** 1918–2002 Irish comedian: in *Independent on Sunday* 20 June 1999

9 Spenser's Ireland
has not altered;—
a place as kind as it is green,
the greenest place I've never seen.

> **Marianne Moore** 1887–1972 American poet: 'Spenser's Ireland' (1941)

10 God made the grass, the air and the rain; and the grass, the air and the rain made the Irish; and the Irish turned the grass, the air and the rain back into God.

> **Sean O'Faolain** 1900–91 Irish writer: in *Holiday* June 1958

11 The moment the very name of Ireland is mentioned, the English seem to bid adieu to common feeling, common prudence, and common sense, and to act with the barbarity of tyrants, and the fatuity of idiots.

> **Sydney Smith** 1771–1845 English clergyman and essayist: *Letters of Peter Plymley* (1807)

12 Out of Ireland have we come.
Great hatred, little room,
Maimed us at the start.

> **W. B. Yeats** 1865–1939 Irish poet: 'Remorse for Intemperate Speech' (1933)

Italy

see also VENICE

1 While stands the Coliseum, Rome shall stand;
When falls the Coliseum, Rome shall fall;
And when Rome falls—the World.

> **Lord Byron** 1788–1824 English poet: *Childe Harold's Pilgrimage* (1812–18)

2 The traveller who has gone to Italy to study the tactile values of Giotto, or the corruption of the Papacy, may return remembering nothing but the blue sky and the men and women under it.

> **E. M. Forster** 1879–1970 English novelist: *A Room with a View* (1908)

3 Italy is a geographical expression.
discussing the Italian question with Palmerston in 1847

> **Prince Metternich** 1773–1859 Austrian statesman: *Mémoires, Documents, etc. de Metternich publiés par son fils* (1883)

4 Lump the whole thing! say that the Creator made Italy from designs by Michael Angelo!

> **Mark Twain** 1835–1910 American writer: *The Innocents Abroad* (1869)

Jazz

1 If you still have to ask . . . shame on you.
when asked what jazz is; sometimes quoted as, 'Man, if you gotta ask you'll never know'

> **Louis Armstrong** 1901–71 American singer and jazz musician: Max Jones et al. *Salute to Satchmo* (1970)

2 Jazz is the only music in which the same note can be played night after night but differently each time.

> **Ornette Coleman** 1930– American jazz musician: W. H. Mellers *Music in a New Found Land* (1964)

3 Playing 'Bop' is like scrabble with all the vowels missing.

> **Duke Ellington** 1899–1974 American jazz musician: in *Look* 10 August 1954

4 A jazz musician is a juggler who uses harmonies instead of oranges.

> **Benny Green** 1927– : *The Reluctant Art* (1962)

5 If you're in jazz and more than ten people like you, you're labelled commercial.

> **Herbie Mann** 1930– American jazz

musician: Henry Pleasants *Serious Music and All That Jazz!* (1969)

6 It don't mean a thing
If it ain't got that swing.

> **Irving Mills** 1894–1985: 'It Don't Mean a Thing' (1932 song; music by Duke Ellington)

7 Jazz music is to be played sweet, soft, plenty rhythm.

> **Jelly Roll Morton** 1885–1941 American jazz musician: *Mister Jelly Roll* (1950)

8 What a terrible revenge by the culture of the Negroes on that of the whites!

> **Ignacy Jan Paderewski** 1860–1941 Polish pianist, composer, and statesman: attributed

9 Jazz will endure, just as long as people hear it through their feet instead of their brains.

> **John Philip Sousa** 1854–1932 American composer and conductor: attributed

Jealousy

see also ENVY

1 Love is strong as death; jealousy is cruel as the grave.

> **Bible**: Song of Solomon

2 Jealousy is no more than feeling alone against smiling enemies.

> **Elizabeth Bowen** 1899–1973 Anglo-Irish novelist: *The House in Paris* (1935)

3 As we all know from witnessing the consuming jealousy of husbands who are never faithful, people do not confine themselves to the emotions to which they are entitled.

> **Quentin Crisp** 1908–99 English writer: *The Naked Civil Servant* (1968)

4 Jealousy is all the fun you *think* they had.

> **Erica Jong** 1942– American novelist: *How to Save Your Own Life* (1977)

5 Though jealousy be produced by love, as ashes are by fire, yet jealousy extinguishes love as ashes smother the flame.

Marguerite d'Angoulême 1492–1549 French writer: *The Heptameron* (1558)

6 To jealousy, nothing is more frightful than laughter.

Françoise Sagan 1935–2004 French novelist: *La Chamade* (1965)

7   Trifles light as air
Are to the jealous confirmations strong
As proofs of holy writ.

William Shakespeare 1564–1616 English dramatist: *Othello* (1602–4)

Journalism

see also NEWS, NEWSPAPERS, PRESS PHOTOGRAPHERS

1 Anyone here been raped and speaks English?

shouted by a British TV reporter in a crowd of Belgian civilians waiting to be airlifted out of the Belgian Congo, c.1960

Anonymous: Edward Behr *Anyone Here been Raped and Speaks English?* (1981)

2 When seagulls follow a trawler, it is because they think sardines will be thrown into the sea.

Eric Cantona 1966– French footballer: to the media at the end of a press conference, 31 March 1995

3 Journalism largely consists in saying 'Lord Jones Dead' to people who never knew that Lord Jones was alive.

G. K. Chesterton 1874–1936 English essayist, novelist, and poet: *Wisdom of Father Brown* (1914)

4 When the legend becomes fact, print the legend.

Willis Goldbeck and **James Warner Bellah** American screenwriters: *The Man who Shot Liberty Valance* (1962 film); see also HEROES 10

5 Go to where the silence is and say something.

accepting an award from Columbia University for her coverage of the 1991 massacre in East Timor by Indonesian troops

Amy Goodman 1957– American journalist: in *Columbia Journalism Review* March/April 1994

6 You furnish the pictures and I'll furnish the war.

message to the artist Frederic Remington in Havana, Cuba, during the Spanish-American War of 1898

William Randolph Hearst 1863–1951 American newspaper publisher: attributed

7 There is one sacred rule of journalism. The writer must not invent. The legend on the licence must read: *None* OF THIS WAS MADE UP.

John Richard Hersey 1914–93 American journalist and novelist: 'The Legend on the Licence' in *Yale Review* vol. 70, 1980

8 A journalist is stimulated by a deadline. He writes worse when he has time.

Karl Kraus 1874–1936 Austrian satirist: *Pro Domo et Mundo* (1912)

9 Listen folks, I'm going to have to stop for a minute, because I've lost my voice—This is the worst thing I've ever witnessed.

eyewitness account of the Hindenburg disaster

Herbert 'Herb' Morrison d. 1989 American radio announcer: recorded broadcast, 6 May 1937

10 Under the modern journalist's code of Olympian objectivity (and total purity of motive), I am absolved of responsibility. We journalists don't have to step on roaches. All we have to do is turn on the kitchen light and watch the critters scurry.

> **P. J. O'Rourke** 1947– American humorous writer: *Parliament of Whores* (1991)

11 Journalists belong in the gutter because that is where the ruling classes throw their guilty secrets.

> **Gerald Priestland** 1927–91 English writer and journalist: in *Observer* 22 May 1988

12 A cynical, mercenary, demagogic, corrupt press will produce in time a people as base as itself.

> **Joseph Pulitzer** 1847–1911 Hungarian-born American newspaper proprietor: inscribed on the gateway to the Columbia School of Journalism in New York

13 The men with the muck-rakes are often indispensable to the well-being of society; but only if they know when to stop raking the muck.

> **Theodore Roosevelt** 1858–1919 American Republican statesman: speech in Washington, 14 April 1906

14 Comment is free, but facts are sacred.

> **C. P. Scott** 1846–1932 British journalist: in *Manchester Guardian* 5 May 1921; see JOURNALISM 15

15 Comment is free but facts are on expenses.

> **Tom Stoppard** 1937– British dramatist: *Night and Day* (1978); see JOURNALISM 14

16 All newspaper and journalistic activity is an intellectual brothel from which there is no retreat.

> **Leo Tolstoy** 1828–1910 Russian novelist: letter to Prince V. P. Meshchersky, 22 August 1871

17 There are laws to protect the freedom of the press's speech, but none that are worth anything to protect the people from the press.

> **Mark Twain** 1835–1910 American writer: 'License of the Press' (1873)

18 Journalism—an ability to meet the challenge of filling the space.

> **Rebecca West** 1892–1983 English novelist and journalist: in *New York Herald Tribune* 22 April 1956

19 You cannot hope
to bribe or twist,
thank God! the
British journalist.
But, seeing what
the man will do
unbribed, there's
no occasion to.

> **Humbert Wolfe** 1886–1940 British poet: 'Over the Fire' (1930)

20 Rock journalism is people who can't write interviewing people who can't talk for people who can't read.

> **Frank Zappa** 1940–93 American rock musician and songwriter: Linda Botts *Loose Talk* (1980)

Justice

see also LAWS, LAWYERS

1 If it falls to me to start a fight to cut out the cancer of bent and twisted journalism in our country with the simple sword of truth and the trusty shield of British fair play, so be it.

> **Jonathan Aitken** 1942– British Conservative politician: statement, London, 10 April 1995

2 *Jedem das Seine.*
To each his own.
often quoted as 'Everyone gets what he deserves'

> **Anonymous**: inscription on the gate of Buchenwald concentration camp, *c.* 1937; see GENOCIDE 2

3 Publicity is the very soul of justice. It is the keenest spur to exertion, and

the surest of all guards against improbity.

> **Jeremy Bentham** 1748–1832 English philosopher: *Publicity in the Courts of Justice* (1843)

4 Life for life,
Eye for eye, tooth for tooth.

> **Bible**: Exodus

5 It is better that ten guilty persons escape than one innocent suffer.

> **William Blackstone** 1723–80 English jurist: *Commentaries on the Laws of England* (1765)

6 When I hear of an 'equity' in a case like this, I am reminded of a blind man in a dark room—looking for a black hat—which isn't there.

> **Lord Bowen** 1835–94 English judge: John Alderson Foote *Pie-Powder* (1911)

7 Justice is truth in action.

> **Benjamin Disraeli** 1804–81 British Tory statesman and novelist: speech, House of Commons, 11 February 1851

8 *Fiat justitia et pereat mundus.*
Let justice be done, though the world perish.

> **Ferdinand I** 1503–64 Holy Roman Emperor: motto; Johannes Manlius *Locorum Communium Collectanea* (1563)

9   Once in a lifetime
The longed-for tidal wave
Of justice can rise up,
And hope and history rhyme.

> **Seamus Heaney** 1939– Irish poet: *The Cure at Troy* (1990)

10 A long line of cases shows that it is not merely of some importance, but is of fundamental importance that justice should not only be done, but should manifestly and undoubtedly be seen to be done.

> **Gordon Hewart** 1870–1943 British lawyer and politician: Rex v Sussex Justices, 9 November 1923

11 Injustice anywhere is a threat to justice everywhere.

> **Martin Luther King** 1929–68 American civil rights leader: letter from Birmingham Jail, Alabama, 16 April 1963

12 I have always found that mercy bears richer fruits than strict justice.

> **Abraham Lincoln** 1809–65 American statesman: remark to Joseph Gillespie, in letter from Gillespie to *Herald and Torch Light* [Hagerstown, MD] 15 March 1876

13 To no man will we sell, or deny, or delay, right or justice.

> **Magna Carta** 1215 Political charter signed by King John: clause 40

14 In England, justice is open to all—like the Ritz Hotel.

> **James Mathew** 1830–1908 Irish judge: R. E. Megarry *Miscellany-at-Law* (1955)

15 Injustice is relatively easy to bear; what stings is justice.

> **H. L. Mencken** 1880–1956 American journalist and literary critic: *Prejudices, Third Series* (1922)

16 The arc of history is long but it bends towards justice.

> **Barack Obama** 1961– American Democratic statesman: speech, George Mason University, 2 February 2007

17 What I say is that 'just' or 'right' means nothing but what is in the interest of the stronger party.
spoken by Thrasymachus

> **Plato** 429–347 BC Greek philosopher: *The Republic*

18 *J'accuse.*
I accuse.
on the Dreyfus affair

> **Émile Zola** 1840–1902 French novelist: title of an open letter to the President of the French Republic in *L'Aurore* 13 January 1898

Kissing

1 A kiss is a lovely trick designed by nature to stop speech when words become superfluous.
   Ingrid Bergman 1915–82 Swedish actress: attributed

2 But indeed, dear, these kisses on paper are scarce worth keeping. You gave me one on my neck that night you were in such good-humour, and one on my lips on some forgotten occasion, that I would not part with for a hundred thousand paper ones.
   Jane Carlyle 1801–66 wife of Thomas Carlyle: letter to Thomas Carlyle, 3 October 1826

3 *when asked what it was like to kiss Marilyn Monroe:*
   It's like kissing Hitler.
   Tony Curtis 1925– American actor: A. Hunter *Tony Curtis* (1985)

4 A fine romance with no kisses.
   A fine romance, my friend, this is.
   Dorothy Fields 1905–74 American songwriter: 'A Fine Romance' (1936 song)

5 To let a fool kiss you is stupid,
   To let a kiss fool you is worse.
   E. Y. Harburg 1898–1981 American songwriter: 'Inscriptions on a Lipstick' (1965)

6 Where do the noses go? I always wondered where the noses would go.
   Ernest Hemingway 1899–1961 American novelist: *For Whom the Bell Tolls* (1940)

7 You must remember this, a kiss is still a kiss,
   A sigh is just a sigh;
   The fundamental things apply,
   As time goes by.
   Herman Hupfeld 1894–1951 American songwriter: 'As Time Goes By' (1931 song)

8 If love is the best thing in life, then the best part of love is the kiss.
   Thomas Mann 1875–1955 German novelist: *Lotte in Weimar* (1939)

9 I wasn't kissing her, I was just whispering in her mouth.
   on being discovered by his wife with a chorus girl
   Chico Marx 1891–1961 American film comedian: Groucho Marx and Richard J. Anobile *Marx Brothers Scrapbook* (1973)

10 A kiss can be a comma, a question mark or an exclamation point. That's basic spelling that every woman ought to know.
   Mistinguett 1875–1956 French dancer: in *Theatre Arts* December 1955

11 O Love, O fire! once he drew
   With one long kiss my whole soul through
   My lips, as sunlight drinketh dew.
   Alfred, Lord Tennyson 1809–92 English poet: 'Fatima' (1832)

Knowledge

see also IGNORANCE, INFORMATION, WISDOM

1 Everyman, I will go with thee, and be thy guide,
   In thy most need to go by thy side.
   spoken by 'Knowledge'
   Anonymous: *Everyman* (c.1509–19)

2 The fox knows many things—the hedgehog one *big* one.
   Archilochus 7th century BC Greek poet: fragment

3 All men by nature desire knowledge.
   Aristotle 384–322 BC Greek philosopher: *Metaphysics*

4 Knowledge itself is power.
   Francis Bacon 1561–1626 English lawyer, courtier, philosopher, and essayist: *Meditationes Sacrae* (1597) 'Of Heresies'

5 He that increaseth knowledge
increaseth sorrow.
Bible: Ecclesiastes

6 It is better to know nothing than to
know what ain't so.
Josh Billings 1818–85 American
humorist: *Proverb* (1874)

7 Knowledge may give weight, but
accomplishments give lustre, and
many more people see than weigh.
Lord Chesterfield 1694–1773 English
writer and politician: *Maxims* (1774)

8 There is no such thing on earth as an
uninteresting subject; the only thing
that can exist is an uninterested
person.
G. K. Chesterton 1874–1936 English
essayist, novelist, and poet: *Heretics*
(1905)

9 Where is the wisdom we have lost in
knowledge?
Where is the knowledge we have lost
in information?
T. S. Eliot 1888–1965 Anglo-American
poet, critic, and dramatist: *The Rock*
(1934)

10 For lust of knowing what should not
be known,
We take the Golden Road to
Samarkand.
James Elroy Flecker 1884–1915 English
poet: *The Golden Journey to Samarkand*
(1913)

11 Action is the proper fruit of
knowledge.
Thomas Fuller 1654–1734 English
writer and physician: *Gnomologia*
(1732)

12 If you wish to advance into the
infinite, explore the finite in all
directions.
Johann Wolfgang von Goethe
1749–1832 German poet, novelist, and
dramatist: epigram, in David Luke
Goethe: Selected Verse (1964)

13 And still they gazed, and still the
wonder grew,
That one small head could carry all
he knew.
Oliver Goldsmith 1728–74 Anglo-Irish
writer, poet, and dramatist: *The
Deserted Village* (1770)

14 We must know,
We will know.
David Hilbert 1862–1943 German
mathematician: epitaph on his
tombstone

15 If a little knowledge is dangerous,
where is the man who has so much
as to be out of danger?
T. H. Huxley 1825–95 English biologist:
'On Elementary Instruction in
Physiology' (written 1877)

16 Knowledge is of two kinds. We know
a subject ourselves, or we know
where we can find information upon
it.
Samuel Johnson 1709–84 English poet,
critic, and lexicographer: James Boswell
Life of Samuel Johnson (1791) 18 April
1775

17 Dare to know! Have the courage to
use your own reason! This is the
motto of the Enlightenment.
Immanuel Kant 1724–1804 German
philosopher: *What is Enlightenment?*
(1784)

18 I keep six honest serving-men
(They taught me all I knew);
Their names are What and Why and
When
And How and Where and Who.
Rudyard Kipling 1865–1936 English
writer and poet: *Just So Stories* (1902)
'The Elephant's Child'

19 We have learned the answers, all the
answers:
It is the question that we do not
know.
Archibald MacLeish 1892–1982
American poet and public official: *The
Hamlet of A. McLeish* (1928)

20 Owl hasn't exactly got Brain, but he
Knows Things.
> **A. A. Milne** 1882–1956 English writer for
> children: *Winnie-the-Pooh* (1926)

21 *Que sais-je?*
What do I know?
on the position of the sceptic
> **Montaigne** 1533–92 French moralist
> and essayist: *Essays* (1580)

22 What I know is enough for me.
> **Persius** AD 34–62 Roman poet: *Satires*

23 A little learning is a dangerous thing;
Drink deep, or taste not the Pierian
spring.
> **Alexander Pope** 1688–1744 English
> poet: *An Essay on Criticism* (1711)

24 There are known knowns; there are
things we know we know. We also
know there are known unknowns;
that is to say we know there are some
things we do not know. But there are
also unknown unknowns—the ones
we don't know we don't know.
> **Donald Rumsfeld** 1932– American
> Republican politician and
> businessman: to a Defense Department
> meeting, February 2002

25 I know nothing except the fact of my
ignorance.
> **Socrates** 469–399 BC Greek philosopher:
> Diogenes Laertius *Lives of the
> Philosophers*

26 Knowledge is good. It does not have
to look good or sound good or even
do good. It is good just by being
knowledge. And the only thing that
makes it knowledge is that it is true.
You can't have too much of it and
there is no little too little to be worth
having.
> **Tom Stoppard** 1937– British dramatist:
> *The Invention of Love* (1997)

27 Knowledge comes, but wisdom
lingers.
> **Alfred, Lord Tennyson** 1809–92 English
> poet: 'Locksley Hall' (1842)

Language

see also GRAMMAR, MEANING, SWEARING,
WORDS

1 A phrase is born into the world both
good and bad at the same time. The
secret lies in a slight, an almost
invisible twist. The lever should rest
in your hand, getting warm, and you
can only turn it once, not twice.
> **Isaac Babel** 1894–1940 Russian short-
> story writer: *Guy de Maupassant* (1932)

2 One picture is worth ten thousand
words.
> **Frederick R. Barnard**: in *Printers' Ink*
> 10 March 1927

3 A definition is the enclosing a
wilderness of idea within a wall of
words.
> **Samuel Butler** 1835–1902 English
> novelist: *Notebooks* (1912)

4 He who understands baboon would
do more towards metaphysics than
Locke.
> **Charles Darwin** 1809–82 English
> natural historian: Notebook M
> (16 August 1838)

5 In language, the ignorant have
prescribed laws to the learned.
> **Richard Duppa** 1770–1831 English
> artist and writer: *Maxims* (1830)

6 Language is fossil poetry.
> **Ralph Waldo Emerson** 1803–82
> American philosopher and poet: *Essays.
> Second Series* (1844) 'The Poet'

7 Where in this small-talking world
can I find
A longitude with no platitude?
> **Christopher Fry** 1907–2005 English

dramatist: *The Lady's not for Burning*
(1949)

8 The chief merit of language is
clearness, and we know that nothing
detracts so much from this as do
unfamiliar terms.

Galen AD 129–199 Greek physician: *On
the Natural Faculties*

9 There's a cool web of language winds
us in,
Retreat from too much joy or too
much fear.

Robert Graves 1895–1985 English poet:
'The Cool Web' (1927)

10 It is hard for a woman to define her
feelings in language which is chiefly
made by men to express theirs.

Thomas Hardy 1840–1928 English
novelist and poet: *Far from the Madding
Crowd* (1874)

11 I believe that political correctness
can be a form of linguistic fascism,
and it sends shivers down the spine
of my generation who went to war
against fascism.

P. D. James 1920– English writer of
detective stories: in *Paris Review* 1995

12 The mystery of language was
revealed to me. I knew then that
'w-a-t-e-r' meant the wonderful cool
something that was flowing over my
hand. That living word awakened my
soul, gave it light, joy, set it free!

Helen Keller 1880–1968 American
writer and social reformer: *The Story of
My Life* (1902)

13 Good heavens! For more than forty
years I have been speaking prose
without knowing it.

Molière 1622–73 French comic
dramatist: *Le Bourgeois Gentilhomme*
(1671)

14 It's very hard to talk quantum using a
language originally designed to tell

other monkeys where the ripe fruit
is.

Terry Pratchett 1948– English science
fiction writer: *Night Watch* (2002)

15 Different persons growing up in the
same language are like different
bushes trimmed and trained to take
the shape of identical elephants. The
anatomical details of twigs and
branches will fulfill the elephantine
form differently from bush to bush,
but the overall outward results are
alike.

W. V. O. Quine 1908–2000 American
philosopher: *Word and Object* (1960)

16 One of our defects as a nation is a
tendency to use what have been
called 'weasel words'. When a weasel
sucks eggs the meat is sucked out of
the egg. If you use a 'weasel word'
after another, there is nothing left of
the other.

Theodore Roosevelt 1858–1919
American Republican statesman:
speech in St Louis, 31 May 1916

17 Slang is a language that rolls up its
sleeves, spits on its hands and goes
to work.

Carl Sandburg 1878–1967 American
poet: in *New York Times* 13 February
1959

18 The limits of my language mean the
limits of my world.

Ludwig Wittgenstein 1889–1951
Austrian-born philosopher: *Tractatus
Logico-Philosophicus* (1922)

Languages

see also TRANSLATION

1 The great breeding people had gone
out and multiplied; colonies in every
clime attest our success; French is

the *patois* of Europe; English is the language of the world.

Walter Bagehot 1826–77 English economist and essayist: in *National Review* January 1856 'Edward Gibbon'

2 *on speaking French fluently rather than correctly:*
It's nerve and brass, *audace* and disrespect, and leaping-before-you-look and what-the-hellism, that must be developed.

Diana Cooper 1892–1986 wife of Duff Cooper: Philip Ziegler *Diana Cooper* (1981)

3 I like to be beholden to the great metropolitan English speech, the sea which receives tributaries from every region under heaven.

Ralph Waldo Emerson 1803–82 American philosopher and poet: *Society and Solitude* (1870)

4 My English text is chaste, and all licentious passages are left in the obscurity of a learned language.
parodied as 'decent obscurity' in the Anti-Jacobin, *1797–8*

Edward Gibbon 1737–94 English historian: *Memoirs of My Life* (1796)

5 He who does not know foreign languages knows nothing of his own.

Johann Wolfgang von Goethe 1749–1832 German poet, novelist, and dramatist: *Maximen und Reflexionen* (1821)

6 I am always sorry when any language is lost, because languages are the pedigree of nations.

Samuel Johnson 1709–84 English poet, critic, and lexicographer: James Boswell *Journal of a Tour to the Hebrides* (1785) 18 September 1773

7 We are walking lexicons. In a single sentence of idle chatter we preserve Latin, Anglo-Saxon, Norse; we carry a museum inside our heads, each

day we commemorate peoples of whom we have never heard.

Penelope Lively 1933– English novelist: *Moon Tiger* (1987)

8 Waiting for the German verb is surely the ultimate thrill.

Flann O'Brien 1911–66 Irish novelist and journalist: *The Hair of the Dogma* (1977)

9 What is not clear is not French.

Antoine de Rivarol 1753–1801 French man of letters: *Discours sur l'Universalité de la Langue Française* (1784)

10 England and America are two countries divided by a common language.

George Bernard Shaw 1856–1950 Irish dramatist: attributed in this and other forms, but not found in Shaw's published writings

11 The English language is nobody's special property. It is the property of the imagination: it is the property of the language itself.

Derek Walcott 1930– West Indian poet and dramatist: Edward Hirsch 'The Art of Poetry' (1986) in R. Hanmer (ed.) *Critical Perspectives on Derek Walcott* (1993)

Last Words

1 *Ave Caesar, morituri te salutant.*
Hail Caesar, those who are about to die salute you.
gladiators saluting the Roman Emperor

Anonymous: Suetonius *Lives of the Caesars* 'Claudius'

2 I lived uncertain, I die doubtful: O thou Being of beings, have mercy upon me!

Aristotle 384–322 BC Greek philosopher: attributed, probably apocryphal; a Latin version was current in the early 17th century

3 I shall hear in heaven.
> **Ludwig van Beethoven** 1770–1827
> German composer: attributed last
> words, almost certainly apocryphal but
> current since the mid nineteenth-
> century

4 Love? What is it? Most natural
painkiller. What there is . . . LOVE.
> **William S. Burroughs** 1914–97
> American novelist: final entry in
> journal, 1 August 1997, the day before
> he died

5 My design is to make what haste I
can to be gone.
> **Oliver Cromwell** 1599–1658 English
> soldier and statesman: John Morley
> *Oliver Cromwell* (1900)

6 All my possessions for a moment of
time.
> **Elizabeth I** 1533–1603 English
> monarch: attributed, but almost
> certainly apocryphal

7 More light!
> **Johann Wolfgang von Goethe**
> 1749–1832 German poet, novelist, and
> dramatist: attributed; actually 'Open the
> second shutter, so that more light can
> come in'

8 Well, I've had a happy life.
> **William Hazlitt** 1778–1830 English
> essayist: W. C. Hazlitt *Memoirs of
> William Hazlitt* (1867)

9 I am about to take my last voyage, a
great leap in the dark.
> **Thomas Hobbes** 1588–1679 English
> philosopher: John Watkins *Anecdotes of
> Men of Learning* (1808)

10 Let me go to the house of the Father.
> **Pope John Paul II** 1920–2005 Polish
> cleric: in *Independent* 19 September
> 2005

11 Such is life.
> *before being hanged, 11 November 1880*
> **Ned Kelly** 1855–80 Australian outlaw:
> Frank Clune *The Kelly Hunters* (1955)

12 Why not, why not, why not. Yeah.
> **Timothy Leary** 1920–96 American
> psychologist: in *Independent* 1 June
> 1996

13 Kiss me, Hardy.
> **Horatio, Lord Nelson** 1758–1805 British
> admiral: Robert Southey *Life of Nelson*
> (1813)

14 I am just going outside and may be
some time.
> **Captain Lawrence Oates** 1880–1912
> English polar explorer: Robert F. Scott's
> diary entry, 16–17 March 1912

15 Die, my dear Doctor, that's the last
thing I shall do!
> **Lord Palmerston** 1784–1865 British
> statesman: E. Latham *Famous Sayings
> and their Authors* (1904)

16 I am going to seek a great
perhaps . . . Bring down the curtain,
the farce is played out.
> **François Rabelais** *c.*1494–*c.*1553 French
> humanist, satirist, and physician:
> attributed, though none of his
> contemporaries authenticated the
> remarks

17 So little done, so much to do.
> *said on the day of his death*
> **Cecil Rhodes** 1853–1902 South African
> statesman: Lewis Michell *Life of Rhodes*
> (1910)

18 Lord take my soul, but the struggle
continues.
> *last words before he was hanged*
> **Ken Saro-Wiwa** 1941–95 Nigerian
> writer and environmentalist: in *Daily
> Telegraph* 13 November 1995

19 For God's sake look after our people.
> **Robert Falcon Scott** 1868–1912 English
> polar explorer: last diary entry,
> 29 March 1912

20 On, on, on.

last words after collapsing on Mont Ventoux in the Tour de France; commonly quoted as, 'Put me back on my bike'

Tom Simpson 1937–67 British cyclist: William Fotheringham *Put Me Back on My Bike* (2002)

21 Just before she [Stein] died she asked, 'What *is* the answer?' No answer came. She laughed and said, 'In that case what is the question?' Then she died.

Gertrude Stein 1874–1946 American writer: Donald Sutherland *Gertrude Stein* (1951)

22 If this is dying, then I don't think much of it.

Lytton Strachey 1880–1932 English biographer: Michael Holroyd *Lytton Strachey* vol. 2 (1968)

23 This is no time for making new enemies.

on being asked to renounce the Devil on his deathbed

Voltaire 1694–1778 French writer and philosopher: attributed

24 Tell them I've had a wonderful life.

Ludwig Wittgenstein 1889–1951 Austrian-born philosopher: Ray Monk *Ludwig Wittgenstein* (1990)

Laws

see also CRIME, JUSTICE, LAWYERS, POLICE, TRIALS

1 Written laws are like spider's webs; they will catch, it is true, the weak and poor, but would be torn in pieces by the rich and powerful.

Anacharsis 6th century BC Scythian prince: Plutarch *Parallel Lives* 'Solon'

2 Laws are like sausages. It's better not to see them being made made.

Otto von Bismarck 1815–98 German statesman: attributed, but not traced and probably apocryphal

3 Bad laws are the worst sort of tyranny.

Edmund Burke 1729–97 Irish-born Whig politician and man of letters: *Speech at Bristol, previous to the Late Election* (1780)

4 *Salus populi suprema est lex.*
The good of the people is the chief law.

Cicero 106–43 BC Roman orator and statesman: *De Legibus*

5 How long soever it hath continued, if it be against reason, it is of no force in law.

Edward Coke 1552–1634 English jurist: *The First Part of the Institutes of the Laws of England* (1628)

6 You know my views about some regulations—they're written for the obedience of fools and the guidance of wise men.

Harry Day British pilot: to Douglas Bader, 1931; Paul Brickhill *Reach for the Sky* (1954)

7 'If the law supposes that,' said Mr Bumble . . . 'the law is a ass—a idiot.'

Charles Dickens 1812–70 English novelist: *Oliver Twist* (1838)

8 The one great principle of the English law is, to make business for itself.

Charles Dickens 1812–70 English novelist: *Bleak House* (1853)

9 Be you never so high, the law is above you.

Thomas Fuller 1654–1734 English writer and physician: *Gnomologia* (1732)

10 A verbal contract isn't worth the paper it is written on.

Sam Goldwyn 1882–1974 American film producer: Alva Johnston *The Great Goldwyn* (1937)

11 I know no method to secure the repeal of bad or obnoxious laws so effective as their stringent execution.

Ulysses S. Grant 1822–85 American Unionist general and statesman: inaugural address, 4 March 1869

12 The people should fight for their law as for their city wall.

Heraclitus *c.*540–*c.*480 BC Greek philosopher: Philip Wheelwright *Heraclitus* (1959) fragment 82

13 The more laws and orders are made prominent,
The more thieves and bandits there will be.

Lao Tzu *c.*604–*c.*531 BC Chinese philosopher: *Tao-te Ching*

14 Loopholes are not always of a fixed dimension. They tend to enlarge as the numbers that pass through wear them away.

Harold Lever 1914–95 British businessman and politician: speech to Finance Bill Committee, 22 May 1968

15 However harmless a thing is, if the law forbids it most people will think it wrong.

W. Somerset Maugham 1874–1965 English novelist: *A Writer's Notebook* (1949) written in 1896

16 Laws were made to be broken.

Christopher North 1785–1854 Scottish literary critic: in *Blackwood's Magazine* (May 1830)

17 Ignorance of the law excuses no man; not that all men know the law, but because 'tis an excuse every man will plead, and no man can tell how to confute him.

John Selden 1584–1654 English historian and antiquary: *Table Talk* (1689) 'Law'

18 The big print giveth, and the fine print taketh away.

Fulton J. Sheen 1895–1979 American Roman Catholic bishop: attributed

19 Everything not forbidden is compulsory.

T. H. White 1906–64 English novelist: *The Sword in the Stone* (1938)

Lawyers

1 No poet ever interpreted nature as freely as a lawyer interprets the truth.

Jean Giraudoux 1882–1944 French dramatist: *La Guerre de Troie n'aura pas lieu* (1935)

2 A lawyer has no business with the justice or injustice of the cause which he undertakes, unless his client asks his opinion, and then he is bound to give it honestly. The justice or injustice of the cause is to be decided by the judge.

Samuel Johnson 1709–84 English poet, critic, and lexicographer: James Boswell *Journal of a Tour to the Hebrides* (1785) 15 August 1773

3 I don't know as I want a lawyer to tell me what I cannot do. I hire him to tell me how to do what I want to do.

John Pierpont Morgan 1837–1913 American financier and philanthropist: Ida M. Tarbell *The Life of Elbert H. Gary* (1925)

4 No brilliance is needed in the law. Nothing but common sense, and relatively clean fingernails.

John Mortimer 1923–2009 English novelist, barrister, and dramatist: *A Voyage Round My Father* (1971)

5 A lawyer with his briefcase can steal more than a hundred men with guns.

Mario Puzo 1920–99 American novelist: *The Godfather* (1969)

6 The Law: It has honoured us, may we honour it.

Daniel Webster 1782–1852 American politician: speech at the Charleston Bar Dinner, 10 May 1847

7 Judges must follow their oaths and do their duty, heedless of editorials, letters, telegrams, threats, petitions, panellists and talk shows.

> **Hiller B. Zobel** 1932– American judge: judicial ruling reducing the conviction of Louise Woodward from murder to manslaughter, 10 November 1997

Leadership

1 I know that the right kind of leader for the Labour Party is a desiccated calculating machine who must not in any way permit himself to be swayed by indignation.

> **Aneurin Bevan** 1897–1960 British Labour politician: Michael Foot *Aneurin Bevan* (1973)

2 They be blind leaders of the blind. And if the blind lead the blind, both shall fall into the ditch.

> **Bible**: St Matthew

3 The art of leadership is saying no, not yes. It is very easy to say yes.

> **Tony Blair** 1953– British Labour statesman: in *Mail on Sunday* 2 October 1994

4 Those who carry on great public schemes must be proof against the most fatiguing delays, the most mortifying disappointments, the most shocking insults, and, worst of all, the presumptuous judgements of the ignorant upon their designs.

> **Edmund Burke** 1729–97 Irish-born Whig politician and man of letters: attributed; Benjamin Ward Richardson 'A Biographical Dissertation' ch. 4 in Edwin Chadwick *The Health of Nations* (1887)

5 Leadership means making people feel good.

> **Jean Chrétien** 1934– Canadian Liberal statesman: in *Toronto Star* 7 June 1984

6 The loyalties which centre upon number one are enormous. If he trips he must be sustained. If he makes mistakes they must be covered. If he sleeps he must not be wantonly disturbed. If he is no good he must be pole-axed. But this last extreme process cannot be carried out every day; and certainly not in the days just after he has been chosen.

> **Winston Churchill** 1874–1965 British Conservative statesman: *The Second World War* vol. 2 (1949)

7 If you desire what is good, the people will be good. The character of a ruler is like wind and that of the people is like grass. In whatever direction the wind blows the grass always bends.

> **Confucius** 551–479 BC Chinese philosopher: *Analects*

8 Leaders should never, ever try to look cool—that's for dictators.

> **Ben Elton** 1959– British writer and performer: in *Radio Times* 18/24 April 1998

9 The art of leadership . . . consists in consolidating the attention of the people against a single adversary and taking care that nothing will split up that attention.

> **Adolf Hitler** 1889–1945 German dictator: *Mein Kampf* (1925)

10 So long as men worship the Caesars and Napoleons, Caesars and Napoleons will duly arise and make them miserable.

> **Aldous Huxley** 1894–1963 English novelist: *Ends and Means* (1937)

11 Leadership is not about being nice. It's about being right and being strong.

> **Paul Keating** 1944– Australian Labor statesman: in *Time* 9 January 1995

12 A leader is best when people barely know he exists . . . He acts without unnecessary speech, and when the work is done the people say 'We did it ourselves'.

Lao Tzu c.604–c.531 BC Chinese philosopher: *Tao-te Ching*

13 The final test of a leader is that he leaves behind him in other men the conviction and the will to carry on.

Walter Lippmann 1889–1974 American journalist: in *New York Herald Tribune* 14 April 1945

14 No human society, from the hunter-gatherer to the postindustrial, has come to the attention of anthropologists that did not have its leaders and the led; and no emergency was ever dealt with effectively by democratic process.

Ian McEwan 1948– English novelist: *Enduring Love* (1998)

15 To grasp and hold a vision, that is the very essence of successful leadership—not only on the movie set where I learned it, but everywhere.

Ronald Reagan 1911–2004 American Republican statesman: in *Wilson Quarterly* Winter 1994; attributed

16 I don't mind how much my Ministers talk, so long as they do what I say.

Margaret Thatcher 1925– British Conservative stateswoman: in *Observer* 27 January 1980

17 At the age of four with paper hats and wooden swords we're all Generals. Only some of us never grow out of it.

Peter Ustinov 1921–2004 British actor, director, and writer: *Romanoff and Juliet* (1956)

18 I used to say of him that his presence on the field made the difference of forty thousand men.

of Napoleon
Duke of Wellington 1769–1852 British

soldier and statesman: Philip Henry Stanhope *Notes of Conversations with the Duke of Wellington* (1888) 2 November 1831

Leisure

see also HOLIDAYS, WORK

1 We combat obstacles in order to get repose, and, when got, the repose is insupportable.

Henry Brooks Adams 1838–1918 American man of letters: *The Education of Henry Adams* (1907)

2 If I am doing nothing, I like to be doing nothing to some purpose. That is what leisure means.

Alan Bennett 1934– English actor and dramatist: *A Question of Attribution* (1989)

3 We are closer to the ants than to the butterflies. Very few people can endure much leisure.

Gerald Brenan 1894–1987 British travel writer and novelist: *Thoughts in a Dry Season* (1978)

4 What is this life if, full of care,
We have no time to stand and stare.

W. H. Davies 1871–1940 Welsh poet: 'Leisure' (1911)

5 Man is so made that he can only find relaxation from one kind of labour by taking up another.

Anatole France 1844–1924 French novelist and man of letters: *The Crime of Sylvestre Bonnard* (1881)

6 It was Einstein who made the real trouble. He announced in 1905 that there was no such thing as absolute rest. After that there never was.

Stephen Leacock 1869–1944 Canadian humorist: *The Boy I Left Behind Me* (1947)

7 Man's heart expands to tinker with his car

For this is Sunday morning, Fate's
great bazaar.
Louis MacNeice 1907–63 British poet,
born in Belfast: 'Sunday Morning'
(1935)

8 To be able to fill leisure intelligently
is the last product of civilization.
Bertrand Russell 1872–1970 British
philosopher and mathematician: *The
Conquest of Happiness* (1930)

9 Repose is a good thing, but boredom
is its brother.
Voltaire 1694–1778 French writer and
philosopher: attributed, 1921

10 The world is too much with us; late
and soon,
Getting and spending, we lay waste
our powers.
William Wordsworth 1770–1850
English poet: 'The world is too much
with us' (1807)

Lending

see also DEBT

1 Never lend books, for no one ever
returns them; the only books I have
in my library are those that other
people have lent me.
Anatole France 1844–1924 French
novelist and man of letters: *La Vie
littéraire* (1888)

2 The human species, according to the
best theory I can form of it, is
composed of two distinct races, *the
men who borrow,* and *the men who
lend.*
Charles Lamb 1775–1834 English
writer: *Essays of Elia* (1823) 'The Two
Races of Men'

3 Neither a borrower, nor a lender be;
For loan oft loses both itself and
friend,

And borrowing dulls the edge of
husbandry.
William Shakespeare 1564–1616
English dramatist: *Hamlet* (1601)

4 Three things I never lends—my 'oss,
my wife, and my name.
R. S. Surtees 1805–64 English sporting
journalist and novelist: *Hillingdon Hall*
(1845)

Lesbianism

see also HOMOSEXUALITY, SEX

1 You're neither unnatural, nor
abominable, nor mad; you're as
much a part of what people call
nature as anyone else; only you're
unexplained as yet—you've not got
your niche in creation.
Radclyffe Hall 1883–1943 English
novelist: *The Well of Loneliness* (1928)

2 I do
And then again
She does
And then sometimes
Neither of us
Wears any trousers at all.
Maria Jastrzebska 1953– : 'Which of Us
Wears the Trousers'

3 Many years ago I chased a woman
for almost two years, only to discover
that her tastes were exactly like
mine: we both were crazy about girls.
Groucho Marx 1890–1977 American
film comedian: letter, 28 March 1955

4 Gay men may seek sex without
emotion; lesbians often end up in
emotion without sex.
Camille Paglia 1947– American writer
and critic: in *Esquire* October 1991

Letters

1 You bid me burn your letters. But I
must forget you first.
John Adams 1735–1826 American

statesman: letter to Abigail Adams,
28 April 1776

2 Letters of thanks, letters from banks,
Letters of joy from girl and boy,
Receipted bills and invitations
To inspect new stock or to visit
relations,
And applications for situations,
And timid lovers' declarations,
And gossip, gossip from all the
nations.
W. H. Auden 1907–73 English poet:
'Night Mail' (1936)

3 She'll vish there wos more, and that's
the great art o' letter writin'.
Charles Dickens 1812–70 English
novelist: *Pickwick Papers* (1837–8)

4 Sir, more than kisses, letters mingle
souls.
John Donne 1572–1631 English poet
and divine: 'To Sir Henry Wotton'
(1597–8)

5 It is wonderful how much news there
is when people write every other day;
if they wait for a month, there is
nothing that seems worth telling.
O. Douglas 1877–1948 Scottish writer:
Penny Plain (1920)

6 I have made this [letter] longer than
usual, only because I have not had
the time to make it shorter.
Blaise Pascal 1623–62 French
mathematician, physicist, and moralist:
Lettres Provinciales (1657)

7 A woman seldom writes her mind
but in her postscript.
Richard Steele 1672–1729 Irish-born
essayist and dramatist: in *The Spectator*
31 May 1711

8 My father spent the last 20 years of
his life writing letters. If someone
thanked him for a present, he
thanked them for thanking him and

there was no end to the exchange but
death.
Evelyn Waugh 1903–66 English novelist:
letter to Lady Mosley, 30 March 1966

9 It is not in my power to tell thee how
I have been affected by this dearest
of all letters—it was so
unexpected—so new a thing to see
the breathing of thy inmost heart
upon paper.
Mary Wordsworth 1782–1859 wife of
William Wordsworth: letter to William
Wordsworth, 1 August 1810

Liberty

1 Liberty is always unfinished
business.
Anonymous: title of 36th Annual Report
of the American Civil Liberties Union,
1 July 1955–30 June 1956

2 Liberty is liberty, not equality or
fairness or justice or human
happiness or a quiet conscience.
Isaiah Berlin 1909–97 British
philosopher: *Two Concepts of Liberty*
(1958)

3 Those who won our
independence . . . believed liberty to
be the secret of happiness and
courage to be the secret of liberty.
Louis D. Brandeis 1856–1941 American
jurist: in *Whitney v California* (1927)

4 The condition upon which God hath
given liberty to man is eternal
vigilance; which condition if he
break, servitude is at once the
consequence of his crime, and the
punishment of his guilt.
John Philpot Curran 1750–1817 Irish
judge: speech on the right of election of
the Lord Mayor of Dublin, 10 July 1790

5 The cost of liberty is less than the price of repression.
> **W. E. B. Du Bois** 1868–1963 American social reformer and political activist: *John Brown* (1909)

6 The moment the slave resolves that he will no longer be a slave, his fetters fall. He frees himself and shows the way to others. Freedom and slavery are mental states.
> **Mahatma Gandhi** 1869–1948 Indian statesman: *Non-Violence in Peace and War* (1949)

7 Freedom is about the willingness of every single human being to cede to lawful authority a great deal of discretion about what you do, and how you do it.
> **Rudy Giuliani** 1944– American politician and lawyer: attributed, in *Independent* 10 July 1999

8 I know not what course others may take; but as for me, give me liberty, or give me death!
> **Patrick Henry** 1736–99 American statesman: speech in Virginia Convention, 23 March 1775

9 The most stringent protection of free speech would not protect a man falsely shouting fire in a theatre and causing a panic.
> *sometimes quoted as 'shouting fire in a crowded theatre'*
> **Oliver Wendell Holmes Jr.** 1841–1935 American lawyer: in *Schenck v. United States* (1919)

10 It is better to die on your feet than to live on your knees.
> **Dolores Ibarruri** 1895–1989 Spanish Communist leader: speech in Paris, 3 September 1936; also attributed to Emiliano Zapata

11 The enemies of Freedom do not argue; they shout and they shoot.
> **William Ralph Inge** 1860–1954 English writer; Dean of St. Paul's, 1911–34: *End of an Age* (1948)

12 The tree of liberty must be refreshed from time to time with the blood of patriots and tyrants. It is its natural manure.
> **Thomas Jefferson** 1743–1826 American Democratic Republican statesman: letter to W. S. Smith, 13 November 1787

13 Liberty is, to the lowest rank of every nation, little more than the choice of working or starving.
> **Samuel Johnson** 1709–84 English poet, critic, and lexicographer: 'The Bravery of the English Common Soldier' (1760)

14 It's often better to be in chains than to be free.
> **Franz Kafka** 1883–1924 Czech novelist: *The Trial* (1925)

15 Let every nation know, whether it wishes us well or ill, that we shall pay any price, bear any burden, meet any hardship, support any friend, oppose any foe to assure the survival and the success of liberty.
> **John F. Kennedy** 1917–63 American Democratic statesman: inaugural address, 20 January 1961

16 Freedom's just another word for nothin' left to lose,
Nothin' ain't worth nothin', but it's free.
> **Kris Kristofferson** 1936– American actor: 'Me and Bobby McGee' (1969 song, with Fred Foster)

17 Liberty is precious—so precious that it must be rationed.
> **Lenin** 1870–1924 Russian revolutionary: Sidney and Beatrice Webb *Soviet Communism* (1936)

18 Freedom is always and exclusively freedom for the one who thinks differently.
> **Rosa Luxemburg** 1871–1919 German revolutionary: *Die Russische Revolution* (1918)

19 If men are to wait for liberty till they become wise and good in slavery, they may indeed wait for ever.

> **Lord Macaulay** 1800–59 English politician and historian: *Essays Contributed to the Edinburgh Review* (1843) 'Milton'

20 I believe there are more instances of the abridgement of freedom of the people by gradual and silent encroachments of those in power than by violent and sudden usurpations.

> **James Madison** 1751–1836 American Democratic Republican statesman: speech in Virginia Convention, 16 June 1788

21 The word 'freedom' means for me not a point of departure but a genuine point of arrival. The point of departure is defined by the word 'order'. Freedom cannot exist without the concept of order.

> **Prince Metternich** 1773–1859 Austrian statesman: *Mein Politisches Testament* (1880)

22 The liberty of the individual must be thus far limited; he must not make himself a nuisance to other people.

> **John Stuart Mill** 1806–73 English philosopher and economist: *On Liberty* (1859)

23 Ask the first man you meet what he means by defending freedom, and he'll tell you privately he means defending the standard of living.

> **Martin Niemöller** 1892–1984 German theologian: address at Augsburg, January 1958

24 Freedom is not something that one people can bestow on another as a gift. They claim it as their own and none can keep it from them.

> **Kwame Nkrumah** 1900–72 Ghanaian statesman: speech in Accra, 10 July 1953

25 Freedom is the freedom to say that two plus two make four. If that is granted, all else follows.

> **George Orwell** 1903–50 English novelist: *Nineteen Eighty-Four* (1949)

26 He that would make his own liberty secure must guard even his enemy from oppression; for if he violates this duty he establishes a precedent that will reach to himself.

> **Thomas Paine** 1737–1809 English political theorist: *Dissertation on First Principles of Government* (1795)

27 Tyranny is always better organized than freedom.

> **Charles Péguy** 1873–1914 French poet and essayist: *Basic Verities* (1943) 'War and Peace'

28 If we choose freedom, then we must be prepared to perish along with it.

> **Karl Popper** 1902–94 Austrian-born philosopher: *All Life is Problem Solving*, first published in *Die Philosophie und die Wissenschaften* (1967)

29 O liberty! O liberty! what crimes are committed in thy name!

> **Mme Roland** 1754–93 French revolutionary: A. de Lamartine *Histoire des Girondins* (1847)

30 Man was born free, and everywhere he is in chains.

> **Jean-Jacques Rousseau** 1712–78 French philosopher and novelist: *Du Contrat social* (1762)

31 I am condemned to be free.

> **Jean-Paul Sartre** 1905–80 French philosopher, novelist, dramatist, and critic: *L'Être et le néant* (1943)

32 Liberty means responsibility. That is why most men dread it.

> **George Bernard Shaw** 1856–1950 Irish dramatist: *Man and Superman* (1903) 'Maxims: Liberty and Equality'

Libraries

see also BOOKS, LENDING, READING

1 I have always imagined Paradise as a kind of library.

Jorge Luis Borges 1899–1986 Argentinian writer: *Seven Nights* (1984) 'Blindness'

2 With awe, around these silent walks I tread;
These are the lasting mansions of the dead.

George Crabbe 1754–1832 English poet: 'The Library' (1808)

3 A man should keep his little brain attic stocked with all the furniture that he is likely to use, and the rest he can put away in the lumber room of his library, where he can get it if he wants it.

Arthur Conan Doyle 1859–1930 Scottish-born writer of detective fiction: *The Adventures of Sherlock Holmes* (1892)

4 No place affords a more striking conviction of the vanity of human hopes, than a public library.

Samuel Johnson 1709–84 English poet, critic, and lexicographer: in *The Rambler* 23 March 1751

5 What is more important in a library than anything else—than everything else—is the fact that it exists.

Archibald MacLeish 1892–1982 American poet and public official: 'The Premise of Meaning' in *American Scholar* 5 June 1972

6 A library is thought in cold storage.

Lord Samuel 1870–1963 British Liberal politician: *A Book of Quotations* (1947)

7 Come, and take choice of all my library,
And so beguile thy sorrow.

William Shakespeare 1564–1616 English dramatist: *Titus Andronicus* (1590)

8 There is in the British Museum an enormous mind. Consider that Plato is there cheek by jowl with Aristotle; and Shakespeare with Marlowe. This great mind is hoarded beyond the power of any single mind to possess it.

Virginia Woolf 1882–1941 English novelist: *Jacob's Room* (1922)

Lies

see also DECEPTION, PROPAGANDA, TRUTH

1 An abomination unto the Lord, but a very present help in time of trouble.
definition of a lie, an amalgamation of Proverbs *12.22 and* Psalms *46.1, often attributed to Adlai Stevenson*

Anonymous: Bill Adler *The Stevenson Wit* (1966)

2 She tells enough white lies to ice a wedding cake.
of Lady Desborough

Margot Asquith 1864–1945 British political hostess: in *Listener* 11 June 1953

3 One sometimes sees more clearly in the man who lies than in the man who tells the truth. Truth, like the light, blinds. Lying, on the other hand, is a beautiful twilight, which gives to each object its value.

Albert Camus 1913–60 French novelist, dramatist, and essayist: attributed; Lord Trevelyan *Diplomatic Channels* (1973)

4 Man's mind is so formed that it is far more susceptible to falsehood than to truth.

Erasmus *c.*1469–1536 Dutch Christian humanist: *In Praise of Folly* (1509)

5 Without lies humanity would perish of despair and boredom.

Anatole France 1844–1924 French novelist and man of letters: *La Vie en fleur* (1922)

6 Whoever would lie usefully should lie seldom.

Lord Hervey 1696–1743 English politician and writer: *Memoirs of the Reign of George II* (ed. J. W. Croker, 1848)

7 The broad mass of a nation . . . will more easily fall victim to a big lie than to a small one.

Adolf Hitler 1889–1945 German dictator: *Mein Kampf* (1925)

8 A little inaccuracy sometimes saves tons of explanation.

Saki 1870–1916 Scottish writer: *The Square Egg* (1924)

9 If you want truth to go round the world you must hire an express train to pull it; but if you want a lie to go round the world, it will fly: it is as light as a feather, and a breath will carry it. It is well said in the old proverb, 'a lie will go round the world while truth is pulling its boots on'.

C. H. Spurgeon 1834–92 English nonconformist preacher: *Gems from Spurgeon* (1859)

10 The cruellest lies are often told in silence.

Robert Louis Stevenson 1850–94 Scottish novelist: *Virginibus Puerisque* (1881)

11 He replied that I must needs be mistaken, or that I *said the thing which was not*. (For they have no word in their language to express lying or falsehood.)

Jonathan Swift 1667–1745 Anglo-Irish poet and satirist: *Gulliver's Travels* (1726)

12 One of the most striking differences between a cat and a lie is that a cat has only nine lives.

Mark Twain 1835–1910 American writer: *Pudd'nhead Wilson* (1894)

13 I can't tell a lie, Pa; you know I can't tell a lie. I did cut it with my hatchet.

George Washington 1732–99 American general and statesman: M. L. Weems *Life of George Washington* (10th ed., 1810)

Life

see also LIFE SCIENCES, LIFESTYLES

1 The Answer to the Great Question Of . . . Life, the Universe and Everything . . . [is] Forty-two.

Douglas Adams 1952–2001 English science fiction writer: *The Hitch Hiker's Guide to the Galaxy* (1979)

2 'Such,' he said, 'O King, seems to me the present life of men on earth, in comparison with that time which to us is uncertain, as if when on a winter's night you sit feasting with your ealdormen and thegns,—a single sparrow should fly swiftly into the hall, and coming in at one door, instantly fly out through another.'

The Venerable Bede AD 673–735 English historian and scholar: *Ecclesiastical History of the English People*

3 Life, you know, is rather like opening a tin of sardines. We are all of us looking for the key. And, I wonder, how many of you here tonight have wasted years of your lives looking behind the kitchen dressers of this life for that key.

Alan Bennett 1934– English actor and dramatist: *Beyond the Fringe* (1961 revue) 'Take a Pew'

4 Life is like playing a violin solo in public and learning the instrument as one goes on.

Samuel Butler 1835–1902 English novelist: speech at the Somerville Club, 27 February 1895

5 Life is a horizontal fall.

Jean Cocteau 1889–1963 French dramatist and film director: *Opium* (1930)

6 Life is an incurable disease.
  Abraham Cowley 1618–67 English poet
  and essayist: 'To Dr Scarborough' (1656)

7 It's a funny old world—a man's lucky
  if he gets out of it alive.
  Walter de Leon and **Paul M. Jones**:
  You're Telling Me (1934 film); spoken by
  W. C. Fields

8 I have measured out my life with
  coffee spoons.
  T. S. Eliot 1888–1965 Anglo-American
  poet, critic, and dramatist: 'The Love
  Song of J. Alfred Prufrock' (1917)

9 Birth, and copulation, and death.
  That's all the facts when you come to
  brass tacks:
  Birth, and copulation, and death.
  I've been born, and once is enough.
  T. S. Eliot 1888–1965 Anglo-American
  poet, critic, and dramatist: *Sweeney
  Agonistes* (1932)

10 All that matters is love and work.
  Sigmund Freud 1856–1939 Austrian
  psychiatrist: attributed

11 Man wants but little here below,
  Nor wants that little long.
  Oliver Goldsmith 1728–74 Anglo-Irish
  writer, poet, and dramatist: 'Edwin and
  Angelina, or the Hermit' (1766)

12 If we find the answer to that [why it is
  that we and the universe exist], it
  would be the ultimate triumph of
  human reason—for then we would
  know the mind of God.
  Stephen Hawking 1942– English
  theoretical physicist: *A Brief History of
  Time* (1988)

13 No arts; no letters; no society; and
  which is worst of all, continual fear
  and danger of violent death; and the
  life of man, solitary, poor, nasty,
  brutish, and short.
  Thomas Hobbes 1588–1679 English
  philosopher: *Leviathan* (1651)

14 Life is just one damned thing after
  another.
  Elbert Hubbard 1859–1915 American
  writer: in *Philistine* December 1909;
  often attributed to Frank Ward
  O'Malley; see LIFE 25

15 Cats and monkeys—monkeys and
  cats—all human life is there!
  Henry James 1843–1916 American
  novelist: *The Madonna of the Future*
  (1879)

16 As far as we can discern, the sole
  purpose of human existence is to
  kindle a light in the darkness of mere
  being.
  Carl Gustav Jung 1875–1961 Swiss
  psychologist: *Erinnerungen, Träume,
  Gedanken* (1962)

17 Life is either a daring adventure or
  nothing.
  Helen Keller 1880–1968 American
  writer and social reformer: *Let Us Have
  Faith* (1940)

18 Life must be understood backwards;
  but . . . it must be lived forwards.
  Sören Kierkegaard 1813–55 Danish
  philosopher: *Journals and Papers* (1843)

19 Life is first boredom, then fear.
  Philip Larkin 1922–85 English poet:
  'Dockery & Son' (1964)

20 Life is like a sewer. What you get out
  of it depends on what you put into it.
  Tom Lehrer 1928– American humorist:
  'We Will All Go Together When We Go'
  (1953 song)

21 Life is just what happens to you,
  while you're busy making other
  plans.
  John Lennon 1940–80 English pop
  singer and songwriter: 'Beautiful Boy'
  (song)

22 Life would be tolerable but for its
  amusements.
  George Cornewall Lewis 1806–63

British Liberal politician and writer: in
The Times 18 September 1872

23 Life is real! Life is earnest!
And the grave is not its goal;
Dust thou art, to dust returnest,
Was not spoken of the soul.
Henry Wadsworth Longfellow 1807–82
American poet: 'A Psalm of Life' (1838)

24 What, knocked a tooth out? Never
mind, dear, laugh it off, laugh it off;
it's all part of life's rich pageant.
Arthur Marshall 1910–89 British
journalist: *The Games Mistress*
(recorded monologue, 1937)

25 It's not true that life is one damn
thing after another—it's one damn
thing over and over.
Edna St Vincent Millay 1892–1950
American poet: letter to Arthur Davison
Ficke, 24 October 1930; see LIFE 14

26 The secret of life is to have a task,
something you devote your entire
life to, something you bring
everything to, every minute of the
day for your whole life. And the most
important thing is—it must be
something you cannot possibly do!
Henry Moore 1898–1986 English
sculptor and draughtsman: attributed,
in Donald Hall *Henry Moore* (1966)
introduction

27 The cradle rocks above an abyss, and
common sense tells us that our
existence is but a brief crack of light
between two eternities of darkness.
Vladimir Nabokov 1899–1977 Russian
novelist: *Speak, Memory* (1951)

28 The world is what it is; men who are
nothing, who allow themselves to
become nothing, have no place in it.
V. S. Naipaul 1932– Trinidadian writer:
A Bend in the River (1979)

29 To live at all is miracle enough.
Mervyn Peake 1911–68 British novelist,
poet, and artist: *The Glassblower* (1950)

30 Real life is elsewhere.
Arthur Rimbaud 1854–91 French poet:
A Season in Hell (1873)

31 My momma always said life was like
a box of chocolates . . . you never
know what you're gonna get.
Eric Roth 1945– American
screenwriter: *Forrest Gump* (1994 film),
based on the novel (1986) by Winston
Groom; spoken by Tom Hanks

32 All the world's a stage,
And all the men and women merely
players:
They have their exits and their
entrances;
And one man in his time plays many
parts,
His acts being seven ages.
William Shakespeare 1564–1616
English dramatist: *As You Like It* (1599)

33 Life's but a walking shadow, a poor
player,
That struts and frets his hour upon
the stage,
And then is heard no more; it is a tale
Told by an idiot, full of sound and
fury,
Signifying nothing.
William Shakespeare 1564–1616
English dramatist: *Macbeth* (1606)

34 Life is not meant to be easy, my
child; but take courage: it can be
delightful.
George Bernard Shaw 1856–1950 Irish
dramatist: *Back to Methuselah* (rev. ed.,
1930); see also ADVERSITY 3

35 Life, like a dome of many-coloured
glass,
Stains the white radiance of Eternity,
Until Death tramples it to fragments.
Percy Bysshe Shelley 1792–1822
English poet: *Adonais* (1821)

36 Not to be born is, past all prizing,
best.
Sophocles *c.*496–406 BC Greek
dramatist: *Oedipus Coloneus*; see LIFE 44

37 Life is a gamble at terrible odds—if it was a bet, you wouldn't take it.

> **Tom Stoppard** 1937– British dramatist: *Rosencrantz and Guildenstern are Dead* (1967)

38 The same stream of life that runs through my veins night and day runs through the world and dances in rhythmic measures.

It is the same life that shoots in joy through the dust of the earth into numberless blades of grass and breaks into tumultuous waves of leaves and flowers.

> **Rabindranath Tagore** 1861–1941 Bengali poet and philosopher: *Gitanjali* (1912)

39 Oh, isn't life a terrible thing, thank God?

> **Dylan Thomas** 1914–53 Welsh poet: *Under Milk Wood* (1954)

40 The mass of men lead lives of quiet desperation.

> **Henry David Thoreau** 1817–62 American writer: *Walden* (1854)

41 Expect nothing. Live frugally on surprise.

> **Alice Walker** 1944– American poet: 'Expect nothing' (1973)

42 This world is a comedy to those that think, a tragedy to those that feel.

> **Horace Walpole** 1717–97 English writer and connoisseur: letter to Anne, Countess of Upper Ossory, 16 August 1776

43 Isn't life a series of images that change as they repeat themselves?

> **Andy Warhol** 1927–87 American artist: Victor Bokris *Andy Warhol* (1989)

44 Never to have lived is best, ancient writers say;
Never to have drawn the breath of life, never to have looked into the eye of day;

The second best's a gay goodnight and quickly turn away.

> **W. B. Yeats** 1865–1939 Irish poet: 'From *Oedipus at Colonus*' (1928); see LIFE 36

45 Life is a rainbow which also includes black.

> **Yevgeny Yevtushenko** 1933– Russian poet: in *Guardian* 11 August 1987

Life Sciences

see also BIOTECHNOLOGY, ENVIRONMENT, HUMAN RACE, LIFE, NATURE, SCIENCE, SCIENCE AND RELIGION, SCIENCE AND SOCIETY

1 What's hit is history, what's missed is mystery.

on the importance of securing a dead specimen of a new species

> **Anonymous**: late 19th-century saying, in *American Naturalist* 1877

2 [The science of life] is a superb and dazzlingly lighted hall which may be reached only by passing through a long and ghastly kitchen.

> **Claude Bernard** 1813–78 French physiologist: *An Introduction to the Study of Experimental Medicine* (1865)

3 It has, I believe, been often remarked that a hen is only an egg's way of making another egg.

> **Samuel Butler** 1835–1902 English novelist: *Life and Habit* (1877)

4 We have discovered the secret of life!

on the discovery of the structure of DNA, 1953

> **Francis Crick** 1916–2004 English biophysicist: James D. Watson *The Double Helix* (1968)

5 Almost all aspects of life are engineered at the molecular level, and without understanding molecules we can only have a very sketchy understanding of life itself.

> **Francis Crick** 1916–2004 English biophysicist: *What Mad Pursuit* (1988)

6 I have called this principle, by which each slight variation, if useful, is preserved, by the term of Natural Selection.

Charles Darwin 1809–82 English natural historian: *On the Origin of Species* (1859)

7 [Natural selection] has no vision, no foresight, no sight at all. If it can be said to play the role of watchmaker in nature, it is the *blind* watchmaker.

referring to William Paley's conception of the world as a watch, made by God

Richard Dawkins 1941– English biologist: *The Blind Watchmaker* (1986)

8 The essence of life is statistical improbability on a colossal scale.

Richard Dawkins 1941– English biologist: *The Blind Watchmaker* (1986)

9 Life is a copiously branching bush, continually pruned by the grim reaper of extinction, not a ladder of predictable progress.

Stephen Jay Gould 1941–2002 American palaeontologist: *Wonderful Life* (1989)

10 I'd lay down my life for two brothers or eight cousins.

J. B. S. Haldane 1892–1964 Scottish mathematical biologist: attributed; in *New Scientist* 8 August 1974

11 Life exists in the universe only because the carbon atom possesses certain exceptional properties.

James Jeans 1877–1946 English astronomer, physicist, and mathematician: *The Mysterious Universe* (1930)

12 There are more animals living in the scum on the teeth in a man's mouth than there are men in a whole kingdom.

on his observations of micro-organisms

Antoni van Leeuwenhoek 1632–1723 Dutch naturalist: letter to Francis Aston, 17 September 1683

13 There are people who do not object to eating a mutton chop—people who do not even object to shooting a pheasant . . . —and yet who consider it something monstrous to introduce under the skin of a guinea pig a little inoculation of some microbe to ascertain its action.

Joseph Lister 1827–1912 English surgeon: in *British Medical Journal* (1897)

14 Population, when unchecked, increases in a geometrical ratio. Subsistence only increases in an arithmetical ratio.

Thomas Robert Malthus 1766–1834 English political economist: *Essay on the Principle of Population* (1798)

15 The microbe is nothing, the terrain is everything.

Louis Pasteur 1822–95 French chemist and bacteriologist: to Professor Rénon, on his deathbed; Hans Seyle *The Stress of Life* (1956)

16 The biologist passes, the frog remains.

sometimes quoted as 'Theories pass. The frog remains'

Jean Rostand 1894–1977 French biologist: *Inquiétudes d'un biologiste* (1967)

17 Water is life's *mater* and *matrix*, mother and medium. There is no life without water.

Albert von Szent-Györgyi 1893–1986 Hungarian-born biochemist: in *Perspectives in Biology and Medicine* Winter 1971

18 The history of the living world can be summarised as the elaboration of ever more perfect eyes within a cosmos in which there is always something more to be seen.

Pierre Teilhard de Chardin 1881–1955 French Jesuit philosopher and palaeontologist: *The Phenomenon of Man* (1959)

19 Evolution advances, not by a priori design, but by the selection of what works best out of whatever choices offer. We are the products of editing, rather than of authorship.

> **George Wald** 1904–97 American biochemist: in *Annals of the New York Academy of Sciences* vol. 69 1957

20 Was it through his grandfather or his grandmother that he claimed his descent from a monkey?

> *addressed to T. H. Huxley in the debate on Darwin's theory of evolution*
>
> **Samuel Wilberforce** 1805–73 English prelate: at a meeting of British Association in Oxford, 30 June 1860; see HUMAN RACE 11 , SCIENCE AND RELIGION 5

Lifestyles

see also LIFE

1 Never play cards with a man called Doc. Never eat at a place called Mom's. Never sleep with a woman whose troubles are worse than your own.

> **Nelson Algren** 1909–81 American novelist: in *Newsweek* 2 July 1956

2 What is the secret of my long life? I really don't know—cigarettes, whisky and wild, wild women!

> *the oldest British survivor of the First World War*
>
> **Henry Allingham** 1896–2009 English airman: in *Sunday Times* 13 November 2005; in *Telegraph* online 10 November 2005

3 I've lived a life that's full, I've travelled each and ev'ry highway And more, much more than this. I did it my way.

> **Paul Anka** 1941– Canadian singer and composer: 'My Way' (1969 song)

4 Love and do what you will.

> **St Augustine of Hippo** AD 354–430 Early Christian theologian: *In Epistolam Joannis ad Parthos* (AD 413)

5 A man hath no better thing under the sun, than to eat, and to drink, and to be merry.

> **Bible**: Ecclesiastes

6 Thou shalt love thy neighbour as thyself.

> **Bible**: Leviticus; see also St Matthew

7 We had better live as we think, otherwise sooner or later we shall end up by thinking as we have lived.

> **Paul Bourget** 1852–1935 French writer: *Le Démon de Midi* (1914)

8 Life is a matter of passing the time enjoyably. There may be other things in life, but I've been too busy passing my time enjoyably to think very deeply about them.

> **Peter Cook** 1937–95 English satirist and actor: in *Guardian* 10 January 1994

9 Do what thou wilt shall be the whole of the Law.

> **Aleister Crowley** 1875–1947 English diabolist: *Book of the Law* (1909)

10 Dream as if you'll live forever. Live as if you'll die today.

> **James Dean** 1931–55 American actor: in 1955, George Perry *James Dean* (2005)

11 Study as if you were to live for ever; live as if you were to die tomorrow.

> **St Edmund of Abingdon** c.1175–1240 English scholar and churchman: John Crozier *St Edmund of Abingdon* (1982)

12 Where is the Life we have lost in living?

> **T. S. Eliot** 1888–1965 Anglo-American poet, critic, and dramatist: *The Rock* (1934)

13 Live in the sunshine, swim the sea, Drink the wild air's salubrity.

> **Ralph Waldo Emerson** 1803–82 American philosopher and poet: *The Conduct of Life* (1860) 'Considerations by the Way'

14 What we do in life echoes in eternity.
> **David Franzoni** 1947– American
> screenwriters: *Gladiator* (2000 film);
> spoken by Russell Crowe

15 Just trust yourself and you'll learn
the art of living.
> **Johann Wolfgang von Goethe**
> 1749–1832 German poet, novelist, and
> dramatist: *Faust* pt. 1 (1808)
> 'Studierzimmer'

16 If I had but two loaves of bread I
would sell one of them, and buy
White Hyacinths to feed my soul.
> **Elbert Hubbard** 1859–1915 American
> writer: *White Hyacinths* (1907)

17 Live all you can; it's a mistake not to.
It doesn't so much matter what you
do in particular, so long as you have
your life. If you haven't had that,
what *have* you had?
> **Henry James** 1843–1916 American
> novelist: *The Ambassadors* (1903)

18 Turn on, tune in and drop out.
> **Timothy Leary** 1920–96 American
> psychologist: lecture, June 1966; *The
> Politics of Ecstasy* (1968)

19 We live, not as we wish to, but as we
can.
> **Menander** 342–*c*.292 BC Greek comic
> dramatist: *The Lady of Andros*

20 Believe me! The secret of reaping the
greatest fruitfulness and the greatest
enjoyment from life is *to live
dangerously*!
> **Friedrich Nietzsche** 1844–1900 German
> philosopher and writer: *Die fröhliche
> Wissenschaft* (1882)

21 Man is born to live, not to prepare for
life.
> **Boris Pasternak** 1890–1960 Russian
> novelist and poet: *Doctor Zhivago*
> (1958)

22 *Fay ce que vouldras.*
Do what you like.
> **François Rabelais** *c*.1494–*c*.1553 French

humanist, satirist, and physician:
Gargantua (1534)

23 You only live once, and the way I live,
once is enough.
> **Frank Sinatra** 1915–98 American singer
> and actor: attributed, in *The Times*
> 16 May 1998

24 [Take] short views of human
life—not further than dinner or tea.
> **Sydney Smith** 1771–1845 English
> clergyman and essayist: letter to Lady
> Georgiana Morpeth, 16 February 1820

25 Keep your eyes open and your
mouth shut.
> **John Steinbeck** 1902–68 American
> novelist: *Sweet Thursday* (1954)

26 Do you want to know the great
drama of my life? It's that I have put
my genius into my life; all I've put
into my works is my talent.
> **Oscar Wilde** 1854–1900 Anglo-Irish
> dramatist and poet: André Gide *Oscar
> Wilde* (1910)

Likes and Dislikes

see also CRITICS, TASTE

1 You don't have to like everything.
proposing a notice for the National Gallery
> **Alan Bennett** 1934– English actor and
> dramatist: in *Independent* 24 May 1995

2 I do not love thee, Dr Fell.
The reason why I cannot tell;
But this I know, and know full well,
I do not love thee, Dr Fell.
> **Thomas Brown** 1663–1704 English
> satirist: translation of an epigram by
> Martial AD *c*.40–*c*.104

3 For I've read in many a novel that,
unless they've souls that grovel,
Folks *prefer* in fact a hovel to your
dreary marble halls.
> **C. S. Calverley** 1831–84 English writer:
> 'In the Gloaming' (1872)

4 The hippies wanted peace and love.
We wanted Ferraris, blondes and
switchblades.

Alice Cooper 1948– American rock
singer: in *Independent* 5 May 2001

5 You're going to like this . . . not a
lot . . . but you'll like it!

Paul Daniels 1938– British conjuror:
catch-phrase used in his conjuring act,
especially on television from
1981 onwards

6 I don't care anything about reasons,
but I know what I like.

Henry James 1843–1916 American
novelist: *Portrait of a Lady* (1881)

7 A little of what you fancy does you
good.

Fred W. Leigh d. 1924 and **George
Arthurs**: title of song (1915)

8 People who like this sort of thing will
find this the sort of thing they like.
judgement of a book

Abraham Lincoln 1809–65 American
Republican statesman: G. W. E. Russell
Collections and Recollections (1898)

9 Tiggers don't like honey.

A. A. Milne 1882–1956 English writer for
children: *House at Pooh Corner* (1928)

10 I bet you if I had met him [Trotsky]
and had a chat with him, I would
have found him a very interesting
and human fellow, for I never yet met
a man that I didn't like.

Will Rogers 1879–1935 American actor
and humorist: in *Saturday Evening Post*
6 November 1926

11 To like and dislike the same things,
that is indeed true friendship.

Sallust 86–35 BC Roman historian:
Catiline

12 Take care to get what you like or you
will be forced to like what you get.

George Bernard Shaw 1856–1950 Irish
dramatist: *Man and Superman* (1903)
'Maxims: Stray Sayings'

13 Do not do unto others as you would
that they should do unto you. Their
tastes may not be the same.

George Bernard Shaw 1856–1950 Irish
dramatist: *Man and Superman* (1903)
'Maxims for Revolutionists: The Golden
Rule'

Literature

see also ART, BOOKS, FICTION, LITERATURE AND
SOCIETY, POETRY, READING, WRITING

1 A losing trade, I assure you, sir:
literature is a drug.

George Borrow 1803–81 English writer:
Lavengro (1851)

2 What literature can and should do is
change the people who teach the
people who don't read the books.

A. S. Byatt 1936– English novelist:
interview in *Newsweek* 5 June 1995

3 Literature is the art of writing
something that will be read twice;
journalism what will be read once.

Cyril Connolly 1903–74 English writer:
Enemies of Promise (1938)

4 He knew everything about literature
except how to enjoy it.

Joseph Heller 1923–99 American
novelist: *Catch-22* (1961)

5 Literature is my Utopia.

Helen Keller 1880–1968 American
writer and social reformer: *The Story of
my Life* (1903)

6 Literature is news that STAYS news.

Ezra Pound 1885–1972 American poet:
The ABC of Reading (1934)

7 Literature is the one place in any
society where, within the secrecy of
our own heads, we can hear *voices
talking about everything in every
possible way.*

Salman Rushdie 1947– Indian-born
British novelist: lecture 'Is Nothing
Sacred' 6 February 1990

8 The illusion of art is to make one believe that great literature is very close to life, but exactly the opposite is true. Life is amorphous, literature is formal.

> **Françoise Sagan** 1935–2004 French novelist: Malcolm Cowley (ed.) *Writers at Work* (1958) 1st series

9 Remarks are not literature.

> **Gertrude Stein** 1874–1946 American writer: *Autobiography of Alice B. Toklas* (1933)

10 Any writer worth his salt knows that only a small proportion of literature does more than partly compensate people for the damage they have suffered in learning to read.

> **Rebecca West** 1892–1983 English novelist and journalist: Peter Vansittart *Path from a White Horse* (1985)

Literature and Society

1 Nothing I wrote in the thirties saved one Jew from Auschwitz.

> **W. H. Auden** 1907–73 English poet: attributed

2 The writer's only responsibility is to his art. He will be completely ruthless if he is a good one. . . . If a writer has to rob his mother, he will not hesitate; the *Ode on a Grecian Urn* is worth any number of old ladies.

> **William Faulkner** 1897–1962 American novelist: in *Paris Review* Spring 1956

3 I am convinced more and more day by day that fine writing is next to fine doing the top thing in the world.

> **John Keats** 1795–1821 English poet: letter to J. H. Reynolds, 24 August 1819

4 One of the things a writer is for is to say the unsayable, speak the unspeakable and ask difficult questions.

> **Salman Rushdie** 1947– Indian-born British novelist: in *Independent on Sunday* 10 September 1995

5 I've used my talents as a writer to enable the Ogoni people to confront their tormentors. I was not able to do it as a politician or a businessman. My writing did it . . . I think I have the moral victory.

> **Ken Saro-Wiwa** 1941–95 Nigerian writer and environmentalist: letter, shortly before his execution in 1995, to William Boyd

6 A writer must refuse, therefore, to allow himself to be transformed into an institution.

> **Jean-Paul Sartre** 1905–80 French philosopher, novelist, dramatist, and critic: refusing the Nobel Prize at Stockholm, 22 October 1964

7 There are various forms of production: artillery, automobiles, lorries. You also produce 'commodities', 'works', 'products'. Such things are highly necessary. Engineering things. For people's souls. 'Products' are highly necessary too. 'Products' are very important for people's souls. You are engineers of human souls.

> **Joseph Stalin** 1879–1953 Soviet dictator: speech to writers at Gorky's house, 26 October 1932; see ART AND SOCIETY 2, ART AND SOCIETY 4

Logic and Reason

1 All that is beautiful and noble is the result of reason and calculation.

> **Charles Baudelaire** 1821–67 French poet and critic: *The Painter of Modern Life* (1863) 'In Praise of Cosmetics'

2 Only reason can convince us of those three fundamental truths without a

recognition of which there can be no
effective liberty: that what we believe
is not necessarily true; that what we
like is not necessarily good; and that
all questions are open.

Clive Bell 1881–1964 English art critic:
Civilization (1928)

3 If we would guide by the light of
reason, we must let our minds be
bold.

Louis D. Brandeis 1856–1941 American
jurist: *Jay Burns Baking Co. v. Bryan*
(1924) (dissenting)

4 'Contrariwise,' continued
Tweedledee, 'if it was so, it might be;
and if it were so, it would be: but as it
isn't, it ain't. That's logic.'

Lewis Carroll 1832–98 English writer
and logician: *Through the Looking-
Glass* (1872)

5 when man determined to destroy
himself he picked the was
of shall and finding only why
smashed it into because.

e. e. cummings 1894–1962 American
poet: *1 x 1* (1944) no. 26

6 'Is there any other point to which
you would wish to draw my
attention?'
'To the curious incident of the dog in
the night-time.'
'The dog did nothing in the night-
time.'
'That was the curious incident,'
remarked Sherlock Holmes.

Arthur Conan Doyle 1859–1930
Scottish-born writer of detective fiction:
The Memoirs of Sherlock Holmes (1894)

7 Reasons are not like garments, the
worse for wearing.

Robert Devereux, Earl of Essex
1566–1601 English soldier and courtier:
letter to Lord Willoughby, 4 January
1599

8 I'll not listen to reason . . . Reason
always means what someone else
has got to say.

Elizabeth Gaskell 1810–65 English
novelist: *Cranford* (1853)

9 A hidden connection is stronger than
an obvious one.

Heraclitus *c.*540–*c.*480 BC Greek
philosopher: Hippolytus *Refutatio*

10 Irrationally held truths may be more
harmful than reasoned errors.

T. H. Huxley 1825–95 English biologist:
Science and Culture and Other Essays
(1881) 'The Coming of Age of the Origin
of Species'

11 Logical consequences are the
scarecrows of fools and the beacons
of wise men.

T. H. Huxley 1825–95 English biologist:
Science and Culture and Other Essays
(1881) 'On the Hypothesis that Animals
are Automata'

12 After all, what was a paradox but a
statement of the obvious so as to
make it sound untrue?

Ronald Knox 1888–1957 English writer
and Roman Catholic priest: *A Spiritual
Aeneid* (1918)

13 You can't think rationally on an
empty stomach, and a whole lot of
people can't do it on a full stomach
either.

Lord Reith 1889–1971 British
administrator and politician: D. Parker
Radio: The Great Years (1977)

14 If I were to suggest that between the
Earth and Mars there is a china
teapot revolving about the sun in an
elliptical orbit, nobody would be
able to disprove my assertion
provided I were careful to add that
the teapot is too small to be revealed
even by our most powerful
telescopes. But if I were to go on to
say that, since my assertion cannot
be disproved, it is intolerable

presumption on the part of human reason to doubt it, I should rightly be thought to be talking nonsense.

> **Bertrand Russell** 1872–1970 British philosopher and mathematician: 'Is There a God?', commissioned (but not published) by *The Illustrated Magazine*, 1952; first published in *Collected Papers* vol. 11 (1997)

15 It is useless to attempt to reason a man out of what he was never reasoned into.

> **Jonathan Swift** 1667–1745 Irish poet and satirist: attributed, but not traced in Swift's works, probably apocryphal

16 Logic must take care of itself.

> **Ludwig Wittgenstein** 1889–1951 Austrian-born philosopher: *Tractatus Logico-Philosophicus* (1922)

London

1 London, thou art the flower of cities all!

> **Anonymous**: 'London' (poem of unknown authorship, previously attributed to William Dunbar, *c*.1465–*c*.1530)

2 *Was für Plunder!*

What rubbish!

of London as seen from the Monument in June 1814; often misquoted as 'Was für plündern [What a place to plunder]*!*'

> **Gebhard Lebrecht Blücher** 1742–1819 Prussian field marshal: Evelyn Princess Blücher *Memoirs of Prince Blücher* (1932)

3 London Pride has been handed down to us.

London Pride is a flower that's free.

London Pride means our own dear town to us,

And our pride it for ever will be.

> **Noël Coward** 1899–1973 English dramatist, actor, and composer: 'London Pride' (1941 song)

4 Maybe it's because I'm a Londoner That I love London so.

> **Hubert Gregg** 1914–2004 English songwriter: 'Maybe It's Because I'm a Londoner' (1947 song)

5 When a man is tired of London, he is tired of life; for there is in London all that life can afford.

> **Samuel Johnson** 1709–84 English poet, critic, and lexicographer: James Boswell *Life of Samuel Johnson* (1791) 20 September 1777

6 I thought of London spread out in the sun,

Its postal districts packed like squares of wheat.

> **Philip Larkin** 1922–85 English poet: 'The Whitsun Weddings' (1964)

7 The parks are the lungs of London.

> **William Pitt, Earl of Chatham** 1708–78 British Whig statesman: speech by William Windham, House of Commons, 30 June 1808

8 Earth has not anything to show more fair:

Dull would he be of soul who could pass by

A sight so touching in its majesty:

This City now doth like a garment wear

The beauty of the morning.

> **William Wordsworth** 1770–1850 English poet: 'Composed upon Westminster Bridge' (1807)

Loneliness

see also SOLITUDE

1 Please fence me in baby the world's too big out here and I don't like it without you.

> **Humphrey Bogart** 1899–1957 American actor: telegram to Lauren Bacall; Lauren Bacall *By Myself* (1978)

2 All the lonely people, where do they
all come from?
John Lennon 1940–80 and **Paul
McCartney** 1942–　English pop singers
and songwriters: 'Eleanor Rigby'
(1966 song)

3 Only the lonely (know the way I feel).
Roy Orbison 1936–88 American singer
and songwriter: title of song (1960, with
Joe Melson)

4 The loneliness of the long-distance
runner.
Alan Sillitoe 1928–　English writer: title
of novel (1959)

5 Oh, no no no, it was too cold always
(Still the dead one lay moaning)
I was much too far out all my life
And not waving but drowning.
Stevie Smith 1902–71 English poet and
novelist: 'Not Waving but Drowning'
(1957)

6 God created man and, finding him
not sufficiently alone, gave him a
companion to make him feel his
solitude more keenly.
Paul Valéry 1871–1945 French poet,
critic, and man of letters: *Tel Quel 1*
(1941)

Love

see also COURTSHIP, FAITHFULNESS, KISSING,
LOVERS, MARRIAGE, RELATIONSHIPS, ROMANCE,
SEX

1 You know very well that love is, above
all, the gift of oneself!
Jean Anouilh 1910–87 French
dramatist: *Ardèle* (1949)

2 Is it prickly to touch as a hedge is,
Or soft as eiderdown fluff?
Is it sharp or quite smooth at the
edges?
O tell me the truth about love.
W. H. Auden 1907–73 English poet: 'Oh
Tell Me the Truth about Love' (1938)

3 How in hell can you handle love
without turning your life upside
down? That's what love does, it
changes everything.
Lauren Bacall 1924–　American actress:
By Myself (1978)

4 Love is just a system for getting
someone to call you darling after sex.
Julian Barnes 1946–　English novelist:
Talking It Over (1991)

5 The fate of love is that it always
seems too little or too much.
Amelia E. Barr 1831–1919 American
writer and journalist: *The Belle of
Bolling Green* (1904)

6 To love someone is to isolate him
from the world, wipe out every trace
of him, dispossess him of his
shadow, drag him into a murderous
future. It is to circle around the other
like a dead star and absorb him into
a black light.
Jean Baudrillard 1929–2007 French
sociologist and cultural critic: *Fatal
Strategies* (1983)

7 With love, you see, even too much is
not enough.
**Pierre-Augustin Caron de
Beaumarchais** 1732–99 French
dramatist: *The Marriage of Figaro* (1784)

8 Love is free; it is not practised as a
way of achieving other ends.
Pope Benedict XVI 1927–　German
cleric: *Deus Caritas Est* (God is Love,
2005)

9 Love is patient and kind; love is not
jealous or boastful; it is not
arrogant or rude.
Love does not insist on its own way;
it is not irritable or resentful;
It does not rejoice at wrong, but
rejoices in the right.
Love bears all things, believes all
things, hopes all things, endures all
things.
Bible: I Corinthians

10 Love seeketh not itself to please,
Nor for itself hath any care;
But for another gives its ease,
And builds a Heaven in Hell's
despair.
> **William Blake** 1757–1827 English poet:
> 'The Clod and the Pebble' (1794)

11 Real love is a pilgrimage. It happens
when there is no strategy, but it is
very rare because most people are
strategists.
> **Anita Brookner** 1928– British novelist
> and art historian: Olga Kenyon (ed.)
> *Women Writers Talk* (1989)

12 In her first passion woman loves her
lover,
In all the others all she loves is love.
> **Lord Byron** 1788–1824 English poet:
> *Don Juan* (1819–24)

13 *when asked if he was 'in love':*
Yes . . . whatever that may mean.
> *after the announcement of his engagement*
> **Charles, Prince of Wales** 1948– British
> prince: interview, 24 February 1981

14 If grass can grow through cement,
love can find you at every time in
your life.
> **Cher** 1946– American singer and
> actress: in *The Times* 30 May 1998

15 Much love much trial, but what an
utter desert is life without love.
> **Charles Darwin** 1809–82 English
> natural historian: letter to Joseph
> Hooker, 27 November 1863

16 Selfhood begins with a walking away,
And love is proved in the letting go.
> **C. Day-Lewis** 1904–72 English poet and
> critic: 'Walking Away' (1962)

17 Love itself is what is left over when
being in love has burned away.
> **Louis de Bernières** 1954– British
> novelist and short-story writer: *Captain
> Corelli's Mandolin* (1994)

18 Love is anterior to life,
Posterior to death,
Initial of creation, and
The exponent of breath.
> **Emily Dickinson** 1830–86 American
> poet: 'Love is anterior to life'

19 The magic of first love is our
ignorance that it can ever end.
> **Benjamin Disraeli** 1804–81 British Tory
> statesman and novelist: *Henrietta
> Temple* (1837)

20 For God's sake hold your tongue, and
let me love.
> **John Donne** 1572–1631 English poet
> and divine: 'The Canonization'

21 There is a kind of love called
maintenance,
Which stores the WD40 and knows
when to use it.
> **U. A. Fanthorpe** 1929–2009 English
> poet: 'Atlas' (1995)

22 Love is a universal migraine.
A bright stain on the vision
Blotting out reason.
> **Robert Graves** 1895–1985 English poet:
> 'Symptoms of Love'

23 What love is, if thou wouldst be
taught,
Thy heart must teach alone—
Two souls with but a single thought,
Two hearts that beat as one.
> **Friedrich Halm** 1806–71 German
> dramatist: *Der Sohn der Wildnis* (1842)

24 When love congeals
It soon reveals
The faint aroma of performing seals,
The double crossing of a pair of
heels.
I wish I were in love again!
> **Lorenz Hart** 1895–1943 American
> songwriter: 'I Wish I Were in Love Again'
> (1937 song)

25 Love is mutually feeding each other,
not one living on another like a
ghoul.
> **Bessie Head** 1937–86 South African-
> born writer: *A Question of Power* (1973)

26 Passion makes the world go round.
Love just makes it a safer place.
   Ice-T 1958– American rap musician:
   The Ice Opinion (1994)

27 Love's like the measles—all the worse
when it comes late in life.
   Douglas Jerrold 1803–57 English
   dramatist and journalist: *The Wit and
   Opinions of Douglas Jerrold* (1859)

28 We love well only once, the first time.
The loves which follow are less
involuntary.
   Jean de la Bruyère 1645–96 French
   satiric moralist: *Les Caractères ou les
   moeurs de ce siècle* (1688) 'Du Coeur'

29 Love. Of course, love. Flames for a
year, ashes for thirty.
   Giuseppe di Lampedusa 1896–1957
   Italian writer: *The Leopard* (1957)

30 What will survive of us is love.
   Philip Larkin 1922–85 English poet: 'An
   Arundel Tomb' (1964)

31 Only the flow matters: live and let
live, love and let love. There is no
point to love and life.
   D. H. Lawrence 1885–1930 English
   novelist and poet: 'Do Women Change?'
   (1930)

32 Love doesn't just sit there, like a
stone, it has to be made, like bread;
remade all the time, made new.
   Ursula K. Le Guin 1929– American
   writer: *The Lathe of Heaven* (1971)

33 How alike are the groans of love to
those of the dying.
   Malcolm Lowry 1909–57 English
   novelist: *Under the Volcano* (1947)

34 Where both deliberate, the love is
slight;
Who ever loved that loved not at first
sight?
   Christopher Marlowe 1564–93 English
   dramatist and poet: *Hero and Leander*
   (1598)

35 The love that lasts longest is the love
that is never returned.
   W. Somerset Maugham 1874–1965
   English novelist: *A Writer's Notebook*
   (1949) written in 1894

36 No, there's nothing half so sweet in
life
As love's young dream.
   Thomas Moore 1779–1852 Irish
   musician and songwriter: 'Love's Young
   Dream' (1807)

37 Love is the extremely difficult
realisation that something other
than oneself is real. Love, and so art
and morals, is the discovery of
reality.
   Iris Murdoch 1919–99 English novelist:
   'The Sublime and the Good' in *Chicago
   Review* 13 (1959)

38 If I can't love Hitler, I can't love at all.
   Rev. A. J. Muste 1885–1967 American
   pacifist: at a Quaker meeting 1940; in
   New York Times 12 February 1967

39 Love is so short, forgetting is so long.
   Pablo Neruda 1904–73 Chilean poet:
   'Tonight I Can Write' (1924)

40 Most people experience love,
without noticing that there is
anything remarkable about it.
   Boris Pasternak 1890–1960 Russian
   novelist and poet: *Doctor Zhivago*
   (1958)

41 Birds do it, bees do it,
Even educated fleas do it.
Let's do it, let's fall in love.
   Cole Porter 1891–1964 American
   songwriter: 'Let's Do It' (1954 song;
   words added to the 1928 original)

42 Love gratified, is love satisfied—and
love satisfied, is indifference begun.
   Samuel Richardson 1689–1761 English
   novelist: *Clarissa* (1751)

43 Love consists in this, that two solitudes protect and touch and greet each other.

> **Rainer Maria Rilke** 1875–1926 German poet: *Letters to a Young Poet* (1929) 14 May 1904 (tr. H. MacLennan)

44 Experience shows us that love does not consist in gazing at each other but in looking together in the same direction.

> **Antoine de Saint-Exupéry** 1900–44 French novelist: *Wind, Sand and Stars* (1939)

45 Love means not ever having to say you're sorry.

> **Erich Segal** 1937– American novelist: *Love Story* (1970)

46 The course of true love never did run smooth.

> **William Shakespeare** 1564–1616 English dramatist: *A Midsummer Night's Dream* (1595–6)

47   To be wise, and love, Exceeds man's might.

> **William Shakespeare** 1564–1616 English dramatist: *Troilus and Cressida* (1602)

48 Let me not to the marriage of true minds Admit impediments. Love is not love Which alters when it alteration finds.

> **William Shakespeare** 1564–1616 English dramatist: sonnet 116

49 To say a man is fallen in love,—or that he is deeply in love,—or up to the ears in love,—and sometimes even over head and ears in it,—carries an idiomatical kind of implication, that love is a thing below a man.

> **Laurence Sterne** 1713–68 English novelist: *Tristram Shandy* (1759–67)

50 Love is the fart Of every heart: It pains a man when 'tis kept close,

And others doth offend, when 'tis let loose.

> **John Suckling** 1609–42 English poet and dramatist: 'Love's Offence' (1646)

51 In the spring a young man's fancy lightly turns to thoughts of love.

> **Alfred, Lord Tennyson** 1809–92 English poet: 'Locksley Hall' (1842)

52 'Tis better to have loved and lost Than never to have loved at all.

> **Alfred, Lord Tennyson** 1809–92 English poet: *In Memoriam A. H. H.* (1850)

53 *Omnia vincit Amor: et nos cedamus Amori.*

Love conquers all things: let us too give in to Love.

> **Virgil** 70–19 BC Roman poet: *Eclogues*

54 Yet each man kills the thing he loves, By each let this be heard, Some do it with a bitter look, Some with a flattering word. The coward does it with a kiss, The brave man with a sword!

> **Oscar Wilde** 1854–1900 Anglo-Irish dramatist and poet: *The Ballad of Reading Gaol* (1898)

55 Even memory is not necessary for love. There is a land of the living and a land of the dead and the bridge is love, the only survival, the only meaning.

> **Thornton Wilder** 1897–1975 American novelist and dramatist: *The Bridge of San Luis Rey* (1927), closing words

56 A woman can be proud and stiff When on love intent; But Love has pitched his mansion in The place of excrement; For nothing can be sole or whole That has not been rent.

> **W. B. Yeats** 1865–1939 Irish poet: 'Crazy Jane Talks with the Bishop' (1932)

Lovers

see also COURTSHIP, LOVE

1 He's more myself than I am.
Whatever our souls are made of his
and mine are the same.
   Emily Brontë 1818–48 English novelist
   and poet: *Wuthering Heights* (1847)

2 If thou must love me, let it be for
nought
Except for love's sake only.
   Elizabeth Barrett Browning 1806–61
   English poet: *Sonnets from the
   Portuguese* (1850) no. 14

3 How do I love thee? Let me count the
ways.
I love thee to the depth and breadth
and height
My soul can reach.
   Elizabeth Barrett Browning 1806–61
   English poet: *Sonnets from the
   Portuguese* (1850) no. 43

4 O, my Luve's like a red, red rose
That's newly sprung in June;
O my Luve's like the melodie
That's sweetly play'd in tune.
   Robert Burns 1759–96 Scottish poet: 'A
   Red Red Rose' (1796); derived from
   various folk-songs

5 When you realize you want to spend
the rest of your life with somebody,
you want the rest of your life to start
as soon as possible.
   Nora Ephron 1941– American
   screenwriter and director: *When Harry
   Met Sally* (1989 film)

6 The ones we choose to love become
our anchor
when the hawser of the blood-tie's
hacked, or frays.
   Tony Harrison 1937– British poet: *v*
   (1985)

7 I can't get no satisfaction
I can't get no girl reaction
   Mick Jagger 1943– and **Keith Richards**

1943– English rock musicians: '(I Can't
Get No) Satisfaction' (1965 song)

8 All you need is love.
   John Lennon 1940–80 and **Paul
   McCartney** 1942– English pop singers
   and songwriters: title of song (1967)

9 The life that I have
Is all that I have
And the life that I have
Is yours.
The love that I have
Of the life that I have
Is yours and yours and yours.
   *given to the British secret agent Violette
   Szabo (1921–45), for use with the Special
   Operations Executive*
   Leo Marks 1920–2001 English
   cryptographer and screenwriter: 'The
   Life that I Have' (written 1943)

10 If I were young and handsome as I
was, instead of old and faded as I am,
and you could lay the empire of the
world at my feet, you should never
share the heart and hand that once
belonged to John, Duke of
Marlborough.
   *refusing an offer of marriage from the
   Duke of Somerset*
   Sarah, Duchess of Marlborough
   1660–1744: W. S. Churchill
   Marlborough: His Life and Times vol. 4
   (1938)

11 I want to do with you what spring
does with the cherry trees.
   Pablo Neruda 1904–73 Chilean poet:
   'Every Day You Play' (1969)

12 By the time you say you're his,
Shivering and sighing
And he vows his passion is
Infinite, undying—
Lady, make a note of this:
One of you is lying.
   Dorothy Parker 1893–1967 American
   critic and humorist: 'Unfortunate
   Coincidence' (1937)

13 I find no peace, and I am not at war,
I fear and hope, and burn and I am
ice.

> **Petrarch** 1304–74 Italian poet:
> *Canzoniere* no. 134 (c.1352) tr. M. Musa

14 It's no longer a burning within my
veins: it's Venus entire latched onto
her prey.

> **Jean Racine** 1639–99 French tragedian:
> *Phèdre* (1677)

15   It were all one
That I should love a bright particular
star
And think to wed it, he is so above
me.

> **William Shakespeare** 1564–1616
> English dramatist: *All's Well that Ends
> Well* (1603–4)

16 Why so pale and wan, fond lover?
Prithee, why so pale?
Will, when looking well can't move
her,
Looking ill prevail?
Prithee, why so pale?

> **John Suckling** 1609–42 English poet
> and dramatist: *Aglaura* (1637)

17 If somebody says 'I love you,' to me, I
feel as though I had a pistol pointed
at my head. What can anybody reply
under such conditions but that
which the pistol-holder requires? 'I
love you, *too*.'

> **Kurt Vonnegut** 1922–2007 American
> novelist and short-story writer:
> *Wampeters, Fama and Granfalloons*
> (1974)

18 Why is it that the most unoriginal
thing we can say to one another is
still the thing we long to hear? 'I love
you' is always a quotation.

> **Jeanette Winterson** 1959– English
> novelist and critic: *Written on the Body*
> (1992)

Loyalty

1 I may be wrong, but I have never
found deserting friends conciliates
enemies.

> **Margot Asquith** 1864–1945 British
> political hostess: *Lay Sermons* (1927)

2 I am not standing by my man, like
Tammy Wynette. I am sitting here
because I love him, I respect him,
and I honour what he's been through
and what we've been through
together.

> **Hillary Rodham Clinton** 1947–
> American lawyer and Republican
> politician: interview on *60 Minutes*,
> CBS-TV, 27 January 1992; see LOYALTY 6

3 I don't want loyalty. I want *loyalty*. I
want him to kiss my ass in Macy's
window at high noon and tell me it
smells like roses. I want his pecker in
my pocket.

> **Lyndon Baines Johnson** 1908–73
> American Democratic statesman: David
> Halberstam *The Best and the Brightest*
> (1972)

4 We are the President's men, and we
must behave accordingly.

> **Henry Kissinger** 1923– American
> politician: M. and B. Kalb *Kissinger*
> (1974)

5 [Grant] stood by me when I was
crazy, and I stood by him when he
was drunk; and now we stand by
each other always.

> **William Sherman** 1820–91 American
> Union general: in 1864; Geoffrey C.
> Ward *The Civil War* (1991)

6 Stand by your man.

> **Tammy Wynette** 1942– American
> country singer: title of song (1968, with
> Billy Sherrill)

Luck

see also CHANCE

1 What we call luck is the inner man externalized. We make things happen to us.
   Robertson Davies 1913–95 Canadian novelist: *What's Bred in the Bone* (1985)

2 There is much good luck in the world, but it is luck. We are none of us safe. We are children, playing or quarrelling on the line.
   E. M. Forster 1879–1970 English novelist: *The Longest Journey* (1907)

3 Care and diligence bring luck.
   Thomas Fuller 1654–1734 English writer and physician: *Gnomologia* (1732)

4 Some folk want their luck buttered.
   Thomas Hardy 1840–1928 English novelist and poet: *The Mayor of Casterbridge* (1886)

5 Watch out w'en you'er gittin all you want. Fattenin' hogs ain't in luck.
   Joel Chandler Harris 1848–1908 American writer: *Uncle Remus: His Songs and His Sayings* (1880)

6 All you know about it [luck] for certain is that it's bound to change.
   Bret Harte 1836–1902 American poet: *The Outcasts of Poker Flat* (1871)

7 now and then
   there is a person born
   who is so unlucky
   that he runs into accidents
   which started to happen
   to somebody else.
   Don Marquis 1878–1937 American poet and journalist: *archys life of mehitabel* (1933)

8 Miracles do happen, but one has to work very hard for them.
   Chaim Weizmann 1874–1952 Russian-born Israeli statesman: Isaiah Berlin *Personal Impressions* (1998)

9 Luck is preparation meeting opportunity.
   Oprah Winfrey 1954– American talk show hostess: interview, Academy of Achievement, 21 February 1991

Luxury

see also WEALTH

1 The saddest thing I can imagine is to get used to luxury.
   Charlie Chaplin 1889–1977 English film actor and director: *My Autobiography* (1964)

2 In the affluent society no useful distinction can be made between luxuries and necessaries.
   J. K. Galbraith 1908–2006 American economist: *The Affluent Society* (1958)

3 I spend my life ministering to the swinish luxury of the rich.
   William Morris 1834–96 English writer, artist, and designer: attributed, *c.*1877; W. R. Lethaby *Philip Webb* (1935)

4 Give us the luxuries of life, and we will dispense with its necessities.
   John Lothrop Motley 1814–77 American historian: Oliver Wendell Holmes *Autocrat of the Breakfast-Table* (1857–8)

5 Walk! Not bloody likely. I am going in a taxi.
   George Bernard Shaw 1856–1950 Irish dramatist: *Pygmalion* (1916)

6 Luxury has been railed at for two thousand years, in verse and in prose, and it has always been loved.
   Voltaire 1694–1778 French writer and philosopher: *Dictionnaire philosophique* (1764)

7 The necessities were going by default to save the luxuries until I hardly knew which were necessities and which luxuries.
   Frank Lloyd Wright 1867–1959

American architect: *Autobiography* (1945)

Madness

see also MENTAL ILLNESS, MIND

1 Dear Sir,—I am in a madhouse and quite forget your name or who you are.
   John Clare 1793–1864 English poet: letter, 1860

2 Babylon in all its desolation is a sight not so awful as that of the human mind in ruins.
   Scrope Davies *c.*1783–1852 English conversationalist: letter to Thomas Raikes, May 1835

3 Mad, is he? Then I hope he will *bite* some of my other generals.
   replying to the Duke of Newcastle, who had complained that General Wolfe was a madman
   George II 1683–1760 British monarch: Henry Beckles Willson *Life and Letters of James Wolfe* (1909)

4 Every one is more or less mad on one point.
   Rudyard Kipling 1865–1936 English writer and poet: *Plain Tales from the Hills* (1888)

5 Madness need not be all breakdown. It may also be break-through.
   R. D. Laing 1927–89 Scottish psychiatrist: *The Politics of Experience* (1967)

6 They called me mad, and I called them mad, and damn them, they outvoted me.
   Nathaniel Lee *c.*1653–92 English dramatist: R. Porter *A Social History of Madness* (1987)

7 Though this be madness, yet there is method in't.
   William Shakespeare 1564–1616 English dramatist: *Hamlet* (1601)

8 O! let me not be mad, not mad, sweet heaven;
   Keep me in temper; I would not be mad!
   William Shakespeare 1564–1616 English dramatist: *King Lear* (1605–6)

9 As an experience, madness is terrific . . . and in its lava I still find most of the things I write about.
   Virginia Woolf 1882–1941 English novelist: letter to Ethel Smyth, 22 June 1930

Majorities

see MINORITIES AND MAJORITIES

Management

see also ADMINISTRATION, CAREERS, ORGANIZATION

1 Some great men owe most of their greatness to the ability of detecting in those they destine for their tools the exact quality of strength that matters for their work.
   Joseph Conrad 1857–1924 Polish-born English novelist: *Lord Jim* (1900)

2 Every organization of today has to build into its very structure the *management of change.*
   Peter F. Drucker 1909– Austrian-born American management consultant, educator, and writer: *Post-Capitalist Society* (1993)

3 Meetings are a great trap . . . However, they are indispensable when you don't want to do anything.
   J. K. Galbraith 1908–2006 Canadian-born American economist: *Ambassador's Journal* (1969) 22 April 1961

4 If you want people motivated to do a good job, give them a good job to do.
   Frederick Herzberg 1923–2000 American management researcher: in *Industry Week* 21 September 1987

5 Every time I make an appointment, I create a hundred malcontents and one ingrate.

> **Louis XIV** 1638–1715 French monarch: Voltaire *Siècle de Louis XIV* (1768 ed.)

6 Perfection of planned layout is achieved only by institutions on the point of collapse.

> **C. Northcote Parkinson** 1909–93 English writer: *Parkinson's Law* (1958)

7 A good plan violently executed *Now* is better than a perfect plan next week.

> **George S. Patton** 1885–1945 American general: *War As I Knew It* (1947)

8 In a hierarchy every employee tends to rise to his level of incompetence.

> **Laurence J. Peter** 1919–90 Canadian writer: *The Peter Principle* (1969)

9 Surround yourself with the best people you can find, delegate authority, and don't interfere.

> **Ronald Reagan** 1911–2004 American Republican statesman: in *Fortune* September 1986

10 There is nothing in the world which does not have its decisive moment, and the masterpiece of good management is to recognize and grasp this moment.

> **Jean-François Paul de Gondi, Cardinal de Retz** 1613–79 French cardinal: *Mémoires* (1717)

11 Try to analyze situations intelligently, anticipate problems and move swiftly to solve them. However, when you're up to your ears in alligators, it is difficult to remember that the reason you're there is to drain the swamp.

> **Donald Rumsfeld** 1932– American Republican politician and businessman: *Rumsfeld's Rules* (2001)

12 You're fired!

in the UK associated with the English businessman Alan Sugar (1947–)

> **Donald Trump** 1946– American businessman: catchphrase on *The Apprentice* NBC TV 2004–

13 Management that wants to change an institution must first show it loves that institution.

> **John Tusa** 1936– British broadcaster and journalist: in *Observer* 27 February 1994

Manners

see also BEHAVIOUR, THANKS

1 Phone for the fish-knives, Norman
As Cook is a little unnerved;
You kiddies have crumpled the serviettes
And I must have things daintily served.

> **John Betjeman** 1906–84 English poet: 'How to get on in Society' (1954)

2 Curtsey while you're thinking what to say. It saves time.

> **Lewis Carroll** 1832–98 English writer and logician: *Through the Looking-Glass* (1872)

3 It is wise to apply the oil of refined politeness to the mechanism of friendship.

> **Colette** 1873–1954 French novelist: *The Pure and the Impure* (1932)

4 The art of pleasing consists in being pleased.

> **William Hazlitt** 1778–1830 English essayist: *The Round Table* (1817) 'On Manner'

5 An insolent reply from a polite person is a bad sign.

> **Hippocrates** *c*.460–357 BC Greek physician: *Prorrhetic*

6 To Americans, English manners are far more frightening than none at all.
> **Randall Jarrell** 1914–65 American poet: *Pictures from an Institution* (1954)

7 When suave politeness, tempering bigot zeal,
Corrected *I believe* to *One does feel*.
> **Ronald Knox** 1888–1957 English writer and Roman Catholic priest: 'Absolute and Abitofhell' (1913)

8 'Always be civil to the girls, you never know who they may marry' is an aphorism which has saved many an English spinster from being treated like an Indian widow.
> **Nancy Mitford** 1904–73 English writer: *Love in a Cold Climate* (1949)

9 If you can't say something nice . . . don't say nothing at all.
> **Larry Morey** 1905–71 American songwriter: *Bambi* (1942 film) spoken by Thumper; from the novel by Felix Salten (1869–1945)

10 Good manners are a combination of intelligence, education, taste, and style mixed together so that you don't need any of those things.
> **P. J. O'Rourke** 1947– American humorous writer: *Modern Manners* (1984)

11 He is the very pineapple of politeness!
> **Richard Brinsley Sheridan** 1751–1816 Anglo-Irish dramatist: *The Rivals* (1775)

12 Good breeding consists in concealing how much we think of ourselves and how little we think of the other person.
> **Mark Twain** 1835–1910 American writer: *Notebooks* (1935)

13 Manners are especially the need of the plain. The pretty can get away with anything.
> **Evelyn Waugh** 1903–66 English novelist: in *Observer* 15 April 1962

Maps

1 Topography displays no favourites; North's as near as West.
More delicate than the historians' are the map-makers' colours.
> **Elizabeth Bishop** 1911–79 American poet: 'The Map' (1946)

2 'What's the good of *Mercator's* North Poles and Equators,
Tropics, Zones and Meridian lines?'
So the Bellman would cry: and the crew would reply,
'They are merely conventional signs!'
> **Lewis Carroll** 1832–98 English writer and logician: *The Hunting of the Snark* (1876)

3 So geographers, in Afric-maps,
With savage-pictures fill their gaps;
And o'er unhabitable downs
Place elephants for want of towns.
> **Jonathan Swift** 1667–1745 Anglo-Irish poet and satirist: 'On Poetry' (1733)

Marriage

see also BACHELORS, COURTSHIP, HUSBANDS, LOVE, SEX, WEDDINGS, WIVES

1 Like everything which is not the involuntary result of fleeting emotion but the creation of time and will, any marriage, happy or unhappy, is infinitely more interesting than any romance, however passionate.
> **W. H. Auden** 1907–73 English poet: *A Certain World* (1970)

2 To have and to hold from this day forward, for better for worse, for richer for poorer, in sickness and in health, to love, cherish, and to obey, till death us do part.
> **The Book of Common Prayer** 1662: *Solemnization of Matrimony* Betrothal

3 Still I can't contradict, what so oft has
  been said,
  'Though women are angels, yet
  wedlock's the devil.'
  Lord Byron 1788–1824 English poet: 'To
  Eliza' (1806)

4 Love and marriage, love and
  marriage,
  Go together like a horse and carriage,
  This I tell ya, brother,
  Ya can't have one without the other.
  Sammy Cahn 1913–93 American
  songwriter: 'Love and Marriage'
  (1955 song)

5 The deep, deep peace of the double-
  bed after the hurly-burly of the
  chaise-longue.
  on her recent marriage
  Mrs Patrick Campbell 1865–1940
  English actress: Alexander Woollcott
  While Rome Burns (1934)

6 I learnt a long time ago that the only
  people who count in any marriage
  are the two that are in it.
  Hillary Rodham Clinton 1947–
  American lawyer and Republican
  politician: television interview with
  NBC, 27 January 1998

7 Marriage is a wonderful invention;
  but, then again, so is a bicycle repair
  kit.
  Billy Connolly 1942– Scottish
  comedian: Duncan Campbell *Billy
  Connolly* (1976)

8 The heart of marriage is memories.
  Bill Cosby 1937– American comedian,
  actor, and producer: *Love and Marriage*
  (1989)

9 The value of marriage is not that
  adults produce children but that
  children produce adults.
  Peter De Vries 1910–93 American
  novelist and humorist: *The Tunnel of
  Love* (1954)

10 There were three of us in this
  marriage, so it was a bit crowded.
  Diana, Princess of Wales 1961–97
  former wife of Charles, Prince of Wales:
  interview on *Panorama*, BBC1 TV,
  20 November 1995

11 I have always thought that every
  woman should marry, and no man.
  Benjamin Disraeli 1804–81 British Tory
  statesman and novelist: *Lothair* (1870)

12 The chains of marriage are so heavy
  that it takes two to bear them, and
  sometimes three.
  Alexandre Dumas 1824–95 French
  writer: Léon Treich *L'Esprit d'Alexandre
  Dumas*

13 Having once embarked upon your
  marital voyage, it is impossible not to
  be aware that you make no way and
  that the sea is not within sight—that
  in fact, you are exploring a closed
  basin.
  George Eliot 1819–80 English novelist:
  Middlemarch (1871–2)

14 Most marriages don't add two people
  together. They subtract one from the
  other.
  Ian Fleming 1908–64 English thriller
  writer: *Diamonds are Forever* (1956)

15 Keep your eyes wide open before
  marriage, half shut afterwards.
  Benjamin Franklin 1706–90 American
  politician, inventor, and scientist: *Poor
  Richard's Almanack* (1738)

16 Do you think your mother and I
  should have lived comfortably so
  long together, if ever we had been
  married?
  John Gay 1685–1732 English poet and
  dramatist: *The Beggar's Opera* (1728)

17 You shall be together when the white
  wings of death scatter your days.
  Ay, you shall be together even in the
  silent memory of God.
  But let there be spaces in your
  togetherness,

And let the winds of the heavens
dance between you.
Kahlil Gibran 1883–1931 Lebanese-
born American writer and painter: *The
Prophet* (1923) 'On Marriage'

18 The concept of two people living
together for 25 years without having
a cross word suggests a lack of spirit
only to be admired in sheep.
A. P. Herbert 1890–1971 English writer
and humorist: in *News Chronicle*, 1940

19 Hogamus, higamous
Man is polygamous
Higamus, hogamous
Woman monogamous.
William James 1842–1910 American
philosopher: attributed

20 The triumph of hope over
experience.
*of a man who remarried immediately after
the death of a wife with whom he had been
unhappy*
Samuel Johnson 1709–84 English poet,
critic, and lexicographer: James Boswell
Life of Samuel Johnson (1791) 1770

21 So they were married—to be the
more together—
And found they were never again so
much together,
Divided by the morning tea,
By the evening paper,
By children and tradesmen's bills.
Louis MacNeice 1907–63 British poet,
born in Belfast: 'Les Sylphides' (1941)

22 The trouble with marriage is that it
ends every night after making love,
and it must be rebuilt every morning
before breakfast.
Gabriel García Márquez 1928–
Colombian novelist: *Love in the Time of
Cholera* (1985)

23 One doesn't have to get anywhere in
a marriage. It's not a public
conveyance.
Iris Murdoch 1919–99 English novelist:
A Severed Head (1961)

24 To keep your marriage brimming
With love in the loving cup,
Whenever you're wrong, admit it,
Whenever you're right, shut up.
Ogden Nash 1902–71 American
humorist: 'A Word to Husbands' (1957)

25 The great secret of a successful
marriage is to treat all disasters as
incidents and none of the incidents
as disasters.
Harold Nicolson 1886–1968 English
diplomat, politician, and writer:
attributed

26 It doesn't much signify whom one
marries, for one is sure to find next
morning that it was someone else.
Samuel Rogers 1763–1855 English poet:
Alexander Dyce (ed.) *Table Talk of
Samuel Rogers* (1860)

27 A young man married is a man that's
marred.
William Shakespeare 1564–1616
English dramatist: *All's Well that Ends
Well* (1603–4)

28 Marriage is popular because it
combines the maximum of
temptation with the maximum of
opportunity.
George Bernard Shaw 1856–1950 Irish
dramatist: *Man and Superman* (1903)
'Maxims: Marriage'

29 Chains do not hold a marriage
together. It is threads, hundreds of
tiny threads which sew people
together through the years. That is
what makes a marriage last—more
than passion or even sex!
Simone Signoret 1921–85 French
actress: in *Daily Mail* 4 July 1978

30 My definition of marriage . . . it
resembles a pair of shears, so joined
that they cannot be separated; often
moving in opposite directions, yet

always punishing anyone who
comes between them.
> **Sydney Smith** 1771–1845 English
> clergyman and essayist: Lady Holland
> *Memoir* (1855)

31 Marriage is like life in this—that it is
a field of battle, and not a bed of
roses.
> **Robert Louis Stevenson** 1850–94
> Scottish novelist: *Virginibus Puerisque*
> (1881)

32 Marriage isn't a word . . . it's a
sentence!
> **King Vidor** 1895–1982 American film
> director: *The Crowd* (1928 film)

33 Marriage is the waste-paper basket
of the emotions.
> **Sidney Webb** 1859–1947 English
> socialist: Bertrand Russell
> *Autobiography* (1967)

34 In married life three is company and
two none.
> **Oscar Wilde** 1854–1900 Anglo-Irish
> dramatist and poet: *The Importance of
> Being Earnest* (1895)

35 Marriage is a bribe to make a
housekeeper think she's a
householder.
> **Thornton Wilder** 1897–1975 American
> novelist and dramatist: *The Merchant of
> Yonkers* (1939)

Masturbation

1 Don't knock masturbation. It's sex
with someone I love.
> **Woody Allen** 1935– American film
> director, writer, and actor: *Annie Hall*
> (1977 film, with Marshall Brickman)

2 Masturbation is the thinking man's
television.
> **Christopher Hampton** 1946– English
> dramatist: *Philanthropist* (1970)

3 Masturbation: the primary sexual
activity of mankind. In the

nineteenth century, it was a disease;
in the twentieth, it's a cure.
> **Thomas Szasz** 1920– Hungarian-born
> psychiatrist: *The Second Sin* (1973)

Mathematics

see also STATISTICS

1 Let no one enter who does not know
geometry [mathematics].
*inscription on Plato's door, probably at the
Academy at Athens*
> **Anonymous**: Elias Philosophus *In
> Aristotelis Categorias Commentaria*

2 If in other sciences we should arrive
at certainty without doubt and truth
without error, it behoves us to place
the foundations of knowledge in
mathematics.
> **Roger Bacon** c.1220–c.92 English
> philosopher and Franciscan monk:
> *Opus Majus*

3 The jury eagerly wrote down all three
dates on their slates, and then added
them up, and reduced the answer to
shillings and pence.
> **Lewis Carroll** 1832–98 English writer
> and logician: *Alice's Adventures in
> Wonderland* (1865)

4 I never could make out what those
damned dots meant.
on decimal points
> **Lord Randolph Churchill** 1849–94
> British Conservative politician: W. S.
> Churchill *Lord Randolph Churchill*
> (1906)

5 It is more important to have beauty
in one's equations than to have them
fit experiment . . . The discrepancy
may well be due to minor
features . . . that will get cleared up
with further developments.
> **Paul Dirac** 1902–84 British theoretical
> physicist: in *Scientific American* May
> 1963

6 There is no 'royal road' to geometry.
Euclid *fl. c.*300 BC Greek mathematician: addressed to Ptolemy I; Proclus *Commentary on the First Book of Euclid's Elementa*

7 The most devilish thing is 8 times 8 and 7 times 7 it is what nature itselfe cant endure.
Marjory Fleming 1803–11 English child writer: *Journals, Letters and Verses* (ed. A. Esdaile, 1934)

8 Prime numbers are what is left when you have taken all the patterns away. I think prime numbers are like life.
Mark Haddon 1962– British novelist: *The Curious Incident of the Dog in the Night-time* (2003)

9 No-one could study mathematics intensively for more than five hours a day and remain sane.
J. B. S. Haldane 1892–1964 Scottish mathematical biologist: in *Perspectives in Biology and Medicine* (1966) 'An Autobiography in Brief'

10 Someone told me that each equation I included in the book would halve the sales.
Stephen Hawking 1942– English theoretical physicist: *A Brief History of Time* (1988)

11 God made the integers, all the rest is the work of man.
Leopold Kronecker 1823–91 German mathematician: *Jahrsberichte der Deutschen Mathematiker Vereinigung*

12 Points
Have no parts or joints
How then can they combine
To form a line?
J. A. Lindon: M. Gardner *Wheels, Life and Other Mathematical Amusements* (1983)

13 In mathematics you don't understand things. You just get used to them.
John von Neumann 1903–57

Hungarian-born American mathematician: Gary Zukav *The Dancing Wu Li Masters* (1979)

14 There are 10 types of people in the country: those who understand binary and those who don't.
Jeremy Paxman 1950– British journalist and broadcaster: in *Sunday Telegraph* 28 December 2003

15 An equation for me has no meaning unless it expresses a thought of God.
Srinivasa Ramanujan 1887–1920 Indian mathematician: Robert Kanigel *The Man Who Knew Infinity* (1992)

16 Mathematics, rightly viewed, possesses not only truth, but supreme beauty—a beauty cold and austere, like that of sculpture.
Bertrand Russell 1872–1970 British philosopher and mathematician: *Philosophical Essays* (1910)

17 Mathematics may be defined as the subject in which we never know what we are talking about, nor whether what we are saying is true.
Bertrand Russell 1872–1970 British philosopher and mathematician: *Mysticism and Logic* (1918)

18 What would life be like without arithmetic, but a scene of horrors?
Sydney Smith 1771–1845 English clergyman and essayist: letter to Miss [Lucie Austen], 22 July 1835

Maturity

see also EXPERIENCE

1 I gave my beauty and my youth to men. I am going to give my wisdom and experience to animals.
Brigitte Bardot 1934– French actress: attributed, June 1987

2 When I was young I hoped that one day I should be able to go into a post office to buy a stamp without feeling nervous and shy: now I realize that I never shall.

> **Edmund Blunden** 1896–1974 English poet: Rupert Hart-Davis, letter to George Lyttelton, 5 August 1956

3 I had always thought that once you grew up you could do anything you wanted—stay up all night or eat ice-cream straight out of the container.

> **Bill Bryson** 1951– American travel writer: *The Lost Continent* (1989)

4 How many roads must a man walk down
Before you can call him a man? . . .
The answer, my friend, is blowin' in the wind,
The answer is blowin' in the wind.

> **Bob Dylan** 1941– American singer and songwriter: 'Blowin' in the Wind' (1962 song)

5 At twenty years of age, the will reigns; at thirty, the wit; and at forty, the judgement.

> **Benjamin Franklin** 1706–90 American politician, inventor, and scientist: *Poor Richard's Almanac* (1741)

6 Immature love says: 'I love you because I need you.' Mature love says: 'I need you because I love you.'

> **Erich Fromm** 1900–80 American philosopher and psychologist: *The Art of Loving* (1956)

7 One of the most obvious facts about grown-ups, to a child, is that they have forgotten what it is like to be a child.

> **Randall Jarrell** 1914–65 American poet: Christina Stead *The Man Who Loved Children* (1965)

8 If you can talk with crowds and keep your virtue,
Or walk with Kings—nor lose the common touch,
If neither foes nor loving friends can hurt you,

If all men count with you, but none too much;
If you can fill the unforgiving minute
With sixty seconds' worth of distance run,
Yours is the Earth and everything that's in it,
And—which is more—you'll be a Man, my son!

> **Rudyard Kipling** 1865–1936 English writer and poet: 'If—' (1910)

9 To be adult is to be alone.

> **Jean Rostand** 1894–1977 French biologist: *Pensées d'un biologiste* (1954)

10 One's prime is elusive. You little girls, when you grow up, must be on the alert to recognise your prime at whatever time of your life it may occur.

> **Muriel Spark** 1918–2006 British novelist: *The Prime of Miss Jean Brodie* (1961)

11 When adults stop being infants, children can be children.

> **Rowan Williams** 1950– British Anglican clergyman, Archbishop of Canterbury: in *Mail on Sunday* 17 April 2005

Meaning

see also WORDS

1 No one means all he says, and yet very few say all they mean, for words are slippery and thought is viscous.

> **Henry Brooks Adams** 1838–1918 American man of letters: *The Education of Henry Adams* (1907)

2 'Then you should say what you mean,' the March Hare went on. 'I do,' Alice hastily replied; 'at least—at least I mean what I say—that's the same thing, you know.' 'Not the same thing a bit!' said the Hatter. 'Why, you might just as well say that "I see

what I eat" is the same thing as "I eat what I see!" '
Lewis Carroll 1832–98 English writer and logician: *Alice's Adventures in Wonderland* (1865)

3 You see it's like a portmanteau—there are two meanings packed up into one word.
Lewis Carroll 1832–98 English writer and logician: *Through the Looking-Glass* (1872)

4 It depends on what the meaning of 'is' is.
Bill Clinton 1946– American Democratic statesman: videotaped evidence to the grand jury; tapes broadcast 21 September 1998

5 If a lady says No, she means Perhaps; if she says Perhaps, she means Yes; if she says Yes, she is no Lady.
If a diplomat says Yes, he means Perhaps; if he says Perhaps, he means No; if he says No, he is no Diplomat.
Lord Dawson of Penn 1864–1945 British physician: Francis Watson *Dawson of Penn* (1950)

6 The meaning doesn't matter if it's only idle chatter of a transcendental kind.
W. S. Gilbert 1836–1911 English writer of comic and satirical verse: *Patience* (1881)

7 It all depends what you mean by . . .
C. E. M. Joad 1891–1953 English philosopher: answering questions on 'The Brains Trust' (formerly 'Any Questions'), BBC radio (1941–8)

8 Any general statement is like a cheque drawn on a bank. Its value depends on what is there to meet it.
Ezra Pound 1885–1972 American poet: *The ABC of Reading* (1934)

9 Egad I think the interpreter is the hardest to be understood of the two!
Richard Brinsley Sheridan 1751–1816 Anglo-Irish dramatist: *The Critic* (1779)

10 The little girl had the making of a poet in her who, being told to be sure of her meaning before she spoke, said, 'How can I know what I think till I see what I say?'
Graham Wallas 1858–1932 British political scientist: *The Art of Thought* (1926)

Means

see WAYS AND MEANS

Medicine

see also HEALTH, SICKNESS

1 I am dying with the help of too many physicians.
Alexander the Great 356–323 BC Greek monarch: attributed

2 Medicinal discovery,
It moves in mighty leaps,
It leapt straight past the common cold
And gave it us for keeps.
Pam Ayres 1947– English writer of humorous verse: 'Oh no, I got a cold' (1976)

3 We all labour against our own cure, for death is the cure of all diseases.
Sir Thomas Browne 1605–82 English writer and physician: *Religio Medici* (1643)

4 If a lot of cures are suggested for a disease, it means that the disease is incurable.
Anton Chekhov 1860–1904 Russian dramatist and short-story writer: *The Cherry Orchard* (1904)

5 Every day, in every way, I am getting better and better.

to be said 15 to 20 times, morning and evening

Émile Coué 1857–1926 French psychologist: *De la suggestion et de ses applications* (1915)

6 The wounded surgeon plies the steel
That questions the distempered part;
Beneath the bleeding hands we feel
The sharp compassion of the healer's art
Resolving the enigma of the fever chart.

T. S. Eliot 1888–1965 Anglo-American poet, critic, and dramatist: *Four Quartets* 'East Coker' (1940)

7 We shall have to learn to refrain from doing things merely because we know how to do them.

Theodore Fox 1899–1989 English doctor: speech to Royal College of Physicians, 18 October 1965

8 Life is short, the art long.

Hippocrates *c.*460–357 BC Greek physician: *Aphorisms*

9 As to diseases, make a habit of two things—to help, or at least to do no harm.

Hippocrates *c.*460–357 BC Greek physician: *Epidemics*

10 I will use treatment to help the sick according to my ability and judgement, but never with a view to injury or wrong-doing. Neither will I administer a poison to anybody when asked to do so, nor will I suggest such a course.

Hippocrates *c.*460–357 BC Greek physician: *The Hippocratic Oath*

11 It may seem a strange principle to enunciate as the very first requirement in a Hospital that it should do the sick no harm.

Florence Nightingale 1820–1910 English nurse: *Notes on Hospitals* (1863 ed.) preface

12 What nursing has to do . . . is to put the patient in the best condition for nature to act upon him.

Florence Nightingale 1820–1910 English nurse: *Notes on Nursing* (1860)

13 One finger in the throat and one in the rectum makes a good diagnostician.

William Osler 1849–1919 Canadian-born physician: *Aphorisms from his Bedside Teachings* (1961)

14 Cured yesterday of my disease,
I died last night of my physician.

Matthew Prior 1664–1721 English poet: 'The Remedy Worse than the Disease' (1727)

15 Throw physic to the dogs; I'll none of it.

William Shakespeare 1564–1616 English dramatist: *Macbeth* (1606)

16 There is at bottom only one genuinely scientific treatment for all diseases, and that is to stimulate the phagocytes.

George Bernard Shaw 1856–1950 Irish dramatist: *The Doctor's Dilemma* (1911)

17 Formerly, when religion was strong and science weak, men mistook magic for medicine; now, when science is strong and religion weak, men mistake medicine for magic.

Thomas Szasz 1920– Hungarian-born psychiatrist: *The Second Sin* (1973)

18 Ah, well, then, I suppose that I shall have to die beyond my means.

at the mention of a huge fee for a surgical operation

Oscar Wilde 1854–1900 Anglo-Irish dramatist and poet: R. H. Sherard *Life of Oscar Wilde* (1906)

Mediocrity

1 Some men are born mediocre, some men achieve mediocrity, and some men have mediocrity thrust upon them. With Major Major it had been all three.
Joseph Heller 1923–99 American novelist: *Catch-22* (1961)

2 If Richard Nixon was second-rate, what in the world *is* third-rate?
Joseph Heller 1923–99 American novelist: *Good as Gold* (1979)

3 Not gods, nor men, nor even booksellers have put up with poets being second-rate.
Horace 65–8 BC Roman poet: *Ars Poetica*

4 There's only one real sin, and that is to persuade oneself that the second-best is anything but the second-best.
Doris Lessing 1919– English writer: *Golden Notebook* (1962)

5 Women want mediocre men, and men are working hard to be as mediocre as possible.
Margaret Mead 1901–78 American anthropologist: in *Quote Magazine* 15 June 1958

6 She has a Rolls body and a Balham mind.
J. B. Morton ('Beachcomber') 1893–1975 British journalist: *Morton's Folly* (1933)

7 It is our national joy to mistake for the first-rate, the fecund rate.
Dorothy Parker 1893–1967 American critic and humorist: in *New Yorker* 16 March 1929

Meeting

see also PARTING

1 Gin a body meet a body
Comin thro' the rye,
Gin a body kiss a body
Need a body cry?
Robert Burns 1759–96 Scottish poet: 'Comin thro' the rye' (1796)

2 Yo, Blair. How are you doing?
the President addresses Tony Blair during a break in the G8 summit in St Petersburg, Russia, 17 July 2006; a microphone had been left on
George W. Bush 1946– American Republican statesman: in *Guardian* 18 July 2006

3 'Is there anybody there?' said the Traveller,
Knocking on the moonlit door.
Walter de la Mare 1873–1956 English poet and novelist: 'The Listeners' (1912)

4 Of all the gin joints in all the towns in all the world, she walks into mine.
Julius J. Epstein 1909–2001: *Casablanca* (1942 film, with Philip G. Epstein and Howard Koch); spoken by Humphrey Bogart

5 Some enchanted evening,
You may see a stranger,
You may see a stranger,
Across a crowded room.
Oscar Hammerstein II 1895–1960 American songwriter: 'Some Enchanted Evening' (1949 song)

6 Not many sounds in life, and I include all urban and all rural sounds, exceed in interest a knock at the door.
Charles Lamb 1775–1834 English writer: *Essays of Elia* (1823) 'Valentine's Day'

7 How d'ye do, and how is the old complaint?
reputed to be his greeting to all those he did not know
Lord Palmerston 1784–1865 British statesman: A. West *Recollections* (1899)

8 We'll meet again, don't know where, Don't know when,

But I know we'll meet again some
sunny day.
Ross Parker 1914–74 and **Hugh Charles**
1907–95 British songwriters: 'We'll Meet
Again' (1939 song)

9 I wish I could remember the first day,
First hour, first moment of your
meeting me,
If bright or dim the season, it might
be
Summer or winter for aught I can
say.
So unrecorded did it slip away.
Christina Rossetti 1830–94 English
poet: 'The First Day'

10 Ill met by moonlight, proud Titania.
William Shakespeare 1564–1616
English dramatist: *A Midsummer Night's
Dream* (1595–6)

11 When shall we three meet again
In thunder, lightning, or in rain?
William Shakespeare 1564–1616
English dramatist: *Macbeth* (1606)

12 Dr Livingstone, I presume?
Henry Morton Stanley 1841–1904
Welsh explorer: *How I found Livingstone*
(1872)

13 Why don't you come up sometime,
and see me?
*usually quoted as 'Why don't you come up
and see me sometime?'*
Mae West 1892–1980 American film
actress: *She Done Him Wrong*
(1933 film)

Memory

1 Memories are hunting horns
Whose sound dies on the wind.
Guillaume Apollinaire 1880–1918
French poet: 'Cors de Chasse' (1912)

2 And we forget because we must
And not because we will.
Matthew Arnold 1822–88 English poet
and essayist: 'Absence' (1852)

3 Think only of the past as its
remembrance gives you pleasure.
Jane Austen 1775–1817 English novelist:
Pride and Prejudice (1813)

4 Someone said that God gave us
memory so that we might have roses
in December.
J. M. Barrie 1860–1937 Scottish writer
and dramatist: Rectorial Address at St
Andrew's, 3 May 1922

5 Memories are not shackles, Franklin,
they are garlands.
Alan Bennett 1934– English actor and
dramatist: *Forty Years On* (1969)

6 We'll tak a cup o' kindness yet,
For auld lang syne.
Robert Burns 1759–96 Scottish poet:
'Auld Lang Syne' (1796)

7 Poor people's memory is less
nourished than that of the rich; it has
fewer landmarks in space because
they seldom leave the place where
they live, and fewer reference points
in time.
Albert Camus 1913–60 French novelist,
dramatist, and essayist: *The First Man*
(1994)

8 Our memories are card-indexes
consulted, and then put back in
disorder by authorities whom we do
not control.
Cyril Connolly 1903–74 English writer:
The Unquiet Grave (1944)

9 I have forgot much, Cynara! gone
with the wind,
Flung roses, roses, riotously, with the
throng,
Dancing, to put thy pale, lost lilies
out of mind.
Ernest Dowson 1867–1900 English
poet: 'Non Sum Qualis Eram' (1896);
also known as 'Cynara'

10 Footfalls echo in the memory
Down the passage which we did not
take

Towards the door we never opened
Into the rose-garden.

> **T. S. Eliot** 1888–1965 Anglo-American
> poet, critic, and dramatist: *Four
> Quartets* 'Burnt Norton' (1936)

11 Everyone seems to remember with
great clarity what they were doing on
November 22nd, 1963, at the precise
moment they heard President
Kennedy was dead.

> **Frederick Forsyth** 1938– English
> novelist: *The Odessa File* (1972)

12 Your memory is a monster; *you*
forget—*it* doesn't. It simply files
things away. It keeps things for you,
or hides things from you—and
summons them to your recall with a
will of its own. You think you have a
memory; but it has you!

> **John Irving** 1942– British novelist: *A
> Prayer for Owen Meany* (1989)

13 The true art of memory is the art of
attention.

> **Samuel Johnson** 1709–84 English poet,
> critic, and lexicographer: *The Idler* no.
> 74 (15 September 1759)

14 We met at nine.
We met at eight.
I was on time.
No, you were late.
Ah yes! I remember it well.

> **Alan Jay Lerner** 1918–86 American
> songwriter: 'I Remember it Well'
> (1958 song)

15 A cigarette that bears a lipstick's
traces,
An airline ticket to romantic places;
And still my heart has wings
These foolish things
Remind me of you.

> **Holt Marvell** 1901–69 English
> songwriter: 'These Foolish Things
> Remind Me of You' (1935 song)

16 And entering with relief some quiet
place

Where never fell his foot or shone his
face
I say, 'There is no memory of him
here!'
And so stand stricken, so
remembering him.

> **Edna St Vincent Millay** 1892–1950
> American poet: 'Time does not bring
> relief'

17 You may break, you may shatter the
vase, if you will,
But the scent of the roses will hang
round it still.

> **Thomas Moore** 1779–1852 Irish
> musician and songwriter:
> 'Farewell!—but whenever' (1807)

18 The memories of long love gather
like drifting snow, poignant as the
mandarin ducks who float side by
side in sleep.

> **Murasaki Shikibu** *c*.978–*c*.1031
> Japanese writer and courtier: *The Tale of
> Genji*

19 What beastly incidents our
memories insist on cherishing! . . .
the ugly and disgusting . . . the
beautiful things we have to keep
diaries to remember!

> **Eugene O'Neill** 1888–1953 American
> dramatist: *Strange Interlude* (1928)

20 And suddenly the memory revealed
itself. The taste was that of the little
piece of madeleine which on Sunday
mornings at Combray . . . my aunt
Léonie used to give me, dipping it
first in her own cup of tea or tisane.

> **Marcel Proust** 1871–1922 French
> novelist: *Swann's Way* (1913, vol. 1 of
> *Remembrance of Things Past*)

21 Better by far you should forget and
smile
Than that you should remember and
be sad.

> **Christina Rossetti** 1830–94 English
> poet: 'Remember' (1862)

22 I've a grand memory for forgetting, David.

> **Robert Louis Stevenson** 1850–94 Scottish novelist: *Kidnapped* (1886)

23 My memory is certainly in my hands. I can remember things only if I have a pencil and I can write with it and play with it. I think your hand concentrates for you.

> **Rebecca West** 1892–1983 English novelist and journalist: George Plimpton (ed.) *The Writer's Chapbook* (1989)

Men

see also BACHELORS, HUSBANDS, MEN AND WOMEN

1 Are all men in disguise except those crying?

> **Dannie Abse** 1923– Welsh-born doctor and poet: 'Encounter at a greyhound bus station' (1986)

2 Men have had every advantage of us in telling their own story. Education has been theirs in so much higher a degree; the pen has been in their hands.

> **Jane Austen** 1775–1817 English novelist: *Persuasion* (1818)

3 Women were brought up to believe that men were the answer. They weren't. They weren't even one of the questions.

> **Julian Barnes** 1946– English novelist: *Staring at the Sun* (1986)

4 Every modern male has, lying at the bottom of his psyche, a large, primitive being covered with hair down to his feet. Making contact with this Wild Man is the step the Eighties male or the Nineties male has yet to take.

> **Robert Bly** 1926– American writer: *Iron John* (1990)

5 Men build bridges and throw railroads across deserts, and yet they contend successfully that the job of sewing on a button is beyond them. Accordingly, they don't have to sew buttons.

> **Heywood Broun** 1888–1939 American journalist: *Seeing Things at Night* (1921)

6 Am I not a man? And is not a man stupid? I'm a man, so I married. Wife, children, house, everything, the full catastrophe

> **Michael Cacoyannis** 1922– Cypriot-born screenwriter and director: *Zorba the Greek* (1964 film); spoken by Anthony Quinn

7 Older men treat women like possessions, which is why I like younger men.

> **Joan Collins** 1933– British actress: in *Times* 27 October 2001

8 Bloody men are like bloody buses—
You wait for about a year
And as soon as one approaches your stop
Two or three others appear.

> **Wendy Cope** 1945– English poet: 'Bloody Men' (1992)

9 Man is to be held only by the *slightest* chains, with the idea that he can break them at pleasure, he submits to them in sport.

> **Maria Edgeworth** 1768–1849 Anglo-Irish novelist: *Letters for Literary Ladies* (1795)

10 Whatever they may be in public life, whatever their relations with men, in their relations with women, all men are rapists, and that's all they are. They rape us with their eyes, their laws, and their codes.

> **Marilyn French** 1929–2009 American writer: *The Women's Room* (1977)

11 We are lads. We have burgled houses and nicked car stereos, and we like

girls and swear and go to the football
and take the piss.
> **Noel Gallagher** 1967– English pop
> singer: interview in *Melody Maker*
> 30 March 1996

12 A man . . . is *so* in the way in the
house!
> **Elizabeth Gaskell** 1810–65 English
> novelist: *Cranford* (1853)

13 Years ago, manhood was an
opportunity for achievement, and
now it is a problem to be overcome.
> **Garrison Keillor** 1942– American
> humorous writer: *The Book of Guys*
> (1994)

14 Give me macho, or give me death.
> **Madonna** 1958– American pop singer
> and actress: in *Sunday Times* 29 July
> 2001

15 If you wish—
 . . . I'll be irreproachably tender;
not a man, but—a cloud in trousers!
> **Vladimir Mayakovsky** 1893–1930
> Russian poet: 'The Cloud in Trousers'
> (1915)

16 Sigh no more, ladies, sigh no more,
Men were deceivers ever.
> **William Shakespeare** 1564–1616
> English dramatist: *Much Ado About
> Nothing* (1598–9)

17 Every man over forty is a scoundrel.
> **George Bernard Shaw** 1856–1950 Irish
> dramatist: *Man and Superman* (1903)
> 'Maxims: Stray Sayings'

18 It's not the men in my life that
counts—it's the life in my men.
> **Mae West** 1892–1980 American film
> actress: *I'm No Angel* (1933 film)

19 A hard man is good to find.
> **Mae West** 1892–1980 American film
> actress: attributed

20 There is, of course, no reason for the
existence of the male sex except that

sometimes one needs help with
moving the piano.
> **Rebecca West** 1892–1983 English
> novelist and journalist: in *Sunday
> Telegraph* 28 June 1970

21 No nice men are good at getting
taxis.
> **Katharine Whitehorn** 1928– English
> journalist: in *Observer* 1977

Men and Women

see also MEN, RELATIONSHIPS, WOMAN'S ROLE,
WOMEN

1 In societies where men are truly
confident of their own worth,
women are not merely tolerated but
valued.
> **Aung San Suu Kyi** 1945– Burmese
> political leader: videotape speech at
> NGO Forum on Women, China, early
> September 1995

2 Women are programmed to love
completely, and men are
programmed to spread it around.
> **Beryl Bainbridge** 1933– English
> novelist: interview in *Daily Telegraph*
> 10 September 1996

3 Men look at women. Women watch
themselves being looked at.
> **John Berger** 1926– British writer and
> art critic: *Ways of Seeing* (1972)

4 Man's love is of man's life a thing
apart,
'Tis woman's whole existence.
> **Lord Byron** 1788–1824 English poet:
> *Don Juan* (1819–24)

5 Women deprived of the company of
men pine, men deprived of the
company of women become stupid.
> **Anton Chekhov** 1860–1904 Russian
> dramatist and short-story writer:
> *Notebooks* (1921)

6 The man's desire is for the woman;
but the woman's desire is rarely other
than for the desire of the man.
Samuel Taylor Coleridge 1772–1834
English poet, critic, and philosopher:
Table Talk (1835) 23 July 1827

7 There is more difference within the
sexes than between them.
Ivy Compton-Burnett 1884–1969
English novelist: *Mother and Son* (1955)

8 In the sex-war thoughtlessness is the
weapon of the male, vindictiveness
of the female.
Cyril Connolly 1903–74 English writer:
The Unquiet Grave (1944)

9 It is not in giving life but in risking
life that man is raised above the
animal; that is why superiority has
been accorded in humanity not to
the sex that brings forth but to that
which kills.
Simone de Beauvoir 1908–86 French
novelist and feminist: *The Second Sex*
(1949)

10 A woman needs a man like a fish
needs a bicycle.
Irina Dunn Australian writer and
politician: graffito written 1970;
attributed by Gloria Steinem in *Time*
9 October 2000

11 A man has every season, while a
woman only has the right to spring.
Jane Fonda 1937– American actress: in
Daily Mail 13 September 1989

12 Women have very little idea of how
much men hate them.
Germaine Greer 1939– Australian
feminist: *The Female Eunuch* (1971)

13 My mother said it was simple to keep
a man, you must be a maid in the
living room, a cook in the kitchen
and a whore in the bedroom. I said
I'd hire the other two and take care of
the bedroom bit.
Jerry Hall 1956– American model: in
Observer 6 October 1985

14 Take my word for it, the silliest
woman can manage a clever man;
but it takes a very clever woman to
manage a fool.
Rudyard Kipling 1865–1936 English
writer and poet: *Plain Tales from the
Hills* (1888)

15 Why can't a woman be more like a
man?
Men are so honest, so thoroughly
square;
Eternally noble, historically fair.
Alan Jay Lerner 1918–86 American
songwriter: 'A Hymn to Him' (1956 song)

16 I think men talk to women so they
can sleep with them and women
sleep with men so they can talk to
them.
Jay McInerney 1955– American writer:
Brightness Falls (1992)

17 A woman can forgive a man for the
harm he does her, but she can never
forgive him for the sacrifices he
makes on her account.
W. Somerset Maugham 1874–1965
English novelist: *The Moon and
Sixpence* (1919)

18 Every woman adores a Fascist,
The boot in the face, the brute
Brute heart of a brute like you.
Sylvia Plath 1932–63 American poet:
'Daddy' (1963)

19 Of all human struggles there is none
so treacherous and remorseless as
the struggle between the artist man
and the mother woman.
George Bernard Shaw 1856–1950 Irish
dramatist: *Man and Superman* (1903)

20 Man is the hunter; woman is his
game.
Alfred, Lord Tennyson 1809–92 English
poet: *The Princess* (1847)

21 Sure he was great, but don't forget that Ginger Rogers did everything he did backwards . . . and in high heels!
caption to 'Frank and Ernest' cartoon showing a Fred Astaire film festival
    Bob Thaves 1924–2006 American cartoonist: Ginger Rogers *Ginger: My Story* (1991)

22 After all these years, I see that I was mistaken about Eve in the beginning; it is better to live outside the Garden with her than inside it without her.
    Mark Twain 1835–1910 American writer: *Adam's Diary*

23 Me Tarzan, you Jane.
summing up his role in Tarzan, the Ape Man *(1932 film)*
    Johnny Weissmuller 1904–84 American film actor: in *Photoplay Magazine* June 1932; the words occur neither in the film nor the original novel, by Edgar Rice Burroughs

24 When women go wrong, men go right after them.
    Mae West 1892–1980 American film actress: *She Done Him Wrong* (1933 film)

25 Whatever women do they must do twice as well as men to be thought half as good.
    Charlotte Whitton 1896–1975 Canadian writer and politician: in *Canada Month* June 1963

26 All women become like their mothers. That is their tragedy. No man does. That's his.
    Oscar Wilde 1854–1900 Anglo-Irish dramatist and poet: *The Importance of Being Earnest* (1895)

27 Women have served all these centuries as looking-glasses possessing the magic and delicious power of reflecting the figure of a man at twice its natural size.
    Virginia Woolf 1882–1941 English novelist: *A Room of One's Own* (1929)

Mental Illness

see also MADNESS, MIND

1 In psychoanalysis nothing is true except the exaggerations.
    Theodor Adorno 1903–69 German philosopher and musicologist: *Minima Moralia* (1951)

2 Psychoanalysis pretends to investigate the Unconscious. The Unconscious by definition is what you are not conscious of. But the Analysts already know what's in it—they should, because they put it all in beforehand.
    Saul Bellow 1915–2005 American novelist: *The Dean's December* (1982)

3 Any man who goes to a psychiatrist should have his head examined.
    Sam Goldwyn 1882–1974 American film producer: Norman Zierold *Moguls* (1969)

4 There was only one catch and that was Catch-22, which specified that a concern for one's own safety in the face of dangers that were real and immediate was the process of a rational mind . . . Orr would be crazy to fly more missions and sane if he didn't, but if he was sane he had to fly them. If he flew them he was crazy and didn't have to; but if he didn't want to he was sane and had to.
    Joseph Heller 1923–99 American novelist: *Catch-22* (1961)

5 Schizophrenia cannot be understood without understanding despair.
    R. D. Laing 1927–89 Scottish psychiatrist: *The Divided Self* (1960)

6 The experience and behaviour that gets labelled schizophrenic is a special strategy that a person invents in order to live in an unlivable situation.

R. D. Laing 1927–89 Scottish psychiatrist: *Politics of Experience* (1967)

7 If the nineteenth century was the age of the editorial chair, ours is the century of the psychiatrist's couch.

Marshall McLuhan 1911–80 Canadian communications scholar: *Understanding Media* (1964)

8 Is there no way out of the mind?

Sylvia Plath 1932–63 American poet: 'Apprehensions' (1971)

9 If you talk to God, you are praying; if God talks to you, you have schizophrenia. If the dead talk to you, you are a spiritualist; if God talks to you, you are a schizophrenic.

Thomas Szasz 1920– Hungarian-born psychiatrist: *The Second Sin* (1973)

Mexico and South America

1 Fatherland, socialism or death—I swear it.

Hugo Chavez 1954– Venezuelan statesman: third inauguration speech, 10 January 2007, in *New York Times* (online edition) 11 January 2007

2 Poor Mexico, so far from God and so close to the United States.

Porfirio Diaz 1830–1915 Mexican revolutionary and statesman: attributed

3 Latins are tenderly enthusiastic. In Brazil they throw flowers at you. In Argentina they throw themselves.

Marlene Dietrich 1901–92 German-born American actress and singer: in *Newsweek* 24 August 1959

4 To be a gringo in Mexico . . . ah, that is euthanasia.

Carlos Fuentes 1928– Mexican novelist and writer: *The Old Gringo* (1985)

5 Night, snow, and sand make up the form
of my thin country,
all silence lies in its long line,
all foam flows from its marine beard,
all coal covers it with mysterious kisses.

Pablo Neruda 1904–73 Chilean poet: 'Discoverers of Chile' (1950)

6 Mexicans are descended from the Aztecs, Peruvians from the Incas and Argentinians from the ships.

Octavio Paz 1914–98 Mexican poet and essayist: attributed, in *Observer* 16 June 1990

7 Brazil—where the nuts come from.

Brandon Thomas 1856–1914 English dramatist: *Charlie's Aunt* (1892)

Middle Age

1 Years ago we discovered the exact point, the dead centre of middle age. It occurs when you are too young to take up golf and too old to rush up to the net.

Franklin P. Adams 1881–1960 American journalist and humorist: *Nods and Becks* (1944)

2 I am past thirty, and three parts iced over.

Matthew Arnold 1822–88 English poet and essayist: letter to Arthur Hugh Clough, 12 February 1853

3 Mr Salteena was an elderly man of 42.

Daisy Ashford 1881–1972 English child writer: *The Young Visiters* (1919)

4 Women over thirty are at their best, but men over thirty are too old to recognize it.

Jean-Paul Belmondo 1933– French film actor: attributed

5 After forty a woman has to choose between losing her figure or her face.

My advice is to keep your face, and stay sitting down.

> **Barbara Cartland** 1901–2000 English writer: in *Times* 6 October 1993

6 At eighteen our convictions are hills from which we look; at forty-five they are caves in which we hide.

> **F. Scott Fitzgerald** 1896–1940 American novelist: 'Bernice Bobs her Hair' (1920)

7 He who thinks to realize when he is older the hopes and desires of youth is always deceiving himself, for every decade of a man's life possesses its own kind of happiness, its own hopes and prospects.

> **Johann Wolfgang von Goethe** 1749–1832 German poet, novelist, and dramatist: *Elective Affinities* (1809)

8 Nobody loves a fairy when she's forty.

> **Arthur W. D. Henley**: title of song (1934)

9 The afternoon of human life must also have a significance of its own and cannot be merely a pitiful appendage to life's morning.

> **Carl Gustav Jung** 1875–1961 Swiss psychologist: *The Stages of Life* (1930)

10 Men at forty
Learn to close softly
The doors to rooms they will not be
Coming back to.

> **Donald Justice** 1925–2004 American poet: 'Men at Forty' (1967)

11 At forty-five,
What next, what next?
At every corner,
I meet my Father,
my age, still alive.

> **Robert Lowell** 1917–77 American poet: 'Middle Age' (1964)

12 The lovely thing about being forty is that you can appreciate twenty-five-year-old men more.

> **Colleen McCullough** 1937– Australian writer: attributed

13 I have a bone to pick with Fate.
Come here and tell me, girlie,
Do you think my mind is maturing late,
Or simply rotted early?

> **Ogden Nash** 1902–71 American humorist: 'Lines on Facing Forty' (1942)

14 One of the pleasures of middle age is to *find out* that one was right, and that one was much righter than one knew at say 17 or 23.

> **Ezra Pound** 1885–1972 American poet: *ABC of Reading* (1934)

15 By the time you hit 50, I reckon you've earned your wrinkles, so why not be proud of them?

> **Twiggy** 1949– English model and actress: in *Observer* 8 September 2002

The Mind

see also COUNSELLING, IDEAS, LOGIC, MADNESS, MENTAL ILLNESS, THINKING

1 A mind lively and at ease, can do with seeing nothing, and can see nothing that does not answer.

> **Jane Austen** 1775–1817 English novelist: *Emma* (1816)

2 It is not enough to have a good mind; the main thing is to use it well.

> **René Descartes** 1596–1650 French philosopher and mathematician: *Le Discours de la méthode* (1637)

3 Minds are like parachutes. They only function when they are open.

> **James Dewar** 1842–1923 Scottish physicist: attributed

4 It is neither death, nor exile, nor toil, nor any such thing that is the cause of our doing, or of our not doing, anything, but only our opinions and the decisions of our will.

> *often quoted as 'Not things, but opinions about things, trouble men'*
>
> **Epictetus** c.AD 50–120 Phrygian Stoic philosopher: *The Discourses*

5 If my mental processes are determined wholly by the motions of atoms in my brain, I have no reason for supposing that my beliefs are true. They may be sound chemically, but that does not make them sound logically. And hence I have no reason for supposing my brain to be composed of atoms.

   J. B. S. Haldane 1892–1964 Scottish mathematical biologist: *Possible Worlds* (1927)

6 On earth there is nothing great but man; in man there is nothing great but mind.

   William Hamilton 1788–1856 Scottish metaphysician: *Lectures on Metaphysics and Logic* (1859)

7 Purple haze is in my brain
   Lately things don't seem the same.
   Jimi Hendrix 1942–70 American rock musician: 'Purple Haze' (1967 song)

8 O the mind, mind has mountains; cliffs of fall
   Frightful, sheer, no-man-fathomed. Hold them cheap
   May who ne'er hung there.
   Gerard Manley Hopkins 1844–89 English poet and priest: 'No worst, there is none' (written 1885)

9 The only means of strengthening one's intellect is to make up one's mind about nothing—to let the mind be a thoroughfare for all thoughts. Not a select party.

   John Keats 1795–1821 English poet: letter to George and Georgiana Keats, 24 September 1819

10 Everyone complains of his memory, and no one complains of his judgement.

   Duc de la Rochefoucauld 1613–80 French moralist: *Maxims* (1678)

11 If the nineteenth century was the age of the editorial chair, ours is the century of the psychiatrist's couch.

   Marshall McLuhan 1911–80 Canadian communications scholar: *Understanding Media* (1964)

12 The mind of man is capable of anything.

   Guy de Maupassant 1850–93 French novelist and short-story writer: 'The Tress of Hair' 1884

13 The mind is its own place, and in itself
   Can make a heaven of hell, a hell of heaven.
   John Milton 1608–74 English poet: *Paradise Lost* (1667)

14 Consciousness . . . is the phenomenon whereby the universe's very existence is made known.

   Roger Penrose 1931– British mathematician: *The Emperor's New Mind* (1989)

15 That's the classical mind at work, runs fine inside but looks dingy on the surface.

   Robert M. Pirsig 1928– American writer: *Zen and the Art of Motorcycle Maintenance* (1974)

16 What is Matter?—Never mind.
   What is Mind?—No matter.
   Punch English humorous weekly periodical: 14 July 1855

17 What a waste it is to lose one's mind, or not to have a mind. How true that is.

   Dan Quayle 1947– American Republican politician: speech to the United Negro College Fund, whose slogan is 'a mind is a terrible thing to waste'; in *Times* 26 May 1989

18 When people will not weed their own minds, they are apt to be overrun with nettles.

   Horace Walpole 1717–97 English writer

and connoisseur: letter to Caroline,
Countess of Ailesbury, 10 July 1779

19 At the very best, a mind enclosed in
language is in prison.
   Simone Weil 1909–43 French essayist
   and philosopher: 'Human Personality'
   (1943)

20 Mind in its purest play is like some
bat
That beats about in caverns all alone,
Contriving by a kind of senseless wit
Not to conclude against a wall of
stone.
   Richard Wilbur 1921– American poet:
   'Mind' (1956)

21 Every human brain is born not as a
blank tablet (a *tabula rasa*) waiting
to be filled in by experience but as
'an exposed negative waiting to be
slipped into developer fluid'.
   on the nature v. nurture debate
   Edward O. Wilson 1929– American
   sociobiologist: attributed

22 To give a sex to mind was not very
consistent with the principles of a
man [Rousseau] who argued so
warmly, and so well, for the
immortality of the soul.
   often quoted as 'Mind has no sex'
   Mary Wollstonecraft 1759–97 English
   feminist: *A Vindication of the Rights of
   Woman* (1792)

Minorities and Majorities

see also DEMOCRACY

1 As for our majority . . . one is
enough.
   Benjamin Disraeli 1804–81 British Tory
   statesman and novelist: *Endymion*
   (1880); now often associated with
   Churchill

2 Nor is the people's judgement always
true:
The most may err as grossly as the
few.
   John Dryden 1631–1700 English poet,
   critic, and dramatist: *Absalom and
   Achitophel* (1681)

3 The majority never has right on its
side. Never I say! That is one of the
social lies that a free, thinking man is
bound to rebel against. Who makes
up the majority in any given
country? Is it the wise men or the
fools? I think we must agree that the
fools are in a terrible overwhelming
majority, all the wide world over. But,
damn it, it can surely never be right
that the stupid should rule over the
clever!
   Henrik Ibsen 1828–1906 Norwegian
   dramatist: *An Enemy of the People*
   (1882)

4 All, too, will bear in mind this sacred
principle, that though the will of the
majority is in all cases to prevail, that
will to be rightful must be
reasonable; that the minority
possess their equal rights, which
equal law must protect, and to
violate would be oppression.
   Thomas Jefferson 1743–1826 American
   Democratic Republican statesman:
   inaugural address, 4 March, 1801

5 A nation is judged by how it treats its
minorities.
   René Lévesque 1922–87 Canadian
   politician: attributed, 1978; John Robert
   Colombo *Colombo's New Canadian
   Quotations* (1987)

6 Minorities . . . are almost always in
the right.
   Sydney Smith 1771–1845 English
   clergyman and essayist: H. Pearson *The
   Smith of Smiths* (1934)

Misfortunes

see also ADVERSITY

1   People will take balls,
Balls will be lost always, little boy,
And no one buys a ball back.
John Berryman 1914–72 American
poet: 'The Ball Poem' (1948)

2 Man is born unto trouble, as the
sparks fly upward.
Bible: Job

3 If Gladstone fell into the Thames,
that would be misfortune; and if
anybody pulled him out, that, I
suppose, would be a calamity.
Benjamin Disraeli 1804–81 British Tory
statesman and novelist: Leon Harris *The
Fine Art of Political Wit* (1965)

4 In the words of one of my more
sympathetic correspondents, it has
turned out to be an 'annus horribilis'.
Elizabeth II 1926– British monarch:
speech at Guildhall, London,
24 November 1992

5 Never cry over spilt milk, because it
may have been poisoned.
W. C. Fields 1880–1946 American
humorist: to Carlotta Monti; Carlotta
Monti with Cy Rice *W. C. Fields and Me*
(1971)

6 I left the room with silent dignity, but
caught my foot in the mat.
George Grossmith 1847–1912 and
Weedon Grossmith 1854–1919 English
writers: *The Diary of a Nobody* (1894)

7 My friends, as I have discovered
myself, there are no disasters, only
opportunities. And, indeed,
opportunities for fresh disasters.
Boris Johnson 1964– British
Conservative politician: in *Daily
Telegraph* 2 December 2004

8 In the misfortune of our best friends,
we always find something which is
not displeasing to us.
Duc de la Rochefoucauld 1613–80
French moralist: *Réflexions ou Maximes
Morales* (1665)

9 boss there is always
a comforting thought
in time of trouble when
it is not our trouble.
Don Marquis 1878–1937 American poet
and journalist: *archy does his part*
(1935)

10 I had never had a piece of toast
Particularly long and wide,
But fell upon the sanded floor,
And always on the buttered side.
James Payn 1830–98 English writer: in
Chambers's Journal 2 February 1884; see
TRANSIENCE 12

11 I never complained at the
vicissitudes of fortune, nor
murmured at the ordinances of
Heaven, excepting once, when my
feet were bare, and I had not the
means of procuring myself shoes. I
entered the great mosque at Cufah
with a heavy heart when I beheld a
man who had no feet. I offered up
praise and thanksgiving to God for
his bounty, and bore with patience
the want of shoes.
*usually quoted as 'I cried because I had no
shoes, until I met a man who had no feet'*
Sadi c.1213–91 Persian poet: *The Rose
Garden* (1258)

12 Misery acquaints a man with strange
bedfellows.
William Shakespeare 1564–1616
English dramatist: *The Tempest* (1611)

13 The fatal law of gravity: when you are
down everything falls on you.
Sylvia Townsend Warner 1893–1978
English writer: attributed

14 One likes people much better when
they're battered down by a

prodigious siege of misfortune than when they triumph.

Virginia Woolf 1882–1941 English novelist: diary, 13 August 1921

Mistakes

1 When people thought the Earth was flat, they were wrong. When people thought the Earth was spherical, they were wrong. But if *you* think that thinking the Earth is spherical is *just as wrong* as thinking the Earth is flat, then your view is wronger than both of them put together.

Isaac Asimov 1920–92 Russian-born biochemist and science fiction writer: *The Relativity of Wrong* (1989)

2 It is worse than a crime, it is a blunder.

on hearing of the execution of the Duc d'Enghien, 1804

Antoine Boulay de la Meurthe 1761–1840 French statesman: C.-A. Sainte-Beuve *Nouveaux Lundis* (1870)

3 We don't just have egg on our face. We have omelette all over our suits.

on the networks' premature calls of a win in Florida in the 2000 presidential election, first to Al Gore and then to George W. Bush

Tom Brokaw 1940– American journalist: in *Atlanta Constitution-Journal* 9 November 2000 (online edition)

4 As she frequently remarked when she made any such mistake, it would be all the same a hundred years hence.

Charles Dickens 1812–70 English novelist: *Nicholas Nickleby* (1839)

5 A stumble may prevent a fall.

Thomas Fuller 1654–1734 English writer and physician: *Gnomologia* (1732)

6 If all else fails, immortality can always be assured by a spectacular error.

J. K. Galbraith 1908–2006 American economist: attributed

7 Mistakes are a fact of life
It is the response to error that counts.

Nikki Giovanni 1943– American poet: 'Of Liberation' (1970)

8 The road to wisdom?—Well, it's plain and simple to express:
Err
and err
and err again
but less
and less
and less.

Piet Hein 1905–96 Danish poet and cartoonist: 'The Road to Wisdom' (1966)

9 Crooked things may be as stiff and unflexible as straight: and men may be as positive in error as in truth.

John Locke 1632–1704 English philosopher: *An Essay concerning Human Understanding* (1690)

10 To err is human, but it feels divine.

Dolly Parton 1946– American singer and songwriter: in *Observer* 7 August 2005; also attributed to Mae West (1892–1980)

11 The man who makes no mistakes does not usually make anything.

Edward John Phelps 1822–1900 American lawyer and diplomat: speech at the Mansion House, London, 24 January 1889

12 One Galileo in two thousand years is enough.

on being asked to proscribe the works of Teilhard de Chardin

Pope Pius XII 1876–1958 Italian cleric: attributed; Stafford Beer *Platform for Change* (1975)

13 'Forward, the Light Brigade!'
Was there a man dismayed?

Not though the soldier knew
Some one had blundered.
Alfred, Lord Tennyson 1809–92 English
poet: 'The Charge of the Light Brigade'
(1854)

14 Well, if I called the wrong number,
why did you answer the phone?
James Thurber 1894–1961 American
humorist: cartoon caption in *New
Yorker* 5 June 1937

15 The report of my death was an
exaggeration.
*usually quoted as 'Reports of my death
have been greatly exaggerated'*
Mark Twain 1835–1910 American
writer: in *New York Journal* 2 June 1897

16 To lose one parent, Mr Worthing,
may be regarded as a misfortune; to
lose both looks like carelessness.
Oscar Wilde 1854–1900 Anglo-Irish
dramatist and poet: *The Importance of
Being Earnest* (1895)

Moderation

1 Nothing in excess.
Anonymous: inscribed on the temple of
Apollo at Delphi, and variously ascribed
to the Seven Wise Men

2 To many, total abstinence is easier
than perfect moderation.
St Augustine of Hippo AD 354–430 Early
Christian theologian: *On the Good of
Marriage* (AD 401)

3 We know what happens to people
who stay in the middle of the road.
They get run down.
Aneurin Bevan 1897–1960 British
Labour politician: in *Observer*
6 December 1953

4 May temperance befriend me,
the gods' most lovely gift.
Euripides *c.*485–*c.*406 BC Greek
dramatist: *Medea*

5 Perhaps too much of everything is as
bad as too little.
Edna Ferber 1887–1968 American
writer: *Giant* (1952)

6 There's nothing in the middle of the
road but yellow stripes and dead
armadillos.
Jim Hightower 1943– American
politician: attributed, 1984

7 You will go most safely by the middle
way.
Ovid 43 BC–*c.*AD 17 Roman poet:
Metamorphoses

8 Above all, gentlemen, not the
slightest zeal.
Charles-Maurice de Talleyrand
1754–1838 French statesman: P. Chasles
*Voyages d'un critique à travers la vie et
les livres* (1868)

9 Use, do not abuse . . . Neither
abstinence nor excess ever renders
man happy.
Voltaire 1694–1778 French writer and
philosopher: *Sept Discours en Vers sur
l'Homme* (1738)

10 Moderation is a fatal thing, Lady
Hunstanton. Nothing succeeds like
excess.
Oscar Wilde 1854–1900 Anglo-Irish
dramatist and poet: *A Woman of No
Importance* (1893)

Money

see also BANKING, ECONOMICS, GREED, POVERTY,
THRIFT, WEALTH

1 The almighty dollar is the only object
of worship.
Anonymous: in *Philadelphia Public
Ledger* 2 December 1836

2 Money is like muck, not good except
it be spread.
Francis Bacon 1561–1626 English
lawyer, courtier, philosopher, and
essayist: *Essays* (1625) 'Of Seditions and
Troubles'

3 Money, it turned out, was exactly like sex, you thought of nothing else if you didn't have it and thought of other things if you did.

James Baldwin 1924–87 American novelist and essayist: in *Esquire* May 1961 'Black Boy looks at the White Boy'

4 Money speaks sense in a language all nations understand.

Aphra Behn 1640–89 English dramatist, poet, and novelist: *The Rover* pt. 2 (1681)

5 I'm tired of Love: I'm still more tired of Rhyme.
But Money gives me pleasure all the time.

Hilaire Belloc 1870–1953 British poet, essayist, historian, novelist, and Liberal politician: 'Fatigued' (1923)

6 The love of money is the root of all evil.

Bible: I Timothy

7 Those who have some means think that the most important thing in the world is love. The poor know that it is money.

Gerald Brenan 1894–1987 British travel writer and novelist: *Thoughts in a Dry Season* (1978)

8 Show me the money!

Cameron Crowe 1957– American film director: *Jerry Maguire* (1996 film), motto given to Tom Cruise as Jerry Maguire by Cuba Golding Jr. as Rod Tidwell

9 Money doesn't talk, it swears.

Bob Dylan 1941– American singer and songwriter: 'It's Alright, Ma (I'm Only Bleeding)' (1965 song)

10 Money makes the world go around.

Fred Ebb 1932–2004 American songwriter: 'Money Money' (1965 song), from the musical *Cabaret*

11 Money is the sinews of love, as of war.

George Farquhar 1678–1707 Irish dramatist: *Love and a Bottle* (1698); see WARFARE 7

12 Money without brains is always dangerous.

Napoleon Hill 1883–1970 American writer: *Think and Grow Rich* (1934)

13 If possible honestly, if not, somehow, make money.

Horace 65–8 BC Roman poet: *Epistles*

14 When a feller says, 'It hain't the money, but th' principle o' th' thing,' it's the money.

Frank McKinney ('Kin') Hubbard 1868–1930 American humorist: *Hoss Sense and Nonsense* (1926)

15 For I don't care too much for money, For money can't buy me love.

John Lennon 1940–80 and **Paul McCartney** 1942– English pop singers and songwriters: 'Can't Buy Me Love' (1964 song)

16 Money is like a sixth sense without which you cannot make a complete use of the other five.

W. Somerset Maugham 1874–1965 English novelist: *Of Human Bondage* (1915)

17 Money couldn't buy friends but you got a better class of enemy.

Spike Milligan 1918–2002 Irish comedian: *Puckoon* (1963)

18 I want the whole of Europe to have one currency; it will make trading much easier.

Napoleon I 1769–1821 French emperor: letter to his brother Louis, 6 May 1807

19 'My boy,' he says, 'always try to rub up against money, for if you rub up against money long enough, some of it may rub off on you.'

Damon Runyon 1884–1946 American writer: in *Cosmopolitan* August 1929, 'A Very Honourable Guy'

20 There's nothing in the world so
demoralizing as money.
Sophocles c.496–406 BC Greek
dramatist: *Antigone*

21 Pennies don't fall from heaven. They
have to be earned on earth.
Margaret Thatcher 1925– British
Conservative stateswoman: in *Observer*
18 November 1979; see OPTIMISM 2

22 You can be young without money
but you can't be old without it.
Tennessee Williams 1911–83 American
dramatist: *Cat on a Hot Tin Roof* (1955)

23 From now the pound abroad is
worth 14 per cent or so less in terms
of other currencies. It does not
mean, of course, that the pound here
in Britain, in your pocket or purse or
in your bank, has been devalued.
Harold Wilson 1916–95 British Labour
statesman: ministerial broadcast,
19 November 1967

Morality

1 It is always easier to fight for one's
principles than to live up to them.
Alfred Adler 1870–1937 Austrian
psychologist and psychiatrist: Phyllis
Bottome *Alfred Adler* (1939)

2 Morality's *not* practical. Morality's a
gesture. A complicated gesture
learned from books.
Robert Bolt 1924–95 English dramatist:
A Man for All Seasons (1960)

3 Food comes first, then morals.
Bertolt Brecht 1898–1956 German
dramatist: *Die Dreigroschenoper* (1928)

4 I learned from my mother and father
that for every opportunity there was
an obligation, for every demand a
duty, for every chance given, a
contribution to be made. And when
they said to me that for every right

there was a responsibility, for them
that was not just words. What they
meant was quite simple and
straightforward, for me my moral
compass.
Gordon Brown 1951– British Labour
statesman: speech, Labour Party
Conference, 26 September 2005

5 I think I did something for the worst
possible reason—just because I
could.
on his relationship with Monica Lewinsky
Bill Clinton 1946– American
Democratic statesman: in *Sunday Times*
20 June 2004

6 The highest possible stage in moral
culture is when we recognize that we
ought to control our thoughts.
Charles Darwin 1809–82 English
natural historian: *The Descent of Man*
(1871)

7 The last temptation is the greatest
treason:
To do the right deed for the wrong
reason.
T. S. Eliot 1888–1965 Anglo-American
poet, critic, and dramatist: *Murder in
the Cathedral* (1935)

8 That action is best, which procures
the greatest happiness for the
greatest numbers.
Francis Hutcheson 1694–1746 Scottish
philosopher: *An Inquiry into the
Original of our Ideas of Beauty and
Virtue* (1725); see SOCIETY 3

9 The end cannot justify the means,
for the simple and obvious reason
that the means employed determine
the nature of the ends produced.
Aldous Huxley 1894–1963 English
novelist: *Ends and Means* (1937)

10 State a moral case to a ploughman
and a professor. The former will
decide it as well, and often better

than the latter, because he has not been led astray by artificial rules.
Thomas Jefferson 1743–1826 American Democratic Republican statesman: letter to Peter Carr, 10 August 1787

11 If people want a sense of purpose, they should get it from their archbishops. They should not hope to receive it from their politicians.
Harold Macmillan 1894–1986 British Conservative statesman: to Henry Fairlie, 1963; H. Fairlie *The Life of Politics* (1968)

12 You can't learn too soon that the most useful thing about a principle is that it can always be sacrificed to expediency.
W. Somerset Maugham 1874–1965 English novelist: *The Circle* (1921)

13 Morality is the herd-instinct in the individual.
Friedrich Nietzsche 1844–1900 German philosopher and writer: *Die fröhliche Wissenschaft* (1882)

14 In olden days a glimpse of stocking
Was looked on as something shocking
Now, heaven knows,
Anything goes.
Cole Porter 1891–1964 American songwriter: 'Anything Goes' (1934 song)

15 There is no good or evil, there is only power, and those too weak to seek it.
J. K. Rowling 1965– English novelist: *Harry Potter and the Philosopher's Stone* (1997)

16 Values are tapes we play on the Walkman of the mind: any tune we choose so long as it does not disturb others.
Jonathan Sacks 1948– British rabbi: *The Persistence of Faith* (1991)

17 The nation's morals are like its teeth: the more decayed they are the more it hurts to touch them.
George Bernard Shaw 1856–1950 Irish dramatist: *The Shewing-up of Blanco Posnet* (1911)

18 If your morals make you dreary, depend upon it they are wrong.
Robert Louis Stevenson 1850–94 Scottish novelist: 'A Christmas Sermon' (1888)

19 The more things are forbidden, the more popular they become.
Mark Twain 1835–1910 American writer: *Mark Twain's Notebook* (1895)

20 Moral indignation is jealousy with a halo.
H. G. Wells 1866–1946 English novelist: *The Wife of Sir Isaac Harman* (1914)

Mothers

see also PARENTS

1 What *do* girls do who haven't any mothers to help them through their troubles?
Louisa May Alcott 1832–88 American novelist: *Little Women* (1869)

2 I like my body better since I became a mother. I feel sexier as a result.
Halle Berry 1968– American actress: in *Esquire* October 2008

3 I have reached the age when a woman begins to perceive that she is growing into the person she least plans to resemble: her mother.
Anita Brookner 1928– British novelist and art historian: *Incidents in the Rue Laugier* (1995)

4 The mother's yearning, that completest type of the life in another life which is the essence of real human love, feels the presence of the cherished child even in the debased, degraded man.
George Eliot 1819–80 English novelist: *Adam Bede* (1859)

5 If I were damned of body and soul,
I know whose prayers would make
me whole,
Mother o' mine, O mother o' mine.
Rudyard Kipling 1865–1936 English
writer and poet: *The Light That Failed*
(1891)

6 Here's to the happiest years of our
lives
Spent in the arms of other men's
wives.
Gentlemen!—Our mothers!
proposing a toast
Edwin Lutyens 1869–1944 English
architect: Clough Williams-Ellis
Architect Errant (1971)

7 No matter how old a mother is she
watches her middle-aged children
for signs of improvement.
Florida Scott-Maxwell: *Measure of my
Days* (1968)

8 My mother had a good deal of
trouble with me, but I think she
enjoyed it.
Mark Twain 1835–1910 American
writer: *Autobiography* (1924)

9 For the hand that rocks the cradle
Is the hand that rules the world.
William Ross Wallace 1819–81
American poet: 'What rules the world'
(1865)

10 Guilt is to motherhood as grapes are
to wine.
Fay Weldon 1931– British novelist and
scriptwriter: *She May Not Leave* (2005)

Mountains

1 The Alps, the Rockies and all other
mountains are related to the earth,
the Himalayas to the heavens.
J. K. Galbraith 1908–2006 American
economist: *A Life in our Times* (1981)

2 There are other Annapurnas in the
lives of men.
Maurice Herzog 1919– French
mountaineer: *Annapurna* (1952)

3 Well, we knocked the bastard off!
on conquering Mount Everest, 1953
Edmund Hillary 1919–2008 New
Zealand mountaineer: *Nothing Venture,
Nothing Win* (1975)

4 It is a fine thing to be out on the hills
alone. A man can hardly be a beast or
a fool alone on a great mountain.
Francis Kilvert 1840–79 English
clergyman and diarist: diary, 29 May
1871

5 Because it's there.
*on being asked why he wanted to climb
Mount Everest*
George Leigh Mallory 1886–1924
British mountaineer: in *New York Times*
18 March 1923

6 To me the only way you achieve a
summit is to come back alive. The
job is half done if you don't get down
again.
son of George Mallory, who died on Everest
John Mallory: in *Independent* 4 May
1999

7 Climb the mountains and get their
good tidings.
John Muir 1838–1914 Scottish-born
American naturalist: in *Atlantic
Monthly* April 1898

8 My mountain did not seem to me a
lifeless thing of rock and ice, but
warm and friendly and living. She
was a mother hen, and the other
mountains were chicks under her
wings.
on Everest
Tenzing Norgay 1914–86 Sherpa
mountaineer: *Man of Everest* (1975)

9 Today I climbed the highest
mountain in this region, which is not
improperly called Ventosus (Windy).

The only motive for my ascent was the wish to see what so great a height had to offer.

of Mont Ventoux in Provence, France
> **Petrarch** 1304–74 Italian poet: letter to Dionisio da Borgo San Sepolcro, *c.*1336 (tr. M. Musa)

10 Do nothing in haste, look well to each step, and from the beginning think what may be the end.
> **Edward Whymper** 1840–1911 English mountaineer: *Scrambles Amongst the Alps* (1871)

Murder

see also DEATH

1 Mordre wol out; that se we day by day.
> **Geoffrey Chaucer** *c.*1343–1400 English poet: *The Canterbury Tales* 'The Nun's Priest's Tale'

2 Thou shalt not kill; but need'st not strive
Officiously to keep alive.
> **Arthur Hugh Clough** 1819–61 English poet: 'The Latest Decalogue' (1862)

3 Murder considered as one of the fine arts.
> **Thomas De Quincey** 1785–1859 English essayist and critic: in *Blackwood's Magazine* February 1827; essay title

4 Assassination has never changed the history of the world.
> **Benjamin Disraeli** 1804–81 British Tory statesman and novelist: speech, House of Commons, 1 May 1865

5 Any man has to, needs to, wants to Once in a lifetime, do a girl in.
> **T. S. Eliot** 1888–1965 Anglo-American poet, critic, and dramatist: *Sweeney Agonistes* (1932)

6 Television has brought back murder into the home—where it belongs.
> **Alfred Hitchcock** 1899–1980 British-born film director: in *Observer* 19 December 1965

7 English law does not permit good persons, as such, to strangle bad persons, as such.
> **T. H. Huxley** 1825–95 English biologist: letter in *Pall Mall Gazette*, 31 October 1866

8 In that case, if we are to abolish the death penalty, let the murderers take the first step.
> **Alphonse Karr** 1808–90 French novelist and journalist: in *Les Guêpes* January 1849

9 Whoso slays a soul not to retaliate for a soul slain, nor for corruption done in the land, shall be as if he had slain mankind altogether.
> **The Koran**: sura 5

10 Roast beef and Yorkshire, or roast pork and apple sauce, followed up by suet pudding and driven home, as it were, by a cup of mahogany-brown tea, have put you in just the right mood. Your pipe is drawing sweetly, the sofa cushions are soft underneath you, the fire is well alight, the air is warm and stagnant. In these blissful circumstances, what is it that you want to read about? Naturally, about a murder.
> **George Orwell** 1903–50 English novelist: 'Decline of the English Murder' (written 1946)

11 Kill a man, and you are an assassin. Kill millions of men, and you are a conqueror. Kill everyone, and you are a god.
> **Jean Rostand** 1894–1977 French biologist: *Pensées d'un biologiste* (1939)

12 Murder most foul, as in the best it is; But this most foul, strange, and unnatural.
> **William Shakespeare** 1564–1616 English dramatist: *Hamlet* (1601)

Museums

1 A country's identity, its value and civilisation resides in its history. If a country's civilisation is looted, as ours has been here, its history ends.
an Iraqi archaeologist on the looting of the National Museum
Raid Abdul Ridhar Mohammed Iraqi archaeologist: in *Times* 14 April 2003

2 An ace caff with quite a nice museum attached.
Advertising slogan: the Victoria and Albert Museum, February 1989

3 Yes
You have come upon the fabled lands where myths
Go when they die.
James Fenton 1949–ββ English poet: 'The Pitt-Rivers Museum' (1983)

4 You've got to have two out of death, sex and jewels.
the ingredients for a successful exhibition
Roy Strong 1935–ββ English art historian: in *Sunday Times* 23 January 1994

Music

see also JAZZ, MUSICAL INSTRUMENTS, MUSICIANS, OPERA, ROCK, SINGING

1 Writing about music is like dancing about architecture.
also found in the form 'Talking about music . . .'
Anonymous: attributed to Elvis Costello, David Bowie, Frank Zappa, and many others, but of unknown origin

2 Good music is that which penetrates the ear with facility and quits the memory with difficulty.
Thomas Beecham 1879–1961 English conductor: speech, *c*.1950; in *New York Times* 9 March 1961

3 Music . . . can name the unnameable, and communicate the unknowable.
Leonard Bernstein 1918–90 American composer, conductor, and pianist: *The Unanswered Question* (1976)

4 Music has charms to soothe a savage breast.
William Congreve 1670–1729 English dramatist: *The Mourning Bride* (1697)

5 The whole problem can be stated quite simply by asking, 'Is there a meaning to music?' My answer to that would be, 'Yes.' And 'Can you state in so many words what the meaning is?' My answer to that would be, 'No.'
Aaron Copland 1900–90 American composer and musician: *What to Listen for in Music* (1939)

6 Extraordinary how potent cheap music is.
Noël Coward 1899–1973 English dramatist, actor, and composer: *Private Lives* (1930)

7 It is only that which cannot be expressed otherwise that is worth expressing in music.
Frederick Delius 1862–1934 English composer: in *Sackbut* September 1920 'At the Crossroads'

8 There is music in the air.
Edward Elgar 1857–1934 English composer: R. J. Buckley *Sir Edward Elgar* (1905)

9 If she can stand it, I can. Play it!
usually misquoted as 'Play it again, Sam'
Julius J. Epstein 1909–2001: *Casablanca* (1942 film, with Philip G. Epstein and Howard Koch); spoken by Humphrey Bogart

10 The hills are alive with the sound of music,
With songs they have sung for a thousand years.

The hills fill my heart with the sound
of music,
My heart wants to sing ev'ry song it
hears.
Oscar Hammerstein II 1895–1960
American songwriter: 'The Sound of
Music' (1959 song)

11 What then is music? . . . It exists
between thought and phenomenon,
like a twilight medium, it stands
between spirit and matter, related to
and yet different from both; it is
spirit, but spirit governed by time; it
is matter, but matter that can
manage without space.
Heinrich Heine 1797–1856 German
poet: *On the French Stage: Intimate
letters to August Lewald* (1857)

12 Classic music is th'kind that we keep
thinkin'll turn into a tune.
Frank McKinney ('Kin') Hubbard
1868–1930 American humorist:
*Comments of Abe Martin and His
Neighbors* (1923)

13 Music is life.
Charles Ives 1874–1954 American
composer: quoted in *American
National Biography* (online edition)

14 A carpenter's hammer, in a warm
summer noon, will fret me into more
than midsummer madness. But
those unconnected, unset sounds
are nothing to the measured malice
of music.
Charles Lamb 1775–1834 English
writer: *Elia* (1823)

15 The symphony must be like the
world. It must embrace everything.
Gustav Mahler 1860–1911 Austrian
composer: remark to Sibelius, Helsinki,
1907

16 Music is spiritual. The music
business is not.
Van Morrison 1945– Irish singer,
songwriter, and musician: in *The Times*
6 July 1990

17 Art is not national. It is international.
Music is not written in red, white and
blue; it is written with the heart's
blood of the composer.
Nellie Melba 1861–1931 Australian
operatic soprano: *Melodies and
Memories* (1925)

18 Melody is the essence of music. I
compare a good melodist to a fine
racer, and counterpoints to hack
post-horses.
Wolfgang Amadeus Mozart 1756–91
Austrian composer: remark to Michael
Kelly, 1786; Michael Kelly *Reminiscences*
(1826)

19 Music is your own experience, your
thoughts, your wisdom. If you don't
live it, it won't come out of your horn.
Charlie Parker 1920–55 American jazz
saxophonist: Nat Shapiro and Nat
Hentoff *Hear Me Talkin' to Ya* (1955)

20 Music begins to atrophy when it
departs too far from the dance . . .
poetry begins to atrophy when it gets
too far from music.
Ezra Pound 1885–1972 American poet:
The ABC of Reading (1934)

21 I am delighted to add another
unplayable work to the repertoire. I
want the Concerto to be difficult and
I want the little finger to become
longer. I can wait.
of his Violin Concerto
Arnold Schoenberg 1874–1951
Austrian-born American composer:
Joseph Machlis *Introduction to
Contemporary Music* (1963)

22 If music be the food of love, play on.
William Shakespeare 1564–1616
English dramatist: *Twelfth Night* (1601)

23 Hell is full of musical amateurs:
music is the brandy of the damned.
George Bernard Shaw 1856–1950 Irish
dramatist: *Man and Superman* (1903)

24 Improvisation is too good to leave to chance.

> **Paul Simon** 1942– American singer and songwriter: in *Observer* 30 December 1990

25 I don't know whether I like it, but it's what I meant.

> *on his 4th symphony*
> **Ralph Vaughan Williams** 1872–1958 English composer: Christopher Headington *Bodley Head History of Western Music* (1974)

26 You just pick a chord, go twang, and you've got music.

> **Sid Vicious** 1957–79 British rock musician: attributed

Musical Instruments

1 There is nothing to it. You only have to hit the right notes at the right time and the instrument plays itself.

> *the organ*
> **Johann Sebastian Bach** 1685–1750 German composer: K. Geiringer *The Bach Family* (1954)

2 Like two skeletons copulating on a corrugated tin roof.

> *the harpsichord*
> **Thomas Beecham** 1879–1961 English conductor: Harold Atkins and Archie Newman *Beecham Stories* (1978)

3 It is like a beautiful woman who has not grown older, but younger with time, more slender, more supple, more graceful.

> *the cello*
> **Pablo Casals** 1876–1973 Spanish cellist, conductor, and composer: in *Time* 29 April 1957

4 The tuba is certainly the most intestinal of instruments—the very lower bowel of music.

> **Peter De Vries** 1910–93 American novelist and humorist: *The Glory of the Hummingbird* (1974)

5 This machine kills fascists.

> **Woody Guthrie** 1912–67 American folksinger and songwriter: slogan on his guitar

6 The piano is the easiest instrument to play in the beginning, and the hardest to master in the end.

> **Vladimir Horowitz** 1904–89 Russian pianist: David Dubal *Evenings with Horowitz* (1992)

7 Is it not strange, that sheeps' guts should hale souls out of men's bodies?

> **William Shakespeare** 1564–1616 English dramatist: *Much Ado About Nothing* (1598–9)

Musicians

see also FAMOUS MUSICIANS, MUSIC, ROCK, AND POP MUSIC

1 Please do not shoot the pianist. He is doing his best.

> *printed notice in a dancing saloon*
> **Anonymous**: Oscar Wilde *Impressions of America* 'Leadville' (*c*.1882–3)

2 There are two golden rules for an orchestra: start together and finish together. The public doesn't give a damn what goes on in between.

> **Thomas Beecham** 1879–1961 English conductor: Harold Atkins and Archie Newman *Beecham Stories* (1978)

3 A musician, if he's a messenger, is like a child who hasn't been handled too many times by man, hasn't had too many fingerprints across his brain.

> **Jimi Hendrix** 1942–70 American rock musician: in *Life Magazine* (1969)

4 Down the road someone is practising scales,
The notes like little fishes vanish with a wink of tails,

> **Louis MacNeice** 1907–63 British poet, born in Belfast: 'Sunday Morning' (1935)

5 We are the music makers,
We are the dreamers of dreams . . .
We are the movers and shakers
Of the world for ever, it seems.
Arthur O'Shaughnessy 1844–81 English
poet: 'Ode' (1874)

6 The notes I handle no better than
many pianists. But the pauses
between the notes—ah, that is where
the art resides!
Artur Schnabel 1882–1951 Austrian-
born pianist: in *Chicago Daily News*
11 June 1958

Names

1 Proper names are poetry in the raw.
Like all poetry they are
untranslatable.
W. H. Auden 1907–73 English poet: *A
Certain World* (1970) 'Names, Proper'

2 I have fallen in love with American
names,
The sharp, gaunt names that never
get fat,
The snakeskin-titles of mining-
claims,
The plumed war-bonnet of Medicine
Hat,
Tucson and Deadwood and Lost
Mule Flat.
Stephen Vincent Benét 1898–1943
American poet and novelist: 'American
Names' (1927)

3 Remember, they only name things
after you when you're dead or really
old.
*at the naming ceremony for the George
Bush Centre for Intelligence*
Barbara Bush 1925– American First
Lady: in *Independent* 28 April 1999

4 With a name like yours, you might be
any shape, almost.
Lewis Carroll 1832–98 English writer
and logician: *Through the Looking-
Glass* (1872)

5 Dear 338171 (May I call you 338?).
Noël Coward 1899–1973 English
dramatist, actor, and composer: letter to
T. E. Lawrence, 25 August 1930

6 Colin is the sort of name you give
your goldfish for a joke.
Colin Firth 1960– British actor: in
Observer 1 September 2002

7 Every Tom, Dick and Harry is called
Arthur.
*to Arthur Hornblow, who was planning to
name his son Arthur*
Sam Goldwyn 1882–1974 American film
producer: Michael Freedland *The
Goldwyn Touch* (1986)

8 A self-made man may prefer a self-
made name.
*on Samuel Goldfish changing his name to
Samuel Goldwyn*
Learned Hand 1872–1961 American
judge: Bosley Crowther *Lion's Share*
(1957)

9 A nickname is the heaviest stone that
the devil can throw at a man.
William Hazlitt 1778–1830 English
essayist: *Sketches and Essays* (1839)
'Nicknames'

10 We've put an accent over the first 'a'
to make it a bit more exotic, and two
'i's at the end just to make it look a
bit different.
on her daughter's name, Princess Tiáamii
Jordan 1978– English model: in
Observer 29 July 2007

11 If you should have a boy do not
christen him John . . . 'Tis a bad
name and goes against a man. If my
name had been Edmund I should
have been more fortunate.
John Keats 1795–1821 English poet:
letter to his sister-in-law, 13 January
1820

12 No, I'm breaking it in for a friend.
when asked if Groucho were his real name
Groucho Marx 1890–1977 American
film comedian: attributed

13 The name of a man is a numbing
blow from which he never recovers.
Marshall McLuhan 1911–80 Canadian
communications scholar:
Understanding Media (1964)

14 What's in a name? that which we call
a rose
By any other name would smell as
sweet.
William Shakespeare 1564–1616
English dramatist: *Romeo and Juliet*
(1595)

Nationality

see also PATRIOTISM

1 INTERVIEWER: You are English, Mr
Beckett?
BECKETT: Au contraire.
Samuel Beckett 1906–89 Irish
dramatist, novelist, and poet: attributed

2 Some people . . . may be Rooshans,
and others may be Prooshans; they
are born so, and will please
themselves. Them which is of other
naturs thinks different.
Charles Dickens 1812–70 English
novelist: *Martin Chuzzlewit* (1844)

3 I may be uninspiring, but I'll be
damned if I'm an alien!
*on H. G. Wells's comment on 'an alien and
uninspiring court'*
George V 1865–1936 British monarch:
Sarah Bradford *George VI* (1989);
attributed, perhaps apocryphal

4 A country is a piece of land
surrounded on all sides by
boundaries, usually unnatural.
Joseph Heller 1923–99 American
novelist: *Catch-22* (1961)

5 A nation is the universality of
citizens speaking the same tongue.
Giuseppe Mazzini 1805–72 Italian
nationalist leader: in *La Giovine Italia*,
1832

6 Grab this land! Take it, hold it, my
brothers, make it, my brothers, shake
it, squeeze it, turn it, twist it, beat it,
kick it, whip it, stomp it, dig it,
plough it, seed it, reap it, rent it, buy
it, sell it, own it, build it, multiply it,
and pass it on—Can you hear me?
Pass it on!
Toni Morrison 1931– American
novelist: *Song of Solomon* (1977)

7 By blood and origin I am Albanian.
My citizenship is Indian. I am a
Catholic nun. As to my calling, I
belong to the whole world. As to my
heart, I belong entirely to the heart of
Jesus.
Mother Teresa 1910–97 Roman Catholic
nun and missionary: in *Independent*
6 September 1997; obituary

8 Because a man is born in a stable,
that does not make him a horse.
*rejecting the view that his Irish birthplace
determined his nationality*
Duke of Wellington 1769–1852 British
soldier and statesman: attributed

Nature

see also EARTH, ENVIRONMENT, LIFE SCIENCES

1 Nature, Mr Allnutt, is what we are
put into this world to rise above.
James Agee 1909–55 American writer:
The African Queen (1951 film); not in
the novel by C. S. Forester

2 The subtlety of nature is greater
many times over than the subtlety of
the senses and understanding.
Francis Bacon 1561–1626 English
lawyer, courtier, philosopher, and
essayist: *Novum Organum* (1620)

3 What a book a devil's chaplain might
write on the clumsy, wasteful,
blundering, low, and horridly cruel
works of nature!
Charles Darwin 1809–82 English
natural historian: letter to J. D. Hooker,
13 July 1856

4 For nature, heartless, witless nature,
Will neither care nor know
What stranger's feet may find the
meadow
And trespass there and go.
   A. E. Housman 1859–1936 English poet:
   Last Poems (1922) no. 40

5 In nature there are neither rewards
nor punishments—there are
consequences.
   Robert G. Ingersoll 1833–99 American
   agnostic: *Some Reasons Why* (1881)

6 'I play for Seasons; not Eternities!'
Says Nature.
   George Meredith 1828–1909 English
   novelist and poet: *Modern Love* (1862)

7 It is far from easy to judge whether
she has proved a kind parent to man
or a harsh step-mother.
on nature
   Pliny the Elder AD 23–79 Roman
   statesman and scholar: *Historia
   Naturalis*

8 Pile the bodies high at Austerlitz and
Waterloo.
Shovel them under and let me
work—
I am the grass; I cover all.
   Carl Sandburg 1878–1967 American
   poet: 'Grass' (1918)

9 And this our life, exempt from public
haunt,
Finds tongues in trees, books in the
running brooks,
Sermons in stones, and good in
everything.
   William Shakespeare 1564–1616
   English dramatist: *As You Like It* (1599)

10 Who trusted God was love indeed
And love Creation's final law—
Though Nature, red in tooth and
claw
With ravine, shrieked against his
creed.
   Alfred, Lord Tennyson 1809–92 English
   poet: *In Memoriam A. H. H.* (1850)

11 Nature is not a temple, but a
workshop, and man's the workman
in it.
   Ivan Turgenev 1818–83 Russian
   novelist: *Fathers and Sons* (1862)

12 I believe a leaf of grass is no less than
the journey-work of the stars,
And the pismire is equally perfect,
and a grain of sand, and the egg of
the wren,
And the tree toad is a chef-d'oeuvre
for the highest,
And the running blackberry would
adorn the parlours of heaven.
   Walt Whitman 1819–92 American poet:
   'Song of Myself' (written 1855)

13 BRICK: Well, they say nature hates a
vacuum, Big Daddy.
BIG DADDY: That's what they say, but
sometimes I think that a vacuum is
a hell of a lot better than some of
the stuff that nature replaces it
with.
   Tennessee Williams 1911–83 American
   dramatist: *Cat on a Hot Tin Roof* (1955)

14 One impulse from a vernal wood
May teach you more of man,
Of moral evil and of good,
Than all the sages can.
   William Wordsworth 1770–1850
   English poet: 'The Tables Turned' (1798)

The Navy

1 A willing foe and sea room.
   Anonymous: naval toast in the time of
   Nelson; W. N. T. Beckett *A Few Naval
   Customs, Expressions, Traditions, and
   Superstitions* (1931)

2 My only great qualification for being
put at the head of the Navy is that I
am very much at sea.
   Edward Carson 1854–1935 British
   lawyer and politician: Ian Colvin *Life of
   Lord Carson* (1936)

3 It is upon the navy under the good Providence of God that the safety, honour, and welfare of this realm do chiefly depend.

> **Charles II** 1630–85 British monarch: 'Articles of War' preamble; Sir Geoffrey Callender *The Naval Side of British History* (1952); probably a modern paraphrase

4 Naval tradition? Monstrous. Nothing but rum, sodomy, prayers, and the lash.

> *often quoted as, 'rum, sodomy, and the lash'*
> **Winston Churchill** 1874–1965 British Conservative statesman: Harold Nicolson, diary, 17 August 1950

5 Heart of oak are our ships,
Heart of oak are our men:
We always are ready;
Steady, boys, steady;
We'll fight and we'll conquer again and again.

> **David Garrick** 1717–79 English actor-manager: 'Heart of Oak' (1759 song)

6 Don't cheer, men; those poor devils are dying.

> **John Woodward ('Jack') Philip** 1840–1900 American naval captain: at the battle of Santiago, 4 July 1898

7 Without a decisive naval force we can do nothing definitive. And with it, everything honorable and glorious.

> **George Washington** 1732–99 American general and statesman: to Lafayette, 15 November 1781

Necessity

see also FATE

1 Must! Is *must* a word to be addressed to princes? Little man, little man! thy father, if he had been alive, durst not have used that word.

> *to Robert Cecil, on his saying she must go to bed*
> **Elizabeth I** 1533–1603 English monarch: J. R. Green *A Short History of the English People* (1874)

2 Nothing have I found stronger than Necessity.

> **Euripides** *c.*485–*c.*406 BC Greek dramatist: *Alcestis*

3 A desperate disease requires a dangerous remedy.

> **Guy Fawkes** 1570–1606 English conspirator: remark, 6 November 1605

4 Necessity never made a good bargain.

> **Benjamin Franklin** 1706–90 American politician, inventor, and scientist: *Poor Richard's Almanac* (1735)

5 Necessity has the face of a dog.

> **Gabriel García Márquez** 1928– Colombian novelist: *In Evil Hour* (1968)

6 Necessity is the plea for every infringement of human freedom: it is the argument of tyrants; it is the creed of slaves.

> **William Pitt** 1759–1806 British Tory statesman: speech, House of Commons, 18 November 1783

7 The superfluous, a very necessary thing.

> **Voltaire** 1694–1778 French writer and philosopher: *Le Mondain* (1736)

Neighbours

1 For what do we live, but to make sport for our neighbours, and laugh at them in our turn?

> **Jane Austen** 1775–1817 English novelist: *Pride and Prejudice* (1813)

2 We make our friends, we make our
enemies; but God makes our next-
door neighbour.
> **G. K. Chesterton** 1874–1936 English
> essayist, novelist, and poet: *Heretics*
> (1905)

3 Your next-door neighbour . . . is not
a man; he is an environment. He is
the barking of a dog; he is the noise
of a pianola; he is a dispute about a
party wall; he is drains that are worse
than yours, or roses that are better
than yours.
> **G. K. Chesterton** 1874–1936 English
> essayist, novelist, and poet: *The Uses of
> Diversity* (1920)

4 If you would be known, and not
know, vegetate in a village; if you
would know, and not be known, live
in a city.
> **Charles Caleb Colton** *c*.1780–1832
> English clergyman and writer: *Lacon*
> (1820)

5 My apple trees will never get across
And eat the cones under his pines, I
tell him.
He only says, 'Good fences make
good neighbours.'
> **Robert Frost** 1874–1963 American poet:
> 'Mending Wall' (1914)

News

see also JOURNALISM, NEWSPAPERS

1 How beautiful upon the mountains
are the feet of him that bringeth
good tidings.
> **Bible**: Isaiah

2 A pseudo event . . . comes about
because someone has planned,
planted, or incited it. Typically, it is
not a train wreck or an earthquake,
but an interview.
> **Daniel J. Boorstin** 1914–2004 American
> writer: *The Image* (1962)

3 If a dog bites a man it is not news,
but if a man bites a dog it is.
> *often attributed to the American journalist
> John B. Bogart (1848–1921)*
>> **Charles A. Dana** 1819–97 American
>> newspaper editor: attributed, in
>> *Bookman* February 1917; earlier sources
>> do not attribute to a specific individual

4 It is now a very good day to get out
anything we want to bury.
> *email sent in the aftermath of the terrorist
> action in America, 11 September 2001;
> popularly quoted as, 'A good day to bury
> bad news'*
>> **Jo Moore** 1963– British government
>> adviser: in *Daily Telegraph* 10 October
>> 2001

5 What news on the Rialto?
> **William Shakespeare** 1564–1616
> English dramatist: *The Merchant of
> Venice* (1596–8)

6 News is what a chap who doesn't
care much about anything wants to
read. And it's only news until he's
read it. After that it's dead.
> **Evelyn Waugh** 1903–66 English novelist:
> *Scoop* (1938)

Newspapers

see also JOURNALISM, NEWS, PRESS
PHOTOGRAPHERS

1 The purchaser [of a newspaper]
desires an article which he can
appreciate at sight; which he can lay
down and say, 'An excellent article,
very excellent; exactly *my own*
sentiments.'
> **Walter Bagehot** 1826–77 English
> economist and essayist: in *National
> Review* July 1856

2 *The Times* has made many
ministries.
> **Walter Bagehot** 1826–77 English
> economist and essayist: *The English
> Constitution* (1867)

3 If I rescued a child from drowning, the Press would no doubt headline the story 'Benn grabs child.'
Tony Benn 1925– British Labour politician: in *Observer* 2 March 1975

4 I read the newspapers avidly. It is my one form of continuous fiction.
Aneurin Bevan 1897–1960 British Labour politician: in *The Times* 29 March 1960

5 Small earthquake in Chile. Not many dead.
the words with which Cockburn claimed to have won a competition at The Times *for the dullest headline*
Claud Cockburn 1904–81 British writer and journalist: *In Time of Trouble* (1956)

6 Let us today drudge on about our inescapably impossible task of providing every week a first rough draft of a history that will never be completed about a world we can never really understand.
Philip Graham 1915–63 American newspaper publisher: remarks to *Newsweek* correspondents, London, 29 April 1963

7 Nothing can now be believed which is seen in a newspaper. Truth itself becomes suspicious by being put into that polluted vehicle.
Thomas Jefferson 1743–1826 American Democratic Republican statesman: letter to John Norvell, 14 June 1807

8 What sells a newspaper? is a question often asked me. The first answer is 'war' . . . a paper has only to be able to put on its placard 'A Great Battle' for its sales to mount up.
Kennedy Jones British journalist: *Fleet Street and Downing Street* (1920)

9 Whenever I see a newspaper I think of the poor trees. As trees they provide beauty, shade and shelter. But as paper all they provide is rubbish.
Yehudi Menuhin 1916–99 American-born British violinist: attributed, 1982

10 A good newspaper, I suppose, is a nation talking to itself.
Arthur Miller 1915–2005 American dramatist: in *Observer* 26 November 1961

11 The power of the press is very great, but not so great as the power of suppress.
Lord Northcliffe 1865–1922 British newspaper proprietor: office message, *Daily Mail* 1918; Reginald Rose and Geoffrey Harmsworth *Northcliffe* (1959)

12 A newspaper should have no friends.
Joseph Pulitzer 1847–1911 Hungarian-born American newspaper proprietor and editor: Don C. Seitz *Joseph Pulitzer: his life and letters* (1926)

13 Well, all I know is what I read in the papers.
Will Rogers 1879–1935 American actor and humorist: in *New York Times* 30 September 1923

14 Ever noticed that no matter what happens in one day, it exactly fits in the newspaper?
Jerry Seinfeld 1954– American comedian: in *Mail on Sunday* 11 February 2007

15 Freedom of the press in Britain means freedom to print such of the proprietor's prejudices as the advertisers don't object to.
Hannen Swaffer 1879–1962 British journalist: Tom Driberg *Swaff* (1974)

New Zealand

see AUSTRALIA AND NEW ZEALAND

Night

see also DAY, EVENING

1 Lighten our darkness, we beseech
thee, O Lord; and by thy great mercy
defend us from all perils and dangers
of this night.
The Book of Common Prayer 1662:
Evening Prayer

2 I cannot walk through the suburbs in
the solitude of the night without
thinking that the night pleases us
because it suppresses idle details,
just as our memory does.
Jorge Luis Borges 1899–1986
Argentinian writer: *Labyrinths* (1962)

3 The Sun's rim dips; the stars rush
out;
At one stride comes the dark.
Samuel Taylor Coleridge 1772–1834
English poet, critic, and philosopher:
'The Rime of the Ancient Mariner'
(1798)

4 The cares that infest the day
Shall fold their tents, like the Arabs,
And as silently steal away.
Henry Wadsworth Longfellow 1807–82
American poet: 'The Day is Done' (1844)

5 'Tis now the very witching time of
night,
When churchyards yawn and hell
itself breathes out
Contagion to this world.
William Shakespeare 1564–1616
English dramatist: *Hamlet* (1601)

6 To begin at the beginning: It is
spring, moonless night in the small
town, starless and bible-black.
Dylan Thomas 1914–53 Welsh poet:
Under Milk Wood (1954)

Nine-Eleven

1 Let's roll.
*heard by telephone operator as Beamer
and other passengers were planning to
storm the cockpit of the hijacked United
Airlines Flight 93, 11 September 2001; the
plane crashed in Pennsylvania minutes
later*
Todd Beamer 1968–2001: in *Washington
Post* 17 September 2001

2 I love you, honey. I know we're all
going to die—but there's three of us
who are going to do something
about it.
*final phone call to his wife from the
hijacked Flight 93, which crashed south of
Pittsburgh, 11 September 2001*
Thomas E. Burnett Jnr 1963–2001
American businessman: in *Independent*
13 September 2001

3 Today we feel what Franklin
Roosevelt called the warm courage
of national unity. This unity against
terror is now extending across the
world.
George W. Bush 1946– American
Republican statesman: address in
Washington National Cathedral,
14 September 2001

4 I didn't capture his death. I captured
part of his life.
*of the picture of a man falling head first
from the World Trade Center, 11 September
2001, known as 'The Falling Man'*
Richard Drew American
photojournalist: quoted in Peter Howe
'Richard Drew' in *Digital Journalist*
2001 (online edition)

5 The number of casualties will be
more than any of us can bear.
Rudolph Giuliani 1944– American
Republican politician: news conference,
New York, 11 September 2001

6 I love you . . . That is what they were
all saying down their phones, from
the hijacked planes and the burning

towers. There is only love, and then oblivion. Love was all they had to set against the hatred of their murderers.

of the last messages sent on 11 September 2001

Ian McEwan 1948– English novelist: in *Guardian* 15 September 2001

7 What do I tell the pilot to do?

in a final telephone conversation to her husband, the US Solicitor-General, from the hijacked plane which crashed into the Pentagon, 11 September 2001

Barbara Olson 1955–2001 American lawyer and broadcaster: in *Daily Telegraph* 14 September 2001, obituary

Northern Ireland

see also IRELAND

1 The whole map of Europe has been changed . . . but as the deluge subsides and the waters fall short we see the dreary steeples of Fermanagh and Tyrone emerging once again.

Winston Churchill 1874–1965 British Conservative statesman: speech, House of Commons, 16 February 1922

2 Ulster will fight; Ulster will be right.

Lord Randolph Churchill 1849–94 British Conservative politician: public letter, 7 May 1886

3 My heart besieged by anger, my mind a gap of danger,
I walked among their old haunts, the home ground where they bled;
And in the dirt lay justice like an acorn in the winter
Till its oak would sprout in Derry where the thirteen men lay dead.

of Bloody Sunday, Londonderry, 30 January 1972

Seamus Heaney 1939– Irish poet: 'The Road to Derry'

4   The famous Northern reticence, the tight gag of place

And times: yes, yes. Of the 'wee six' I sing.

Seamus Heaney 1939– Irish poet: 'Whatever You Say Say Nothing' (1975)

5 My war is over. My job as a political leader is to prevent war.

Martin McGuinness 1950– Northern Irish politician: in *Daily Telegraph* 30 October 2002

6 A disease in the family that is never mentioned.

of the troubles in Northern Ireland

William Trevor 1928– Anglo-Irish novelist and short story writer: in *Observer* 18 November 1990

Old Age

see also AGEING, MIDDLE AGE, RETIREMENT

1 To me old age is always fifteen years older than I am.

Bernard Baruch 1870–1965 American financier: in *Newsweek* 29 August 1955

2 If I'd known I was gonna live this long, I'd have taken better care of myself.

on reaching the age of 100

Eubie Blake 1883–1983 American ragtime pianist: in *Observer* 13 February 1983

3 What is called the serenity of age is only perhaps a euphemism for the fading power to feel the sudden shock of joy or sorrow.

Arthur Bliss 1891–1975 English composer: *As I Remember* (1970)

4 Although I am 92, my brain is 30 years old.

Alfred Eisenstaedt 1898–1995 German-born American photographer: to a reporter in 1991; in *Life* 24 August 1995

5 As Groucho Marx once said, 'Anyone can get old—all you have to do is to live long enough.'

Elizabeth II 1926– British monarch:

speech at her official 80th birthday
lunch, 15 June 2006

6 There's a fascination frantic
In a ruin that's romantic;
Do you think you are sufficiently
   decayed?
   W. S. Gilbert 1836–1911 English writer
   of comic and satirical verse: *The Mikado*
   (1885)

7 Age does not make us childish, as
   men tell,
It merely finds us children still at
   heart.
   Johann Wolfgang von Goethe
   1749–1832 German poet, novelist, and
   dramatist: *Faust* pt. 1 (1808)

8 What one wishes for in youth, one
   has in abundance in old age.
   Johann Wolfgang von Goethe
   1749–1832 German poet, novelist, and
   dramatist: *Poetry and Truth* (1812)

9 How happy he who crowns in shades
   like these,
A youth of labour with an age of ease.
   Oliver Goldsmith 1728–74 Anglo-Irish
   writer, poet, and dramatist: *The
   Deserted Village* (1770)

10 It is better to be seventy years young
   than forty years old!
   Oliver Wendell Holmes 1809–94
   American physician, poet, and essayist:
   reply to invitation from Julia Ward Howe
   to her seventieth birthday party, 27 May
   1889

11 When I am an old woman I shall
   wear purple
With a red hat which doesn't go, and
   doesn't suit me.
And I shall spend my pension on
   brandy and summer gloves
And satin sandals, and say we've got
   no money for butter.
   Jenny Joseph 1932– English poet:
   'Warning' (1974)

12 Will you still need me, will you still
   feed me,

When I'm sixty four?
   John Lennon 1940–80 and **Paul
   McCartney** 1942– English pop singers
   and songwriters: 'When I'm Sixty Four'
   (1967 song)

13 In one old people's home they
   changed the words of the song to
   'When I'm 84' as they considered
   64 to be young. I might do that.
   Paul McCartney 1942– : in *Times*
   14 October 2006

14 From the earliest times the old have
   rubbed it into the young that they
   are wiser than they, and before the
   young had discovered what
   nonsense this was they were old too,
   and it profited them to carry on the
   imposture.
   W. Somerset Maugham 1874–1965
   English novelist: *Cakes and Ale* (1930)

15 I woke up this morning and I was still
   alive, so I am pretty cheerful.
   on being 79
   Spike Milligan 1918–2002 Irish
   comedian: in *Irish Times* 8 November
   1997

16   Last scene of all,
That ends this strange eventful
   history,
Is second childishness, and mere
   oblivion,
Sans teeth, sans eyes, sans taste, sans
   everything.
   William Shakespeare 1564–1616
   English dramatist: *As You Like It* (1599)

17 Old age is the most unexpected of all
   things that happen to a man.
   Leon Trotsky 1879–1940 Russian
   revolutionary: diary, 8 May 1935

18 Those that desire to write or say
   anything to me have no time to lose;
   for time has shaken me by the hand
   and death is not far behind.
   John Wesley 1703–91 English preacher:
   letter to Ezekiel Cooper, 1 February 1791

19 When you are old and grey and full of
 sleep,
 And nodding by the fire, take down
 this book,
 And slowly read, and dream of the
 soft look
 Your eyes had once, and of their
 shadows deep.
> **W. B. Yeats** 1865–1939 Irish poet: 'When
> You Are Old' (1893)

20 An aged man is but a paltry thing,
 A tattered coat upon a stick, unless
 Soul clap its hands and sing, and
 louder sing
 For every tatter in its mortal dress.
> **W. B. Yeats** 1865–1939 Irish poet:
> 'Sailing to Byzantium' (1928)

Olympic Games

1 *Citius, altius, fortius.*
 Swifter, higher, stronger.
> **Anonymous**: motto of the Olympic
> Games

2 When I competed, no one ever
 thought it would be possible to make
 money from doing something you
 enjoyed so much.
> **Fanny Blankers-Koen** 1918–2004
> Dutch athlete: quoted in *Independent*
> 27 January 2004

3 I just blew my mind. And I blew the
 world's mind.
> *on winning the 200m at the Beijing
> Olympics*
> **Usain Bolt** 1986– Jamaican athlete: in
> *Independent* 21 August 2008

4 I skated for pure enjoyment. That's
 how I wanted my Olympic moment
 to be.
> **Sarah Hughes** 1985– American skater:
> in *Newsweek* 4 March 2002

5 I say to the Chinese and I say to the
 world—ping pong is coming home.
> *on the 2012 London Olympics*
> **Boris Johnson** 1964– British

Conservative politician: at the
conclusion of the Beijing Olympics; in
Independent 25 August 2008

6 These are the Olympics—you die for
 them.
> *before winning a gold medal while injured*
> **Al Oerter** 1936–2007 American discus
> thrower: at the Tokyo Olymics, 1964; in
> *Times* 4 October 2007

7 Eat, sleep and swim. That's all I can
 do.
> *attributing his record number of Olympic
> gold medals to his high-calorie diet*
> **Michael Phelps** 1985– American
> swimmer: in *Observer* 17 August 2008

Opera

see also CULTURE, MUSIC, SINGING

1 No opera plot can be sensible, for in
 sensible situations people do not
 sing. An opera plot must be, in both
 senses of the word, a melodrama.
> **W. H. Auden** 1907–73 English poet: in
> *Times Literary Supplement* 2 November
> 1967

2 People are wrong when they say that
 the opera isn't what it used to be. It is
 what it used to be—that's what's
 wrong with it.
> **Noël Coward** 1899–1973 English
> dramatist, actor, and composer: *Design
> for Living* (1933)

3 Opera is when a guy gets stabbed in
 the back and, instead of bleeding, he
 sings.
> **Ed Gardner** 1901–63 American radio
> comedian: in *Duffy's Tavern* (US radio
> programme, 1940s)

4 An unalterable and unquestioned
 law of the musical world required
 that the German text of French
 operas sung by Swedish artists
 should be translated into Italian for

the clearer understanding of English-speaking audiences.

> **Edith Wharton** 1862–1937 American novelist: *The Age of Innocence* (1920)

Opinion

see also ARGUMENT

1 Why should you mind being wrong if someone can show you that you are?
> **A. J. Ayer** 1910–89 English philosopher: attributed

2 I've never had a humble opinion. If you've got an opinion, why be humble about it?
> **Joan Baez** 1941– American singer and songwriter: in *Observer* 29 February 2004

3 The being without an opinion is so painful to human nature that most people will leap to a hasty opinion rather than undergo it.
> **Walter Bagehot** 1826–77 English economist and essayist: in *The Economist* 4 December 1875

4 He that complies against his will,
Is of his own opinion still.
> **Samuel Butler** 1612–80 English poet: *Hudibras* pt. 3 (1680)

5 The public buys its opinions as it buys its meat, or takes in its milk, on the principle that it is cheaper to do this than to keep a cow. So it is, but the milk is more likely to be watered.
> **Samuel Butler** 1835–1902 English novelist: *Notebooks* (1912)

6 You might very well think that. I couldn't possibly comment.
the Chief Whip's habitual response to questioning
> **Michael Dobbs** 1948– British novelist and broadcaster: *House of Cards* (televised 1990)

7 People seem not to see that their opinion of the world is also a confession of character.
> **Ralph Waldo Emerson** 1803–82 American philosopher and poet: *The Conduct of Life* (1860) 'Worship'

8 Every man has a right to utter what he thinks truth, and every other man has a right to knock him down for it. Martyrdom is the test.
> **Samuel Johnson** 1709–84 English poet, critic, and lexicographer: James Boswell *Life of Samuel Johnson* (1791) 1780

9 There are nine and sixty ways of constructing tribal lays,
And—every—single—one—of—them—is—right!
> **Rudyard Kipling** 1865–1936 English writer and poet: 'In the Neolithic Age' (1893)

10 Thank God, in these days of enlightenment and establishment, everyone has a right to his own opinions, and chiefly to the opinion that nobody else has a right to theirs.
> **Ronald Knox** 1888–1957 English writer and Roman Catholic priest: *Reunion All Round* (1914)

11 If all mankind minus one were of one opinion, and only one person were of the contrary opinion, mankind would be no more justified in silencing that one person, than he, if he had the power, would be justified in silencing mankind.
> **John Stuart Mill** 1806–73 English philosopher and economist: *On Liberty* (1859)

12 Opinion in good men is but knowledge in the making.
> **John Milton** 1608–74 English poet: *Areopagitica* (1644)

13 Some praise at morning what they blame at night;

But always think the last opinion right.

Alexander Pope 1688–1744 English poet: *An Essay on Criticism* (1711)

14 The opinions that are held with passion are always those for which no good ground exists; indeed the passion is the measure of the holder's lack of rational conviction.

Bertrand Russell 1872–1970 British philosopher and mathematician: *Sceptical Essays* (1928)

15 A man can brave opinion, a woman must submit to it.

Mme de Staël 1766–1817 French writer: *Delphine* (1802)

16 INTERVIEWER: I hear you have strong political views.
TAYLOR: No. Extreme views, weakly held.

A. J. P. Taylor 1906–90 British historian: letter to Eva Haraszti Taylor, 16 July 1970

17 It were not best that we should all think alike; it is difference of opinion that makes horse-races.

Mark Twain 1835–1910 American writer: *Pudd'nhead Wilson* (1894)

18 An intellectual hatred is the worst, So let her think opinions are accursed.

W. B. Yeats 1865–1939 Irish poet: 'A Prayer for My Daughter' (1920)

Opportunity

1 Never the time and the place And the loved one all together!

Robert Browning 1812–89 English poet: 'Never the Time and the Place' (1883)

2 We must beat the iron while it is hot, but we may polish it at leisure.

John Dryden 1631–1700 English poet, critic, and dramatist: *Aeneis* (1697)

3 She's got a ticket to ride, but she don't care.

John Lennon 1940–80 and **Paul McCartney** 1942– English pop singers and songwriters: 'Ticket to Ride' (1965 song)

4 *La carrière ouverte aux talents.*
The career open to the talents.

Napoleon I 1769–1821 French emperor: Barry E. O'Meara *Napoleon in Exile* (1822)

5 If only I could get down to Sidcup! I've been waiting for the weather to break. He's got my papers, this man I left them with, it's got it all down there, I could prove everything.

Harold Pinter 1930–2008 English dramatist: *The Caretaker* (1960)

6 I could have had class. I could have been a contender.

Budd Schulberg 1914–2009 American writer: *On the Waterfront* (1954 film); spoken by Marlon Brando

7 There is a tide in the affairs of men, Which, taken at the flood, leads on to fortune;
Omitted, all the voyage of their life Is bound in shallows and in miseries.

William Shakespeare 1564–1616 English dramatist: *Julius Caesar* (1599)

Optimism

see also HOPE, PESSIMISM

1 The lark's on the wing; The snail's on the thorn: God's in his heaven— All's right with the world!

Robert Browning 1812–89 English poet: *Pippa Passes* (1841)

2 Every time it rains, it rains Pennies from heaven. Don't you know each cloud contains Pennies from heaven?

Johnny Burke 1908–64 American

songwriter: 'Pennies from Heaven'
(1936 song)

3 I have known him come home to
supper with a flood of tears, and a
declaration that nothing was now
left but a jail; and go to bed making a
calculation of the expense of putting
bow-windows to the house, 'in case
anything turned up,' which was his
favourite expression.
of Mr Micawber
   Charles Dickens 1812–70 English
   novelist: *David Copperfield* (1850)

4 Grab your coat, and get your hat,
Leave your worry on the doorstep,
Just direct your feet
To the sunny side of the street.
   Dorothy Fields 1905–74 American
   songwriter: 'On the Sunny Side of the
   Street' (1930 song)

5 Cheer up! the worst is yet to come!
   Philander Chase Johnson 1866–1939:
   in *Everybody's Magazine* May 1920

6 but wotthehell archy wotthehell
jamais triste archy jamais triste
that is my motto.
   Don Marquis 1878–1937 American poet
   and journalist: *archy and mehitabel*
   (1927)

7 You've got to ac-cent-tchu-ate the
positive
Elim-my-nate the negative
Latch on to the affirmative
Don't mess with Mister In-between.
   Johnny Mercer 1909–76 American
   songwriter: 'Ac-cent-tchu-ate the
   Positive' (1944 song)

8 Things can only get better.
   Jamie Petrie and **Peter Cunnah** British
   singers and songwriters: title of song
   (1994); used as a Labour Party
   campaign slogan, 1997

9 Everything's coming up roses.
   Stephen Sondheim 1930– American
   songwriter: title of song (1959)

10 In this best of possible worlds . . . all
is for the best.
   *usually quoted as 'All is for the best in the
   best of all possible worlds'*
   Voltaire 1694–1778 French writer and
   philosopher: *Candide* (1759)

Organization

see also MANAGEMENT, READINESS AND
PREPARATION

1 A place for everything and
everything in its place.
   Isabella Beeton 1836–65 English writer:
   The Book of Household Management
   (1861); often attributed to Samuel
   Smiles

2 This island is made mainly of coal
and surrounded by fish. Only an
organizing genius could produce a
shortage of coal and fish at the same
time.
   Aneurin Bevan 1897–1960 British
   Labour politician: speech at Blackpool,
   24 May 1945

3 Oh, the Germans classify, but the
French arrange!
   Willa Cather 1873–1947 American
   novelist: *Death Comes For the
   Archbishop* (1927))

4 First things first, second things
never.
   Shirley Conran 1932–   English writer:
   Superwoman (1975)

5 All organization is and must be
grounded on the idea of exclusion
and prohibition just as two objects
cannot occupy the same space.
   Arthur Miller 1915–2005 American
   dramatist: *The Crucible* (1953)

6 The shortest way to do many things
is to do only one thing at once.
   Samuel Smiles 1812–1904 English
   writer: *Self-Help* (1859)

Originality

see also PLAGIARISM

1 The truth is that the propensity of man to imitate what is before him is one of the strongest parts of his nature.
Walter Bagehot 1826–77 English economist and essayist: *Physics and Politics* (1872)

2 Be daring, be different, be impractical, be anything that will assert integrity of purpose and imaginative vision against the play-it-safers, the creatures of the commonplace, the slaves of the ordinary.
Cecil Beaton 1904–80 English photographer: in *Theatre Arts* May 1957

3 It is sometimes necessary to repeat what we all know. All mapmakers should place the Mississippi in the same location, and avoid originality.
Saul Bellow 1915–2005 American novelist: *Mr Sammler's Planet* (1969)

4 The original writer is not he who refrains from imitating others, but he who can be imitated by none.
François-René Chateaubriand 1768–1848 French writer and diplomat: *Le Génie du Christianisme* (1802)

5 Every public action, which is not customary, either is wrong, or, if it is right, is a dangerous precedent. It follows that nothing should ever be done for the first time.
Francis M. Cornford 1874–1943 English academic: *Microcosmographia Academica* (1908)

6 Let's have some new clichés.
Sam Goldwyn 1882–1974 American film producer: attributed, perhaps apocryphal

7 When people are free to do as they please, they usually imitate each other. Originality is deliberate and forced, and partakes of the nature of a protest.
Eric Hoffer 1902–83 American philosopher: *Passionate State of Mind* (1955)

8 What is originality? Undetected plagiarism.
William Ralph Inge 1860–1954 English writer; Dean of St. Paul's, 1911–34: *Labels and Libels* (1929)

9 Posterity weaves no garlands for the actor.
often quoted as 'Posterity weaves no garlands for imitators'
Friedrich von Schiller 1759–1805 German dramatist and poet: *Wallenstein's Camp* (1798) prologue

10 Nothing has yet been said that's not been said before.
Terence *c.*190–159 BC Roman comic dramatist: *Eunuchus*

11 What a good thing Adam had. When he said a good thing he knew nobody had said it before.
Mark Twain 1835–1910 American writer: *Notebooks* (1935)

12 Never forget what I believe was observed to you by Coleridge, that every great and original writer, in proportion as he is great and original, must himself create the taste by which he is to be relished.
William Wordsworth 1770–1850 English poet: letter to Lady Beaumont, 21 May 1807

Oxford

1 Beautiful city! so venerable, so lovely, so unravaged by the fierce intellectual life of our century, so serene! . . . whispering from her towers the last enchantments of the Middle Age . . . Home of lost causes,

and forsaken beliefs, and unpopular names, and impossible loyalties!

>   **Matthew Arnold** 1822–88 English poet and essayist: *Essays in Criticism* First Series (1865)

2 And that sweet City with her dreaming spires,
She needs not June for beauty's heightening.

>   **Matthew Arnold** 1822–88 English poet and essayist: 'Thyrsis' (1866)

3 Towery city and branchy between towers;
Cuckoo-echoing, bell-swarmèd, lark-charmèd, rook-racked, river-rounded.

>   **Gerard Manley Hopkins** 1844–89 English poet and priest: 'Duns Scotus's Oxford' (written 1879)

Pacifism

see also PEACE, VIOLENCE

1 I ain't got no quarrel with the Viet Cong.
refusing to be drafted to fight in Vietnam

>   **Muhammad Ali** 1942– American boxer: at a press conference in Miami, Florida, February 1966

2 Pale Ebenezer thought it wrong to fight,
But Roaring Bill (who killed him) thought it right.

>   **Hilaire Belloc** 1870–1953 British poet, essayist, historian, novelist, and Liberal politician: 'The Pacifist' (1938)

3 Resist not evil: but whosoever shall smite thee on thy right cheek, turn to him the other also.

>   **Bible**: St Matthew

4 I am not only a pacifist but a militant pacifist. I am willing to fight for peace. Nothing will end war unless the people themselves refuse to go to war.

>   **Albert Einstein** 1879–1955 German-

born theoretical physicist: interview with G. S. Viereck, January 1931

5 Non-violence is the first article of my faith. It is also the last article of my creed.

>   **Mahatma Gandhi** 1869–1948 Indian statesman: speech at Shahi Bag, 18 March 1922, on a charge of sedition

6 CHAIRMAN OF MILITARY TRIBUNAL: What would you do if you saw a German soldier trying to violate your sister?
STRACHEY: I would try to get between them.
otherwise rendered as, 'I should interpose my body'

>   **Lytton Strachey** 1880–1932 English biographer: Robert Graves *Good-bye to All That* (1929)

7 The quietly pacifist peaceful always die
to make room for men who shout.

>   **Alice Walker** 1944– American poet: 'The QPP' (1973)

Painting

see also ART, FAMOUS ARTISTS, COLOURS, DRAWING

1 Not a day without a line.
proverbial summary of his philosophy

>   **Apelles** Greek painter of the 4th century BC: Pliny the Elder *Historia Naturalis*

2 The spray can is a tool that can be used for good or ill . . . I always try to leave a wall looking better than I found it.

>   **Banksy** British graffiti artist: in *Sunday Times* 14 June 2009

3 A product of the untalented, sold by the unprincipled to the utterly bewildered.
on abstract art

>   **Al Capp** 1907–79 American cartoonist: in *National Observer* 1 July 1963

4 A picture equals a movement in space.

> **Emily Carr** 1871–1945 Canadian artist: *Hundreds and Thousands: The Journals of Emily Carr* (1966) August 1935

5 Good painters imitate nature, bad ones spew it up.

> **Cervantes** 1547–1616 Spanish novelist: *El Licenciado Vidriera* (1613)

6 I will astonish Paris with an apple.

> **Paul Cézanne** 1839–1906 French painter: Gustave Geffroy *Claude Monet* (1894)

7 Treat nature in terms of the cylinder, the sphere, the cone, all in perspective.

> **Paul Cézanne** 1839–1906 French painter: letter to Emile Bernard, 1904; Emile Bernard *Paul Cézanne* (1925)

8 A remarkable example of modern art. It certainly combines force with candour.

> *on the notorious 80th birthday portrait by Graham Sutherland, later destroyed by Lady Churchill*
>
> **Winston Churchill** 1874–1965 British Conservative statesman: Martin Gilbert *Churchill: A Life* (1991)

9 The sound of water escaping from mill-dams, etc., willows, old rotten planks, slimy posts, and brickwork . . . those scenes made me a painter and I am grateful.

> **John Constable** 1776–1837 English painter: letter to John Fisher, 23 October 1821

10 I am just returned . . . with a deep conviction of Sir Joshua Reynolds' observation that there is no easy way of becoming a good painter. It can only be obtained by long contemplation and incessant labour.

> **John Constable** 1776–1837 English painter: letter to John Dunthorne, 29 May 1802; R. G. W. Clive *John Constable* (1903)

11 There are only two styles of portrait painting; the serious and the smirk.

> **Charles Dickens** 1812–70 English novelist: *Nicholas Nickleby* (1839)

12 For my part the famous smile has always seemed to me to be the smile of a woman who has just dined off her husband.

> *of the Mona Lisa*
>
> **Lawrence Durrell** 1912–90 English novelist, poet, and travel writer: *Justine* (1957)

13 If I were alive in Rubens's time, I'd be celebrated as a model. Kate Moss would be used as a paint brush.

> **Dawn French** 1957– British comedy actress: in *Sunday Times* 13 August 2006

14 I would wish my portraits to be *of* the people, not *like* them. Not having a look of the sitter, *being* them.

> **Lucian Freud** 1922– German-born British painter: Lawrence Gowing *Lucian Freud* (1982)

15 All painting, no matter what you're painting, is abstract in that it's got to be organized.

> **David Hockney** 1937– British artist: *David Hockney* (1976)

16 Maybe I'm not very human. What I wanted to do was to paint sunlight on the side of the house.

> **Edward Hopper** 1882–1967 American artist: interview with Lloyd Goodrich, 20 April 1946; S. Wagstaff (ed.) *Edward Hopper* (2004)

17 I don't want justice, I want mercy.

> *on having his portrait painted*
>
> **William Morris 'Billy' Hughes** 1862–1952 British-born Australian statesman: John Thompson *On the Lips of Living Men* (1962)

18 I paint my own reality.

> **Frida Kahlo** 1907–54 Mexican painter: Hayden Herrera *Frida* (1983)

19 Art does not reproduce the visible;
rather, it makes visible.

Paul Klee 1879–1940 Swiss painter:
Inward Vision (1958) 'Creative Credo'
(1920)

20 *Ceci n'est pas une pipe.*

This is not a pipe.

René Magritte 1898–1967 Belgian
surrealist painter: on a painting of a
tobacco pipe

21 What I dream of is an art of balance,
of purity and serenity devoid of
troubling or depressing subject
matter . . . a soothing, calming
influence on the mind, rather like a
good armchair which provides
relaxation from physical fatigue.

Henri Matisse 1869–1954 French
painter: *Notes d'un peintre* (1908)

22 You should not paint the chair, but
only what someone has felt about it.

Edvard Munch 1863–1944 Norwegian
painter and engraver: written *c.*1891; R.
Heller *Munch* (1984)

23 No, painting is not made to decorate
apartments. It's an offensive and
defensive weapon against the
enemy.

Pablo Picasso 1881–1973 Spanish
painter: interview with Simone Téry,
24 March 1945

24 There was a reviewer a while back
who wrote that my pictures didn't
have any beginning or any end. He
didn't mean it as a compliment, but
it was. It was a fine compliment.

Jackson Pollock 1912–56 American
painter: Francis V. O'Connor *Jackson
Pollock* (1967)

25 An imitation in lines and colours on
any surface of all that is to be found
under the sun.

of painting

Nicolas Poussin 1594–1665 French
painter: letter to M. de Chambray, 1665

26 Do not judge this movement kindly.
It is not just another amusing stunt.
It is defiant—the desperate act of
men too profoundly convinced of
the rottenness of our civilization to
want to save a shred of its
respectability.

Herbert Read 1893–1968 English art
historian: International Surrealist
Exhibition Catalogue, London 1936

27 It's with my brush that I make love.

often quoted as 'I paint with my prick'

Pierre Auguste Renoir 1841–1919
French painter: A. André *Renoir* (1919)

28 A mere copier of nature can never
produce anything great.

Joshua Reynolds 1723–92 English
painter: *Discourses on Art* 14 December
1770

29 Every time I paint a portrait I lose a
friend.

John Singer Sargent 1856–1925
American painter: N. Bentley and E.
Esar *Treasury of Humorous Quotations*
(1951)

30 I am a painter and I nail my pictures
together.

Kurt Schwitters 1887–1948 German
painter: R. Hausmann *Am Anfang war
Dada* (1972)

31 Painting is saying 'Ta' to God.

Stanley Spencer 1891–1959 English
painter: letter from Spencer's daughter
Shirin to *Observer* 7 February 1988

The Paranormal

see also SUPERNATURAL

1 It's life, Jim, but not as we know it.

Anonymous: saying associated with the
television series *Star Trek* (1966–),
created by Gene Roddenberry
(1921–91); the saying does not occur in
the series but derives from the
1987 song 'Star Trekkin' ' sung by The
Firm

2 I always knew the living talked rot, but it's nothing to the rot the dead talk.

on spiritualism

> **Margot Asquith** 1864–1945 British political hostess: Chips Channon, diary, 20 December 1937

3 The truth is out there.

> **Chris Carter** 1957– American producer and director: catchphrase; *The X Files* (American television series, 1993–)

4 I don't believe in astrology; I'm a Sagittarius and we're sceptical.

> **Arthur C. Clarke** 1917–2008 English science fiction writer: attributed; Nigel Rees *Cassell Dictionary of Humorous Quotations* (1999)

5 From the astrologer came the astronomer, from the alchemist the chemist, from the mesmerist the experimental psychologist. The quack of yesterday is the professor of tomorrow.

> **Arthur Conan Doyle** 1859–1930 Scottish-born writer of detective fiction: *Tales of Terror and Mystery* (1922)

6 No testimony is sufficient to establish a miracle, unless the testimony be of such a kind, that its falsehood would be more miraculous than the fact which it endeavours to establish.

> **David Hume** 1711–76 Scottish philosopher: 'Of Miracles' (1748)

7 Mr Geller may have psychic powers by means of which he can bend spoons; if so, he appears to be doing it the hard way.

> **James Randi** 1928– Canadian-born American conjuror: *The Supernatural A-Z: the truth and the lies* (1995)

8 There are more things in heaven and earth, Horatio,

Than are dreamt of in your philosophy.

> **William Shakespeare** 1564–1616 English dramatist: *Hamlet* (1601)

9 About astrology and palmistry: they are good because they make people vivid and full of possibilities. They are communism at its best. Everybody has a birthday and almost everybody has a palm.

> **Kurt Vonnegut** 1922–2007 American novelist and short-story writer: *Wampeters, Foma and Granfalloons* (1974)

Parents

see also BABIES, CHILDREN, FAMILY, FATHERS, MOTHERS

1 Children always assume the sexual lives of their parents come to a grinding halt at their conception.

> **Alan Bennett** 1934– English actor and dramatist: *Getting On* (1972)

2 Diogenes struck the father when the son swore.

> **Robert Burton** 1577–1640 English clergyman and scholar: *The Anatomy of Melancholy* (1621–51)

3 Having one child makes you a parent; having two you are a referee.

> **David Frost** 1939– English broadcaster and writer: in *Independent* 16 September 1989

4 My father was frightened of his mother; I was frightened of my father, and I am damned well going to see to it that my children are frightened of me.

> **George V** 1865–1936 British monarch: attributed, perhaps apocryphal; Randolph S. Churchill *Lord Derby* (1959)

5 Your children are not your children. They are the sons and daughters of Life's longing for itself.

They came through you but not from you
And though they are with you yet they belong not to you.

Kahlil Gibran 1883–1931 Lebanese-born American writer and painter: *The Prophet* (1923) 'On Children'

6 Do they know they're old,
These two who are my father and my mother
Whose fire from which I came, has now grown cold?

Elizabeth Jennings 1926–2001 English poet: 'One Flesh.' (1967)

7 Nothing has a stronger influence on their children than the unlived lives of their parents.

Carl Gustav Jung 1875–1961 Swiss psychologist: attributed; in *Boston Magazine* June 1978

8 They fuck you up, your mum and dad.
They may not mean to, but they do.
They fill you with the faults they had
And add some extra, just for you.

Philip Larkin 1922–85 English poet: 'This Be The Verse' (1974)

9 Love crawls with the baby, walks with the toddler, runs with the child, then stands aside to let the youth walk into adulthood.

Jo Ann Merrell: 'Love: A Variation on a Theme'

10 Children aren't happy with nothing to ignore,
And that's what parents were created for.

Ogden Nash 1902–71 American humorist: 'The Parent' (1933)

11 Oh, what a tangled web do parents weave
When they think that their children are naïve.

Ogden Nash 1902–71 American humorist: 'Baby, What Makes the Sky Blue' (1940); see DECEPTION 10

12 The affection you get back from children is sixpence given as change for a sovereign.

Edith Nesbit 1858–1924 English writer: J. Briggs *A Woman of Passion* (1987)

13 If you bungle raising your children I don't think whatever else you do well matters very much.

Jacqueline Kennedy Onassis 1929–94 wife of John Fitzgerald Kennedy: Theodore C. Sorenson *Kennedy* (1965)

14 A Jewish man with parents alive is a fifteen-year-old boy, and will remain a fifteen-year-old boy until *they die*!

Philip Roth 1933– American novelist: *Portnoy's Complaint* (1967)

15 The natural term of the affection of the human animal for its offspring is six years.

George Bernard Shaw 1856–1950 Irish dramatist: *Heartbreak House* (1919)

16 Parentage is a very important profession, but no test of fitness for it is ever imposed in the interest of the children.

George Bernard Shaw 1856–1950 Irish dramatist: *Everybody's Political What's What?* (1944)

17 Parents learn a lot from their children about coping with life.

Muriel Spark 1918–2006 British novelist: *The Comforters* (1957)

18 You shouldn't sit in judgment of your parents. We did the best we could while being people too.

John Updike 1932–2009 American novelist and short-story writer: *Rabbit at Rest* (1990)

19 Parents are the bones on which children sharpen their teeth.

Peter Ustinov 1921–2004 British actor, director, and writer: attributed, in *Times* 30 March 2004

20 Children begin by loving their parents; after a time they judge

them; rarely, if ever, do they forgive
them.

Oscar Wilde 1854–1900 Anglo-Irish
dramatist and poet: *A Woman of No
Importance* (1893)

21 A slavish bondage to parents cramps
every faculty of the mind.

Mary Wollstonecraft 1759–97 English
feminist: *A Vindication of the Rights of
Woman* (1792)

Parliament

1 The British House of Lords is the
British Outer Mongolia for retired
politicians.

Tony Benn 1925– British Labour
politician: in *Observer* 4 February 1962

2 Your representative owes you, not his
industry only, but his judgement;
and he betrays, instead of serving
you, if he sacrifices it to your
opinion.

Edmund Burke 1729–97 Irish-born
Whig politician and man of letters:
speech, Bristol, 3 November 1774

3 The only safe pleasure for a
parliamentarian is a bag of boiled
sweets.

Julian Critchley 1930–2000 British
Conservative politician and journalist:
in *Listener* 10 June 1982

4 The duty of an Opposition [is] very
simple . . . to oppose everything, and
propose nothing.

Edward Stanley, 14th Earl of Derby
1799–1869 British Conservative
statesman: quoting 'Mr Tierney, a great
Whig authority', in House of Commons,
4 June 1841

5 Think of it! A second Chamber
selected by the Whips. A seraglio of
eunuchs.

Michael Foot 1913– British Labour
politician: speech, House of Commons,
3 February 1969

6 When in that House MPs divide,
If they've a brain and cerebellum too,
They have to leave that brain
outside,
And vote just as their leaders tell 'em
to.

W. S. Gilbert 1836–1911 English writer
of comic and satirical verse: *Iolanthe*
(1882)

7 Your business is not to govern the
country but it is, if you think fit, to
call to account those who do govern
it.

W. E. Gladstone 1809–98 British Liberal
statesman: speech to the House of
Commons, 29 January 1855

8 Though we cannot out-vote them we
will out-argue them.
*on the practical value of speeches in the
House of Commons*

Samuel Johnson 1709–84 English poet,
critic, and lexicographer: James Boswell
Life of Samuel Johnson (1791) 3 April
1778

9 I have neither eye to see, nor tongue
to speak here, but as the House is
pleased to direct me.
*on being asked if he had seen any of the five
MPs whom the King had ordered to be
arrested*

William Lenthall 1591–1662 Speaker of
the House of Commons: to Charles I,
4 January 1642

10 Being an MP feeds your vanity and
starves your self-respect.

Matthew Parris 1949– British
journalist and former politician: in *The
Times* 9 February 1994

11 Parliament itself would not exist in
its present form had people not
defied the law.

Arthur Scargill 1938– British trades-
union leader: evidence to House of
Commons Select Committee on
Employment, 2 April 1980

12 The longest running farce in the West
End.
of the House of Commons
  Cyril Smith 1928– British Liberal
  politician: *Big Cyril* (1977)

13 It is, I think, good evidence of life
after death.
*on the quality of debate in the House of
Lords*
  Donald Soper 1903–98 British
  Methodist minister: in *Listener*
  17 August 1978

14 The House of Lords, an illusion to
which I have never been able to
subscribe—responsibility without
power, the prerogative of the eunuch
throughout the ages.
  Tom Stoppard 1937– British dramatist:
  Lord Malquist and Mr Moon (1966); see
  RESPONSIBILITY 2

Parties

see also HOSTS AND GUESTS

1 The sooner every party breaks up the
better.
  Jane Austen 1775–1817 English novelist:
  Emma (1816)

2 Like other parties of the kind, it was
first silent, then talky, then
argumentative, then disputatious,
then unintelligible, then altogethery,
then inarticulate, and then drunk.
  Lord Byron 1788–1824 English poet:
  letter to Thomas Moore, 31 October
  1815

3 The best number for a dinner party
is two—myself and a dam' good head
waiter.
  Nubar Gulbenkian 1896–1972 British
  industrialist and philanthropist: in
  Daily Telegraph 14 January 1965

4 The true essentials of a feast are only
fun and feed.
  Oliver Wendell Holmes 1809–94

American physician, poet, and essayist:
'Nux Postcoenatica' (1849)

5 The tumult and the shouting dies,
The captains and the kings depart,
And we are left with large supplies
Of cold blancmange and rhubarb
tart.
  Ronald Knox 1888–1957 English writer
  and Roman Catholic priest: 'After the
  Party' (1959); see HUMILITY 4

6 At every party there are two kinds of
people—those who want to go home
and those who don't. The trouble is,
they are usually married to each
other.
  Ann Landers 1918–2002 American
  advice columnist: in *International
  Herald Tribune* 19 June 1991

7 A successful party is a creative act,
and creation is always painful.
  Phyllis McGinley 1905–78 American
  poet: *Sixpence in her Shoe* (1964)

8 At a dinner party one should eat
wisely but not too well, and talk well
but not too wisely.
  W. Somerset Maugham 1874–1965
  English novelist: *Writer's Notebook*
  (1949); written in 1896

9 Candy
Is dandy
But liquor
Is quicker.
  Ogden Nash 1902–71 American
  humorist: 'Reflections on Ice-breaking'
  (1931)

10 An office party is not, as is
sometimes supposed, the Managing
Director's chance to kiss the tea-girl.
It is the tea-girl's chance to kiss the
Managing Director.
  Katharine Whitehorn 1928– English
  journalist: *Roundabout* (1962) 'The
  Office Party'

11 If one plays good music, people don't listen and if one plays bad music people don't talk.

> **Oscar Wilde** 1854–1900 Anglo-Irish dramatist and poet: *The Importance of Being Earnest* (1895)

Parting

see also MEETING

1 I leave before being left. I decide.

> **Brigitte Bardot** 1934– French actress: in *Newsweek* 5 March 1973

2 CORBETT: It's goodnight from me.
BARKER: And it's goodnight from him.

> **Ronnie Barker** 1929–2005 and **Ronnie Corbett** 1930– English comedians: in *The Two Ronnies*, 1971–87 BBC television series

3 Friends part
forever—wild geese
lost in cloud.

> **Matsuo Basho** 1644–94 Japanese poet: translated by Lucien Stryk

4 I wish everyone, friend or foe, well. That is that. The end.

> **Tony Blair** 1953– British Labour statesman: on leaving the House of Commons, 27 June 2007

5 I'll be back.

> **James Cameron** 1954– Canadian-born American film director: *The Terminator* (1984 film, with Gale Anne Hurd); spoken by Arnold Schwarzenegger

6 *Atque in perpetuum, frater, ave atque vale.*

And so, my brother, hail, and farewell evermore!

> **Catullus** *c.*84–*c.*54 BC Roman poet: *Carmina*

7 Parting is all we know of heaven, And all we need of hell.

> **Emily Dickinson** 1830–86 American poet: 'My life closed twice before its close'

8 Since there's no help, come let us kiss and part,
Nay, I have done: you get no more of me.

> **Michael Drayton** 1563–1631 English poet: *Idea* (1619) sonnet 61

9 And ever has it been that love knows not its own depth until the hour of separation.

> **Kahlil Gibran** 1883–1931 Lebanese-born American writer and painter: *The Prophet* (1923)

10 If you can't leave in a taxi you can leave in a huff. If that's too soon, you can leave in a minute and a huff.

> **Bert Kalmar** 1884–1947: *Duck Soup* (1933 film); spoken by Groucho Marx

11 She said she always believed in the old addage, 'Leave them while you're looking good.'

> **Anita Loos** 1893–1981 American writer: *Gentlemen Prefer Blondes* (1925)

12 We're drinking my friend,
To the end of a brief episode,
Make it one for my baby
And one more for the road.

> **Johnny Mercer** 1909–76 American songwriter: 'One For My Baby' (1943 song)

13 Now this is the last day of our acquaintance.

> **Sinéad O'Connor** 1966– Irish singer and songwriter: 'The Last Day of Our Acquaintance' (1990 song)

14 But how strange the change from major to minor
Every time we say goodbye.

> **Cole Porter** 1891–1964 American songwriter: 'Every Time We Say Goodbye' (1944 song)

15 Don't have nightmares. Do sleep well.

> **Nick Ross** 1947– British television presenter: habitual closing words for BBC1's *Crimewatch* (1984–)

16 Good-night, good-night! parting is
such sweet sorrow
That I shall say good-night till it be
morrow.
   William Shakespeare 1564–1616
   English dramatist: *Romeo and Juliet*
   (1595)

The Past

see also HISTORY, MEMORY, PRESENT, TRADITION

1 Even a god cannot change the past.
   *literally 'The one thing which even God
   cannot do is to make undone what has
   been done'*
   Agathon b. *c.*445 Greek tragic poet:
   Aristotle *Nicomachaean Ethics*

2 In every age 'the good old days' were
a myth. No one ever thought they
were good at the time. For every age
has consisted of crises that seemed
intolerable to the people who lived
through them.
   Brooks Atkinson 1894–1984 American
   journalist and critic: *Once Around the
   Sun* (1951)

3 Stands the Church clock at ten to
three?
And is there honey still for tea?
   Rupert Brooke 1887–1915 English poet:
   'The Old Vicarage, Grantchester' (1915)

4 We cannot reform our forefathers.
   George Eliot 1819–80 English novelist:
   Adam Bede (1859)

5 The past is never dead. It's not even
past.
   William Faulkner 1897–1962 American
   novelist: *Requiem for a Nun* (1951)

6 The moving finger writes; and,
having writ,
Moves on: nor all thy piety nor wit
Shall lure it back to cancel half a line,
Nor all thy tears wash out a word of
it.
   Edward Fitzgerald 1809–83 English

scholar and poet: *The Rubáiyát of Omar
Khayyám* (1859)

7 It is not the literal past, the 'facts' of
history, that shape us, but images of
the past embodied in language . . .
we must never cease renewing those
images; because once we do, we
fossilize.
   Brian Friel 1929– Irish dramatist:
   Translations (1980)

8 The past is a foreign country: they do
things differently there.
   L. P. Hartley 1895–1972 English novelist:
   The Go-Between (1953)

9 By despising all that has preceded us,
we teach others to despise ourselves.
   William Hazlitt 1778–1830 English
   essayist: 'On Reading New Books' (1827)

10 What are those blue remembered
hills,
What spires, what farms are those?
That is the land of lost content,
I see it shining plain,
The happy highways where I went
And cannot come again.
   A. E. Housman 1859–1936 English poet:
   A Shropshire Lad (1896)

11 Yesterday, all my troubles seemed so
far away,
Now it looks as though they're here
to stay.
Oh I believe in yesterday.
   John Lennon 1940–80 and **Paul
   McCartney** 1942– English pop singers
   and songwriters: 'Yesterday' (1965 song)

12 Think of it, soldiers; from the
summit of these pyramids, forty
centuries look down upon you.
   Napoleon I 1769–1821 French emperor:
   speech, 21 July 1798, before the Battle of
   the Pyramids

13 Things ain't what they used to be.
   Ted Persons: title of song (1941)

14 I tell you the past is a bucket of ashes.
> **Carl Sandburg** 1878–1967 American poet: 'Prairie' (1918)

15 Those who cannot remember the past are condemned to repeat it.
> **George Santayana** 1863–1952 Spanish-born philosopher and critic: *The Life of Reason* (1905)

16 O! call back yesterday, bid time return.
> **William Shakespeare** 1564–1616 English dramatist: *Richard II* (1595)

17 People who are always praising the past
> And especially the times of faith as best
> Ought to go and live in the Middle Ages
> And be burnt at the stake as witches and sages.
> **Stevie Smith** 1902–71 English poet and novelist: 'The Past' (1957)

18 The past is the only dead thing that smells sweet.
> **Edward Thomas** 1878–1917 English poet: 'Early one morning in May I set out' (1917)

19 *Mais où sont les neiges d'antan?*
> But where are the snows of yesteryear?
> **François Villon** c.1431–after 1463 French poet: *Le Grand Testament* (1461) 'Ballade des dames du temps jadis'

20 Hindsight is always twenty-twenty.
> **Billy Wilder** 1906–2002 American screenwriter and director: J. R. Columbo *Wit and Wisdom of the Moviemakers* (1979)

Patience

see also DELAY, PERSISTENCE, WAITING

1 We had better wait and see.
> **Herbert Asquith** 1852–1928 British Liberal statesman: phrase used repeatedly in speeches in 1910; Roy Jenkins *Asquith* (1964)

2 Our patience will achieve more than our force.
> **Edmund Burke** 1729–97 Irish-born Whig politician and man of letters: *Reflections on the Revolution in France* (1790)

3 Beware the fury of a patient man.
> **John Dryden** 1631–1700 English poet, critic, and dramatist: *Absalom and Achitophel* (1681)

4 Patience, that blending of moral courage with physical timidity.
> **Thomas Hardy** 1840–1928 English novelist and poet: *Tess of the d'Urbervilles* (1891)

5 Patience and tenacity of purpose are worth more than twice their weight of cleverness.
> **T. H. Huxley** 1825–95 English biologist: 'On Medical Education' (address at University College, 1870)

6 There is only one cardinal sin: impatience. Because of impatience we were driven out of Paradise; because of impatience we cannot return.
> **Franz Kafka** 1883–1924 Czech novelist: *Collected Aphorisms* no. 3

7 They also serve who only stand and wait.
> **John Milton** 1608–74 English poet: 'When I consider how my light is spent' (1673)

8 Patience is a bitter thing, but its fruit is sweet.
> **Sadi** c.1213–91 Persian poet: 'Rose Garden'

9 Let nothing trouble you, nothing frighten you. All things are passing; God never changes. Patient endurance attains all things.
> **St Teresa of Ávila** 1512–82 Spanish

Carmelite nun and mystic: 'St Teresa's Bookmark'; found in her breviary after her death

10 I am extraordinarily patient, provided I get my own way in the end.
Margaret Thatcher 1925– British Conservative stateswoman: in *Observer* 4 April 1989

11 The strongest of all warriors are these two—time and patience.
Leo Tolstoy 1828–1910 Russian novelist: *War and Peace* (1865–9)

Patriotism

see also NATIONALITY

1 Patriotism is a lively sense of collective responsibility. Nationalism is a silly cock crowing on its own dunghill.
Richard Aldington 1892–1962 English poet, novelist, and biographer: *The Colonel's Daughter* (1931)

2 If I should die, think only this of me: That there's some corner of a foreign field
That is for ever England.
Rupert Brooke 1887–1915 English poet: 'The Soldier' (1914)

3 Standing, as I do, in view of God and eternity, I realize that patriotism is not enough. I must have no hatred or bitterness towards anyone.
on the eve of her execution for helping Allied soldiers to escape from occupied Belgium
Edith Cavell 1865–1915 English nurse: in *The Times* 23 October 1915

4 'My country, right or wrong', is a thing that no patriot would think of saying except in a desperate case. It is like saying, 'My mother, drunk or sober'.
G. K. Chesterton 1874–1936 English

essayist, novelist, and poet: *Defendant* (1901) 'Defence of Patriotism'

5 Our country! In her intercourse with foreign nations, may she always be in the right; but our country, right or wrong.
Stephen Decatur 1779–1820 American naval officer: toast at Norfolk, Virginia, April 1816; see PATRIOTISM 17

6 Never was patriot yet, but was a fool.
John Dryden 1631–1700 English poet, critic, and dramatist: *Absalom and Achitophel* (1681)

7 If I had to choose between betraying my country and betraying my friend, I hope I should have the guts to betray my country.
E. M. Forster 1879–1970 English novelist: *Two Cheers for Democracy* (1951)

8 You think you are dying for your country; you die for the industrialists.
Anatole France 1844–1924 French novelist and man of letters: in *L'Humanité* 18 July 1922

9 That this House will in no circumstances fight for its King and Country.
D. M. Graham 1911–99: motion worded by Graham for a debate at the Oxford Union, 9 February 1933 (passed by 275 votes to 153)

10 I only regret that I have but one life to lose for my country.
prior to his execution by the British for spying
Nathan Hale 1755–76 American revolutionary: Henry Phelps Johnston *Nathan Hale, 1776* (1914)

11 *Dulce et decorum est pro patria mori.*
Lovely and honourable it is to die for one's country.
Horace 65–8 BC Roman poet: *Odes*; see WARFARE 7

12 Patriotism is the last refuge of a scoundrel.

> **Samuel Johnson** 1709–84 English poet, critic, and lexicographer: James Boswell *Life of Samuel Johnson* (1791) 7 April 1775

13 And so, my fellow Americans: ask not what your country can do for you—ask what you can do for your country.

> **John F. Kennedy** 1917–63 American Democratic statesman: inaugural address, 20 January 1961

14 I would die for my country but I could never let my country die for me.

> **Neil Kinnock** 1942– British Labour politician: speech at Labour Party Conference, 30 September 1986

15 These are the times that try men's souls. The summer soldier and the sunshine patriot will, in this crisis, shrink from the service of their country; but he that stands it *now*, deserves the love and thanks of men and women.

> **Thomas Paine** 1737–1809 English political theorist: *The Crisis* (December 1776)

16 I worry that patriotism run amok will trample the very values that the country seeks to defend.

> **Dan Rather** 1931– American journalist: in *Independent* 18 May 2002

17 My country, right or wrong; if right, to be kept right; and if wrong, to be set right!

> **Carl Schurz** 1829–1906 American soldier and politician: speech, US Senate, 29 February 1872; see PATRIOTISM 5

18 Breathes there the man, with soul so dead,
Who never to himself hath said,
This is my own, my native land!

> **Sir Walter Scott** 1771–1832 Scottish

novelist and poet: *The Lay of the Last Minstrel* (1805)

19 You'll never have a quiet world till you knock the patriotism out of the human race.

> **George Bernard Shaw** 1856–1950 Irish dramatist: *O'Flaherty V.C.* (1919)

20 I vow to thee, my country—all earthly things above—
Entire and whole and perfect, the service of my love.

> **Cecil Spring-Rice** 1859–1918 British diplomat: 'I Vow to Thee, My Country' (1918)

21 The cricket test—which side do they cheer for? . . . Are you still looking back to where you came from or where you are?

on the loyalties of Britain's immigrant population

> **Norman Tebbit** 1931– British Conservative politician: interview in *Los Angeles Times*; in *Daily Telegraph* 20 April 1990

Peace

see also PACIFISM, WAR

1 They shall beat their swords into plowshares, and their spears into pruninghooks: nation shall not lift up sword against nation, neither shall they learn war any more.

> **Bible**: Isaiah

2 The peace of God, which passeth all understanding, shall keep your hearts and minds through Christ Jesus.

> **Bible**: Philippians

3 Give peace in our time, O Lord.

> **The Book of Common Prayer** 1662: *Morning Prayer*

4 One observes, they have gone too long without a war here. Where is

morality to come from in such a case, I ask? Peace is nothing but slovenliness, only war creates order.
Bertolt Brecht 1898–1956 German dramatist: *Mother Courage* (1939)

5 This is the second time in our history that there has come back from Germany to Downing Street peace with honour. I believe it is peace for our time.
Neville Chamberlain 1869–1940 British Conservative statesman: speech from 10 Downing Street, 30 September 1938

6 Go placidly amid the noise and the haste, and remember what peace there may be in silence.
often wrongly dated to 1692, the date of foundation of a church in Baltimore whose vicar circulated the poem in 1956
Max Ehrmann 1872–1945: 'Desiderata' (1948)

7 I think that people want peace so much that one of these days governments had better get out of the way and let them have it.
Dwight D. Eisenhower 1890–1969 American general and Republican statesman: broadcast discussion, 31 August 1959

8 Lord, make me an instrument of Your peace!
Where there is hatred let me sow love.
St Francis of Assisi 1181–1226 Italian monk: 'Prayer of St Francis'; attributed

9 I have many times asked myself whether there can be more potent advocates of peace upon earth through the years to come than this massed multitude of silent witnesses to the desolation of war.
George V 1865–1936 British monarch: message read at Terlincthun Cemetery, Boulogne, 13 May 1922

10 War makes rattling good history; but Peace is poor reading.
Thomas Hardy 1840–1928 English novelist and poet: *The Dynasts* (1904)

11 'Peace upon earth!' was said. We sing it,
And pay a million priests to bring it.
After two thousand years of mass
We've got as far as poison-gas.
Thomas Hardy 1840–1928 English novelist and poet: 'Christmas: 1924' (1928)

12 Give peace a chance.
John Lennon 1940–80 and **Paul McCartney** 1942– English pop singers and songwriters: title of song (1969)

13 Peace is indivisible.
Maxim Litvinov 1876–1951 Soviet diplomat: note to the Allies, 25 February 1920

14 A war can perhaps be won single-handedly. But peace—lasting peace—cannot be secured without the support of all.
Luiz Inácio Lula da Silva 1945– Brazilian statesman: speech, United Nations, 23 September 2003

15 War appears to be as old as mankind, but peace is a modern invention.
Henry Maine 1822–88 English jurist: lecture delivered in Cambridge, 1887, in *International Law* (1888)

16 You can't separate peace from freedom because no one can be at peace unless he has his freedom.
Malcolm X 1925–65 American civil rights campaigner: speech in New York, 7 January 1965

17 You can't switch on peace like a light.
Mo Mowlam 1949–2005 British Labour politician: in *Independent* 6 September 1999

18 The grim fact is that we prepare for war like precocious giants and for peace like retarded pygmies.
> **Lester Pearson** 1897–1972 Canadian Liberal statesman: speech in Toronto, 14 March 1955

19 Enough of blood and tears. Enough.
> **Yitzhak Rabin** 1922–95 Israeli statesman: at the signing of the Israel-Palestine Declaration, Washington, 13 September 1993

20 The work, my friend, is peace. More than an end of this war—an end to the beginnings of all wars.
> **Franklin D. Roosevelt** 1882–1945 American Democratic statesman: undelivered address for Jefferson Day, 13 April 1945 (the day after Roosevelt died)

21 They make a wilderness and call it peace.
> **Tacitus** AD c.56–after 117 Roman senator and historian: *Agricola*

People

see FAMOUS PEOPLE

Perfection

see also EXCELLENCE

1 Pictures of perfection as you know make me sick and wicked.
> **Jane Austen** 1775–1817 English novelist: letter to Fanny Knight, 23 March 1817

2 Faultless to a fault.
> **Robert Browning** 1812–89 English poet: *The Ring and the Book* (1868–9)

3 It's a delightful thing to think of perfection; but it's vastly more amusing to talk of errors and absurdities.
> **Fanny Burney** 1752–1840 English novelist and diarist: *Camilla* (1796)

4 Forget your perfect offering
There is a crack in everything
That's how the light gets in.
> **Leonard Cohen** 1934– Canadian singer and writer: 'Anthem' (1992 song)

5 No one ever approaches perfection except by stealth, and unknown to himself.
> **William Hazlitt** 1778–1830 English essayist: 'On Taste' (1818)

6 Nothing is an unmixed blessing.
> **Horace** 65–8 BC Roman poet: *Odes*

7 Trifles make perfection, and perfection is no trifle.
> **Michelangelo** 1475–1564 Italian sculptor, painter, architect, and poet: attributed; Samuel Smiles *Self-Help* (1859)

8 To live is to change, and to be perfect is to have changed often.
> **John Henry Newman** 1801–90 English theologian and cardinal: *An Essay on the Development of Christian Doctrine* (1845)

9 Perfection is terrible, it cannot have children.
> **Sylvia Plath** 1932–63 American poet: 'The Munich Mannequins' (1965)

10 Perfection is finally attained not when there is no longer anything to add but when there is no longer anything to take away, when a body has been stripped down to its nakedness.
> **Antoine de Saint-Exupéry** 1900–44 French novelist: *Wind, Sand and Stars* (1939)

11 Finality is death. Perfection is finality.
Nothing is perfect. There are lumps in it.
> **James Stephens** 1882–1950 Irish poet and writer: *The Crock of Gold* (1912)

12 Faultily faultless, icily regular, splendidly null,

Dead perfection, no more.
Alfred, Lord Tennyson 1809–92 English poet: *Maud* (1855)

13 The intellect of man is forced to choose
Perfection of the life, or of the work.
W. B. Yeats 1865–1939 Irish poet: 'The Choice' (1933)

Persistence

see also DETERMINATION, PATIENCE

1 'If seven maids with seven mops
Swept it for half a year,
Do you suppose,' the Walrus said,
'That they could get it clear?'
'I doubt it,' said the Carpenter,
And shed a bitter tear.
Lewis Carroll 1832–98 English writer and logician: *Through the Looking-Glass* (1872)

2 The comeback kid!
Bill Clinton 1946– American Democratic statesman: description of himself after coming second in the New Hampshire primary, 1992

3 Nothing in the world can take the place of persistence. Talent will not; nothing is more common than unsuccessful men with talent. Genius will not; unrewarded genius is almost a proverb. Education will not; the world is full of educated derelicts. Persistence and determination are omnipotent. The slogan 'press on' has solved and always will solve the problems of the human race.
Calvin Coolidge 1872–1933 American Republican statesman: attributed in the programme of a memorial service for Coolidge in 1933

4 Ride on! Rough-shod if need be, smooth-shod if that will do, but ride

on! Ride on over all obstacles, and win the race!
Charles Dickens 1812–70 English novelist: *David Copperfield* (1850)

5 There must be a beginning of any great matter, but the continuing unto the end until it be thoroughly finished yields the true glory.
Francis Drake *c*.1540–96 English sailor and explorer: dispatch to Sir Francis Walsingham, 17 May 1587

6 Pick yourself up,
Dust yourself off,
Start all over again.
Dorothy Fields 1905–74 American songwriter: 'Pick Yourself Up' (1936 song)

7 If at first you don't succeed, try, try again. Then quit. No use being a damn fool about it.
W. C. Fields 1880–1946 American humorist: attributed

8 But above all
we have
the ability
to sort peas,
to cup water in our hands,
to seek
the right screw
under the sofa
for hours.
Miroslav Holub 1923–98 Czech poet: 'Wings' (1967)

9 The drop of rain maketh a hole in the stone, not by violence, but by oft falling.
Hugh Latimer *c*.1485–1555 English Protestant martyr: *The Second Sermon preached before the King's Majesty*, 19 April 1549

10 Keep right on to the end of the road,
Keep right on to the end.
Tho' the way be long, let your heart be strong,

Keep right on round the bend.
> **Harry Lauder** 1870–1950 Scottish music-hall entertainer: 'The End of the Road' (1924 song)

11 The capacity women have for just hanging on is depressing to contemplate.
> **Stevie Smith** 1902–71 English poet and novelist: in *Tribune* c.1945

12 What is the victory of a cat on a hot tin roof?—I wish I knew . . . Just staying on it, I guess, as long as she can.
> **Tennessee Williams** 1911–83 American dramatist: *Cat on a Hot Tin Roof* (1955)

Pessimism

see also DESPAIR, HOPE, OPTIMISM

1 I feel that life is—is divided up into the horrible and the miserable.
> **Woody Allen** 1935– American film director, writer, and actor: *Annie Hall* (1977 film, with Marshall Brickman)

2 The optimist proclaims that we live in the best of all possible worlds; and the pessimist fears this is true.
> **James Branch Cabell** 1879–1958 American novelist and essayist: *The Silver Stallion* (1926); see OPTIMISM 10

3 I don't consider myself a pessimist. I think of a pessimist as someone who is waiting for it to rain. And I feel soaked to the skin.
> **Leonard Cohen** 1934– Canadian singer and writer: in *Observer* 2 May 1993

4 There are bad times just around the corner,
There are dark clouds travelling through the sky
And it's no good whining
About a silver lining
For we know from experience that they won't roll by.
> **Noël Coward** 1899–1973 English

dramatist, actor, and composer: 'There are Bad Times Just Around the Corner' (1953 song)

5 It is wisdom in prosperity, when all is as thou wouldst have it, to fear and suspect the worst.
> **Erasmus** c.1469–1536 Dutch Christian humanist: *Proverbs or Adages* (1545 ed.)

6 If way to the Better there be, it exacts a full look at the worst.
> **Thomas Hardy** 1840–1928 English novelist and poet: 'De Profundis' (1902)

7 Nothing to do but work,
Nothing to eat but food,
Nothing to wear but clothes
To keep one from going nude.
> **Benjamin Franklin King** 1857–94 American poet: 'The Pessimist'

8 If we see light at the end of the tunnel,
It's the light of the oncoming train.
> **Robert Lowell** 1917–77 American poet: 'Since 1939' (1977)

9 'Twixt the optimist and pessimist
The difference is droll:
The optimist sees the doughnut
But the pessimist sees the hole.
> **McLandburgh Wilson** b. 1892: *Optimist and Pessimist* (c.1915)

10 Pessimism is a luxury that a Jew can never allow himself.
> **Golda Meir** 1898–1978 Israeli stateswoman: in *Observer* 29 December 1974

Philosophy

see also LOGIC

1 To ask the hard question is simple.
> **W. H. Auden** 1907–73 English poet: title of poem (1933)

2 The Socratic manner is not a game at which two can play.
> **Max Beerbohm** 1872–1956 English

critic, essayist, and caricaturist: *Zuleika Dobson* (1911)

3 Metaphysics is the finding of bad reasons for what we believe upon instinct; but to find these reasons is no less an instinct.

F. H. Bradley 1846–1924 English philosopher: *Appearance and Reality* (1893)

4 There is nothing so absurd but some philosopher has said it.

Cicero 106–43 BC Roman orator and statesman: *De Divinatione*

5 I have tried too in my time to be a philosopher; but, I don't know how, cheerfulness was always breaking in.

Oliver Edwards 1711–91 English lawyer: James Boswell *Life of Samuel Johnson* (1791) 17 April 1778

6 When philosophy paints its grey on grey, then has a shape of life grown old. By philosophy's grey on grey it cannot be rejuvenated but only understood. The owl of Minerva spreads its wings only with the falling of the dusk.

G. W. F. Hegel 1770–1831 German idealist philosopher: *Philosophy of Right* (1821)

7 The philosophers have only interpreted the world in various ways; the point is to change it.

Karl Marx 1818–83 German political philosopher: *Theses on Feuerbach* (written 1845, published 1888)

8 No more things should be presumed to exist than are absolutely necessary.

known as 'Occam's razor'

William of Occam *c*.1285–1349 English philosopher and friar: not found in this form in his writings, although he frequently used similar expressions, e.g. 'Plurality should not be assumed unnecessarily'; *Quodlibeta* (c.1324)

9 Apart from the known and the unknown, what else is there?

Harold Pinter 1930–2008 English dramatist: *The Homecoming* (1965)

10 The unexamined life is not worth living.

Socrates 469–399 BC Greek philosopher: Plato *Apology*

11 Superstition sets the whole world in flames; philosophy quenches them.

Voltaire 1694–1778 French writer and philosopher: *Dictionnaire philosophique* (1764) 'Superstition'

12 The safest general characterization of the European philosophical tradition is that it consists of a series of footnotes to Plato.

Alfred North Whitehead 1861–1947 English philosopher and mathematician: *Process and Reality* (1929)

13 What is your aim in philosophy?—To show the fly the way out of the fly-bottle.

Ludwig Wittgenstein 1889–1951 Austrian-born philosopher: *Philosophische Untersuchungen* (1953)

Photography

see also ART, PRESS PHOTOGRAPHERS

1 A photograph is a secret about a secret. The more it tells you the less you know.

Diane Arbus 1923–71 American photographer: Patricia Bosworth *Diane Arbus: a Biography* (1985)

2 It takes a lot of imagination to be a good photographer. You need less imagination to be a painter, because you can invent things. But in photography everything is so ordinary; it takes a lot of looking before you learn to see the ordinary.

David Bailey 1938– English photographer: interview in *The Face* December 1984

3 Most things in life are moments of pleasure and a lifetime of embarrassment; photography is a moment of embarrassment and a lifetime of pleasure.

> **Tony Benn** 1925– British Labour politician: in *Independent* 21 October 1989

4 In photography you've got to be quick, quick, quick, like an animal and a prey.

> **Henri Cartier-Bresson** 1908–2004 French photographer and artist: interview, 1979

5 It's more important to click with people than to click the shutter.

> **Alfred Eisenstaedt** 1898–1995 German-born American photographer: in *Life* 24 August 1995

6 All you can do with most ordinary photographs is stare at them—they stare back, blankly—and presently your concentration begins to fade. They stare you down. I mean, photography is all right if you don't mind looking at the world from the point of view of a paralysed cyclops—*for a split second.*

> **David Hockney** 1937– British artist: as told to Lawrence Weschler, *Cameraworks* (1984)

7 Photography deals exquisitely with appearances, but nothing is what it appears to be.

> **Duane Michals** 1932– American photographer: attributed

8 The photographer is like the cod which produces a million eggs in order that one may reach maturity.

> **George Bernard Shaw** 1856–1950 Irish dramatist: introduction to the catalogue for an exhibition at the Royal Photographic Society, 1906

9 The camera makes everyone a tourist in other people's reality, and eventually in one's own.

> **Susan Sontag** 1933– American writer: in *New York Review of Books* 18 April 1974

10 My idea of a good picture is one that's in focus and of a famous person doing something unfamous. It's being in the right place at the wrong time.

> **Andy Warhol** 1927–87 American artist: *Andy Warhol's Exposures* (1979)

Physics

see also SCIENCE

1 There is no democracy in physics. We can't say that some second-rate guy has as much right to opinion as Fermi.

> **Luis Walter Alvarez** 1911–88 American physicist: D. S. Greenberg *The Politics of Pure Science* (1969)

2 Anybody who is not shocked by this subject has failed to understand it.
of quantum mechanics

> **Niels Bohr** 1885–1962 Danish physicist: attributed

3 There was a young lady named Bright,
Whose speed was far faster than light;
She set out one day
In a relative way
And returned on the previous night.

> **Arthur Buller** 1874–1944 British botanist and mycologist: 'Relativity' (1923)

4 If someone points out to you that your pet theory of the universe is in disagreement with Maxwell's equations—then so much the worse for Maxwell's equations. If it is found to be contradicted by observation—well, these experimentalists do bungle things sometimes. But if your theory is found to be against the second law of thermodynamics I can give you no hope; there is nothing for it but to collapse in deepest humiliation.

> **Arthur Eddington** 1882–1944 British astrophysicist: *The Nature of the Physical World* (1928)

5 If I could remember the names of all these particles I'd be a botanist.

> **Enrico Fermi** 1901–54 Italian-born American atomic physicist: R. L. Weber *More Random Walks in Science* (1973)

6 Heat won't pass from a cooler to a hotter,
You can try it if you like but you'd far better notter.

> **Michael Flanders** 1922–75 and **Donald Swann** 1923–94 English songwriters: 'The First and Second Law' (1956 song)

7 If we assume that the last breath of, say, Julius Caesar has by now become thoroughly scattered through the atmosphere, then the chances are that each of us inhales one molecule of it with every breath we take.

> **James Jeans** 1877–1946 English astronomer, physicist, and mathematician: *An Introduction to the Kinetic Theory of Gases* (1940)

8 I remembered the line from the Hindu scripture, the *Bhagavad Gita* . . . 'I am become death, the destroyer of worlds.'
on the explosion of the first atomic bomb near Alamogordo, New Mexico, 16 July 1945

> **J. Robert Oppenheimer** 1904–67 American physicist: Len Giovannitti and Fred Freed *The Decision to Drop the Bomb* (1965)

9 In some sort of crude sense which no vulgarity, no humour, no overstatement can quite extinguish, the physicists have known sin; and this is a knowledge which they cannot lose.

> **J. Robert Oppenheimer** 1904–67 American physicist: lecture at Massachusetts Institute of Technology, 25 November 1947

10 Neutrinos, they are very small
They have no charge and have no mass
And do not interact at all.

> **John Updike** 1932–2009 American novelist and short-story writer: 'Cosmic Gall ' (1964)

11 It would be a poor thing to be an atom in a world without physicists. And physicists are made of atoms. A physicist is an atom's way of knowing about atoms.

> **George Wald** 1904–97 American biochemist: foreword to L. J. Henderson *The Fitness of the Environment* (1958)

Plagiarism

see also ORIGINALITY

1 They lard their lean books with the fat of others' works.

> **Robert Burton** 1577–1640 English clergyman and scholar: *The Anatomy of Melancholy* (1621–51)

2 Immature poets imitate; mature poets steal.

> **T. S. Eliot** 1888–1965 Anglo-American poet, critic, and dramatist: *The Sacred Wood* (1920) 'Philip Massinger'

3 When a thing has been said and well said, have no scruple: take it and copy it.

> **Anatole France** 1844–1924 French novelist and man of letters: 'The Creed', in Jean Jacques Brousson and John Pollock *Anatole France Himself: A Boswellian Record* (1925)

4 No plagiarist can excuse the wrong by showing how much of his work he did not pirate.

> **Learned Hand** 1872–1961 American judge: *Sheldon v. Metro-Goldwyn Pictures Corp.* 1936

5 When 'Omer smote 'is bloomin' lyre,
He'd 'eard men sing by land an' sea;
An' what he thought 'e might require,
'E went an' took—the same as me!

> **Rudyard Kipling** 1865–1936 English writer and poet: 'When 'Omer smote 'is bloomin' lyre' (1896)

6 If you steal from one author, it's plagiarism; if you steal from many, it's research.

> **Wilson Mizner** 1876–1933 American dramatist: Alva Johnston *The Legendary Mizners* (1953)

7 It could be said of me that in this book I have only made up a bunch of other men's flowers, providing of my own only the string that ties them together.

> **Montaigne** 1533–92 French moralist and essayist: *Essays* (1580)

8 So, naturalists observe, a flea
Hath smaller fleas that on him prey;
And these have smaller fleas to bite 'em,
And so proceed *ad infinitum*.

> **Jonathan Swift** 1667–1745 Anglo-Irish poet and satirist: 'On Poetry' (1733)

Pleasure

see also HAPPINESS

1 No pleasure is worth giving up for the sake of two more years in a geriatric home in Weston-super-Mare.

> **Kingsley Amis** 1922–95 English novelist and poet: in *The Times* 21 June 1994; attributed

2 A fool bolts pleasure, then complains of moral indigestion.

> **Minna Antrim** 1861–1950 American writer: *Naked Truth and Veiled Allusions* (1902)

3 The prudent man aspires not to pleasure, but to the absence of pain.

> **Aristotle** 384–322 BC Greek philosopher: *Nicomachean Ethics*

4 One half of the world cannot understand the pleasures of the other.

> **Jane Austen** 1775–1817 English novelist: *Emma* (1816)

5 The great pleasure in life is doing what people say you cannot do.

> **Walter Bagehot** 1826–77 English economist and essayist: in *Prospective Review* 1853 'Shakespeare'

6 Let us have wine and women, mirth and laughter,
Sermons and soda-water the day after.

> **Lord Byron** 1788–1824 English poet: *Don Juan* (1819–24)

7 In love, as in gluttony, pleasure is a matter of the utmost precision.

> **Italo Calvino** 1923–85 Italian novelist and short-story writer: Charles Fourier *Theory of the Four Movements* (1971)

8 Lying in bed would be an altogether perfect and supreme experience if only one had a coloured pencil long enough to draw on the ceiling.

> **G. K. Chesterton** 1874–1936 English essayist, novelist, and poet: *Tremendous Trifles* (1909) 'On Lying in Bed'

9 There's no greater bliss in life than when the plumber eventually comes to unblock your drains. No writer can give that sort of pleasure.

> **Victoria Glendinning** 1937– English biographer and novelist: in *Observer* 3 January 1993

10 People must not do things for fun. We are not here for fun. There is no reference to fun in any Act of Parliament.

> **A. P. Herbert** 1890–1971 English writer and humorist: *Uncommon Law* (1935)

11 The less we indulge our pleasures the more we enjoy them.

> **Juvenal** AD *c*.60–*c*.130 Roman satirist: *Satires* no. 11 (tr. N. Rudd)

12 The greatest pleasure I know, is to do a good action by stealth, and to have it found out by accident.

> **Charles Lamb** 1775–1834 English writer: 'Table Talk by the late Elia' in *The Athenaeum* 4 January 1834

13 Who loves not woman, wine, and song
Remains a fool his whole life long.

> **Martin Luther** 1483–1546 German Protestant theologian: attributed; later inscribed in the Luther room in the Wartburg, but with no proof of authorship

14 The Puritan hated bear-baiting, not because it gave pain to the bear, but because it gave pleasure to the spectators.

> **Lord Macaulay** 1800–59 English politician and historian: *History of England* vol. 1 (1849)

15 Pleasure chews and grinds us.

> **Montaigne** 1533–92 French moralist and essayist: *Essays* (1580)

16 It is a curious thing that people only ask if you are enjoying yourself when you aren't.

> **Edith Nesbit** 1858–1924 English writer: *Five of Us, and Madeline* (1925)

17 I admit it is better fun to punt than to be punted, and that a desire to have all the fun is nine-tenths of the law of chivalry.

> **Dorothy L. Sayers** 1893–1957 English writer of detective fiction: *Gaudy Night* (1935)

18 Pleasure is nothing else but the intermission of pain.

> **John Selden** 1584–1654 English historian and antiquary: *Table Talk* (1689) 'Pleasure'

19 Nothing is so perfectly amusement as a total change of ideas.

> **Laurence Sterne** 1713–68 English novelist: *Tristram Shandy* (1759–67)

20 All the things I really like to do are either illegal, immoral, or fattening.

> **Alexander Woollcott** 1887–1943 American writer: R. E. Drennan *Wit's End* (1973)

21 It's always the good feel rotten. Pleasure's for those who are bad.

> **Sergei Yesenin** 1895–1925 Russian poet: 'Pleasure's for the Bad' (1923)

Poetry

see also FAMOUS POETS, WRITING

1 It is barbarous to write a poem after Auschwitz.

> **Theodor Adorno** 1903–69 German philosopher and musicologist: I. Buruma *Wages of Guilt* (1994)

2 A poet's hope: to be,
like some valley cheese,
local, but prized elsewhere.

> **W. H. Auden** 1907–73 English poet: 'Shorts II' (1976)

3 Prose is when all the lines except the last go on to the end. Poetry is when some of them fall short of it.

> **Jeremy Bentham** 1748–1832 English philosopher: M. St J. Packe *The Life of John Stuart Mill* (1954)

4 Some rhyme a neebor's name to lash;
Some rhyme (vain thought!) for needfu' cash;
Some rhyme to court the countra clash,
An' raise a din;

For me, an aim I never fash;
I rhyme for fun.
> **Robert Burns** 1759–96 Scottish poet:
> 'To J. S[mith]' (1786)

5 All poets are mad.
> **Robert Burton** 1577–1640 English
> clergyman and scholar: *The Anatomy of
> Melancholy* (1621–51)

6 There's nothing in the world for
which a poet will give up writing, not
even when he is a Jew and the
language of his poems is German.
> **Paul Celan** 1920–70 German poet: letter
> to relatives, 2 August 1948

7 The worst tragedy for a poet is to be
admired through being
misunderstood.
> **Jean Cocteau** 1889–1963 French
> dramatist and film director: *Le Rappel à
> l'ordre* (1926)

8 That willing suspension of disbelief
for the moment, which constitutes
poetic faith.
> **Samuel Taylor Coleridge** 1772–1834
> English poet, critic, and philosopher:
> *Biographia Literaria* (1817)

9 Prose = words in their best
order;—poetry = the *best* words in
the best order.
> **Samuel Taylor Coleridge** 1772–1834
> English poet, critic, and philosopher:
> *Table Talk* (1835) 12 July 1827

10 I am two fools, I know,
For loving, and for saying so
In whining poetry.
> **John Donne** 1572–1631 English poet
> and divine: 'The Triple Fool'

11 Poetry is not a turning loose of
emotion, but an escape from
emotion; it is not the expression of
personality but an escape from
personality.
> **T. S. Eliot** 1888–1965 Anglo-American
> poet, critic, and dramatist: *The Sacred
> Wood* (1920)

12 Poetry's a mere drug, Sir.
> **George Farquhar** 1678–1707 Irish
> dramatist: *Love and a Bottle* (1698)

13 I'd as soon write free verse as play
tennis with the net down.
> **Robert Frost** 1874–1963 American poet:
> Edward Lathem *Interviews with Robert
> Frost* (1966)

14 As soon as war is declared it will be
impossible to hold the poets back.
Rhyme is still the most effective
drum.
> **Jean Giraudoux** 1882–1944 French
> dramatist: *La Guerre de Troie n'aura pas
> lieu* (1935)

15   What
ought a poem be? Answer, *a sad
and angry consolation.*
> **Geoffrey Hill** 1932– English poet: *The
> Triumph of Love* (1999)

16 Experience has taught me, when I
am shaving of a morning, to keep
watch over my thoughts, because, if
a line of poetry strays into my
memory, my skin bristles so that the
razor ceases to act . . . The seat of
this sensation is the pit of the
stomach.
> **A. E. Housman** 1859–1936 English poet:
> lecture at Cambridge, 9 May 1933

17 If poetry comes not as naturally as
the leaves to a tree it had better not
come at all.
> **John Keats** 1795–1821 English poet:
> letter to John Taylor, 27 February 1818

18 The notion of expressing sentiments
in short lines having similar sounds
at their ends seems as remote as
mangoes on the moon.
> **Philip Larkin** 1922–85 English poet:
> letter to Barbara Pym, 22 January 1975

19 For twenty years I've stared my level
best
To see if evening—any evening
—would suggest

A patient etherized upon a table;
In vain. I simply wasn't able.
on contemporary poetry

> **C. S. Lewis** 1898–1963 English literary
> scholar: 'A Confession' (1964); see
> EVENING 1

20 A poem should not mean
But be.
> **Archibald MacLeish** 1892–1982
> American poet and public official: 'Ars
> Poetica' (1926)

21 Most people ignore most poetry
because
most poetry ignores most people.
> **Adrian Mitchell** 1932–2008 English
> poet, novelist, and dramatist: *Poems*
> (1964)

22 All that is not prose is verse; and all
that is not verse is prose.
> **Molière** 1622–73 French comic
> dramatist: *Le Bourgeois Gentilhomme*
> (1671)

23 All a poet can do today is warn.
> **Wilfred Owen** 1893–1918 English poet:
> preface (written 1918) in *Poems* (1963)

24 Poetry is the achievement of the
synthesis of hyacinths and biscuits.
> **Carl Sandburg** 1878–1967 American
> poet: in *Atlantic Monthly* March 1923

25 Poets are the unacknowledged
legislators of the world.
> **Percy Bysshe Shelley** 1792–1822
> English poet: *A Defence of Poetry*
> (written 1821)

26 Poetry is not the most important
thing in life . . . I'd much rather lie in
a hot bath reading Agatha Christie
and sucking sweets.
> **Dylan Thomas** 1914–53 Welsh poet:
> Joan Wyndham *Love is Blue* (1986) 6 July
> 1943

27 In this
most Christian of worlds all poets
are Jews.
> **Marina Tsvetaeva** 1892–1941 Russian
> poet: 'Poem of the End' (1924)

28 A poem is never finished; it's always
an accident that puts a stop to it—i.e.
gives it to the public.
*often quoted as paraphrased by W. H.
Auden: 'A poem is never finished, only
abandoned'*

> **Paul Valéry** 1871–1945 French poet,
> critic, and man of letters: *Littérature*
> (1930)

29 Poetry is the spontaneous overflow
of powerful feelings: it takes its
origin from emotion recollected in
tranquillity.
> **William Wordsworth** 1770–1850
> English poet: *Lyrical Ballads* (2nd ed.,
> 1802)

30 I said 'a line will take us hours
maybe;
Yet if it does not seem a moment's
thought,
Our stitching and unstitching has
been naught.'
> **W. B. Yeats** 1865–1939 Irish poet:
> 'Adam's Curse' (1904)

31 We make out of the quarrel with
others, rhetoric, but of the quarrel
with ourselves, poetry.
> **W. B. Yeats** 1865–1939 Irish poet: *Essays*
> (1924) 'Anima Hominis'

32 I think poetry should be alive. You
should be able to dance it.
> **Benjamin Zephaniah** 1958– British
> poet: in *Sunday Times* 23 August 1987

Police

see also LAWS

1 When constabulary duty's to be
done,
A policeman's lot is not a happy one.
> **W. S. Gilbert** 1836–1911 English writer
> of comic and satirical verse: *The Pirates
> of Penzance* (1879)

2 They always get their man.
unofficial motto of the Royal Canadian Mounted Police

John J. Healy 1840–1908 American newspaperman and whiskey trader: attributed, 1877

3 Every society gets the kind of criminal it deserves. What is equally true is that every community gets the kind of law enforcement it insists on.

Robert Kennedy 1925–68 American Democratic politician: *The Pursuit of Justice* (1964)

4 The South African police would leave no stone unturned to see that nothing disturbed the even terror of their lives.

Tom Sharpe 1928– British novelist: *Indecent Exposure* (1973)

5 A liberal is a conservative who has been arrested.

Tom Wolfe 1931– American writer: *The Bonfire of the Vanities* (1987)

Political Parties

see also COMMUNISM, POLITICIANS, POLITICS

1 The language of priorities is the religion of Socialism.

Aneurin Bevan 1897–1960 British Labour politician: speech at Labour Party Conference in Blackpool, 8 June 1949

2 Fascism is not in itself a new order of society. It is the future refusing to be born.

Aneurin Bevan 1897–1960 British Labour politician: Leon Harris *The Fine Art of Political Wit* (1965)

3 One of the things I'm writing about is that I'm convinced the further left you go, the more right wing you become.

Alan Bleasdale 1946– British dramatist and novelist: in *Independent* 2 May 1990

4 God will not always be a Tory.

Lord Byron 1788–1824 English poet: letter, 2 February 1821

5 Then raise the scarlet standard high!
Within its shade we'll live or die.
Tho' cowards flinch and traitors sneer,
We'll keep the red flag flying here.

James M. Connell 1852–1929 Irish socialist songwriter: 'The Red Flag' (1889 song)

6 Damn your principles! Stick to your party.

Benjamin Disraeli 1804–81 British Tory statesman and novelist: attributed to Disraeli and believed to have been said to Edward Bulwer-Lytton; E. Latham *Famous Sayings and their Authors* (1904)

7 There are some of us . . . who will fight and fight and fight again to save the Party we love.

Hugh Gaitskell 1906–63 British Labour politician: speech at Labour Party Conference, 5 October 1960

8 I always voted at my party's call,
And I never thought of thinking for myself at all.

W. S. Gilbert 1836–1911 English writer of comic and satirical verse: *HMS Pinafore* (1878)

9 Conservatives do not believe that the political struggle is the most important thing in life . . . The simplest of them prefer fox-hunting—the wisest religion.

Lord Hailsham 1907–2001 British Conservative politician: *The Case for Conservatism* (1947)

10 We are all socialists now.
during the passage of the 1888 budget, noted for the reduction of the National Debt

William Harcourt 1827–1904 British Liberal politician: attributed; Hubert Bland 'The Outlook' in G. B. Shaw (ed.) *Fabian Essays in Socialism* (1889)

11 A dead or dying beast lying across a railway line and preventing other trains from getting through.
of the Labour Party
> **Roy Jenkins** 1920–2003 British politician: in *Guardian* 16 May 1987

12 I am a free man, an American, a United States Senator, and a Democrat, in that order.
> **Lyndon Baines Johnson** 1908–73 American Democratic statesman: in *Texas Quarterly* Winter 1958

13 The longest suicide note in history.
on the Labour Party's election manifesto New Hope for Britain *(1983)*
> **Gerald Kaufman** 1930– British Labour politician: Denis Healey *The Time of My Life* (1989)

14 When in office, the Liberals forget their principles and the Tories remember their friends.
> **Thomas Kettle** 1880–1916 Irish economist and poet: Nicholas Mansergh *The Irish Question* (ed. 3, 1975)

15 Loyalty is the Tory's secret weapon.
> **Lord Kilmuir** 1900–67 British Conservative politician and lawyer: Anthony Sampson *Anatomy of Britain* (1962)

16 As usual the Liberals offer a mixture of sound and original ideas. Unfortunately none of the sound ideas is original and none of the original ideas is sound.
> **Harold Macmillan** 1894–1986 British Conservative statesman: speech to London Conservatives, 7 March 1961

17 You know what some people call us: the nasty party.
> **Theresa May** 1956– British Conservative politician: speech to the Conservative Conference, 7 October 2002

18 Under democracy one party always devotes its energies to trying to prove that the other party is unfit to rule—and both commonly succeed and are right.
> **H. L. Mencken** 1880–1956 American journalist and literary critic: *Minority Report* (1956)

19 Socialism is what the Labour Government does.
> **Herbert Morrison** 1888–1965 British Labour politician: attributed

20 I fear my Socialism is purely cerebral; I do not like the masses in the flesh.
> **Harold Nicolson** 1886–1968 English diplomat, politician, and writer: letter to Vita Sackville-West, 7 May 1948

21 I have only one firm belief about the American political system, and that is this: God is a Republican and Santa Claus is a Democrat.
> **P. J. O'Rourke** 1947– American humorous writer: *Parliament of Whores* (1991)

22 To the ordinary working man, the sort you would meet in any pub on Saturday night, Socialism does not mean much more than better wages and shorter hours and nobody bossing you about.
> **George Orwell** 1903–50 English novelist: *The Road to Wigan Pier* (1937)

23 The Labour Party owes more to Methodism than to Marxism.
> **Morgan Phillips** 1902–63 British Labour politician: James Callaghan *Time and Chance* (1987); coined by Denis Healey (1917–) as speechwriter for Phillips at the Socialist International Conference, Copenhagen, 1953

24 I am reminded of four definitions: A Radical is a man with both feet firmly planted—in the air. A Conservative is a man with two perfectly good legs who, however, has never learned to walk forward. A Reactionary is a somnambulist walking backwards. A Liberal is a man who uses his legs and his hands at the behest—at the command—of his head.

> **Franklin D. Roosevelt** 1882–1945 American Democratic statesman: radio address, 26 October 1939

25 If they [the Republicans] will stop telling lies about the Democrats, we will stop telling the truth about them.

> **Adlai Stevenson** 1900–65 American Democratic politician: speech during 1952 Presidential campaign; J. B. Martin *Adlai Stevenson and Illinois* (1976)

26 An independent is a guy who wants to take the politics out of politics.

> **Adlai Stevenson** 1900–65 American Democratic politician: Bill Adler *The Stevenson Wit* (1966)

27 Socialism can only arrive by bicycle.

> **José Antonio Viera Gallo** 1943– Chilean politician: Ivan Illich *Energy and Equity* (1974) epigraph

28 This party is a moral crusade or it is nothing.

> **Harold Wilson** 1916–95 British Labour statesman: speech at the Labour Party Conference, 1 October 1962

Politicians

see also FAMOUS POLITICIANS, POLITICAL PARTIES, POLITICS, PRESIDENCY, PRIME MINISTERS, SPEECHES

1 A political leader must keep looking over his shoulder all the time to see if the boys are still there. If they aren't still there, he's no longer a political leader.

> **Bernard Baruch** 1870–1965 American financier: in *New York Times* 21 June 1965

2 I am not going to spend any time whatsoever in attacking the Foreign Secretary . . . If we complain about the tune, there is no reason to attack the monkey when the organ grinder is present.

during a debate on the Suez crisis

> **Aneurin Bevan** 1897–1960 British Labour politician: speech, House of Commons, 16 May 1957

3 An honest politician is one who when he's bought stays bought.

> **Simon Cameron** 1799–1889 American politician: attributed

4 A minister who moves about in society is in a position to read the signs of the times even in a festive gathering, but one who remains shut up in his office learns nothing.

> **Duc de Choiseul** 1719–85 French politician: Jack F. Bernard *Talleyrand* (1973)

5 The ability to foretell what is going to happen tomorrow, next week, next month, and next year. And to have the ability afterwards to explain why it didn't happen.

describing the qualifications desirable in a prospective politician

> **Winston Churchill** 1874–1965 British Conservative statesman: B. Adler *Churchill Wit* (1965)

6 a politician is an arse upon which everyone has sat except a man.

> **e. e. cummings** 1894–1962 American poet: *1 x 1* (1944) no. 10

7 'Do you pray for the senators, Dr Hale?' 'No, I look at the senators and I pray for the country.'

> **Edward Everett Hale** 1822–1909 American Unitarian clergyman: Van Wyck Brooks *New England Indian Summer* (1940)

8 If you want to succeed in politics, you must keep your conscience well under control.

> **David Lloyd George** 1863–1945 British Liberal statesman: Lord Riddell, diary, 23 April 1919

9 Forever poised between a cliché and an indiscretion.

on the life of a Foreign Secretary

   Harold Macmillan 1894–1986 British Conservative statesman: in *Newsweek* 30 April 1956

10 did you ever
notice that when
a politician
does get an idea
he usually
gets it all wrong.

   Don Marquis 1878–1937 American poet and journalist: *archys life of mehitabel* (1933)

11 What I want is men who will support me when I am in the wrong.

replying to a politician who said 'I will support you as long as you are in the right'

   Lord Melbourne 1779–1848 British Whig statesman: Lord David Cecil *Lord M* (1954)

12 The greatest gift of any statesman rests not in knowing what concessions to make, but recognising when to make them.

   Prince Metternich 1773–1859 Austrian statesman: *Concessionen und Nichtconcessionen* (1852)

13 Anyone who campaigns for public office becomes disqualified for holding any office at all.

   Thomas More 1478–1535 English scholar and saint: *Utopia* (1516)

14 The city in which those who are to rule are least eager to hold office must needs be the best governed and freest from strife.

   Plato 429–347 BC Greek philosopher: *The Republic*

15 A statesman is a politician who places himself at the service of the nation. A politician is a statesman who places the nation at his service.

   Georges Pompidou 1911–74 French statesman: in *Observer* 30 December 1973

16 All political lives, unless they are cut off in midstream at a happy juncture, end in failure, because that is the nature of politics and of human affairs.

   Enoch Powell 1912–98 British Conservative politician: *Joseph Chamberlain* (1977)

17 He may be a son of a bitch, but he's our son of a bitch.

on President Somoza of Nicaragua, 1938

   Franklin D. Roosevelt 1882–1945 American Democratic statesman: attributed

18 He knows nothing; and he thinks he knows everything. That points clearly to a political career.

   George Bernard Shaw 1856–1950 Irish dramatist: *Major Barbara* (1907)

19 Someone must fill the gap between platitudes and bayonets.

   Adlai Stevenson 1900–65 American Democratic politician: Leon Harris *The Fine Art of Political Wit* (1965)

20 In politics, if you want anything said, ask a man. If you want anything done, ask a woman.

   Margaret Thatcher 1925– British Conservative stateswoman: in 1970; in *People* (New York) 15 September 1975

21 A politician is a man who understands government, and it takes a politician to run a government. A statesman is a politician who's been dead 10 or 15 years.

   Harry S. Truman 1884–1972 American Democratic statesman: in *New York World Telegram and Sun* 12 April 1958

Politics

1 The trouble with this country is that there are too many politicians who believe, with a conviction based on experience, that you can fool all of the people all of the time.
   Franklin P. Adams 1881–1960 American journalist and humorist: *Nods and Becks* (1944); see DECEPTION 6

2 Politics, as a practice, whatever its professions, has always been the systematic organization of hatreds.
   Henry Brooks Adams 1838–1918 American man of letters: *The Education of Henry Adams* (1907)

3 I agree with you that in politics the middle way is none at all.
   John Adams 1735–1826 American statesman: letter to Horatio Gates, 23 March 1776

4 The personal is political.
   Anonymous: 1970s feminist slogan, attributed to Carol Hanisch (1945–)

5 Man is by nature a political animal.
   Aristotle 384–322 BC Greek philosopher: *Politics*

6 A statesman . . . must wait until he hears the steps of God sounding through events; then leap up and grasp the hem of his garment.
   Otto von Bismarck 1815–98 German statesman: A. J. P. Taylor *Bismarck* (1955)

7 Politics is the art of the possible.
   Otto von Bismarck 1815–98 German statesman: in conversation with Meyer von Waldeck, 11 August 1867

8 The liberals can understand everything but people who don't understand them.
   Lenny Bruce 1925–66 American comedian: John Cohen (ed.) *The Essential Lenny Bruce* (1967)

9 In politics you must always keep running with the pack. The moment that you falter and they sense that you are injured, the rest will turn on you like wolves.
   R. A. Butler 1902–82 British Conservative politician: Dennis Walters *Not Always with the Pack* (1989)

10 In politics, there is no use looking beyond the next fortnight.
   Joseph Chamberlain 1836–1914 British Liberal politician: letter from A. J. Balfour to 3rd Marquess of Salisbury, 24 March 1886

11 The art of politics is learning to walk with your back to the wall, your elbows high, and a smile on your face. It's a survival game played under the glare of lights.
   Jean Chrétien 1934– Canadian Liberal statesman: *Straight from the Heart* (1985)

12 Politics are almost as exciting as war and quite as dangerous. In war you can only be killed once, but in politics—many times.
   Winston Churchill 1874–1965 British Conservative statesman: attributed

13 There are no true friends in politics. We are all sharks circling, and waiting, for traces of blood to appear in the water.
   Alan Clark 1928–99 British Conservative politician: diary, 30 November 1990

14 If something makes you cry, you have to do something about it. That's the difference between politics and guilt.
   Bill Clinton 1946– American Democratic statesman: *On the Make* (1994)

15 International life is right-wing, like nature. The social contract is left-wing, like humanity.
  Régis Debray 1940– French Marxist theorist: *Charles de Gaulle* (1994)

16 Politics are too serious a matter to be left to the politicians.
  replying to Attlee's remark that 'De Gaulle is a very good soldier and a very bad politician'
  Charles de Gaulle 1890–1970 French soldier and statesman: Clement Attlee *A Prime Minister Remembers* (1961)

17 Finality is not the language of politics.
  Benjamin Disraeli 1804–81 British Tory statesman and novelist: speech, House of Commons, 28 February 1859

18 I never dared be radical when young For fear it would make me conservative when old.
  Robert Frost 1874–1963 American poet: 'Precaution' (1936)

19 Politics is not the art of the possible. It consists in choosing between the disastrous and the unpalatable.
  J. K. Galbraith 1908–2006 American economist: letter to President Kennedy, 2 March 1962; see POLITICS 7

20 In politics, being ridiculous is more damaging than being extreme.
  Roy Hattersley 1932– British Labour politician: in *Evening Standard* 9 May 1989

21 Healey's first law of politics: when you're in a hole, stop digging.
  Denis Healey 1917– British Labour politician: attributed

22 Politics is a marathon, not a sprint.
  Ken Livingstone 1945– British Labour politician: in *New Statesman* 10 October 1997

23 The opposition of events.
  on his biggest problem in politics;
  popularly quoted as, 'Events, dear boy. Events'
  Harold Macmillan 1894–1986 British Conservative statesman: David Dilks *The Office of Prime Minister in Twentieth Century Britain* (1993)

24 Politics is war without bloodshed while war is politics with bloodshed.
  Mao Zedong 1893–1976 Chinese statesman: lecture, 1938

25 All reactionaries are paper tigers. In appearance, the reactionaries are terrifying, but in reality they are not so powerful. From a long-term point of view, it is not the reactionaries but the people who are really powerful.
  Mao Zedong 1893–1976 Chinese statesman: interview with Anne Louise Strong, August 1946

26 Never doubt that a small group of thoughtful committed citizens can change the world. In fact, it's the only thing that ever has.
  Margaret Mead 1901–78 American anthropologist: attributed; Mary Bowman-Kruhm *Margaret Mead: a biography* (2003)

27 Political language . . . is designed to make lies sound truthful and murder respectable, and to give an appearance of solidity to pure wind.
  George Orwell 1903–50 English novelist: *Shooting an Elephant* (1950) 'Politics and the English Language'

28 Men enter local politics solely as a result of being unhappily married.
  C. Northcote Parkinson 1909–93 English writer: *Parkinson's Law* (1958)

29 Politics is supposed to be the second oldest profession. I have come to realize that it bears a very close resemblance to the first.
  Ronald Reagan 1911–2004 American Republican statesman: at a conference in Los Angeles, 2 March 1977

30 What is morally wrong cannot be politically right.

> **Donald Soper** 1903–98 British Methodist minister: speech, House of Lords, 1966

31 A week is a long time in politics.

> *probably first said at the time of the 1964 sterling crisis*
> **Harold Wilson** 1916–95 British Labour statesman: Nigel Rees *Sayings of the Century* (1984)

Pollution

see also EARTH, ENVIRONMENT, NATURE

1 And did the Countenance Divine
Shine forth upon our clouded hills?
And was Jerusalem builded here
Among these dark Satanic mills?

> **William Blake** 1757–1827 English poet: *Milton* (1804–10) 'And did those feet in ancient time'

2 Over increasingly large areas of the United States, spring now comes unheralded by the return of the birds, and the early mornings are strangely silent where once they were filled with the beauty of bird song.

> **Rachel Carson** 1907–64 American zoologist: *The Silent Spring* (1962)

3 The river Rhine, it is well known,
Doth wash your city of Cologne;
But tell me, Nymphs, what power divine
Shall henceforth wash the river Rhine?

> **Samuel Taylor Coleridge** 1772–1834 English poet, critic, and philosopher: 'Cologne' (1834)

4 The sea is the universal sewer.

> **Jacques Cousteau** 1910–97 French underwater explorer: testimony before the House Committee on Science and Astronautics, 28 January 1971

5 Clear the air! clean the sky! wash the wind!

> **T. S. Eliot** 1888–1965 Anglo-American poet, critic, and dramatist: *Murder in the Cathedral* (1935)

6 The sanitary and mechanical age we are now entering makes up for the mercy it grants to our sense of smell by the ferocity with which it assails our sense of hearing. As usual, what we call 'progress' is the exchange of one nuisance for another nuisance.

> **Havelock Ellis** 1859–1939 English sexologist: *Impressions and Comments* (1914)

7 Dirt is only matter out of place.

> **John Chipman Gray** 1839–1915 American lawyer: *Restraints on the Alienation of Property* (2nd ed., 1895)

8 And all is seared with trade; bleared, smeared with toil;
And wears man's smudge and shares man's smell.

> **Gerard Manley Hopkins** 1844–89 English poet and priest: 'God's Grandeur' (written 1877)

9 Forget six counties overhung with smoke,
Forget the snorting steam and piston stroke,
Forget the spreading of the hideous town;
Think rather of the pack-horse on the down,
And dream of London, small and white and clean,
The clear Thames bordered by its gardens green.

> **William Morris** 1834–96 English writer, artist, and designer: *The Earthly Paradise* (1868–70)

10 We have met the enemy and he is us.

> *the cartoon-strip character, Pogo the opossum, looking at litter under a tree; used as an Earth Day poster in 1971*
> **Walt Kelly** 1913–73 American cartoonist: *Pogo* cartoon, 1970

11 It goes so heavily with my
disposition that this goodly frame,
the earth, seems to me a sterile
promontory; this most excellent
canopy, the air, look you, this brave
o'erhanging firmament, this
majestical roof fretted with golden
fire, why, it appears no other thing to
me but a foul and pestilent
congregation of vapours.
   William Shakespeare 1564–1616
   English dramatist: *Hamlet* (1601)

12 I do wonder whether there will come
a time when we can no longer afford
our wastefulness—chemical wastes
in the rivers, metal wastes
everywhere, and atomic wastes
buried deep in the earth or sunk in
the sea. When an Indian village
became too deep in its own filth, the
inhabitants moved. And we have no
place to which to move.
   John Steinbeck 1902–68 American
   novelist: *Travels With Charley* (1962)

Pop Music

see ROCK AND POP MUSIC

Pornography

1 A widespread taste for pornography
means that nature is alerting us to
some threat of extinction.
   J. G. Ballard 1930–2009 British writer:
   Myths of the Near Future (1982)

2 Pornography is rather like trying to
find out about a Beethoven
symphony by having somebody tell
you about it and perhaps hum a few
bars.
   Robertson Davies 1913–95 Canadian
   novelist: in 1972; *The Enthusiasms of
   Robertson Davies* (1990)

3 Pornography is the attempt to insult
sex, to do dirt on it.
   D. H. Lawrence 1885–1930 English

novelist and poet: *Phoenix* (1936)
'Pornography and Obscenity'

4 It is obvious that 'obscenity' is not a
term capable of exact legal
definition; in the practice of the
Courts, it means 'anything that
shocks the magistrate'.
   Bertrand Russell 1872–1970 British
   philosopher and mathematician:
   Sceptical Essays (1928) 'The
   Recrudescence of Puritanism'

5 What pornography is really about,
ultimately, isn't sex but death.
   Susan Sontag 1933– American writer:
   in *Partisan Review* Spring 1967

Possessions

1 The goal of all inanimate objects is to
resist man and ultimately to defeat
him.
   Russell Baker 1925– American
   journalist and columnist: in *New York
   Times* 18 June 1968

2 For we brought nothing into this
world, and it is certain we can carry
nothing out.
   Bible: I Timothy

3 There are only two families in the
world, as a grandmother of mine
used to say: the haves and the have-
nots.
   Cervantes 1547–1616 Spanish novelist:
   Don Quixote (1605)

4 People don't resent having nothing
nearly as much as too little.
   Ivy Compton-Burnett 1884–1969
   English novelist: *A Family and a Fortune*
   (1939)

5 The moon belongs to everyone,
The best things in life are free.
   Buddy De Sylva 1895–1950 and **Lew
   Brown** 1893–1958: 'The Best Things in
   Life are Free' (1927 song)

6 Property has its duties as well as its rights.

> **Thomas Drummond** 1797–1840 British government official: letter to the Earl of Donoughmore, 22 May 1838

7 Well! some people talk of morality, and some of religion, but give me a little snug property.

> **Maria Edgeworth** 1768–1849 Anglo-Irish novelist: *The Absentee* (1812)

8 People who get through life dependent on other people's possessions are always the first to lecture you on how little possessions count.

> **Ben Elton** 1959– British writer and performer: *Stark* (1989)

9 Things are in the saddle,
And ride mankind.

> **Ralph Waldo Emerson** 1803–82 American philosopher and poet: 'Ode' Inscribed to W. H. Channing (1847)

10 Man must choose whether to be rich in things or in the freedom to use them.

> **Ivan Illich** 1926–2002 American sociologist: *Deschooling Society* (1971)

11 Have nothing in your houses that you do not know to be useful, or believe to be beautiful.

> **William Morris** 1834–96 English writer, artist, and designer: *Hopes and Fears for Art* (1882)

12 Property is theft.

> **Pierre-Joseph Proudhon** 1809–65 French social reformer: *Qu'est-ce que la propriété?* (1840)

13 How many things I can do without!
on looking at a multitude of wares exposed for sale

> **Socrates** 469–399 BC Greek philosopher: Diogenes Laertius *Lives of the Philosophers*

Poverty

see also MONEY, WEALTH

1 She was poor but she was honest
Victim of a rich man's game.
First he loved her, then he left her,
And she lost her maiden name . . .
It's the same the whole world over,
It's the poor wot gets the blame,
It's the rich wot gets the gravy.
Ain't it all a bleedin' shame?

> **Anonymous**: 'She was Poor but she was Honest'; sung by British soldiers in the First World War

2 Make poverty history.

> **Anonymous**: slogan of a campaign launched in 2005 by a coalition of charities and other groups to pressure governments to take action to reduce poverty

3 Anyone who has ever struggled with poverty knows how extremely expensive it is to be poor.

> **James Baldwin** 1924–87 American novelist and essayist: *Nobody Knows My Name* (1961)

4 Come away; poverty's catching.

> **Aphra Behn** 1640–89 English dramatist, poet, and novelist: *The Rover* pt. 2 (1681)

5 The poor always ye have with you.

> **Bible**: St John

6 When I give food to the poor they call me a saint. When I ask why the poor have no food they call me a communist.

> **Helder Camara** 1909–99 Brazilian priest: attributed

7 The poor are Europe's blacks.

> **Nicolas-Sébastien Chamfort** 1741–94 French writer: *Maximes et Pensées* (1796)

8 They [the poor] have to labour in the face of the majestic equality of the law, which forbids the rich as well as the poor to sleep under bridges, to beg in the streets, and to steal bread.

Anatole France 1844–1924 French novelist and man of letters: *Le Lys rouge* (1894)

9 Laws grind the poor, and rich men rule the law.

Oliver Goldsmith 1728–74 Anglo-Irish writer, poet, and dramatist: *The Traveller* (1764)

10 Let not ambition mock their useful toil,
Their homely joys, and destiny obscure;
Nor grandeur hear with a disdainful smile,
The short and simple annals of the poor.

Thomas Gray 1716–71 English poet: *Elegy Written in a Country Churchyard* (1751)

11 Brother can you spare a dime?

E. Y. Harburg 1898–1981 American songwriter: title of song (1932)

12 I want there to be no peasant in my kingdom so poor that he is unable to have a chicken in his pot every Sunday.

Henri IV 1553–1610 French monarch: Hardouin de Péréfixe *Histoire de Henry le Grand* (1681); see PROGRESS 11

13 Oh! God! that bread should be so dear,
And flesh and blood so cheap!

Thomas Hood 1799–1845 English poet and humorist: 'The Song of the Shirt' (1843)

14 Resolve not to be poor: whatever you have, spend less. Poverty is a great enemy to human happiness; it certainly destroys liberty, and it makes some virtues impracticable, and others extremely difficult.

Samuel Johnson 1709–84 English poet, critic, and lexicographer: letter to Boswell, 7 December 1782

15 The misfortunes of poverty carry with them nothing harder to bear than that it makes men ridiculous.

Juvenal AD *c.*60–*c.*130 Roman satirist: *Satires*

16 There's nothing surer,
The rich get rich and the poor get children.

Gus Kahn 1886–1941 and **Raymond B. Egan** 1890–1952 American songwriters: 'Ain't We Got Fun' (1921 song)

17 Overcoming poverty is not a gesture of charity. It is an act of justice.

Nelson Mandela 1918– South African statesman: speech in Trafalgar Square, London, 3 February 2005

18 Poverty is a lot like childbirth—you know it is going to hurt before it happens, but you'll never know how much until you experience it.

J. K. Rowling 1965– English novelist: in *Mail on Sunday* 16 June 2002

19 The greatest of evils and the worst of crimes is poverty.

George Bernard Shaw 1856–1950 Irish dramatist: *Major Barbara* (1907)

20 Born down in a dead man's town
The first kick I took was when I hit the ground.

Bruce Springsteen 1949– American rock singer and songwriter: 'Born in the USA' (1984 song)

Power

see also POLITICS, STRENGTH

1 Power tends to corrupt and absolute power corrupts absolutely.

Lord Acton 1834–1902 British historian: letter to Bishop Mandell Creighton, 3 April 1887

2 When he laughed, respectable senators burst with laughter,

And when he cried the little children died in the streets.

W. H. Auden 1907–73 English poet: 'Epitaph on a Tyrant' (1940)

3 Whatever happens we have got
The Maxim Gun, and they have not.

Hilaire Belloc 1870–1953 British poet, essayist, historian, novelist, and Liberal politician: *The Modern Traveller* (1898)

4 *questions habitually asked on meeting somebody in power:*
What power have you got? Where did you get it from? In whose interests do you exercise it? To whom are you accountable? How do we get rid of you?

Tony Benn 1925– British Labour politician: 'The Independent Mind', lecture at Nottingham, 18 June 1993

5 Every dictator uses religion as a prop to keep himself in power.

Benazir Bhutto 1953–2007 Pakistani stateswoman: interview on *60 Minutes*, CBS-TV, 8 August 1986

6 Authority without wisdom is like a heavy axe without an edge, fitter to bruise than polish.

Anne Bradstreet *c.*1612–72 English-born American poet: *The Tenth Muse* (1650) 'Meditations Divine and Moral'

7 The tyrant grinds down his slaves and they don't turn against him, they crush those beneath them.

Emily Brontë 1818–48 English novelist and poet: *Wuthering Heights* (1847)

8 'The question is,' said Humpty Dumpty, 'which is to be master—that's all.'

Lewis Carroll 1832–98 English writer and logician: *Through the Looking-Glass* (1872); see POWER 21

9 I shall be an autocrat: that's my trade. And the good Lord will forgive me: that's his.

Catherine the Great 1729–96 Russian empress: attributed

10 Nature has left this tincture in the blood,
That all men would be tyrants if they could.

Daniel Defoe 1660–1731 English novelist and journalist: *The History of the Kentish Petition* (1712–13)

11 Power concedes nothing without a demand. It never did, and it never will.

Frederick Douglass *c.*1818–95 American former slave and civil rights campaigner: letter to Gerrit Smith, 30 March 1849

12 A fly, Sir, may sting a stately horse and make him wince; but one is but an insect, and the other is a horse still.

Samuel Johnson 1709–84 English poet, critic, and lexicographer: James Boswell *Life of Samuel Johnson* (1791) 1754

13 What is needed is a realization that power without love is reckless and abusive, and love without power is sentimental and anaemic. Power at its best is love implementing the demands of justice.

Martin Luther King 1929–68 American civil rights leader: *Where Do We Go From Here?* (1967)

14 Power is the great aphrodisiac.

Henry Kissinger 1923– American politician: in *New York Times* 19 January 1971

15 The struggle of man against power is the struggle of memory against forgetting.

Milan Kundera 1929– Czech novelist: *The Book of Laughter and Forgetting* (1979)

16 I claim not to have controlled events, but confess plainly that events have controlled me.

Abraham Lincoln 1809–65 American Republican statesman: letter to A. G. Hodges, 4 April 1864

17 Power? It's like a Dead Sea fruit. When you achieve it, there is nothing there.

> **Harold Macmillan** 1894–1986 British Conservative statesman: Anthony Sampson *The New Anatomy of Britain* (1971)

18 Every Communist must grasp the truth, 'Political power grows out of the barrel of a gun'.

> **Mao Zedong** 1893–1976 Chinese statesman: speech, 6 November 1938

19 When you make your peace with authority, you become an authority.

> **Jim Morrison** 1943–71 American rock singer and songwriter: Andrew Doe and John Tobler *In Their Own Words: The Doors* (1988)

20 Who controls the past controls the future: who controls the present controls the past.

> **George Orwell** 1903–50 English novelist: *Nineteen Eighty-Four* (1949)

21 'But,' said Alice, 'the question is whether you can make a word mean different things.' 'Not so,' said Humpty-Dumpty, 'the question is which is to be the master. That's all.' We are the masters at the moment, and not only at the moment, but for a very long time to come.

> *often quoted as 'We are the masters now'*
>
> **Hartley Shawcross** 1902–2003 British Labour politician: speech, House of Commons, 2 April 1946; see POWER 8

22 You only have power over people as long as you don't take *everything* away from them. But when you've robbed a man of *everything* he's no longer in your power — he's free again.

> **Alexander Solzhenitsyn** 1918–2008 Russian novelist: *The First Circle* (1968)

Practicality

1 It's grand, and you canna expect to be baith grand and comfortable.

> **J. M. Barrie** 1860–1937 Scottish writer and dramatist: *The Little Minister* (1891)

2 Put your trust in God, my boys, and keep your powder dry.

> **Valentine Blacker** 1728–1823 Anglo-Indian soldier: 'Oliver's Advice'; often attributed to Oliver Cromwell himself

3 Whenever our neighbour's house is on fire, it cannot be amiss for the engines to play a little on our own.

> **Edmund Burke** 1729–97 Irish-born Whig politician and man of letters: *Reflections on the Revolution in France* (1790)

4 Life is too short to stuff a mushroom.

> **Shirley Conran** 1932– English writer: *Superwoman* (1975)

5 Common sense is the best distributed commodity in the world, for every man is convinced that he is well supplied with it.

> **René Descartes** 1596–1650 French philosopher and mathematician: *Le Discours de la méthode* (1637)

6 Common sense is nothing more than a deposit of prejudices laid down in the mind before you reach eighteen.

> **Albert Einstein** 1879–1955 German-born theoretical physicist: Lincoln Barnett *The Universe and Dr Einstein* (1950 ed.)

7 Praise the Lord and pass the ammunition.

> *moving along a line of sailors passing ammunition by hand to the deck*
>
> **Howell Forgy** 1908–83 American naval chaplain: at Pearl Harbor, 7 December 1941; later the title of a song by Frank Loesser, 1942

8 A dead woman bites not.
pressing for the execution of Mary Queen of Scots in 1587
> **Patrick, Lord Gray** d. 1612: oral tradition; William Camden *Annals of the Reign of Queen Elizabeth* (1615)

9 So I really think that American gentlemen are the best after all, because kissing your hand may make you feel very very good but a diamond and safire bracelet lasts forever.
> **Anita Loos** 1893–1981 American writer: *Gentlemen Prefer Blondes* (1925)

10 Be nice to people on your way up because you'll meet 'em on your way down.
> **Wilson Mizner** 1876–1933 American dramatist: Alva Johnston *The Legendary Mizners* (1953)

11 And he gave it for his opinion, that whoever could make two ears of corn or two blades of grass to grow upon a spot of ground where only one grew before, would deserve better of mankind, and do more essential service to his country than the whole race of politicians put together.
> **Jonathan Swift** 1667–1745 Anglo-Irish poet and satirist: *Gulliver's Travels* (1726) 'A Voyage to Brobdingnag'

12 Common sense is not so common.
> **Voltaire** 1694–1778 French writer and philosopher: *Dictionnaire philosophique* (1765) 'Sens Commun'

Praise

see also FLATTERY

1 The advantage of doing one's praising for oneself is that one can lay it on so thick and exactly in the right places.
> **Samuel Butler** 1835–1902 English novelist: *The Way of All Flesh* (1903)

2 It would be nice if sometimes the kind things I say were considered worthy of quotation. It isn't difficult, you know, to be witty or amusing when one has something to say that is destructive, but damned hard to be clever and quotable when you are singing someone's praises.
> **Noël Coward** 1899–1973 English dramatist, actor, and composer: William Marchant *The Pleasure of His Company* (1981)

3 Nothing so soon the drooping spirits can raise
As praises from the men, whom all men praise.
> **Abraham Cowley** 1618–67 English poet and essayist: 'Ode upon a Copy of Verses of My Lord Broghill's' (1663)

4 How light, how small is the thing which casts down or restores a mind greedy for praise.
> **Horace** 65–8 BC Roman poet: *Epistles*

5 And even the ranks of Tuscany Could scarce forbear to cheer.
> **Lord Macaulay** 1800–59 English politician and historian: *Lays of Ancient Rome* (1842) 'Horatius'

6 Of whom to be dispraised were no small praise.
> **John Milton** 1608–74 English poet: *Paradise Regained* (1671)

7 Damn with faint praise, assent with civil leer,
And without sneering, teach the rest to sneer.
of Addison
> **Alexander Pope** 1688–1744 English poet: 'An Epistle to Dr Arbuthnot' (1735)

Prayer

1 O God, if there be a God, save my soul, if I have a soul!
prayer of a common soldier before the battle of Blenheim, 1704
   Anonymous: in *Notes and Queries* 9 October 1937

2 O Lord! thou knowest how busy I must be this day: if I forget thee, do not thou forget me.
prayer before the Battle of Edgehill, 1642
   Jacob Astley 1579–1652 English soldier and Royalist: Sir Philip Warwick *Memoires* (1701)

3 The wish for prayer is a prayer in itself.
   Georges Bernanos 1888–1948 French novelist and essayist: *Journal d'un curé de campagne* (1936)

4 Ask, and it shall be given you; seek, and ye shall find; knock, and it shall be opened unto you.
   Bible: St Matthew

5 And lips say, 'God be pitiful,' Who ne'er said, 'God be praised.'
   Elizabeth Barrett Browning 1806–61 English poet: 'The Cry of the Human' (1844)

6 He prayeth well, who loveth well Both man and bird and beast.
   He prayeth best, who loveth best All things both great and small.
   Samuel Taylor Coleridge 1772–1834 English poet, critic, and philosopher: 'The Rime of the Ancient Mariner' (1798)

7 I throw myself down in my Chamber, and I call in, and invite God, and his Angels thither, and when they are there, I neglect God and his Angels, for the noise of a fly, for the rattling of a coach, for the whining of a door.
   John Donne 1572–1631 English poet and divine: *LXXX Sermons* (1640) 12 December 1626

8 To lift up the hands in prayer gives God glory, but a man with a dungfork in his hand, a woman with a slop-pail, give him glory too. He is so great that all things give him glory if you mean they should.
   Gerard Manley Hopkins 1844–89 English poet and priest: 'The Principle or Foundation' (1882)

9 Often when I pray I wonder if I am not posting letters to a non-existent address.
   C. S. Lewis 1898–1963 English literary scholar: letter to Arthur Greeves, 24 December 1930

10 Hush! Hush! Whisper who dares! Christopher Robin is saying his prayers.
   A. A. Milne 1882–1956 English writer for children: 'Vespers' (1924)

11 Christ beside me,
   Christ before me,
   Christ behind me,
   Christ within me,
   Christ beneath me,
   Christ above me.
   St Patrick *fl.* 5th cent. patron saint and Apostle of Ireland: 'St Patrick's Breastplate'

12 I am just going to pray for you at St Paul's, but with no very lively hope of success.
   Sydney Smith 1771–1845 English clergyman and essayist: H. Pearson *The Smith of Smiths* (1934)

13 More things are wrought by prayer Than this world dreams of.
   Alfred, Lord Tennyson 1809–92 English poet: *Idylls of the King* 'The Passing of Arthur' (1869)

14 Prayer in my opinion is nothing else than an intimate sharing between friends.
   St Teresa of Ávila 1512–82 Spanish Carmelite nun and mystic: *Life of the Mother Teresa of Jesus* (1611)

15 Whatever a man prays for, he prays for a miracle. Every prayer reduces itself to this: Great God, grant that twice two be not four.

> **Ivan Turgenev** 1818–83 Russian novelist: *Poems in Prose* (1881) 'Prayer'

16 You can't pray a lie.

> **Mark Twain** 1835–1910 American writer: *Adventures of Huckleberry Finn* (1885)

17 I have always made one prayer to God, a very short one. Here it is, 'My God, make our enemies very ridiculous!'

> **Voltaire** 1694–1778 French writer and philosopher: letter to Étienne-Noel Damilaville, 16 May 1767

Pregnancy

see also BIRTH, BIRTH CONTROL

1 Abortions will not let you forget. You remember the children you got that you did not get . . .

> **Gwendolyn Brooks** 1917–2000 American poet: 'The Mother' (1945)

2 If men had to have babies, they would only ever have one each.

> **Diana, Princess of Wales** 1961–97 former wife of Charles, Prince of Wales: in *Observer* 29 July 1984

3 If men could get pregnant, abortion would be a sacrament.

> **Florynce Kennedy** 1916–2001 American lawyer: in *Ms.* March 1973

4 I am not yet born; O fill me
With strength against those who would freeze my
humanity, would dragoon me into a lethal automaton,
would make me a cog in a machine, a thing with
one face, a thing.

> **Louis MacNeice** 1907–63 British poet, born in Belfast: 'Prayer Before Birth' (1944)

5 Let them not make me a stone and let them not spill me,
Otherwise kill me.

> **Louis MacNeice** 1907–63 British poet, born in Belfast: 'Prayer Before Birth' (1944)

6 In the dark womb where I began
My mother's life made me a man.
Through all the months of human birth
Her beauty fed my common earth.
I cannot see, nor breathe, nor stir,
But through the death of some of her.

> **John Masefield** 1878–1967 English poet: 'C. L. M.' (1910)

7 I wish either my father or my mother, or indeed both of them, as they were in duty both equally bound to it, had minded what they were about when they begot me.

> **Laurence Sterne** 1713–68 English novelist: *Tristram Shandy* (1759–67)

Prejudice

see also IMPARTIALITY, RACISM, TOLERANCE

1 Prejudices, it is well known, are most difficult to eradicate from the heart whose soil has never been loosened or fertilised by education.

> **Charlotte Brontë** 1816–55 English novelist: *Jane Eyre* (1847)

2 Bigotry may be roughly defined as the anger of men who have no opinions.

> **G. K. Chesterton** 1874–1936 English essayist, novelist, and poet: *Heretics* (1905)

3 If my theory of relativity is proven correct, Germany will claim me as a German and France will declare that I am a citizen of the world. Should my theory prove untrue, France will say that I am a German and Germany will declare that I am a Jew.

> **Albert Einstein** 1879–1955 German-

born theoretical physicist: address at the Sorbonne, Paris, possibly early December 1929; in *New York Times* 16 February 1930

4 Drive out prejudices through the door, and they will return through the window.

Frederick the Great 1712–86 Prussian monarch: letter to Voltaire, 19 March 1771

5 Intolerance of groups is often, strangely enough, exhibited more strongly against small differences than against fundamental ones.

Sigmund Freud 1856–1939 Austrian psychiatrist: *Moses and Monotheism* (1938)

6 Prejudice is the child of ignorance.

William Hazlitt 1778–1830 English essayist: 'On Prejudice' (1830)

7 Oh who is that young sinner with the handcuffs on his wrists?
And what has he been after that they groan and shake their fists?
And wherefore is he wearing such a conscience-stricken air?
Oh they're taking him to prison for the colour of his hair.

A. E. Housman 1859–1936 English poet: *Collected Poems* (1939) 'Additional Poems' no. 18

8 PLEASE ACCEPT MY RESIGNATION. I DON'T WANT TO BELONG TO ANY CLUB THAT WILL ACCEPT ME AS A MEMBER.

Groucho Marx 1890–1977 American film comedian: *Groucho and Me* (1959)

9 Four legs good, two legs bad.

George Orwell 1903–50 English novelist: *Animal Farm* (1945)

10 Who's 'im, Bill?
A stranger!
'Eave 'arf a brick at 'im.

Punch English humorous weekly periodical: 25 February 1854

11 Bigotry tries to keep truth safe in its hand
With a grip that kills it.

Rabindranath Tagore 1861–1941 Bengali poet and philosopher: *Fireflies* (1928)

The Present

see also PAST

1 To-morrow for the young the poets exploding like bombs,
The walks by the lake, the weeks of perfect communion;
To-morrow the bicycle races
Through the suburbs on summer evenings: but to-day the struggle.

W. H. Auden 1907–73 English poet: 'Spain 1937' (1937)

2 Take therefore no thought for the morrow: for the morrow shall take thought for the things of itself. Sufficient unto the day is the evil thereof.

Bible: St Matthew

3 Few people can say: I am here. They look for themselves in the past and see themselves in the future.

Georges Braque 1882–1963 French painter: Alex Danchev *Georges Braque* (2005)

4 Exhaust the little moment. Soon it dies.
And be it gash or gold it will not come
Again in this identical disguise.

Gwendolyn Brooks 1917–2000 American poet: 'Exhaust the little moment' (1949)

5 The rule is, jam to-morrow and jam yesterday—but never jam today.

Lewis Carroll 1832–98 English writer and logician: *Through the Looking-Glass* (1872)

6 The present is the funeral of the past,
And man the living sepulchre of life.
> **John Clare** 1793–1864 English poet:
> 'The present is the funeral of the past'
> (written 1845)

7 Ah, fill the cup:—what boots it to
repeat
How time is slipping underneath our
feet:
Unborn TO-MORROW, and dead
YESTERDAY,
Why fret about them if TO-DAY be
sweet!
> **Edward Fitzgerald** 1809–83 English
> scholar and poet: *The Rubáiyát of Omar
> Khayyám* (1859)

8 *Carpe diem, quam minimum credula
postero.*
Seize the day, put no trust in the
future.
> **Horace** 65–8 BC Roman poet: *Odes*

9 When it's three o'clock in New York,
it's still 1938 in London.
> **Bette Midler** 1945– American actress:
> attributed

10 Things are both more trivial than
they ever were, and more important
than they ever were, and the
difference between the trivial and
the important doesn't seem to
matter. But the nowness of
everything is absolutely wondrous.
> *on his heightened awareness of things, in
> the face of his imminent death*
> **Dennis Potter** 1935–94 English
> television dramatist: *Seeing the Blossom*
> (1994)

11 The New Age? It's just the old age
stuck in a microwave oven for fifteen
seconds.
> **James Randi** 1928– American
> magician: in *Observer* 14 April 1991

12 Life is one tenth Here and Now, nine-
tenths a history lesson. For most of
the time the Here and Now is neither
now nor here.
> **Graham Swift** 1949– British writer:
> *Waterland* (1984)

The Presidency

see also FAMOUS POLITICIANS, POLITICIANS,
UNITED STATES

1 Anybody that wants the presidency
so much that he'll spend two years
organizing and campaigning for it is
not to be trusted with the office.
> **David Broder** 1929– American
> columnist: in *Washington Post* 18 July
> 1973

2 The US presidency is a Tudor
monarchy plus telephones.
> **Anthony Burgess** 1917–93 English
> novelist and critic: George Plimpton
> (ed.) *Writers at Work* 4th Series (1977)

3 Somewhere out in this audience may
even be someone who will one day
follow in my footsteps, and preside
over the White House as the
President's spouse. I wish him well!
> **Barbara Bush** 1925– American First
> Lady: remarks at Wellesley College
> Commencement, 1 June 1990

4 I had rather be right than be
President.
> **Henry Clay** 1777–1852 American
> politician: S. W. McCall *Life of Thomas
> Brackett Reed* (1914)

5 Although we weren't able to shatter
that highest, hardest glass ceiling
this time, thanks to you, it has about
18 million cracks in it.
> **Hillary Rodham Clinton** 1947–
> American lawyer and Republican
> politician: speech to her supporters,
> conceding the Democratic party
> presidential nomination to Barack
> Obama, 7 June 2008

6 When I was a boy I was told that anybody could become President. I'm beginning to believe it.

> **Clarence Darrow** 1857–1938 American lawyer: Irving Stone *Clarence Darrow for the Defence* (1941)

7 No easy problems ever come to the President of the United States. If they are easy to solve, somebody else has solved them.

> **Dwight D. Eisenhower** 1890–1969 American general and Republican statesman: in *Parade Magazine* 8 April 1962

8 The vice-presidency isn't worth a pitcher of warm piss.

> **John Nance Garner** 1868–1967 American Democratic politician: O. C. Fisher *Cactus Jack* (1978)

9 There can be no whitewash at the White House.

> *on Watergate*
>
> **Richard Nixon** 1913–94 American Republican statesman: television speech, 30 April 1973

10 When the President does it, that means that it is not illegal.

> **Richard Nixon** 1913–94 American Republican statesman: David Frost *I Gave Them a Sword* (1978)

11 The one thing I do not want to be called is First Lady. It sounds like a saddle horse.

> **Jacqueline Kennedy Onassis** 1929–94 wife of John Fitzgerald Kennedy: Peter Colier and David Horowitz *The Kennedys* (1984)

12 If the President has a bully pulpit, then the First Lady has a white glove pulpit . . . more refined, restricted, ceremonial, but it's a pulpit all the same.

> **Nancy Reagan** 1923– American actress: in *New York Times* 10 March 1988; see PRESIDENCY 13

13 I have got such a bully pulpit!

> **Theodore Roosevelt** 1858–1919 American Republican statesman: in *Outlook* (New York) 27 February 1909

14 Log-cabin to White House.

> **William Roscoe Thayer** 1859–1923 American biographer and historian: title of biography (1910) of James Garfield (1831–81)

15 He'll sit right here and he'll say do this, do that! And nothing will happen. Poor Ike—it won't be a bit like the Army.

> **Harry S. Truman** 1884–1972 American Democratic statesman: *Harry S. Truman* (1973)

Press Photographers

see also JOURNALISM, NEWSPAPERS

1 [A] frozen flash of history.

> *Pulitzer Prize (1945) citation on the photograph by American photographer Joe Rosenthal (1911–2006) of US Marines raising the flag at Iwo Jima*
>
> **Anonymous**: quoted in *New York Times* 9 May 1945

2 If your pictures aren't good enough, you aren't close enough.

> **Robert Capa** 1913–54 Hungarian-born American photojournalist: Russell Miller *Magnum: Fifty years at the Front Line of History* (1997)

3 I took the photo. The Marines took Iwo Jima.

> *of his award-winning picture of US Marines raising the flag at Iwo Jima*
>
> **Joe Rosenthal** 1911–2006 American photographer: attributed

4 I always believed the press would kill her in the end. But not even I could believe they would take such a direct hand in her death as seems to be the case . . . Every proprietor and editor of every publication that has paid for intrusive and exploitative photographs of her . . . has blood on their hands today.

on the death of his sister, Diana, Princess of Wales, in a car crash while being pursued by photographers

> **Lord Spencer** 1964– English peer: in *Daily Telegraph* 1 September 1997

Pride

see also HUMILITY, SELF-ESTEEM

1 Pride goeth before destruction, and an haughty spirit before a fall.
> **Bible**: Proverbs

2 Proud people breed sad sorrows for themselves.
> **Emily Brontë** 1818–48 English novelist and poet: *Wuthering Heights* (1847)

3 And the Devil did grin, for his darling sin
Is pride that apes humility.
> **Samuel Taylor Coleridge** 1772–1834 English poet, critic, and philosopher: 'The Devil's Thoughts' (1799)

4 As soon as there were two, there was pride.
> **John Donne** 1572–1631 English poet and divine: sermon, 19 December 1619

5 Pride helps us; and pride is not a bad thing when it only urges us to hide our own hurts, not to hurt others.
> **George Eliot** 1819–80 English novelist: *Middlemarch* (1871–2)

Prime Ministers

see also FAMOUS POLITICIANS

1 There are three classes which need sanctuary more than others—birds, wild flowers, and Prime Ministers.
> **Stanley Baldwin** 1867–1947 British Conservative statesman: in *Observer* 24 May 1925

2 I think a Prime Minister has to be a butcher and know the joints. That is perhaps where I have not been quite competent, in knowing all the ways that you can cut up a carcass.
> **R. A. Butler** 1902–82 British Conservative politician: in *Listener* 28 June 1966

3 Nearly all Prime Ministers are dissatisfied with their successors, perhaps even more so if they come from their own party.
> **Roy Jenkins** 1920–2003 British politician: *Gladstone* (1995)

4 We all know that Prime Ministers are wedded to the truth, but like other married couples they sometimes live apart.
> **Saki** 1870–1916 Scottish writer: *The Unbearable Bassington* (1912)

5 Every Prime Minister needs a Willie.
at the farewell dinner to Lord Whitelaw
> **Margaret Thatcher** 1925– British Conservative stateswoman: in *Guardian* 7 August 1991

Prison

see also LAWS

1 *reply to a prison visitor who asked if he were sewing:*
No, reaping.
> **Horatio Bottomley** 1860–1933 British newspaper proprietor and financier: S. T. Felstead *Horatio Bottomley* (1936)

2 Jails and prisons are designed to break human beings, to convert the population into specimens in a zoo—obedient to our keepers, but dangerous to each other.
> **Angela Davis** 1944– American political activist: *An Autobiography* (1974)

3 A lot of gangsters and Radio 4.
describing life in prison
> **Pete Doherty** 1979– English pop singer and songwriter: in *Sunday Times* 11 May 2008

4 Stone walls do not a prison make,
Nor iron bars a cage.
Richard Lovelace 1618–58 English poet:
'To Althea, From Prison' (1649)

5 The thoughts of a prisoner—they're
not free either. They keep returning
to the same things.
Alexander Solzhenitsyn 1918–2008
Russian novelist: *One Day in the Life of
Ivan Denisovich* (1962)

6 I want to see the word laogai in every
dictionary in every language in the
world. I want to see the laogai ended.
Before 1974, the word 'gulag' did not
appear in any dictionary. Today, this
single word conveys the meaning of
Soviet political violence and its
labour camp system. 'Laogai' also
deserves a place in our dictionaries.
the laogai *are Chinese labour camps*
Harry Wu 1937– Chinese-born
American political activist: in
Washington Post 26 May 1996

Problems and Solutions

see also WAYS AND MEANS

1 Probable impossibilities are to be
preferred to improbable
possibilities.
Aristotle 384–322 BC Greek
philosopher: *Poetics*

2 It isn't that they can't see the
solution. It is that they can't see the
problem.
G. K. Chesterton 1874–1936 English
essayist, novelist, and poet: *Scandal of
Father Brown* (1935)

3 Let me have the best solution
worked out. Don't argue the matter.
The difficulties will argue for
themselves.
on the Mulberry floating harbours
Winston Churchill 1874–1965 British

Conservative statesman: minute to Lord
Mountbatten, 30 May 1942

4 What we're saying today is that
you're either part of the solution or
you're part of the problem.
Eldridge Cleaver 1935–98 American
political activist: speech in San
Francisco, 1968

5 How often have I said to you that
when you have eliminated the
impossible, whatever remains,
however improbable, must be the
truth?
Arthur Conan Doyle 1859–1930
Scottish-born writer of detective fiction:
The Sign of Four (1890)

6 Most of life's problems can be solved
By running fast and kicking
something.
U. A. Fanthorpe 1929–2009 English
poet: 'Autumn Offer' (2000)

7 Don't let us make imaginary evils,
when you know we have so many
real ones to encounter.
Oliver Goldsmith 1728–74 Irish writer,
poet, and dramatist: *The Good-Natured
Man* (1768)

8 Problems worthy
of attack
prove their worth
by hitting back.
Piet Hein 1905–96 Danish poet and
cartoonist: 'Problems' (1969)

9 Another nice mess you've gotten me
into.
Stan Laurel 1890–1965 American film
comedian, born in Britain: *Another Fine
Mess* (1930 film) and many other Laurel
and Hardy films; spoken by Oliver
Hardy

10 Houston, we've had a problem.
James Lovell 1928– American
astronaut: on Apollo 13 space mission,
14 April 1970

11 There is always a well-known solution to every human problem—neat, plausible, and wrong.

> **H. L. Mencken** 1880–1956 American journalist and literary critic: *Prejudices* 2nd series (1920)

12 One hears only those questions for which one is able to find answers.

> **Friedrich Nietzsche** 1844–1900 German philosopher and writer: *The Gay Science* (1882)

13 We haven't got the money, so we've got to think!

> **Ernest Rutherford** 1871–1937 New Zealand physicist: in *Bulletin of the Institute of Physics* (1962)

14 The fascination of what's difficult Has dried the sap of my veins, and rent Spontaneous joy and natural content Out of my heart.

> **W. B. Yeats** 1865–1939 Irish poet: 'The Fascination of What's Difficult' (1910)

Progress

see also CHANGE

1 The new growth in the plant swelling against the sheath, which at the same time imprisons and protects it, must still be the truest type of progress.

> **Jane Addams** 1860–1935 American social worker: *Democracy and Social Ethics* (1907)

2 We are like dwarfs on the shoulders of giants, so that we can see more than they, and things at a greater distance, not by virtue of any sharpness of sight on our part, or any physical distinction, but because we are carried high and raised up by their giant size.

> **Bernard of Chartres** d. *c.*1130 French philosopher: John of Salisbury *The Metalogicon* (1159); see PROGRESS 15

3 The march of social progress is like a long and straggling parade, with the seers and prophets at its head and a smug minority bringing up the rear.

> **Pierre Berton** 1920–2004 Canadian writer: *The Smug Minority* (1968)

4 Want is one only of five giants on the road of reconstruction . . . the others are Disease, Ignorance, Squalor and Idleness.

> **William Henry Beveridge** 1879–1963 British economist: *Social Insurance and Allied Services* (1942)

5 The thing that hath been, it is that which shall be; and that which is done is that which shall be done: and there is no new thing under the sun.

> **Bible**: Ecclesiastes

6 Nothing in progression can rest on its original plan. We may as well think of rocking a grown man in the cradle of an infant.

> **Edmund Burke** 1729–97 Irish-born Whig politician and man of letters: *Letter to the Sheriffs of Bristol* (1777)

7 What have the Romans ever done for us?

> **Graham Chapman** 1941–89 and **John Cleese** 1939– British comedy writers and actors: *Monty Python's Life of Brian* (1983 film, with Terry Gilliam, Eric Idle, Terry Jones, and Michael Palin)

8 pity this busy monster, manunkind, not. Progress is a comfortable disease.

> **e. e. cummings** 1894–1962 American poet: *1 x 1* (1944) no. 14

9 The European talks of progress because by an ingenious application of some scientific acquirements he has established a society which has mistaken comfort for civilization.

> **Benjamin Disraeli** 1804–81 British Tory statesman and novelist: *Tancred* (1847)

10 The slogan of progress is changing from the full dinner pail to the full garage.

sometimes paraphrased as, 'a car in every garage and a chicken in every pot'

Herbert Hoover 1874–1964 American Republican statesman: speech in New York, 22 October 1928; see POVERTY 12

11 There's only one corner of the universe you can be certain of improving, and that's your own self.

Aldous Huxley 1894–1963 English novelist: *Time Must Have a Stop* (1944)

12 Is it progress if a cannibal uses knife and fork?

Stanislaw Lec 1909–66 Polish writer: *Unkempt Thoughts* (1962)

13 One step forward two steps back.

Lenin 1870–1924 Russian revolutionary: title of book (1904)

14 Let us be frank about it: most of our people have never had it so good.

Harold Macmillan 1894–1986 British Conservative statesman: speech at Bedford, 20 July 1957; 'You Never Had It So Good' was the Democratic Party slogan during the 1952 US election campaign

15 If I have seen further it is by standing on the shoulders of giants.

Isaac Newton 1642–1727 English mathematician and physicist: letter to Robert Hooke, 5 February 1676; see PROGRESS 2

16 'Change' is scientific, 'progress' is ethical; change is indubitable, whereas progress is a matter of controversy.

Bertrand Russell 1872–1970 British philosopher and mathematician: *Unpopular Essays* (1950) 'Philosophy and Politics'

17 The reasonable man adapts himself to the world: the unreasonable one persists in trying to adapt the world to himself. Therefore all progress depends on the unreasonable man.

George Bernard Shaw 1856–1950 Irish dramatist: *Man and Superman* (1903)

Promises

1 If [human life] depends on anything, it is on this frail cord, flung from the forgotten hills of yesterday to the invisible mountains of tomorrow.

on the promise

G. K. Chesterton 1874–1936 English essayist, novelist, and poet: *The Appetite of Tyranny* (1915)

2 You always pay too much. Particularly for promises. There ain't no such thing as a bargain promise.

Cormac McCarthy 1933– American novelist: *No Country For Old Men* (2005)

3 A promise made is a debt unpaid, and the trail has its own stern code.

Robert W. Service 1874–1958 Canadian poet: 'The Cremation of Sam McGee' (1907)

4 Promises and pie-crust are made to be broken.

Jonathan Swift 1667–1745 Irish poet and satirist: *Polite Conversation* (1738)

5 To promise not to do a thing is the surest way in the world to make a body want to go and do that very thing.

Mark Twain 1835–1910 American writer: *The Adventures of Tom Sawyer* (1876)

Propaganda

1 When war is declared, Truth is the first casualty.

Anonymous: epigraph to Arthur Ponsonby's *Falsehood in Wartime* (1928); attributed also to Hiram Johnson, speaking in the US Senate,

1918, but not recorded in his speech; possibly based on a passage by Samuel Johnson in *The Idler* 11 November 1758

2 Propaganda is a soft weapon: hold it in your hands too long, and it will move about like a snake, and strike the other way.

Jean Anouilh 1910–87 French dramatist: *The Lark* (adapted by Lillian Hellman, 1955)

3 In wartime . . . truth is so precious that she should always be attended by a bodyguard of lies.

Winston Churchill 1874–1965 British Conservative statesman: *The Second World War* vol. 5 (1951)

4 That branch of the art of lying which consists in very nearly deceiving your friends without quite deceiving your enemies.

Francis M. Cornford 1874–1943 English academic: *Microcosmographia Academica* (1922 ed.)

5 The greatest triumphs of propaganda have been accomplished, not by doing something, but by refraining from doing. 'Great is the truth', but still greater . . . is silence about truth.

Aldous Huxley 1894–1963 English novelist: *Brave New World* (1946)

6 A false report, if believed during three days, may be of great service to a government.

Catherine de' Medici 1518–89 French queen consort: Isaac D'Israeli *Curiosities of Literature* Second Series vol. 2 (1849)

7 In our country the lie has become not just a moral category but a pillar of the State.

Alexander Solzhenitsyn 1918–2008 Russian novelist: 1974 interview, in *The Oak and the Calf* (1975)

Protest

see also POLITICS, REVOLUTION

1 Even a purely moral act that has no hope of any immediate and visible political effect can gradually and indirectly, over time, gain in political significance.

Václav Havel 1936– Czech dramatist and statesman: letter to Alexander Dubček, August 1969

2 She sat down in order that we all might stand up—and the walls of segregation came down.

of the American civil rights activist Rosa Parks (1913–2005)

Jesse Jackson 1941– American Democratic politician and clergyman: in *BBC News* (online edition) 25 October 2005

3 Ev'rywhere I hear the sound of marching, charging feet, boy,
'Cause summer's here and the time is right for fighting in the street, boy.

Mick Jagger 1943– and **Keith Richards** 1943– English rock musicians: 'Street Fighting Man' (1968 song)

4 One-fifth of the people are against everything all the time.

Robert Kennedy 1925–68 American Democratic politician: speech, University of Pennsylvania, 6 May 1964

5 I'm interested in anything about revolt, disorder, chaos, especially activity that appears to have no meaning. It seems to me to be the road toward freedom.

Jim Morrison 1943–71 American rock singer and songwriter: in *Time* 24 January 1968

6 I've always had the impression that real militants are like cleaning women, doing a thankless, daily but necessary job.

François Truffaut 1932–84 French film director: letter to Jean-Luc Godard, May-June 1973

Publishing

see also BOOKS

1 Publishers are in business to make money, and if your books do well they don't care whether you are male, female, or an elephant.
   Margaret Atwood 1939– Canadian novelist: Graeme Gibson *Eleven Canadian Novelists* (1973) 'Dissecting the Way a Writer Works'

2 The poem will please if it is lively—if it is stupid it will fail—but I will have none of your damned cutting and slashing.
   Lord Byron 1788–1824 English poet: letter to his publisher John Murray, 6 April 1819

3 Now Barabbas was a publisher.
   alteration in a Bible of the verse 'Now Barabbas was a robber'
   Thomas Campbell 1777–1844 Scottish poet: attributed, in Samuel Smiles *A Publisher and his Friends* (1891); also attributed, wrongly, to Byron

4 Of all the literary scenes
   Saddest this sight to me:
   The graves of little magazines
   Who died to make verse free.
   Keith Preston 1884–1927 American poet: 'The Liberators'

5 Publish and be damned.
   replying to Harriette Wilson's blackmail threat, c. 1825
   Duke of Wellington 1769–1852 British soldier and statesman: attributed

6 Being published by the Oxford University Press is rather like being married to a duchess: the honour is almost greater than the pleasure.
   G. M. Young 1882–1959 English historian: Rupert Hart-Davis, letter to George Lyttelton, 29 April 1956

Punctuality

see also WAITING

1 The only way of catching a train I have ever discovered is to miss the train before.
   G. K. Chesterton 1874–1936 English essayist, novelist, and poet: *Tremendous Trifles* (1909)

2 We've been waiting 700 years, you can have the seven minutes.
   on arriving at Dublin Castle for the handover by British forces on 16 January 1922, and being told that he was seven minutes late
   Michael Collins 1880–1922 Irish revolutionary: Tim Pat Coogan *Michael Collins* (1990); attributed, perhaps apocryphal

3 Recollect that painting and punctuality mix like oil and vinegar, and that genius and regularity are utter enemies, and must be to the end of time.
   Thomas Gainsborough 1727–88 English painter: letter to Edward Stratford, 1 May 1772

4 Punctuality is the politeness of kings.
   Louis XVIII 1755–1824 French monarch: *Souvenirs de J. Lafitte* (1844); attributed

5 I have noticed that the people who are late are often so much jollier than the people who have to wait for them.
   E. V. Lucas 1868–1938 English journalist, essayist, and critic: *365 Days and One More* (1926)

6 We must leave exactly on time . . . From now on everything must function to perfection.
   to a station-master
   Benito Mussolini 1883–1945 Italian Fascist dictator: Giorgio Pini *Mussolini* (1939)

7 Never be a pioneer. It's the Early
Christian that gets the fattest lion.
Saki 1870–1916 Scottish writer:
Reginald (1904) 'Reginald's Choir Treat'

8 You come most carefully upon your
hour.
William Shakespeare 1564–1616
English dramatist: *Hamlet* (1601)

9 Punctuality is the virtue of the bored.
Evelyn Waugh 1903–66 English novelist:
diary, 26 March 1962

10 My Aunt Minnie would always be
punctual and never hold up
production, but who would pay to
see my Aunt Minnie?
on Marilyn Monroe's unpunctuality
Billy Wilder 1906–2002 American
screenwriter and director: P. F. Boller
and R. L. Davis *Hollywood Anecdotes*
(1988)

Punishment

see also CRIME, LAWS, PRISON

1 All punishment is mischief: all
punishment in itself is evil.
Jeremy Bentham 1748–1832 English
philosopher: *Principles of Morals and
Legislation* (1789)

2 He that spareth his rod hateth his
son.
Bible: Proverbs

3 Hanging is too good for him, said Mr
Cruelty.
John Bunyan 1628–88 English writer
and Nonconformist preacher: *The
Pilgrim's Progress* (1678)

4 Cameron's empty idea seems to be
'let's hug a hoodie', whatever they
have done.
*commenting on the text of a forthcoming
speech by British Conservative politician
David Cameron (1966–); often wrongly
attributed to Cameron*
Vernon Coaker 1953– British Labour
politician: in *Observer* 9 July 2006

5 Excessive bail shall not be required,
nor excessive fines imposed, nor
cruel and unusual punishment
inflicted.
Constitution of the United States 1787:
Eighth Amendment (1791)

6 Better build schoolrooms for 'the
boy',
Than cells and gibbets for 'the man'.
Eliza Cook 1818–89 English poet: 'A
Song for the Ragged Schools' (1853)

7 To crush, to annihilate a man utterly,
to inflict on him the most terrible
punishment so that the most
ferocious murderer would shudder
at it beforehand, one need only give
him work of an absolutely,
completely useless and irrational
character.
Fedor Dostoevsky 1821–81 Russian
novelist: *House of the Dead* (1862)

8 Punishment is not for revenge, but to
lessen crime and reform the
criminal.
Elizabeth Fry 1780–1845 English
Quaker prison reformer: Rachel E.
Cresswell and Katharine Fry *Memoir of
the Life of Elizabeth Fry* (1848)

9 Whenever the offence inspires less
horror than the punishment, the
rigour of penal law is obliged to give
way to the common feelings of
mankind.
Edward Gibbon 1737–94 English
historian: attributed

10 My object all sublime
I shall achieve in time—
To let the punishment fit the crime—
The punishment fit the crime.
W. S. Gilbert 1836–1911 English writer
of comic and satirical verse: *The Mikado*
(1885)

11 Men are not hanged for stealing
horses, but that horses may not be
stolen.
Lord Halifax 1633–95 English politician

and essayist: *Political, Moral, and Miscellaneous Thoughts and Reflections* (1750) 'Of Punishment'

12 This is the first of punishments, that no guilty man is acquitted if judged by himself.

Juvenal AD c.60–c.130 Roman satirist: *Satires*

13 Society needs to condemn a little more and understand a little less.

John Major 1943– British Conservative statesman: interview with *Mail on Sunday* 21 February 1993

14 For de little stealin' dey gits you in jail soon or late. For de big stealin' dey makes you Emperor and puts you in de Hall o' Fame when you croaks.

Eugene O'Neill 1888–1953 American dramatist: *The Emperor Jones* (1921)

15 Lay then the axe to the root, and teach governments humanity. It is their sanguinary punishments which corrupt mankind.

Thomas Paine 1737–1809 English political theorist: *The Rights of Man* (1791)

16 I'm all for bringing back the birch, but only between consenting adults.

Gore Vidal 1925– American novelist and critic: in *Sunday Times Magazine* 16 September 1973

Quotations

1 The surest way to make a monkey of a man is to quote him.

Robert Benchley 1889–1945 American humorist: *My Ten Years in a Quandary* (1936)

2 It is a good thing for an uneducated man to read books of quotations.

Winston Churchill 1874–1965 British Conservative statesman: *My Early Life* (1930)

3 I hate quotation. Tell me what you know.

Ralph Waldo Emerson 1803–82 American philosopher and poet: diary, May 1849

4 Next to the originator of a good sentence is the first quoter of it.

Ralph Waldo Emerson 1803–82 American philosopher and poet: *Letters and Social Aims* (1876)

5 Windbags can be right. Aphorists can be wrong. It is a tough world.

James Fenton 1949– English poet: in *Times* 21 February 1985

6 People who like quotations love meaningless generalizations.

Graham Greene 1904–91 English novelist: *Travels With My Aunt* (1969)

7 He wrapped himself in quotations—as a beggar would enfold himself in the purple of emperors.

Rudyard Kipling 1865–1936 English writer and poet: *Many Inventions* (1893)

8 Misquotation is, in fact, the pride and privilege of the learned. A widely-read man never quotes accurately, for the rather obvious reason that he has read too widely.

Hesketh Pearson 1887–1964 English actor and biographer: *Common Misquotations* (1934)

9 An anthology is like all the plums and orange peel picked out of a cake.

Walter Raleigh 1861–1922 English lecturer and critic: letter to Mrs Robert Bridges, 15 January 1915

10 A proverb is one man's wit and all men's wisdom.

Lord John Russell 1792–1878 British Whig statesman: R. J. Mackintosh *Sir James Mackintosh* (1835)

11 I always have a quotation for everything—it saves original thinking.

> **Dorothy L. Sayers** 1893–1957 English writer of detective fiction: *Have His Carcase* (1932)

12 OSCAR WILDE: How I wish I had said that.
WHISTLER: You will, Oscar, you will.

> **James McNeill Whistler** 1834–1903 American-born painter: R. Ellman *Oscar Wilde* (1987)

13 The nice thing about quotes is that they give us a nodding acquaintance with the originator which is often socially impressive.

> **Kenneth Williams** 1926–88 English actor: *Acid Drops* (1980)

Race

see also RACISM

1 The gentleman will please remember that when his half-civilized ancestors were hunting the wild boar in Silesia, mine were princes of the earth.

> *in reply to a taunt by a Senator of German descent*
>
> **Judah Benjamin** 1811–84 American politician and lawyer: B. Perley Poore *Perley's Reminiscences* (1886)

2 When I recovered a little I found some black people about me . . . I asked them if we were not to be eaten by those white men with horrible looks, red faces, and loose hair.

> **Olaudah Equiano** c.1745–c.97 African writer and former slave: *Narrative of the Life of Olaudah Equiano* (1789)

3 The so-called white races are really pinko-grey.

> **E. M. Forster** 1879–1970 English novelist: *A Passage to India* (1924)

4 Irish Americans are about as Irish as black Americans are African.

> **Bob Geldof** 1954– Irish rock musician: in *Observer* 22 June 1986

5 Though it be a thrilling and marvellous thing to be merely young and gifted in such times, it is doubly so, doubly dynamic—to be young, gifted and *black*.

> **Lorraine Hansberry** 1930–65 American dramatist: *To be young, gifted and black: Lorraine Hansberry in her own words* (1969) adapted by Robert Nemiroff

6 When I look out at this convention, I see the face of America, red, yellow, brown, black, and white. We are all precious in God's sight—the real rainbow coalition.

> **Jesse Jackson** 1941– American Democratic politician and clergyman: speech at Democratic National Convention, Atlanta, 19 July 1988

7 There are no 'white' or 'coloured' signs on the foxholes or graveyards of battle.

> **John F. Kennedy** 1917–63 American Democratic statesman: message to Congress on proposed Civil Rights Bill, 19 June 1963

8 In the joy of a new beginning, we ask you to help us work for that day when black will not be asked to get back, when brown can stick around – [laughter] – when yellow will be mellow – [laughter] – when the red man can get ahead, man – [laughter] – and when white will embrace what is right.

> **Joseph Lowery** 1924– American Methodist minister: benediction at the inauguration of President Barack Obama, 20 January 2009

9 But I'll tell instead of brave and fine
When lives of black and white entwine.
And men in brotherhood combine,

This would I tell you, son of mine.
Oodgeroo Noonuccal 1920–93
Australian poet: 'Son of Mine (To
Denis)' (1964)

10 Growing up, I came up with this
name: I'm a Cablinasian.
*explaining his rejection of 'African-
American' as the term to describe his
Caucasian, Afro-American, Native
American, Thai, and Chinese ancestry*
Tiger Woods 1975– American golfer:
interviewed by Oprah Winfrey, 21 April
1997

Racism

see also EQUALITY, GENOCIDE, PREJUDICE, RACE,
TOLERANCE

1 It comes as a great shock around the
age of 5, 6 or 7 to discover that the
flag to which you have pledged
allegiance, along with everybody
else, has not pledged allegiance to
you. It comes as a great shock to see
Gary Cooper killing off the Indians
and, although you are rooting for
Gary Cooper, that the Indians are
you.
*speaking for the proposition that 'The
American Dream is at the expense of the
American Negro'*
James Baldwin 1924–87 American
novelist and essayist: Cambridge Union,
England, 17 February 1965

2 The basic tenet of Black
consciousness is that the Black man
must reject all value systems that
seek to make him a foreigner in the
country of his birth and reduce his
basic human dignity.
Steve Biko 1946–77 South African anti-
apartheid campaigner: statement as
witness, 3 May 1976

3 Being a star has made it possible for
me to get insulted in places where

the average Negro could never *hope*
to go and get insulted.
Sammy Davis Jnr. 1925–90 American
entertainer: *Yes I Can* (1965)

4 You have seen how a man was made
a slave; you shall see how a slave was
made a man.
Frederick Douglass *c.*1818–95
American former slave and civil rights
campaigner: *Narrative of the Life of
Frederick Douglass* (1845)

5 Because a man has a black face and a
different religion from our own,
there is no reason why he should be
treated as a brute.
Edward VII 1841–1910 British monarch:
letter to Lord Granville, 30 November
1875

6 How odd
Of God
To choose
The Jews.
*to which Cecil Browne replied: 'But not so
odd/As those who choose/A Jewish God/
But spurn the Jews.'*
William Norman Ewer 1885–1976
British writer: *Week-End Book* (1924)

7 You've got to be taught to be afraid
Of people whose eyes are oddly
made,
Of people whose skin is a different
shade.
You've got to be carefully taught.
Oscar Hammerstein II 1895–1960
American songwriter: 'You've Got to be
Carefully Taught' (1949)

8 The Gypsies are a litmus test not of
democracy but of civil society.
Václav Havel 1936– Czech dramatist
and statesman: attributed

9 And if the white man thought that
Asians were a low, filthy nation,
Asians could still smile with
relief—at least, they were not
Africans. And if the white man
thought that Africans were a low,

filthy nation, Africans in southern
Africa could still smile—at least, they
were not bushmen. They all have
their monsters.

> **Bessie Head** 1937–86 South African-
> born writer: *Maru* (1971)

10 Southern trees bear strange fruit,
Blood on the leaves and blood at the
root,
Black bodies swinging in the
Southern breeze,
Strange fruit hanging from the
poplar trees.

> **Billie Holiday** 1915–59 American
> singer: 'Strange Fruit' (1939 song)

11 You can be up to your boobies in
white satin, with gardenias in your
hair and no sugar cane for miles, but
you can still be working on a
plantation.

> **Billie Holiday** 1915–59 American
> singer: *Lady Sings the Blues* (1956, with
> William Duffy)

12 I, too, sing America.
I am the darker brother.
They send me to eat in the kitchen
When company comes.

> **Langston Hughes** 1902–67 American
> writer and poet: 'I, Too' (1925)

13 I want to be the white man's brother,
not his brother-in-law.

> **Martin Luther King** 1929–68 American
> civil rights leader: in *New York Journal-
> American* 10 September 1962

14 As I look ahead, I am filled with
foreboding. Like the Roman, I seem
to see 'the River Tiber foaming with
much blood'.

> *on the probable consequences of
> immigration*
> **Enoch Powell** 1912–98 British
> Conservative politician: speech,
> Birmingham, 20 April 1968

15 The only good Indian is a dead
Indian.

> *at Fort Cobb, January 1869*
> **Philip Henry Sheridan** 1831–88
> American cavalry commander:
> attributed

16 Segregation now, segregation
tomorrow and segregation forever!

> **George Wallace** 1919–98 American
> Democratic politician: inaugural
> speech as Governor of Alabama,
> 14 January 1963

17 Am I not a man and a brother.

> *legend on Wedgwood cameo, depicting a
> kneeling Negro slave in chains*
> **Josiah Wedgwood** 1730–95 English
> potter: E. Darwin *The Botanic Garden*
> pt. 1 (1791)

Railways

1 This is the Night Mail crossing the
Border,
Bringing the cheque and the postal
order,
Letters for the rich, letters for the
poor,
The shop at the corner, the girl next
door.
Pulling up Beattock, a steady climb:
The gradient's against her, but she's
on time.

> **W. H. Auden** 1907–73 English poet:
> 'Night Mail' (1936)

2 Railways and the Church have their
critics, but both are the best ways of
getting a man to his ultimate
destination.

> **Revd W. Awdry** 1911–97 English writer
> of children's books: in *Daily Telegraph*
> 22 March 1997; obituary

3 Railway termini. They are our gates
to the glorious and the unknown.
Through them we pass out into

adventure and sunshine, to them,
alas! we return.

> **E. M. Forster** 1879–1970 English
> novelist: *Howards End* (1910)

4 Sir, Saturday morning, although
recurring at regular and well-
foreseen intervals, always seems to
take this railway by surprise.

> **W. S. Gilbert** 1836–1911 English writer
> of comic and satirical verse: letter to the
> station-master at Baker Street, on the
> Metropolitan line; John Julius Norwich
> *Christmas Crackers* (1980)

5 That life-quickening atmosphere of a
big railway station where everything
is something trembling on the brink
of something else.

> **Vladimir Nabokov** 1899–1977 Russian
> novelist: *Spring in Fialta and other
> stories* (1956)

6 After the first powerful plain
  manifesto
The black statement of pistons,
  without more fuss
But gliding like a queen, she leaves
  the station.

> **Stephen Spender** 1909–95 English poet:
> 'The Express' (1933)

7 I have seldom heard a train go by and
not wished I was on it. Those
whistles sing bewitchment: railways
are irresistible bazaars, snaking
along perfectly level no matter what
the landscape, improving your mood
with speed, and never upsetting your
drink.

> **Paul Theroux** 1941– American novelist
> and travel writer: *The Great Railway
> Bazaar* (1975)

Rain

1 Rainy days—
silkworms droop
on mulberries.

> **Matsuo Basho** 1644–94 Japanese poet:
> translated by Lucien Stryk

2 The rain, it raineth on the just
And also on the unjust fella:
But chiefly on the just, because
The unjust steals the just's umbrella.

> **Lord Bowen** 1835–94 English judge:
> Walter Sichel *Sands of Time* (1923); see
> EQUALITY 3

3 It is impossible to live in a country
which is continually under
hatches . . . Rain! Rain! Rain!

> **John Keats** 1795–1821 English poet:
> letter to J. H. Reynolds from Devon,
> 10 April 1818

4 Rain is grace; rain is the sky
condescending to the earth; without
rain, there would be no life.

> **John Updike** 1932–2009 American
> novelist and short-story writer: *Self-
> Consciousness: Memoirs* (1989)

Readiness and Preparation

see also ORGANIZATION

1 The scouts' motto is founded on my
initials, it is: BE PREPARED, which
means, you are always to be in a state
of readiness in mind and body to do
your duty.

> **Robert Baden-Powell** 1857–1941
> English soldier; founder of the Boy
> Scouts: *Scouting for Boys* (1908)

2 We are ready for any unforeseen
event which may or may not happen.

> **George W. Bush** 1946– American
> Republican statesman: in *Guardian*
> 30 December 2000

3 Barkis is willin'.

> **Charles Dickens** 1812–70 English
> novelist: *David Copperfield* (1850)

4 In preparing for battle I have always
found that plans are useless, but
planning is indispensable.

> **Dwight D. Eisenhower** 1890–1969
> American general and Republican

statesman: attributed; Richard Nixon
Six Crises (1962)

5 The man who has planned badly, if
fortune is on his side, may have had
a stroke of luck; but his plan was a
bad one nonetheless.
Herodotus *c.*485–*c.*425 BC Greek
historian: *Histories*

6 I think the necessity of being *ready*
increases. Look to it.
Abraham Lincoln 1809–65 American
Republican statesman: the whole of a
letter to Governor Andrew Curtin of
Pennsylvania, 8 April 1861

7 No time like the present.
Mrs Manley 1663–1724 English novelist
and dramatist: *The Lost Lover* (1696)

8 No plan of operations reaches with
any certainty beyond the first
encounter with the enemy's main
force.
*usually quoted as 'No plan survives first
contact with the enemy'*
Helmuth von Moltke 1800–91 Prussian
military commander:
Kriegsgechichtiche Einzelschriften
(1880)

9 Go ahead, make my day.
Joseph C. Stinson 1947– : *Sudden
Impact* (1983 film); spoken by Clint
Eastwood

10 If we had had more time for
discussion we should probably have
made a great many more mistakes.
Leon Trotsky 1879–1940 Russian
revolutionary: *My Life* (1930)

Reading

see also BOOKS, LITERATURE

1 The world may be full of fourth-rate
writers but it's also full of fourth-rate
readers.
Stan Barstow 1928– English novelist:
in *Daily Mail* 15 August 1989

2 History shows that the less people
read, the more books they buy.
Albert Camus 1913–60 French novelist,
dramatist, and essayist: *Jonas, or the
Artist at Work* (1957)

3 Choose an author as you choose a
friend.
Wentworth Dillon, Lord Roscommon
*c.*1633–85 Irish poet and critic: *Essay on
Translated Verse* (1684)

4 When I want to read a novel, I write
one.
Benjamin Disraeli 1804–81 British Tory
statesman and novelist: W. Monypenny
and G. Buckle *Life of Benjamin Disraeli*
vol. 6 (1920)

5 What do we ever get nowadays from
reading to equal the excitement and
the revelation in those first fourteen
years?
Graham Greene 1904–91 English
novelist: *The Lost Childhood and Other
Essays* (1951)

6 A man ought to read just as
inclination leads him; for what he
reads as a task will do him little good.
Samuel Johnson 1709–84 English poet,
critic, and lexicographer: James Boswell
Life of Samuel Johnson (1791) 14 July
1763

7 [*The Compleat Angler*] is
acknowledged to be one of the
world's books. Only the trouble is
that the world doesn't read its books,
it borrows a detective story instead.
Stephen Leacock 1869–1944 Canadian
humorist: *The Boy I Left Behind Me*
(1947)

8 Curiously enough, one cannot *read* a
book: one can only reread it. A good
reader, a major reader, an active and
creative reader is a rereader.
Vladimir Nabokov 1899–1977 Russian
novelist: *Lectures on Literature* (1980)

9 Much reading is an oppression of the
mind, and extinguishes the natural

candle, which is the reason of so many senseless scholars in the world.

> **William Penn** 1644–1718 English Quaker: *Fruits of a Father's Love* (1726)

10 What really knocks me out is a book that, when you're all done reading it, you wish the author that wrote it was a terrific friend of yours and you could call him up on the phone whenever you felt like it.

> **J. D. Salinger** 1919– American novelist and short-story writer: *Catcher in the Rye* (1951)

11 POLONIUS: What do you read, my lord?
HAMLET: Words, words, words.

> **William Shakespeare** 1564–1616 English dramatist: *Hamlet* (1601)

12 People say that life is the thing, but I prefer reading.

> **Logan Pearsall Smith** 1865–1946 American-born man of letters: *Afterthoughts* (1931)

13 Reading is to the mind what exercise is to the body.

> **Richard Steele** 1672–1729 Irish-born essayist and dramatist: in *The Tatler* 18 March 1710

14 Digressions, incontestably, are the sunshine;—they are the life, the soul of reading;—take them out of this book for instance,—you might as well take the book along with them.

> **Laurence Sterne** 1713–68 English novelist: *Tristram Shandy* (1759–67)

Reality

see also APPEARANCE, FACTS

1 Reality is that which, when you stop believing in it, doesn't go away.

> **Philip K. Dick** 1928–82 American science fiction writer and novelist: *I Hope I Shall Arrive Soon* (1986) 'How to Build a Universe That Doesn't Fall Apart Two Days Later'

2 Perhaps the rare and simple pleasure of being seen for what one is compensates for the misery of being it.

> **Margaret Drabble** 1939– English novelist: *A Summer Bird-Cage* (1963)

3 Between the idea
And the reality
Between the motion
And the act
Falls the Shadow.

> **T. S. Eliot** 1888–1965 Anglo-American poet, critic, and dramatist: 'The Hollow Men' (1925)

4 All theory, dear friend, is grey, but the golden tree of actual life springs ever green.

> **Johann Wolfgang von Goethe** 1749–1832 German poet, novelist, and dramatist: *Faust* pt. 1 (1808)

5 I refute it *thus*.
kicking a large stone by way of refuting Bishop Berkeley's theory of the non-existence of matter

> **Samuel Johnson** 1709–84 English poet, critic, and lexicographer: James Boswell *Life of Samuel Johnson* (1791) 6 August 1763

6 I'm up to my neck in the real world, every day. Just you try doing your VAT return with a head full of goblins.

> **Terry Pratchett** 1948– English science fiction writer: in *Sunday Times* 27 February 2000

7 Do you think that the things people make fools of themselves about are any less real and true than the things they behave sensibly about? They are more true: they are the only things that are true.

> **George Bernard Shaw** 1856–1950 Irish dramatist: *Candida* (1898)

8 They said, 'You have a blue guitar,
You do not play things as they are.'
The man replied, 'Things as they are
Are changed upon the blue guitar.'
> **Wallace Stevens** 1879–1955 American
> poet: 'The Man with the Blue Guitar'
> (1937)

9 It is the spirit of the age to believe
that any fact, no matter how suspect,
is superior to any imaginative
exercise, no matter how true.
> **Gore Vidal** 1925– American novelist
> and critic: in *Encounter* December 1967

10 The nineteenth century dislike of
Realism is the rage of Caliban seeing
his own face in the glass.
> **Oscar Wilde** 1854–1900 Anglo-Irish
> dramatist and poet: *The Picture of
> Dorian Gray* (1891)

11 BLANCHE: I don't want realism.
MITCH: Naw, I guess not.
BLANCHE: I'll tell you what I want.
Magic!
> **Tennessee Williams** 1911–83 American
> dramatist: *A Streetcar Named Desire*
> (1947)

Reason

see LOGIC AND REASON

Relationships

see also FRIENDSHIP, HATRED, LOVE, SEX

1 He who has a thousand friends has
not a friend to spare,
And he who has one enemy will meet
him everywhere.
> **Ali ibn-Abi-Talib** *c.*602–661 fourth
> Islamic caliph: *A Hundred Sayings*

2 Almost all of our relationships begin
and most of them continue as forms
of mutual exploitation, a mental or
physical barter, to be terminated
when one or both parties run out of
goods.
> **W. H. Auden** 1907–73 English poet: *The
> Dyer's Hand* (1963)

3 In necessary things, unity; in
doubtful things, liberty; in all things,
charity.
> **Richard Baxter** 1615–91 English divine:
> motto

4 Am I my brother's keeper?
> **Bible**: Genesis

5 Love is like the wild rose-briar;
Friendship like the holly-tree:
The holly is dark when the rose-briar
blooms,
But which will bloom most
constantly?
> **Emily Brontë** 1818–48 English novelist
> and poet: 'Love and Friendship' (1846)

6 Now the whole dizzying and
delirious range of sexual possibilities
has been boiled down to that one
big, boring, bulimic word.
RELATIONSHIP.
> **Julie Burchill** 1960– English journalist
> and writer: *Sex and Sensibility* (1992)

7 Love, friendship, respect do not
unite people as much as common
hatred for something.
> **Anton Chekhov** 1860–1904 Russian
> dramatist and short-story writer:
> *Notebooks* (1921)

8 Men love women, women love
children; children love
hamsters—it's quite hopeless.
> **Alice Thomas Ellis** 1932–2005 English
> novelist: attributed, 1987

9 Personal relations are the important
thing for ever and ever, and not this
outer life of telegrams and anger.
> **E. M. Forster** 1879–1970 English
> novelist: *Howards End* (1910)

10 The soul is not where it lives, but
where it loves.
> **Thomas Fuller** 1654–1734 English

writer and physician: *Gnomologia*
(1732)

11 When we take people, thou wouldst
say, merely as they are, we make
them worse; when we treat them as if
they were what they should be, we
improve them as far as they can be
improved.

*sometimes quoted as 'Treat a man as he is,
and that is what he remains. Treat a man
as he can be, and that is what he becomes'*

Johann Wolfgang von Goethe
1749–1832 German poet, novelist, and
dramatist: *Wilhelm Meisters Lehrjare*
(1795–6) tr. Carlyle

12 In human relations kindness and lies
are worth a thousand truths.
Graham Greene 1904–91 English
novelist: *The Heart of the Matter* (1948)

13 Their relationship consisted
In discussing if it existed.
Thom Gunn 1929–2004 English poet:
'Jamesian' (1992)

14 Three things in human life are
important. The first is to be kind. The
second is to be kind. And the third is
to be kind.
Henry James 1843–1916 American
novelist: in 1902; Leon Edel *Henry
James: A Life* vol. 5 (1972)

15 The meeting of two personalities is
like the contact of two chemical
substances: if there is any reaction,
both are transformed.
Carl Gustav Jung 1875–1961 Swiss
psychologist: *Modern Man in Search of
a Soul* (1933)

16 It is easier to know man in general
than to know one man in particular.
Duc de la Rochefoucauld 1613–80
French moralist: *Maxims* (1678)

17 We've got this gift of love, but love is
like a precious plant. You can't just
accept it and leave it in the cupboard
or just think it's going to get on by
itself. You've got to keep watering it.
You've got to really look after it and
nurture it.
John Lennon 1940–80 English pop
singer and songwriter: television
interview, 30 December 1969

18 Ships that pass in the night, and
speak each other in passing;
Only a signal shown and a distant
voice in the darkness;
So on the ocean of life we pass and
speak one another,
Only a look and a voice; then
darkness again and a silence.
Henry Wadsworth Longfellow 1807–82
American poet: *Tales of a Wayside Inn*
pt. 3 (1874)

19 Difficult or easy, pleasant or bitter,
you are the same you: I cannot live
with you—or without you.
Martial AD *c*.40–*c*.104 Roman
epigrammatist: *Epigrammata*

20 I love her too, but our neuroses just
don't match.
Arthur Miller 1915–2005 American
dramatist: *The Ride Down Mount
Morgan* (1991)

21 I believe a little incompatibility is the
spice of life, particularly if he has
income and she is pattable.
Ogden Nash 1902–71 American
humorist: 'I Do, I Will, I Have' (1949)

22 Human relationships don't belong to
engineering, mathematics, chess,
which offer problems that can be
perfectly solved. Human
relationships grow, like trees.
J. B. Priestley 1894–1984 English
novelist, dramatist, and critic: *Journey
Down a Rainbow* (with Jacquetta
Hawkes) (1957 rev. ed.)

23 I hold this to be the highest task for a
bond between two people: that each
protects the solitude of the other.
Rainer Maria Rilke 1875–1926 German
poet: letter to Paula Modersohn-Becker,
12 February 1902

24 The time to make up your mind
about people is never.
> **Donald Ogden Stewart** 1894–1980
> American screenwriter: *The
> Philadelphia Story* (1940 film) from the
> play by Philip Barry, spoken by
> Katharine Hepburn as Tracy Lord

25 We would never love anybody if we
could see past our invention.
> **Tom Stoppard** 1937–   British dramatist:
> *The Invention of Love* (1997)

26 Love and sex can go together and sex
and unlove can go together and love
and unsex can go together. But
personal love and personal sex is
bad.
> **Andy Warhol** 1927–87 American artist:
> *Philosophy of Andy Warhol* (*From A to B
> and Back Again*) (1975)

Religion

see also BIBLE, CHRISTIANITY, CHURCH, CLERGY,
FAITH, GOD, PRAYER, SCIENCE AND RELIGION

1 Render therefore unto Caesar the
things which are Caesar's; and unto
God the things that are God's.
> **Bible**: St Matthew

2 One religion is as true as another.
> **Robert Burton** 1577–1640 English
> clergyman and scholar: *The Anatomy of
> Melancholy* (1621–51)

3 'Sensible men are all of the same
religion.' 'And pray what is that?' . . .
'Sensible men never tell.'
> **Benjamin Disraeli** 1804–81 British Tory
> statesman and novelist: *Endymion*
> (1880)

4 So long as man remains free he
strives for nothing so incessantly and
so painfully as to find someone to
worship.
> **Fedor Dostoevsky** 1821–81 Russian
> novelist: *The Brothers Karamazov*
> (1879–80)

5 All religions must be tolerated and
the sole concern of officials is to
ensure that one denomination does
not interfere with another, for here
everyone can seek salvation in the
manner that seems best to him.
> **Frederick the Great** 1712–86 Prussian
> monarch: scribbled in the margin of an
> official reply to an enquiry from the
> General Directory on the civic rights of
> Roman Catholics, June 1740

6 To become a popular religion, it is
only necessary for a superstition to
enslave a philosophy.
> **William Ralph Inge** 1860–1954 English
> writer; Dean of St Paul's, 1911–34: *Idea
> of Progress* (1920)

7 I go into the Muslim mosque and the
Jewish synagogue and the Christian
church and I see one altar.
> **Jalal ad-Din ar-Rumi** 1207–73 Persian
> poet and Sufi mystic: Coleman Barks
> and John Moyne (eds.) *The Essential
> Rumi* (1999)

8 Religion's in the heart, not in the
knee.
> **Douglas Jerrold** 1803–57 English
> dramatist and journalist: *The Devil's
> Ducat* (1830)

9 It is our first duty to serve society,
and, after we have done that, we may
attend wholly to the salvation of our
own souls. A youthful passion for
abstracted devotion should not be
encouraged.
> **Samuel Johnson** 1709–84 English poet,
> critic, and lexicographer: James Boswell
> *Life of Samuel Johnson* (1791) February
> 1766

10 Religion is the frozen thought of men
out of which they build temples.
> **Jiddu Krishnamurti** 1895–1986 Indian
> spiritual philosopher: in *Observer*
> 22 April 1928

11 I count religion but a childish toy,
And hold there is no sin but
ignorance.

Christopher Marlowe 1564–93 English
dramatist and poet: *The Jew of Malta*
(c.1592)

12 Religion . . . is the opium of the
people.

Karl Marx 1818–83 German political
philosopher: *A Contribution to the
Critique of Hegel's Philosophy of Right*
(1843–4)

13 Things have come to a pretty pass
when religion is allowed to invade
the sphere of private life.
on hearing an evangelical sermon

Lord Melbourne 1779–1848 British
Whig statesman: G. W. E. Russell
Collections and Recollections (1898)

14 There's no reason to bring religion
into it. I think we ought to have as
great a regard for religion as we can,
so as to keep it out of as many things
as possible.

Sean O'Casey 1880–1964 Irish
dramatist: *The Plough and the Stars*
(1926)

15 My country is the world, and my
religion is to do good.

Thomas Paine 1737–1809 English
political theorist: *The Rights of Man* pt.
2 (1792)

16 Any system of religion that has any
thing in it that shocks the mind of a
child cannot be a true system.

Thomas Paine 1737–1809 English
political theorist: *The Age of Reason* pt. 1
(1794)

17 To be furious in religion, is to be
irreligiously religious.

William Penn 1644–1718 English
Quaker: *Some Fruits of Solitude* (1693)

18 Religion to me has always been the
wound, not the bandage.

Dennis Potter 1935–94 English

television dramatist: *Seeing the Blossom*
(1994)

19 Religion, which may in most of its
forms be defined as the belief that
the gods are on the side of the
Government.

Bertrand Russell 1872–1970 British
philosopher and mathematician:
Marriage and Morals (1929)

20 Had I but served my God with half
the zeal
I served my king, he would not in
mine age
Have left me naked to mine enemies.

William Shakespeare 1564–1616
English dramatist: *Henry VIII* (1613)

21 We have just enough religion to
make us hate, but not enough to
make us love one another.

Jonathan Swift 1667–1745 Anglo-Irish
poet and satirist: *Thoughts on Various
Subjects* (1711)

22 Orthodoxy is my doxy; heterodoxy is
another man's doxy.

William Warburton 1698–1779 English
theologian: to Lord Sandwich; Joseph
Priestley *Memoirs* (1807)

23 Zen . . . does not confuse spirituality
with thinking about God while one is
peeling potatoes. Zen spirituality is
just to peel the potatoes.

Alan Watts 1915–73 American teacher
and writer: *The Way of Zen* (1957)

24 I went to America to convert the
Indians; but oh, who shall convert
me?

John Wesley 1703–91 English preacher:
diary, 24 January 1738

25 So many gods, so many creeds,
So many paths that wind and wind,
While just the art of being kind
Is all the sad world needs.

Ella Wheeler Wilcox 1855–1919
American poet: 'The World's Need'

Reputation

see also FAME

1　Woe unto you, when all men shall speak well of you!
　　Bible: St Luke

2　The devil's most devilish when respectable.
　　Elizabeth Barrett Browning 1806–61 English poet: *Aurora Leigh* (1857)

3　Caesar's wife must be above suspicion.
　　Julius Caesar 100–44 BC Roman general and statesman: oral tradition, based on Plutarch *Parallel Lives* 'Julius Caesar'

4　The reputation which the world bestows
　　is like the wind, that shifts now here now there,
　　its name changed with the quarter whence it blows.
　　Dante Alighieri 1265–1321 Italian poet: *Divina Commedia* 'Purgatorio'

5　You can't shame or humiliate modern celebrities. What used to be called shame and humiliation is now called publicity.
　　P. J. O'Rourke 1947– American humorous writer: *Give War a Chance* (1992)

6　Honour is like a match, you can only use it once.
　　Marcel Pagnol 1895–1974 French dramatist and film-maker: *Marius* (1946)

7　What is merit? The opinion one man entertains of another.
　　Lord Palmerston 1784–1865 British statesman: Thomas Carlyle *Shooting Niagara: and After?* (1867)

8　He that filches from me my good name
　　Robs me of that which not enriches him,

And makes me poor indeed.
　　William Shakespeare 1564–1616 English dramatist: *Othello* (1602–4)

9　We owe respect to the living; to the dead we owe only truth.
　　Voltaire 1694–1778 French writer and philosopher: 'Première Lettre sur Oedipe' in *Oeuvres* (1785)

10　I'm the girl who lost her reputation and never missed it.
　　Mae West 1892–1980 American film actress: P. F. Boller and R. L. Davis *Hollywood Anecdotes* (1988)

Research

see also EXPERIMENT, SCIENCE, THEORY

1　Basic research is what I am doing when I don't know what I am doing.
　　Wernher von Braun 1912–77 German-born American rocket engineer: R. L. Weber *A Random Walk in Science* (1973)

2　If politics is the art of the possible, research is surely the art of the soluble. Both are immensely practical-minded affairs.
　　Peter Medawar 1915–87 English immunologist and writer: in *New Statesman* 19 June 1964; see POLITICS 7

3　In research the horizon recedes as we advance, and is no nearer at sixty than it was at twenty. As the power of endurance weakens with age, the urgency of the pursuit grows more intense . . . And research is always incomplete.
　　Mark Pattison 1813–84 English educationist: *Isaac Casaubon* (1875)

4　He had been eight years upon a project for extracting sun-beams out of cucumbers, which were to be put into vials hermetically sealed, and let out to warm the air in raw inclement summers.
　　Jonathan Swift 1667–1745 Anglo-Irish

poet and satirist: *Gulliver's Travels*
(1726)

5 The outcome of any serious research
can only be to make two questions
grow where one question grew
before.

Thorstein Veblen 1857–1929 American
economist and social scientist:
University of California Chronicle (1908)

6 No more impressive warning can be
given to those who would confine
knowledge and research to what is
apparently useful, than the reflection
that conic sections were studied for
eighteen hundred years merely as an
abstract science, without regard to
any utility other than to satisfy the
craving for knowledge on the part of
mathematicians, and that then at the
end of this long period of abstract
study, they were found to be the
necessary key with which to attain
the knowledge of the most important
laws of nature.

Alfred North Whitehead 1861–1947
English philosopher and
mathematician: *Introduction to
Mathematics* (1911)

Responsibility

see also DUTY

1 When a man assumes a public trust,
he should consider himself as public
property.

Thomas Jefferson 1743–1826 American
Democratic Republican statesman: to
Baron von Humboldt, 1807; B. L. Rayner
Life of Jefferson (1834)

2 Power without responsibility: the
prerogative of the harlot throughout
the ages.

*summing up Lord Beaverbrook's political
standpoint as a newspaper editor; Stanley
Baldwin, Kipling's cousin, subsequently
obtained permission to use the phrase in a
speech*

Rudyard Kipling 1865–1936 English

writer and poet: in *Kipling Journal*
December 1971

3 The buck stops here.

Harry S. Truman 1884–1972 American
Democratic statesman: unattributed
motto on Truman's desk

Retirement

1 Once I leave, I leave. I am not going
to speak to the man on the bridge,
and I am not going to spit on the
deck.

on resigning

Stanley Baldwin 1867–1947 British
Conservative statesman: statement to
the Cabinet, 28 May 1937

2 I go to Bournemouth in lieu of
Paradise.

on retiring from Eton

Lord Hugh Cecil 1869–1956 British
Conservative politician and clergyman,
Provost of Eton: in *Dictionary of
National Biography*

3 The transition from Who's Who to
Who's He.

*view of the former Governor of the Bank of
England*

Eddie George 1938–2009 English
banker: in *Independent* 29 December
2003

4 When you get done, you get done.

announcing his retirement from writing

Stephen King 1947– American writer:
in *Times* 2 February 2002

5 Learn to live well, or fairly make your
will;
You've played, and loved, and ate,
and drunk your fill:
Walk sober off; before a sprightlier
age
Comes tittering on, and shoves you
from the stage.

Alexander Pope 1688–1744 English
poet: *Imitations of Horace* (1737)

6 As to that leisure evening of life, I must say that I do not want it. I can conceive of no contentment of which toil is not to be the immediate parent.
Anthony Trollope 1815–82 English novelist: letter, 8 June 1876

Revenge

1 Revenge is a kind of wild justice, which the more man's nature runs to, the more ought law to weed it out.
Francis Bacon 1561–1626 English lawyer, courtier, philosopher, and essayist: *Essays* (1625) 'Of Revenge'

2 Vengeance is mine; I will repay, saith the Lord.
Bible: Romans

3 You can't be fuelled by bitterness. It can eat you up, but it cannot drive you.
Benazir Bhutto 1953–2007 Pakistani stateswoman: *Daughter of Destiny* (1989)

4 Sweet is revenge—especially to women.
Lord Byron 1788–1824 English poet: *Don Juan* (1819–24)

5 Heaven has no rage, like love to hatred turned,
Nor Hell a fury, like a woman scorned.
William Congreve 1670–1729 English dramatist: *The Mourning Bride* (1697)

6 Cancel the kitchen scraps for lepers and orphans. No more merciful beheadings. And call off Christmas!
Pen Densham and **John Watson**: *Robin Hood, Prince of Thieves* (1991 film); spoken by Alan Rickman

7 The Germans, if this Government is returned, are going to pay every penny; they are going to be squeezed as a lemon is squeezed—until the pips squeak.
Eric Geddes 1875–1937 British politician and administrator: speech at Cambridge, 10 December 1918

8 Nobody ever forgets where he buried a hatchet.
Frank McKinney ('Kin') Hubbard 1868–1930 American humorist: *Abe Martin's Broadcast* (1930)

9 Get your retaliation in first.
Carwyn James 1929–83 Welsh Rugby Football coach: attributed, 1971

10 Indeed, revenge is always the pleasure of a paltry, feeble, tiny mind.
Juvenal AD *c.*60–*c.*130 Roman satirist: *Satires*

11 Men should be either treated generously or destroyed, because they take revenge for slight injuries—for heavy ones they cannot.
Niccolò Machiavelli 1469–1527 Florentine statesman and political philosopher: *The Prince* (written 1513)

12 Beware of the man who does not return your blow: he neither forgives you nor allows you to forgive yourself.
George Bernard Shaw 1856–1950 Irish dramatist: *Man and Superman* (1903)

13 Two wrongs don't make a right, but they make a good excuse.
Thomas Szasz 1920– Hungarian-born psychiatrist: *The Second Sin* (1973)

Reviews

see also CRITICS

1 A bad review may spoil your breakfast but you shouldn't allow it to spoil your lunch.
Kingsley Amis 1922–95 English novelist

and poet: attributed; Giles Gordon *Aren't We Due a Royalty Statement?* (1993)

2 One cannot review a bad book without showing off.

W. H. Auden 1907–73 English poet: *The Dyer's Hand* (1963) 'Reading'

3 When the reviews are bad I tell my staff that they can join me as I cry all the way to the bank.

Liberace 1919–87 American showman: *Autobiography* (1973); coined in the mid-1950s

4 From the moment I picked up your book until I laid it down, I was convulsed with laughter. Some day I intend reading it.

blurb written for S. J. Perelman's book Dawn Ginsberg's Revenge *(1928)*

Groucho Marx 1890–1977 American film comedian: Hector Arce *Groucho* (1979)

5 I am sitting in the smallest room of my house. I have your review before me. In a moment it will be behind me.

responding to a savage review by Rudolph Louis in Münchener Neueste Nachrichten, *7 February 1906*

Max Reger 1873–1916 German composer: Nicolas Slonimsky *Lexicon of Musical Invective* (1953)

6 I never read a book before reviewing it; it prejudices a man so.

Sydney Smith 1771–1845 English clergyman and essayist: H. Pearson *The Smith of Smiths* (1934)

Revolution

see also POLITICS, PROTEST

1 The most radical revolutionary will become a conservative on the day after the revolution.

Hannah Arendt 1906–75 American political philosopher: in *New Yorker* 12 September 1970

2 Those who have served the cause of the revolution have ploughed the sea.

Simón Bolívar 1783–1830 Venezuelan patriot and statesman: attributed

3 Revolutions are celebrated when they are no longer dangerous.

Pierre Boulez 1925– French conductor and composer: in *Guardian* 13 January 1989

4 Would it not be easier
In that case for the government
To dissolve the people
And elect another?

on the 1953 uprising in East Germany

Bertolt Brecht 1898–1956 German dramatist: 'The Solution' (1953)

5 All modern revolutions have ended in a reinforcement of the State.

Albert Camus 1913–60 French novelist, dramatist, and essayist: *L'Homme révolté* (1951)

6 What is a rebel? A man who says no.

Albert Camus 1913–60 French novelist, dramatist, and essayist: *L'Homme révolté* (1951)

7 History will absolve me.

Fidel Castro 1927– Cuban statesman: title of pamphlet (1953)

8 The Revolution is made by man, but man must forge his revolutionary spirit from day to day.

Ernesto ('Che') Guevara 1928–67 Argentinian revolutionary: *Socialism and Man in Cuba* (1968)

9 When the people contend for their liberty, they seldom get anything by their victory but new masters.

Lord Halifax 1633–95 English politician and essayist: *Political, Moral, and Miscellaneous Thoughts and Reflections* (1750) 'Of Prerogative, Power and Liberty'

10 Maximilien Robespierre was nothing but the hand of Jean Jacques

Rousseau, the bloody hand that drew from the womb of time the body whose soul Rousseau had created.

Heinrich Heine 1797–1856 German poet: *Zur Geschichte der Religion und Philosophie in Deutschland* (1834)

11 I will die like a true-blue rebel. Don't waste any time in mourning—organize.

prior to his death by firing squad

Joe Hill 1879–1915 Swedish-born American labour leader: farewell telegram to Bill Haywood, 18 November 1915

12 Revolution's delightful in the preliminary stages. So long as it's a question of getting rid of people at the top.

Aldous Huxley 1894–1963 English novelist: *Eyeless in Gaza* (1936)

13 A little rebellion now and then is a good thing.

Thomas Jefferson 1743–1826 American Democratic Republican statesman: letter to James Madison, 30 January 1787

14 Those who make peaceful revolution impossible will make violent revolution inevitable.

John F. Kennedy 1917–63 American Democratic statesman: speech at the White House, 13 March 1962

15 A revolution does not last more than fifteen years, the period which coincides with the flourishing of a generation.

José Ortega y Gasset 1883–1955 Spanish writer and philosopher: *The Revolt of the Masses* (1930)

16 A share in two revolutions is living to some purpose.

Thomas Paine 1737–1809 English political theorist: Eric Foner *Tom Paine and Revolutionary America* (1976)

17 Revolutions are not made; they come. A revolution is as natural a growth as an oak. It comes out of the past. Its foundations are laid far back.

Wendell Phillips 1811–84 American abolitionist: speech 8 January 1852

18 *Après nous le déluge.*

After us the deluge.

Madame de Pompadour 1721–64 favourite of Louis XV of France: Madame du Hausset *Mémoires* (1824)

19 I know, and all the world knows, that revolutions never go backward.

William Seward 1801–72 American politician: speech at Rochester, 25 October 1858

20 Revolutions have never lightened the burden of tyranny: they have only shifted it to another shoulder.

George Bernard Shaw 1856–1950 Irish dramatist: *Man and Superman* (1903) 'The Revolutionist's Handbook' foreword

21 The social order destroyed by a revolution is almost always better than that which immediately preceded it, and experience shows that the most dangerous moment for a bad government is generally that in which it sets about reform.

Alexis de Tocqueville 1805–59 French historian and politician: *L'Ancien régime* (1856)

22 Bliss was it in that dawn to be alive, But to be young was very heaven!

William Wordsworth 1770–1850 English poet: 'The French Revolution, as it Appeared to Enthusiasts' (1809)

Risk

see also DANGER, SECURITY

1 He either fears his fate too much, Or his deserts are small, That puts it not unto the touch To win or lose it all.

James Graham, Marquess of Montrose

1612–50 Scottish general and poet: 'My
Dear and Only Love' (written *c.*1642)

2 Hesitation increases in relation to
risk in equal proportion to age.
 Ernest Hemingway 1899–1961
 American novelist: A. E. Hotchner *Papa
 Hemingway* (1966)

3 My inclination to go by Air Express is
confirmed by the crash they had
yesterday, which will make them
careful in the immediate future.
 A. E. Housman 1859–1936 English poet:
 letter, 17 August 1920

4 Where there is no risk there can be
no pride in achievement and
consequently no happiness.
 Ray Kroc 1902–84 American
 businessman: *Grinding It Out* (1977)

5 To sail is necessary; to live is not.
 insisting on setting sail during a storm
 Pompey the Great 106–48 BC Roman
 general and statesman: Plutarch
 Parallel Lives 'Pompey'

6 BETTER DROWNED THAN DUFFERS IF
NOT DUFFERS WONT DROWN.
 Arthur Ransome 1884–1967 English
 writer: *Swallows and Amazons* (1930)

7 We took risks, we knew we took
them; things have come out against
us, and therefore we have no cause
for complaint.
 Robert Falcon Scott 1868–1912 English
 polar explorer: 'The Last Message' in
 Scott's Last Expedition (1913)

8 A sheltered life can be a daring life as
well. For all serious daring starts
from within.
 Eudora Welty 1909–2001 American
 writer: *One Writer's Beginnings* (1984)

Rivers

1 Says Tweed to Till—
'What gars ye rin sae still?'

Says Till to Tweed—
'Though ye rin with speed
And I rin slaw,
For ae man that ye droon
I droon twa.'
 Anonymous: traditional rhyme

2 The Thames is liquid history.
 *to an American who had compared the
 Thames disparagingly with the Mississippi*
 John Burns 1858–1943 British Liberal
 politician: in *Daily Mail* 25 January 1943

3 I do not know much about gods; but
I think that the river
Is a strong brown god—sullen,
untamed and intractable.
 T. S. Eliot 1888–1965 Anglo-American
 poet, critic, and dramatist: *Four
 Quartets* 'The Dry Salvages' (1941)

4 Ol' man river, dat ol' man river,
He must know sumpin', but don't say
nothin',
He jus' keeps rollin',
He jus' keeps rollin' along.
 Oscar Hammerstein II 1895–1960
 American songwriter: 'Ol' Man River'
 (1927 song)

5 I've known rivers:
I've known rivers ancient as the
world and older than the flow of
human blood in human veins.
 Langston Hughes 1902–67 American
 writer and poet: 'The Negro Speaks of
 Rivers' (1921)

6 I bathed in the Euphrates when
dawns were young.
I built my hut near the Congo and it
lulled me to sleep.
I looked upon the Nile and raised the
pyramids above it.
I heard the singing of the Mississippi
when Abe Lincoln went down to
New Orleans, and I've seen its
muddy bosom turn all golden in
the sunset.
 Langston Hughes 1902–67 American
 writer and poet: 'The Negro Speaks of
 Rivers' (1921)

7 Then I saw the Congo, creeping
through the black,
Cutting through the forest with a
golden track.
Vachel Lindsay 1879–1931 American
poet: 'The Congo' (1914)

8 Sabrina fair,
Listen where thou art sitting
Under the glassy, cool, translucent
wave,
In twisted braids of lilies knitting
The loose train of thy amber-
dropping hair.
Sabrina, the nymph of the River Severn
John Milton 1608–74 English poet:
Comus (1637)

9 Sweet Thames, run softly, till I end
my song.
Edmund Spenser *c.*1552–99 English
poet: *Prothalamion* (1596)

10 I come from haunts of coot and
hern,
I make a sudden sally
And sparkle out among the fern,
To bicker down a valley.
Alfred, Lord Tennyson 1809–92 English
poet: 'The Brook' (1855)

Rock and Pop Music

see also MUSIC

1 The filth and the fury.
*following a notorious interview with the
Sex Pistols broadcast live on Thames
Television*
Anonymous: headline in *Daily Mirror*,
2 December 1976

2 Rock is like a battery that must
always go back to blues to get
recharged.
Eric Clapton 1945– English rock
musician: attributed; M. Palmer *Small
Talk, Big Names* (1993)

3 I thought punk was a good idea—like
someone shaking an apple tree until

all the bad ones fell off and you'd just
got the good ones left.
Phil Collins 1951– British rock
musician: D. Bowler and D. Dray
Genesis: a biography (1992)

4 Hardly anyone bought the Velvets'
albums when they were originally
released, but everyone who did
formed a band.
*of the American rock group Velvet
Underground, formed in 1965*
Brian Eno 1948– British musician and
record producer: attributed

5 I would hope we mean more to
people than putting money in a
church basket and saying ten Hail
Marys on a Sunday. Has God played
Knebworth recently?
on the drawing power of Oasis
Noel Gallagher 1967– English pop
singer: in *New Musical Express* 12 July
1997

6 Most people get into bands for three
very simple rock and roll reasons: to
get laid, to get fame, and to get rich.
Bob Geldof 1954– Irish rock musician:
in *Melody Maker* 27 August 1977

7 I'm dealing in rock'n'roll. I'm, like,
I'm not a bona fide human being.
Phil Spector 1940– American record
producer and songwriter: attributed

Romance

1 One is never too old for romance.
Ingrid Bergman 1915–82 Swedish
actress: in *Sunday Mirror* 5 May 1974

2 The essence of romantic love is that
wonderful beginning, after which
sadness and impossibility may
become the rule.
Anita Brookner 1928– British novelist
and art historian: *A Friend From
England* (1987)

3 Personally, I can't see why it would
be any less romantic to find a

husband in a nice four-colour catalogue than in the average downtown bar at happy hour.

> **Barbara Ehrenreich** 1941– American sociologist and writer: *The Worst Years of Our Lives* (1991)

4 I have met with women whom I really think would like to be married to a poem and to be given away by a novel.

> **John Keats** 1795–1821 English poet: letter to Fanny Brawne, 8 July 1819

5 It's our *own* story *exactly*! He bold as a hawk, she soft as the dawn.

> **James Thurber** 1894–1961 American humorist: cartoon caption in *New Yorker* 25 February 1939

6 Men are so romantic, don't you think? They look for a perfect partner when what they should be looking for is perfect love.

> **Fay Weldon** 1931– British novelist and scriptwriter: in *Sunday Times* 6 September 1987

The Royal Family

1 When I appear in public people expect me to neigh, grind my teeth, paw the ground and swish my tail—none of which is easy.

> **Anne, Princess Royal** 1950– British princess: in *Observer* 22 May 1977

2 She was the People's Princess, and that is how she will stay . . . in our hearts and in our memories forever.

> **Tony Blair** 1953– British Labour statesman: on hearing of the death of Diana, Princess of Wales, 31 August 1997

3 I'd like to be a queen in people's hearts but I don't see myself being Queen of this country.

> **Diana, Princess of Wales** 1961–97 former wife of Charles, Prince of Wales:

interview on *Panorama*, BBC1 TV, 20 November 1995

4 I declare before you all that my whole life, whether it be long or short, shall be devoted to your service and the service of our great Imperial family to which we all belong.

> **Elizabeth II** 1926– British monarch: broadcast speech to the Commonwealth from Cape Town, 21 April 1947

5 I think everybody really will concede that on this, of all days, I should begin my speech with the words 'My husband and I'.

> **Elizabeth II** 1926– British monarch: speech at Guildhall, London, on her 25th wedding anniversary, 20 November 1972

6 The family firm.
description of the British monarchy

> **George VI** 1895–1952 British monarch: attributed

7 The personality conveyed by the utterances which are put into her mouth is that of a priggish schoolgirl, captain of the hockey team, a prefect, and a recent candidate for confirmation. It is not thus that she will be able to come into her own as an independent and distinctive character.
of Queen Elizabeth II

> **John Grigg** 1924– British writer and journalist: in *National and English Review* August 1957

8 And it seems to me you lived your life
Like a candle in the wind:
Never fading with the sunset
When the rain set in.
of Diana, Princess of Wales

> **Elton John** 1947– and **Bernie Taupin** 1950– English pop singer and songwriter; songwriter: 'Candle in the Wind' (song, revised version, 1997)

9 For seventeen years he did nothing at all but kill animals and stick in stamps.
of King George V
> **Harold Nicolson** 1886–1968 English diplomat, politician, and writer: diary, 17 August 1949

Royalty

see also ROYAL FAMILY

1 Above all things our royalty is to be reverenced, and if you begin to poke about it you cannot reverence it . . . Its mystery is its life. We must not let in daylight upon magic.
> **Walter Bagehot** 1826–77 English economist and essayist: *The English Constitution* (1867)

2 The Sovereign has, under a constitutional monarchy such as ours, three rights—the right to be consulted, the right to encourage, the right to warn.
> **Walter Bagehot** 1826–77 English economist and essayist: *The English Constitution* (1867)

3 To be Prince of Wales is not a position. It is a predicament.
> **Alan Bennett** 1934– English actor and dramatist: *The Madness of King George* (1995 film)

4 A subject and a sovereign are clean different things.
> **Charles I** 1600–49 British monarch: speech on the scaffold, 30 January 1649

5 The influence of the Crown has increased, is increasing, and ought to be diminished.
> **John Dunning** 1731–83 English lawyer and politician: resolution passed in the House of Commons, 6 April 1780

6 At long last I am able to say a few words of my own . . . you must believe me when I tell you that I have found it impossible to carry the heavy burden of responsibility and to discharge my duties as King as I would wish to do without the help and support of the woman I love.
> **Edward VIII** 1894–1972 British monarch: radio broadcast following his abdication, 11 December 1936

7 I know I have the body of a weak and feeble woman, but I have the heart and stomach of a king, and of a king of England too.
> **Elizabeth I** 1533–1603 English monarch: speech to the troops at Tilbury on the approach of the Armada, 1588

8 To be a king and wear a crown is a thing more glorious to them that see it than it is pleasant to them that bear it.
> **Elizabeth I** 1533–1603 English monarch: The Golden Speech, 1601

9 I've danced with a man who's danced with a girl
Who's danced with the Prince of Wales!
> **Herbert Farjeon** 1887–1945 English writer and theatre critic: 'I've danced with a man who's danced with a girl'; first written for Elsa Lanchester and sung at private parties; later sung on stage by Mimi Crawford (1928)

10 The whole world is in revolt. Soon there will be only five Kings left—the King of England, the King of Spades, the King of Clubs, the King of Hearts and the King of Diamonds.
> **King Farouk** 1920–65 Egyptian monarch: addressed to the author at a conference in Cairo, 1948; Lord Boyd-Orr *As I Recall* (1966)

11 Whoso pulleth out this sword of this stone and anvil is rightwise King born of all England.
> **Thomas Malory** d. 1471 English writer: *Le Morte D'Arthur* (1470)

12 Royalty is the gold filling in a
mouthful of decay.

John Osborne 1929–94 English
dramatist: 'They call it cricket' in T.
Maschler (ed.) *Declaration* (1957)

13 I see it is impossible for the King to
have things done as cheap as other
men.

Samuel Pepys 1633–1703 English
diarist: diary, 21 July 1662

14 Uneasy lies the head that wears a
crown.

William Shakespeare 1564–1616
English dramatist: *Henry IV, Part 2*
(1597)

15 Monarchy is only the string that ties
the robber's bundle.

Percy Bysshe Shelley 1792–1822
English poet: *A Philosophical View of
Reform* (written 1819–20)

16 I will be good.

*on being shown a chart of the line of
succession, 11 March 1830*

Queen Victoria 1819–1901 British
monarch: Theodore Martin *The Prince
Consort* (1875)

Russia

see also COMMUNISM

1 Every country has its own
constitution; ours is absolutism
moderated by assassination.

Anonymous: Ernst Friedrich Herbert,
Count Münster, quoting 'an intelligent
Russian', in *Political Sketches of the State
of Europe, 1814–1867* (1868)

2 [Russian Communism is] the
illegitimate child of Karl Marx and
Catherine the Great.

Clement Attlee 1883–1967 British
Labour statesman: speech at Aarhus
University, 11 April 1956

3 The Lord God has given us vast
forests, immense fields, wide
horizons; surely we ought to be
giants, living in such a country as
this.

Anton Chekhov 1860–1904 Russian
dramatist and short-story writer: *The
Cherry Orchard* (1904)

4 I cannot forecast to you the action of
Russia. It is a riddle wrapped in a
mystery inside an enigma.

Winston Churchill 1874–1965 British
Conservative statesman: radio
broadcast, 1 October 1939

5 Petersburg, the most abstract and
premeditated city on earth.

Fedor Dostoevsky 1821–81 Russian
novelist: *Notes from Underground*
(1864)

6 A land that does not like doing things
by halves.

of Russia

Nikolai Gogol 1809–52 Russian writer:
Dead Souls (1842)

7 The idea of restructuring
[perestroika] . . . combines
continuity and innovation, the
historical experience of Bolshevism
and the contemporaneity of
socialism.

Mikhail Sergeevich Gorbachev 1931–
Soviet statesman: speech on the
seventieth anniversary of the Russian
Revolution, 2 November 1987

8 Russia has two generals in whom she
can confide—Generals Janvier
[January] and Février [February].

Nicholas I 1796–1855 Russian emperor:
attributed; *Punch* 10 March 1855

9 Moscow: those syllables can start
A tumult in the Russian heart.

Alexander Pushkin 1799–1837 Russian
poet: *Eugene Onegin* (1833)

10 Through reason Russia can't be
known,
No common yardstick can avail you:
She has a nature all her own —

Have faith in her, all else will fail you.
F. I. Tyutchev 1803–73 Russian writer:
'Through reason Russia can't be known'
(1866)

11 God of frostbite, God of famine,
beggars, cripples by the yard,
farms with no crops to examine—
that's him, that's your Russian God.
Prince Peter Vyazemsky 1792–1878
Russian poet: 'The Russian God' (1828)

12 Today is the last day of an era past.
*at a Berlin ceremony to end the Soviet
military presence in Germany*
Boris Yeltsin 1931–2007 Russian
statesman: in *Guardian* 1 September
1994

Sacrifice

see also SELF-INTEREST, SUFFERING

1 Greater love hath no man than this,
that a man lay down his life for his
friends.
Bible: St John

2 I have nothing to offer but blood,
toil, tears and sweat.
Winston Churchill 1874–1965 British
Conservative statesman: speech, House
of Commons, 13 May 1940

3 It is a far, far better thing that I do,
than I have ever done; it is a far, far
better rest that I go to, than I have
ever known.
*Sydney Carton's thoughts on the steps of the
guillotine, taking the place of Charles
Darnay whom he has smuggled out of
prison*
Charles Dickens 1812–70 English
novelist: *A Tale of Two Cities* (1859)

4 I gave my life for freedom — This I
know:
For those who bade me fight had told
me so.
William Norman Ewer 1885–1976
British writer: 'Five Souls' (1917)

5 She's the sort of woman who lives for
others—you can always tell the
others by their hunted expression.
C. S. Lewis 1898–1963 English literary
scholar: *The Screwtape Letters* (1942)

6 To gain that which is worth having, it
may be necessary to lose everything
else.
Bernadette Devlin McAliskey 1947–
Northern Irish politician: preface to *The
Price of My Soul* (1969)

7 I do not think you have ever realised
the shock, which the attitude you
took up caused your family and the
whole nation. It seemed
inconceivable to those who had
made such sacrifices during the war
that you, as their King, refused a
lesser sacrifice.
Queen Mary 1867–1953 British Queen
Consort: letter to the Duke of Windsor,
July 1938

8 A woman will always sacrifice herself
if you give her the opportunity. It is
her favourite form of self-
indulgence.
W. Somerset Maugham 1874–1965
English novelist: *The Circle* (1921)

9 Self-sacrifice enables us to sacrifice
other people without blushing.
George Bernard Shaw 1856–1950 Irish
dramatist: *Man and Superman* (1903)
'Maxims: Self-Sacrifice'

Saints

1 SAINT, *n.* A dead sinner revised and
edited.
Ambrose Bierce 1842–*c.*1914 American
writer: *The Devil's Dictionary* (1911)

2 Saints should always be judged
guilty until they are proved innocent.
George Orwell 1903–50 English
novelist: *Shooting an Elephant* (1950)
'Reflections on Gandhi'

3 If you can't bear the thought of messing up your nice clean soul, you'd better give up the whole idea of life and become a saint. Because you'll never make it as a human being. It's either this world or the next.

> **John Osborne** 1929–94 English dramatist: *Look Back in Anger* (1956)

4 It is easier to make a saint out of a libertine than out of a prig.

> **George Santayana** 1863–1952 Spanish-born philosopher and critic: *The Life of Reason* (1905)

5 The only difference between the saint and the sinner is that every saint has a past, and every sinner has a future.

> **Oscar Wilde** 1854–1900 Anglo-Irish dramatist and poet: *A Woman of No Importance* (1893)

Satire

see WIT AND SATIRE

Schools

see also CHILDREN, EDUCATION, TEACHING

1 The dread of beatings! Dread of being late!
And, greatest dread of all, the dread of games!

> **John Betjeman** 1906–84 English poet: *Summoned by Bells* (1960)

2 Forty years on, when afar and asunder
Parted are those who are singing to-day.

> **E. E. Bowen** 1836–1901 English schoolmaster: 'Forty Years On' (Harrow School Song, published 1886)

3 The day of the bog-standard comprehensive is over.

> **Alastair Campbell** 1957– British

journalist: press briefing, 12 February 2001

4 Headmasters have powers at their disposal with which Prime Ministers have never yet been invested.

> **Winston Churchill** 1874–1965 British Conservative statesman: *My Early Life* (1930)

5 You send your child to the schoolmaster, but 'tis the schoolboys who educate him.

> **Ralph Waldo Emerson** 1803–82 American philosopher and poet: *Conduct of Life* (1860)

6 The dawn of legibility in his handwriting has revealed his utter inability to spell.

> **Ian Hay** 1876–1952 Scottish novelist and dramatist: attributed; perhaps used in a dramatization of *The Housemaster* (1938)

7 As we read the school reports on our children we realize a sense of relief that . . . nobody is reporting in this fashion on us!

> **J. B. Priestley** 1894–1984 English novelist, dramatist, and critic: in *Reader's Digest* June 1964

8 Make the boy interested in natural history if you can; it is better than games.

> **Robert Falcon Scott** 1868–1912 English polar explorer: last letter to his wife, in *Scott's Last Expedition* (1913)

9 For every person who wants to teach there are approximately thirty who don't want to learn—much.

> **W. C. Sellar** 1898–1951 and **R. J. Yeatman** 1898–1968 British writers: *And Now All This* (1932)

10 I am putting old heads on your young shoulders . . . all my pupils are the crème de la crème.

> **Muriel Spark** 1918–2006 British novelist: *The Prime of Miss Jean Brodie* (1961)

Science

see also ARTS AND SCIENCES, BIOTECHNOLOGY, CHEMISTRY, EXPERIMENT, FACTS, INVENTIONS, LIFE SCIENCES, PHYSICS, RESEARCH, SCIENCE AND RELIGION, SCIENCE AND SOCIETY, TECHNOLOGY, THEORY

1 The aim of science is not to open the door to infinite wisdom, but to set a limit to infinite error.
   Bertolt Brecht 1898–1956 German dramatist: *Life of Galileo* (1939)

2 The scientific method, as far as it is a method, is nothing more than doing one's damnedest with one's mind, no holds barred.
   Percy Williams Bridgeman 1882–1961 American physicist: *Reflections of a Physicist* (1955)

3 The essence of science: ask an impertinent question, and you are on the way to a pertinent answer.
   Jacob Bronowski 1908–74 Polish-born mathematician and humanist: *The Ascent of Man* (1973)

4 In science the credit goes to the man who convinces the world, not to the man to whom the idea first occurs.
   Francis Darwin 1848–1925 English botanist: in *Eugenics Review* April 1914 'Francis Galton'

5 I ask you to look both ways. For the road to a knowledge of the stars leads through the atom; and important knowledge of the atom has been reached through the stars.
   Arthur Eddington 1882–1944 British astrophysicist: *Stars and Atoms* (1928)

6 The world looks so different after learning science. For example, trees are made of air, primarily. When they are burned, they go back to air, and in the flaming heat is released the flaming heat of the sun which was bound in to convert the air into tree.
   Richard Phillips Feynman 1918–88

American theoretical physicist: speech to the 15th annual meeting of the National Science Teachers Association, New York City, 1966

7 The importance of a scientific work can be measured by the number of previous publications it makes it superfluous to read.
   David Hilbert 1862–1943 German mathematician: attributed; Lewis Wolpert *The Unnatural Nature of Science* (1993)

8 Science is nothing but trained and organized common sense, differing from the latter only as a veteran may differ from a raw recruit: and its methods differ from those of common sense only as far as the guardsman's cut and thrust differ from the manner in which a savage wields his club.
   T. H. Huxley 1825–95 English biologist: *Collected Essays* (1893–4) 'The Method of Zadig'

9 When you can measure what you are speaking about, and express it in numbers, you know something about it; but when you cannot measure it, when you cannot express it in numbers, your knowledge is of a meagre and unsatisfactory kind: it may be the beginning of knowledge, but you have scarcely, in your thoughts, advanced to the stage of *science*, whatever the matter may be.
   often quoted as 'If you cannot measure it, then it is not science'
   Lord Kelvin 1824–1907 British scientist: 'Electrical Units of Measurement', lecture delivered 3 May 1883

10 Scientific truth should be presented in different forms, and should be regarded as equally scientific whether it appears in the robust form and the vivid colouring of a physical illustration, or in the tenuity

and paleness of a symbolic expression.

James Clerk Maxwell 1831–79 Scottish physicist: attributed

11 To mistrust science and deny the validity of the scientific method is to resign your job as a human. You'd better go look for work as a plant or wild animal.

P. J. O'Rourke 1947– American humorous writer: *Parliament of Whores* (1991)

12 There are no such things as applied sciences, only applications of science.

Louis Pasteur 1822–95 French chemist and bacteriologist: address, Lyons, 11 September 1872

13 A new scientific truth does not triumph by convincing its opponents and making them see the light, but rather because its opponents eventually die, and a new generation grows up that is familiar with it.

Max Planck 1858–1947 German physicist: *A Scientific Autobiography* (1949)

14 Science is built up of facts, as a house is built of stones; but an accumulation of facts is no more a science than a heap of stones is a house.

Henri Poincaré 1854–1912 French mathematician and philosopher: *Science and Hypothesis* (1905)

15 Nature, and Nature's laws lay hid in night.
God said, *Let Newton be!* and all was light.

Alexander Pope 1688–1744 English poet: 'Epitaph: Intended for Sir Isaac Newton' (1730); see SCIENCE 17

16 All science is either physics or stamp collecting.

Ernest Rutherford 1871–1937 New

Zealand physicist: J. B. Birks *Rutherford at Manchester* (1962)

17 It did not last: the Devil howling 'Ho! Let Einstein be!' restored the status quo.

J. C. Squire 1884–1958 English man of letters: 'In continuation of Pope on Newton' (1926); see SCIENCE 15

18 There is something fascinating about science. One gets such wholesale returns of conjecture out of such a trifling investment of fact.

Mark Twain 1835–1910 American writer: *Life on the Mississippi* (1883)

19 Science is a cemetery of dead ideas.

Miguel de Unamuno 1864–1937 Spanish philosopher and writer: *The Tragic Sense of Life* (1913)

Science and Religion

1 The atoms of Democritus
And Newton's particles of light
Are sands upon the Red sea shore
Where Israel's tents do shine so bright.

William Blake 1757–1827 English poet: *MS Note-Book*

2 We have grasped the mystery of the atom and rejected the Sermon on the Mount.

Omar Bradley 1893–1981 American general: speech on Armistice Day, 1948

3 Science without religion is lame, religion without science is blind.

Albert Einstein 1879–1955 German-born theoretical physicist: *Science, Philosophy and Religion: a Symposium* (1941)

4 In disputes about natural phenomena one must begin not with the authority of Scriptural passage but with sensory experience and necessary demonstrations. For the

Holy Scripture and nature derive equally from the Godhead, the former as the dictation of the Holy Spirit and the latter as the most obedient executrix of God's orders.

Galileo Galilei 1564–1642 Italian astronomer and physicist: letter to Christina Lotharinga, Archduchess of Tuscany

5 If ignorance of nature gave birth to the Gods, knowledge of nature is destined to destroy them.

Paul Henri, Baron d'Holbach 1723–89 French philosopher: *Système de la Nature* (1770)

6 I asserted—and I repeat—that a man has no reason to be ashamed of having an ape for his grandfather. If there were an ancestor whom I should feel shame in recalling it would rather be a *man*—a man of restless and versatile intellect—who, not content with an equivocal success in his own sphere of activity, plunges into scientific questions with which he has no real acquaintance, only to obscure them by an aimless rhetoric, and distract the attention of his hearers from the real point at issue by eloquent digressions and skilled appeals to religious prejudice.

replying to Bishop Samuel Wilberforce in the debate on Darwin's theory of evolution

T. H. Huxley 1825–95 English biologist: at a meeting of the British Association in Oxford, 30 June 1860; see LIFE SCIENCES 18

7 The means by which we live have outdistanced the ends for which we live. Our scientific power has outrun our spiritual power. We have guided missiles and misguided men.

Martin Luther King 1929–68 American civil rights leader: *Strength to Love* (1963)

8 The scientist who yields anything to theology, however slight, is yielding

to ignorance and false pretences, and as certainly as if he granted that a horse-hair put into a bottle of water will turn into a snake.

H. L. Mencken 1880–1956 American journalist and literary critic: *Minority Report* (1956)

9 The Buddha, the Godhead, resides quite as comfortably in the circuits of a digital computer or the gears of a cycle transmission as he does at the top of a mountain or in the petals of a flower.

Robert M. Pirsig 1928– American writer: *Zen and the Art of Motorcycle Maintenance* (1974)

10 Science is for the cultivation of religion, not for worldly enjoyment.

Sadi *c.*1213–91 Persian poet: *The Rose Garden* (1258)

11 How is it that hardly any major religion has looked at science and concluded, 'This is better than we thought! The Universe is much bigger than our prophets said, grander, more subtle, more elegant'?

Carl Sagan 1934–96 American astronomer: *Pale Blue Dot* (1995)

12 There is no evil in the atom; only in men's souls.

Adlai Stevenson 1900–65 American Democratic politician: speech at Hartford, Connecticut, 18 September 1952

Science and Society

see also BIOTECHNOLOGY

1 In science, we must be interested in things, not in persons.

Marie Curie 1867–1934 Polish-born French physicist: to an American journalist, *c.*1904; Eve Curie *Madame Curie* (1937)

2 One must divide one's time between politics and equations. But our

equations are much more important to me.

Albert Einstein 1879–1955 German-born theoretical physicist: C. P. Snow 'Einstein' in M. Goldsmith et al. (eds.) *Einstein* (1980)

3 Science is an integral part of culture. It's not this foreign thing, done by an arcane priesthood. It's one of the glories of human intellectual tradition.

Stephen Jay Gould 1941–2002 American palaeontologist: in *Independent* 24 January 1990

4 Science knows no country, because knowledge belongs to humanity.

Louis Pasteur 1822–95 French chemist and bacteriologist: toast at banquet of the International Congress of Sericulture, Milan, 1876, in Maurice B. Strauss *Familiar Medical Quotations* (1968)

5 I almost think it is the ultimate destiny of science to exterminate the human race.

Thomas Love Peacock 1785–1866 English novelist and poet: *Gryll Grange* (1861)

6 The priest persuades humble people to endure their hard lot; the politician urges them to rebel against it; and the scientist thinks of a method that does away with the hard lot altogether.

Max Perutz 1914–2002 Austrian-born scientist: *Is Science Necessary* (1989)

7 Every day I saw the huge material, intellectual and nervous resources of thousands of people being poured into the creation of a means of total destruction, something capable of annihilating all human civilization. I noticed that the control levers were in the hands of people who, though talented in their own ways, were cynical.

Andrei Sakharov 1921–89 Russian

nuclear physicist: *Sakharov Speaks* (1974)

Science Fiction

see also FANTASY

1 Science Fiction is no more written for scientists than ghost stories are written for ghosts.

Brian Aldiss 1925– English science fiction writer: introduction to *Penguin Science Fiction* (1962)

2 The only genuine consciousness-expanding drug.

on science fiction

Arthur C. Clarke 1917–2008 English science fiction writer: letter claiming coinage in *New Scientist* 2 April 1994

3 What you get in science fiction is what someone once called 'the view from a distant star'. It helps us to see our world from outside.

Frederik Pohl 1919– American science fiction writer: Stan Nicholls (ed.) *Wordsmiths of Wonder* (1993)

Scotland

1 O ye'll tak' the high road, and I'll tak' the low road,
And I'll be in Scotland afore ye,
But me and my true love will never meet again,
On the bonnie, bonnie banks o' Loch Lomon'.

Anonymous: 'The Bonnie Banks of Loch Lomon' (traditional song)

2 There are few more impressive sights in the world than a Scotsman on the make.

J. M. Barrie 1860–1937 Scottish writer and dramatist: *What Every Woman Knows* (1918)

3 Scotland, land of the omnipotent No.

Alan Bold 1943– Scottish poet: 'A Memory of Death' (1969)

4 My heart's in the Highlands, my
heart is not here;
My heart's in the Highlands
a-chasing the deer.
Robert Burns 1759–96 Scottish poet:
'My Heart's in the Highlands' (1790)

5 Scots, wha hae wi' Wallace bled,
Scots, wham Bruce has aften led,
Welcome to your gory bed,—
Or to victorie.
Robert Burns 1759–96 Scottish poet:
'Robert Bruce's March to Bannockburn'
(1799) (also known as 'Scots, Wha Hae')

6 I don't want a Stormont. I don't want
a wee pretendy government in
Edinburgh.
*on the prospective Scottish Parliament;
often quoted as 'a wee pretendy
Parliament'*
Billy Connolly 1942– Scottish
comedian: interview on *Breakfast with
Frost* (BBC TV), 9 February 1997

7 From the lone shieling of the misty
island
Mountains divide us, and the waste
of seas—
Yet still the blood is strong, the heart
is Highland,
And we in dreams behold the
Hebrides!
John Galt 1779–1839 Scottish writer:
'Canadian Boat Song' (1829); translated
from the Gaelic; attributed

8 The noblest prospect which a
Scotchman ever sees, is the high
road that leads him to England!
Samuel Johnson 1709–84 English poet,
critic, and lexicographer: James Boswell
Life of Samuel Johnson (1791) 6 July
1763

9 Who owns this landscape?
The millionaire who bought it or
the poacher staggering downhill in
the early morning
with a deer on his back?
Norman McCaig 1910–96 Scottish poet:
'A Man in Assynt' (1969)

10 Scotland small? Our multiform, our
infinite Scotland *small*?
Only as a patch of hillside may be a
cliché corner
To a fool who cries 'Nothing but
heather!' . . .
Hugh MacDiarmid 1892–1978 Scottish
poet and nationalist: *Direadh* 1 (1974)

11 O Caledonia! stern and wild,
Meet nurse for a poetic child!
Sir Walter Scott 1771–1832 Scottish
novelist and poet: *The Lay of the Last
Minstrel* (1805)

12 It's ill taking the breeks aff a wild
Highlandman.
Sir Walter Scott 1771–1832 Scottish
novelist and poet: *The Fortunes of Nigel*
(1822)

13 Stands Scotland where it did?
William Shakespeare 1564–1616
English dramatist: *Macbeth* (1606)

14 It's nae good blamin' it oan the
English fir colonising us. Ah don't
hate the English. They're just
wankers. We can't even pick a decent
vibrant, healthy culture to be
colonised by.
Irvine Welsh 1957– Scottish novelist:
Trainspotting (1994)

15 O flower of Scotland, when will we
see your like again,
that fought and died for your wee bit
hill and glen
and stood against him, proud
Edward's army,
and sent him homeward tae think
again.
unofficial Scottish Nationalist anthem
Roy Williamson 1936–90 Scottish
folksinger and musician: 'O Flower of
Scotland' (1968)

16 It is never difficult to distinguish
between a Scotsman with a
grievance and a ray of sunshine.
P. G. Wodehouse 1881–1975 English

writer: *Blandings Castle and Elsewhere* (1935)

Sculpture

see also ART

1 Why don't they stick to murder and leave art to us?
   on hearing that his statue of Lazarus in New College chapel, Oxford, kept Khrushchev awake at night
   Jacob Epstein 1880–1959 British sculptor: attributed

2 Carving is interrelated masses conveying an emotion: a perfect relationship between the mind and the colour, light and weight which is the stone, made by the hand which feels.
   Barbara Hepworth 1903–75 English sculptor: Herbert Read (ed.) *Unit One* (1934)

3 When smashing monuments, save the pedestals—they always come in handy.
   Stanislaw Lec 1909–66 Polish writer: *Unkempt Thoughts* (1962)

4 The marble not yet carved can hold the form
   Of every thought the greatest artist has.
   Michelangelo 1475–1564 Italian sculptor, painter, and architect: Sonnet 15

5 The first hole made through a piece of stone is a revelation.
   Henry Moore 1898–1986 English sculptor and draughtsman: in *Listener* 18 August 1937

The Sea

see also BOATS, NAVY

1 They that go down to the sea in ships: and occupy their business in great waters;

These men see the works of the Lord: and his wonders in the deep.
   Bible: Psalm 107

2 Roll on, thou deep and dark blue Ocean—roll!
   Ten thousand fleets sweep over thee in vain;
   Man marks the earth with ruin—his control
   Stops with the shore.
   Lord Byron 1788–1824 English poet: *Childe Harold's Pilgrimage* (1812–18)

3 Water, water, everywhere,
   And all the boards did shrink;
   Water, water, everywhere,
   Nor any drop to drink.
   Samuel Taylor Coleridge 1772–1834 English poet, critic, and philosopher: 'The Rime of the Ancient Mariner' (1798)

4 They didn't think much to the Ocean:
   The waves, they were fiddlin' and small,
   There was no wrecks and nobody drownded,
   Fact, nothing to laugh at at all.
   Marriott Edgar 1880–1951: 'The Lion and Albert' (1932)

5 The dragon-green, the luminous, the dark, the serpent-haunted sea.
   James Elroy Flecker 1884–1915 English poet: 'The Gates of Damascus' (1913)

6 The snotgreen sea. The scrotumtightening sea.
   James Joyce 1882–1941 Irish novelist: *Ulysses* (1922)

7 It is an interesting biological fact that all of us have in our veins the exact same percentage of salt in our blood that exists in the ocean, and therefore, we have salt in our blood, in our sweat, in our tears. We are tied to the ocean. And when we go back to the sea—whether it is to sail or to

watch it—we are going back from whence we came.

> **John F. Kennedy** 1917–63 American Democratic statesman: speech, Newport, Rhode Island, 14 September 1962

8 When you are up there, it's like trying to hang on to a telegraph pole in an earthquake.

> *90 feet up the mast of her boat* Kingfisher
> **Ellen MacArthur** 1976– English yachtswoman: in *Daily Telegraph* 16 February 2001

9 I must go down to the sea again, to the lonely sea and the sky,
And all I ask is a tall ship and a star to steer her by,
And the wheel's kick and the wind's song and the white sail's shaking,
And a grey mist on the sea's face and a grey dawn breaking.

> **John Masefield** 1878–1967 English poet: 'Sea Fever'; 'I must down to the seas' in the original of 1902, possibly a misprint

10 Meditation and water are wedded for ever.

> **Herman Melville** 1819–91 American novelist and poet: *Moby Dick* (1851)

11 It [the Channel] is a mere ditch, and will be crossed as soon as someone has the courage to attempt it.

> **Napoleon I** 1769–1821 French emperor: letter to Consul Cambacérès, 16 November 1803

12 The sea hates a coward!

> **Eugene O'Neill** 1888–1953 American dramatist: *Mourning becomes Electra* (1931)

13 The sea has such extraordinary moods that sometimes you feel this is the only sort of life—and 10 minutes later you're praying for death.

> **Prince Philip, Duke of Edinburgh** 1921– husband of Elizabeth II: in *Independent* 31 December 1998

14 Whosoever commands the sea commands the trade; whosoever commands the trade of the world commands the riches of the world, and consequently the world itself.

> **Walter Ralegh** *c.*1552–1618 English explorer and courtier: 'A Discourse of the Invention of Ships, Anchors, Compass, &c.'

15 The sea is as near as we come to another world.

> **Anne Stevenson** 1933– English poet: 'North Sea off Carnoustie' (1977)

16 'A man who is not afraid of the sea will soon be drownded,' he said 'for he will be going out on a day he shouldn't. But we do be afraid of the sea, and we do only be drownded now and again.'

> **John Millington Synge** 1871–1909 Irish dramatist: *The Aran Islands* (1907)

17 Break, break, break,
On thy cold grey stones, O Sea!
And I would that my tongue could utter
The thoughts that arise in me.

> **Alfred, Lord Tennyson** 1809–92 English poet: 'Break, Break, Break' (1842)

18 Rocked in the cradle of the deep.

> **Emma Hart Willard** 1787–1870 American pioneer of women's education: title of song (1840), inspired by a prospect of the Bristol Channel

Secrecy

1 A Company for carrying on an undertaking of Great Advantage, but no one to know what it is.

> **Anonymous**: Company Prospectus at the time of the South Sea Bubble (1711)

2 I shall be but a short time tonight. I have seldom spoken with greater regret, for my lips are not yet unsealed. Were these troubles over I

would make a case, and I guarantee that not a man would go into the lobby against us.

on the Abyssinian crisis; usually quoted as 'My lips are sealed'

> **Stanley Baldwin** 1867–1947 British Conservative statesman: speech, House of Commons, 10 December 1935

3 Let not thy left hand know what thy right hand doeth.

> **Bible**: St Matthew

4 Secrecy lies at the very core of power.

> **Elias Canetti** 1905–94 Bulgarian-born writer and novelist: *Crowds and Power* (1960)

5 After the first silence the small man said to the other: 'Where does a wise man hide a pebble?' And the tall man answered in a low voice: 'On the beach.' The small man nodded, and after a short silence said: 'Where does a wise man hide a leaf?' And the other answered: 'In the forest.'

> **G. K. Chesterton** 1874–1936 English essayist, novelist, and poet: *The Innocence of Father Brown* (1911)

6 The best leaks always take place in the urinal.

> **John Cole** 1927– Northern Irish journalist and broadcaster: in *Independent* 3 June 1996

7 I know that's a secret, for it's whispered every where.

> **William Congreve** 1670–1729 English dramatist: *Love for Love* (1695)

8 Secrets with girls, like loaded guns with boys,
Are never valued till they make a noise.

> **George Crabbe** 1754–1832 English poet: *Tales of the Hall* (1819) 'The Maid's Story'

9 We never knows wot's hidden in each other's hearts; and if we had glass winders there, we'd need keep the

shutters up, some on us, I do assure you!

> **Charles Dickens** 1812–70 English novelist: *Martin Chuzzlewit* (1844)

10 I would not open windows into men's souls.

> **Elizabeth I** 1533–1603 English monarch: oral tradition, the words very possibly originating in a letter drafted by Bacon; J. B. Black *Reign of Elizabeth 1558–1603* (1936)

11 A secret in the Oxford sense: you may tell it to only one person at a time.

> **Lord Franks** 1905–92 British philosopher and administrator: in *Sunday Telegraph* 30 January 1977

12 We dance round in a ring and suppose,
But the Secret sits in the middle and knows.

> **Robert Frost** 1874–1963 American poet: 'The Secret Sits' (1942)

13 Once the toothpaste is out of the tube, it is awfully hard to get it back in.

on the Watergate affair

> **H. R. Haldeman** 1929–93 Presidential assistant to Richard Nixon: to John Dean, 8 April 1973

14 And whatsoever I shall see or hear in the course of my profession, as well as outside my profession in my intercourse with men, if it be what should not be published abroad, I will never divulge holding such things to be holy secrets.

> **Hippocrates** c.460–357 BC Greek physician: *The Hippocratic Oath*

15 Stolen sweets are always sweeter,
Stolen kisses much completer,
Stolen looks are nice in chapels,
Stolen, stolen, be your apples.

> **Leigh Hunt** 1784–1859 English poet and essayist: 'Song of Fairies Robbing an Orchard' (1830)

16 Nothing weighs so heavy as a secret; women find it difficult to carry one far. And I know a lot of men who are just like women about this.

> **Jean de la Fontaine** 1621–95 French poet: *Fables* bk. 8 (1678–9) 'The Women and the Secret'

17 That's another of those irregular verbs, isn't it? I give confidential briefings; you leak; he has been charged under Section 2a of the Official Secrets Act.

> **Jonathan Lynn** 1943– and **Antony Jay** 1930– English writers: *Yes Prime Minister* (1987) vol. 2 'Man Overboard'

18 It is wise to disclose what cannot be concealed.

> **Friedrich von Schiller** 1759–1805 German dramatist and poet: *Don Carlos* (1787)

19 A secret may be sometimes best kept by keeping the secret of its being a secret.

> **Henry Taylor** 1800–86 English poet and public servant: *The Statesman* (1836)

Security

see also RISK

1 In my view, stability is a sexy thing.

> **Tony Blair** 1953– British Labour statesman: in *The Week* 28 November 1998

2 Security is when everything is settled, when nothing can happen to you; security is the denial of life.

> **Germaine Greer** 1939– Australian feminist: *The Female Eunuch* (1970)

3 Security is mostly a superstition. It does not exist in nature, nor do the children of men as a whole experience it. Avoiding danger is no safer in the long run than outright exposure. Life is either a daring adventure, or nothing.

> **Helen Keller** 1880–1968 American

writer and social reformer: *The Open Door* (1957)

4 He had grown up in a country run by politicians who sent the pilots to man the bombers to kill the babies to make the world safer for children to grow up in.

> **Ursula K. Le Guin** 1929– American writer: *The Lathe of Heaven* (1971)

Seduction

see also SEX

1 He said it was artificial respiration, but now I find I am to have his child.

> **Anthony Burgess** 1917–93 English novelist and critic: *Inside Mr Enderby* (1963)

2 A little still she strove, and much repented,
And whispering 'I will ne'er consent'—consented.

> **Lord Byron** 1788–1824 English poet: *Don Juan* (1819–24)

3 Seduction is often difficult to distinguish from rape. In seduction, the rapist bothers to buy a bottle of wine.

> **Andrea Dworkin** 1946–2005 American feminist and writer: speech to women at *Harper & Row*, 1976; in *Letters from a War Zone* (1988)

4 He in a few minutes ravished this fair creature, or at least would have ravished her, if she had not, by a timely compliance, prevented him.

> **Henry Fielding** 1707–54 English novelist and dramatist: *Jonathan Wild* (1743)

5 Pursuit and seduction are the essence of sexuality. It's part of the sizzle.

> **Camille Paglia** 1947– American writer and critic: in *Playboy* October 1991

The Self

see also INDIVIDUALITY, SELF-KNOWLEDGE

1 Whatever you are is never enough;
you must find a way to accept
something however small from the
other to make you whole.
> **Chinua Achebe** 1930– Nigerian
> novelist: *Anthills of the Savannah* (1987)

2 My one regret in life is that I am not
someone else.
> **Woody Allen** 1935– American film
> director, writer, and actor: Eric Lax
> *Woody Allen and his Comedy* (1975)

3 The image of myself which I try to
create in my own mind in order that I
may love myself is very different
from the image which I try to create
in the minds of others in order that
they may love me.
> **W. H. Auden** 1907–73 English poet: *The
> Dyer's Hand* (1963) 'Hic et Ille'

4 Some thirty inches from my nose
The frontier of my Person goes,
And all the untilled air between
Is private *pagus* or demesne.
Stranger, unless with bedroom eyes
I beckon you to fraternize,
Beware of rudely crossing it:
I have no gun, but I can spit.
> **W. H. Auden** 1907–73 English poet:
> 'Prologue: the Birth of Architecture'
> (1966)

5 In the greatest confusion there is still
an open channel to the soul. It may
be difficult to find because by midlife
it is overgrown, and some of the
wildest thickets that surround it
grow out of what we describe as our
education. But the channel is always
there, and it is our business to keep it
open, to have access to the deepest
part of ourselves.
> **Saul Bellow** 1915–2005 American
> novelist: Allan Bloom *The Closing of the
> American Mind* (1987)

6 Through the Thou a person becomes
I.
> **Martin Buber** 1878–1965 Austrian-born
> religious philosopher: *Ich und Du*
> (1923)

7 The men who really believe in
themselves are all in lunatic asylums.
> **G. K. Chesterton** 1874–1936 English
> essayist, novelist, and poet: *Orthodoxy*
> (1908)

8 I am—yet what I am, none cares or
knows;
My friends forsake me like a memory
lost:
I am the self-consumer of my woes.
> **John Clare** 1793–1864 English poet: 'I
> Am' (1848)

9 We are all serving a life-sentence in
the dungeon of self.
> **Cyril Connolly** 1903–74 English writer:
> *The Unquiet Grave* (1944)

10 'You' your joys and your sorrows,
your memories and ambitions, your
sense of personal identity and free
will, are in fact no more than the
behaviour of a vast assembly of
nerve cells and their associated
molecules.
> **Francis Crick** 1916–2004 English
> biophysicist: *The Astonishing
> Hypothesis: The Scientific Search for the
> Soul* (1994)

11 But I do nothing upon my self, and
yet I am mine own *Executioner*.
> **John Donne** 1572–1631 English poet
> and divine: *Devotions upon Emergent
> Occasions* (1624)

12 The worth of a soul cannot be told.
> **Olaudah Equiano** *c.*1745–*c.*97 African
> writer and former slave: *Narrative of the
> Life of Olaudah Equiano* (1789)

13 It matters not how strait the gate,
How charged with punishments the
scroll,
I am the master of my fate:

I am the captain of my soul.
W. E. Henley 1849–1903 English poet and dramatist: 'Invictus. In Memoriam R.T.H.B.' (1888)

14 If I am not for myself who is for me; and being for my own self what am I? If not now when?
Hillel 'The Elder' *c*.60 BC–*c*.AD 9 Jewish scholar and teacher: *Pirqe Aboth*

15 It is not contrary to reason to prefer the destruction of the whole world to the scratching of my finger.
David Hume 1711–76 Scottish philosopher: *A Treatise upon Human Nature* (1739)

16 He that overvalues himself will undervalue others, and he that undervalues others will oppress them.
Samuel Johnson 1709–84 English poet, critic, and lexicographer: Sermon 6

17 I am not a number, I am a free man!
Patrick McGoohan 1928–2009 American actor: Number Six, in *The Prisoner* (TV series 1967–68)

18 A man should keep for himself a little back shop, all his own, quite unadulterated, in which he establishes his true freedom and chief place of seclusion and solitude.
Montaigne 1533–92 French moralist and essayist: *Essays* (1580)

19 Every man's ordure well to his own sense doth smell.
Montaigne 1533–92 French moralist and essayist: *Essays* (1580, Florio's translation of 1603), quoting the Latin of Erasmus (1469–1536)

20 When a man points a finger at someone else, he should remember that four of his fingers are pointing to himself.
Louis Nizer 1902–94 British-born American lawyer: *My Life in Court* (1963)

21 I am I plus my surroundings, and if I do not preserve the latter I do not preserve myself.
José Ortega y Gasset 1883–1955 Spanish writer and philosopher: *Meditaciones del Quijote* (1914)

22 The self is hateful.
Blaise Pascal 1623–62 French mathematician, physicist, and moralist: *Pensées* (1670)

23 The whole human way of life has been destroyed and ruined. All that's left is the bare, shivering human soul, stripped to the last shred, the naked force of the human psyche for which nothing has changed because it was always cold and shivering and reaching out to its nearest neighbour, as cold and lonely as itself.
Boris Pasternak 1890–1960 Russian novelist and poet: *Doctor Zhivago* (1958)

24 Personal isn't the same as important.
Terry Pratchett 1948– English science fiction writer: *Men at Arms* (1993)

25 This above all: to thine own self be true,
And it must follow, as the night the day,
Thou canst not then be false to any man.
William Shakespeare 1564–1616 English dramatist: *Hamlet* (1601)

26 Whatever people think I am or say I am, that's what I'm not.
Alan Sillitoe 1928– English writer: *Saturday Night and Sunday Morning* (1958)

27 Rose is a rose is a rose is a rose, is a rose.
Gertrude Stein 1874–1946 American writer: *Sacred Emily* (1913)

28 Each had his past shut in him like the leaves of a book known to him by

heart; and his friends could only read the title.

> **Virginia Woolf** 1882–1941 English novelist: *Jacob's Room* (1922)

Self-Esteem and Assertiveness

see also HUMILITY, PRIDE

1 I'm the greatest.

> **Muhammad Ali** 1942– American boxer: catch-phrase used from 1962, in *Louisville Times* 16 November 1962

2 His opinion of himself, having once risen, remained at 'set fair'.

> **Arnold Bennett** 1867–1931 English novelist: *The Card* (1911)

3 Anything you can do, I can do better, I can do anything better than you.

> **Irving Berlin** 1888–1989 American songwriter: 'Anything You Can Do' (1946 song)

4 That's it baby, when you got it, flaunt it.

> **Mel Brooks** 1926– American film director and actor: *The Producers* (1968 film)

5 How shall we expect charity towards others when we are uncharitable to ourselves?

> **Sir Thomas Browne** 1605–82 English writer and physician: *Religio Medici* (1643)

6 I know of no case where a man added to his dignity by standing on it.

> **Winston Churchill** 1874–1965 British Conservative statesman: attributed

7 Pretentious? *Moi*?

> **John Cleese** 1939– and **Connie Booth**: *Fawlty Towers* 'The Psychiatrist' (BBC TV programme, 1979)

8 You must stir it and stump it, And blow your own trumpet,

Or trust me, you haven't a chance.

> **W. S. Gilbert** 1836–1911 English writer of comic and satirical verse: *Ruddigore* (1887)

9 It's easy to be independent when you've got money. But to be independent when you haven't got a thing—that's the Lord's test.

> **Mahalia Jackson** 1911–72 American singer: *Movin' On Up* (with Evan McLoud Wylie 1966)

10 Shyness is egotism out of its depth.

> **Penelope Keith** 1940– British actress: in *Daily Mail* 27 June 1988

11 Our mistreatment was just not right, and I was tired of it.

> *of her refusal, on 1 December 1955, to surrender her seat on a segregated bus in Alabama to a white man*
> **Rosa Parks** 1913–2005 American civil rights activist: *Quiet Strength* (1994)

12 He fell in love with himself at first sight and it is a passion to which he has always remained faithful.

> **Anthony Powell** 1905–2000 English novelist: *The Acceptance World* (1955)

13 No one can make you feel inferior without your consent.

> **Eleanor Roosevelt** 1884–1962 American humanitarian and diplomat: in *Catholic Digest* August 1960

14 It is easy—terribly easy— to shake a man's faith in himself. To take advantage of that to break a man's spirit is devil's work.

> **George Bernard Shaw** 1856–1950 Irish dramatist: *Candida* (1898)

15 I have often wished I had time to cultivate modesty . . . But I am too busy thinking about myself.

> **Edith Sitwell** 1887–1964 English poet and critic: in *Observer* 30 April 1950

16 As for conceit, what man will do any good who is not conceited? Nobody

holds a good opinion of a man who
has a low opinion of himself.
> **Anthony Trollope** 1815–82 English
> novelist: *Orley Farm* (1862)

17 Our deepest fear is not that we are
inadequate. Our deepest fear is that
we are powerful beyond measure. It
is our light, not our darkness, that
most frightens us.
> **Marianne Williamson** 1953– American
> writer and philanthropist: *A Return to
> Love* (1992)

Self-Interest

see also SACRIFICE

1 And this is law, I will maintain,
Unto my dying day, Sir,
That whatsoever King shall reign,
I will be the Vicar of Bray, sir!
> **Anonymous**: 'The Vicar of Bray'
> (1734 song)

2 Men are nearly always willing to
believe what they wish.
> **Julius Caesar** 100–44 BC Roman general
> and statesman: *De Bello Gallico*

3 It's the first time in recorded history
that turkeys have been known to
vote for an early Christmas.
*on the collapse of the pact between Labour
and the Liberals*
> **James Callaghan** 1912–2005 British
> Labour statesman: in the House of
> Commons, 28 March 1979

4 We are all special cases. We all want
to appeal against something!
> **Albert Camus** 1913–60 French novelist,
> dramatist, and essayist: *La Chute* (1956)

5 *Cui bono?*
To whose profit?
> **Cicero** 106–43 BC Roman orator and
> statesman: *Pro Roscio Amerino*; quoting
> L. Cassius Longinus Ravilla

6 All sensible people are selfish, and
nature is tugging at every contract to
make the terms of it fair.
> **Ralph Waldo Emerson** 1803–82
> American philosopher and poet: *The
> Conduct of Life* (1860)

7 Every man, in his own opinion,
forms an exception to the ordinary
rules of morality.
> **William Hazlitt** 1778–1830 English
> essayist: *Characteristics* (1823)

8 Fourteen heart attacks and he had to
die in my week. In MY week.
*when ex-President Eisenhower's death
prevented her photograph appearing on
the cover of* Newsweek
> **Janis Joplin** 1943–70 American singer:
> in *New Musical Express* 12 April 1969

9 He would, wouldn't he?
*on being told that Lord Astor claimed that
her allegations, concerning himself and his
house parties at Cliveden, were untrue*
> **Mandy Rice-Davies** 1944– English
> model and showgirl: at the trial of
> Stephen Ward, 29 June 1963

10 We are now in the Me
Decade—seeing the upward roll
of . . . the third great religious wave
in American history . . . and this one
has the mightiest, holiest roll of all,
the beat that goes . . . *Me . . . Me . . .
Me . . . Me.*
> **Tom Wolfe** 1931– American writer:
> *Mauve Gloves and Madmen* (1976)

Self-Knowledge

see also SELF

1 Know thyself.
> **Anonymous**: inscribed on the temple of
> Apollo at Delphi; Plato ascribes the
> saying to the Seven Wise Men

2 Between the ages of twenty and forty
we are engaged in the process of
discovering who we are, which

involves learning the difference between accidental limitations which it is our duty to outgrow and the necessary limitations of our nature beyond which we cannot trespass with impunity.

> **W. H. Auden** 1907–73 English poet: *The Dyer's Hand* (1963) 'Reading'

3 The tragedy of a man who has found himself out.

> **J. M. Barrie** 1860–1937 Scottish writer and dramatist: *What Every Woman Knows* (1918)

4 The one self-knowledge worth having is to know one's own mind.

> **F. H. Bradley** 1846–1924 English philosopher: *Appearance and Reality* (1893)

5 No, when the fight begins within himself,
A man's worth something.

> **Robert Browning** 1812–89 English poet: 'Bishop Blougram's Apology' (1855)

6 O wad some Pow'r the giftie gie us
To see oursels as others see us!
It wad frae mony a blunder free us,
And foolish notion.

> **Robert Burns** 1759–96 Scottish poet: 'To a Louse' (1786)

7 How little do we know that which we are!
How less what we may be!

> **Lord Byron** 1788–1824 English poet: *Don Juan* (1819–24)

8 To study the self is to forget the self.
To forget the self is to be authenticated by the myriad things.
often quoted as ' . . . to become one with the ten thousand things'

> **Dogen Kigen** 1200–53 Japanese Buddhist monk: William R. LaFleur (ed.) *Dogen Studies* (1985)

9 I do not know myself, and God forbid that I should.

> **Johann Wolfgang von Goethe**

1749–1832 German poet, novelist, and dramatist: J. P. Eckermann *Gespräche mit Goethe* (1836–48) 10 April 1829

10 He who knows others is wise;
He who knows himself is enlightened.
He who conquers others has physical strength.
He who conquers himself is strong.

> **Lao Tzu** *c.*604–*c.*531 BC Chinese philosopher: *Tao-te Ching*

11 There are few things more painful than to recognise one's own faults in others.

> **John Wells** 1936– British actor, comedian, and writer: in *Observer* 23 May 1982

12 At thirty a man suspects himself a fool;
Knows it at forty, and reforms his plan;
At fifty chides his infamous delay,
Pushes his prudent purpose to resolve;
In all the magnanimity of thought
Resolves; and re-resolves; then dies the same.

> **Edward Young** 1683–1765 English poet and dramatist: *Night Thoughts* (1742–5)

13 I do not know whether I was then a man dreaming I was a butterfly, or whether I am now a butterfly dreaming I am a man.

> **Zhuangzi** *c.*369–286 BC Chinese philosopher: *Chuang Tzu* (1889)

The Senses

see also BODY

1   Any nose
May ravage with impunity a rose.

> **Robert Browning** 1812–89 English poet: *Sordello* (1840)

2 By convention there is colour, by convention sweetness, by

convention bitterness, but in reality there are atoms and space.
Democritus c.460–c.370 BC Greek philosopher: fragment 125

3 Friday I tasted life. It was a vast morsel. A Circus passed the house—still I feel the red in my mind though the drums are out. The Lawn is full of south and the odours tangle, and I hear to-day for the first time the river in the tree.
Emily Dickinson 1830–86 American poet: letter to Mrs J. G. Holland, May 1866

4 You see, but you do not observe.
Arthur Conan Doyle 1859–1930 Scottish-born writer of detective fiction: *The Adventures of Sherlock Holmes* (1892)

5 The important thing is not the camera but the eye.
Alfred Eisenstaedt 1898–1995 German-born American photographer: in *New York Times* 26 September 1994

6 Eyes and ears are bad witnesses to men if they have souls that understand not their language.
often quoted as '. . . poor witnesses to people if they have uncultured souls'
Heraclitus c.540–c.480 BC Greek philosopher: fragment 42 in H. Ritter and L. Preller *Historia Philosophiae Graecae* (1898)

7 Whatever withdraws us from the power of our senses; whatever makes the past, the distant, or the future predominate over the present, advances us in the dignity of thinking beings.
Samuel Johnson 1709–84 English poet, critic, and lexicographer: *A Journey to the Western Islands of Scotland* (1775)

8 O for a life of sensations rather than of thoughts!
John Keats 1795–1821 English poet: letter to Benjamin Bailey, 22 November 1817

9 Fortissimo at last!
on seeing Niagara Falls
Gustav Mahler 1860–1911 Austrian composer: K. Blaukopf *Gustav Mahler* (1973)

10 I test my bath before I sit,
And I'm always moved to wonderment
That what chills the finger not a bit
Is so frigid upon the fundament.
Ogden Nash 1902–71 American humorist: 'Samson Agonistes' (1942)

11 Each day I live in a glass room
Unless I break it with the thrusting
Of my senses and pass through
The splintered walls to the great landscape.
Mervyn Peake 1911–68 British novelist, poet, and artist: 'Each day I live in a glass room' (1967)

12 Is this a dagger which I see before me,
The handle toward my hand? Come, let me clutch thee:
I have thee not, and yet I see thee still.
William Shakespeare 1564–1616 English dramatist: *Macbeth* (1606)

Sex

see also CELIBACY, HOMOSEXUALITY, LESBIANISM, LOVE, MARRIAGE, MASTURBATION, PORNOGRAPHY, RELATIONSHIPS, SEDUCTION

1 Is sex dirty? Only if it's done right.
Woody Allen 1935– American film director, writer, and actor: *Everything You Always Wanted to Know about Sex* (1972 film)

2 That [sex] was the most fun I ever had without laughing.
Woody Allen 1935– American film director, writer, and actor: *Annie Hall* (1977 film, with Marshall Brickman)

3 On bisexuality: It immediately doubles your chances for a date on Saturday night.

> **Woody Allen** 1935– American film director, writer, and actor: in *New York Times* 1 December 1975

4 Give me chastity and continency—but not yet!

> **St Augustine of Hippo** AD 354–430 Early Christian theologian: *Confessions* (AD 397–8)

5 I don't know what I am, darling. I've tried several varieties of sex. The conventional position makes me claustrophobic. And the others give me either stiff neck or lockjaw.

> **Tallulah Bankhead** 1903–68 American actress: Lee Israel *Miss Tallulah Bankhead* (1972)

6 *at the age of ninety-seven, Blake was asked at what age the sex drive goes:*
You'll have to ask somebody older than me.

> **Eubie Blake** 1883–1983 American ragtime pianist: in *Ned Sherrin in his Anecdotage* (1993)

7 It doesn't matter what you do in the bedroom as long as you don't do it in the street and frighten the horses.

> **Mrs Patrick Campbell** 1865–1940 English actress: Daphne Fielding *The Duchess of Jermyn Street* (1964)

8 The pleasure is momentary, the position ridiculous, and the expense damnable.

> **Lord Chesterfield** 1694–1773 English writer and politician: attributed

9 I have never yet seen anyone whose desire to build up his moral power was as strong as sexual desire.

> **Confucius** 551–479 BC Chinese philosopher: *Analects*

10 License my roving hands, and let them go,
Behind, before, above, between, below.

O my America, my new found land,
My kingdom, safeliest when with one man manned.

> **John Donne** 1572–1631 English poet and divine: 'To His Mistress Going to Bed' (*c.*1595)

11 I'll have what she's having.

> *woman to waiter, seeing Sally acting an orgasm*

> **Nora Ephron** 1941– American writer and journalist: *When Harry Met Sally* (1989 film)

12 Personally I know nothing about sex because I've always been married.

> **Zsa Zsa Gabor** 1919– Hungarian-born film actress: in *Observer* 16 August 1987

13 But did thee feel the earth move?

> **Ernest Hemingway** 1899–1961 American novelist: *For Whom the Bell Tolls* (1940)

14 When I hear his steps outside my door I lie down on my bed, close my eyes, open my legs, and think of England.

> **Lady Hillingdon** 1857–1940: diary 1912 (original untraced, perhaps apocryphal); J. Gathorne-Hardy *The Rise and Fall of the British Nanny* (1972)

15 I'll come no more behind your scenes, David; for the silk stockings and white bosoms of your actresses excite my amorous propensities.

> **Samuel Johnson** 1709–84 English poet, critic, and lexicographer: James Boswell *Life of Samuel Johnson* (1791) 1750

16 The only unnatural sex act is that which you cannot perform.

> **Alfred Kinsey** 1894–1956 American zoologist and sex researcher: attributed; in *Time* 21 January 1966

17 'Tisn't beauty, so to speak, nor good talk necessarily. It's just It. Some

women'll stay in a man's memory if they once walked down a street.
> **Rudyard Kipling** 1865–1936 English writer and poet: *Traffics and Discoveries* (1904)

18 Sexual intercourse began
In nineteen sixty-three
(Which was rather late for me) —
Between the end of the *Chatterley* ban
And the Beatles' first LP.
> **Philip Larkin** 1922–85 English poet: 'Annus Mirabilis' (1974)

19   While we think of it, and talk of it
Let us leave it alone, physically, keep apart.
For while we have sex in the mind, we truly have none in the body.
> **D. H. Lawrence** 1885–1930 English novelist and poet: 'Leave Sex Alone' (1929)

20 There is nothing safe about sex. There never will be.
> **Norman Mailer** 1923–2007 American novelist and essayist: in *International Herald Tribune* 24 January 1992

21 The Duke returned from the wars today and did pleasure me in his top-boots.
> **Sarah, Duchess of Marlborough** 1660–1744: oral tradition, attributed in various forms

22 Continental people have sex life; the English have hot-water bottles.
> **George Mikes** 1912–87 Hungarian-born writer: *How to be an Alien* (1946)

23 The orgasm has replaced the Cross as the focus of longing and the image of fulfilment.
> **Malcolm Muggeridge** 1903–90 British journalist: *Tread Softly* (1966)

24 Lolita, light of my life, fire of my loins. My sin, my soul.
> **Vladimir Nabokov** 1899–1977 Russian novelist: *Lolita* (1955)

25 Not tonight, Josephine.
> **Napoleon I** 1769–1821 French emperor: attributed, but probably apocryphal

26 Love is two minutes fifty-two seconds of squishing noises.
> **Johnny Rotten** 1957–   British rock singer: in *Daily Mirror*, 1983

27 Is it not strange that desire should so many years outlive performance?
> **William Shakespeare** 1564–1616 English dramatist: *Henry IV, Part 2* (1597)

28 Someone asked Sophocles, 'How is your sex-life now? Are you still able to have a woman?' He replied, 'Hush, man; most gladly indeed am I rid of it all, as though I had escaped from a mad and savage master.'
> **Sophocles** *c.*496–406 BC Greek dramatist: Plato *Republic*

29 Traditionally, sex has been a very private, secretive activity. Herein perhaps lies its powerful force for uniting people in a strong bond. As we make sex less secretive, we may rob it of its power to hold men and women together.
> **Thomas Szasz** 1920–   Hungarian-born psychiatrist: *The Second Sin* (1973)

30 Give a man a free hand and he'll try to put it all over you.
> **Mae West** 1892–1980 American film actress: *Klondike Annie* (1936 film)

31 Is that a gun in your pocket, or are you just glad to see me?
usually quoted as 'Is that a pistol in your pocket . . . '
> **Mae West** 1892–1980 American film actress: Joseph Weintraub *Peel Me a Grape* (1975)

William Shakespeare

1 Others abide our question. Thou art free.

We ask and ask: Thou smilest and art still,
Out-topping knowledge.
  Matthew Arnold 1822–88 English poet and essayist: 'Shakespeare' (1849)

2 Shakespeare is so tiring. You never get a chance to sit down unless you're a king.
  Josephine Hull ?1886–1957 American actress: in *Time* 16 November 1953

3 He was not of an age, but for all time!
  Ben Jonson c.1573–1637 English dramatist and poet: 'To the Memory of My Beloved, the Author, Mr William Shakespeare' (1623)

4 Thou hadst small Latin, and less Greek.
  Ben Jonson c.1573–1637 English dramatist and poet: 'To the Memory of My Beloved, the Author, Mr William Shakespeare' (1623)

5 When I read Shakespeare I am struck with wonder
That such trivial people should muse and thunder
In such lovely language.
  D. H. Lawrence 1885–1930 English novelist and poet: 'When I Read Shakespeare' (1929)

6 Shakespeare—the nearest thing in incarnation to the eye of God.
  Laurence Olivier 1907–89 English actor and director: in *Kenneth Harris Talking To* (1971) 'Sir Laurence Olivier'

7 Brush up your Shakespeare,
Start quoting him now.
Brush up your Shakespeare
And the women you will wow.
  Cole Porter 1891–1964 American songwriter: 'Brush Up your Shakespeare' (1948 song)

8 With the single exception of Homer, there is no eminent writer, not even Sir Walter Scott, whom I can despise so entirely as I despise Shakespeare

when I measure my mind against his.
  George Bernard Shaw 1856–1950 Irish dramatist: in *Saturday Review* 26 September 1896

9 Scorn not the Sonnet; Critic, you have frowned,
Mindless of its just honours; with this key
Shakespeare unlocked his heart.
  William Wordsworth 1770–1850 English poet: 'Scorn not the Sonnet' (1827)

Shopping

see also CONSUMER SOCIETY

1 We used to build civilizations. Now we build shopping malls.
  Bill Bryson 1951– American travel writer: *Neither Here Nor There* (1991)

2 Pile it high, sell it cheap.
  John Cohen 1898–1979 British businessman: slogan associated with his company Tesco

3 What peaches and what penumbras! Whole families shopping at night! Aisles full of husbands! Wives in the avocados, babies in the tomatoes!—and you, Garcia Lorca what were you doing down by the watermelons?
  Allen Ginsberg 1926–97 American poet and novelist: 'A Supermarket in California' (1956)

4 The car, the furniture, the wife, the children—everything has to be disposable. Because you see the main thing today is—shopping.
  Arthur Miller 1915–2005 American dramatist: *The Price* (1968)

5 Buying is much more American than thinking and I'm as American as they come.
  Andy Warhol 1927–87 American artist: *Philosophy of Andy Warhol* (*From A to B and Back Again*) (1975)

Sickness

see also AIDS, ALZHEIMER'S, CANCER, HEALTH, MEDICINE, MENTAL ILLNESS

1 I know the colour rose, and it is
  lovely,
  But not when it ripens in a tumour;
  And healing greens, leaves and grass,
    so springlike,
  In limbs that fester are not
    springlike.
    Dannie Abse 1923– Welsh-born doctor
    and poet: 'Pathology of Colours' (1968)

2 A man's illness is his private territory
  and, no matter how much he loves
  you and how close you are, you stay
  an outsider. You are healthy.
    Lauren Bacall 1924– American actress:
    By Myself (1978)

3 'Ye can call it influenza if ye like,' said
  Mrs Machin. 'There was no influenza
  in my young days. We called a cold a
  cold.'
    Arnold Bennett 1867–1931 English
    novelist: *The Card* (1911)

4 All diseases run into one, old age.
    Ralph Waldo Emerson 1803–82
    American philosopher and poet:
    Journals, 1840

5 It's all about losing your brain
  without losing your mind.
  on his fight against Parkinson's disease
    Michael J. Fox 1961– Canadian actor:
    in *The Times* 16 September 2000

6 When two pains occur together, but
  not in the same place, the more
  violent obscures the other.
    Hippocrates *c.*460–357 BC Greek
    physician: *Aphorisms*

7 It is a most extraordinary thing, but I
  never read a patent medicine
  advertisement without being
  impelled to the conclusion that I am
  suffering from the particular disease

therein dealt with in its most virulent
form.
  Jerome K. Jerome 1859–1927 English
  writer: *Three Men in a Boat* (1889)

8 Illness is not something a person
  has; it's another way of *being*.
    Jonathan Miller 1934– English writer
    and director: *The Body in Question*
    (1978)

9 Illness is the doctor to whom we pay
  most heed; to kindness, to
  knowledge, we make promise only;
  pain we obey.
    Marcel Proust 1871–1922 French
    novelist: *Cities of the Plain* (1922)

10 You matter because you are you, and
  you matter to the last moment of
  your life. We will do all that we can
  not only to help you die peacefully,
  but also to live until you die.
    Cicely Saunders 1916–2005 English
    founder of St Christopher's Hospice,
    London: quoted in Robert Twycross 'A
    Tribute to Dame Cicely Saunders',
    Memorial Service, 8 March 2006

11 I enjoy convalescence. It is the part
  that makes illness worth while.
    George Bernard Shaw 1856–1950 Irish
    dramatist: *Back to Methuselah* (1921)

12 Illness is the night-side of life, a more
  onerous citizenship. Everyone who is
  born holds dual citizenship, in the
  kingdom of the well and in the
  kingdom of the sick.
    Susan Sontag 1933– American writer:
    in *New York Review of Books* 26 January
    1978

13 The biggest disease today is not
  leprosy or tuberculosis, but rather
  the feeling of being unwanted,
  uncared for and deserted by
  everybody.
    Mother Teresa 1910–97 Roman Catholic
    nun and missionary: in *The Observer*
    3 October 1971

Silence

1 Under all speech that is good for anything there lies a silence that is better. Silence is deep as Eternity; speech is shallow as Time.

Thomas Carlyle 1795–1881 Scottish historian and political philosopher: *Critical and Miscellaneous Essays* (1838) 'Sir Walter Scott'

2 No voice; but oh! the silence sank Like music on my heart.

Samuel Taylor Coleridge 1772–1834 English poet, critic, and philosopher: 'The Rime of the Ancient Mariner' (1798)

3 Blessed is the man who, having nothing to say, abstains from giving us wordy evidence of the fact.

George Eliot 1819–80 English novelist: *The Impressions of Theoprastus Such* (1879)

4 Speech is often barren; but silence also does not necessarily brood over a full nest. Your still fowl, blinking at you without remark, may all the while be sitting on one addled egg; and when it takes to cackling will have nothing to announce but that addled delusion.

George Eliot 1819–80 English novelist: *Felix Holt* (1866)

5 Elected Silence, sing to me And beat upon my whorlèd ear.

Gerard Manley Hopkins 1844–89 English poet and priest: 'The Habit of Perfection' (written 1866)

6 Thou still unravished bride of quietness, Thou foster-child of silence and slow time.

John Keats 1795–1821 English poet: 'Ode on a Grecian Urn' (1820)

7 *Aut tace aut loquere meliora silentio.* Be silent, unless your speech is better than silence.

Salvator Rosa 1615–73 Italian painter and etcher: inscription on self portrait in the National Gallery, London

8 Shallow brooks murmur most, deep silent slide away.

Philip Sidney 1554–86 English soldier, poet, and courtier: *Arcadia* (1581)

9 People talking without speaking People hearing without listening . . . 'Fools,' said I, 'You do not know Silence like a cancer grows.'

Paul Simon 1942– American singer and songwriter: 'Sound of Silence' (1964 song)

Similarity and Difference

1 In one and the same fire, clay grows hard and wax melts.

Francis Bacon 1561–1626 English lawyer, courtier, philosopher, and essayist: *History of Life and Death* (1623)

2 One of the most common defects of half-instructed minds is to think much of that in which they differ from others, and little of that in which they agree with others.

Walter Bagehot 1826–77 English economist and essayist: in *Economist* 11 June 1870

3 Not merely a chip of the old 'block', but the old block itself.

on the younger Pitt's maiden speech, February 1781

Edmund Burke 1729–97 Irish-born Whig politician and man of letters: N. W. Wraxall *Historical Memoirs of My Own Time* (1904 ed.)

4 The road up and the road down are one and the same.

Heraclitus c.540–c.480 BC Greek philosopher: fragment 60

5 If we cannot end now our differences, at least we can help make the world safe for diversity.
   John F. Kennedy 1917–63 American Democratic statesman: address at American University, Washington, DC, 10 June 1963

6 When Greeks joined Greeks, then was the tug of war!
   Nathaniel Lee *c.*1653–92 English dramatist: *The Rival Queens* (1677)

7 World is crazier and more of it than we think,
   Incorrigibly plural. I peel and portion
   A tangerine and spit the pips and feel
   The drunkenness of things being various.
   Louis MacNeice 1907–63 British poet, born in Belfast: 'Snow' (1935)

8 There never were in the world two opinions alike, no more than two hairs or two grains; the most universal quality is diversity.
   Montaigne 1533–92 French moralist and essayist: *Essays* (1580)

9 Comparisons are odorous.
   William Shakespeare 1564–1616 English dramatist: *Much Ado About Nothing* (1598–9)

10 No caparisons, Miss, if you please!—Caparisons don't become a young woman.
   Richard Brinsley Sheridan 1751–1816 Anglo-Irish dramatist: *The Rivals* (1775)

11 Without deviation from the norm, progress is not possible.
   Frank Zappa 1940–93 American rock musician and songwriter: attributed, in *New York* 20 June 1994

Simplicity

1 Simplicity is not a goal, but one arrives at simplicity in spite of oneself, as one approaches the real meaning of things.
   Constantin Brancusi 1876–1957 Romanian sculptor: Ionel Jianou *Brancusi* (1963)

2 Out of intense complexities intense simplicities emerge.
   Winston Churchill 1874–1965 British Conservative statesman: *The World Crisis* (1923–9)

3 Less is more.
   Mies van der Rohe 1886–1969 German-born architect and designer: P. Johnson *Mies van der Rohe* (1947); see ARCHITECTURE 13

4 Simplicity is light, carefree, neat, and loving—not a self-punishing ascetic trip.
   Gary Snyder 1930–   American poet: *A Place in Space* (1995)

5 Our life is frittered away by detail . . . Simplify, simplify.
   Henry David Thoreau 1817–62 American writer: *Walden* (1854)

6 The guiding motto in the life of every natural philosopher should be, Seek simplicity and distrust it.
   Alfred North Whitehead 1861–1947 English philosopher and mathematician: *The Concept of Nature* (1920)

Sin

see also EVIL, TEMPTATION

1 All sin tends to be addictive, and the terminal point of addiction is what is called damnation.
   W. H. Auden 1907–73 English poet: *A Certain World* (1970) 'Hell'

2 With love for mankind and hatred of sins.
   often quoted as 'Love the sinner but hate the sin'
   St Augustine of Hippo AD 354–430 Early

Christian theologian: letter 211; J.-P. Migne (ed.) *Patrologiae Latinae* (1845)

3 Be sure your sin will find you out.
Bible: Numbers

4 The wages of sin is death.
Bible: Romans

5 We have left undone those things which we ought to have done; And we have done those things which we ought not to have done; And there is no health in us.
The Book of Common Prayer 1662: *Morning Prayer* General Confession

6 We have erred, and strayed from thy ways like lost sheep. We have followed too much the devices and desires of our own hearts.
The Book of Common Prayer 1662: *Morning Prayer* General Confession

7 I waive the quantum o' the sin;
The hazard of concealing;
But och! it hardens a' within,
And petrifies the feeling!
Robert Burns 1759–96 Scottish poet: 'Epistle to a Young Friend' (1786)

8 There are different kinds of wrong. The people sinned against are not always the best.
Ivy Compton-Burnett 1884–1969 English novelist: *The Mighty and their Fall* (1961)

9 *when asked by Mrs Coolidge what a sermon had been about:*
'Sins,' he said. 'Well, what did he say about sin?' 'He was against it.'
Calvin Coolidge 1872–1933 American Republican statesman: John H. McKee *Coolidge: Wit and Wisdom* (1933); perhaps apocryphal

10 For the sin ye do by two and two ye must pay for one by one!
Rudyard Kipling 1865–1936 English writer and poet: 'Tomlinson' (1892)

11 Shoot all the bluejays you want, if you can hit 'em, but remember it's a sin to kill a mockingbird.
Harper Lee 1926– American novelist: *To Kill a Mockingbird* (1960)

12 It is public scandal that constitutes offence, and to sin in secret is not to sin at all.
Molière 1622–73 French comic dramatist: *Le Tartuffe* (1669)

13 She [the Catholic Church] holds that it were better for sun and moon to drop from heaven, for the earth to fail, and for all the many millions who are upon it to die of starvation in extremest agony, as far as temporal affliction goes, than that one soul, I will not say, should be lost, but should commit one single venial sin, should tell one wilful untruth . . . or steal one poor farthing without excuse.
John Henry Newman 1801–90 English theologian and cardinal: *Lectures on Anglican Difficulties* (1852)

14 Sins become more subtle as you grow older. You commit sins of despair rather than lust.
Piers Paul Read 1941– English novelist: in *Daily Telegraph* 3 October 1990

15   Commit
The oldest sins the newest kind of ways.
William Shakespeare 1564–1616 English dramatist: *Henry IV, Part 2* (1597)

16 All sins are attempts to fill voids.
Simone Weil 1909–43 French essayist and philosopher: *La Pesanteur et la grâce* (1948)

17 When I'm good, I'm very, very good, but when I'm bad, I'm better.
Mae West 1892–1980 American film actress: *I'm No Angel* (1933 film)

Singing

see also MUSIC, OPERA

1 Nothing is capable of being well set to music that is not nonsense.
Joseph Addison 1672–1719 English poet, dramatist, and essayist: in *The Spectator* 21 March 1711

2 The exercise of singing is delightful to Nature, and good to preserve the health of man. It doth strengthen all parts of the breast, and doth open the pipes.
William Byrd 1543–1623 English composer: *Psalms, Sonnets and Songs* (1588)

3 He was an average guy who could carry a tune.
Crosby's own suggestion for his epitaph
Bing Crosby 1903–77 American singer and film actor: in *Newsweek* 24 October 1977

4 Every tone [of the songs of the slaves] was a testimony against slavery, and a prayer to God for deliverance from chains.
Frederick Douglass c.1818–95 American former slave and civil rights campaigner: *Narrative of the Life of Frederick Douglass* (1845)

5 In writing songs I've learned as much from Cézanne as I have from Woody Guthrie.
Bob Dylan 1941– American singer and songwriter: Clinton Heylin *Dylan: Behind the Shades* (1991)

6 Maybe the most that you can expect from a relationship that goes bad is to come out of it with a few good songs.
Marianne Faithfull 1946– British singer: *Faithfull* (1994)

7 A good lyric should be rhymed conversation.
Ira Gershwin 1896–1983 American songwriter: Philip Furia *Ira Gershwin* (1966)

8 I only know two tunes. One of them is 'Yankee Doodle' and the other isn't.
Ulysses S. Grant 1822–85 American Unionist general and statesman: attributed

9 Words make you think a thought. Music makes you feel a feeling. A song makes you feel a thought.
E. Y. Harburg 1898–1981 American songwriter: lecture given at the New York YMCA in 1970

10 It's the only song I've ever written where I get goose bumps every time I play it.
of 'Candle in the Wind'
Elton John 1947– English pop singer and songwriter: in *Daily Telegraph* 9 September 1997; see FAMOUS PEOPLE 4, ROYAL FAMILY 8

11 You think that's noise—you ain't heard nuttin' yet!
first said in a café, competing with the din from a neighbouring building site, in 1906; subsequently an aside in the 1927 film The Jazz Singer
Al Jolson 1886–1950 American singer: Martin Abramson *The Real Story of Al Jolson* (1950); also the title of a Jolson song, 1919, in the form 'You Ain't Heard Nothing Yet'

12 Tenors get women by the score.
James Joyce 1882–1941 Irish novelist: *Ulysses* (1922)

13 Sentimentally I am disposed to harmony. But organically I am incapable of a tune.
Charles Lamb 1775–1834 English writer: *Essays of Elia* (1823) 'A Chapter on Ears'

14 Everyone suddenly burst out singing;
And I was filled with such delight

As prisoned birds must find in
  freedom.
  Siegfried Sassoon 1886–1967 English
  poet: 'Everyone Sang' (1919)

15 Nothing can be more disgusting than
  an oratorio. How absurd to see
  500 people fiddling like madmen
  about Israelites in the Red Sea!
  Sydney Smith 1771–1845 English
  clergyman and essayist: Hesketh
  Pearson *The Smith of Smiths* (1934)

Situation

see CIRCUMSTANCE AND SITUATION

The Skies

see also SPACE, UNIVERSE

1 We have seen
  The moon in lonely alleys make
  A grail of laughter of an empty ash
    can.
  Hart Crane 1899–1932 American poet:
  'Chaplinesque' (1926)

2 Slowly, silently, now the moon
  Walks the night in her silver shoon.
  Walter de la Mare 1873–1956 English
  poet and novelist: 'Silver' (1913)

3 Busy old fool, unruly sun,
  Why dost thou thus,
  Through windows, and through
    curtains call on us?
  John Donne 1572–1631 English poet
  and divine: 'The Sun Rising'

4 The moon is nothing
  But a circumambulating aphrodisiac
  Divinely subsidized to provoke the
    world
  Into a rising birth-rate.
  Christopher Fry 1907–2005 English
  dramatist: *The Lady's not for Burning*
  (1949)

5 But it does move.
  *after his recantation, that the earth moves
  around the sun, in 1632*
  Galileo Galilei 1564–1642 Italian
  astronomer and physicist: attributed

6 It may be that the stars of heaven
  appear to us fair and pure simply
  because we are at such a distance
  from them, and know nothing of
  their private life.
  Heinrich Heine 1797–1856 German
  poet: *The Romantic School* (1833)

7 Look at the stars! look, look up at the
    skies!
  O look at all the fire-folk sitting in the
    air!
  The bright boroughs, the circle-
    citadels there!
  Gerard Manley Hopkins 1844–89
  English poet and priest: 'The Starlight
  Night' (written 1877)

8 The heaventree of stars hung with
  humid nightblue fruit.
  James Joyce 1882–1941 Irish novelist:
  Ulysses (1922)

9   The evening star,
  Love's harbinger.
  John Milton 1608–74 English poet:
  Paradise Lost (1667)

10   The moon's an arrant thief,
  And her pale fire she snatches from
    the sun.
  William Shakespeare 1564–1616
  English dramatist: *Timon of Athens*
  (c.1607)

11 I am the daughter of Earth and
    Water,
  And the nursling of the Sky;
  I pass through the pores of the ocean
    and shores;
  I change, but I cannot die.
  Percy Bysshe Shelley 1792–1822
  English poet: 'The Cloud' (1819)

12 I have loved the stars too fondly to be fearful of the night.
Sarah Williams 1837–68 British writer: 'The Old Astronomer to His Pupil' (1920)

Sleep

see also DREAMS

1 The cool kindliness of sheets, that soon
Smooth away trouble; and the rough male kiss
Of blankets.
Rupert Brooke 1887–1915 English poet: 'The Great Lover' (1914)

2 Care-charmer Sleep, son of the sable Night,
Brother to Death, in silent darkness born.
Samuel Daniel 1563–1619 English poet and dramatist: *Delia* (1592) sonnet 54

3 Sleep is when all the unsorted stuff comes flying out as from a dustbin upset in a high wind.
William Golding 1911–93 English novelist: *Pincher Martin* (1956)

4 I love sleep because it is both pleasant and safe to use.
Fran Lebowitz 1946– American writer: *Metropolitan Life* (1978)

5 What hath night to do with sleep?
John Milton 1608–74 English poet: *Comus* (1637)

6 And so to bed.
Samuel Pepys 1633–1703 English diarist: diary, 20 April 1660

7 Not to be a-bed after midnight is to be up betimes.
William Shakespeare 1564–1616 English dramatist: *Twelfth Night* (1601)

8 Methought I heard a voice cry, 'Sleep no more!
Macbeth does murder sleep,' the innocent sleep,

Sleep that knits up the ravelled sleave of care.
William Shakespeare 1564–1616 English dramatist: *Macbeth* (1606)

9 In winter I get up at night
And dress by yellow candle-light.
In summer, quite the other way,—
I have to go to bed by day.
Robert Louis Stevenson 1850–94 Scottish novelist: 'Bed in Summer' (1885)

10 Must we to bed indeed? Well then, Let us arise and go like men,
And face with an undaunted tread
The long black passage up to bed.
Robert Louis Stevenson 1850–94 Scottish novelist: 'North-West Passage. Good-Night' (1885)

11 Early to rise and early to bed makes a male healthy and wealthy and dead.
James Thurber 1894–1961 American humorist: 'The Shrike and the Chipmunks' in *New Yorker* 18 February 1939

12 'Tis the voice of the sluggard; I heard him complain,
'You have waked me too soon, I must slumber again'.
As the door on its hinges, so he on his bed,
Turns his sides and his shoulders and his heavy head.
Isaac Watts 1674–1748 English hymn-writer: 'The Sluggard' (1715)

13 Tired Nature's sweet restorer, balmy sleep!
Edward Young 1683–1765 English poet and dramatist: *Night Thoughts* (1742–5)

Smoking

1 More doctors smoke Camels than any other cigarette.
Advertising slogan: Camel cigarettes, 1940s-50s

2 The pipe with solemn interposing
 puff,
Makes half a sentence at a time
 enough;
The dozing sages drop the drowsy
 strain,
Then pause, and puff—and speak,
 and pause again.
> **William Cowper** 1731–1800 English
> poet: 'Conversation' (1782)

3 The wretcheder one is, the more one
smokes; and the more one smokes,
the wretcheder one gets—a vicious
circle!
> **George du Maurier** 1834–96 French-
> born cartoonist and novelist: *Peter
> Ibbetson* (1892)

4 The roots of tobacco plants must go
clear through to hell.
> **Thomas Alva Edison** 1847–1931
> American inventor: in *American
> Heritage* 12 July 1885

5 A custom loathsome to the eye,
hateful to the nose, harmful to the
brain, dangerous to the lungs, and in
the black, stinking fume thereof,
nearest resembling the horrible
Stygian smoke of the pit that is
bottomless.
> **James I** 1566–1625 (James VI of
> Scotland): *A Counterblast to Tobacco*
> (1604)

6 I do hold it, and will affirm it (before
any prince in Europe) to be the most
sovereign and precious weed that
ever the earth tendered to the use of
man.
of tobacco
> **Ben Jonson** c.1573–1637 English
> dramatist and poet: *Every Man in His
> Humour* (1598)

7 This very night I am going to leave
off tobacco! Surely there must be
some other world in which this
unconquerable purpose shall be
realized.
> **Charles Lamb** 1775–1834 English

writer: letter to Thomas Manning,
26 December 1815

8 He who lives without tobacco is not
worthy to live.
> **Molière** 1622–73 French comic
> dramatist: *Don Juan* (performed 1665)

9 I smoked my first cigarette and
kissed my first woman on the same
day. I have never had time for
tobacco since.
> **Arturo Toscanini** 1867–1957 Italian
> conductor: in *Observer* 30 June 1946

10 A cigarette is the perfect type of a
perfect pleasure. It is exquisite, and it
leaves one unsatisfied. What more
can one want?
> **Oscar Wilde** 1854–1900 Anglo-Irish
> dramatist and poet: *The Picture of
> Dorian Gray* (1891)

Snow

1 British Rail, which last week
predicted that it was ready for the
worst the weather could do, now
blames the near-total dislocation of
its services on 'the wrong sort of
snow'.
> **Anonymous**: leader in *Evening
> Standard* 12 February 1991; see SNOW 5

2 When men were all asleep the snow
 came flying,
In large white flakes falling on the
 city brown,
Stealthily and perpetually settling
 and loosely lying,
Hushing the latest traffic of the
 drowsy town.
> **Robert Bridges** 1844–1930 English poet:
> 'London Snow' (1890)

3 Whose woods these are I think I
 know.
His house is in the village though;
He will not see me stopping here

To watch his woods fill up with snow.

Robert Frost 1874–1963 American poet: 'Stopping by Woods on a Snowy Evening' (1923)

4 The first fall of snow is not only an event, but it is a magical event. You go to bed in one kind of world and wake up to find yourself in another quite different, and if this is not enchantment, then where is it to be found?

J. B. Priestley 1894–1984 English novelist, dramatist, and critic: *Apes and Angels* (1928) 'First Snow'

5 We are having particular problems on this occasion with the type of snow, which is very dry and powdery and is actually penetrating all the protection we had on some of our locomotives.

explaining disruption on British Rail; popularly summarized as 'the wrong sort of snow'; see SNOW 1

Terry Worrall *fl.* 1991 British spokesman for British Rail: in *Evening Standard* 11 February 1991

Society

see also ART AND SOCIETY, GOVERNMENT, HUMAN RACE, LITERATURE AND SOCIETY, SCIENCE AND SOCIETY

1 There is no such thing as the State
And no one exists alone;
Hunger allows no choice
To the citizen or the police;
We must love one another or die.

W. H. Auden 1907–73 English poet: 'September 1, 1939' (1940)

2 We started off trying to set up a small anarchist community, but people wouldn't obey the rules.

Alan Bennett 1934– English actor and dramatist: *Getting On* (1972)

3 The greatest happiness of the greatest number is the foundation of morals and legislation.

Jeremy Bentham 1748–1832 English philosopher: *The Commonplace Book*; Bentham claimed that either Joseph Priestley (1733–1804) or Cesare Beccaria (1738–94) passed on the 'sacred truth'

4 No man is an Island, entire of it self; every man is a piece of the Continent, a part of the main.

John Donne 1572–1631 English poet and divine: *Devotions upon Emergent Occasions* (1624)

5 Economics is all about how people make choices. Sociology is all about why they don't have any choices to make.

James Stemble Duesenberry 1918– American economist: *Demographic and Economic Change in the Developed World* (1960)

6 No man can have society upon his own terms. If he seeks it, he must serve it too.

Ralph Waldo Emerson 1803–82 American philosopher and poet: *Journal* 28 May 1833

7 Only in the state does man have a rational existence . . . Man owes his entire existence to the state, and has his being within it alone. Whatever worth and spiritual reality he possesses are his solely by virtue of the state.

G. W. F. Hegel 1770–1831 German idealist philosopher: *Lectures on the Philosophy of World History: Introduction* (1830)

8 In your time we have the opportunity to move not only toward the rich society and the powerful society, but upward to the Great Society.

Lyndon Baines Johnson 1908–73 American Democratic statesman:

speech at University of Michigan, 22 May 1964

9 If a free society cannot help the many who are poor, it cannot save the few who are rich.
John F. Kennedy 1917–63 American Democratic statesman: inaugural address, 20 January 1961

10 From each according to his abilities, to each according to his needs.
Karl Marx 1818–83 German political philosopher: *Critique of the Gotha Programme* (written 1875, but of earlier origin)

11 When society requires to be rebuilt, there is no use in attempting to rebuild it on the old plan.
John Stuart Mill 1806–73 English philosopher and economist: *Dissertations and Discussions* vol. 1 (1859) 'Essay on Coleridge'

12 There is no such thing as Society. There are individual men and women, and there are families.
Margaret Thatcher 1925– British Conservative stateswoman: in *Woman's Own* 31 October 1987

13 Wherever a man goes, men will pursue him and paw him with their dirty institutions, and, if they can, constrain him to belong to their desperate oddfellow society.
Henry David Thoreau 1817–62 American writer: *Walden* (1854) 'The Village'

14 The Social Contract is nothing more or less than a vast conspiracy of human beings to lie to and humbug themselves and one another for the general Good. Lies are the mortar that bind the savage individual man into the social masonry.
H. G. Wells 1866–1946 English novelist: *Love and Mr Lewisham* (1900)

Solitude

see also LONELINESS

1 He who is unable to live in society, or who has no need because he is sufficient for himself, must be either a beast or a god.
Aristotle 384–322 BC Greek philosopher: *Politics*

2 [Barrymore] would quote from Genesis the text which says, 'It is not good for man to be alone,' and then add, 'But O my God, what a relief.'
John Barrymore 1882–1942 American actor: Alma Power-Waters *John Barrymore* (1941)

3 To fly from, need not be to hate, mankind.
Lord Byron 1788–1824 English poet: *Childe Harold's Pilgrimage* (1812–18)

4 You come into the world alone and you go out of the world alone yet it seems to me you are more alone while living than even going and coming.
Emily Carr 1871–1945 Canadian artist: *Hundreds and Thousands: The Journals of Emily Carr* (1966) 16 July 1933

5 We live, as we dream—alone.
Joseph Conrad 1857–1924 Polish-born English novelist: *Heart of Darkness* (1902)

6 Anythin' for a quiet life, as the man said wen he took the sitivation at the lighthouse.
Charles Dickens 1812–70 English novelist: *Pickwick Papers* (1837)

7 How does it feel
To be on your own
With no direction home
Like a complete unknown
Like a rolling stone?
Bob Dylan 1941– American singer and songwriter: *Like a Rolling Stone* (1965 song)

8 I want to be alone.

Greta Garbo 1905–90 Swedish film actress: *Grand Hotel* (1932 film), the phrase already being associated with Garbo

9 Conversation enriches the understanding, but solitude is the school of genius.

Edward Gibbon 1737–94 English historian: *The Decline and Fall of the Roman Empire* (1776–88)

10 Down to Gehenna or up to the Throne,
He travels the fastest who travels alone.

Rudyard Kipling 1865–1936 English writer and poet: 'The Winners' (*The Story of the Gadsbys*, 1890)

11 My heart is a lonely hunter that hunts on a lonely hill.

Fiona McLeod 1855–1905 Scottish writer: 'The Lonely Hunter' (1896); reworked by Carson McCullers as 'The heart is a lonely hunter' for the title of a novel, 1940

12 Man goes into the noisy crowd to drown his own clamour of silence.

Rabindranath Tagore 1861–1941 Bengali poet and philosopher: 'Stray Birds' (1916)

13 We're all of us sentenced to solitary confinement inside our own skins, for life!

Tennessee Williams 1911–83 American dramatist: *Orpheus Descending* (1958)

14 I will arise and go now, and go to Innisfree,
And a small cabin build there, of clay and wattles made;
Nine bean rows will I have there, a hive for the honey bee,
And live alone in the bee-loud glade.

W. B. Yeats 1865–1939 Irish poet: 'The Lake Isle of Innisfree' (1893)

Solutions

see PROBLEMS AND SOLUTIONS ·

Sorrow

see also BEREAVEMENT, DEPRESSION, SUFFERING, UNHAPPINESS

1 Sob, heavy world,
Sob as you spin
Mantled in mist, remote from the happy.

W. H. Auden 1907–73 English poet: *The Age of Anxiety* (1947)

2 By the waters of Babylon we sat down and wept: when we remembered thee, O Sion.

Bible: Psalm 137

3 I tell you, hopeless grief is passionless.

Elizabeth Barrett Browning 1806–61 English poet: 'Grief' (1844)

4 All my joys to this are folly,
Naught so sweet as Melancholy.

Robert Burton 1577–1640 English clergyman and scholar: *The Anatomy of Melancholy* (1621–51)

5 . . . *Nessun maggior dolore,*
Che ricordarsi del tempo felice
Nella miseria.

There is no greater pain than to remember a happy time when one is in misery.

Dante Alighieri 1265–1321 Italian poet: *Divina Commedia* 'Inferno'; see UNHAPPINESS 2

6 *Adieu tristesse*
Bonjour tristesse
Tu es inscrite dans les lignes du plafond.

Farewell sadness
Good-day sadness
You are inscribed in the lines of the ceiling.

Paul Éluard 1895–1952 French poet: 'À peine défigurée' (1932)

7 Yes, he thought, between grief and nothing I will take grief.

> **William Faulkner** 1897–1962 American novelist: *The Wild Palms* (1931) 'Wild Palms'

8 Now laughing friends deride tears I cannot hide,
So I smile and say 'When a lovely flame dies,
Smoke gets in your eyes.'

> **Otto Harbach** 1873–1963 American songwriter: 'Smoke Gets in your Eyes' (1933 song)

9 Áh! ás the heart grows older
It will come to such sights colder
By and by, nor spare a sigh
Though worlds of wanwood leafmeal lie;
And yet you *will* weep and know why.

> **Gerard Manley Hopkins** 1844–89 English poet and priest: 'Spring and Fall: to a young child' (written 1880)

10 Grief is a species of idleness.

> **Samuel Johnson** 1709–84 English poet, critic, and lexicographer: letter to Mrs Thrale, 17 March 1773

11 No one ever told me that grief felt so like fear.

> **C. S. Lewis** 1898–1963 English literary scholar: *A Grief Observed* (1961)

12 Nothing is here for tears.

> **John Milton** 1608–74 English poet: *Samson Agonistes* (1671)

13 Small sorrows speak; great ones are silent.

> **Seneca ('the Younger')** *c.*4 BC–AD 65 Roman philosopher and poet: *Hippolytus*

14 If you have tears, prepare to shed them now.

> **William Shakespeare** 1564–1616 English dramatist: *Julius Caesar* (1599)

15 When sorrows come, they come not single spies,

But in battalions.

> **William Shakespeare** 1564–1616 English dramatist: *Hamlet* (1601)

16 Tears, idle tears, I know not what they mean,
Tears from the depth of some divine despair.

> **Alfred, Lord Tennyson** 1809–92 English poet: *The Princess* (1850 ed.)

17 Pure and complete sorrow is as impossible as pure and complete joy.

> **Leo Tolstoy** 1828–1910 Russian novelist: *War and Peace* (1865)

18 *Sunt lacrimae rerum et mentem mortalia tangunt.*
There are tears shed for things even here and mortality touches the heart.

> **Virgil** 70–19 BC Roman poet: *Aeneid*

19 We think caged birds sing, when indeed they cry.

> **John Webster** *c.*1580–*c.*1625 English dramatist: *The White Devil* (1612)

20 Laugh and the world laughs with you;
Weep, and you weep alone;
For the sad old earth must borrow its mirth,
But has trouble enough of its own.

> **Ella Wheeler Wilcox** 1855–1919 American poet: 'Solitude'

South America

see MEXICO AND SOUTH AMERICA

Space

see also SKIES, UNIVERSE

1 We are not alone.

> **Anonymous**: advertising slogan for *Close Encounters of the Third Kind* (1977 film)

2 Houston, Tranquillity Base here. The Eagle has landed.

Neil Armstrong 1930– American astronaut: landing on the moon, 20 July 1969

3 Don't tell me that man doesn't belong out there. Man belongs wherever he wants to go—and he'll do plenty well when he gets there.

Wernher von Braun 1912–77 German-born American rocket engineer: in *Time* 17 February 1958

4 The fancy that extraterrestrial life is by definition of a higher order than our own is one that soothes all children, and many writers.

Joan Didion 1934– American writer: *The White Album* (1979)

5 But where is everybody?
on the existence of extra-terrestrials, known as the Fermi paradox

Enrico Fermi 1901–54 Italian-born American atomic physicist: attributed, *c.*1950

6 We won't find anywhere as nice as Earth unless we go to another star system.
on colonizing space

Stephen Hawking 1942– English theoretical physicist: in *Mail on Sunday* 18 June 2006

7 *on Felix Bloch's stating that space was the field of linear operations:*
Nonsense. Space is blue and birds fly through it.

Werner Heisenberg 1901–76 German mathematical physicist: Felix Bloch 'Heisenberg and the early days of quantum mechanics', in *Physics Today* December 1976

8 Space isn't remote at all. It's only an hour's drive away if your car could go straight upwards.

Fred Hoyle 1915–2001 English astrophysicist: in *Observer* 9 September 1979

9 Cosmologists are often in error, but never in doubt.

Lev Landau 1908–68 Russian physicist: attributed in Simon Singh *Big Bang* (2004)

10 The pursuit of the good and evil are now linked in astronomy as in almost all science . . . The fate of human civilization will depend on whether the rockets of the future carry the astronomer's telescope or a hydrogen bomb.

Bernard Lovell 1913– British astronomer: *The Individual and the Universe* (1959)

11 The eternal silence of these infinite spaces [the heavens] terrifies me.

Blaise Pascal 1623–62 French mathematician, physicist, and moralist: *Pensées* (1670)

12 Space is almost infinite. As a matter of fact, we think it is infinite.

Dan Quayle 1947– American Republican politician: in *Daily Telegraph* 8 March 1989

13 We will never forget them, nor the last time we saw them this morning, as they prepared for the journey and waved goodbye and 'slipped the surly bonds of earth' to 'touch the face of God.'
after the loss of the space shuttle Challenger *with all its crew*

Ronald Reagan 1911–2004 American Republican statesman: broadcast from the Oval Office, 28 January 1986; see AIR FORCE 4

Speech

see also CONVERSATION, GRAMMAR, LANGUAGE, SILENCE

1 Sentence structure is innate but whining is acquired.

Woody Allen 1935– American film director, writer, and actor: 'Remembering Needleman' (1976)

2 Never express yourself more clearly than you think.

> **Niels Bohr** 1885–1962 Danish physicist: Abraham Pais *Einstein Lived Here* (1994)

3 Take care of the sense, and the sounds will take care of themselves.

> **Lewis Carroll** 1832–98 English writer and logician: *Alice's Adventures in Wonderland* (1865)

4 Somwhat he lipsed, for his wantownesse,
To make his Englissh sweete upon his tonge.

> **Geoffrey Chaucer** c.1343–1400 English poet: *The Canterbury Tales* 'The General Prologue'

5 *when asked if he found his stammering very inconvenient:*
No, Sir, because I have time to think before I speak, and don't ask impertinent questions.

> **Erasmus Darwin** 1731–1802 English physician: Francis Darwin 'Reminiscences of My Father's Everyday Life', in Charles Darwin *Autobiography* (1877 ed.)

6 Half the sorrows of women would be averted if they could repress the speech they know to be useless; nay, the speech they have resolved not to make.

> **George Eliot** 1819–80 English novelist: *Felix Holt* (1866)

7   Speech impelled us
To purify the dialect of the tribe
And urge the mind to aftersight and foresight.

> **T. S. Eliot** 1888–1965 Anglo-American poet, critic, and dramatist: *Four Quartets* 'Little Gidding' (1942)

8 Human speech is like a cracked kettle on which we tap crude rhythms for bears to dance to, while we long to make music that will melt the stars.

> **Gustave Flaubert** 1821–80 French novelist: *Madame Bovary* (1857)

9 It has been well said, that heart speaks to heart, whereas language only speaks to the ears.

> **St Francis de Sales** 1567–1622 French bishop: letter to the Archbishop of Bourges, 5 October 1604, paraphrased by John Henry Newman as '*cor ad cor loquitur* [heart speaks to heart]'

10 He could make men weep or tremble by his varied utterances of the word 'Mesopotamia'.

> *on the moving voice of the English Methodist preacher George Whitefield (1714–70); Garrick is also said to have remarked 'I would give a hundred guineas if I could say "Oh" like Mr Whitefield'*
>
> **David Garrick** 1717–79 English actor-manager: A. C. H. Seymour *The Life and Times of Selina, Countess of Huntingdon* (1840)

11 You like potato and I like po-tah-to,
You like tomato and I like to-mah-to;
Potato, po-tah-to, tomato, to-mah-to—
Let's call the whole thing off!

> **Ira Gershwin** 1896–1983 American songwriter: 'Let's Call the Whole Thing Off' (1937 song)

12 Most men make little other use of their speech than to give evidence against their own understanding.

> **Lord Halifax** 1633–95 English politician and essayist: *Political, Moral, and Miscellaneous Thoughts and Reflections* (1750)

13 If, sir, I possessed, as you suggest, the power of conveying unlimited sexual attraction through the potency of my voice, I would not be reduced to accepting a miserable pittance from the BBC for interviewing a faded female in a damp basement.

> *reply to Mae West's manager who asked 'Can't you sound a bit more sexy when you interview her?'*
>
> **Gilbert Harding** 1907–60 British broadcaster: S. Grenfell *Gilbert Harding by his Friends* (1961)

14 A tart temper never mellows with age, and a sharp tongue is the only edged tool that grows keener with constant use.
   Washington Irving 1783–1859 American writer: *The Sketch Book* (1820)

15 Speech is civilisation itself. The word, even the most contradictory word, preserves contact — it is silence which isolates.
   Thomas Mann 1875–1955 German novelist: *The Magic Mountain* (1924)

16 Continual eloquence is tedious.
   Blaise Pascal 1623–62 French mathematician, physicist, and moralist: *Pensées* (1670)

17 I do not much dislike the matter, but The manner of his speech.
   William Shakespeare 1564–1616 English dramatist: *Antony and Cleopatra* (1606–7)

18 Nagging is the repetition of unpalatable truths.
   Edith Summerskill 1901–80 British Labour politician: speech to the Married Women's Association, House of Commons, 14 July 1960

19 Faith, that's as well said, as if I had said it myself.
   Jonathan Swift 1667–1745 Anglo-Irish poet and satirist: *Polite Conversation* (1738)

20 What can be said at all can be said clearly; and whereof one cannot speak thereof one must be silent.
   Ludwig Wittgenstein 1889–1951 Austrian-born philosopher: *Tractatus Logico-Philosophicus* (1922)

21 The reason why we have two ears and only one mouth is that we may listen the more and talk the less.
   Zeno 333–261 BC Greek philosopher: Diogenes Laertius *Lives of the Philosophers*

Speeches

1 Give brief orders; speeches that are too long are likely to be forgotten.
   Abu Bakr 573–634 Arab ruler: advice to his army, R. W. Maqsood *Sayings of Abu Bakr* (1989)

2 I do not object to people looking at their watches when I am speaking. But I strongly object when they start shaking them to make certain they are still going.
   Lord Birkett 1883–1962 English barrister and judge: in *Observer* 30 October 1960

3 I take the view, and always have, that if you cannot say what you are going to say in twenty minutes you ought to go away and write a book about it.
   Lord Brabazon 1884–1964 British aviator and politician: speech, House of Lords, 21 June 1955

4 Grasp the subject, the words will follow.
   Cato the Elder 234–149 BC Roman statesman, orator, and writer: Caius Julius Victor *Ars Rhetorica*

5 And adepts in the speaking trade Keep a cough by them ready made.
   Charles Churchill 1731–64 English poet: *The Ghost* (1763)

6 He is one of those orators of whom it was well said, 'Before they get up, they do not know what they are going to say; when they are speaking, they do not know what they are saying; and when they have sat down, they do not know what they have said.'
   of Lord Charles Beresford
   Winston Churchill 1874–1965 British Conservative statesman: speech, House of Commons, 20 December 1912

7 It was the nation and the race dwelling all round the globe that had the lion's heart. I had the luck to be called upon to give the roar. I also hope that I sometimes suggested to the lion the right place to use his claws.

Winston Churchill 1874–1965 British Conservative statesman: speech at Westminster Hall, 30 November 1954

8 If you don't say anything, you won't be called on to repeat it.

Calvin Coolidge 1872–1933 American Republican statesman: attributed

9 When asked what was first in oratory, [he] replied to his questioner, 'action,' what second, 'action,' and again third, 'action'.

Demosthenes c.384–c.322 BC Athenian orator and statesman: Cicero *Brutus*

10 The finest eloquence is that which gets things done and the worst is that which delays them.

David Lloyd George 1863–1945 British Liberal statesman: speech at Paris Peace Conference, 18 January 1919

11 But all was false and hollow; though his tongue
Dropped manna, and could make the worse appear
The better reason.

John Milton 1608–74 English poet: *Paradise Lost* (1667)

12 Poor George, he can't help it—he was born with a silver foot in his mouth.
of George Bush

Ann Richards 1933–2006 American Democratic politician: keynote speech at the Democratic convention, in *Independent* 20 July 1988

13 Friends, Romans, countrymen, lend me your ears.

William Shakespeare 1564–1616 English dramatist: *Julius Caesar* (1599)

14 The Right Honourable gentleman is indebted to his memory for his jests, and to his imagination for his facts.

Richard Brinsley Sheridan 1751–1816

Anglo-Irish dramatist: T. Moore *Life of Sheridan* (1825)

15 Do you remember that in classical times when Cicero had finished speaking, the people said, 'How well he spoke', but when Demosthenes had finished speaking, they said, 'Let us march.'

Adlai Stevenson 1900–65 American Democratic politician: introducing John F. Kennedy in 1960; Bert Cochran *Adlai Stevenson* (1969)

16 Preach not because you have to say something, but because you have something to say.

Richard Whately 1787–1863 English philosopher and theologian: *Apophthegms* (1854)

17 If I am to speak for ten minutes, I need a week for preparation; if fifteen minutes, three days; if half an hour, two days; if an hour, I am ready now.

Woodrow Wilson 1856–1924 American Democratic statesman: Josephus Daniels *The Wilson Era* (1946)

Speed

see also DELAY

1 *Festina lente.*
Make haste slowly.

Augustus 63 BC–AD 14 Roman emperor: Suetonius *Lives of the Caesars* 'Divus Augustus'

2 Men travel faster now, but I do not know if they go to better things.

Willa Cather 1873–1947 American novelist: *Death Comes for the Archbishop* (1927)

3 Get there first with the most men.
often quoted as 'Git thar fustest with the mostest', though there is no evidence that non-standard speech was characteristic of Forrest

Nathan B. Forrest 1821–77 American Confederate general: attributed

4 There is more to life than increasing its speed.

    Mahatma Gandhi 1869–1948 Indian statesman: attributed

5 Home James, and don't spare the horses.

    Fred Hillebrand 1893–1963: title of song (1934)

6 What good is speed if the brain has oozed out on the way?

    Karl Kraus 1874–1936 Austrian satirist: in *Die Fackel* September 1909

7 I'll put a girdle round about the earth In forty minutes.

    William Shakespeare 1564–1616 English dramatist: *A Midsummer Night's Dream* (1595–6)

8 Though I am always in haste, I am never in a hurry.

    John Wesley 1703–91 English preacher: letter to Miss March, 10 December 1777

Sports and Games

see also BASEBALL, BOXING, CRICKET, FOOTBALL, FIELD SPORTS, FISHING, GOLF, HUNTING, OLYMPIC GAMES, TENNIS, WINNING

1 This is a hard tour and hard work wins it. Vive Le Tour.

on winning his seventh consecutive Tour de France

    Lance Armstrong 1971– American cyclist: in *Independent* 25 July 2005

2 In America, it is sport that is the opiate of the masses.

    Russell Baker 1925– American journalist and columnist: in *New York Times* 3 October 1967

3 Sports do not build character. They reveal it.

    Heywood Hale Broun 1918–2001 American sports commentator: attributed; James Michener *Sports in America* (1976)

4 What I know most surely about morality and the duty of man I owe to sport.

often quoted as, '. . . I owe to football'

    Albert Camus 1913–60 French novelist, dramatist, and essayist: Herbert R. Lottman *Albert Camus* (1979)

5 There is plenty of time to win this game, and to thrash the Spaniards too.

receiving news of the Armada while playing bowls on Plymouth Hoe

    Francis Drake c.1540–96 English sailor and explorer: attributed

6 I called off his players' names as they came marching up the steps behind him . . . All nice guys. They'll finish last. Nice guys. Finish last.

usually quoted as 'Nice guys finish last'

    Leo Durocher 1906–91 American baseball coach: casual remark at a practice ground, July 1946

7 I hated the easy assumption that girls had to be slower than boys.

    Dawn Fraser 1937– Australian swimmer: attributed; Colin Jarman *Guinness Dictionary of Sports Quotations* (1990)

8 All pro athletes are bilingual. They speak English and profanity.

    Gordie Howe 1928– Canadian ice-hockey player: in *Toronto Star* 27 May 1975

9 The thing about sport, any sport, is that swearing is very much part of it.

    Jimmy Greaves 1940– English footballer: in *Observer* 1 January 1989

10 I skate to where the puck is going to be, not where it's been.

    Wayne Gretzky 1961– Canadian ice-hockey player: attributed, 1985; John Robert Colombo *Colombo's New Canadian Quotations* (1987)

11 He shoots! He scores!

    Foster William Hewitt 1902–85

Canadian broadcaster: catchphrase used at ice-hockey games; first said over the radio 4 April 1933 at the game between the Toronto Maple Leafs and the Boston Bruins

12 The only athletic sport I ever mastered was backgammon.
   Douglas Jerrold 1803–57 English dramatist and journalist: Walter Jerrold *Douglas Jerrold* (1914)

13 I am sorry I have not learned to play at cards. It is very useful in life: it generates kindness and consolidates society.
   Samuel Johnson 1709–84 English poet, critic, and lexicographer: James Boswell *Journal of a Tour to the Hebrides* (1785) 21 November 1773

14 Then ye returned to your trinkets; then ye contented your souls
   With the flannelled fools at the wicket or the muddied oafs at the goals.
   Rudyard Kipling 1865–1936 English writer and poet: 'The Islanders' (1903)

15 Rugby shows men how they like to see themselves—noble warriors, primitive god-monsters—whereas soccer shows men as women see them: competitive, full of greedy ego and with that mummy-watch-me-jump need to impress.
   Nigella Lawson 1960– British journalist and cookery writer: in *Evening Standard* 26 May 2009

16   Chaos umpire sits,
   And by decision more embroils the fray.
   John Milton 1608–74 English poet: *Paradise Lost* (1667)

17 And it's not for the sake of a ribboned coat,
   Or the selfish hope of a season's fame,
   But his Captain's hand on his shoulder smote—

'Play up! play up! and play the game!'
   Henry Newbolt 1862–1938 English lawyer, poet, and man of letters: 'Vitaï Lampada' (1897)

18 Serious sport has nothing to do with fair play. It is bound up with hatred, jealousy, boastfulness, and disregard of all the rules.
   George Orwell 1903–50 English novelist: *Shooting an Elephant* (1950) 'I Write as I Please'

19 Don't look back. Something may be gaining on you.
   a baseball pitcher's advice
   Leroy ('Satchel') Paige 1906–82 American baseball player: in *Collier's* 13 June 1953

20 The theory and practice of gamesmanship or The art of winning games without actually cheating.
   Stephen Potter 1900–69 British writer: title of book (1947)

21 All you need to run is good shoes.
   Paula Radcliffe 1973– British long-distance runner: in *Observer* 6 November 2005

22 To play billiards well is a sign of an ill-spent youth.
   Charles Roupell: attributed; D. Duncan *Life of Herbert Spencer* (1908)

23 I can't see who's in the lead but it's either Oxford or Cambridge.
   John Snagge 1904–96 English sports commentator: commentary on the 1949 Boat Race

24 What a sad old age you are preparing for yourself.
   to a young diplomat who boasted of his ignorance of whist
   Charles-Maurice de Talleyrand 1754–1838 French statesman: J. Amédée Pichot *Souvenirs Intimes sur M. de Talleyrand* (1870)

25 Jogging is for people who aren't intelligent enough to watch television.

> **Victoria Wood** 1953– British writer and comedienne: *Mens Sana in Thingummy Doodah* (1990)

Spring

1 It is about five o'clock in an evening that the first hour of spring strikes—autumn arrives in the early morning, but spring at the close of a winter day.

> **Elizabeth Bowen** 1899–1973 Anglo-Irish novelist: *The Death of the Heart* (1938)

2 Oh, to be in England
Now that April's there,
And whoever wakes in England
Sees, some morning, unaware,
That the lowest boughs and the brushwood sheaf
Round the elm-tree bole are in tiny leaf,
While the chaffinch sings on the orchard bough
In England—now!

> **Robert Browning** 1812–89 English poet: 'Home-Thoughts, from Abroad' (1845)

3 April is the cruellest month, breeding
Lilacs out of the dead land, mixing
Memory and desire, stirring
Dull roots with spring rain.

> **T. S. Eliot** 1888–1965 Anglo-American poet, critic, and dramatist: *The Waste Land* (1922)

4 We need spring. We need it desperately and, usually, we need it before God is willing to give it to us.

> **Peter John Gzowski** 1934–2002 Canadian broadcaster: *Peter Gzowski's Spring Tonic* (1979)

5 And since to look at things in bloom
Fifty springs are little room,
About the woodlands I will go

To see the cherry hung with snow.

> **A. E. Housman** 1859–1936 English poet: *A Shropshire Lad* (1896)

6 Work seethes in the hands of spring,
That strapping dairymaid.

> **Boris Pasternak** 1890–1960 Russian novelist and poet: *Doctor Zhivago* (1958) 'Zhivago's Poems: March'

Spying

1 The licence to kill for the Secret Service, the double-0 prefix, was a great honour.

> *popularly quoted as 'Licensed to kill', referring to the status of Secret Service agent James Bond, 007*
>
> **Ian Fleming** 1908–64 English thriller writer: *Dr No* (1958)

2 It's easy to forget what intelligence consists of: luck and speculation. Here and there a windfall, here and there a scoop.

> **John le Carré** 1931– English thriller writer: *The Looking-Glass War* (1965)

3 The necessity of procuring good intelligence is apparent and need not be further urged.

> **George Washington** 1732–99 American statesman: letter, 26 July 1777

4 Having watched the form of our traitors for a number of years, I cannot think that espionage can be recommended as a technique for building an impressive civilization. It's a lout's game.

> **Rebecca West** 1892–1983 English novelist and journalist: *The Meaning of Treason* (1982 ed.)

Statistics

see also MATHEMATICS

1 [The War Office kept three sets of figures:] one to mislead the public, another to mislead the Cabinet, and the third to mislead itself.

> **Herbert Asquith** 1852–1928 British Liberal statesman: Alistair Horne *Price of Glory* (1962)

2 Every moment dies a man,
Every moment 1¹⁄₁₆ is born.

> **Charles Babbage** 1791–1871 English mathematician and inventor: parody of Tennyson's 'Vision of Sin' in an unpublished letter to the poet; in *New Scientist* 4 December 1958; see STATISTICS 14

3 One of the thieves was saved. (*Pause*)
It's a reasonable percentage.

> **Samuel Beckett** 1906–89 Irish dramatist, novelist, and poet: *Waiting for Godot* (1955)

4 Statistics are the triumph of the quantitative method, and the quantitative method is the victory of sterility and death.

> **Hilaire Belloc** 1870–1953 British poet, essayist, historian, novelist, and Liberal politician: *The Silence of the Sea* (1941)

5 A witty statesman said, you might prove anything by figures.

> **Thomas Carlyle** 1795–1881 Scottish historian and political philosopher: *Chartism* (1839)

6 Long and painful experience has taught me one great principle in managing business for other people, viz., if you want to inspire confidence, *give plenty of statistics.*

> **Lewis Carroll** 1832–98 English writer and logician: C. L. Dodgson *Three Years in a Curatorship by One Whom It Has Tried* (1886)

7 There are three kinds of lies: lies, damned lies and statistics.

> **Benjamin Disraeli** 1804–81 British Tory statesman and novelist: attributed; Mark Twain *Autobiography* (1924)

8 From the fact that there are 400,000 species of beetles on this planet, but only 8,000 species of mammals, he [Haldane] concluded that the Creator, if He exists, has a special preference for beetles.

> **J. B. S. Haldane** 1892–1964 Scottish mathematical biologist: report of lecture, 7 April 1951

9 We are just statistics, born to consume resources.

> **Horace** 65–8 BC Roman poet: *Epistles*

10 He uses statistics as a drunken man uses lampposts—for support rather than for illumination.

> **Andrew Lang** 1844–1912 Scottish man of letters: attributed

11 You cannot feed the hungry on statistics.

> **David Lloyd George** 1863–1945 British Liberal statesman: speech, House of Commons, 1904

12 You mean, your statistics are facts, but my facts are just statistics.

> **Jonathan Lynn** 1943– and **Antony Jay** 1930– English writers: *Yes Prime Minister* (1986) vol. 1

13 If your experiment needs statistics, you ought to have done a better experiment.

> **Ernest Rutherford** 1871–1937 New Zealand physicist: Norman T. J. Bailey *The Mathematical Approach to Biology and Medicine* (1967)

14 Every moment dies a man,
Every moment one is born.

> **Alfred, Lord Tennyson** 1809–92 English poet: 'The Vision of Sin' (1842); see STATISTICS 2

15 The so-called science of poll-taking is not a science at all but a mere necromancy. People are unpredictable by nature, and although you can take a nation's pulse, you can't be sure that the

nation hasn't just run up a flight of stairs.

> **E. B. White** 1899–1985 American humorist: in *New Yorker* 13 November 1948

Strength and Weakness

see also DETERMINATION

1 Our cock won't fight.

> *of Edward VIII, said to Winston Churchill during the abdication crisis of 1936*
> **Lord Beaverbrook** 1879–1964 Canadian-born British newspaper proprietor and Conservative politician: Frances Donaldson *Edward VIII* (1974)

2 For the good that I would I do not: but the evil which I would not, that I do.

> **Bible**: Romans

3 If God be for us, who can be against us?

> **Bible**: Romans

4 The weak have one weapon: the errors of those who think they are strong.

> **Georges Bidault** 1899–1983 French politician: in *Observer* 15 July 1962

5 The most potent weapon in the hands of the oppressor is the mind of the oppressed.

> **Steve Biko** 1946–77 South African anti-apartheid campaigner: statement as witness, 3 May 1976

6 The weak are strong because they are reckless. The strong are weak because they have scruples.

> **Otto von Bismarck** 1815–98 German statesman: quoted by Henry Kissinger to James Callaghan, 1975; James Callaghan *Time and Chance* (1987)

7 It is the nature, and the advantage, of strong people that they can bring out the crucial questions and form a clear opinion about them. The weak always have to decide between alternatives that are not their own.

> **Dietrich Bonhoeffer** 1906–45 German Lutheran theologian: *Resistance and Submission* (1951)

8 The concessions of the weak are the concessions of fear.

> **Edmund Burke** 1729–97 Irish-born Whig politician and man of letters: *On Conciliation with America* (1775)

9 As you know, God is usually on the side of the big squadrons against the small.

> *often quoted as 'Providence is always on the side of the big battalions'*
> **Comte de Bussy-Rabutin** 1618–93 French soldier and poet: letter to the Comte de Limoges, 18 October 1677; see STRENGTH 19

10 Toughness doesn't have to come in a pinstripe suit.

> **Dianne Feinstein** 1933– American Democratic politician: in *Time* 4 June 1984

11 Nothing is wasted, nothing is in vain: The seas roll over but the rocks remain.

> **A. P. Herbert** 1890–1971 English writer and humorist: *Tough at the Top* (operetta c.1949)

12 The thing is, you see, that the strongest man in the world is the man who stands most alone.

> **Henrik Ibsen** 1828–1906 Norwegian dramatist: *An Enemy of the People* (1882)

13 All the world knows that the weak overcomes the strong and the soft overcomes the hard.
But none can practice it.

> **Lao Tzu** c.604–c.531 BC Chinese philosopher: *Tao-te Ching*

14 Strength through joy.
> **Robert Ley** 1890–1945 German Nazi:
> German Labour Front slogan from 1933

15 One is never weaker than when one appears to have everybody's support.
> **Émile Ollivier** 1825–1913 French politician: *L'Empire libéral* (1894)

16 Choose rather to be strong in soul than strong of body.
> **Pythagoras** 580–500 BC Greek philosopher: Stobaeus *Sententiae*

17 You are the weakest link . . . goodbye.
> **Anne Robinson** 1944– British television presenter: catchphrase used on the television game-show *The Weakest Link* (2000–)

18 This is the law of the Yukon, that only the Strong shall thrive;
> That surely the Weak shall perish, and only the Fit survive.
> **Robert W. Service** 1874–1958 Canadian poet: 'The Law of the Yukon' (1907)

19 The gods are on the side of the stronger.
> **Tacitus** AD c.56–after 117 Roman senator and historian: *Histories*; see STRENGTH 9

20 If you can't stand the heat, get out of the kitchen.
> **Harry S. Truman** 1884–1972 American Democratic statesman: in *Time* 28 April 1952; associated with Truman, but attributed by him to Harry Vaughan, his 'military jester'

21 Limitation makes for power: the strength of the genie comes of his being confined in a bottle.
> **Richard Wilbur** 1921– American poet: 'The Genie in the Bottle' in John Ciardi (ed.) *Mid-Century American Poets* (1950)

Style

see also LANGUAGE

1 People think that I can teach them style. What stuff it all is! Have something to say, and say it as clearly as you can. That is the only secret of style.
> **Matthew Arnold** 1822–88 English poet and essayist: G. W. E. Russell *Collections and Recollections* (1898)

2 No iron can stab the heart with such force as a full stop put just at the right place.
> **Isaac Babel** 1894–1940 Russian short-story writer: *Guy de Maupassant* (1932)

3 These things [subject matter] are external to the man; style is the man.
> **Comte de Buffon** 1707–88 French naturalist: *Discours sur le style*; address given to the Académie Française, 25 August 1753

4 The Mandarin style . . . is beloved by literary pundits, by those who would make the written word as unlike as possible to the spoken one.
> **Cyril Connolly** 1903–74 English writer: *Enemies of Promise* (1938)

5 Style is life! It is the very life-blood of thought!
> **Gustave Flaubert** 1821–80 French novelist: letter to Louise Colet, 7 September 1853

6 I strive to be brief, and I become obscure.
> **Horace** 65–8 BC Roman poet: *Ars Poetica*

7 When we see a natural style, we are quite surprised and delighted, for we expected to see an author and we find a man.
> **Blaise Pascal** 1623–62 French mathematician, physicist, and moralist: *Pensées* (1670)

8 True wit is Nature to advantage dressed,

What oft was thought, but ne'er so well expressed.
Alexander Pope 1688–1744 English poet: *An Essay on Criticism* (1711)

9 More matter with less art.
William Shakespeare 1564–1616 English dramatist: *Hamlet* (1601)

10 Proper words in proper places, make the true definition of a style.
Jonathan Swift 1667–1745 Anglo-Irish poet and satirist: *Letter to a Young Gentleman lately entered into Holy Orders* 9 January 1720

11 As to the Adjective: when in doubt, strike it out.
Mark Twain 1835–1910 American writer: *Pudd'nhead Wilson* (1894)

12 'Feather-footed through the plashy fen passes the questing vole' . . . 'Yes,' said the Managing Editor. 'That must be good style.'
Evelyn Waugh 1903–66 English novelist: *Scoop* (1938)

13 Style is the dress of thought; a modest dress,
Neat, but not gaudy, will true critics please.
Samuel Wesley 1662–1735 English clergyman and poet: 'An Epistle to a Friend concerning Poetry' (1700)

14 It's not what I do, but the way I do it.
It's not what I say, but the way I say it.
Mae West 1892–1980 American film actress: G. Eells and S. Musgrove *Mae West* (1989)

15 I don't wish to sign my name, though I am afraid everybody will know who the writer is: one's style is one's signature always.
Oscar Wilde 1854–1900 Anglo-Irish dramatist and poet: letter to the *Daily Telegraph*, 2 February 1891

Success

see also DEFEAT, FAILURE, WINNING

1 'Tis not in mortals to command success,
But we'll do more, Sempronius; we'll deserve it.
Joseph Addison 1672–1719 English poet, dramatist, and essayist: *Cato* (1713)

2 For what shall it profit a man, if he shall gain the whole world, and lose his own soul?
Bible: St Mark

3 It was roses, roses, all the way.
Robert Browning 1812–89 English poet: 'The Patriot' (1855)

4 At the end of your life you will never regret not having passed one more test, winning one more verdict or not closing one more deal. You will regret time not spent with a husband, a child, a friend or a parent.
Barbara Bush 1925– American Fisrt Lady: in *Washington Post* 2 June 1990

5 *Veni, vidi, vici.*
I came, I saw, I conquered.
Julius Caesar 100–44 BC Roman general and statesman: inscription displayed in Caesar's Pontic triumph, according to Suetonius *Lives of the Caesars* 'Divus Julius'; or, according to Plutarch *Parallel Lives* 'Julius Caesar', written in a letter by Caesar, announcing the victory of Zela which concluded the Pontic campaign

6 How to win friends and influence people.
Dale Carnegie 1888–1955 American writer and lecturer: title of book (1936)

7 Success took me to her bosom like a maternal boa constrictor.
Noël Coward 1899–1973 English dramatist, actor, and composer: Sheridan Morley *A Talent to Amuse* (1969)

8 Success is counted sweetest
By those who ne'er succeed.
To comprehend a nectar
Requires sorest need.
> **Emily Dickinson** 1830–86 American
> poet: 'Success is counted sweetest'
> (1859)

9 In the United States there's a Puritan
ethic and a mythology of success. He
who is successful is good. In Latin
countries, in Catholic countries, a
successful person is a sinner.
> **Umberto Eco** 1932– Italian novelist
> and semiotician: in *International
> Herald Tribune* 14 December 1988

10 If *A* is a success in life, then *A* equals
x plus *y* plus *z*. Work is *x*; *y* is play;
and *z* is keeping your mouth shut.
> **Albert Einstein** 1879–1955 German-
> born theoretical physicist: in *Observer*
> 15 January 1950

11 Success is relative:
It is what we can make of the mess
we have made of things.
> **T. S. Eliot** 1888–1965 Anglo-American
> poet, critic, and dramatist: *The Family
> Reunion* (1939)

12 Success is more dangerous than
failure, the ripples break over a wider
coastline.
> **Graham Greene** 1904–91 English
> novelist: in *The Independent* 4 April
> 1991

13 The moral flabbiness born of the
exclusive worship of the bitch-
goddess *success*.
> **William James** 1842–1910 American
> philosopher: letter to H. G. Wells,
> 11 September 1906

14 Sweet smell of success.
> **Ernest Lehman** 1920–2005 American
> screenwriter: title of book and film
> (1957)

15 In most things success depends on
knowing how long it takes to
succeed.
> **Montesquieu** 1689–1755 French
> political philosopher: *Pensées et
> fragments inédits . . .* vol. 1 (1901) no.
> 630

16 Is it possible to succeed without any
act of betrayal?
> **Jean Renoir** 1894–1979 French film
> director: *My Life and My Films* (1974)

17 The world continues to offer
glittering prizes to those who have
stout hearts and sharp swords.
> **F. E. Smith** 1872–1930 British
> Conservative politician and lawyer:
> Rectorial Address, Glasgow University,
> 7 November 1923

18 Success makes life easier. It doesn't
make *living* easier.
> **Bruce Springsteen** 1949– American
> rock singer and songwriter: in *Q
> Magazine* August 1992

19 He has achieved success who has
lived well, laughed often, and loved
much; who has enjoyed the trust of
pure women, the respect of
intelligent men, and the love of little
children; . . . whose life was an
inspiration, whose memory a
benediction.
> **Bessie Anderson Stanley** *fl.* 1905
> American writer: 'What Constitutes
> Success', in *Modern Women* December
> 1905, and often wrongly attributed to
> Ralph Waldo Emerson or Robert Louis
> Stevenson; in *Notes and Queries* July
> 1976

20 Success to me is having ten
honeydew melons and eating only
the top half of each one.
> **Barbra Streisand** 1942– American
> singer, actress, and film director: in *Life*
> 20 September 1963

21 All you need in this life is ignorance and confidence; then success is sure.

> **Mark Twain** 1835–1910 American writer: letter to Mrs Foote, 2 December 1887

22 Whenever a friend succeeds, a little something in me dies.

> **Gore Vidal** 1925– American novelist and critic: in *Sunday Times Magazine* 16 September 1973

Suffering

see also COMPASSION, SACRIFICE, SORROW, TRAGEDY

1 Children's talent to endure stems from their ignorance of alternatives.

> **Maya Angelou** 1928– American writer: *I Know Why The Caged Bird Sings* (1969)

2 About suffering they were never wrong,
The Old Masters: how well they understood
Its human position; how it takes place
While someone else is eating or opening a window or just walking dully along.

> **W. H. Auden** 1907–73 English poet: 'Musée des Beaux Arts' (1940)

3 Nothing happens to anybody which he is not fitted by nature to bear.

> **Marcus Aurelius** AD 121–180 Roman emperor: *Meditations*

4 Misery such as mine has no pride. I care not who knows that I am wretched.

> **Jane Austen** 1775–1817 English novelist: *Sense and Sensibility* (1811)

5   For frequent tears have run
The colours from my life.

> **Elizabeth Barrett Browning** 1806–61 English poet: *Sonnets from the Portuguese* (1850)

6 After great pain, a formal feeling comes—
The Nerves sit ceremonious, like Tombs.

> **Emily Dickinson** 1830–86 American poet: 'After great pain, a formal feeling comes' (1862)

7 The beginning of hardship is like the first taste of bitter food—it seems for a moment unbearable; yet, if there is nothing else to satisfy our hunger, we take another bite and find it possible to go on.

> **George Eliot** 1819–80 English novelist: *Adam Bede* (1859)

8 To each his suff'rings, all are men,
Condemned alike to groan;
The tender for another's pain,
Th' unfeeling for his own.

> **Thomas Gray** 1716–71 English poet: *Ode on a Distant Prospect of Eton College* (1747)

9 The fool learns by suffering.

> **Hesiod** *fl. c.* 700 BC Greek poet: *Works and Days*

10 Pity is the feeling which arrests the mind in the presence of whatsoever is grave and constant in human sufferings and unites it with the human sufferer. Terror is the feeling which arrests the mind in the presence of whatsoever is grave and constant in human sufferings and unites it with the secret cause.

> **James Joyce** 1882–1941 Irish novelist: *A Portrait of the Artist as a Young Man* (1916)

11 Fade far away, dissolve, and quite forget
What thou among the leaves hast never known,
The weariness, the fever, and the fret
Here, where men sit and hear each other groan.

> **John Keats** 1795–1821 English poet: 'Ode to a Nightingale' (1820)

12 The toad beneath the harrow knows
Exactly where each tooth-point goes;

The butterfly upon the road
Preaches contentment to that toad.
Rudyard Kipling 1865–1936 English
writer and poet: 'Pagett, MP' (1886)

13 Sorrow and silence are strong, and
patient endurance is godlike.
Henry Wadsworth Longfellow 1807–82
American poet: *Evangeline* (1847)

14 Scars have the strange power to
remind us that our past is real.
Cormac McCarthy 1933– American
writer: *All the Pretty Horses* (1993)

15 It is not true that suffering ennobles
the character; happiness does that
sometimes, but suffering, for the
most part, makes men petty and
vindictive.
W. Somerset Maugham 1874–1965
English novelist: *The Moon and
Sixpence* (1919)

16 Willy Loman never made a lot of
money. His name was never in the
paper. He's not the finest character
that ever lived. But he's a human
being, and a terrible thing is
happening to him. So attention must
be paid.
Arthur Miller 1915–2005 American
dramatist: *Death of a Salesman* (1949)

17 What does not kill me makes me
stronger.
Friedrich Nietzsche 1844–1900 German
philosopher and writer: *Twilight of the
Idols* (1889)

18 We can't all be happy, we can't all be
rich, we can't all be lucky . . . Some
must cry so that others may be able
to laugh the more heartily.
Jean Rhys *c.*1890–1979 British novelist
and short-story writer: *Good Morning,
Midnight* (1939)

19 Suffering is only intolerable when
nobody cares.
Cicely Saunders 1916–2005 English
founder of St Christopher's Hospice,
London: 'The Management of Patients
in the Terminal Stage' in *Cancer*
1960 vol. 6

20 Pain is an inconsiderable thing if not
reinforced by opinion.
Seneca ('the Younger') *c.*4 BC–AD 65
Roman philosopher and poet: *Epistulae
ad Lucilium*

21 He jests at scars, that never felt a
wound.
William Shakespeare 1564–1616
English dramatist: *Romeo and Juliet*
(1595)

22   The worst is not,
So long as we can say, 'This is the
worst.'
William Shakespeare 1564–1616
English dramatist: *King Lear* (1605–6)

23 How can you expect a man who's
warm to understand one who's cold?
Alexander Solzhenitsyn 1918–2008
Russian novelist: *One Day in the Life of
Ivan Denisovich* (1962)

24 Nothing begins, and nothing ends,
That is not paid with moan;
For we are born in other's pain,
And perish in our own.
Francis Thompson 1859–1907 English
poet: 'Daisy' (1913)

25 Suffering is permanent, obscure and
dark,
And shares the nature of infinity.
William Wordsworth 1770–1850
English poet: *The Borderers* (1842)

26 Too long a
sacrifice
Can make a
stone of the
heart.
W. B. Yeats 1865–1939 Irish poet: 'Easter,
1916' (1921)

Suicide

1 Without the possibility of suicide, I
would have killed myself long ago.
E. M. Cioran 1911–95 Romanian-born
French philosopher: in *Independent*
2 December 1989

2 Suicide is our way of saying to God: 'You can't fire me. I quit'.

> **Bill Maher** 1956– American comedian: *Politically Incorrect* (American TV show, 1993–2002)

3 A suicide kills two people, Maggie, that's what it's for!

> **Arthur Miller** 1915–2005 American dramatist: *After the Fall* (1964)

4 The thought of suicide is a great source of comfort: with it a calm passage is to be made across many a bad night.

> **Friedrich Nietzsche** 1844–1900 German philosopher and writer: *Jenseits von Gut und Böse* (1886)

5 Guns aren't lawful;
Nooses give;
Gas smells awful;
You might as well live.

> **Dorothy Parker** 1893–1967 American critic and humorist: 'Résumé' (1937)

6 If I cannot give consent to my own death, then whose body is this? Who owns my life?

> **Sue Rodriguez** 1951–94 Canadian euthanasia activist: appealing to a subcomittee of the Canadian Commons, November 1992

7 But suicides have a special language. Like carpenters they want to know *which tools*.
They never ask *why build*.

> **Anne Sexton** 1928–74 American poet: 'Wanting to Die' (1966)

8 For who would bear the whips and scorns of time,
The oppressor's wrong, the proud man's contumely,
The pangs of disprized love, the law's delay,
The insolence of office, and the spurns
That patient merit of the unworthy takes,

When he himself might his quietus make
With a bare bodkin?

> **William Shakespeare** 1564–1616 English dramatist: *Hamlet* (1601)

9   Nor at all can tell
Whether I mean this day to end myself,
Or lend an ear to Plato where he says,
That men like soldiers may not quit the post
Allotted by the Gods.

> **Alfred, Lord Tennyson** 1809–92 English poet: 'Lucretius' (1868)

10 It's better to burn out
Than to fade away.

> *quoted by Kurt Cobain in his suicide note, 8 April 1994*
>
> **Neil Young** 1945– Canadian singer and songwriter: 'My My, Hey Hey (Out of the Blue)' (1978 song, with Jeff Blackburn)

Summer

1 Sumer is icumen in,
Lhude sing cuccu!
Groweth sed, and bloweth med,
And springth the wude nu.

> **Anonymous**: 'Cuckoo Song' (*c*.1250)

2 Summer has set in with its usual severity.

> **Samuel Taylor Coleridge** 1772–1834 English poet, critic, and philosopher: letter from Charles Lamb to Vincent Novello, 9 May 1826

3 June is bustin' out all over.

> **Oscar Hammerstein II** 1895–1960 American songwriter: title of song (1945)

4 Summer time an' the livin' is easy,
Fish are jumpin' an' the cotton is high.

> **Du Bose Heyward** 1885–1940 and **Ira Gershwin** 1896–1983 American songwriters: 'Summertime' (1935 song)

5 August creates as she slumbers,
replete and satisfied.
> **Joseph Wood Krutch** 1893–1970
> American critic and naturalist: *Twelve
> Seasons* (1949)

6 The way to ensure summer in
England is to have it framed and
glazed in a comfortable room.
> **Horace Walpole** 1717–97 English writer
> and connoisseur: letter to Revd William
> Cole, 28 May 1774

The Supernatural

see also PARANORMAL

1 Up the airy mountain,
Down the rushy glen,
We daren't go a-hunting,
For fear of little men.
> **William Allingham** 1824–89 Irish poet:
> 'The Fairies' (1850)

2 From ghoulies and ghosties and
long-leggety beasties
And things that go bump in the
night,
Good Lord, deliver us!
> **Anonymous**: 'The Cornish or West
> Country Litany'; Francis T.
> Nettleinghame *Polperro Proverbs and
> Others* (1926)

3 There is a superstition in avoiding
superstition.
> **Francis Bacon** 1561–1626 English
> lawyer, courtier, philosopher, and
> essayist: *Essays* (1625) 'Of Superstition'

4 Every time a child says 'I don't
believe in fairies' there is a little fairy
somewhere that falls down dead.
> **J. M. Barrie** 1860–1937 Scottish writer
> and dramatist: *Peter Pan* (1928)

5 For we wrestle not against flesh and
blood, but against principalities,
against powers, against the rulers of
the darkness of this world, against
spiritual wickedness in high places.
> **Bible**: Ephesians

6 The twilight is the crack between the
worlds. It is the door to the
unknown.
> **Carlos Castaneda** 1925–98: *Tales of
> Power* (1974)

7 Go, and catch a falling star,
Get with child a mandrake root,
Tell me, where all past years are,
Or who cleft the Devil's foot.
> **John Donne** 1572–1631 English poet
> and divine: 'Song: Go and catch a falling
> star'

8 There are fairies at the bottom of our
garden!
> **Rose Fyleman** 1877–1957 English writer
> for children: 'The Fairies' (1918)

9 Superstition is the poetry of life.
> **Johann Wolfgang von Goethe**
> 1749–1832 German poet, novelist, and
> dramatist: *Maximen und Reflexionen*
> (1819)

10 All argument is against it; but all
belief is for it.
of the existence of ghosts
> **Samuel Johnson** 1709–84 English poet,
> critic, and lexicographer: James Boswell
> *Life of Samuel Johnson* (1791) 31 March
> 1778

11 Double, double toil and trouble;
Fire burn and cauldron bubble.
> **William Shakespeare** 1564–1616
> English dramatist: *Macbeth* (1606)

Surprise

1 Surprises are foolish things. The
pleasure is not enhanced, and the
inconvenience is often considerable.
> **Jane Austen** 1775–1817 English novelist:
> *Emma* (1816)

2 'Curiouser and curiouser!' cried
Alice.
> **Lewis Carroll** 1832–98 English writer
> and logician: *Alice's Adventures in
> Wonderland* (1865)

3 Nobody expects the Spanish Inquisition!

> **Graham Chapman** 1941–89 and **John Cleese** 1939– British comedy writers and actors: *Monty Python's Flying Circus* (BBC TV programme, 1970, with Terry Gilliam, Eric Idle, Terry Jones, and Michael Palin)

4 It was quite the most incredible event that has ever happened to me in my life. It was almost as incredible as if you fired a 15-inch shell at a piece of tissue paper and it came back and hit you.

on the back-scattering effect of metal foil on alpha-particles

> **Ernest Rutherford** 1871–1937 New Zealand physicist: E. N. da C. Andrade *Rutherford and the Nature of the Atom* (1964)

5 O wonderful, wonderful, and most wonderful wonderful! and yet again wonderful, and after that, out of all whooping!

> **William Shakespeare** 1564–1616 English dramatist: *As You Like It* (1599)

6 I turned to Aunt Agatha, whose demeanour was now rather like that of one who, picking daisies on the railway, has just caught the down express in the small of the back.

> **P. G. Wodehouse** 1881–1975 English writer: *The Inimitable Jeeves* (1923)

Swearing

1 Expletive deleted.

> **Anonymous**: *Submission of Recorded Presidential Conversations to the Committee on the Judiciary of the House of Representatives by President Richard M. Nixon* 30 April 1974

2 Don't swear, boy. It shows a lack of vocabulary.

> **Alan Bennett** 1934– English actor and dramatist: *Forty Years On* (1969)

3 The man who first abused his fellows with swear-words instead of bashing their brains out with a club should be counted among those who laid the foundations of civilization.

> **John Cohen** 1911– : in *Observer* 21 November 1965

4 Though 'Bother it' I may
Occasionally say,
I never use a big, big D—

> **W. S. Gilbert** 1836–1911 English writer of comic and satirical verse: *HMS Pinafore* (1878)

5 You taught me language; and my profit on't
Is, I know how to curse: the red plague rid you,
For learning me your language!

> **William Shakespeare** 1564–1616 English dramatist: *The Tempest* (1611)

6 If ever I utter an oath again may my soul be blasted to eternal damnation!

> **George Bernard Shaw** 1856–1950 Irish dramatist: *Saint Joan* (1924)

Tact

1 The tribute which intelligence pays to humbug.

> **St John Brodrick** 1856–1942 British Conservative politician: Lady Ribblesdale to Lord Curzon 3 April 1891; Kenneth Rose *Superior Person* (1969)

2 Euphemisms are unpleasant truths wearing diplomatic cologne.

> **Quentin Crisp** 1908–99 English writer: *Manners from Heaven* (1984)

3 'Not to put too fine a point upon it'—a favourite apology for plain-speaking with Mr Snagsby.

> **Charles Dickens** 1812–70 English novelist: *Bleak House* (1853)

4 BISHOP: I'm afraid you've got a bad egg, Mr Jones.

CURATE: Oh no, my Lord, I assure you!
Parts of it are excellent!
Punch English humorous weekly
periodical: 11 May 1895

5 Up to a point, Lord Copper.
meaning no
Evelyn Waugh 1903–66 English novelist:
Scoop (1938)

Taste

see also VULGARITY

1 Good taste is better than bad taste,
but bad taste is better than no taste,
and men without individuality have
no taste—at any rate no taste that
they can impose on their publics.
Arnold Bennett 1867–1931 English
novelist: in *Evening Standard* 21 August
1930

2 A difference of taste in jokes is a great
strain on the affections.
George Eliot 1819–80 English novelist:
Daniel Deronda (1876)

3 Taste is the feminine of genius.
Edward Fitzgerald 1809–83 English
scholar and poet: letter to J. R. Lowell,
October 1877

4 Our tastes greatly alter. The lad does
not care for the child's rattle, and the
old man does not care for the young
man's whore.
Samuel Johnson 1709–84 English poet,
critic, and lexicographer: James Boswell
Life of Samuel Johnson (1791) Spring
1766

5 Nowhere probably is there more true
feeling, and nowhere worse taste,
than in a churchyard.
Benjamin Jowett 1817–93 English
classicist: Evelyn Abbott and Lewis
Campbell (eds.) *Letters of Benjamin
Jowett* (1899)

6 The kind of people who always go on
about whether a thing is in good
taste invariably have very bad taste.
Joe Orton 1933–67 English dramatist: in
Transatlantic Review Spring 1967

7 Could we teach taste or genius by
rules, they would be no longer taste
and genius.
Joshua Reynolds 1723–92 English
painter: *Discourses on Art* 14 December
1770

8 The play, I remember, pleased not
the million; 'twas caviare to the
general.
William Shakespeare 1564–1616
English dramatist: *Hamlet* (1601)

9 *of the wallpaper in the room where he was
dying:*
One of us must go.
Oscar Wilde 1854–1900 Anglo-Irish
dramatist and poet: attributed,
probably apocryphal

Taxes

1 Can't pay, won't pay.
Anonymous: anti-Poll Tax slogan,
*c.*1990

2 To tax and to please, no more than to
love and to be wise, is not given to
men.
Edmund Burke 1729–97 Irish-born
Whig politician and man of letters: *On
American Taxation* (1775)

3 Read my lips: no new taxes.
George Bush 1924– American
Republican statesman: campaign
pledge on taxation, in *New York Times*
19 August 1988

4 The art of taxation consists in so
plucking the goose as to obtain the
largest possible amount of feathers
with the smallest possible amount of
hissing.
Jean-Baptiste Colbert 1619–83 French
statesman: attributed

5 In this world nothing can be said to be certain, except death and taxes.
Benjamin Franklin 1706–90 American politician, inventor, and scientist: letter to Jean Baptiste Le Roy, 13 November 1789

6 Only the little people pay taxes.
Leona Helmsley c.1920–2007 American hotelier: addressed to her housekeeper in 1983, and reported at her trial for tax evasion; in *New York Times* 12 July 1989

7 *Excise.* A hateful tax levied upon commodities.
Samuel Johnson 1709–84 English poet, critic, and lexicographer: *A Dictionary of the English Language* (1755)

8 Death is the most convenient time to tax rich people.
David Lloyd George 1863–1945 British Liberal statesman: in *Lord Riddell's Intimate Diary of the Peace Conference and After, 1918–23* (1933)

9 The Chancellor of the Exchequer is a man whose duties make him more or less of a taxing machine. He is intrusted with a certain amount of misery which it is his duty to distribute as fairly as he can.
Robert Lowe 1811–92 British Liberal politician: speech, House of Commons, 11 April 1870

10 Taxation without representation is tyranny.
James Otis 1725–83 American politician: watchword (c.1761) of the American Revolution; in *Dictionary of American Biography*

11 Taxation is just a sophisticated way of demanding money with menaces.
Terry Pratchett 1948– English science fiction writer: *Night Watch* (2002)

12 Income Tax has made more Liars out of the American people than Golf.
Will Rogers 1879–1935 American actor and humorist: *The Illiterate Digest*

(1924) 'Helping the Girls with their Income Taxes'

13 There is no art which one government sooner learns of another than that of draining money from the pockets of the people.
Adam Smith 1723–90 Scottish philosopher and economist: *Wealth of Nations* (1776)

14 It is the part of the good shepherd to shear his flock, not skin it.
to governors who recommended burdensome taxes
Tiberius 42 BC–AD 37 Roman emperor: Suetonius *Lives of the Caesars* 'Tiberius'

15 Money has no smell.
quashing an objection to a tax on public lavatories
Vespasian AD 9–79 Roman emperor: traditional summary; Suetonius *Lives of the Caesars* 'Vespasian'

Teaching

see also EDUCATION, SCHOOLS

1 A teacher affects eternity; he can never tell where his influence stops.
Henry Brooks Adams 1838–1918 American man of letters: *The Education of Henry Adams* (1907)

2 There is no such whetstone, to sharpen a good wit and encourage a will to learning, as is praise.
Roger Ascham 1515–68 English scholar, writer, and courtier: *The Schoolmaster* (1570)

3 That is the difference between good teachers and great teachers: good teachers make the best of a pupil's means: great teachers foresee a pupil's ends.
Maria Callas 1923–77 American-born operatic soprano: *Kenneth Harris Talking To* (1971) 'Maria Callas'

4 A man who reviews the old so as to find out the new is qualified to teach others.

   Confucius 551–479 BC Chinese philosopher: *Analects*

5 C-l-e-a-n, clean, verb active, to make bright, to scour. W-i-n, win, d-e-r, der, winder, a casement. When the boy knows this out of the book, he goes and does it.

   Charles Dickens 1812–70 English novelist: *Nicholas Nickleby* (1839)

6 Technology is just a tool. In terms of getting the kids working together and motivating them, the teacher is the most important.

   Bill Gates 1955– American computer entrepreneur: in *Independent on Sunday* 12 October 1997

7 It is no matter what you teach them [children] first, any more than what leg you shall put into your breeches first.

   Samuel Johnson 1709–84 English poet, critic, and lexicographer: James Boswell *Life of Samuel Johnson* (1791) 26 July 1763

8 I hope you enjoy the absence of pupils . . . the total oblivion of them for definite intervals is a necessary condition for doing them justice at the proper time.

   James Clerk Maxwell 1831–79 Scottish physicist: letter to Lewis Campbell, 21 April 1862

9 We teachers can only help the work going on, as servants wait upon a master.

   Maria Montessori 1870–1952 Italian educationist: *The Absorbent Mind* (1949)

10 Discussion in class, which means letting twenty young blockheads and two cocky neurotics discuss something that neither their teacher nor they know.

   Vladimir Nabokov 1899–1977 Russian novelist: *Pnin* (1957)

11 Men must be taught as if you taught them not,
And things unknown proposed as things forgot.

   Alexander Pope 1688–1744 English poet: *An Essay on Criticism* (1711)

12 Few have been taught to any purpose who have not been their own teachers.

   Joshua Reynolds 1723–92 English painter: *Discourses on Art* 11 December 1769

13 Even while they teach, men learn.

   Seneca ('the Younger') c.4 BC–AD 65 Roman philosopher and poet: *Epistulae Morales*

14 He who can, does. He who cannot, teaches.

   George Bernard Shaw 1856–1950 Irish dramatist: *Man and Superman* (1903)

15 A teacher should have maximal authority and minimal power.

   Thomas Szasz 1920– Hungarian-born psychiatrist: *The Second Sin* (1973) 'Education'

16 Delightful task! to rear the tender thought,
To teach the young idea how to shoot.

   James Thomson 1700–48 Scottish poet: *The Seasons* (1746) 'Spring'

17 Knowledge has to be sucked into the brain, not pushed into it.

   Victor Weisskopf 1908–2002 American physicist: *The Privilege of Being a Physicist* (1989)

Technology

see also INVENTIONS, SCIENCE

1 Science finds, industry applies, man conforms.
   Anonymous: subtitle of guidebook to 1933 Chicago World's Fair

2 The three fundamental Rules of Robotics . . . One, a robot may not injure a human being, or, through inaction, allow a human being to come to harm . . . Two . . . a robot must obey the orders given it by human beings except where such orders would conflict with the First Law . . . three, a robot must protect its own existence as long as such protection does not conflict with the First or Second Laws.
   Isaac Asimov 1920–92 Russian-born biochemist and science fiction writer: *I, Robot* (1950) 'Runaround'

3 Inanimate objects are classified scientifically into three major categories—those that don't work, those that break down, and those that get lost.
   Russell Baker 1925– American journalist and columnist: in *New York Times* 18 June 1968

4 I am a sundial, and I make a botch Of what is done much better by a watch.
   Hilaire Belloc 1870–1953 British poet, essayist, historian, novelist, and Liberal politician: 'On a Sundial' (1938)

5 The biggest obstacle to professional writing is the necessity for changing a typewriter ribbon.
   Robert Benchley 1889–1945 American humorist: *Chips off the old Benchley* (1949) 'Learn to Write'

6 Your worship is your furnaces, Which, like old idols, lost obscenes, Have molten bowels; your vision is

Machines for making more machines.
   Gordon Bottomley 1874–1948 English poet and dramatist: 'To Ironfounders and Others' (1912)

7 I sell here, Sir, what all the world desires to have—POWER.
   of his engineering works
   Matthew Boulton 1728–1809 British engineer: James Boswell *Life of Samuel Johnson* (1791) 22 March 1776

8 Man is a tool-using animal . . . Without tools he is nothing, with tools he is all.
   Thomas Carlyle 1795–1881 Scottish historian and political philosopher: *Sartor Resartus* (1834)

9 Any sufficiently advanced technology is indistinguishable from magic.
   Arthur C. Clarke 1917–2008 English science fiction writer: *Profiles of the Future* (1962)

10 The first rule of intelligent tinkering is to save all the parts.
   Paul Ralph Ehrlich 1932– American biologist: in *Saturday Review* 5 June 1971

11 For a successful technology, reality must take precedence over public relations, for nature cannot be fooled.
   Richard Phillips Feynman 1918–88 American theoretical physicist: Appendix to the *Rogers Commission Report on the Space Shuttle Challenger Accident* 6 June 1986

12 Technology . . . the knack of so arranging the world that we need not experience it.
   Max Frisch 1911–91 Swiss novelist and dramatist: *Homo Faber* (1957)

13 Technology happens. It's not good, it's not bad. Is steel good or bad?
   Andrew Grove 1936– American

businessman: in *Time* 29 December 1997

14 The thing with high-tech is that you always end up using scissors.
David Hockney 1937– British artist: in *Observer* 10 July 1994

15 This is not the age of pamphleteers. It is the age of the engineers. The spark-gap is mightier than the pen.
Lancelot Hogben 1895–1975 English scientist: *Science for the Citizen* (1938)

16 One machine can do the work of fifty ordinary men. No machine can do the work of one extraordinary man.
Elbert Hubbard 1859–1915 American writer: *Thousand and One Epigrams* (1911)

17 When this circuit learns your job, what are you going to do?
Marshall McLuhan 1911–80 Canadian communications scholar: *The Medium is the Massage* (1967)

18 The medium is the message.
Marshall McLuhan 1911–80 Canadian communications scholar: *Understanding Media* (1964)

19 Gutenberg made everybody a reader. Xerox makes everybody a publisher.
Marshall McLuhan 1911–80 Canadian communications scholar: in *Guardian Weekly* 12 June 1977

20 When you see something that is technically sweet, you go ahead and do it and you argue about what to do about it only after you have had your technical success. That is the way it was with the atomic bomb.
J. Robert Oppenheimer 1904–67 American physicist: in *In the Matter of J. Robert Oppenheimer, USAEC Transcript of Hearing Before Personnel Security Board* (1954)

21 Machines are worshipped because they are beautiful, and valued because they confer power; they are hated because they are hideous, and loathed because they impose slavery.
Bertrand Russell 1872–1970 British philosopher and mathematician: *Sceptical Essays* (1928) 'Machines and Emotions'

22 It has been said that an engineer is a man who can do for ten shillings what any fool can do for a pound.
Nevil Shute 1899–1960 British novelist: *Slide Rule* (1954)

23 The things I want to show are mechanical. Machines have less problems. I'd like to be a machine, wouldn't you?
Andy Warhol 1927–87 American artist: Mike Wrenn *Andy Warhol: In His Own Words* (1991)

24 The Britain that is going to be forged in the white heat of this revolution will be no place for restrictive practices or for outdated methods on either side of industry.
usually quoted as 'the white heat of the technological revolution'
Harold Wilson 1916–95 British Labour statesman: speech at the Labour Party Conference, 1 October 1963

Teetotalism

1 One reason why I don't drink is because I wish to know when I am having a good time.
Nancy Astor 1879–1964 American-born British Conservative politician: in *Christian Herald* June 1960

2 Our country has deliberately undertaken a great social and economic experiment, noble in motive and far-reaching in purpose.
on the Eighteenth Amendment enacting Prohibition
Herbert Hoover 1874–1964 American Republican statesman: letter to Senator W. H. Borah, 23 February 1928

3 No verse can give pleasure for long,
nor last, that is written by drinkers of
water.

> **Horace** 65–8 BC Roman poet: *Epistles*

4 Prohibition makes you want to cry
into your beer and denies you the
beer to cry into.

> **Don Marquis** 1878–1937 American poet
> and journalist: *Sun Dial Time* (1936)

5 I'd hate to be a teetotaller. Imagine
getting up in the morning and
knowing that's as good as you're
going to feel all day.

> **Dean Martin** 1917– American singer
> and actor: attributed; also attributed to
> Jimmy Durante

6 I'm only a beer teetotaller, not a
champagne teetotaller.

> **George Bernard Shaw** 1856–1950 Irish
> dramatist: *Candida* (1898)

7 Your lips, on my own, when they
printed 'Farewell',
Had never been soiled by the
'beverage of hell';
But they come to me now with the
bacchanal sign,
And the lips that touch liquor must
never touch mine.

> **George W. Young** 1846–1919: 'The Lips
> That Touch Liquor Must Never Touch
> Mine' (*c.* 1870); also attributed, in a
> different form, to Harriet A. Glazebrook,
> 1874

Television

1 TV—a clever contraction derived
from the words Terrible
Vaudeville . . . we call it a medium
because nothing's well done.

> **Goodman Ace** 1899–1982 American
> humorist: letter to Groucho Marx,
> *c.*1953

2 Adams' first law of television: the
weight of the backside is greater than
the force of the intellect.

> **Philip Adams** 1939– Australian film
> director and producer: in 1970;
> attributed, Stephen Murray-Smith (ed.)
> *The Dictionary of Australian Quotations*
> (1984)

3 So much chewing gum for the eyes.
*small boy's definition of certain television
programmes*

> **Anonymous**: James Beasley Simpson
> *Best Quotes of '50, '55, '56* (1957)

4 Television . . . thrives on unreason,
and unreason thrives on
television . . . [It] strikes at the
emotions rather than the intellect.

> **Robin Day** 1923–2000 British
> broadcaster: *Grand Inquisitor* (1989)

5 Let's face it, there are no plain
women on television.

> **Anna Ford** 1943– English journalist
> and broadcaster: in *Observer*
> 23 September 1979

6 Television is simultaneously blamed,
often by the same people, for
worsening the world and for being
powerless to change it.

> **Clive James** 1939– Australian critic and
> writer: *Glued to the Box* (1981)

7 Television brought the brutality of
war into the comfort of the living
room. Vietnam was lost in the living
rooms of America—not the
battlefields of Vietnam.

> **Marshall McLuhan** 1911–80 Canadian
> communications scholar: in *Montreal
> Gazette* 16 May 1975

8 When the politicians complain that
TV turns their proceedings into a
circus, it should be made plain that
the circus was already there, and that
TV has merely demonstrated that
not all the performers are well
trained.

> **Ed Murrow** 1908–65 American

broadcaster and journalist: attributed, 1959

9 Television is actually closer to reality than anything in books. The madness of TV is the madness of human life.

Camille Paglia 1947– American writer and critic: in *Harper's Magazine* March 1991

10 Television has made dictatorship impossible, but democracy unbearable.

Shimon Peres 1923– Israeli statesman: at a Davos meeting, in *Financial Times* 31 January 1995

11 He who prides himself on giving what he thinks the public wants is often creating a fictitious demand for lower standards which he will then satisfy.

Lord Reith 1889–1971 British administrator and politician: memo to Crawford Committee 1926; Andrew Boyle *Only the Wind Will Listen* (1972)

12 Nation shall speak peace unto nation.

Montague John Rendall 1862–1950 English headmaster: motto of the BBC; see PEACE 2

13 Radio and television . . . have succeeded in lifting the manufacture of banality out of the sphere of handicraft and placed it in that of a major industry.

Nathalie Sarraute 1902–99 French novelist: in *Times Literary Supplement* 10 June 1960

14 *Television*? The word is half Greek, half Latin. No good can come of it.

C. P. Scott 1846–1932 British journalist: Asa Briggs *The BBC: the First Fifty Years* (1985)

15 57 channels (and nothin' on).

Bruce Springsteen 1949– American rock singer and songwriter: title of song, 1992

16 A terminal blight has hit the TV industry nipping fun in the bud and stunting our growth. This blight is management—the dreaded Four M's: male, middle class, middle-aged and mediocre.

Janet Street-Porter 1946– English broadcaster and programme-maker: MacTaggart Lecture, Edinburgh Television Festival, 25 August 1995

17 Like having a licence to print your own money.
on the profitability of commercial television in Britain

Roy Thomson 1894–1976 Canadian-born British newspaper proprietor: R. Braddon *Roy Thomson* (1965)

18 I hate television. I hate it as much as peanuts. But I can't stop eating peanuts.

Orson Welles 1915–85 American actor and film director: in *New York Herald Tribune* 12 October 1956

19 It used to be that we in films were the lowest form of art. Now we have something to look down on.
of television

Billy Wilder 1906–2002 American screenwriter and director: A. Madsen *Billy Wilder* (1968)

20 Television contracts the imagination and radio expands it.

Terry Wogan 1938– Irish broadcaster: attributed, 1984

Temptation

1 Watch and pray, that ye enter not into temptation: the spirit indeed is willing but the flesh is weak.

Bible: St Matthew

2 What's done we partly may compute, But know not what's resisted.

Robert Burns 1759–96 Scottish poet: 'Address to the Unco Guid' (1787)

3 I've looked on a lot of women with lust. I've committed adultery in my heart many times. This is something that God recognizes I will do — and I have done it — and God forgives me for it.

Jimmy Carter 1924– American Democratic statesman: in *Playboy* November 1976

4 The Lord above made liquor for temptation
To see if man could turn away from sin.
The Lord above made liquor for temptation—but
With a little bit of luck,
With a little bit of luck,
When temptation comes you'll give right in!

Alan Jay Lerner 1918–86 American songwriter: 'With a Little Bit of Luck' (1956 song)

5 He that but looketh on a plate of ham and eggs to lust after it, hath already committed breakfast with it in his heart.

C. S. Lewis 1898–1963 English literary scholar: letter, 10 March 1954

6 Temptations came to him, in middle age, tentatively and without insistence, like a neglected butcher-boy who asks for a Christmas box in February for no more hopeful reason than that he didn't get one in December.

Saki 1870–1916 Scottish writer: *The Chronicles of Clovis* (1911)

7   Is this her fault or mine?
The tempter or the tempted, who sins most?

William Shakespeare 1564–1616 English dramatist: *Measure for Measure* (1604)

8 It may almost be a question whether such wisdom as many of us have in our mature years has not come from

the dying out of the power of temptation, rather than as the results of thought and resolution.

Anthony Trollope 1815–82 English novelist: *The Small House at Allington* (1864)

9 There are several good protections against temptations, but the surest is cowardice.

Mark Twain 1835–1910 American writer: *Following the Equator* (1897)

10 I can resist everything except temptation.

Oscar Wilde 1854–1900 Anglo-Irish dramatist and poet: *Lady Windermere's Fan* (1892)

Tennis

1 Love-thirty, love-forty, oh! weakness of joy,
The speed of a swallow, the grace of a boy,
With carefullest carelessness, gaily you won,
I am weak from your loveliness, Joan Hunter Dunn.

John Betjeman 1906–84 English poet: 'A Subaltern's Love-Song' (1945)

2 I call tennis the McDonald's of sport—you go in, they make a quick buck out of you, and you're out.

Pat Cash 1965– Australian tennis player: in *Independent on Sunday* 4 July 1999

3 New Yorkers love it when you spill your guts out there. Spill your guts at Wimbledon and they make you stop and clean it up.

Jimmy Connors 1952– American tennis player: at Flushing Meadow, 1984

4 You cannot be serious!

John McEnroe 1959– American tennis player: said to tennis umpire at Wimbledon, early 1980s

5 Do what you love and love what you do and everything else is detail.
Martina Navratilova 1956– Czech-born American tennis player: in *The Times* 3 July 2004

6 If you can keep playing tennis when somebody is shooting a gun down the street, that's concentration. I didn't grow up playing at the country club.
Serena Williams 1981– American tennis player: in *Sunday Times* 2 June 2002

Terrorism
see also NINE-ELEVEN, VIOLENCE

1 We will make no distinction between terrorists who committed these acts and those who harbour them.
after the terrorist attacks of 11 September
George W. Bush 1946– American Republican statesman: televised address, 12 September 2001

2 How much blood must be spilled? How many tears shall we cry? How many mothers' hearts must be maimed?
mother of Anthony Fatayi-Williams, killed in the London bombings of 7 July 2005
Marie Fatayi-Williams Nigerian mother: speech near Tavistock Square, London, 11 July 2005

3 This was not a terrorist attack against the mighty and the powerful. It was not aimed at Presidents or Prime Ministers. It was aimed at ordinary, working-class Londoners, black and white, Muslim and Christian, Hindu and Jew, young and old. It was an indiscriminate attempt to slaughter, irrespective of any considerations for age, for class, for religion.
on the suicide bombings in London, 7 July 2005
Ken Livingstone 1945– British Labour

politician: speech, Singapore, 7 July 2005; in *Observer* 10 July 2005

4 We are especially not going to tolerate these attacks from outlaw states run by the strangest collection of misfits, Looney Tunes, and squalid criminals since the advent of the Third Reich.
Ronald Reagan 1911–2004 American Republican statesman: speech following the hijack of a US plane, 8 July 1985

5 It is of little use trying to suppress terrorism if the production of deadly devices continues to be deemed a legitimate employment of man's creative powers.
E. F. Schumacher 1911–77 German-born economist: *Small is Beautiful* (1973)

6 We must try to find ways to starve the terrorist and the hijacker of the oxygen of publicity on which they depend.
Margaret Thatcher 1925– British Conservative stateswoman: speech, 15 July 1985

7 The terrible thing about terrorism is that ultimately it destroys those who practise it. Slowly but surely, as they try to extinguish life in others, the light within them dies.
Terry Waite 1939– British religious adviser: in *Guardian* 20 February 1992

Thanks
see also GRATITUDE, MANNERS

1 No duty is more urgent than that of returning thanks.
St Ambrose *c.*339–397 French-born bishop of Milan: attributed

2 They say late thanks are ever best.
Francis Bacon 1561–1626 English lawyer, courtier, philosopher, and

essayist: letter to Robert, Lord Cecil, July 1603

3 A joyful and pleasant thing it is to be thankful.
Bible: Psalm 147

4 When I'm not thanked at all, I'm thanked enough,
I've done my duty, and I've done no more.
Henry Fielding 1707–54 English novelist and dramatist: *Tom Thumb the Great* (1731)

5 For this relief much thanks.
William Shakespeare 1564–1616 English dramatist: *Hamlet* (1601)

The Theatre

see also ACTING, ACTORS, SHAKESPEARE

1 There's no business like show business.
Irving Berlin 1888–1989 American songwriter: title of song (1946)

2 Things on stage should be as complicated and as simple as in life. People dine, just dine, while their happiness is made and their lives are smashed. If in Act 1 you have a pistol hanging on the wall, then it must fire in the last act.
Anton Chekhov 1860–1904 Russian dramatist and short-story writer: attributed; Donald Rayfield *Anton Chekhov* (1997)

3 *Étonne-moi.*
Astonish me.
to Jean Cocteau
Sergei Diaghilev 1872–1929 Russian ballet impresario: Wallace Fowlie (ed.) *Journals of Jean Cocteau* (1956)

4 Shaw is like a train. One just speaks the words and sits in one's place. But Shakespeare is like bathing in the sea—one swims where one wants.
Vivien Leigh 1913–67 English actress:

letter from Harold Nicolson to Vita Sackville-West, 1 February 1956

5 Don't clap too hard—it's a very old building.
John Osborne 1929–94 English dramatist: *The Entertainer* (1957)

6 The weasel under the cocktail cabinet.
on being asked what his plays were about
Harold Pinter 1930–2008 English dramatist: J. Russell Taylor *Anger and After* (1962)

7 You've got to perform in a role hundreds of times. In keeping it fresh one can become a large, madly humming, demented refrigerator.
Ralph Richardson 1902–83 English actor: in *Time* 21 August 1978

8 The play-bill, which is said to have announced the tragedy of Hamlet, the character of the Prince of Denmark being left out.
commonly alluded to as 'Hamlet without the Prince'
Sir Walter Scott 1771–1832 Scottish novelist and poet: *The Talisman* (1825)

9   Can this cockpit hold
The vasty fields of France? or may we cram
Within this wooden O the very casques
That did affright the air at Agincourt?
William Shakespeare 1564–1616 English dramatist: *Henry V* (1599)

10 I can do you blood and love without the rhetoric, and I can do you blood and rhetoric without the love, and I can do you all three concurrent or consecutive, but I can't do you love and rhetoric without the blood. Blood is compulsory—they're all blood, you see.
Tom Stoppard 1937– British dramatist: *Rosencrantz and Guildenstern are Dead* (1967)

11 I've never much enjoyed going to plays . . . The unreality of painted people standing on a platform saying things they've said to each other for months is more than I can overlook.

> **John Updike** 1932–2009 American novelist and short-story writer: George Plimpton (ed.) *Writers at Work* 4th Series (1977)

12 We never closed.

> *of the Windmill Theatre, London, during the Second World War*
>
> **Vivian van Damm** *c.*1889–1960 British theatre manager: *Tonight and Every Night* (1952)

13 Four trestles, four boards, two actors, a passion.

> *all he needed to create a play*
>
> **Lope de Vega** 1562–1635 Spanish dramatist and poet: attributed; James Fitzmaurice-Kelly *Lope de Vega and the Spanish Drama* (1902)

14 It's a sound you can't get in the movies or television . . . the sound of a wonderful, deep silence that means you've hit them where they live.

> **Shelley Winters** 1922–2006 American actress: in *Theatre Arts* June 1956

Theory

see also EXPERIMENT, FACTS, IDEAS, SCIENCE

1 When, however, the lay public rallies around an idea that is denounced by distinguished but elderly scientists and supports that idea with great fervour and emotion—the distinguished but elderly scientists are then, after all, probably right.

> *corollary to Arthur C. Clarke's law; see* THEORY 2
>
> **Isaac Asimov** 1920–92 Russian-born biochemist and science fiction writer: Arthur C. Clarke 'Asimov's Corollary' in K. Frazier (ed.) *Paranormal Borderlands of Science* (1981)

2 If an elderly but distinguished scientist says that something is possible he is almost certainly right, but if he says that it is impossible he is very probably wrong.

> **Arthur C. Clarke** 1917–2008 English science fiction writer: in *New Yorker* 9 August 1969; see THEORY 1

3 False views, if supported by some evidence, do little harm, for everyone takes a salutary pleasure in proving their falseness.

> **Charles Darwin** 1809–82 English natural historian: *The Descent of Man* (1871)

4 It is a capital mistake to theorize before you have all the evidence. It biases the judgement.

> **Arthur Conan Doyle** 1859–1930 Scottish-born writer of detective fiction: *A Study in Scarlet* (1888)

5 The grand aim of all science [is] to cover the greatest number of empirical facts by logical deduction from the smallest possible number of hypotheses or axioms.

> **Albert Einstein** 1879–1955 German-born theoretical physicist: Lincoln Barnett *The Universe and Dr Einstein* (1950 ed.)

6 The great tragedy of Science—the slaying of a beautiful hypothesis by an ugly fact.

> **T. H. Huxley** 1825–95 English biologist: *Collected Essays* (1893–4) 'Biogenesis and Abiogenesis'

7 It is a good morning exercise for a research scientist to discard a pet hypothesis every day before breakfast. It keeps him young.

> **Konrad Lorenz** 1903–89 Austro-German zoologist: *Das Sogenannte Böse* (1963; translated by Marjorie Latzke as *On Aggression*, 1966)

8 No *good* model ever accounted for *all* the facts since some data was

bound to be misleading if not plain wrong.

> **James D. Watson** 1928– American biologist: Francis Crick *Some Mad Pursuit* (1988)

Thinking

see also IDEAS, MIND

1 Think different.

> **Advertising slogan**: Apple Computers, 1997

2 To change your mind and to follow him who sets you right is to be nonetheless the free agent that you were before.

> **Marcus Aurelius** AD 121–180 Roman emperor: *Meditations*

3 He can't think without his hat.

> **Samuel Beckett** 1906–89 Irish dramatist, novelist, and poet: *Waiting for Godot* (1955)

4 Stung by the splendour of a sudden thought.

> **Robert Browning** 1812–89 English poet: 'A Death in the Desert' (1864)

5 What was once thought can never be unthought.

> **Friedrich Dürrenmatt** 1921–90 Swiss writer: *The Physicists* (1962)

6 *Je pense, donc je suis.*
I think, therefore I am.

> *usually quoted as,* 'Cogito, ergo sum', *from the 1641 Latin edition*
> **René Descartes** 1596–1650 French philosopher and mathematician: *Le Discours de la méthode* (1637)

7 It is quite a three-pipe problem, and I beg that you won't speak to me for fifty minutes.

> **Arthur Conan Doyle** 1859–1930 Scottish-born writer of detective fiction: *The Adventures of Sherlock Holmes* (1892)

8 How can I tell what I think till I see what I say?

> **E. M. Forster** 1879–1970 English novelist: *Aspects of the Novel* (1927)

9 It is a far, far better thing to have a firm anchor in nonsense than to put out on the troubled seas of thought.

> **J. K. Galbraith** 1908–2006 American economist: *The Affluent Society* (1958)

10 A man of action forced into a state of thought is unhappy until he can get out of it.

> **John Galsworthy** 1867–1933 English novelist: *Maid in Waiting* (1931)

11 Three minutes' thought would suffice to find this out; but thought is irksome and three minutes is a long time.

> **A. E. Housman** 1859–1936 English poet: *D. Iunii Iuvenalis Saturae* (1905) preface

12 Two things fill the mind with ever new and increasing wonder and awe, the more often and the more seriously reflection concentrates upon them: the starry heaven above me and the moral law within me.

> **Immanuel Kant** 1724–1804 German philosopher: *Critique of Practical Reason* (1788)

13 *I think, therefore I am* is the statement of an intellectual who underrates toothaches.

> **Milan Kundera** 1929– Czech novelist: *Immortality* (1991); see THINKING 6

14 She did her work with the thoroughness of a mind which reveres details and never quite understands them.

> **Sinclair Lewis** 1885–1951 American novelist: *Babbitt* (1922)

15 Pooh began to feel a little more comfortable, because when you are a Bear of Very Little Brain, and you Think of Things, you find sometimes that a Thing which seemed very Thingish inside you is quite different when it gets out into the open and has other people looking at it.

> **A. A. Milne** 1882–1956 English writer for children: *The House at Pooh Corner* (1928)

16 *Doublethink* means the power of holding two contradictory beliefs in one's mind simultaneously, and accepting both of them.

> **George Orwell** 1903–50 English novelist: *Nineteen Eighty-Four* (1949)

17 I don't mind your thinking slowly: I mind your publishing faster than you think.

> **Wolfgang Pauli** 1900–58 Austrian-born American physicist: attributed

18 Sometimes I sits and thinks, and then again I just sits.

> **Punch** English humorous weekly periodical: 24 October 1906

19 Many people would sooner die than think. In fact they do.

> **Bertrand Russell** 1872–1970 British philosopher and mathematician: attributed

20 The real question is not whether machines think but whether men do.

> **B. F. Skinner** 1904–90 American psychologist: *Contingencies of Reinforcement* (1969)

21 How often misused words generate misleading thoughts.

> **Herbert Spencer** 1820–1903 English philosopher: *Principles of Ethics* (1879)

22 The important thing is not to think much but to love much.

> **St Teresa of Ávila** 1512–82 Spanish Carmelite nun and mystic: *The Interior Castle* (1588)

23 Heretics are the only bitter remedy against the entropy of human thought.

> **Yevgeny Zamyatin** 1884–1937 Russian

writer: 'Literature, Revolution and Entropy' quoted in *The Dragon and other Stories* (1967) introduction

Thrift

see also MONEY

1 We could have saved sixpence. We have saved fivepence. (*Pause*) But at what cost?

> **Samuel Beckett** 1906–89 Irish dramatist, novelist, and poet: *All That Fall* (1957)

2 Economy is going without something you do want in case you should, some day, want something you probably won't want.

> **Anthony Hope** 1863–1933 English novelist: *The Dolly Dialogues* (1894)

3 Take care of the pence, and the pounds will take care of themselves.

> **William Lowndes** 1652–1724 English politician: Lord Chesterfield *Letters to his Son* (1774) 5 February 1750

4 Thrift, thrift, Horatio! the funeral baked meats
Did coldly furnish forth the marriage tables.

> **William Shakespeare** 1564–1616 English dramatist: *Hamlet* (1601)

Time

see also FUTURE, PAST, PRESENT, TRANSIENCE

1 Time is an illusion. Lunchtime doubly so.

> **Douglas Adams** 1952–2001 English science fiction writer: *The Hitch Hiker's Guide to the Galaxy* (1979)

2 Every instant of time is a pinprick of eternity.

> **Marcus Aurelius** AD 121–180 Roman emperor: *Meditations*

3 Days and months are travellers of eternity. So are the years that pass by.
> **Matsuo Basho** 1644–94 Japanese poet: *The Narrow Road to the Deep North*, tr. Nobuyuki Yuasa

4 VLADIMIR: That passed the time.
ESTRAGON: It would have passed in any case.
VLADIMIR: Yes, but not so rapidly.
> **Samuel Beckett** 1906–89 Irish dramatist, novelist, and poet: *Waiting for Godot* (1955)

5 Time is a great teacher but unfortunately it kills all its pupils.
> **Hector Berlioz** 1803–69 French composer: attributed; in *Almanach des lettres françaises et étrangères* (1924) 11 May

6 I am Time grown old to destroy the world,
Embarked on the course of world annihilation.
> **Bhagavad Gita** 250 BC–AD 250 Hindu poem: ch. 11

7 Men talk of killing time, while time quietly kills them.
> **Dion Boucicault** 1820–90 Irish dramatist: *London Assurance* (1841)

8 He said, 'What's time? Leave Now for dogs and apes!
Man has Forever.'
> **Robert Browning** 1812–89 English poet: 'A Grammarian's Funeral' (1855)

9 I recommend to you to take care of minutes: for hours will take care of themselves.
> **Lord Chesterfield** 1694–1773 English writer and politician: *Letters to his Son* (1774) 6 November 1747

10 Time is the great physician.
> **Benjamin Disraeli** 1804–81 British Tory statesman and novelist: *Henrietta Temple* (1837)

11 The distinction between past, present and future is only an illusion, however persistent.
> **Albert Einstein** 1879–1955 German-born theoretical physicist: letter to Michelangelo Besso, 21 March 1955

12 Time present and time past
Are both perhaps present in time future,
And time future contained in time past.
> **T. S. Eliot** 1888–1965 Anglo-American poet, critic, and dramatist: *Four Quartets* 'Burnt Norton' (1936)

13 Remember that time is money.
> **Benjamin Franklin** 1706–90 American politician, inventor, and scientist: *Advice to a Young Tradesman* (1748)

14 Time is . . . Time was . . . Time is past.
> **Robert Greene** *c.*1560–92 English poet and dramatist: *Friar Bacon and Friar Bungay* (1594)

15 Time, you old gipsy man,
Will you not stay,
Put up your caravan
Just for one day?
> **Ralph Hodgson** 1871–1962 English poet: 'Time, You Old Gipsy Man' (1917)

16 He that runs against Time has an antagonist not subject to casualties.
> **Samuel Johnson** 1709–84 English poet, critic, and lexicographer: *Lives of the English Poets* (1779–81) 'Pope'

17 Time cools, time clarifies; no mood can be maintained quite unaltered through the course of hours.
> **Thomas Mann** 1875–1955 German novelist: *The Magic Mountain* (1924) tr. H. T. Lowe-Porter

18 But at my back I always hear
Time's wingèd chariot hurrying near:
And yonder all before us lie
Deserts of vast eternity.
> **Andrew Marvell** 1621–78 English poet: 'To His Coy Mistress' (1681)

19 *Tempus edax rerum.*
Time the devourer of everything.
> **Ovid** 43 BC–*c*.AD 17 Roman poet: *Metamorphoses*

20 Wait for the wisest of all counsellors, Time.
> **Pericles** *c*.495–429 BC Greek statesman and Athenian general: Plutarch *Parallel Lives* 'Pericles'

21 Even such is Time, which takes in trust
Our youth, our joys, and all we have,
And pays us but with age and dust.
> **Walter Ralegh** *c*.1552–1618 English explorer and courtier: written the night before his death, and found in his Bible in the Gate-house at Westminster

22 Half our life is spent trying to find something to do with the time we have rushed through life trying to save.
> **Will Rogers** 1879–1935 American actor and humorist: letter in *New York Times* 29 April 1930

23 Three o'clock is always too late or too early for anything you want to do.
> **Jean-Paul Sartre** 1905–80 French philosopher, novelist, dramatist, and critic: *La Nausée* (1938)

24 Ah! the clock is always slow;
It is later than you think.
> **Robert W. Service** 1874–1958 Canadian poet: 'It Is Later Than You Think' (1921)

25 To-morrow, and to-morrow, and to-morrow,
Creeps in this petty pace from day to day,
To the last syllable of recorded time;
And all our yesterdays have lighted fools
The way to dusty death.
> **William Shakespeare** 1564–1616 English dramatist: *Macbeth* (1606)

26 Eternity's a terrible thought. I mean, where's it all going to end?
> **Tom Stoppard** 1937– British dramatist: *Rosencrantz and Guildenstern are Dead* (1967)

27 As if you could kill time without injuring eternity.
> **Henry David Thoreau** 1817–62 American writer: *Walden* (1854) 'Economy'

28 Time is
Too slow for those who wait,
Too swift for those who fear,
Too long for those who grieve,
Too short for those who rejoice;
But for those who love,
Time is eternity.
> **Henry Van Dyke** 1852–1933 American Presbyterian minister and writer: 'Time is too slow for those who wait' (1905), read at the funeral of Diana, Princess of Wales; the original form of the last line is 'Time is not'

29 *Sed fugit interea, fugit inreparabile tempus.*
But meanwhile it is flying, irretrievable time is flying.
> *usually quoted as* 'tempus fugit *[time flies]*'
> **Virgil** 70–19 BC Roman poet: *Georgics*

30 The years like great black oxen tread the world,
And God the herdsman goads them on behind,
And I am broken by their passing feet.
> **W. B. Yeats** 1865–1939 Irish poet: *The Countess Cathleen* (1895)

Titles

see also ARISTOCRACY, CLASS

1 Not a reluctant peer but a persistent commoner.
> *of his ultimately successful fight to disclaim his inherited title of Viscount Stansgate*
> **Tony Benn** 1925– British Labour politician: at a press conference, 23 November 1960

2 Tyndall, I must remain plain Michael Faraday to the last; and let me now tell you, that if I accepted the honour which the Royal Society desires to confer upon me, I would not answer for the integrity of my intellect for a single year.

on being offered the Presidency of the Royal Society

Michael Faraday 1791–1867 English physicist and chemist: J. Tyndall *Faraday as a Discoverer* (1868)

3 What I like about the Order of the Garter is that there is no damned merit about it.

Lord Melbourne 1779–1848 British Whig statesman: Lord David Cecil *The Young Melbourne* (1939)

4 When I want a peerage, I shall buy it like an honest man.

Lord Northcliffe 1865–1922 British newspaper proprietor: Tom Driberg *Swaff* (1974)

5 There is no stronger craving in the world than that of the rich for titles, except perhaps that of the titled for riches.

Hesketh Pearson 1887–1964 English actor and biographer: *The Pilgrim Daughters* (1961)

6 Titles distinguish the mediocre, embarrass the superior, and are disgraced by the inferior.

George Bernard Shaw 1856–1950 Irish dramatist: *Man and Superman* (1903)

7 She needed no royal title to continue to generate her particular brand of magic.

of his sister, Diana, Princess of Wales

Lord Spencer 1964–   English peer: tribute at her funeral, 7 September 1997

8 What harm have I ever done to the Labour Party?

declining the offer of a peerage

R. H. Tawney 1880–1962 British

economic historian: in *Evening Standard* 18 January 1962

Toasts

1 Here's tae us; wha's like us? Gey few, and they're a' deid.

Anonymous

2 Here's looking at you, kid.

Julius J. Epstein 1909–2001: *Casablanca* (1942 film, with Philip G. Epstein and Howard Koch); spoken by Humphrey Bogart

3 Lang may yer lum reek!

long may your chimney smoke

Scottish Proverb

4 May you live all the days of your life.

Jonathan Swift 1667–1745 Irish poet and satirist: *Polite Conversation* (1738)

Tolerance

see also COMPROMISE, IMPARTIALITY, PREJUDICE

1 Hear the other side.

St Augustine of Hippo AD 354–430 Early Christian theologian: *De Duabus Animabus contra Manicheos*

2 Judge not, that ye be not judged.

Bible: St Matthew

3 There is, however, a limit at which forbearance ceases to be a virtue.

Edmund Burke 1729–97 Irish-born Whig politician and man of letters: *Observations on a late Publication on the Present State of the Nation* (2nd ed., 1769)

4 Human diversity makes tolerance more than a virtue, it makes it a requirement for survival.

René Dubos 1901–82 French-born American microbiologist : *Celebrations of Life* (1981)

5 Make hatred hated!

Anatole France 1844–1924 French

novelist and man of letters: speech to public school teachers in Tours, August 1919

6 Tolerance is only another name for indifference.

W. Somerset Maugham 1874–1965 English novelist: *A Writer's Notebook* (1949) written in 1896

7 We should therefore claim, in the name of tolerance, the right not to tolerate the intolerant.

Karl Popper 1902–94 Austrian-born philosopher: *The Open Society and Its Enemies* (1945)

8 You might as well fall flat on your face as lean over too far backward.

James Thurber 1894–1961 American humorist: 'The Bear Who Let It Alone' in *New Yorker* 29 April 1939

Trade Unions

see also EMPLOYMENT, WORK

1 Had the employers of past generations all of them dealt fairly with their men there would have been no unions.

Stanley Baldwin 1867–1947 British Conservative statesman: speech in Birmingham, 14 January 1931

2 The most conservative man in this world is the British Trade Unionist when you want to change him.

Ernest Bevin 1881–1951 British Labour politician and trade unionist: speech, Trades Union Congress, 8 September 1927

3 I had known it was going to be a 'winter of discontent'.

echoing Shakespeare's Richard III

James Callaghan 1912–2005 British Labour statesman: television interview, 8 February 1979

4 Not a penny off the pay, not a second on the day.

often quoted with 'minute' substituted for 'second'

A. J. Cook 1885–1931 English labour leader: speech at York, 3 April 1926

5 Industrial relations are like sexual relations. It's better between two consenting parties.

Vic Feather 1908–76 British trade unionist: in *Guardian Weekly* 8 August 1976

6 You don't get me I'm part of the union.

John Ford 1948– and **Richard Hudson** 1948– English singers and songwriters: 'Part of the Union' (1974 song)

Tradition

1 One can't carry one's father's corpse about everywhere.

Guillaume Apollinaire 1880–1918 French poet: *Les peintres cubistes* (1965)

2 Tradition means giving votes to the most obscure of all classes, our ancestors. It is the democracy of the dead.

G. K. Chesterton 1874–1936 English essayist, novelist, and poet: *Orthodoxy* (1908)

3 I confess myself to be a great admirer of tradition. The longer you can look back, the farther you can look forward.

Winston Churchill 1874–1965 British Conservative statesman: speech, March 1944

4 The tradition of all the dead generations weighs like a nightmare on the brain of the living.

Karl Marx 1818–83 German political philosopher: *The Eighteenth Brumaire of Louis Bonaparte* (1852)

5 But to my mind,—though I am native here,

And to the manner born,—it is a custom
More honoured in the breach than the observance.
William Shakespeare 1564–1616 English dramatist: *Hamlet* (1601)

6 Far from implying the repetition of what has been, tradition presupposes the reality of what endures.
Igor Stravinsky 1882–1971 Russian composer: *Poetics of Music* (1947)

Tragedy

see also SUFFERING

1 Tragedy is clean, it is restful, it is flawless.
Jean Anouilh 1910–87 French dramatist: *Antigone* (1944)

2 Tragedy is thus a representation of an action that is worth serious attention, complete in itself and of some amplitude . . . by means of pity and fear bringing about the purgation of such emotions.
Aristotle 384–322 BC Greek philosopher: *Poetics*

3 What the American public always wants is a tragedy with a happy ending.
William Dean Howells 1837–1920 American novelist and critic: to Edith Wharton in October 1906

4 That was how his life happened. No mad hooves galloping in the sky, But the weak, washy way of true tragedy—
A sick horse nosing around the meadow for a clean place to die.
Patrick Kavanagh 1904–67 Irish poet: 'The Great Hunger' (1947)

5 Tragedy ought really to be a great kick at misery.
D. H. Lawrence 1885–1930 English

novelist and poet: letter to A. W. McLeod, 6 October 1912

6 The bad end unhappily, the good unluckily. That is what tragedy means.
Tom Stoppard 1937– British dramatist: *Rosencrantz and Guildenstern are Dead* (1967)

7 The composition of a tragedy requires *testicles*.
on being asked why no woman had ever written 'a tolerable tragedy'
Voltaire 1694–1778 French writer and philosopher: letter from Byron to John Murray, 2 April 1817

8 You get tragedy where the tree, instead of bending, breaks.
Ludwig Wittgenstein 1889–1951 Austrian-born philosopher: *Culture and Value* (1929)

Transience

see also OPPORTUNITY, TIME

1 All flesh is as grass, and all the glory of man as the flower of grass. The grass withereth, and the flower thereof falleth away.
Bible: I Peter

2 He who binds to himself a joy Doth the winged life destroy But he who kisses the joy as it flies Lives in Eternity's sunrise.
William Blake 1757–1827 English poet: *MS Note-Book*

3 *Pourvu que ça dure!*
Let's hope it lasts!
on her son becoming Emperor, 1804
Laetitia Bonaparte 1750–1836 French mother of Napoleon Bonaparte: attributed, possibly apocryphal

4 Treaties, you see, are like girls and roses: they last while they last.
Charles de Gaulle 1890–1970 French

soldier and statesman: speech at Elysée Palace, 2 July 1963

5 Look thy last on all things lovely,
Every hour.
Walter de la Mare 1873–1956 English poet and novelist: 'Fare Well' (1918)

6 They are not long, the days of wine and roses:
Out of a misty dream
Our path emerges for a while, then closes
Within a dream.
Ernest Dowson 1867–1900 English poet: 'Vitae Summa Brevis' (1896)

7 Gather ye rosebuds while ye may,
Old Time is still a-flying:
And this same flower that smiles to-day,
To-morrow will be dying.
Robert Herrick 1591–1674 English poet and clergyman: 'To the Virgins, to Make Much of Time' (1648)

8 Like that of leaves is a generation of men.
Homer *fl. c.*750 BC Greek poet: *The Iliad*

9 He will be just like the scent on a pocket handkerchief.
on being asked what place Arthur Balfour would have in history
David Lloyd George 1863–1945 British Liberal statesman: Thomas Jones diary, 9 June 1922

10 The sunlight on the garden
Hardens and grows cold,
We cannot cage the minute
Within its net of gold.
Louis MacNeice 1907–63 British poet, born in Belfast: 'Sunlight on the Garden' (1938)

11 The spider weaves the curtains in the palace of the Caesars;
The owl calls the watches in the towers of Afrasiab.
quoting an anonymous Persian poet at the
ruins of the Old Sacred Palace in Constantinople, 1453
Mehmed II 1430–81 Ottoman sultan: attributed; Steven Runciman *Fall of Constantinople* (1965)

12 I never nursed a dear gazelle,
To glad me with its soft black eye,
But when it came to know me well,
And love me, it was sure to die!
Thomas Moore 1779–1852 Irish musician and songwriter: *Lalla Rookh* (1817) 'The Fire-Worshippers'; see DISILLUSION 2 , VALUE 4

13 Ev'ry day a little death
On the lips and in the eyes,
In the murmurs, in the pauses,
In the gestures, in the sighs.
Ev'ry day a little dies.
Stephen Sondheim 1930– American songwriter: 'Every Day a Little Death' (1973 song)

14 The butterfly counts not months but moments,
And has time enough.
Rabindranath Tagore 1861–1941 Bengali poet and philosopher: *Fireflies* (1928)

15 The rainbow comes and goes,
And lovely is the rose.
William Wordsworth 1770–1850 English poet: 'Ode. Intimations of Immortality' (1807)

Translation

1 The original is unfaithful to the translation.
on Henley's translation of Beckford's Vathek
Jorge Luis Borges 1899–1986 Argentinian writer: *Sobre el 'Vathek' de William Beckford* (1974)

2 Translations (like wives) are seldom strictly faithful if they are in the least attractive.
Roy Campbell 1901–57 South African poet: in *Poetry Review* June-July 1949

3 The vanity of translation; it were as wise to cast a violet into a crucible that you might discover the formal principle of its colour and odour, as seek to transfuse from one language to another the creations of a poet. The plant must spring again from its seed, or it will bear no flower.

Percy Bysshe Shelley 1792–1822 English poet: *A Defence of Poetry* (written 1821)

4 Like playing Beethoven on the kazoo.
on his translation of Shakespeare into text messages

John Sutherland 1938– English writer: in *Mail on Sunday* 20 November 2005

5 A translation is no translation unless it will give you the music of a poem along with the words of it.

John Millington Synge 1871–1909 Irish dramatist: *The Aran Islands* (1907)

Travel

see also EXPLORATION, HOLIDAYS, MAPS

1 Travel, in the younger sort, is a part of education; in the elder, a part of experience. He that travelleth into a country before he hath some entrance into the language, goeth to school, and not to travel.

Francis Bacon 1561–1626 English lawyer, courtier, philosopher, and essayist: *Essays* (1625) 'Of Travel'

2 In America there are two classes of travel—first class, and with children.

Robert Benchley 1889–1945 American humorist: *Pluck and Luck* (1925)

3 What an odd thing tourism is. You fly off to a strange land, eagerly abandoning all the comforts of home, and then expend vast quantities of time and money in a largely futile attempt to recapture the comforts that you wouldn't have lost if you hadn't left home in the first place.

Bill Bryson 1951– American travel writer: *Neither Here Nor There* (1991)

4 See one promontory (said Socrates of old), one mountain, one sea, one river, and see all.

Robert Burton 1577–1640 English clergyman and scholar: *The Anatomy of Melancholy* (1621–51)

5 When you set out for Ithaka ask that your way be long.

Constantine Cavafy 1863–1933 Greek poet: 'Ithaka' (1911)

6 Why do the wrong people travel, travel, travel,
When the right people stay back home?

Noël Coward 1899–1973 English dramatist, actor, and composer: 'Why do the Wrong People Travel?' (1961 song)

7 A wise traveller never despises his own country.

Carlo Goldoni 1707–93 Italian dramatist: *Pamela* (1749)

8 Some minds improve by travel, others, rather
Resemble copper wire, or brass,
Which gets the narrower by going farther!

Thomas Hood 1799–1845 English poet and humorist: 'Ode to Rae Wilson, Esq.'

9 Worth seeing, yes; but not worth going to see.
on the Giant's Causeway

Samuel Johnson 1709–84 English poet, critic, and lexicographer: James Boswell *Life of Samuel Johnson* (1791) 12 October 1779

10 Of all noxious animals, too, the most noxious is a tourist. And of all tourists the most vulgar, ill-bred, offensive and loathsome is the British tourist.

Francis Kilvert 1840–79 English

clergyman and diarist: diary, 5 April
1870

11 Thanks to the interstate highway
system, it is now possible to travel
from coast to coast without seeing
anything.
Charles Kuralt 1934–97 American
journalist and broadcaster: *On the Road*
(1980)

12 A good traveller leaves no track or
trace.
*often quoted as 'A good traveller has no
fixed plans'*
Lao Tzu *c.*604–*c.*531 BC Chinese
philosopher: *Tao Te Ching*

13 A good traveller is one who does not
know where he is going to, and a
perfect traveller does not know
where he came from.
Lin Yutang 1895–1976 Chinese writer
and philologist: *The Importance of
Living* (1938)

14 I have not told even half of the things
that I have seen.
*when asked if he wished to deny any of his
stories of his travels*
Marco Polo *c.*1254–*c.*1324 Italian
traveller: attributed, but probably
apocryphal

15 Frogs . . . are slightly better than
Huns or Wops, but abroad is
unutterably bloody and foreigners
are fiends.
Nancy Mitford 1904–73 English writer:
The Pursuit of Love (1945)

16 A man travels the world in search of
what he needs and returns home to
find it.
George Moore 1852–1933 Anglo-Irish
novelist: *The Brook Kerith* (1916)

17 In the middle ages people were
tourists because of their religion,
whereas now they are tourists
because tourism is their religion.
Robert Runcie 1921–99 English

Protestant clergyman; Archbishop of
Canterbury: speech in London,
6 December 1988

18 For my part, I travel not to go
anywhere, but to go. I travel for
travel's sake. The great affair is to
move.
Robert Louis Stevenson 1850–94
Scottish novelist: *Travels with a Donkey*
(1879)

19 To travel hopefully is a better thing
than to arrive, and the true success is
to labour.
Robert Louis Stevenson 1850–94
Scottish novelist: *Virginibus Puerisque*
(1881)

20 It is not worthwhile to go around the
world to count the cats in Zanzibar.
Henry David Thoreau 1817–62
American writer: *Walden* (1854)
'Conclusion'

21 Travel is fatal to prejudice, bigotry,
and narrow-mindedness.
Mark Twain 1835–1910 American
writer: *The Innocents Abroad* (1869)

22 Commuter—one who spends his life
In riding to and from his wife;
A man who shaves and takes a train,
And then rides back to shave again.
E. B. White 1899–1985 American
humorist: 'The Commuter' (1982)

Trees

1 A culture is no better than its woods.
W. H. Auden 1907–73 English poet:
'Woods' (1958)

2 The tree which moves some to tears
of joy is in the eyes of others only a
green thing that stands in the way.
William Blake 1757–1827 English poet:
letter to Rev. Dr Trusler, 23 August 1799

3 I am for the woods against the world,
But are the woods for me?

> **Edmund Blunden** 1896–1974 English
> poet: 'The Kiss' (1931)

4 Generations pass while some trees
stand, and old families last not three
oaks.

> **Sir Thomas Browne** 1605–82 English
> writer and physician: *Hydriotaphia*
> (Urn Burial, 1658)

5 I like trees because they seem more
resigned to the way they have to live
than other things do.

> **Willa Cather** 1873–1947 American
> novelist: *O Pioneers!* (1913)

6 For pines are gossip pines the wide
world through
And full of runic tales to sigh or sing.

> **James Elroy Flecker** 1884–1915 English
> poet: *Golden Journey to Samarkand*
> (1913) 'Brumana'

7 The woods are lovely, dark and deep.
But I have promises to keep,
And miles to go before I sleep,
And miles to go before I sleep.

> **Robert Frost** 1874–1963 American poet:
> 'Stopping by Woods on a Snowy
> Evening' (1923)

8 He that plants trees loves others
beside himself.

> **Thomas Fuller** 1654–1734 English
> writer and physician: *Gnomologia*
> (1732)

9 Loveliest of trees, the cherry now
Is hung with bloom along the bough,
And stands about the woodland ride
Wearing white for Eastertide.

> **A. E. Housman** 1859–1936 English poet:
> *A Shropshire Lad* (1896)

10 I think that I shall never see
A poem lovely as a tree.

> **Joyce Kilmer** 1886–1918 American poet:
> 'Trees' (1914); see ENVIRONMENT 13

11 Of all the trees that grow so fair,
Old England to adorn,

Greater are none beneath the Sun,
Than Oak, and Ash, and Thorn.

> **Rudyard Kipling** 1865–1936 English
> writer and poet: *Puck of Pook's Hill*
> (1906) 'A Tree Song'

12 Woodman, spare that tree!
Touch not a single bough!
In youth it sheltered me,
And I'll protect it now.

> **George Pope Morris** 1802–64 American
> poet: 'Woodman, Spare That Tree'
> (1830)

13 Willows whiten, aspens quiver,
Little breezes dusk and shiver.

> **Alfred, Lord Tennyson** 1809–92 English
> poet: 'The Lady of Shalott' (1832,
> revised 1842)

14 Laburnums, dropping-wells of fire.

> **Alfred, Lord Tennyson** 1809–92 English
> poet: *In Memoriam A. H. H.* (1850)

15 In every wood, in every spring,
there is a different green.

> **J. R. R. Tolkien** 1892–1973 British
> philologist and writer: *The Fellowship of
> the Ring* (1954)

Trials

see also JUSTICE, LAWS

1 Who breaks a butterfly on a wheel?
*defending Mick Jagger after his arrest for
cannabis possession*

> **Anonymous**: leader in *The Times* 1 June
> 1967, written by William Rees-Mogg; see
> FUTILITY 11

2 If ever there was a case of clearer
evidence than this of persons acting
together, this case is that case.

> **William Arabin** 1773–1841 English
> judge: H. B. Churchill *Arabiniana* (1843)

3 If this is justice, I am a banana.
*on the libel damages awarded against
Private Eye to Sonia Sutcliffe*

> **Ian Hislop** 1960– English satirical
> journalist: comment, 24 May 1989

4 That four great nations, flushed with victory and stung with injury, stay the hands of vengeance and voluntarily submit their captive enemies to the judgement of the law, is one of the most significant tributes that Power has ever paid to Reason.
Robert H. Jackson 1892–1954 American lawyer and judge: opening statement for the prosecution, International Military Tribunal in Nuremberg, 21 November 1945

5 We are not final because we are infallible, but we are infallible only because we are final.
of the Supreme Court
Robert H. Jackson 1892–1954 American lawyer and judge: *Brown v. Allen* (1953)

6 You may object that it is not a trial at all; you are quite right, for it is only a trial if I recognize it as such.
Franz Kafka 1883–1924 Czech novelist: *The Trial* (1925)

7 The art of cross-examination is not the art of examining crossly. It's the art of leading the witness through a line of propositions he agrees to until he's forced to agree to the *one fatal question.*
Clifford Mortimer d. 1960 English barrister: John Mortimer *Clinging to the Wreckage* (1982)

8 Not only did we play the race card, we played it from the bottom of the deck.
on the defence's conduct of the O. J. Simpson trial
Robert Shapiro 1942– American lawyer: interview, 3 October 1995

9 Asking the ignorant to use the incomprehensible to decide the unknowable.
on the jury system
Hiller B. Zobel 1932– American judge: 'The Jury on Trial' in *American Heritage* July–August 1995

Trust

see also BETRAYAL, FAITHFULNESS

1 Would you buy a used car from this man?
Anonymous: campaign slogan directed against Richard Nixon, 1968

2 Suspicions amongst thoughts are like bats amongst birds, they ever fly by twilight.
Francis Bacon 1561–1626 English lawyer, courtier, philosopher, and essayist: *Essays* (1625) 'Of Suspicion'

3 The thing on the blind side of the heart,
On the wrong side of the door,
The green plant groweth, menacing
Almighty lovers in the Spring;
There is always a forgotten thing,
And love is not secure.
G. K. Chesterton 1874–1936 English essayist, novelist, and poet: *The Ballad of the White Horse* (1911)

4 Frankly speaking it is difficult to trust the Chinese. Once bitten by a snake you feel suspicious even when you see a piece of rope.
Dalai Lama 1935– Spiritual head of Tibetan Buddhism: attributed, 1981

5 To trust people is a luxury in which only the wealthy can indulge; the poor cannot afford it.
E. M. Forster 1879–1970 English novelist: *Howards End* (1910)

6 It is better to suffer wrong than to do it, and happier to be sometimes cheated than not to trust.
Samuel Johnson 1709–84 English poet, critic, and lexicographer: in *Rambler* 18 December 1750

7 *Quis custodiet ipsos custodes?*
Who is to guard the guards themselves?
Juvenal AD *c.*60–*c.*130 Roman satirist: *Satires*

8 It is more shameful to doubt one's friends than to be duped by them.
Duc de la Rochefoucauld 1613–80 French moralist: *Maximes* (1678)

9 We have listened to the wisdom in an old Russian maxim. And I'm sure you're familiar with it, Mr General Secretary. The maxim is . . . 'trust, but verify'.
Ronald Reagan 1911–2004 American Republican statesman: at the signing of the INF treaty on arms limitation, 8 December 1987, and used frequently thereafter

10 A man who does not trust himself will never really trust anybody.
Jean-François Paul de Gondi, Cardinal de Retz 1613–79 French cardinal: *Mémoires* (1717)

11 And trust me not at all or all in all.
Alfred, Lord Tennyson 1809–92 English poet: *Idylls of the King* 'Merlin and Vivien' (1859)

12 We have to distrust each other. It's our only defence against betrayal.
Tennessee Williams 1911–83 American dramatist: *Camino Real* (1953)

13 He trusted neither of them as far as he could spit, and he was a poor spitter, lacking both distance and control.
P. G. Wodehouse 1881–1975 English writer: *Money in the Bank* (1946)

Truth

see also HONESTY, LIES

1 The truth is often a terrible weapon of aggression. It is possible to lie, and even to murder, for the truth.
Alfred Adler 1870–1937 Austrian psychologist and psychiatrist: *The Problems of Neurosis* (1929)

2 The truth which makes men free is for the most part the truth which men prefer not to hear.
Herbert Agar 1897–1980 American poet and writer: *A Time for Greatness* (1942)

3 It contains a misleading impression, not a lie. It was being economical with the truth.
the phrase 'economy of truth' was earlier used by Edmund Burke (1729–97)
Robert Armstrong 1927– British civil servant: referring to a letter during the 'Spycatcher' trial, Supreme Court, New South Wales, in *Daily Telegraph* 19 November 1986

4 What is truth? said jesting Pilate; and would not stay for an answer.
Francis Bacon 1561–1626 English lawyer, courtier, philosopher, and essayist: *Essays* (1625) 'Of Truth'

5 A platitude is simply a truth repeated until people get tired of hearing it.
Stanley Baldwin 1867–1947 British Conservative statesman: speech, House of Commons, 29 May 1924

6 And ye shall know the truth, and the truth shall make you free.
Bible: St John

7 A truth that's told with bad intent Beats all the lies you can invent.
William Blake 1757–1827 English poet: 'Auguries of Innocence' (*c.*1803)

8 One of the favourite maxims of my father was the distinction between the two sorts of truths, profound truths recognized by the fact that the opposite is also a profound truth, in contrast to trivialities where opposites are obviously absurd.
Niels Bohr 1885–1962 Danish physicist: S. Rozental *Niels Bohr* (1967)

9 Many from . . . an inconsiderate zeal unto truth, have too rashly charged

the troops of error, and remain as trophies unto the enemies of truth.

> **Sir Thomas Browne** 1605–82 English writer and physician: *Religio Medici* (1643)

10 'Tis strange—but true; for truth is always strange;
Stranger than fiction.

> **Lord Byron** 1788–1824 English poet: *Don Juan* (1819–24)

11 What I tell you three times is true.

> **Lewis Carroll** 1832–98 English writer and logician: *The Hunting of the Snark* (1876)

12 An exaggeration is a truth that has lost its temper.

> **Kahlil Gibran** 1883–1931 Lebanese-born American writer and painter: *Sand and Foam* (1926)

13 Believe those who are seeking the truth; doubt those who find it.

> **André Gide** 1869–1951 French novelist and critic: *So Be It* (1960)

14 Truth, like a torch, the more it's shook it shines.

> **William Hamilton** 1788–1856 Scottish metaphysician: *Discussions on Philosophy* (1852)

15 It is the customary fate of new truths to begin as heresies and to end as superstitions.

> **T. H. Huxley** 1825–95 English biologist: *Science and Culture and Other Essays* (1881) 'The Coming of Age of the Origin of Species'

16 Truth is a pathless land, and you cannot approach it by any path whatsoever, by any religion, by any sect.

> **Jiddu Krishnamurti** 1895–1986 Indian spiritual philosopher: speech in Holland, 3 August 1929

17 It is one thing to show a man that he is in error, and another to put him in possession of truth.

> **John Locke** 1632–1704 English philosopher: *An Essay concerning Human Understanding* (1690)

18 He who does not bellow the truth when he knows the truth makes himself the accomplice of liars and forgers.

> **Charles Péguy** 1873–1914 French poet and essayist: *Basic Verities* (1943) 'Lettre du Provincial' 21 December 1899

19 But, my dearest Agathon, it is truth which you cannot contradict; you can without any difficulty contradict Socrates.

> **Socrates** 469–399 BC Greek philosopher: Plato *Symposium*

20 Rather than love, than money, than fame, give me truth.

> **Henry David Thoreau** 1817–62 American writer: *Walden* (1854) 'Conclusion'

21 There are no whole truths; all truths are half-truths. It is trying to treat them as whole truths that plays the devil.

> **Alfred North Whitehead** 1861–1947 English philosopher and mathematician: *Dialogues* (1954)

22 The truth is rarely pure, and never simple.

> **Oscar Wilde** 1854–1900 Anglo-Irish dramatist and poet: *The Importance of Being Earnest* (1895)

23 Truth is on the march, and nothing will stop it.
on the Dreyfus affair

> **Émile Zola** 1840–1902 French novelist: in *Le Figaro* 25 November 1897

Twentieth Century

1 Everything is becoming science fiction. From the margins of an

almost invisible literature has sprung the intact reality of the 20th century.
> **J. G. Ballard** 1930–2009 British writer: 'Fictions of Every Kind' in *Books and Bookmen* February 1971

2 What we may be witnessing is not just the end of the Cold War but the end of history as such: that is, the end point of man's ideological evolution and the universalism of Western liberal democracy.
> **Francis Fukuyama** 1952– American historian: in *Independent* 20 September 1989

3 For 80 per cent of humanity the Middle Ages ended suddenly in the 1950s; or perhaps better still, they were *felt* to end in the 1960s.
> **Eric Hobsbawm** 1917– British historian: *Age of Extremes* (1994)

4 It was in 1915 the old world ended.
> **D. H. Lawrence** 1885–1930 English novelist and poet: *Kangaroo* (1923)

5 We close the century with most people still languishing in poverty, subjected to hunger, preventable disease, illiteracy and insufficient shelter.
> **Nelson Mandela** 1918– South African statesman: at a ceremony at his former prison cell on Robben Island; in *Observer* 2 January 2000

6 Our gadget-filled paradise suspended in a hell of international insecurity.
> **Reinhold Niebuhr** 1892–1971 American theologian: *Pious and Secular America* (1957)

7 After the suffering of decades of violence and oppression, the human soul longs for higher things, warmer and purer than those offered by today's mass living habits, introduced as by a calling card by the revolting invasion of commercial advertising, by TV stupor and by intolerable music.
> **Alexander Solzhenitsyn** 1918–2008 Russian novelist: speech in Cambridge, Massachusetts, 8 June 1978

8 The twentieth century will be remembered chiefly, not as an age of political conflicts and technical inventions, but as an age in which human society dared to think of the health of the whole human race as a practical objective.
> **Arnold Toynbee** 1889–1975 English historian: attributed

9 The twentieth century really belongs to those who will build it. The future can be promised to no one.
> **Pierre Trudeau** 1919–2000 Canadian Liberal statesman: in 1968; see CANADA 12

Twenty-first Century

1 The intelligent minority of this world will mark 1 January 2001 as the real beginning of the 21st century and the Third Millennium.
> **Arthur C. Clarke** 1917–2008 English science fiction writer: in *Newsweek* 8 January 2001

2 The American century—and the European half millennium—is coming to an end. The world century is beginning.
> **Rosabeth Moss Kanter** 1943– American management consultant and writer: *World Class* (1995)

Unemployment

1 Machines are the new proletariat. The working class is being given its walking papers.
> **Jacques Attali** 1943– French economist and writer: *Millenium: Winners and Losers in the Coming World Order* (1991)

2 When a great many people are unable to find work, unemployment results.

> **Calvin Coolidge** 1872–1933 American Republican statesman: attributed

3 Naturally, the workers are perfectly free; the manufacturer does not force them to take his materials and his cards, but he says to them . . . 'If you don't like to be frizzled in my frying-pan, you can take a walk into the fire'.

> **Friedrich Engels** 1820–95 German socialist: *The Condition of the Working Class in England in 1844* (1892)

4 Give a man a dole and you save his body and destroy his spirit. Give him a job and you save both body and spirit.

> **Harry Lloyd Hopkins** 1890–1946 American government official and presidential adviser: in 1934

5 Recession is when you have to tighten the belt. Depression is when there is no belt to tighten. We are probably in the next degree of collapse when there are no trousers as such.

> **Boris Pankin** 1931– Russian diplomat: in *Independent* 25 July 1992

6 I grew up in the Thirties with our unemployed father. He did not riot, he got on his bike and looked for work.

> **Norman Tebbit** 1931– British Conservative politician: speech at Conservative Party Conference, 15 October 1981

7 It's a recession when your neighbour loses his job; it's a depression when you lose yours.

> **Harry S. Truman** 1884–1972 American Democratic statesman: in *Observer* 13 April 1958

Unhappiness

see also DEPRESSION, HAPPINESS, SORROW

1 It is a miserable state of mind to have few things to desire, and many things to fear.

> **Francis Bacon** 1561–1626 English lawyer, courtier, philosopher, and essayist: *Essays* (1625) 'Of Empire'

2 For in every ill-turn of fortune the most unhappy sort of unfortunate man is the one who has been happy.

> **Boethius** c.AD 476–524 Roman statesman and philosopher: *De Consolatione Philosophiae*; see SORROW 5

3 MEDVEDENKO: Why do you wear black all the time?
MASHA: I'm in mourning for my life, I'm unhappy.

> **Anton Chekhov** 1860–1904 Russian dramatist and short-story writer: *The Seagull* (1896)

4 He felt the loyalty we all feel to unhappiness—the sense that that is where we really belong.

> **Graham Greene** 1904–91 English novelist: *The Heart of the Matter* (1948)

5 One is never as unhappy as one thinks, nor as happy as one hopes.

> **Duc de la Rochefoucauld** 1613–80 French moralist: *Sentences et Maximes de Morale* (1664)

6 I was looking for a job, and then I found a job
And heaven knows I'm miserable now.

> **Morrissey** 1959– English singer and songwriter: 'Heaven Knows I'm Miserable Now' (1984 song)

7 Men who are unhappy, like men who sleep badly, are always proud of the fact.

> **Bertrand Russell** 1872–1970 British philosopher and mathematician: *The Conquest of Happiness* (1930)

United States

see also AMERICAN CITIES

1 America! America!
God shed His grace on thee
And crown thy good with
   brotherhood
From sea to shining sea!
> **Katherine Lee Bates** 1859–1929
> American writer and educationist:
> 'America the Beautiful' (1893)

2 God bless America,
Land that I love,
Stand beside her and guide her
Thru the night with a light from
   above.
From the mountains to the prairies,
To the oceans white with foam,
God bless America,
My home sweet home.
> **Irving Berlin** 1888–1989 American
> songwriter: 'God Bless America'
> (1939 song)

3 We are a nation of communities, of
tens and tens of thousands of ethnic,
religious, social, business, labour
union, neighbourhood, regional and
other organizations, all of them
varied, voluntary, and unique . . . a
brilliant diversity spread like stars,
like a thousand points of light in a
broad and peaceful sky.
> **George Bush** 1924– American
> Republican statesman: acceptance
> speech at the Republican National
> Convention in New Orleans, 18 August
> 1988

4 There is nothing wrong with America
that cannot be fixed by what is right
with America.
> **Bill Clinton** 1946– American
> Democratic statesman: 1993 inaugural
> address

5 I'm a Yankee Doodle Dandy,
A Yankee Doodle, do or die;
A real live nephew of my Uncle
Sam's,

Born on the fourth of July.
> **George M. Cohan** 1878–1942 American
> songwriter, dramatist, and producer:
> 'Yankee Doodle Boy' (1904 song)

6 The chief business of the American
people is business.
> **Calvin Coolidge** 1872–1933 American
> Republican statesman: speech in
> Washington, 17 January 1925

7 'next to of course god america i
love you land of the pilgrims' and so
   forth oh
say can you see by the dawn's early
   my
country 'tis of centuries come and go
> **e. e. cummings** 1894–1962 American
> poet: *is 5* (1926)

8 The thing that impresses me most
about America is the way parents
obey their children.
> **Edward VIII** 1894–1972 British
> monarch: in *Look* 5 March 1957

9 Isn't this a billion dollar country?
*responding to a Democratic gibe about a
'million dollar Congress'*
> **Charles Foster** 1828–1904 American
> politician: at the 51st Congress, in *North
> American Review* March 1892; also
> attributed to Thomas B. Reed

10 Yes, America is gigantic, but a
gigantic mistake.
> **Sigmund Freud** 1856–1939 Austrian
> psychiatrist: Peter Gay *Freud: A Life for
> Our Time* (1988)

11 Go West, young man, and grow up
with the country.
> **Horace Greeley** 1811–72 American
> newspaper editor: *Hints toward Reforms*
> (1850)

12 This land is your land, this land is my
   land,
From California to the New York
   Island.
From the redwood forest to the Gulf
   Stream waters

This land was made for you and me.

> **Woody Guthrie** 1912–67 American folksinger and songwriter: 'This Land is Your Land' (1956 song)

13 The American system of rugged individualism.

> **Herbert Hoover** 1874–1964 American Republican statesman: speech in New York City, 22 October 1928

14 America is not a lie, it is a disappointment. But it can be a disappointment only because it is also a hope.

> **Samuel Huntington** 1927–2008 American political scientist: *American Politics: the Promise of Disharmony* (1981)

15 'Tis the star-spangled banner; O long may it wave
O'er the land of the free, and the home of the brave!

> **Francis Scott Key** 1779–1843 American lawyer and verse-writer: 'The Star-Spangled Banner' (1814)

16 Give me your tired, your poor,
Your huddled masses yearning to breathe free.

> *inscription on the Statue of Liberty, New York*
>
> **Emma Lazarus** 1849–87 American poet: 'The New Colossus' (1883)

17 The immense popularity of American movies abroad demonstrates that Europe is the unfinished negative of which America is the proof.

> **Mary McCarthy** 1912–89 American novelist: *On the Contrary* (1961)

18 Our national flower is the concrete cloverleaf.

> **Lewis Mumford** 1895–1990 American sociologist: in *Quote Magazine* 8 October 1961

19 There's not a black America and white America and Latino America and Asian America; there's the United States of America.

> **Barack Obama** 1961– American Democratic statesman: Democratic National Convention keynote address, 27 July 2004

20 I pledge you, I pledge myself, to a new deal for the American people.

> **Franklin D. Roosevelt** 1882–1945 American Democratic statesman: speech to the Democratic Convention in Chicago, 2 July 1932, accepting the presidential nomination

21 There is no room in this country for hyphenated Americanism . . . The one absolutely certain way of bringing this nation to ruin, of preventing all possibility of its continuing to be a nation at all, would be to permit it to become a tangle of squabbling nationalities.

> **Theodore Roosevelt** 1858–1919 American Republican statesman: speech in New York, 12 October 1915

22 What law have I broken? Is it wrong for me to love my own? Is it wicked for me because my skin is red? Because I am Sioux; because I was born where my fathers lived; because I would die for my people and my country?

> **Sitting Bull** *c.*1831–90 Hunkpapa Sioux leader: to Major Brotherton, recorded July 1881; Gary C. Anderson *Sitting Bull* (1996)

23 I like to be in America!
O.K. by me in America!
Ev'rything free in America
For a small fee in America!

> **Stephen Sondheim** 1930– American songwriter: 'America' (1957 song)

24 In the United States there is more space where nobody is than where anybody is. That is what makes America what it is.

Gertrude Stein 1874–1946 American writer: *The Geographical History of America* (1936)

25 Where today are the Pequot? Where are the Narragansett, the Mohican, the Pokanoket, and many other once powerful tribes of our people? They have vanished before the avarice and oppression of the white man, as snow before the summer sun.

Tecumseh 1768–1813 Shawnee leader: Dee Brown *Bury My Heart at Wounded Knee* (1970)

26 America is a vast conspiracy to make you happy.

John Updike 1932–2009 American novelist and short-story writer: *Problems* (1980)

27 The United States themselves are essentially the greatest poem.

Walt Whitman 1819–92 American poet: *Leaves of Grass* (1855)

28 America is God's Crucible, the great Melting-Pot where all the races of Europe are melting and re-forming!

Israel Zangwill 1864–1926 Jewish spokesman and writer: *The Melting Pot* (1908)

The Universe

see also EARTH, SKIES, SPACE

1 Had I been present at the Creation, I would have given some useful hints for the better ordering of the universe.
on studying the Ptolemaic system
Alfonso 'the Wise' 1221–84 Spanish monarch: attributed

2 We are the children of chaos, and the deep structure of change is decay. At root, there is only corruption, and the unstemmable tide of chaos.

Gone is purpose; all that is left is direction. This is the bleakness we have to accept as we peer deeply and dispassionately into the heart of the Universe.

Peter Atkins 1940– British chemist: *The Second Law* (1984)

3 For one of those gnostics, the visible universe was an illusion or, more precisely, a sophism. Mirrors and fatherhood are abominable because they multiply it and extend it.

Jorge Luis Borges 1899–1986 Argentinian writer: *Tlön, Uqbar, Orbis Tertius* (1941)

4 *on hearing that Margaret Fuller 'accepted the universe':*
Gad! she'd better!

Thomas Carlyle 1795–1881 Scottish historian and political philosopher: William James *Varieties of Religious Experience* (1902)

5 The eternal mystery of the world is its comprehensibility . . . The fact that it is comprehensible is a miracle.
usually quoted as 'The most incomprehensible fact about the universe is that it is comprehensible'
Albert Einstein 1879–1955 German-born theoretical physicist: in *Franklin Institute Journal* March 1936 'Physics and Reality'

6 The world is disgracefully managed, one hardly knows to whom to complain.

Ronald Firbank 1886–1926 English novelist: *Vainglory* (1915)

7 It is often said that there is no such thing as a free lunch. The Universe, however, is a free lunch.

Alan Guth 1947– American physicist: in *Harpers* November 1994

8 Now, my own suspicion is that the universe is not only queerer than we suppose, but queerer than we *can* suppose . . . I suspect that there are

more things in heaven and earth than are dreamed of, or can be dreamed of, in any philosophy.

> **J. B. S. Haldane** 1892–1964 Scottish mathematical biologist: *Possible Worlds and Other Essays* (1927) 'Possible Worlds'; see SUPERNATURAL 11

9 What is it that breathes fire into the equations and makes a universe for them to describe . . . Why does the universe go to all the bother of existing?

> **Stephen Hawking** 1942– English theoretical physicist: *A Brief History of Time* (1988)

10 This, now, is the judgement of our scientific age—the third reaction of man upon the universe! This universe is not hostile, nor yet is it friendly. It is simply indifferent.

> **John H. Holmes** 1879–1964 American Unitarian minister: *The Sensible Man's View of Religion* (1932)

11 There is a coherent plan to the universe, though I don't know what it's a plan for.

> **Fred Hoyle** 1915–2001 English astrophysicist: attributed

12 From the intrinsic evidence of his creation, the Great Architect of the Universe now begins to appear as a pure mathematician.

> **James Jeans** 1877–1946 English astronomer, physicist, and mathematician: *The Mysterious Universe* (1930)

13 The Universe is not obliged to conform to what we consider comfortable or plausible.

> **Carl Sagan** 1934–96 American scientist and writer: *Pale Blue Dot* (1995)

14 The world is everything that is the case.

> **Ludwig Wittgenstein** 1889–1951 Austrian-born philosopher: *Tractatus Logico-Philosophicus* (1922)

Universities

see also EDUCATION, TEACHING

1 The delusion that there are thousands of young people about who are capable of benefiting from university training, but have somehow failed to find their way there, is . . . a necessary component of the expansionist case . . . More will mean worse.

> **Kingsley Amis** 1922–95 English novelist and poet: in *Encounter* July 1960

2 There is one thing that a professor can be absolutely certain of: almost every student entering the university believes, or says he believes, that truth is relative.

> **Allan Bloom** 1930–92 American writer and educator: *The Closing of the American Mind* (1987)

3 Gentlemen: I have not had your advantages. What poor education I have received has been gained in the University of Life.

> **Horatio Bottomley** 1860–1933 British newspaper proprietor and financier: speech at the Oxford Union, 2 December 1920

4 The true University of these days is a collection of books.

> **Thomas Carlyle** 1795–1881 Scottish historian and political philosopher: *On Heroes, Hero-Worship, and the Heroic* (1841)

5 A University should be a place of light, of liberty, and of learning.

> **Benjamin Disraeli** 1804–81 British Tory statesman and novelist: speech, House of Commons, 11 March 1873

6 The value of an education in a liberal arts college is not the learning of many facts but the training of the

mind to think something that cannot be learned from textbooks.

> **Albert Einstein** 1879–1955 German-born theoretical physicist: in 1921; Philipp Frank *Einstein: His Life and Times* (1947)

7 The most prominent requisite to a lecturer, though perhaps not really the most important, is a good delivery; for though to all true philosophers science and nature will have charms innumerable in every dress, yet I am sorry to say that the generality of mankind cannot accompany us one short hour unless the path is strewed with flowers.

> **Michael Faraday** 1791–1867 English physicist and chemist: *Advice to a Lecturer* (1960); from his letters and notebook written at age 21

8 Why am I the first Kinnock in a thousand generations to be able to get to a university?

> *later plagiarized by the American politician Joe Biden*
>
> **Neil Kinnock** 1942– British Labour politician: speech in party political broadcast, 21 May 1987

9 Our American professors like their literature clear and cold and pure and very dead.

> **Sinclair Lewis** 1885–1951 American novelist: Nobel Prize Address, 12 December 1930

10 Universities never reform themselves; everyone knows that.

> **Lord Melbourne** 1779–1848 British Whig statesman: speech, House of Lords, 11 April 1837

11 A whaleship was my Yale College and my Harvard.

> **Herman Melville** 1819–91 American novelist and poet: *Moby Dick* (1851)

12 The discipline of colleges and universities is in general contrived, not for the benefit of the students, but for the interest, or more properly speaking, for the ease of the masters.

> **Adam Smith** 1723–90 Scottish philosopher and economist: *Wealth of Nations* (1776)

13 A classic lecture, rich in sentiment,
With scraps of thundrous epic lilted out
By violet-hooded Doctors, elegies
And quoted odes, and jewels five-words-long,
That on the stretched forefinger of all Time
Sparkle for ever.

> **Alfred, Lord Tennyson** 1809–92 English poet: *The Princess* (1847)

Value

1 Nothing that costs only a dollar is worth having.

> **Elizabeth Arden** 1876–1966 Canadian-born American businesswoman: attributed; in *Fortune* October 1973

2 There is less in this than meets the eye.

> *on a revival of Maeterlinck's play 'Aglavaine and Selysette'*
>
> **Tallulah Bankhead** 1903–68 American actress: Alexander Woollcott *Shouts and Murmurs* (1922)

3 A living dog is better than a dead lion.

> **Bible**: Ecclesiastes

4 I never loved a dear Gazelle—
*Nor anything that cost me much:
High prices profit those who sell,
But why should I be fond of such?*

> **Lewis Carroll** 1832–98 English writer and logician: *Phantasmagoria* (1869) 'Theme with Variations'; see TRANSIENCE 12

5 Men do not weigh the stalk for that it was,

When once they find her flower, her glory, pass.

Samuel Daniel 1563–1619 English poet and dramatist: *Delia* (1592) sonnet 32

6 It has long been an axiom of mine that the little things are infinitely the most important.

Arthur Conan Doyle 1859–1930 Scottish-born writer of detective fiction: *Adventures of Sherlock Holmes* (1892)

7 Every man is wanted, and no man is wanted much.

Ralph Waldo Emerson 1803–82 American philosopher and poet: *Essays. Second Series* (1844) 'Nominalist and Realist'

8   Then on the shore
Of the wide world I stand alone and think
Till love and fame to nothingness do sink.

John Keats 1795–1821 English poet: 'When I have fears that I may cease to be' (written 1818)

9 Thirty spokes share the wheel's hub;
It is the centre hole that makes it useful.
Shape clay into a vessel;
It is the space within that makes it useful.
Cut doors and windows for a room;
It is the holes which make it useful.
Therefore profit comes from what is there;
Usefulness from what is not there.

Lao Tzu *c*.604–*c*.531 BC Chinese philosopher: *Tao-Tê-Ching*

10 An acre in Middlesex is better than a principality in Utopia.

Lord Macaulay 1800–59 English politician and historian: *Essays Contributed to the Edinburgh Review* (1843) 'Lord Bacon'

11 The thing that is important is the thing that is not seen.

Antoine de Saint-Exupéry 1900–44 French novelist: *The Little Prince* (1943)

12 O monstrous! but one half-pennyworth of bread to this intolerable deal of sack!

William Shakespeare 1564–1616 English dramatist: *Henry IV, Part 1* (1597)

13 I cannot help it that my pictures do not sell. Nevertheless the time will come when people will see that they are worth more than the price of the paint.

Vincent Van Gogh 1853–90 Dutch painter: letter to his brother Theo, 20 October 1888

14 It is not that pearls fetch a high price *because* men have dived for them; but on the contrary, men dive for them because they fetch a high price.

Richard Whately 1787–1863 English philosopher and theologian: *Introductory Lectures on Political Economy* (1832)

Venice

1 STREETS FLOODED. PLEASE ADVISE.
telegraph message on arriving in Venice
Robert Benchley 1889–1945 American humorist: R. E. Drennan (ed.) *Wits End* (1973)

2 Venice is like eating an entire box of chocolate liqueurs in one go.

Truman Capote 1924–84 American writer and novelist: in *Observer* 26 November 1961

3 Sun-girt city, thou hast been
Ocean's child, and then his queen;
Now is come a darker day,
And thou soon must be his prey.

Percy Bysshe Shelley 1792–1822 English poet: 'Lines written amongst the Euganean Hills' (1818)

Vietnam War

1 It became necessary to destroy the town to save it.
statement by unidentified US Army Major, referring to Ben Tre in Vietnam
Anonymous: Associated Press Report, *New York Times* 8 February 1968

2 I love the smell of napalm in the morning. It smells like victory.
Francis Ford Coppola 1939– American film director, writer, and producer: *Apocalypse Now* (1979 film, with John Milius)

3 Kissinger brought peace to Vietnam the same way Napoleon brought peace to Europe: by losing.
Joseph Heller 1923–99 American novelist: *Good as Gold* (1979)

4 We are not about to send American boys 9 or 10,000 miles away from home to do what Asian boys ought to be doing for themselves.
Lyndon Baines Johnson 1908–73 American Democratic statesman: speech at Akron University, 21 October 1964

5 They've got to draw in their horns and stop their aggression, or we're going to bomb them back into the Stone Age.
on the North Vietnamese
Curtis E. LeMay 1906–90 US air-force officer: *Mission with LeMay* (1965)

6 I don't object to it's being called 'McNamara's War' . . . It is a very important war and I am pleased to be identified with it and do whatever I can to win it.
Robert McNamara 1916–2009 American Democratic politician: in *New York Times* 25 April 1964

7 We . . . acted according to what we thought were the principles and traditions of this nation. We were wrong. We were terribly wrong.
of the conduct of the Vietnam War by the Kennedy and Johnson administrations
Robert McNamara 1916–2009 American Democratic politician: speaking in Washington, just before the twentieth anniversary of the American withdrawal from Vietnam, April 1995

8 Let us understand: North Vietnam cannot defeat or humiliate the United States. Only Americans can do that.
Richard Nixon 1913–94 American Republican statesman: broadcast, 3 November 1969

Violence

see also PACIFISM, TERRORISM

1 Keep violence in the mind
Where it belongs.
Brian Aldiss 1925– English science fiction writer: *Barefoot in the Head* (1969) 'Charteris'

2 The only thing that's been a worse flop than the organization of non-violence has been the organization of violence.
Joan Baez 1941– American singer and songwriter: *Daybreak* (1970)

3 All they that take the sword shall perish with the sword.
Bible: St Matthew

4 Force is not a remedy.
John Bright 1811–89 English Liberal politician and reformer: speech to the Birmingham Junior Liberal Club, 16 November 1880

5 I say violence is necessary. It is as American as cherry pie.
H. Rap Brown 1943– American Black Power leader: speech at Washington, 27 July 1967

6 Certain women should be struck
regularly, like gongs.

> **Noël Coward** 1899–1973 English
> dramatist, actor, and composer: *Private
> Lives* (1930)

7 Not hard enough.

> *when asked how hard she had slapped a
> policeman*
> **Zsa Zsa Gabor** 1919– Hungarian-born
> film actress: in *Independent*
> 21 September 1989

8 Wisdom has taught us to be calm
and meek,
To take one blow, and turn the other
cheek;
It is not written what a man shall do
If the rude caitiff smite the other too!

> **Oliver Wendell Holmes** 1809–94
> American physician, poet, and essayist:
> 'Non-Resistance' (1861)

9 Force, unaided by judgement,
collapses through its own weight.

> **Horace** 65–8 BC Roman poet: *Odes*

10 A man may build himself a throne of
bayonets, but he cannot sit on it.

> *quoted by Boris Yeltsin at the time of the
> failed military coup in Russia, August 1991*
> **William Ralph Inge** 1860–1954 English
> writer; Dean of St. Paul's, 1911–34:
> *Philosophy of Plotinus* (1923)

11 A riot is at bottom the language of
the unheard.

> **Martin Luther King** 1929–68 American
> civil rights leader: *Where Do We Go From
> Here?* (1967)

12 In violence, we forget who we are.

> **Mary McCarthy** 1912–89 American
> novelist: *On the Contrary* (1961)
> 'Characters in Fiction'

13 If you strike a child take care that you
strike it in anger, even at the risk of
maiming it for life. A blow in cold

blood neither can nor should be
forgiven.

> **George Bernard Shaw** 1856–1950 Irish
> dramatist: *Man and Superman* (1903)
> 'Maxims: How to Beat Children'

14 Not believing in force is the same
thing as not believing in gravitation.

> **Leon Trotsky** 1879–1940 Russian
> revolutionary: G. Maximov *The
> Guillotine at Work* (1940)

15 Where force is necessary, there it
must be applied boldly, decisively
and completely. But one must know
the limitations of force; one must
know when to blend force with a
manoeuvre, a blow with an
agreement.

> **Leon Trotsky** 1879–1940 Russian
> revolutionary: *What Next?* (1932)

Vulgarity

1 Vulgarity has its uses. Vulgarity often
cuts ice which refinement scrapes at
vainly.

> **Max Beerbohm** 1872–1956 English
> critic, essayist, and caricaturist: letter,
> 21 May 1921

2 Very notable was his distinction
between coarseness and vulgarity
(coarseness, revealing something;
vulgarity, concealing something).

> **E. M. Forster** 1879–1970 English
> novelist: *The Longest Journey* (1907)

3 None among us is superman enough
to escape kitsch completely. No
matter how we scorn it, kitsch is an
integral part of the human
condition.

> **Milan Kundera** 1929– Czech novelist:
> *The Unbearable Lightness of Being*
> (1984)

4 It's worse than wicked, my dear, it's vulgar.

Punch English humorous weekly periodical: Almanac (1876)

Waiting

see also DELAY, PUNCTUALITY

1 ESTRAGON: Charming spot. Inspiring prospects. Let's go.
VLADIMIR: We can't.
ESTRAGON: Why not?
VLADIMIR: We're waiting for Godot.

Samuel Beckett 1906–89 Irish dramatist, novelist, and poet: *Waiting for Godot* (1955)

2 I think we ought to let him hang there. Let him twist slowly, slowly in the wind.

opposing the nomination of Patrick Gray as director of the FBI

John Ehrlichman 1925–99 Presidential assistant to Richard Nixon: telephone conversation with John Dean, in *Washington Post* 27 July 1973

3 There was a pause—just long enough for an angel to pass, flying slowly.

Ronald Firbank 1886–1926 English novelist: *Vainglory* (1915)

4 If anyone believes that our smiles involve abandonment of the teaching of Marx, Engels and Lenin he deceives himself. Those who wait for that must wait until a shrimp learns to whistle.

Nikita Khrushchev 1894–1971 Soviet statesman: speech in Moscow, 17 September 1955

5 How men hate waiting while their wives shop for clothes and trinkets; how women hate waiting, often for much of their lives, while their husbands shop for fame and glory.

Thomas Szasz 1920– Hungarian-born psychiatrist: *The Second Sin* (1973)

Wales

1 It profits a man nothing to give his soul for the whole world . . . But for Wales—!

Robert Bolt 1924–95 English dramatist: *A Man for All Seasons* (1960)

2 The English have forgot that they ever conquered the Welsh, but some ages will elapse before the Welsh forget that the English have conquered them.

George Borrow 1803–81 English writer: *Wild Wales* (1854)

3 Who dare compare the English, the most degraded of all the races under heaven, with the Welsh?

Giraldus Cambrensis *c.*1146–*c.*1220 Welsh cleric and historian: attributed

4 Wales, Wales, sweet are thy hills and vales,
Thy speech, thy song,
To thee belong,
O may they live ever in Wales.

Evan James 1809–78 Welsh bard: 'Land of My Fathers' (1856)

5 Among our ancient mountains,
And from our lovely vales,
Oh, let the prayer re-echo:
'God bless the Prince of Wales!'

George Linley 1798–1865 English songwriter: 'God Bless the Prince of Wales' (1862 song); translated from the Welsh original by J. C. Hughes (1837–87)

6 Everyday when I wake up, I thank the Lord I'm Welsh.

Cerys Matthews 1969– Welsh singer: 'International Velvet' (1998 song)

7 The land of my fathers. My fathers can have it.

Dylan Thomas 1914–53 Welsh poet: in *Adam* December 1953

8 I wanted a play that would paint the full face of sensuality, rebellion and

revivalism. In South Wales these three phenomena have played second fiddle only to Rugby Union which is a distillation of all three.

Gwyn Thomas 1913–81 Welsh novelist and dramatist: introduction to *Jackie the Jumper* (1962)

9 There is no present in Wales,
And no future;
There is only the past,
Brittle with relics . . .
And an impotent people,
Sick with inbreeding,
Worrying the carcase of an old song.

R. S. Thomas 1913–2000 Welsh poet and clergyman: 'Welsh Landscape' (1955)

10 'I often think,' he continued, 'that we can trace almost all the disasters of English history to the influence of Wales!'

Evelyn Waugh 1903–66 English novelist: *Decline and Fall* (1928)

War

see also AIR FORCE, AMERICAN CIVIL WAR, AMERICAN WAR OF INDEPENDENCE, ARMY, FALKLANDS, GULF WAR, IRAQ WAR, NAVY, PEACE, VIETNAM WAR, WARFARE, WATERLOO, WEAPONS, WORLD WAR I, WORLD WAR II

1 We make war that we may live in peace.

Aristotle 384–322 BC Greek philosopher: *Nicomachean Ethics*

2 In war there is no second prize for the runner-up.

Omar Bradley 1893–1981 American general: in *Military Review* February 1950

3 War always finds a way.

Bertolt Brecht 1898–1956 German dramatist: *Mother Courage* (1939)

4 In war, whichever side may call itself the victor, there are no winners, but all are losers.

Neville Chamberlain 1869–1940 British Conservative statesman: speech at Kettering, 3 July 1938

5 In war: resolution. In defeat: defiance. In victory: magnanimity. In peace: goodwill.

Winston Churchill 1874–1965 British Conservative statesman: *The Second World War* vol. 1 (1948)

6 Laws are silent in time of war.

Cicero 106–43 BC Roman orator and statesman: *Pro Milone*

7 The sinews of war, unlimited money.

Cicero 106–43 BC Roman orator and statesman: *Fifth Philippic*

8 Everything is very simple in war, but the simplest thing is difficult. These difficulties accumulate and produce a friction which no man can imagine exactly who has not seen war.

Karl von Clausewitz 1780–1831 Prussian soldier and military theorist: *On War* (1832–4)

9 War is nothing but a continuation of politics with the admixture of other means.

commonly rendered as 'War is the continuation of politics by other means'

Karl von Clausewitz 1780–1831 Prussian soldier and military theorist: *On War* (1832–4)

10 War is too serious a matter to entrust to military men.

Georges Clemenceau 1841–1929 French statesman: attributed to Clemenceau, but also to Briand and Talleyrand

11 There never was a good war, or a bad peace.

Benjamin Franklin 1706–90 American politician, inventor, and scientist: letter to Josiah Quincy, 11 September 1783

12 What difference does it make to the dead, the orphans and the homeless, whether the mad destruction is wrought under the name of totalitarianism or the holy name of liberty or democracy?

> **Mahatma Gandhi** 1869–1948 Indian statesman: *Non-Violence in Peace and War* (1942)

13 War is hell, and all that, but it has a good deal to recommend it. It wipes out all the small nuisances of peace-time.

> **Ian Hay** 1876–1952 Scottish novelist and dramatist: *The First Hundred Thousand* (1915)

14 War is the father of all and the king of all.

> **Heraclitus** *c.*540–*c.*480 BC Greek philosopher: *On the Universe* fragment 44

15 Older men declare war. But it is youth who must fight and die.

> **Herbert Hoover** 1874–1964 American Republican statesman: speech at the Republican National Convention, Chicago, 27 June 1944

16 Mankind must put an end to war or war will put an end to mankind.

> **John F. Kennedy** 1917–63 American Democratic statesman: speech to United Nations General Assembly, 25 September 1961

17 The conventional army loses if it does not win. The guerrilla wins if he does not lose.

> **Henry Kissinger** 1923– American politician: in *Foreign Affairs* January 1969

18 It is well that war is so terrible. We should grow too fond of it.

> **Robert E. Lee** 1807–70 American Confederate general: after the battle of Fredericksburg, December 1862; attributed

19 I have never met anyone who wasn't against war. Even Hitler and Mussolini were, according to themselves.

> **David Low** 1891–1963 British political cartoonist: in *New York Times Magazine* 10 February 1946

20 He knew that the essence of war is violence, and that moderation in war is imbecility.

> **Lord Macaulay** 1800–59 English politician and historian: *Essays Contributed to the Edinburgh Review* (1843) 'John Hampden'

21 Wars begin when you will, but they do not end when you please.

> **Niccolò Machiavelli** 1469–1527 Florentine statesman and political philosopher: *History of Florence* (1521–4)

22 There are not fifty ways of fighting, there's only one, and that's to win. Neither revolution nor war consists in doing what one pleases.

> **André Malraux** 1901–76 French novelist, essayist, and art critic: *L'Espoir* (1937)

23 War is a necessary part of God's arrangement of the world . . . Without war the world would deteriorate into materialism.

> **Helmuth von Moltke** 1800–91 Prussian military commander: letter to Dr J. K. Bluntschli, 11 December 1880

24 Strategy is a system of expedients; it is more than a mere scholarly discipline.

> **Helmuth von Moltke** 1800–91 Prussian military commander: D. J. Hughes (ed.) *Moltke on the Art of War* (1993)

25 Rule 1, on page 1 of the book of war, is: 'Do not march on Moscow' . . . [Rule 2] is: 'Do not go fighting with your land armies in China.'

> **Lord Montgomery** 1887–1976 British field marshal: speech, House of Lords, 30 May 1962

26 In war, three-quarters turns on personal character and relations; the balance of manpower and materials counts only for the remaining quarter.

> **Napoleon I** 1769–1821 French emperor: 'Observations sur les affaires d'Espagne, Saint-Cloud, 27 août 1808'

27 The quickest way of ending a war is to lose it.

> **George Orwell** 1903–50 English novelist: in *Polemic* May 1946

28 My subject is War, and the pity of War.
The Poetry is in the pity.

> **Wilfred Owen** 1893–1918 English poet: preface (written 1918) in *Poems* (1963)

29 History is littered with the wars which everybody knew would never happen.

> **Enoch Powell** 1912–98 British Conservative politician: speech to the Conservative Party Conference, 19 October 1967

30 I have seen war. I have seen war on land and sea. I have seen blood running from the wounded. I have seen men coughing out their gassed lungs. I have seen the dead in the mud. I have seen cities destroyed. I have seen 200 limping, exhausted men come out of line—the survivors of a regiment of 1,000 that went forward 48 hours before. I have seen children starving. I have seen the agony of mothers and wives. I hate war.

> **Franklin D. Roosevelt** 1882–1945 American Democratic statesman: speech at Chautauqua, NY, 14 August 1936

31 Sometime they'll give a war and nobody will come.

> **Carl Sandburg** 1878–1967 American poet: *The People, Yes* (1936); 'Suppose They Gave a War and Nobody Came?' was the title of a 1970 film

32 There is many a boy here to-day who looks on war as all glory, but, boys, it is all hell.

> **William Sherman** 1820–91 American Union general: speech at Columbus, Ohio, 11 August 1880

33 War is capitalism with the gloves off and many who go to war know it but they go to war because they don't want to be a hero.

> **Tom Stoppard** 1937– British dramatist: *Travesties* (1975)

34 Waste of Blood, and waste of Tears,
Waste of youth's most precious years,
Waste of ways the saints have trod,
Waste of Glory, waste of God,
War!

> **G. A. Studdert Kennedy** 1883–1929 British poet: 'Waste' (1919)

35 Know the enemy and know yourself; in a hundred battles you will never be defeated.

> **Sun Tzu** *fl. c.*400–320 BC Chinese general and military theorist: *The Art of War*

36 Dead battles, like dead generals, hold the military mind in their dead grip and Germans, no less than other peoples, prepare for the last war.

> **Barbara W. Tuchman** 1912–89 American writer: *August 1914* (1962)

37 God is on the side not of the heavy battalions, but of the best shots.

> **Voltaire** 1694–1778 French writer and philosopher: 'The Piccini Notebooks' (*c.*1735–50); see STRENGTH 9

38 Next to a battle lost, the greatest misery is a battle gained.

> **Duke of Wellington** 1769–1852 British soldier and statesman: in *Diary of Frances, Lady Shelley 1787–1817* (ed. R. Edgcumbe)

39 All the business of war, and indeed all the business of life, is to endeavour to find out what you don't know by what you do; that's what I called 'guessing what was at the other side of the hill'.

Duke of Wellington 1769–1852 British soldier and statesman: in *The Croker Papers* (1885)

40 Once lead this people into war and they will forget there ever was such a thing as tolerance.

Woodrow Wilson 1856–1924 American Democratic statesman: John Dos Passos *Mr Wilson's War* (1917)

41 One to destroy, is murder by the law;
And gibbets keep the lifted hand in awe;
To murder thousands, takes a specious name,
'War's glorious art', and gives immortal fame.

Edward Young 1683–1765 English poet and dramatist: *The Love of Fame* (1725–8)

Warfare

see also WAR

1 War is the most exciting and dramatic thing in life. In fighting to the death you feel terribly relaxed when you manage to come through.

Moshe Dayan 1915–81 Israeli statesman and general: in *Observer* 13 February 1972

2 I fear we have only awakened a sleeping giant, and his reaction will be terrible.

of the attack on Pearl Harbor
Larry Forrester, **Hideo Oguni**, and **Ryuzo Kikushima** screenwriters: *Tora! Tora! Tora!* (1970 film); said by the Japanese admiral Isoruko Yamamoto, although there is no evidence that Yamamoto used these words; see WARFARE 10

3 When you're in the battlefield, survival is all there is. Death is the only great emotion.

Sam Fuller 1911–97 American film director: in *Guardian* 26 February 1991

4 Gentlemen of France, fire first.
said before the Battle of Fontenoy, 1745
Lord Charles Hay *c.*1700–60 Scottish army officer: Voltaire *Siècle de Louis XIV* (1751), where the wording is given as 'Gentlemen of the French guards, open fire'

5 Always mystify, mislead, and surprise the enemy, if possible.
his strategic motto during the Civil War
Thomas Jonathan 'Stonewall' Jackson 1824–63 American Confederate general: M. Miner and H. Rawson *American Heritage Dictionary of American Quotations* (1997)

6 Come and see the blood
in the streets!
Pablo Neruda 1904–73 Chilean poet: 'I'm Explaining a Few Things' (1947)

7 If you could hear, at every jolt, the blood
Come gargling from the froth-corrupted lungs,
Obscene as cancer, bitter as the cud
Of vile, incurable sores on innocent tongues,—
My friend, you would not tell with such high zest
To children ardent for some desperate glory,
The old Lie: Dulce et decorum est
Pro patria mori.
Wilfred Owen 1893–1918 English poet: 'Dulce et Decorum Est'; see PATRIOTISM 11

8 Once more unto the breach, dear friends, once more;
Or close the wall up with our English dead!
In peace there's nothing so becomes a man
As modest stillness and humility:

But when the blast of war blows in
  our ears,
Then imitate the action of the tiger;
Stiffen the sinews, summon up the
  blood,
Disguise fair nature with hard-
  favoured rage.
>   **William Shakespeare** 1564–1616
>   English dramatist: *Henry V* (1599)

9 I hae brocht ye to the ring, now see
gif ye can dance.
>   **William Wallace** *c.*1270–1305 Scottish
>   national hero: before the battle of
>   Falkirk, 1298; attributed in varying
>   forms, including ' . . . hop if ye can';
>   James MacKay *William Wallace: Brave
>   Heart* (1996)

10 A military man can scarcely pride
himself on having 'smitten a sleeping
enemy'; in fact, to have it pointed
out is more a matter of shame.
>   **Isoroku Yamamoto** 1884–1943
>   Japanese admiral: letter, 9 January 1942;
>   Hirosuki Asawa *The Reluctant Admiral*
>   (1979); see WARFARE 2

Waterloo 1815

1 *La Garde meurt, mais ne se rend pas.*
The Guards die but do not surrender.
*when called upon to surrender at Waterloo,
1815*
>   **Pierre, Baron de Cambronne**
>   1770–1842 French general: attributed to
>   Cambronne, but later denied by him

2 Probably the battle of Waterloo *was*
won on the playing-fields of Eton,
but the opening battles of all
subsequent wars have been lost
there.
>   **George Orwell** 1903–50 English
>   novelist: *The Lion and the Unicorn*
>   (1941) 'England Your England'; see
>   WATERLOO 5

3 Up Guards and at them!
>   **Duke of Wellington** 1769–1852 British

soldier and statesman: in *The Battle of
Waterloo* by a Near Observer [J. Booth]
(1815); later denied by Wellington

4 Hard pounding this, gentlemen; let's
see who will pound longest.
>   **Duke of Wellington** 1769–1852 British
>   soldier and statesman: Sir Walter Scott
>   *Paul's Letters* (1816)

5 The battle of Waterloo was won on
the playing fields of Eton.
>   **Duke of Wellington** 1769–1852 British
>   soldier and statesman: oral tradition,
>   but not found in this form of words; C. F.
>   R. Montalembert *De l'avenir politique
>   de l'Angleterre* (1856); see WATERLOO 2

Ways and Means

1 It is in life as it is in ways, the shortest
way is commonly the foulest, and
surely the fairer way is not much
about.
>   **Francis Bacon** 1561–1626 English
>   lawyer, courtier, philosopher, and
>   essayist: *The Advancement of Learning*
>   (1605)

2 A servant's too often a negligent elf;
—If it's business of consequence, DO
IT YOURSELF!
>   **R. H. Barham** 1788–1845 English
>   clergyman: 'The Ingoldsby
>   Penance!—Moral' (1842)

3 They sought it with thimbles, they
  sought it with care;
They pursued it with forks and hope;
They threatened its life with a
  railway-share;
They charmed it with smiles and
  soap.
>   **Lewis Carroll** 1832–98 English writer
>   and logician: *The Hunting of the Snark*
>   (1876)

4 The colour of the cat doesn't matter
as long as it catches the mice.
quoting a Chinese proverb

> **Deng Xiaoping** 1904–97 Chinese
> Communist statesman: in *Financial
> Times* 18 December 1986

5 The way is long if one follows
precepts, but short and helpful if one
follows patterns.

> **Seneca ('the Younger')** *c.*4 BC–AD 65
> Roman philosopher and poet: *Epistulae
> ad Lucilium*

6 *Dans ce pays-ci il est bon de tuer de
temps en temps un amiral pour
encourager les autres.*
In this country [England] it is
thought well to kill an admiral from
time to time to encourage the others.
*referring to the controversial execution of
Admiral John Byng, 1757*

> **Voltaire** 1694–1778 French writer and
> philosopher: *Candide* (1759)

Weakness

see STRENGTH AND WEAKNESS

Wealth

see also LUXURY, MONEY

1 If you really want to make a
million . . . the quickest way is to
start your own religion.

> **Anonymous**: previously attributed to L.
> Ron Hubbard 1911–86 in B. Corydon
> and L. Ron Hubbard Jr. *L. Ron Hubbard*
> (1987), but attribution subsequently
> rejected by L. Ron Hubbard Jr., who also
> dissociated himself from the book

2 Riches are for spending.

> **Francis Bacon** 1561–1626 English
> lawyer, courtier, philosopher, and
> essayist: *Essays* (1625) 'Of Expense'

3 People say I wasted my money. I say
90 per cent went on women, fast cars
and booze. The rest I wasted.

> **George Best** 1946–2005 Northern Irish

footballer: in *Daily Telegraph*
29 December 1990

4 It is easier for a camel to go through
the eye of a needle, than for a rich
man to enter into the kingdom of
God.

> **Bible**: St Matthew

5 A very rich person should leave his
kids enough to do anything but not
enough to do nothing.

> **Warren Buffett** 1930– American
> businessman: quoted in *Fortune
> Magazine* (online edition) 25 June 2006

6 The man who dies . . . rich dies
disgraced.

> **Andrew Carnegie** 1835–1919 American
> industrialist and philanthropist: in
> *North American Review* June 1889
> 'Wealth'

7 To be clever enough to get all that
money, one must be stupid enough
to want it.

> **G. K. Chesterton** 1874–1936 English
> essayist, novelist, and poet: *Wisdom of
> Father Brown* (1914)

8 The minute you walked in the joint,
I could see you were a man of
distinction,
A real big spender . . .
Hey! big spender, spend a little time
with me.

> **Dorothy Fields** 1905–74 American
> songwriter: 'Big Spender' (1966 song)

9 Let me tell you about the very rich.
They are different from you and me.

> **F. Scott Fitzgerald** 1896–1940 American
> novelist: *All the Sad Young Men* (1926);
> to which Ernest Hemingway replied,
> 'Yes, they have more money', in *Esquire*
> August 1936

10 In every well-governed state, wealth
is a sacred thing; in democracies it is
the only sacred thing.

> **Anatole France** 1844–1924 French
> novelist and man of letters: *L'Île des
> pingouins* (1908)

11 The greater the wealth, the thicker
will be the dirt.
J. K. Galbraith 1908–2006 American
economist: *The Affluent Society* (1958)

12 If you can actually count your
money, then you are not really a rich
man.
J. Paul Getty 1892–1976 American
industrialist: in *Observer* 3 November
1957

13 We are not here to sell a parcel of
boilers and vats, but the potentiality
of growing rich, beyond the dreams
of avarice.
at the sale of Thrale's brewery
Samuel Johnson 1709–84 English poet,
critic, and lexicographer: James Boswell
Life of Samuel Johnson (1791) 6 April
1781

14   I glory
More in the cunning purchase of my
wealth
Than in the glad possession.
Ben Jonson c.1573–1637 English
dramatist and poet: *Volpone* (1606)

15 Will the people in the cheaper seats
clap your hands? All the rest of you, if
you'll just rattle your jewellery.
John Lennon 1940–80 English pop
singer and songwriter: at the Royal
Variety Performance, 4 November 1963

16 I want to spend, and spend, and
spend.
*said to reporters on arriving to collect her
husband's football pools winnings of
£152,000*
Vivian Nicholson 1936– : in *Daily
Herald* 28 September 1961

17 Get place and wealth, if possible,
with grace;
If not, by any means get wealth and
place.
Alexander Pope 1688–1744 English
poet: *Imitations of Horace* (1738)

18 Having money is rather like being a
blonde. It is more fun but not vital.
Mary Quant 1934– English fashion
designer: in *Observer* 2 November 1986

19 A kiss on the hand may be quite
continental,
But diamonds are a girl's best friend.
Leo Robin 1900–84 American
songwriter: 'Diamonds are a Girl's Best
Friend' (1949 song)

20 The chief enjoyment of riches
consists in the parade of riches.
Adam Smith 1723–90 Scottish
philosopher and economist: *Wealth of
Nations* (1776)

21 To suppose, as we all suppose, that
we could be rich and not behave as
the rich behave, is like supposing
that we could drink all day and keep
absolutely sober.
Logan Pearsall Smith 1865–1946
American-born man of letters:
Afterthoughts (1931)

22 I've been rich and I've been poor:
rich is better.
Sophie Tucker 1884–1966 American
vaudeville artiste: attributed

Weapons

1 Weapons are like money; no one
knows the meaning of *enough*.
Martin Amis 1949– English novelist:
Einstein's Monsters (1987)

2 A bigger bang for a buck.
Anonymous: Charles E. Wilson's
defence policy, in *Newsweek* 22 March
1954

3 Every gun that is made, every
warship launched, every rocket fired
signifies, in the final sense, a theft
from those who hunger and are not
fed, those who are cold and are not
clothed. This world in arms is not

spending money alone. It is spending the sweat of its labourers, the genius of its scientists, the hopes of its children.

> **Dwight D. Eisenhower** 1890–1969 American general and Republican statesman: speech in Washington, 16 April 1953

4 We can manage without butter but not, for example, without guns. If we are attacked we can only defend ourselves with guns not with butter.

> **Joseph Goebbels** 1897–1945 German Nazi leader: speech in Berlin, 17 January 1936

5 We have no butter . . . but I ask you—would you rather have butter or guns? . . . preparedness makes us powerful. Butter merely makes us fat.

> **Hermann Goering** 1893–1946 German Nazi leader: speech at Hamburg, 1936; W. Frischauer *Goering* (1951)

6 58% Don't Want Pershing.

> **Katharine Hamnett** 1947– British fashion designer: anti-nuclear weapons slogan on T-shirt worn when she attended a drinks party at 10 Downing Street in 1984

7 History could hang in the balance tonight. Give us bombs for peace.

> *on the need to maintain military pressure on Serbia*
>
> **Richard Holbrooke** 1941– American diplomat: telegram to State Department, summer 1995

8 We have not yet found shiny, pointy things that I would call a weapon.

> *as weapons inspector in Iraq 1991–2 and 2003–4*
>
> **David Kay** American official: interview, CNN *Late Edition* 5 October 2003

9 If the Third World War is fought with nuclear weapons, the fourth will be fought with bows and arrows.

> **Lord Mountbatten** 1900–79 British

sailor, soldier, and statesman: in *Maclean's* 17 November 1975

10 Wars may be fought with weapons, but they are won by men.

> **George S. Patton** 1885–1945 American general: in *Cavalry Journal* September 1933

11 You can't say civilization don't advance, however, for in every war they kill you in a new way.

> **Will Rogers** 1879–1935 American actor and humorist: in *New York Times* 23 December 1929

12 Cannon to right of them,
Cannon to left of them,
Cannon in front of them
Volleyed and thundered.

> **Alfred, Lord Tennyson** 1809–92 English poet: 'The Charge of the Light Brigade' (1854)

13 Spare us all word of the weapons, their force and range,
The long numbers that rocket the mind.

> **Richard Wilbur** 1921– American poet: 'Advice to a Prophet' (1961)

Weather

see also FOG, RAIN, SNOW, WIND

1 What dreadful hot weather we have! It keeps one in a continual state of inelegance.

> **Jane Austen** 1775–1817 English novelist: letter, 18 September 1796

2 Wet spring had merged imperceptibly into bleak autumn. For months the sky had remained a depthless grey. Sometimes it rained, but mostly it was just dull . . . It was like living inside Tupperware.

> **Bill Bryson** 1951– American travel writer: *The Lost Continent* (1989)

3 The frost performs its secret ministry,

Unhelped by any wind.
Samuel Taylor Coleridge 1772–1834 English poet, critic, and philosopher: 'Frost at Midnight' (1798)

4 I believe we should all behave quite differently if we lived in a warm, sunny climate all the time.
Noël Coward 1899–1973 English dramatist, actor, and composer: *Brief Encounter* (1945)

5 It ain't a fit night out for man or beast.
W. C. Fields 1880–1946 American humorist: adopted by Fields but claimed by him not to be original; letter, 8 February 1944

6 A woman rang to say she heard there was a hurricane on the way. Well don't worry, there isn't.
weather forecast on the night before serious gales in southern England
Michael Fish 1944– British weather forecaster: BBC TV, 15 October 1987

7 This is the weather the cuckoo likes, And so do I;
When showers betumble the chestnut spikes,
And nestlings fly.
Thomas Hardy 1840–1928 English novelist and poet: 'Weathers' (1922)

8 The weather is like the Government, always in the wrong.
Jerome K. Jerome 1859–1927 English writer: *Idle Thoughts of an Idle Fellow* (1889)

9 When two Englishmen meet, their first talk is of the weather.
Samuel Johnson 1709–84 English poet, critic, and lexicographer: in *The Idler* 24 June 1758

10 Thank heavens, the sun has gone in, and I don't have to go out and enjoy it.
Logan Pearsall Smith 1865–1946 American-born man of letters: *Afterthoughts* (1931)

11 There is no such thing as bad weather. All weather is good because it is God's.
St Teresa of Ávila 1512–82 Spanish Carmelite nun and mystic: attributed; H. Ward and J. Wild (eds.) *The Lion Christian Quotation Collection* (1997)

12 There is a sumptuous variety about the New England weather that compels the stranger's admiration—and regret. The weather is always doing something there; always attending strictly to business; always getting up new designs and trying them on the people to see how they will go.
Mark Twain 1835–1910 American writer: speech to New England Society, 22 December 1876

13 The best sun we have is made of Newcastle coal.
Horace Walpole 1717–97 English writer and connoisseur: letter to George Montagu, 15 June 1768

Weddings

see also MARRIAGE

1 If it were not for the presents, an elopement would be preferable.
George Ade 1866–1944 American humorist and dramatist: *Forty Modern Fables* (1901)

2 Oh! how many torments lie in the small circle of a wedding-ring!
Colley Cibber 1671–1757 English dramatist: *The Double Gallant* (1707)

3 It's pretty easy. Just say 'I do' whenever anyone asks you a question.
Richard Curtis 1956– New Zealand-born writer: *Four Weddings and a Funeral* (1994 film)

4 I'm getting married in the morning, Ding dong! The bells are gonna chime.

Pull out the stopper;
Let's have a whopper;
But get me to the church on time!

> **Alan Jay Lerner** 1918–86 American
> songwriter: 'Get Me to the Church on
> Time' (1956 song)

5 Fair Concord, ever abide by their
couch, and to so well-matched a pair
may Venus ever be propitious.

> **Martial** AD *c.*40–*c.*104 Roman
> epigrammatist: *Epigrams*

6 What woman, however old, has not
the bridal-favours and raiment
stowed away, and packed in
lavender, in the inmost cupboards of
her heart?

> **William Makepeace Thackeray**
> 1811–63 English novelist: *The Virginians*
> (1857–9)

7 What a holler there would be if
people had to pay the minister as
much to marry them as they have to
pay a lawyer to get them a divorce.

> **Claire Trevor** American actress: in *New
> York Journal-American* 12 October 1960

The West Indies

1 The architecture of our future is not
only unfinished; the scaffolding has
hardly gone up.

> **George Lamming** 1927– Barbados-
> born novelist and poet: 'The West
> Indian People' (1966) in Andrew Salkey
> (ed.) *Caribbean Essays* (1973); quoted by
> Owen Arthur, Prime Minister of
> Barbados, symposium 28–30 June 2006

2 History is built around creation and
achievement, and nothing was
created in the West Indies.

> **V. S. Naipaul** 1932– Trinidadian writer:
> *The Middle Passage* (1962); see WEST
> INDIES 3

3 Nothing will always be created in the
West Indies for quite long time,

because what will come out of there
is like nothing one has ever seen
before.

> *in response to V. S. Naipaul's comment; see*
> WEST INDIES 2
>
> **Derek Walcott** 1930– West Indian poet
> and dramatist: 'The Caribbean: Culture
> or Mimicry?' in *Journal of Interamerican
> Studies and World Affairs* February 1974

4 Visual surprise is natural in the
Caribbean; it comes with the
landscape, and faced with its beauty,
the sigh of History dissolves.

> **Derek Walcott** 1930– West Indian poet
> and dramatist: 'The Antilles: Fragments
> of an Epic Memory' (1992)

Wind

1   We just sit tight while wind dives
And strafes invisibly. Space is a salvo,
We are bombarded by the empty air.
Strange, it is a huge nothing that we
fear.

> **Seamus Heaney** 1939– Irish poet:
> 'Storm on the Island' (1966)

2 On Wenlock Edge the wood's in
trouble;
His forest fleece the Wrekin heaves;
The gale, it plies the saplings double,
And thick on Severn snow the leaves.

> **A. E. Housman** 1859–1936 English poet:
> *A Shropshire Lad* (1896)

3 Welcome, wild North-easter!
Shame it is to see
Odes to every zephyr;
Ne'er a verse to thee.

> **Charles Kingsley** 1819–75 English
> writer and clergyman: 'Ode to the
> North-East Wind' (1858)

4 No one can tell me,
Nobody knows,
Where the wind comes from,
Where the wind goes.

> **A. A. Milne** 1882–1956 English writer for
> children: 'Wind on the Hill' (1927)

5 O wild West Wind, thou breath of
     Autumn's being,
   Thou, from whose unseen presence
     the leaves dead
   Are driven, like ghosts from an
     enchanter fleeing,
   Yellow, and black, and pale, and
     hectic red,
   Pestilence-stricken multitudes.
   Percy Bysshe Shelley 1792–1822
   English poet: 'Ode to the West Wind'
   (1819)

Winning

see also AWARDS, DEFEAT, FAILURE, SUCCESS

1 Anybody can Win, unless there
   happens to be a Second Entry.
   George Ade 1866–1944 American
   humorist and dramatist: *Fables in Slang*
   (1900)

2 EVERYBODY has won, and all must
   have prizes.
   Lewis Carroll 1832–98 English writer
   and logician: *Alice's Adventures in
   Wonderland* (1865)

3 What's lost upon the roundabouts
   we pulls up on the swings!
   Patrick Reginald Chalmers 1872–1942
   British banker and writer:
   'Roundabouts and Swings' (1912)

4 What is our aim? . . . Victory, victory
   at all costs, victory in spite of all
   terror; victory, however long and
   hard the road may be; for without
   victory, there is no survival.
   Winston Churchill 1874–1965 British
   Conservative statesman: speech, House
   of Commons, 13 May 1940

5 The important thing in life is not the
   victory but the contest; the essential
   thing is not to have won but to have
   fought well.
   Baron Pierre de Coubertin 1863–1937
   French sportsman and educationist:
   speech on the Olympic Games, London,
   24 July 1908

6 Winning is everything. The only ones
   who remember you when you come
   second are your wife and your dog.
   Damon Hill 1960– English motor-
   racing driver: in *Sunday Times*
   18 December 1994

7 When in doubt, win the trick.
   Edmond Hoyle 1672–1769 English
   writer on card-games: *Hoyle's Games
   Improved* (ed. Charles Jones, 1790)
   'Twenty-four Short Rules for Learners'
   (though attributed to Hoyle, this may
   well have been an editorial addition by
   Jones, since it is not found in earlier
   editions)

8 The politicians of New York . . . see
   nothing wrong in the rule, that to the
   victor belong the spoils of the enemy.
   William Learned Marcy 1786–1857
   American politician: speech to the
   Senate, 25 January 1832

9 The moment of victory is much too
   short to live for that and nothing
   else.
   Martina Navratilova 1956– Czech-
   born American tennis player: in
   Independent 21 June 1989

10 Eclipse first, the rest nowhere.
    *comment on a horse-race at Epsom, 3 May
    1769*
    Dennis O'Kelly *c.*1720–87 Irish
    racehorse-owner: in *Annals of Sporting*
    (1822); *Dictionary of National
    Biography* gives the occasion as the
    Queen's Plate at Winchester, 1769

11 One more such victory and we are
    lost.
    *on defeating the Romans at Asculum, 279
    BC*
    Pyrrhus 319–272 BC Greek monarch:
    Plutarch *Parallel Lives* 'Pyrrhus'

12 Sure, winning isn't everything. It's the
    only thing.
    Henry 'Red' Sanders: in *Sports
    Illustrated* 26 December 1955; often
    attributed to Vince Lombardi

13 Winning isn't everything. It's the money you make doing it that's everything.

Lee Trevino 1939– American golfer: in *sport.telegraph* 30 December 2003 'Quotes of the Year'

Winter

1 The English winter—ending in July,
To recommence in August.

Lord Byron 1788–1824 English poet: *Don Juan* (1819–24)

2 Winter lies too long in country towns; hangs on until it is stale and shabby, old and sullen.

Willa Cather 1873–1947 American novelist: *My Ántonia* (1918)

3 No warmth, no cheerfulness, no healthful ease,
No comfortable feel in any member—
No shade, no shine, no butterflies, no bees,
No fruits, no flowers, no leaves, no birds,—
November!

Thomas Hood 1799–1845 English poet and humorist: 'No!' (1844)

4 Winter is icummen in,
Lhude sing Goddamm,
Raineth drop and staineth slop,
And how the wind doth ramm!
Sing: Goddamm.

Ezra Pound 1885–1972 American poet: 'Ancient Music' (1917); see SUMMER 1

5 A tedious season they await
Who hear November at the gate.

Alexander Pushkin 1799–1837 Russian poet: *Eugene Onegin* (1833)

6   O, Wind,
If Winter comes, can Spring be far behind?

Percy Bysshe Shelley 1792–1822 English poet: 'Ode to the West Wind' (1819)

7 She has made me in love with a cold climate, and frost and snow, with a northern moonlight.

on Mary Wollstonecraft's letters from Sweden and Norway

Robert Southey 1774–1843 English poet and writer: letter to his brother Thomas, 28 April 1797

8 Let no man boast himself that he has got through the perils of winter till at least the seventh of May.

Anthony Trollope 1815–82 English novelist: *Doctor Thorne* (1858)

Wisdom

see also KNOWLEDGE

1 Justice inclines her scales so that wisdom comes at the price of suffering.

Aeschylus *c.*525–456 BC Greek tragedian: *Agamemnon*

2 The price of wisdom is above rubies.

Bible: Job

3 Does the eagle know what is in the pit?
Or wilt thou go ask the mole:
Can wisdom be put in a silver rod?
Or love in a golden bowl?

William Blake 1757–1827 English poet: *The Book of Thel* (1789) 'Thel's Motto'

4 Mere cleverness is not wisdom.

Euripides *c.*485–*c.*406 BC Greek dramatist: *Bacchae*

5 Wisdom is not the purchase of a day.

Thomas Paine 1737–1809 English political theorist: *The Crisis* (December 1776)

6 No man is wise at all times.

Pliny the Elder AD 23–79 Roman statesman and scholar: *Natural History*

7 One would need to be already wise, in order to love wisdom.

Friedrich von Schiller 1759–1805

German dramatist and poet: *On the Aesthetic Education of Man* (1795)

Wit and Satire

see also HUMOUR, WORDPLAY

1 Wit is educated insolence.
Aristotle 384–322 BC Greek philosopher: *The Art of Rhetoric*

2 A thing well said will be wit in all languages.
John Dryden 1631–1700 English poet, critic, and dramatist: *An Essay of Dramatic Poesy* (1668)

3 Wit is the salt of conversation, not the food.
William Hazlitt 1778–1830 English essayist: *Lectures on the English Comic Writers* (1819)

4 Impropriety is the soul of wit.
W. Somerset Maugham 1874–1965 English novelist: *The Moon and Sixpence* (1919)

5 Satire is a lesson, parody is a game.
Vladimir Nabokov 1899–1977 Russian novelist: *Strong Opinions* (1974)

6 Wit is the epitaph of an emotion.
Friedrich Nietzsche 1844–1900 German philosopher and writer: *Menschliches, Allzumenschliches* (1867–80)

7 There's a hell of a distance between wise-cracking and wit. Wit has truth in it; wise-cracking is simply callisthenics with words.
Dorothy Parker 1893–1967 American critic and humorist: in *Paris Review* Summer 1956

8 I am not only witty in myself, but the cause that wit is in other men.
William Shakespeare 1564–1616 English dramatist: *Henry IV, Part 2* (1597)

9 Brevity is the soul of wit.
William Shakespeare 1564–1616 English dramatist: *Hamlet* (1601)

10 There's no possibility of being witty without a little ill-nature; the malice of a good thing is the barb that makes it stick.
Richard Brinsley Sheridan 1751–1816 Anglo-Irish dramatist: *The School for Scandal* (1777)

11 Satire is a sort of glass, wherein beholders do generally discover everybody's face but their own.
Jonathan Swift 1667–1745 Anglo-Irish poet and satirist: *The Battle of the Books* (1704)

Wives

see also MARRIAGE, WOMEN

1 Wives are young men's mistresses, companions for middle age, and old men's nurses.
Francis Bacon 1561–1626 English lawyer, courtier, philosopher, and essayist: *Essays* (1625) 'Of Marriage and the Single Life'

2 A man's mother is his misfortune, but his wife is his fault.
on being urged to marry by his mother
Walter Bagehot 1826–77 English economist and essayist: in Norman St John Stevas *Works of Walter Bagehot* (1986) vol. 15 'Walter Bagehot's Conversation'

3 Meek wifehood is no part of my profession;
I am your friend, but never your possession.
Vera Brittain 1893–1970 English writer: 'Married Love'

4 If you want to know about a man you can find out an awful lot by looking at who he married.
Kirk Douglas 1916– American film actor and producer: in *Daily Mail* 9 September 1988

5 Man's best possession is a sympathetic wife.

> **Euripides** c.485–c.406 BC Greek dramatist: fragment no. 164

6 What man thinks of changing himself so as to suit his wife? And yet men expect that women shall put on altogether new characters when they are married, and girls think that they can do so.

> **Anthony Trollope** 1815–82 English novelist: *Phineas Redux* (1874)

Woman's Role

see also MEN AND WOMEN

1 In the new code of laws which I suppose it will be necessary for you to make I desire you would remember the ladies, and be more generous and favourable to them than your ancestors. Do not put such unlimited power into the hands of the husbands. Remember all men would be tyrants if they could.

> **Abigail Adams** 1744–1818 American letter writer: letter to John Adams, 31 March 1776

2 The sadness of the women's movement is that they don't allow the necessity of love. See, I don't personally trust any revolution where love is not allowed.

> **Maya Angelou** 1928– American writer: in *California Living* 14 May 1975

3 If all men are born free, how is it that all women are born slaves?

> **Mary Astell** 1668–1731 English poet and feminist: *Some Reflections upon Marriage* (1706 ed.)

4 The only position for women in SNCC is prone.

> **Stokely Carmichael** 1941–98 American Black Power leader: response to a question about the position of women at a Student Nonviolent Coordinating Committee conference, November 1964

5 I could have stayed home and baked cookies and had teas. But what I decided was to fulfil my profession, which I entered before my husband was in public life.

> **Hillary Rodham Clinton** 1947– American lawyer and Republican politician: comment on questions raised by rival Democratic contender Edmund G. Brown Jr.; in *Albany Times-Union* 17 March 1992

6 I want to be something so much worthier than the doll in the doll's house.

> **Charles Dickens** 1812–70 English novelist: *Our Mutual Friend* (1865)

7 Today the problem that has no name is how to juggle work, love, home and children.

> **Betty Friedan** 1921–2006 American feminist: *The Second Stage* (1987)

8 I didn't fight to get women out from behind the vacuum cleaner to get them onto the board of Hoover.

> **Germaine Greer** 1939– Australian feminist: in *Guardian* 27 October 1986

9 De nigger woman is de mule uh de world.

> **Zora Neale Hurston** c.1901–60 American writer: *Their Eyes Were Watching God* (1937)

10 A woman's preaching is like a dog's walking on his hinder legs. It is not done well; but you are surprised to find it done at all.

> **Samuel Johnson** 1709–84 English poet, critic, and lexicographer: James Boswell *Life of Samuel Johnson* (1791) 31 July 1763

11 A man is in general better pleased when he has a good dinner upon his table, than when his wife talks Greek.

> **Samuel Johnson** 1709–84 English poet, critic, and lexicographer: John Hawkins (ed.) *The Works of Samuel Johnson* (1787) 'Apophthegms, Sentiments, Opinions, etc.'

12 I'm furious about the women's liberationists. They keep getting up on soap boxes and proclaiming that women are brighter than men. That's true, but it should be kept very quiet or it ruins the whole racket.

   Anita Loos 1893–1981 American writer: attributed

13 But if God had wanted us to think just with our wombs, why did He give us a brain?

   Clare Booth Luce 1903–87 American diplomat, politician, and writer: in *Life* 16 October 1970

14 Women's Liberation is just a lot of foolishness. It's the men who are discriminated against. They can't bear children. And no-one's likely to do anything about that.

   Golda Meir 1898–1978 Israeli stateswoman: in *Newsweek* 23 October 1972

15 Religion is an all-important matter in a public school for girls. Whatever people say, it is the mother's safeguard, and the husband's. What we ask of education is not that girls should think, but that they should believe.

   Napoleon I 1769–1821 French emperor: 'Note sur L'Établissement D'Écouen' 15 May 1807

16 Woman is the nigger of the world.

   Yoko Ono 1933– Japanese poet and songwriter: remark made in a 1968 interview for *Nova* magazine and adopted by John Lennon as the title of a song (1972)

17 We are here to claim our right as women, not only to be free, but to fight for freedom. That it is our right as well as our duty.

   Christabel Pankhurst 1880–1958 English suffragette: in *Votes for Women* 31 March 1911

18 The one point on which all women are in furious secret rebellion against the existing law is the saddling of the right to a child with the obligation to become the servant of a man.

   George Bernard Shaw 1856–1950 Irish dramatist: *Getting Married* (1911)

19 We are becoming the men we wanted to marry.

   Gloria Steinem 1934– American journalist: in *Ms* July/August 1982

20 Feminism is the most revolutionary idea there has ever been. Equality for women demands a change in the human psyche more profound than anything Marx dreamed of. It means valuing parenthood as much as we value banking.

   Polly Toynbee 1946– English journalist: in *Guardian* 19 January 1987

21 That little man . . . he says women can't have as much rights as men, cause Christ wasn't a woman. Where did your Christ come from? From God and a woman. Man had nothing to do with Him.

   Sojourner Truth *c.*1797–1883 American evangelist and reformer: speech at Women's Rights Convention, Akron, Ohio, 1851

22 The Queen is most anxious to enlist every one who can speak or write to join in checking this mad, wicked folly of 'Woman's Rights', with all its attendant horrors, on which her poor feeble sex is bent, forgetting every sense of womanly feeling and propriety.

   Queen Victoria 1819–1901 British monarch: letter to Theodore Martin, 29 May 1870

23 Womanist is to feminist as purple to lavender.

   Alice Walker 1944– American poet: *In Search of Our Mother's Gardens* (1983)

24 I myself have never been able to find
out precisely what feminism is: I only
know that people call me a feminist
whenever I express sentiments that
differentiate me from a doormat or a
prostitute.
  Rebecca West 1892–1983 English
  novelist and journalist: in *The Clarion*
  14 November 1913

25 I do not wish them [women] to have
power over men; but over
themselves.
  Mary Wollstonecraft 1759–97 English
  feminist: *A Vindication of the Rights of
  Woman* (1792)

Women

see also MEN AND WOMEN, WIVES, WOMAN'S
ROLE

1 All the privilege I claim for my own
sex . . . is that of loving longest, when
existence or when hope is gone.
  Jane Austen 1775–1817 English novelist:
  Persuasion (1818)

2 Women—one half the human race at
least—care fifty times more for a
marriage than a ministry.
  Walter Bagehot 1826–77 English
  economist and essayist: *The English
  Constitution* (1867) 'The Monarchy'

3 Who can find a virtuous woman? for
her price is far above rubies.
  Bible: Proverbs

4 Women have no wilderness in them,
They are provident instead,
Content in the tight hot cell of their
    hearts
To eat dusty bread.
  Louise Bogan 1897–1970 American
  poet: 'Women' (1923)

5 The freedom women were supposed
to have found in the Sixties largely
boiled down to easy contraception

and abortion: things to make life
easier for men, in fact.
  Julie Burchill 1960– English journalist
  and writer: *Damaged Goods* (1986)
  'Born Again Cows'

6 Auld nature swears, the lovely dears
Her noblest work she classes, O;
Her prentice han' she tried on man,
An' then she made the lasses, O.
  Robert Burns 1759–96 Scottish poet:
  'Green Grow the Rashes' (1787)

7 If *Miss* means respectably
unmarried, and *Mrs* respectably
married, then *Ms* means nudge,
nudge, wink, wink.
  Angela Carter 1940–92 English novelist:
  'The Language of Sisterhood' in
  Christopher Ricks (ed.) *The State of the
  Language* (1980)

8 The prime truth of woman, the
universal mother . . . that if a thing is
worth doing, it is worth doing badly.
  G. K. Chesterton 1874–1936 English
  essayist, novelist, and poet: *What's
  Wrong with the World* (1910) 'Folly and
  Female Education'

9 One is not born a woman: one
becomes one.
  Simone de Beauvoir 1908–86 French
  novelist and feminist: *Le deuxième sexe*
  (1949)

10 Women never have young minds.
They are born three thousand years
old.
  Shelagh Delaney 1939– English
  dramatist: *A Taste of Honey* (1959)

11 She knows her man, and when you
rant and swear,
Can draw you to her *with a single
hair.*
  John Dryden 1631–1700 English poet,
  critic, and dramatist: translation of
  Persius *Satires*

12 She takes just like a woman, yes, she
does

She makes love just like a woman,
yes, she docs
And she aches just like a woman
But she breaks like a little girl.

> **Bob Dylan** 1941– American singer and
> songwriter: 'Just Like a Woman'
> (1966 song)

13 I am a woman and my business is to
hold things together.

> **F. Scott Fitzgerald** 1896–1940 American
> novelist: *Tender is the Night* (1934)

14 The great question that has never
been answered and which I have not
yet been able to answer, despite my
thirty years of research into the
feminine soul, is 'What does a
woman want?'

> **Sigmund Freud** 1856–1939 Austrian
> psychiatrist: to Marie Bonaparte; Ernest
> Jones *Sigmund Freud: Life and Work*
> (1955)

15 Eternal Woman draws us upward.

> **Johann Wolfgang von Goethe**
> 1749–1832 German poet, novelist, and
> dramatist: *Faust* pt. 2 (1832)
> 'Hochgebirg'

16 You can now see the Female Eunuch
the world over . . . spreading herself
wherever blue jeans and Coca-Cola
may go. Wherever you see nail
varnish, lipstick, brassieres, and high
heels, the Eunuch has set up her
camp.

> **Germaine Greer** 1939– Australian
> feminist: *The Female Eunuch* (20th
> anniversary ed., 1991)

17 There is nothin' like a dame.

> **Oscar Hammerstein II** 1895–1960
> American songwriter: title of song
> (1949)

18 Whoever has a daughter and does
not bury her alive, nor insult her nor
favour his son over her, Allah will
enter him into Paradise.

> **Ahmad ibn Hanbal** 780–855 Arab
> scholar: Musnad no. 1957

19 When you get to a man in the case,
They're like as a row of pins—
For the Colonel's Lady an' Judy
O'Grady
Are sisters under their skins!

> **Rudyard Kipling** 1865–1936 English
> writer and poet: 'The Ladies' (1896)

20 The female of the species is more
deadly than the male.

> **Rudyard Kipling** 1865–1936 English
> writer and poet: 'The Female of the
> Species' (1919)

21 Being a woman is of special interest
only to aspiring male transsexuals.
To actual women, it is merely a good
excuse not to play football.

> **Fran Lebowitz** 1946– American writer:
> *Metropolitan Life* (1978)

22 I got a twenty dollar piece says
There ain't nothin' I can't do.
I can make a dress out of a feed bag
an' I can make a man out of you.
'Cause I'm a woman
W-O-M-A-N
I'll say it again.

> **Jerry Leiber** 1933– American
> songwriter: 'I'm a Woman' (1962 song)

23 Thank heaven for little girls!
For little girls get bigger every day.

> **Alan Jay Lerner** 1918–86 American
> songwriter: 'Thank Heaven for Little
> Girls' (1958 song)

24 Sisterhood is powerful.

> **Robin Morgan** 1941– American
> feminist: title of book (1970)

25 If she never learns how to be a
daughter, she can't never learn how
to be a woman.

> **Toni Morrison** 1931– American
> novelist: *Tar Baby* (1981)

26 Woman was God's second blunder.

> **Friedrich Nietzsche** 1844–1900 German
> philosopher and writer: *Der Antichrist*
> (1888)

27 There is no female Mozart because there is no female Jack the Ripper.
>**Camille Paglia** 1947– American writer and critic: in *International Herald Tribune* 26 April 1991

28 The perpetual hunger to be beautiful and that thirst to be loved which is the real curse of Eve.
>**Jean Rhys** *c.*1890–1979 British novelist and short-story writer: *The Left Bank* (1927) 'Illusion'

29 Only the male intellect, clouded by sexual impulse, could call the undersized, narrow-shouldered, broad-hipped, and short-legged sex the fair sex.
>**Arthur Schopenhauer** 1788–1860 German philosopher: 'On Women' (1851)

30 O Woman! in our hours of ease,
Uncertain, coy, and hard to please,
And variable as the shade
By the light quivering aspen made;
When pain and anguish wring the brow,
A ministering angel thou!
>**Sir Walter Scott** 1771–1832 Scottish novelist and poet: *Marmion* (1808)

31 Frailty, thy name is woman!
>**William Shakespeare** 1564–1616 English dramatist: *Hamlet* (1601)

32 Here's to the maiden of bashful fifteen
Here's to the widow of fifty
Here's to the flaunting, extravagant quean;
And here's to the housewife that's thrifty.
>**Richard Brinsley Sheridan** 1751–1816 Anglo-Irish dramatist: *The School for Scandal* (1777)

33 The great and almost only comfort about being a woman is that one can always pretend to be more stupid than one is and no one is surprised.
>**Freya Stark** 1893–1993 English writer

and traveller: *The Valleys of the Assassins* (1934)

34   The woman is so hard
Upon the woman.
>**Alfred, Lord Tennyson** 1809–92 English poet: *The Princess* (1847)

35 From birth to 18 a girl needs good parents. From 18 to 35, she needs good looks. From 35 to 55, good personality. From 55 on, she needs good cash.
>**Sophie Tucker** 1884–1966 American vaudeville artiste: Michael Freedland *Sophie* (1978)

36 When once a woman has given you her heart, you can never get rid of the rest of her body.
>**John Vanbrugh** 1664–1726 English architect and dramatist: *The Relapse* (1696)

37 One should never trust a woman who tells one her real age. A woman who would tell one that, would tell one anything.
>**Oscar Wilde** 1854–1900 Anglo-Irish dramatist and poet: *A Woman of No Importance* (1893)

Wordplay

see also WIT

1 The *t* is silent, as in *Harlow.*
to Jean Harlow, who had been mispronouncing 'Margot'
>**Margot Asquith** 1864–1945 British political hostess: T. S. Matthews *Great Tom* (1973)

2 Apt Alliteration's artful aid.
>**Charles Churchill** 1731–64 English poet: *The Prophecy of Famine* (1763)

3 What is an Epigram? a dwarfish whole,
Its body brevity, and wit its soul.
>**Samuel Taylor Coleridge** 1772–1834 English poet, critic, and philosopher: 'Epigram' (1809)

4 A man who could make so vile a pun
would not scruple to pick a pocket.
John Dennis 1657–1734 English critic,
poet, and dramatist: editorial note in
The Gentleman's Magazine (1781)

5 [A pun] is a pistol let off at the ear;
not a feather to tickle the intellect.
Charles Lamb 1775–1834 English
writer: *Last Essays of Elia* (1833)
'Popular Fallacies'

6 The conclusion of your syllogism, I
said lightly, is fallacious, being based
upon licensed premises.
Flann O'Brien 1911–66 Irish novelist
and journalist: *At Swim-Two-Birds*
(1939)

7 If, with the literate, I am
Impelled to try an epigram,
I never seek to take the credit;
We all assume that Oscar said it.
Dorothy Parker 1893–1967 American
critic and humorist: 'A Pig's-Eye View of
Literature' (1937)

8 If I reprehend any thing in this world,
it is the use of my oracular tongue,
and a nice derangement of epitaphs!
Richard Brinsley Sheridan 1751–1816
Anglo-Irish dramatist: *The Rivals* (1775)

9 I summed up all systems in a phrase,
and all existence in an epigram.
Oscar Wilde 1854–1900 Anglo-Irish
dramatist and poet: letter, from Reading
Prison, to Lord Alfred Douglas,
January–March 1897

Words

see also DICTIONARIES, GRAMMAR, LANGUAGE,
MEANING, NAMES, WORDS AND DEEDS

1 The Greeks had a word for it.
Zoë Akins 1886–1958 American poet
and dramatist: title of play (1930)

2 There is no use indicting words, they
are no shoddier than what they
peddle.
Samuel Beckett 1906–89 Irish

dramatist, novelist, and poet: *Malone
Dies* (1958)

3 Words easy to be understood do
often hit the mark; when high and
learned ones do only pierce the air.
John Bunyan 1628–88 English writer
and Nonconformist preacher: *The Holy
City* (1665)

4 'When *I* use a word,' Humpty
Dumpty said in a rather scornful
tone, 'it means just what I choose it
to mean—neither more nor less.'
Lewis Carroll 1832–98 English writer
and logician: *Through the Looking-
Glass* (1872)

5 'Do you spell it with a "V" or a "W"?'
inquired the judge. 'That depends
upon the taste and fancy of the
speller, my Lord,' replied Sam
[Weller].
Charles Dickens 1812–70 English
novelist: *Pickwick Papers* (1837)

6 I gotta use words when I talk to you.
T. S. Eliot 1888–1965 Anglo-American
poet, critic, and dramatist: *Sweeney
Agonistes* (1932)

7 Words strain,
Crack and sometimes break, under
the burden,
Under the tension, slip, slide, perish,
Decay with imprecision, will not stay
in place,
Will not stay still.
T. S. Eliot 1888–1965 Anglo-American
poet, critic, and dramatist: *Four
Quartets* 'Burnt Norton' (1936)

8 Some word that teems with hidden
meaning—like Basingstoke.
W. S. Gilbert 1836–1911 English writer
of comic and satirical verse: *Ruddigore*
(1887)

9 It's exactly where a thought is lacking
That, just in time, a word shows up
instead.
Johann Wolfgang von Goethe
1749–1832 German poet, novelist, and
dramatist: *Faust* (1808)

10 Words are chameleons, which reflect
the colour of their environment.
Learned Hand 1872–1961 American
judge: in *Commissioner v. National
Carbide Corp.* (1948)

11 And once sent out a word takes wing
beyond recall.
Horace 65–8 BC Roman poet: *Epistles*

12 Summer afternoon—summer
afternoon . . . the two most beautiful
words in the English language.
Henry James 1843–1916 American
novelist: Edith Wharton *A Backward
Glance* (1934)

13 I am not yet so lost in lexicography as
to forget that words are the
daughters of earth, and that things
are the sons of heaven. Language is
only the instrument of science, and
words are but the signs of ideas: I
wish, however, that the instrument
might be less apt to decay, and that
signs might be permanent, like the
things which they denote.
Samuel Johnson 1709–84 English poet,
critic, and lexicographer: *A Dictionary
of the English Language* (1755)

14 I fear those big words, Stephen said,
which make us so unhappy.
James Joyce 1882–1941 Irish novelist:
Ulysses (1922)

15 Words are, of course, the most
powerful drug used by mankind.
Rudyard Kipling 1865–1936 English
writer and poet: speech, 14 February
1923

16 In my youth there were words you
couldn't say in front of a girl; now
you can't say 'girl'.
Tom Lehrer 1928– American humorist:
interview in *The Oldie*, 1996

17 My spelling is Wobbly. It's good
spelling but it Wobbles, and the
letters get in the wrong places.
A. A. Milne 1882–1956 English writer for
children: *Winnie-the-Pooh* (1926)

18 Whatever we have words for, that we
have already got beyond.
Friedrich Nietzsche 1844–1900 German
philosopher and writer: *Twilight of the
Idols* (1889) 'Skirmishes of an Untimely
Man'

19 MIKE: There's no word in the Irish
language for what you were doing.
WILSON: In Lapland they have no
word for snow.
Joe Orton 1933–67 English dramatist:
The Ruffian on the Stair (rev. ed. 1967)

20 Words are like leaves; and where they
most abound,
Much fruit of sense beneath is rarely
found.
Alexander Pope 1688–1744 English
poet: *An Essay on Criticism* (1711)

21 In a world full of audio visual
marvels, may words matter to you
and be full of magic.
Godfrey Smith 1926– English
journalist and columnist: letter to a new
grandchild, in *Sunday Times* 5 July 1987

22 Man does not live by words alone,
despite the fact that he sometimes
has to eat them.
Adlai Stevenson 1900–65 American
Democratic politician: *The Wit and
Wisdom of Adlai Stevenson* (1965)

Words and Deeds

1 When a man says he approves of
something in principle, it means he

hasn't the slightest intention of putting it into practice.
> **Otto von Bismarck** 1815–98 German statesman: attributed

2 Because half a dozen grasshoppers under a fern make the field ring with their importunate chink, whilst thousands of great cattle, reposed beneath the shadow of the British oak, chew the cud and are silent, pray do not imagine that those who make the noise are the only inhabitants of the field.
> **Edmund Burke** 1729–97 Irish-born Whig politician and man of letters: *Reflections on the Revolution in France* (1790)

3 The end of man is an action and not a thought, though it were the noblest.
> **Thomas Carlyle** 1795–1881 Scottish historian and political philosopher: *Sartor Resartus* (1834)

4 This is very true: for my words are my own, and my actions are my ministers'.
> *reply to Lord Rochester's epitaph*
> **Charles II** 1630–85 British monarch: in *Thomas Hearne: Remarks and Collections* (1885–1921) 17 November 1706; see WORDS AND DEEDS 9

5 An ass may bray a good while before he shakes the stars down.
> **George Eliot** 1819–80 English novelist: *Romola* (1863)

6 It is by acts and not by ideas that people live.
> **Anatole France** 1844–1924 French novelist and man of letters: *La Vie littéraire* (1888) 'Sérénus'

7 Words without actions are the assassins of idealism.
> **Herbert Hoover** 1874–1964 American Republican statesman: attributed, in *Capital Times* (Madison, Wisconsin) 15 April 1930

8 Considering how foolishly people act and how pleasantly they prattle, perhaps it would be better for the world if they talked more and did less.
> **W. Somerset Maugham** 1874–1965 English novelist: *A Writer's Notebook* (1949) written in 1892

9 Here lies a great and mighty king
Whose promise none relies on;
He never said a foolish thing,
Nor ever did a wise one.
> *on Charles II*
> **Lord Rochester** 1647–80 English poet: 'The King's Epitaph' (alternatively 'Here lies our sovereign lord the King'); see WORDS AND DEEDS 4

10 Do not, as some ungracious pastors do,
Show me the steep and thorny way to heaven,
Whiles, like a puffed and reckless libertine,
Himself the primrose path of dalliance treads,
And recks not his own rede.
> **William Shakespeare** 1564–1616 English dramatist: *Hamlet* (1601)

Work

see also CAREERS, EMPLOYMENT, IDLENESS, LEISURE, TRADE UNIONS, UNEMPLOYMENT

1 *Arbeit macht frei.*
Work liberates.
> **Anonymous**: words inscribed on the gates of Dachau concentration camp, 1933, and subsequently on those of Auschwitz

2 If any would not work, neither should he eat.
> **Bible**: II Thessalonians

3 Who built Thebes of the seven gates?
In the books you will find the names of kings.
Did the kings haul up the lumps of rock? . . .

Where, the evening that the wall of
China was finished
Did the masons go?

Bertolt Brecht 1898–1956 German
dramatist: 'Questions From A Worker
Who Reads' (1935)

4 Without work, all life goes rotten, but
when work is soulless, life stifles and
dies.

Albert Camus 1913–60 French novelist,
dramatist, and essayist: attributed; E. F.
Schumacher *Good Work* (1979)

5 It has been my experience that one
cannot, in any shape or form,
depend on human relations for
lasting reward. It is only work that
truly satisfies.

Bette Davis 1908–89 American actress:
The Lonely Life (1962)

6 My life is one demd horrid grind!

Charles Dickens 1812–70 English
novelist: *Nicholas Nickleby* (1839)

7 Work is love made visible.

Kahlil Gibran 1883–1931 Syrian writer
and painter: *The Prophet* (1923)

8 I have long been of the opinion that
if work were such a splendid thing
the rich would have kept more of it
for themselves.

Bruce Grocott 1940– British Labour
politician: in *Observer* 22 May 1988

9 Generations have trod, have trod,
have trod;
And all is seared with trade; bleared,
smeared with toil.

Gerard Manley Hopkins 1844–89
English poet and priest: 'God's
Grandeur' (written 1877)

10 I like work: it fascinates me. I can sit
and look at it for hours. I love to keep
it by me: the idea of getting rid of it
nearly breaks my heart.

Jerome K. Jerome 1859–1927 English
writer: *Three Men in a Boat* (1889)

11 For men must work, and women
must weep,
And there's little to earn, and many
to keep,
Though the harbour bar be
moaning.

Charles Kingsley 1819–75 English
writer and clergyman: 'The Three
Fishers' (1858)

12 Who first invented work—and tied
the free
And holy-day rejoicing spirit down
To the ever-haunting importunity
Of business?

Charles Lamb 1775–1834 English
writer: letter to Bernard Barton,
11 September 1822

13 Why should I let the toad *work*
Squat on my life?
Can't I use my wit as a pitchfork
And drive the brute off?

Philip Larkin 1922–85 English poet:
'Toads' (1955)

14 Blessèd are the horny hands of toil!

James Russell Lowell 1819–91
American poet: 'A Glance Behind the
Curtain' (1844)

15 Work expands so as to fill the time
available for its completion.

C. Northcote Parkinson 1909–93
English writer: *Parkinson's Law* (1958)

16 We spend our midday sweat, our
midnight oil;
We tire the night in thought, the day
in toil.

Francis Quarles 1592–1644 English
poet: *Emblems* (1635)

17 It's true hard work never killed
anybody, but I figure why take the
chance?

Ronald Reagan 1911–2004 American
Republican statesman: interview,
Guardian 31 March 1987

18 If you have great talents, industry
will improve them: if you have but

moderate abilities, industry will supply their deficiency.
> **Joshua Reynolds** 1723–92 English painter: *Discourses on Art* 11 December 1769

19 Labour without joy is base. Labour without sorrow is base. Sorrow without labour is base. Joy without labour is base.
> **John Ruskin** 1819–1900 English art and social critic: *Time and Tide* (1867)

20 The labour we delight in physics pain.
> **William Shakespeare** 1564–1616 English dramatist: *Macbeth* (1606)

21 Work was like a stick. It had two ends. When you worked for the knowing you gave them quality; when you worked for a fool you simply gave him eye-wash.
> **Alexander Solzhenitsyn** 1918–2008 Russian novelist: *One Day in the Life of Ivan Denisovich* (1962)

22 Work to survive, survive by consuming, survive to consume: the hellish cycle is complete.
> **Raoul Vaneigem** 1934– Belgian philosopher: *The Revolution of Everyday Life* (1967)

23 Work saves us from three great evils: boredom, vice and need.
> **Voltaire** 1694–1778 French writer and philosopher: *Candide* (1759)

24 Work is the curse of the drinking classes.
> **Oscar Wilde** 1854–1900 Anglo-Irish dramatist and poet: H. Pearson *Life of Oscar Wilde* (1946)

World War I

see also ARMY, WAR

1 Your country needs you.
with picture of Lord Kitchener pointing
> **Advertising slogan**: on First World War recruitment poster, 1914, designed by Alfred Leete (1882–1933)

2 *Ils ne passeront pas.*
They shall not pass.
> **Anonymous**: slogan used by the French army at the defence of Verdun in 1916; variously attributed to Marshal Pétain and to General Robert Nivelle

3 The Somme is like the Holocaust. It revealed things about mankind that we cannot come to terms with and cannot forget. It can never become the past.
> **Pat Barker** 1943– English novelist: on winning the Booker Prize, November 1995

4 Now, God be thanked Who has matched us with His hour,
And caught our youth, and wakened us from sleeping.
> **Rupert Brooke** 1887–1915 English poet: 'Peace' (1914)

5 My home policy: I wage war; my foreign policy: I wage war. All the time I wage war.
> **Georges Clemenceau** 1841–1929 French statesman: speech to French Chamber of Deputies, 8 March 1918

6 Over there, over there,
Send the word, send the word over there
That the Yanks are coming, the Yanks are coming . . .
We'll be over, we're coming over
And we won't come back till it's over, over there.
> **George M. Cohan** 1878–1942 American songwriter, dramatist, and producer: 'Over There' (1917 song)

7 See that little stream—we could walk to it in two minutes. It took the British a month to walk it—a whole empire walking very slowly, dying in front and pushing forward behind. And another empire walked very slowly backward a few inches a day, leaving the dead like a million bloody rugs.

> **F. Scott Fitzgerald** 1896–1940 American novelist: *Tender is the Night* (1934)

8 My centre is giving way, my right is retreating, situation excellent, I am attacking.

> **Ferdinand Foch** 1851–1929 French Marshal: message sent during the first Battle of the Marne, September 1914; R. Recouly *Foch* (1919)

9 This is not a peace treaty, it is an armistice for twenty years.

> **Ferdinand Foch** 1851–1929 French Marshal: at the signing of the Treaty of Versailles, 1919; Paul Reynaud *Mémoires* (1963)

10 *Gott strafe England!*

God punish England!

> **Alfred Funke** 1869–1941 German writer: *Schwert und Myrte* (1914)

11 The lamps are going out all over Europe; we shall not see them lit again in our lifetime.

> **Edward Grey** 1862–1933 British Liberal politician: remark on the eve of the First World War, *25 Years* (1925)

12 The war has used up words.

> **Henry James** 1843–1916 American novelist: in *New York Times* 21 March 1915

13 Do your duty bravely. Fear God. Honour the King.

> **Lord Kitchener** 1850–1916 British soldier and statesman: message to soldiers of the British Expeditionary Force, August 1914

14 At eleven o'clock this morning came to an end the cruellest and most terrible war that has ever scourged mankind. I hope we may say that thus, this fateful morning, came to an end all wars.

> **David Lloyd George** 1863–1945 British Liberal statesman: speech, House of Commons, 11 November 1918

15 In Flanders fields the poppies blow Between the crosses, row on row.

> **John McCrae** 1872–1918 Canadian poet and military physician: 'In Flanders Fields' (1915)

16 All quiet on the western front.

> **Erich Maria Remarque** 1898–1970 German novelist: English title of *Im Westen nichts Neues* (1929 novel)

17 Oh! we don't want to lose you but we think you ought to go
For your King and your Country both need you so.

> **Paul Alfred Rubens** 1875–1917 English songwriter: 'Your King and Country Want You' (1914 song)

18 You are all a lost generation.

of the young who served in the First World War

> **Gertrude Stein** 1874–1946 American writer: phrase borrowed (in translation) from a French garage mechanic, whom Stein heard address it disparagingly to an incompetent apprentice; epigraph to Ernest Hemingway *The Sun Also Rises* (1926)

World War II

see also GENOCIDE, WAR

1 I think we might be going a bridge too far.

expressing reservations about the Arnhem 'Market Garden' operation

> **Frederick ('Boy') Browning** 1896–1965 British soldier: to Field Marshal Montgomery on 10 September 1944

2 How horrible, fantastic, incredible it is that we should be digging trenches and trying on gas-masks here because of a quarrel in a far away country between people of whom we know nothing.

on Germany's annexation of the Sudetenland

> **Neville Chamberlain** 1869–1940 British Conservative statesman: radio broadcast, 27 September 1938

3 We shall not flag or fail. We shall go on to the end. We shall fight in France, we shall fight on the seas and oceans, we shall fight with growing confidence and growing strength in the air, we shall defend our island, whatever the cost may be. We shall fight on the beaches, we shall fight on the landing grounds, we shall fight in the fields and in the streets, we shall fight in the hills; we shall never surrender.

> **Winston Churchill** 1874–1965 British Conservative statesman: speech, House of Commons, 4 June 1940

4 Let us therefore brace ourselves to our duty, and so bear ourselves that, if the British Empire and its Commonwealth lasts for a thousand years, men will still say, 'This was their finest hour.'

> **Winston Churchill** 1874–1965 British Conservative statesman: speech, House of Commons, 18 June 1940

5 It may almost be said, 'Before Alamein we never had a victory. After Alamein we never had a defeat.'

> **Winston Churchill** 1874–1965 British Conservative statesman: *Second World War* (1951)

6 Don't let's be beastly to the Germans When our Victory is ultimately won.

> **Noël Coward** 1899–1973 English dramatist, actor, and composer: 'Don't Let's Be Beastly to the Germans' (1943 song)

7 France has lost a battle. But France has not lost the war!

> **Charles de Gaulle** 1890–1970 French soldier and statesman: proclamation, 18 June 1940

8 I'm glad we've been bombed. It makes me feel I can look the East End in the face.

> **Queen Elizabeth, the Queen Mother** 1900–2002 British Queen Consort: to a London policeman, 13 September 1940

9 I would not regard the whole of the remaining cities of Germany as worth the bones of one British Grenadier.

supporting the continued strategic bombing of German cities

> **Arthur Harris** 1892–1984 British Air Force Marshal: letter to Norman Bottomley, deputy Chief of Air Staff, 29 March 1945; Max Hastings *Bomber Command* (1979)

10 We're gonna hang out the washing on the Siegfried Line.

> **Jimmy Kennedy** and **Michael Carr** British songwriters: title of song (1939)

11 I came through and I shall return.

on reaching Australia, having broken through Japanese lines en route from Corregidor

> **Douglas MacArthur** 1880–1964 American general: statement in Adelaide, 20 March 1942

12 Who do you think you are kidding, Mister Hitler?
If you think we're on the run?
We are the boys who will stop your little game
We are the boys who will make you think again.

> **Jimmy Perry** 1923– British songwriter: 'Who do you think you are kidding, Mister Hitler' (theme song of *Dad's Army*, BBC television, 1968–77)

13 This little steamer, like all her brave and battered sisters, is immortal. She'll go sailing proudly down the years in the epic of Dunkirk. And our great-grand-children, when they learn how we began this war by snatching glory out of defeat, and then swept on to victory, may also learn how the little holiday steamers made an excursion to hell and came back glorious.

> **J. B. Priestley** 1894–1984 English novelist, dramatist, and critic: radio broadcast, 5 June 1940

14 We have the men—the skill—the
wealth—and above all, the will . . .
We must be the great arsenal of
democracy.
   Franklin D. Roosevelt 1882–1945
   American Democratic statesman:
   'Fireside Chat' radio broadcast,
   29 December 1940

15 Yesterday, December 7, 1941—a date
which will live in infamy—the
United States of America was
suddenly and deliberately attacked
by naval and air forces of the Empire
of Japan.
   Franklin D. Roosevelt 1882–1945
   American Democratic statesman:
   address to Congress, 8 December 1941

Worry

1 What's the use of worrying?
It never was worth while,
So, pack up your troubles in your old
kit-bag,
And smile, smile, smile.
   George Asaf 1880–1951 British
   songwriter: 'Pack up your Troubles'
   (1915 song)

2 In trouble to be troubled
Is to have your trouble doubled.
   Daniel Defoe 1660–1731 English
   novelist and journalist: *The Farther
   Adventures of Robinson Crusoe* (1719)

3 Nothing puzzles me more than time
and space; and yet nothing troubles
me less, as I never think about them.
   Charles Lamb 1775–1834 English
   writer: letter to Thomas Manning,
   2 January 1810

4 O polished perturbation! golden
care!
That keep'st the ports of slumber
open wide
To many a watchful night!
   William Shakespeare 1564–1616
   English dramatist: *Henry IV, Part 2*
   (1597)

5 Neurosis is the way of avoiding non-
being by avoiding being.
   Paul Tillich 1886–1965 German-born
   Protestant theologian: *The Courage To
   Be* (1952)

6 A neurosis is a secret you don't know
you're keeping.
   Kenneth Tynan 1927–80 English theatre
   critic: Kathleen Tynan *Life of Kenneth
   Tynan* (1987)

Writing

see also BOOKS, FAMOUS WRITERS, FICTION,
LITERATURE, ORIGINALITY, POETRY, STYLE, WORDS

1 If you can't annoy somebody with
what you write, I think there's little
point in writing.
   Kingsley Amis 1922–95 English novelist
   and poet: in *Radio Times* 1 May 1971

2 Let other pens dwell on guilt and
misery. I quit such odious subjects as
soon as I can.
   Jane Austen 1775–1817 English novelist:
   Mansfield Park (1814)

3 Writers, like teeth, are divided into
incisors and grinders.
   Walter Bagehot 1826–77 English
   economist and essayist: *Estimates of
   some Englishmen and Scotchmen* (1858)
   'The First Edinburgh Reviewers'

4 The writer must be universal in
sympathy and an outcast by nature:
only then can he see clearly.
   Julian Barnes 1946– English novelist:
   Flaubert's Parrot (1984)

5 It is a foolish thing to make a long
prologue, and to be short in the story
itself.
   Bible: II Maccabees

6 Of every four words I write, I strike
out three.
   Nicolas Boileau 1636–1711 French
   critic and poet: *Satire* (2). *A M. Molière*
   (1665)

7 Manuscripts don't burn.
  Mikhail Bulgakov 1891–1940 Russian
  writer: *The Master and Margarita*
  (1966–67)

8 Beneath the rule of men entirely
  great
  The pen is mightier than the sword.
  Edward Bulwer-Lytton 1803–73 British
  novelist and politician: *Richelieu* (1839)

9 A writer must be as objective as a
  chemist: he must abandon the
  subjective line; he must know that
  dung-heaps play a very reasonable
  part in a landscape, and that evil
  passions are as inherent in life as
  good ones.
  Anton Chekhov 1860–1904 Russian
  dramatist and short-story writer: letter
  to M. V. Kiselev, 14 January 1887

10 They shut me up in prose—
  As when a little girl
  They put me in the closet—
  Because they liked me 'still'.
  Emily Dickinson 1830–86 American
  poet: 'They shut me up in prose'
  (*c.*1862)

11 My theory of writing I can sum up in
  one sentence. An author ought to
  write for the youth of his own
  generation, the critics of the next,
  and the schoolmasters of ever after.
  F. Scott Fitzgerald 1896–1940 American
  novelist: letter to the Booksellers'
  Convention, April 1920

12 Only connect! . . . Only connect the
  prose and the passion, and both will
  be exalted, and human love will be
  seen at its height.
  E. M. Forster 1879–1970 English
  novelist: *Howards End* (1910)

13 Another damned, thick, square book!
  Always scribble, scribble, scribble!
  Eh! Mr Gibbon?
  William Henry, Duke of Gloucester
  1743–1805: Henry Best *Personal and
  Literary Memorials* (1829); also

attributed to the Duke of Cumberland
and King George III

14 Any fool may write a most valuable
  book by chance, if he will only tell us
  what he heard and saw with veracity.
  Thomas Gray 1716–71 English poet:
  letter to Horace Walpole, 25 February
  1768

15 There is a splinter of ice in the heart
  of a writer.
  Graham Greene 1904–91 English
  novelist: *A Sort of Life* (1971)

16 The business of the poet and novelist
  is to show the sorriness underlying
  the grandest things, and the
  grandeur underlying the sorriest
  things.
  Thomas Hardy 1840–1928 English
  novelist and poet: notebook entry for
  19 April 1885

17 The most essential gift for a good
  writer is a built-in, shock-proof shit
  detector. This is the writer's radar
  and all great writers have had it.
  Ernest Hemingway 1899–1961
  American novelist: in *Paris Review*
  Spring 1958

18 I am a camera with its shutter open,
  quite passive, recording, not
  thinking.
  Christopher Isherwood 1904–86
  English novelist: *Goodbye to Berlin*
  (1939) 'Berlin Diary' Autumn 1930

19 Read over your compositions, and
  where ever you meet with a passage
  which you think is particularly fine,
  strike it out.
  Samuel Johnson 1709–84 English poet,
  critic, and lexicographer: quoting a
  college tutor; James Boswell *Life of
  Samuel Johnson* (1791) 30 April 1773

20 No man but a blockhead ever wrote,
  except for money.
  Samuel Johnson 1709–84 English poet,
  critic, and lexicographer: James Boswell

Life of Samuel Johnson (1791) 5 April 1776

21 A writer's ambition should be . . . to trade a hundred contemporary readers for ten readers in ten years' time and for one reader in a hundred years.
Arthur Koestler 1905–83 Hungarian-born writer: in *New York Times Book Review* 1 April 1951

22 When my sonnet was rejected, I exclaimed, 'Damn the age; I will write for Antiquity!'
Charles Lamb 1775–1834 English writer: letter to B. W. Proctor, 22 January 1829

23   What in me is dark
Illumine, what is low raise and support;
That to the height of this great argument
I may assert eternal providence,
And justify the ways of God to men.
John Milton 1608–74 English poet: *Paradise Lost* (1667)

24 Good prose is like a window-pane.
George Orwell 1903–50 English novelist: *Collected Essays* (1968) vol. 1 'Why I Write'

25 The last thing one knows in constructing a work is what to put first.
Blaise Pascal 1623–62 French mathematician, physicist, and moralist: *Pensées* (1670)

26 The tip's a good one, as for literature It gives no man a sinecure.
And no one knows, at sight, a masterpiece.
And give up verse, my boy,
There's nothing in it.
Ezra Pound 1885–1972 American poet: *Hugh Selwyn Mauberley* (1920) 'Mr Nixon'

27 If writing did not exist, what terrible depressions we should suffer from.
Sei Shōnagon *c.*966–*c.*1013 Japanese diarist and writer: *The Pillow Book of Sei Shōnagon*

28 And, as imagination bodies forth
The forms of things unknown, the poet's pen
Turns them to shapes, and gives to airy nothing
A local habitation and a name.
William Shakespeare 1564–1616 English dramatist: *A Midsummer Night's Dream* (1595–6)

29 You write with ease, to show your breeding,
But easy writing's vile hard reading.
Richard Brinsley Sheridan 1751–1816 Anglo-Irish dramatist: 'Clio's Protest' (written 1771, published 1819)

30 Writing is not a profession but a vocation of unhappiness.
Georges Simenon 1903–89 Belgian novelist: interview in *Paris Review* Summer 1955

31 Writing, when properly managed (as you may be sure I think mine is) is but a different name for conversation.
Laurence Sterne 1713–68 English novelist: *Tristram Shandy* (1759–67)

32 How vain it is to sit down to write when you have not stood up to live.
Henry David Thoreau 1817–62 American writer: diary, 19 August 1851

33 The shelf life of the modern hardback writer is somewhere between the milk and the yoghurt.
Calvin Trillin 1935– American journalist and writer: in *Sunday Times* 9 June 1991; attributed

34 Three hours a day will produce as much as a man ought to write.
Anthony Trollope 1815–82 English novelist: *Autobiography* (1883)

35 Writing saved me from the sin and *inconvenience* of violence.

> **Alice Walker** 1944– American poet: 'One Child of One's Own' in Janet Sternburg *The Writer on her Work* (1980)

36 A woman must have money and a room of her own if she is to write fiction.

> **Virginia Woolf** 1882–1941 English novelist: *A Room of One's Own* (1929)

Youth

see also CHILDREN, GENERATION GAP

1 Youth would be an ideal state if it came a little later in life.

> **Herbert Asquith** 1852–1928 British Liberal statesman: in *Observer* 15 April 1923

2 I'm not young enough to know everything.

> **J. M. Barrie** 1860–1937 Scottish writer and dramatist: *The Admirable Crichton* (performed 1902, published 1914)

3 We have created a child who will be so exposed to the media that he will be lost to his parents by the time he is 12.

> **David Bowie** 1947– English rock musician: in *Melody Maker* 22 January 1972

4 It's that second time you hear your love song sung,
Makes you think perhaps, that
Love like youth is wasted on the young.

> **Sammy Cahn** 1913–93 American songwriter: 'The Second Time Around' (1960 song)

5 Youth is something very new: twenty years ago no one mentioned it.

> **Coco Chanel** 1883–1971 French couturière: Marcel Haedrich *Coco Chanel, Her Life, Her Secrets* (1971)

6 I remember my youth and the feeling that will never come back any more—the feeling that I could last for ever, outlast the sea, the earth, and all men; the deceitful feeling that lures us on to joys, to perils, to love, to vain effort—to death; the triumphant conviction of strength, the heat of life in the handful of dust, the glow in the heart that with every year grows dim, grows cold, grows small, and expires—and expires, too soon, too soon—before life itself.

> **Joseph Conrad** 1857–1924 Polish-born English novelist: *Youth* (1902)

7 It is better to waste one's youth than to do nothing with it at all.

> **Georges Courteline** 1858–1929 French writer and dramatist: *La Philosophie de Georges Courteline* (1948)

8 The Youth of a Nation are the trustees of Posterity.

> **Benjamin Disraeli** 1804–81 British Tory statesman and novelist: *Sybil* (1845)

9 Youth is happy because it has the ability to see beauty.

> **Franz Kafka** 1883–1924 Czech novelist: *Conversations with Kafka*

10 Remember that as a teenager you are at the last stage in your life when you will be happy to hear that the phone is for you.

> **Fran Lebowitz** 1946– American writer: *Social Studies* (1981)

11 Youth is vivid rather than happy, but memory always remembers the happy things.

> **Bernard Lovell** 1913– British astronomer: in *The Times* 20 August 1993

12 Whom the gods love dies young.

> **Menander** 342–c.292 BC Greek comic dramatist: *Dis Exapaton*

13 The atrocious crime of being a young man . . . I shall neither attempt to palliate nor deny.

William Pitt, Earl of Chatham 1708–78 British Whig statesman: speech, House of Commons, 2 March 1741

14 Should I live for centuries, the sweet period of my youth would not be reborn, nor effaced from my memory.

Jean-Jacques Rousseau 1712–78 French philosopher and novelist: *Julie, ou la nouvelle Hélöise* (1761)

15 In delay there lies no plenty;
Then come kiss me, sweet and twenty,
Youth's a stuff will not endure.

William Shakespeare 1564–1616 English dramatist: *Twelfth Night* (1601)

16 What music is more enchanting than the voices of young people, when you can't hear what they say?

Logan Pearsall Smith 1865–1946 American-born man of letters: *Afterthoughts* (1931) 'Age and Death'

17 Live as long as you may, the first twenty years are the longest half of your life.

Robert Southey 1774–1843 English poet and writer: *The Doctor* (1812)

18 Make me young, make me young, make me young!

Kurt Vonnegut 1922–2007 American novelist and short-story writer: *Breakfast of Champions* (1973)

19 Heaven lies about us in our infancy!
Shades of the prison-house begin to close
Upon the growing boy,

William Wordsworth 1770–1850 English poet: 'Ode. Intimations of Immortality' (1807)

20 The only way to stay young is to avoid old people.

James D. Watson 1928– American biologist: in *The Times* 9 March 2002

Author Index

Amis, Kingsley (1922-95)
Alcohol 1, Death 1, Fat 1,
Pleasure 1, Reviews 1,
Universities 1, Writing 1

Amis, Martin (1949-)
Weapons 1

Anacharsis (6th century BC)
Laws 1

Anderson, Maxwell
(1888-1959)
Autumn 1, Fame 1

Angelou, Maya (1928-)
Defiance 1, Human Race 2,
Suffering 1, Woman's Role 2

Anka, Paul (1941-)
Lifestyles 3

Anne, Princess Royal
(1950-)
Royal Family 1

Anonymous
Action 1, Actors 1, Alcohol 2,
Animal Rights 1, Animals 1,
Appearance 2, Army 1, 2, Awards
1, Bereavement 1, Caution 1,
Censorship 1, Communism 1,
Computers 1, Cricket 1, 2, Crises
3, 4, Defiance 2, Determination 1,
Disability 1, Disasters 1, Dogs 1,
Drugs 1, Economics 1, Elections 1,
Environment 1, Epitaphs 2, 3, 4,
5, 6, 7, Experience 2, Falklands 1,
Famous People 1, Famous
Politicians 2, 3, Fear 1, Fools 1,
Friendship 2, God 2, Heroes 2,
Human Rights 1, 2, 3, Innocence
1, Iraq War 2, Journalism 1,
Justice 2, Knowledge 1, Last
Words 1, Liberty 1, Lies 1, Life
Sciences 1, London 1,
Mathematics 1, Moderation 1,
Money 1, Music 1, Musicians 1,
Navy 1, Olympic Games 1,
Paranormal 1, Politics 4, Poverty
1, 2, Prayer 1, Press
Photographers 1, Propaganda 1,
Rivers 1, Rock 1, Russia 1,
Scotland 1, Secrecy 1, Self-
Interest 1, Self-Knowledge 1,
Snow 1, Space 1, Summer 1,
Supernatural 2, Swearing 1, Taxes
1, Technology 1, Television 3,
Toasts 1, Trials 1, Trust 1, Vietnam
War 1, Wealth 1, Weapons 2,
Work 1, World War I 2

Anouilh, Jean (1910-87)
Commitment 1, Fate 1, France 1,
Love 1, Propaganda 2, Tragedy 1

Anthony, Susan Brownell
(1820-1906)
Human Rights 4

Antrim, Minna (1861-1950)
Pleasure 2

Apelles
Painting 1

Apollinaire, Guillaume
(1880-1918)
Inventions 1, Memory 1, Tradition
1

Appleton, Thomas Gold
(1812-84)
American Cities 2

Arabin, William (1773-1841)
Trials 2

Arafat, Yasser (1929-2004)
International Relations 1

Arbus, Diane (1923-71)
Fear 2, Photography 1

Archilochus (7th century BC)
Knowledge 2

Archimedes (c.287-212 BC)
Inventions 2

Arden, Elizabeth (1876-1966)
Value 1

Ardrey, Robert (1908-80)
Human Race 3

Arendt, Hannah (1906-75)
Action 2, Evil 1, Revolution 1

Aristophanes (c.450-c.385
BC)
Futility 1

Aristotle (384-322 BC)
Causes 1, Choice 1, Democracy 2,
Education 2, Famous Writers 2,
Friendship 3, Habit 2, Hosts and
Guests 1, Knowledge 3, Last
Words 2, Pleasure 3, Politics 5,
Problems 1, Solitude 1, Tragedy 2,
War 1, Wit 1

Armistead, Lewis Addison
(1817-63)
American Civil War 1

Armour, Richard (1906-89)
Food 1

Armstrong, Lance (1971-)
Sports 1

Armstrong, Louis (1901-71)
Jazz 1

Armstrong, Neil (1930-)
Achievement 1, Space 2

Armstrong, Robert (1927-)
Truth 3

Arnald-Amaury (d. 1225)
Cynicism 1

Arnold, George (1834-65)
Charity 1

Arnold, Matthew (1822-88)
Faith 1, Famous Poets 1, 2,
Memory 2, Middle Age 2, Oxford
1, 2, Shakespeare 1, Style 1

Arthurs, George see **Leigh,
Fred W.** and **Arthurs, George**

Asaf, George (1880-1951)
Worry 1

Ascham, Roger (1515-68)
Teaching 2

Ashford, Daisy (1881-1972)
Middle Age 3

Asimov, Isaac (1920-92)
Diets 2, Foresight 1, Mistakes 1,
Technology 2, Theory 1

Asquith, Herbert
(1852-1928)
Patience 1, Statistics 1, Youth 1

Asquith, Margot (1864-1945)
Famous Politicians 4, Lies 2,
Loyalty 1, Paranormal 2, Wordplay
1

Astell, Mary (1668-1731)
Woman's Role 3

Astley, Jacob (1579-1652)
Prayer 2

Astor, Nancy (1879-1964)
Teetotalism 1

Atatürk, Kemal (1881-1938)
Army 3

Atkins, Peter (1940-)
Universe 2

Atkinson, Brooks
(1894-1984)
Capitalism 1, Democracy 3, Past 2

Atkinson, E. L. (1882-1929)
and **Cherry-Garrard, Apsley**
(1882-1959)
Epitaphs 8

Attali, Jacques (1943-)
Unemployment 1

Attlee, Clement (1883-1967)
Democracy 4, Famous Politicians
5, Russia 2

Atwood, Margaret (1939-)
Canada 2, Celibacy 1, Divorce 1,
Gratitude 1, Publishing 1
Auden, W. H. (1907-73)
Army 4, Art 1, Arts and Sciences 1,
Behaviour 2, Belief 1,
Bereavement 2, Books 1, Defeat
1, Drugs 2, Emotions 1, Evil 2,
Exile 1, Face 1, Faithfulness 1,
Famous People 2, Famous Poets
3, Futility 2, Genius 2, Habit 3,
Ignorance 1, Intellectuals 1,
Intelligence 1, Letters 2, Literature
and Society 1, Love 2, Marriage 1,
Names 1, Opera 1, Philosophy 1,
Poetry 2, Power 2, Present 1,
Railways 1, Relationships 2,
Reviews 2, Self 3, 4, Self-
Knowledge 2, Sin 1, Society 1,
Sorrow 1, Suffering 2, Trees 1
Augarten, Stan
Computers 2
Augustine (AD 354-430)
Lifestyles 4, Moderation 2, Sex 4,
Sin 2, Tolerance 1
Augustus (63 BC-AD 14)
Speed 1
Aung San Suu Kyi (1945-)
Fear 3, Men and Women
Aurelius, Marcus (AD
121-180)
Body 2, Change 1, Goodness 1,
Suffering 3, Thinking 2, Time 2
Austen, Jane (1775-1817)
Advice 2, Bachelors 1, British
Cities 1, 2, Choice 2, Compassion
1, Conversation 1, Famous Writers
3, Food 2, Forgiveness 1, Gossip
1, Happiness 1, Hosts and Guests
2, Idleness 1, Ignorance 2,
Impulsiveness 1, Memory 3, Men
2, Mind 1, Neighbours 1, Parties
1, Perfection 1, Pleasure 4,
Suffering 4, Surprise 1, Weather 1,
Women 1, Writing 2
Awdry, Revd W. (1911-97)
Railways 2
Ayckbourn, Alan (1939-)
Flattery 1, Insults 1
Ayer, A. J. (1910-89)
Opinion 1
Ayesha (*fl.* 1492)
Defeat 2

Ayres, Pam (1947-)
Medicine 2

Babbage, Charles
(1791-1871)
Statistics 2
Babel, Isaac (1894-1940)
Fear 4, Language 1, Style 2
Bacall, Lauren (1924-)
Face 2, Love 3, Sickness 2
Bach, Johann Sebastian
(1685-1750)
Musical Instruments 1
Bach, Richard (1936-)
Achievement 2
Bacon, Francis (1561-1626)
Ability 1, Action 3, Advice 3, Belief
2, Bible 1, Books 2, Change 2,
Children 1, Doubt 1, Family 1,
Gardens 1, 2, Indifference 1,
Knowledge 4, Money 2, Nature 2,
Revenge 1, Similarity 1,
Supernatural 3, Thanks 2, Travel 1,
Trust 2, Truth 4, Unhappiness 1,
Ways 1, Wealth 2, Wives 1
Bacon, Francis (1909-92)
Friendship 4
Bacon, Roger (*c.*1220-*c.*92)
Mathematics 2
Baden-Powell, Robert
(1857-1941)
Readiness and Preparation 1
Baez, Joan (1941-)
Opinion 2, Violence 2
Bagehot, Walter (1826-77)
Bureaucracy 1, Equality 1, Family
2, Famous Writers 4, Human
Nature 1, International Relations
2, Languages 1, Newspapers 1, 2,
Opinion 3, Originality 1, Pleasure
5, Royalty 1, 2, Similarity 2, Wives
2, Women 2, Writing 3
Bailey, David (1938-)
Fashion 1, Photography 2
Bainbridge, Beryl (1933-)
Men and Women 2
Bairnsfather, Bruce
(1888-1959)
Advice 4
Baker, Russell (1925-)
Possessions 1, Sports 2,
Technology 3

Bakunin, Michael (1814-76)
Creativity 1, Famous Musicians 1
Baldwin, James (1924-87)
Money 3, Poverty 3, Racism 1
Baldwin, Stanley (1867-1947)
Air Force 1, International
Relations 3, Prime Ministers 1,
Retirement 1, Secrecy 2, Trade
Unions 1, Truth 5
Balfour, Arthur James
(1848-1930)
Cynicism 2, Famous Politicians 6,
Forgiveness 2, Hunting 1
Ballard, J. G. (1930-2009)
Awards 2, Cars 1, Culture 2,
Pornography 1, Twentieth Century
1
Balliett, Whitney (1926-2007)
Critics 1
Balmain, Pierre (1914-82)
Clothes 2
Balzac, Honoré de
(1799-1850)
Compassion 2, Equality 2,
Faithfulness 2
Bankhead, Tallulah
(1903-68)
Drugs 3, Education 3, Goodness
2, Sex 5, Value 2
Banks, Joseph (1743-1820)
Australia 1
Banks-Smith, Nancy
Architecture 1
Banksy
Painting 2
Baraka, Imamu Amiri
(1934-)
God 3
Baratynsky, Yevgeny
(1800-44)
Hope 1
Bardot, Brigitte (1934-)
Faithfulness 3, Maturity 1, Parting
1
Barham, R. H. (1788-1845)
Ways 2
Barker, Joel Arthur
Action 4
Barker, Pat (1943-)
World War I 3
Barker, Ronnie (1929-2005)
Humour 2
Barker, Ronnie (1929-2005)
and **Corbett, Ronnie** (1930-)

Parting 2

Barnard, Frederick R.
Language 2

Barnes, Julian (1946-)
Art 2, Books 3, Children 2, History 1, Love 4, Men 3, Writing 4

Barnier, Michel (1951-)
International Relations 4

Barnum, Phineas T.
(1810-91)
Fools 2

Barr, Amelia E. (1831-1919)
Love 5

Barr, Roseanne (1953-)
God 4, Husbands 1

Barrie, J. M. (1860-1937)
Birth 1, Celebrations 1, Charm 1, Courage 1, Dying 2, Human Nature 2, Memory 4, Practicality 1, Scotland 2, Self-Knowledge 3, Supernatural 4, Youth 2

Barry, Sebastian (1955-)
Ireland 1

Barrymore, Ethel
(1879-1959)
Actors 2

Barrymore, John (1882-1942)
Solitude 2

Barstow, Stan (1928-)
Reading 1

Barth, Karl (1886-1968)
Famous Musicians 2

Barthes, Roland (1915-80)
Cars 2

Baruch, Bernard (1870-1965)
Elections 2, Old Age 1, Politicians 1

Basho, Matsuo (1644-94)
Animals 2, Autumn 2, Education 4, Parting 3, Rain 1, Time 3

Bates, Katherine Lee
(1859-1929)
United States 1

Batten, Jean (1909-82)
Air Travel 1

Baudelaire, Charles
(1821-67)
Beauty 2, Class 2, Logic 1

Baudrillard, Jean
(1929-2007)
Information 1, Love 6

Bauer, Lord (1915-2002)
Aid 1

Bauer, Yehuda (1926-)
Indifference 2

Bavasi, Buzzie (1914-2008)
Baseball 1

Baxter, Richard (1615-91)
Relationships 3

Bayley, John (1925-)
Alzheimer's 1

Beamer, Todd (1968-2001)
Nine-Eleven 1

Beaton, Cecil (1904-80)
Originality 2

Beatty, Warren (1937-)
Faithfulness 4

Beaumarchais, Pierre-Augustin Caron de (1732-99)
Human Race 4, Humour 3, Love 7

Beaverbrook, Lord
(1879-1964)
Fame 2, Famous Politicians 7, Indecision 1, Strength 1

Beckett, Samuel (1906-89)
Boredom 1, Death 2, Failure 1, Futility 3, Habit 4, Human Nature 3, Nationality 1, Statistics 3, Thinking 3, Thrift 1, Time 4, Waiting 1, Words 2

Beckham, Victoria (1974-)
Exercise 1

Becque, Henry (1837-99)
Equality 3

Bede, The Venerable (AD 673-735)
Life 2

Bee, Barnard Elliott
(1823-61)
American Civil War 2

Beecham, Thomas
(1879-1961)
Famous Musicians 3, Music 2, Musical Instruments 2, Musicians 2

Beerbohm, Max (1872-1956)
Conformity 1, Cosmetics 2, Critics 2, Dreams 1, Excellence 1, Fantasy 1, Hosts and Guests 3, Philosophy 2, Vulgarity 1

Beers, Ethel Lynn (1827-79)
American Civil War 3

Beethoven, Ludwig van
(1770-1827)
Art and Society 1, Cooking 1, Famous Musicians 4, Fate 2, Last Words 3

Beeton, Isabella (1836-65)
Housework 1, Organization 1

Behan, Brendan (1923-64)
Absence 1, Fame 3

Behn, Aphra (1640-89)
Money 4, Poverty 4

Bell, Clive (1881-1964)
Logic 2

Bell, Daniel (1919-)
Communism 2

Bellah, James Warner see
Goldbeck, Willis and **Bellah, James Warner**

Belloc, Hilaire (1870-1953)
Animals 3, 4, Caution 2, Cooking 2, Doubt 2, Elections 3, Employment 2, Epitaphs 9, Money 5, Pacifism 2, Power 3, Statistics 4, Technology 4

Bellow, Saul (1915-2005)
Mental Illness 2, Originality 3, Self 5

Belmondo, Jean-Paul
(1933-)
Middle Age 4

Benchley, Robert
(1889-1945)
Quotations 1, Technology 5, Travel 2, Venice 1

Benda, Julien (1867-1956)
Intellectuals 2

Benedict XVI, Pope (1927-)
Love 8

Benét, Stephen Vincent
(1898-1943)
Biography 1, Names 2

Ben-Gurion, David
(1886-1973)
Honesty 1

Benjamin, Judah (1811-84)
Race 1

Benn, Tony (1925-)
Communism 3, Faith 2, Foresight 2, Newspapers 3, Parliament 1, Photography 3, Power 4, Titles 1

Bennett, Alan (1934-)
Crime Fiction 1, Europe 1, Family 3, Famous Writers 5, Humour 4, Leisure 2, Life 3, Likes 1, Memory 5, Parents 1, Royalty 3, Society 2, Swearing 2

Bennett, Arnold (1867-1931)
Husbands 2, Idealism 1, Self-Esteem 2, Sickness 3, Taste 1

Bennett, Brian see **Welch, Bruce** and **Bennett, Brian**
Bennett, Jill (1931-90)
Husbands 3
Bentham, Jeremy
(1748-1832)
Animal Rights 2, Censorship 2, Human Rights 5, Justice 3, Poetry 3, Punishment 1, Society 3
Bentley, Edmund Clerihew
(1875-1956)
Biography 2, Corruption 1
Beresford, Lord Charles
(1846-1919)
Apology 2
Berger, John (1926-)
Men and Women 3
Bergman, Ingrid (1915-82)
Kissing 1, Romance 1
Bergson, Henri (1859-1941)
Causes 2
Berlin, Irving (1888-1989)
Beauty 3, Christmas 1, Courtship 1, Dance 1, 2, Idleness 2, Self-Esteem 3, Theatre 1, United States 2
Berlin, Isaiah (1909-97)
Character 3, Liberty 2
Berlioz, Hector (1803-69)
Time 5
Berlusconi, Silvio (1936-)
Disasters 2
Bernal, J. D. (1901-71)
Biotechnology 1
Bernall, Cassie (1981-99)
Faith 3
Bernanos, Georges
(1888-1948)
Hell 1, Prayer 3
Bernard, Claude (1813-78)
Arts and Sciences 2, Experiment 1, Ideas 2, Life Sciences 2
Bernard of Chartres
(d. c.1130)
Progress 2
Bernbach, Bill (1911-82)
Advertising 1
Berners, Lord (1883-1950)
Fame 4
Berners-Lee, Tim (1955-)
Internet 1
Bernstein, Leonard
(1918-90)
Music 3

Berra, Yogi (1925-)
Baseball 2, 3, Ending 1, Foresight 3, Future 4
Berry, Halle (1968-)
Beauty 4, Mothers 2
Berry, Wendell (1934-)
Earth 1
Berryman, John (1914-72)
Boredom 2, Fear 5, Misfortunes 1
Berton, Pierre (1920-2004)
Canada 3, Progress 3
Best, George (1946-2005)
Wealth 3
Betjeman, John (1906-84)
British Cities 3, Childhood 1, Christmas 2, England 1, Manners 1, Schools 1, Tennis 1
Bevan, Aneurin (1897-1960)
Corruption 2, International Relations 5, 6, Leadership 1, Moderation 3, Newspapers 4, Organization 2, Political Parties 1, 2, Politicians 2
Beveridge, William Henry
(1879-1963)
Ignorance 3, Progress 4
Bevin, Ernest (1881-1951)
Enemies 1, Europe 2, International Relations 7, Trade Unions 2
Beza, Theodore (1519-1605)
Church 1
Bhagavad Gita (250 BC-AD 250)
Time 6
Bhutto, Benazir (1953-2007)
Power 5, Revenge 3
Bibesco, Elizabeth
(1897-1945)
Certainty 2
Bible
Achievement 3, Anger 1, Animal Rights 2, Beauty 5, Beginning 1, Belief 3, Bereavement 3, Books 4, Business 3, Careers 1, Causes 3, Change 3, Choice 3, Christmas 3, Circumstance 1, Cities 1, Cooperation 2, 3, Death 3, Despair 2, Doubt 3, Ending 2, Enemies 2, 3, Environment 2, Epitaphs 10, Equality 4, Face 3, Faith 4, Familiarity 1, Fate 3, Friendship 5, Futility 4, Gifts 1, God 5, 6, Guilt 1, Humility 1,

Idealism 2, Innocence 2, Jealousy 1, Justice 4, Knowledge 5, Leadership 2, Lifestyles 5, 6, Love 9, Misfortunes 2, Money 6, News 1, Pacifism 3, Peace 1, 2, Possessions 2, Poverty 5, Prayer 4, Present 2, Pride 1, Progress 5, Punishment 2, Relationships 4, Religion 1, Reputation 1, Revenge 2, Sacrifice 1, Sea 1, Secrecy 3, Sin 3, 4, Sorrow 2, Strength 2, 3, Success 2, Supernatural 5, Temptation 1, Thanks 3, Tolerance 2, Transience 1, Truth 6, Value 3, Violence 3, Wealth 4, Wisdom 2, Women 3, Work 2, Writing 5
Bidault, Georges (1899-1983)
Strength 4
Bierce, Ambrose
(1842-c.1914)
Cynicism 3, Saints 1
Biko, Steve (1946-77)
Racism 2, Strength 5
Billings, Josh (1818-85)
Knowledge 6
Binyon, Laurence
(1869-1943)
Autumn 3, Epitaphs 11
Bion (c.325-c.255 BC)
Cruelty 1
Birkett, Lord (1883-1962)
Speeches 4
Birney, Earle (1904-95)
Canada 4
Birrell, Augustine
(1850-1933)
History 2
Bishop, Billy (1894-1956)
Air Travel 2
Bishop, Elizabeth (1911-79)
American Cities 3, Dreams 2, Maps 1
Bismarck, Otto von
(1815-98)
Africa 1, Balkans 1, 2, Diplomacy 1, Europe 3, Famous Politicians 8, International Relations 8, Laws 2, Politics 6, 7, Strength 6, Words and Deeds 1
Blacker, Valentine
(1728-1823)
Practicality 2
Blackstone, William
(1723-80)

Braque, Georges (1882-1963)
Arts and Sciences 3, Present 3
Braun, Wernher von (1912-77)
Research 1, Space 3
Brecht, Bertolt (1898-1956)
Banking 1, Charity 2, Clothes 3, Death 6, Delay 1, Goodness 3, 4, Heroes 4, Morality 3, Peace 4, Revolution 4, Science 1, War 3, Work 3
Brenan, Gerald (1894-1987)
Leisure 3, Money 7
Brenner, Sydney (1927-)
Computers 3
Bridgeman, Percy Williams (1882-1961)
Science 2
Bridges, Robert (1844-1930)
Snow 2
Bright, John (1811-89)
Violence 4
Brillat-Savarin, Anthelme (1755-1826)
Alcohol 3, Cooking 3, Eating 1, Inventions 3
Brittain, Vera (1893-1970)
Wives 3
Brockbank, Russell (1913-79)
Europe 4
Broder, David (1929-)
Presidency 1
Brodrick, St John (1856-1942)
Tact 1
Brokaw, Tom (1940-)
Fishing 1, Mistakes 3
Bronowski, Jacob (1908-74)
Action 5, Counselling 1, Cruelty 2, Failure 2, Science 3
Brontë, Charlotte (1816-55)
Action 6, Hypocrisy 1, Prejudice 1
Brontë, Emily (1818-48)
Courage 2, Lovers 1, Power 7, Pride 2, Relationships 5
Brooke, Rupert (1887-1915)
England 3, Flowers 1, History 3, Past 3, Patriotism 2, Sleep 1, World War I 4
Brookner, Anita (1928-)
Guilt 2, Love 11, Mothers 3, Romance 2

Brooks, Gwendolyn (1917-2000)
Pregnancy 1, Present 4
Brooks, J.
Animals 6
Brooks, Mel (1926-)
Self-Esteem 4
Brougham, Lord (1778-1868)
Education 7
Broun, Heywood (1888-1939)
Censorship 3, Fanaticism 1, Men 5
Broun, Heywood Hale (1918-2001)
Sports 3
Brown, Frederic (1906-72)
Fantasy 2
Brown, Gordon (1951-)
Banking 2, Fathers 1, Morality 4
Brown, H. Rap (1943-)
Violence 5
Brown, Lew (1893-1958) see **De Sylva, Buddy** and **Brown, Lew**
Brown, Thomas (1663-1704)
Likes 2
Browne, Sir Thomas (1605-82)
Human Race 5, Medicine 3, Self-Esteem 5, Trees 4, Truth 9
Browning, Elizabeth Barrett (1806-61)
Change 4, Famous Writers 6, Genius 3, Lovers 2, 3, Prayer 5, Reputation 2, Sorrow 3, Suffering 5
Browning, Frederick ('Boy') (1896-1965)
World War II 1
Browning, Robert (1812-89)
Achievement 4, Ambition 3, Belief 5, Betrayal 1, Bible 2, Birds 1, Choice 4, Defiance 3, Despair 3, Disillusion 1, Ignorance 4, Opportunity 1, Optimism 1, Perfection 2, Self-Knowledge 5, Senses 1, Spring 2, Success 3, Thinking 4, Time 8
Bruce, Lenny (1925-66)
Circumstance 3, Drugs 4, Politics 8
Brundtland, Gro Harlem (1939-)
Environment 3

Bruno, Frank (1961-)
Boxing 2, Insight 3
Bryan, William Jennings (1860-1925)
Greed 2
Bryant, Anita (1940-)
Homosexuality 2
Bryson, Bill (1951-)
American Cities 5, Animals 7, Maturity 3, Shopping 1, Travel 3, Weather 2
Buber, Martin (1878-1965)
Self 6
Buchan, John (1875-1940)
Atheism 2, Civilization 1, Determination 3, Education 8, Happiness 2
Buchman, Frank (1878-1961)
Greed 3
Buck, Pearl S. (1892-1973)
Asia 1
Buffett, Warren (1930-)
Wealth 5
Buffon, Comte de (1707-88)
Style 3
Bulgakov, Mikhail (1891-1940)
Writing 7
Buller, Arthur (1874-1944)
Physics 3
Bulwer-Lytton, Edward (1803-73)
Arts and Sciences 4, Writing 8
Bunting, Basil (1900-85)
Culture 3
Buñuel, Luis (1900-83)
Atheism 3
Bunyan, John (1628-88)
Causes 4, Hell 2, Humility 2, Punishment 3, Words 3
Burchill, Julie (1960-)
Relationships 6, Women 5
Burgess, Anthony (1917-93)
Books 5, Presidency 2, Seduction 1
Burgon, John William (1813-88)
Asia 2
Burke, Edmund (1729-97)
Ambition 4, Compromise 1, Cooperation 4, Custom 1, Danger 1, Enemies 4, Evil 3, Failure 3, Family 4, Fear 6, Foresight 5, Future 5, Laws 3, Leadership 4,

Parliament 2, Patience 2,
Practicality 3, Progress 6,
Similarity 3, Strength 8, Taxes 2,
Tolerance 3, Words and Deeds 2

Burke, Johnny (1908-64)
Optimism 2

Burnett, Frances Hodgson
(1849-1924)
Gardens 3

Burnett, Thomas E., Jnr.
(1963-2001)
Nine-Eleven 2

Burney, Fanny (1752-1840)
Indifference 3, Perfection 3

Burns, George (1896-1996)
Experts 1

Burns, John (1858-1943)
Rivers 2

Burns, Robert (1759-96)
Alcohol 4, Aristocracy 1, Cruelty
3, Eating 2, Education 9, Equality
5, Fear 7, Food 3, Foresight 6,
Friendship 9, Lovers 4, Meeting 1,
Memory 6, Poetry 4, Scotland 4,
5, Self-Knowledge 6, Sin 7,
Temptation 2, Women 6

Burroughs, William S.
(1914-97)
Drugs 5, Evil 4, Homosexuality 3,
Last Words 4

Burton, Robert (1577-1640)
Birds 2, Parents 2, Plagiarism 1,
Poetry 5, Religion 2, Sorrow 4,
Travel 4

Bush, Barbara (1925-)
Names 3, Presidency 3, Success 4

Bush, George (1924-)
Boredom 3, Family 5, Food 4,
Future 6, Idealism 3, Taxes 3,
United States 3

Bush, George W. (1946-)
Achievement 5, International
Relations 10, Meeting 2, Nine-
Eleven 3, Readiness and
Preparation 2, Terrorism 1

Bussy-Rabutin, Comte de
(1618-93)
Strength 9

Butler, Nicholas Murray
(1862-1947)
Experts 2

Butler, R. A. (1902-82)
Politics 9, Prime Ministers 2

Butler, Samuel (1612-80)
Cynicism 4, Deception 2, Opinion
4

Butler, Samuel (1835-1902)
Animals 8, Art 4, Bible 3, Canada
6, Conscience 1, Dogs 2, Eating 3,
Faith 5, Famous Poets 5,
Friendship 10, History 4,
Language 3, Life 4, Life Sciences
3, Opinion 5, Praise 1

Butler, William (1535-1618)
Food 5

Byatt, A. S. (1936-)
Literature 2

Byrd, William (1543-1623)
Singing 2

Byron, Lord (1788-1824)
Advice 5, Beauty 6, Censorship 4,
Children 4, Christianity 1, Critics
3, Cruelty 4, Dance 3, Debt 1,
Dogs 3, Ending 3, Fame 6,
Familiarity 2, Fiction 1, Friendship
11, Greece 1, Hatred 1, Hope 2,
In-Laws 1, Italy 1, Love 12,
Marriage 3, Men and Women 4,
Parties 2, Pleasure 6, Political
Parties 4, Publishing 2, Revenge
4, Sea 2, Seduction 2, Self-
Knowledge 7, Solitude 3, Truth
10, Winter 1

Byron, Robert (1905-41)
Buildings 1

Cabell, James Branch
(1879-1958)
Pessimism 2

Cacoyannis, Michael
(1922-)
Men 6

Caesar, Julius (100-44 BC)
Ambition 5, Betrayal 2, Crises 5,
Reputation 3, Self-Interest 2,
Success 5

Cahn, Sammy (1913-93)
Marriage 4, Youth 4

Caine, Michael (1933-)
Awards 3, Information 2

Caligula (AD 12-41)
Cruelty 5

Callaghan, James
(1912-2005)
Idealism 4, Self-Interest 3, Trade
Unions 3

Callas, Maria (1923-77)
Teaching 3

Calverley, C. S. (1831-84)
Likes 3

Calvino, Italo (1923-85)
Fantasy 3, Pleasure 7

Camara, Helder (1909-99)
Poverty 6

**Cambronne, Pierre, Baron
de** (1770-1842)
Waterloo 1

Cameron, David (1966-)
Disability 2

Cameron, James (1954-)
Parting 5

Cameron, Simon
(1799-1889)
Politicians 3

Campbell, Alastair (1957-)
God 7, Schools 3

Campbell, Jane Montgomery
(1817-78)
Farming 1

Campbell, Mrs Patrick
(1865-1940)
Marriage 5, Sex 7

Campbell, Roy (1901-57)
Human Race 6, Translation 2

Campbell, Thomas
(1777-1844)
Country 1, Publishing 3

Camus, Albert (1913-60)
Adversity 1, Autumn 4, Charm 2,
Honesty 2, Imagination 2,
Intellectuals 3, Lies 3, Memory 7,
Reading 2, Revolution 5, 6, Self-
Interest 4, Sports 4, Work 4

Canetti, Elias (1905-94)
Crime 2, Dreams 3, Secrecy 4

Canning, George
(1770-1827)
Friendship 12

Cantona, Eric (1966-)
Journalism 2

Capa, Robert (1913-54)
Press Photographers 2

Capone, Al (1899-1947)
Crime 3

Capote, Truman (1924-84)
Venice 2

Capp, Al (1907-79)
Painting 3

Capra, Frank (1897-1991)
Cinema 2

Beauty 7, Murder 1, Speech 4

Chavez, Hugo (1954-)
Mexico 1

Chayefsky, Paddy (1923-81)
Anger 3

Chekhov, Anton (1860-1904)
Beauty 8, Environment 4, Friendship 13, Medicine 4, Men and Women 5, Relationships 7, Russia 3, Theatre 2, Unhappiness 3, Writing 9

Cher (1946-)
Love 14

Cherry-Garrard, Apsley (1882-1959)
Exploration 2

Cherry-Garrard, Apsley (1882-1959) see **Atkinson, E. L.** and **Cherry-Garrard, Apsley**

Chesterfield, Lord (1694-1773)
Advice 6, Behaviour 4, Chance 1, Conversation 5, Idleness 4, Insults 2, Knowledge 7, Sex 8, Time 9

Chesterton, G. K. (1874-1936)
Animals 9, Arts and Sciences 5, Atheism 4, Change 6, Christianity 2, Crime 5, Emotions 2, Famous Poets 6, Famous Writers 8, Fiction 2, Food 6, Government 4, Happiness 4, Imagination 3, Insight 4, Ireland 3, Journalism 3, Knowledge 8, Neighbours 2, 3, Patriotism 5, Pleasure 8, Prejudice 2, Problems 2, Promises 1, Punctuality 1, Secrecy 5, Self 7, Tradition 2, Trust 3, Wealth 7, Women 8

Chevalier, Maurice (1888-1972)
Ageing 3

Chifley, Joseph Benedict 'Ben' (1885-1951)
Australia 3

Child, Lydia Maria (1802-80)
Celebrations 2

Chirac, Jacques (1932-)
Britain 2

Choiseul, Duc de (1719-85)
Politicians 4

Chomsky, Noam (1928-)
Grammar 2, Internet 3

Chrétien, Jean (1934-)
Leadership 5, Politics 11

Christie, Agatha (1890-1976)
Archaeology 2, Experience 5, Intelligence 2

Chuo Wen-chun (c.179-117 BC)
Husbands 4

Church, Francis Pharcellus (1839-1906)
Christmas 4

Churchill, Charles (1731-64)
Excellence 2, Hypocrisy 2, Speeches 5, Wordplay 2

Churchill, Lord Randolph (1849-94)
Mathematics 4, Northern Ireland 2

Churchill, Winston (1874-1965)
Achievement 6, Air Force 2, Alcohol 6, Animals 10, Architecture 2, Awards 4, Babies 1, Betrayal 3, Britain 3, Character 6, Colours 1, Communism 5, Courage 3, Crises 7, Culture 5, Democracy 5, Determination 5, Diplomacy 2, 3, Drunkenness 1, Education 10, Ending 4, Examinations 1, Famous People 3, Famous Politicians 9, 10, Fanaticism 2, Food 7, Grammar 3, Impartiality 1, International Relations 12, Leadership 6, Navy 4, Northern Ireland 1, Painting 8, Politicians 5, Politics 12, Problems 3, Propaganda 3, Quotations 2, Russia 4, Sacrifice 2, Schools 4, Self-Esteem 6, Simplicity 2, Speeches 6, 7, Tradition 3, War 5, Winning 4, World War II 3, 4, 5

Ciano, Count Galeazzo (1903-44)
Defeat 3

Cibber, Colley (1671-1757)
Weddings 2

Cicero (106-43 BC)
Behaviour 5, Farming 2, History 5, Laws 4, Philosophy 4, Self-Interest 5, War 6, 7

Cioran, E. M. (1911-95)
Idleness 5, Suicide 1

Clapton, Eric (1945-)
Rock 2

Clare, John (1793-1864)
Madness 1, Present 6, Self 8

Clark, Alan (1928-99)
Politics 13

Clarke, Arthur C. (1917-2008)
Earth 2, Paranormal 4, Science Fiction 2, Technology 9, Theory 2, Twenty-first Century 1

Clarke, Kenneth (1940-)
Generation Gap 1

Clausewitz, Karl von (1780-1831)
War 8, 9

Clay, Henry (1777-1852)
Diplomacy 4, Presidency 4

Clayton, Tubby (1885-1972)
Charity 3

Cleaver, Eldridge (1935-98)
Conversation 6, Problems 4

Cleese, John (1939-) and **Booth, Connie**
Europe 5, Holidays 1, Self-Esteem 7

Cleese, John (1939-) see **Chapman, Graham** and **Cleese, John**

Clemenceau, Georges (1841-1929)
Ageing 4, War 10, World War I 5

Cliff, Clarice (1899-1972)
Colours 2

Clinton, Bill (1946-)
Drugs 6, Elections 4, Forgiveness 4, Meaning 4, Morality 5, Persistence 2, Politics 14, United States 4

Clinton, Hillary Rodham (1947-)
Children 5, Loyalty 2, Marriage 6, Presidency 5, Woman's Role 5

Clooney, George (1961-)
Actors 4, Cinema 5, Genocide 2

Clough, Arthur Hugh (1819-61)
Crime 6, Effort 3, Envy 2, Failure 4, God 8, Hope 3, Murder 2

Coaker, Vernon (1953-)
Punishment 4

Cockburn, Claud (1904-81)
Newspapers 5

Cocteau, Jean (1889-1963)
Behaviour 6, Choice 5, Dictionaries 1, Life 5, Poetry 7

Coetzee, J. M. (1940-)
Dreams 4

Cohan, George M.
(1878-1942)
Fame 7, United States 5, World
War I 6

Cohen, John (1898-1979)
Shopping 2

Cohen, John (1911-)
Swearing 3

Cohen, Leonard (1934-)
Body 4, Canada 7, Perfection 4,
Pessimism 3

Coke, Edward (1552-1634)
Laws 5

Colbert, Jean-Baptiste
(1619-83)
Taxes 4

Colbert, Stephen (1964-)
Books 7

Cole, John (1927-)
Secrecy 6

Coleman, Ornette (1930-)
Jazz 2

Coleridge, Samuel Taylor
(1772-1834)
Christianity 3, Experience 6,
Famous Poets 7, Men and Women
6, Night 3, Poetry 8, 9, Pollution
3, Prayer 6, Pride 3, Sea 3, Silence
2, Summer 2, Weather 3,
Wordplay 3

Colette (1873-1954)
Emotions 3, Manners 3

Collins, Joan (1933-)
Husbands 5, Men 7

Collins, Michael (1880-1922)
Punctuality 2

Collins, Phil (1951-)
Rock 3

Collins, Tim (1960-)
Iraq War 5

Colombo, John Robert
(1936-)
Canada 8

Colton, Charles Caleb
(c.1780-1832)
Examinations 2, Neighbours 4

Columbus, Christopher
(1451-1506)
Exploration 3

Comden, Betty (1917-2006)
and **Green, Adolph**
(1915-2002)
American Cities 8, Ending 5

Compton-Burnett, Ivy
(1884-1969)
Cruelty 6, Habit 5, Men and
Women 7, Possessions 4, Sin 8

Confucius (551-479 BC)
Commitment 2, Education 11,
Human Nature 4, Leadership 7,
Sex 9, Teaching 4

Congreve, William
(1670-1729)
Behaviour 7, Courtship 2, Music
4, Revenge 5, Secrecy 7

Connell, James M.
(1852-1929)
Political Parties 5

Connolly, Billy (1942-)
Fishing 2, Marriage 7, Scotland 6

Connolly, Cyril (1903-74)
Cities 2, Critics 4, Famous Writers
9, Fat 2, Generation Gap 2,
Literature 3, Memory 8, Men and
Women 8, Self 9, Style 4

Connolly, James (1868-1916)
Capitalism 2

Connors, Jimmy (1952-)
Tennis 3

Conrad, Joseph (1857-1924)
Action 7, Ambition 6, Arts and
Sciences 6, Enemies 5, Fear 8,
Human Nature 5, Management 1,
Solitude 5, Youth 6

Conran, Shirley (1932-)
Housework 2, Organization 4,
Practicality 4

Constable, John (1776-1837)
Beauty 9, Famous Artists 2,
Painting 9, 10

Constant, Benjamin
(1767-1834)
Art 5

**Constitution of the United
States** (1787)
Punishment 5

Cook, A. J. (1885-1931)
Trade Unions 4

Cook, Eliza (1818-89)
Punishment 6

Cook, James (1728-79)
Australia 4, Exploration 4

Cook, Peter (1937-95)
Lifestyles 8

Cook, Robin (1946-2005)
Iraq War 6

Coolidge, Calvin (1872-1933)
Chemistry 1, Debt 2, Persistence
3, Sin 9, Speeches 8,
Unemployment 2, United States 6

Cooper, Alice (1948-)
Likes 4

Cooper, Diana (1892-1986)
Languages 2

Cooper, Jilly (1937-)
In-Laws 2

Cooper, Susie (1902-95)
Design 1

Cope, Wendy (1945-)
Men 8

Copland, Aaron (1900-90)
Music 5

Coppola, Francis Ford
(1939-)
Vietnam War 2

Corbett, Ronnie (1930-) see
Barker, Ronnie and **Corbett,
Ronnie**

Corelli, Marie (1855-1924)
Husbands 6

Corneille, Pierre (1606-84)
Danger 2, Duty 1, Impulsiveness 2

Cornfeld, Bernard (1927-95)
Ambition 7

Cornford, Francis M.
(1874-1943)
Committees 2, Originality 5,
Propaganda 4

Cornuel, Mme (1605-94)
Heroes 6

Cory, William (1823-92)
Boats 1

Cosby, Bill (1937-)
Marriage 8

Coubertin, Baron Pierre de
(1863-1937)
Winning 5

Coué, Émile (1857-1926)
Medicine 5

Coupland, Douglas (1961-)
Careers 2, Individuality 1

Courteline, Georges
(1858-1929)
Youth 7

Cousteau, Jacques (1910-97)
Environment 5, Pollution 4

Coward, Noël (1899-1973)
Acting 2, Actors 5, Aristocracy 2,
England 5, Holidays 2, London 3,
Music 6, Names 5, Opera 2,

Pessimism 4, Praise 2, Success 7, Travel 6, Violence 6, Weather 4, World War II 6

Cowley, Abraham (1618-67)
Life 6, Praise 3

Cowper, William (1731-1800)
Caution 4, Change 7, Cities 3, Fools 5, Friendship 14, God 9, Inventions 4, Smoking 2

Crabbe, George (1754-1832)
Defeat 4, Habit 6, Libraries 2, Secrecy 8

Craig, Maurice James (1919-)
British Cities 4

Crane, Hart (1899-1932)
Famous Poets 8, Skies 1

Creighton, Mandell (1843-1901)
Goodness 5

Crick, Francis (1916-2004)
Inventions 5, Life Sciences 4, 5, Self 10

Crisp, Quentin (1908-99)
Autobiography 1, Homosexuality 4, Housework 3, Jealousy 3, Tact 2

Critchley, Julian (1930-2000)
Famous Politicians 11, Parliament 3

Cromwell, Oliver (1599-1658)
Achievement 7, Action 8, Certainty 3, Honesty 3, Last Words 5

Cronenberg, David (1943-)
Canada 9, Fear 9

Crosby, Bing (1903-77)
Singing 3

Cross, Amanda (1926-2003)
Guilt 3

Cross, Douglas
American Cities 9

Crossman, Richard (1907-74)
Civil Service 1

Crowe, Cameron (1957-)
Greatness 1, Money 8

Crowe, Russell (1964-)
Fathers 2

Crowley, Aleister (1875-1947)
Lifestyles 9

cummings, e. e. (1894-1962)
Beginning 3, Belief 7, Body 5,

Logic 5, Politicians 6, Progress 8, United States 7

Cunnah, Peter see **Petrie, Jamie** and **Cunnah, Peter**

Cunningham, Allan (1784-1842)
Boats 2

Cuomo, Mario (1932-)
Elections 5

Cupitt, Don (1934-)
Christmas 5

Curie, Marie (1867-1934)
Fear 10, Science and Society 1

Curnow, Allen (1911-2001)
Australia 5

Curran, John Philpot (1750-1817)
Appearance 4, Liberty 4

Curtis, Richard (1956-)
Faithfulness 5, Weddings 3

Curtis, Tony (1925-)
Kissing 3

Curzon, Lord (1859-1925)
Class 3

Cyprian, St (AD c.200-258)
Church 3

Dalai Lama (1935-)
Compassion 4, Trust 4

Dali, Salvador (1904-89)
Ambition 8, Famous Artists 3

Dana, Charles A. (1819-97)
News 3

Daniel, Samuel (1563-1619)
Sleep 2, Value 5

Daniels, Paul (1938-)
Likes 5

Dante (1265-1321)
Hell 3, Reputation 4, Sorrow 5

Danton, Georges Jacques (1759-94)
Courage 4

Darion, Joe (1917-2001)
Idealism 5

Darnell, Bill
Environment 6

Darrow, Clarence (1857-1938)
Belief 8, Human Rights 6, Presidency 6

Darwin, Charles (1809-82)
Animal Rights 5, Animals 11, Appearance 5, Beginning 4,

Human Race 7, Language 4, Life Sciences 6, Love 15, Morality 6, Nature 3, Theory 3

Darwin, Erasmus (1731-1802)
Speech 5

Darwin, Erasmus (1804-81)
Facts 2

Darwin, Francis (1848-1925)
Science 4

David, Elizabeth (1913-92)
Cooking 4

Davies, Robertson (1913-95)
Canada 10, Luck 1, Pornography 2

Davies, Scrope (c.1783-1852)
Madness 2

Davies, W. H. (1871-1940)
Birds 3, Leisure 4

Davis, Angela (1944-)
Prison 2

Davis, Bette (1908-89)
Work 5

Davis, Sammy, Jnr. (1925-90)
Racism 3

Dawkins, Richard (1941-)
Africa 3, Life Sciences 7, 8

Dawson, Christopher (1889-1970)
Evil 5

Dawson of Penn, Lord (1864-1945)
Meaning 5

Day, Harry
Laws 6

Day, Robin (1923-2000)
Television 4

Dayan, Moshe (1915-81)
Warfare 1

Day-Lewis, C. (1904-72)
Love 16

Dean, James (1931-55)
Cars 3, Lifestyles 10

de Beauvoir, Simone (1908-86)
Housework 4, Men and Women 9, Women 9

de Bernières, Louis (1954-)
Emotions 4, Love 17

Debray, Régis (1940-)
Politics 15

Debs, Eugene Victor (1855-1926)
Equality 6

Frayn, Michael (1933-)
Guilt 5
Frazer, James George
(1854-1941)
In-Laws 3
Frederick the Great
(1712-86)
Army 9, Prejudice 4, Religion 5
Freeman, Cathy (1973-)
Australia 6
Freeman, E. A. (1823-92)
History 8
French, Dawn (1957-)
Painting 13
French, Marilyn (1929-2009)
Family 6, Housework 5, Men 10
Freud, Lucian (1922-)
Painting 14
Freud, Sigmund (1856-1939)
Body 7, Circumstance 4,
Depression 1, Dreams 5, Honesty
5, Life 10, Prejudice 5, United
States 10, Women 14
Friedan, Betty (1921-2006)
Individuality 2, Woman's Role 7
Friedman, Milton
(1912-2006)
Administration 2, Capitalism 3,
Economics 3
Friel, Brian (1929-)
Past 7
Frisch, Max (1911-91)
Technology 12
Fromm, Erich (1900-80)
Discontent 4, Maturity 6
Frost, David (1939-)
Achievement 10, Parents 3
Frost, Robert (1874-1963)
Banking 4, Birthdays 1, Careers 6,
Change 10, Choice 9, Creativity 5,
Determination 6, Disillusion 3,
Education 12, Ending 8, Fear 12,
God 14, Happiness 8, Home 2,
Neighbours 5, Poetry 13, Politics
18, Secrecy 12, Snow 3, Trees 7
Fry, Christopher (1907-2005)
Body 8, Bureaucracy 5, Goodness
6, Home 3, Language 7, Skies 4
Fry, Elizabeth (1780-1845)
Punishment 8
Fry, Stephen (1957-)
Internet 4
Frye, Mary E. (1905-2004)
Bereavement 6

Fuentes, Carlos (1928-)
Mexico 4
Fukuyama, Francis (1952-)
Computers 4, Twentieth Century 2
Fuller, R. Buckminster
(1895-1983)
Earth 3, God 15
Fuller, Sam (1911-97)
Warfare 3
Fuller, Thomas (1608-61)
Architecture 4
Fuller, Thomas (1654-1734)
Knowledge 11, Laws 9, Luck 3,
Mistakes 5, Relationships 10,
Trees 8
Funke, Alfred (1869-1941)
World War I 10
Fyleman, Rose (1877-1957)
Supernatural 8

Gabor, Zsa Zsa (1919-)
Bachelors 2, Divorce 2, Hatred 3,
Husbands 7, Sex 12, Violence 7
Gainsborough, Thomas
(1727-88)
Punctuality 3
Gaitskell, Hugh (1906-63)
Country 3, European Union 1,
Political Parties 7
Galbraith, J. K. (1908-2006)
Advertising 4, Business 8,
Conformity 6, Consumer Society
1, Crises 8, Delay 3, Economics 4,
5, Honesty 6, Luxury 2,
Management 3, Mistakes 6,
Mountains 1, Politics 19, Thinking
9, Wealth 11
Galen (AD 129-199)
Experiment 4, Language 8
Galileo Galilei (1564-1642)
Inventions 3, Science and
Religion 4, Skies 5
Gallagher, Noel (1967-)
Action 9, Drugs 8, Men 11, Rock
5
Galsworthy, John
(1867-1933)
Beauty 13, Ignorance 5, Thinking
10
Galt, John (1779-1839)
Exile 3, Scotland 7
Galton, Ray (1930-) and
Simpson, Alan (1929-)

Body 9, Censorship 6
Gandhi, Indira (1917-84)
Asia 4, International Relations 14
Gandhi, Mahatma
(1869-1948)
Capitalism 4, Change 11,
Civilization 5, Evil 8, Liberty 6,
Pacifism 5, Speed 4, War 12
Garbo, Greta (1905-90)
Solitude 8
García Lorca, Federico
(1899-1936)
Colours 3
Gardner, Ed (1901-63)
Opera 3
Garner, John Nance
(1868-1967)
Presidency 8
Garrick, David (1717-79)
Navy 5, Speech 10
Gaskell, Elizabeth (1810-65)
Fools 7, Logic 8, Men 12
Gates, Bill (1955-)
Teaching 6
Gay, John (1685-1732)
Choice 10, Deception 4, Epitaphs
14, Marriage 16
Geddes, Eric (1875-1937)
Revenge 7
Gehry, Frank (1929-)
Architecture 5
Geldof, Bob (1954-)
Diets 4, Race 4, Rock 6
Geldof, Bob (1954-) and
Ure, Midge (1953-)
Aid 2
Genet, Jean (1910-86)
Betrayal 4, Ideas 4
Gentle, Rose
Iraq War 8
George II (1683-1760)
Madness 3
George V (1865-1936)
British Cities 5, Nationality 3,
Parents 4, Peace 9
George VI (1895-1952)
Diplomacy 6, Royal Family 6
George, Dan (1899-1981)
Canada 12
George, Eddie (1938-2009)
Retirement 3
Geronimo (c.1829-1909)
Defeat 5

Hewitt, Foster William
(1902-85)
Sports 11

Hewson, John (1946-)
Insults 5

Heyward, Du Bose
(1885-1940) and **Gershwin,
Ira** (1896-1983)
Bible 4, Summer 4

Hicks, J. R. (1904-89)
Economics 9

Hicks, Seymour (1871-1949)
Ageing 6

Hightower, Jim (1943-)
Moderation 6

Hilbert, David (1862-1943)
Knowledge 14, Science 7

Hill, Aaron (1685-1750)
Courage 9

Hill, Damon (1960-)
Winning 6

Hill, Geoffrey (1932-)
Innocence 6, Poetry 15

Hill, Joe (1879-1915)
Future 10, Revolution 11

Hill, Napoleon (1883-1970)
Money 12

Hillary, Edmund (1919-2008)
Mountains 3

Hillebrand, Fred (1893-1963)
Speed 5

Hillel 'The Elder' (*c.*60 BC-
*c.*AD 9)
Self 14

Hillingdon, Lady (1857-1940)
Sex 14

Hilton, Paris (1981-)
Clothes 9

Hinshelwood, Cyril
(1897-1967)
Chemistry 2

Hippocrates (*c.*460-357 BC)
Manners 5, Medicine 8, 9, 10,
Secrecy 14, Sickness 6

Hirohito, Emperor (1901-89)
Defeat 7

Hirst, Damien (1965-)
Famous Artists 4

Hislop, Ian (1960-)
Trials 3

Hitchcock, Alfred
(1899-1980)
Actors 7, Cinema 14, Fear 13,
Murder 6

Hitler, Adolf (1889-1945)
Betrayal 7, Colours 4, Fate 6,
Genocide 4, Leadership 9, Lies 7

Hobbes, Thomas (1588-1679)
Apology 5, Conscience 5, Humour
9, Last Words 9, Life 13

Hobsbawm, Eric (1917-)
Twentieth Century 3

Hockney, David (1937-)
Design 2, Painting 15,
Photography 6, Technology 14

Hoddle, Glenn (1957-)
Disability 5

Hodgkin, Dorothy (1910-94)
Chemistry 3

Hodgson, Ralph (1871-1962)
Animal Rights 6, Time 15

Hoffer, Eric (1902-83)
Originality 7

Hofmannsthal, Hugo von
(1874-1929)
Friendship 20

Hogben, Lancelot
(1895-1975)
Technology 15

**Holbach, Paul Henri, Baron
d'** (1723-89)
Science and Religion 5

Holbrooke, Richard (1941-)
Weapons 7

Holiday, Billie (1915-59)
Drugs 10, Racism 10, 11

Holland, Henry Scott
(1847-1918)
Death 14

Holmes, John H. (1879-1964)
Universe 10

Holmes, Oliver Wendell
(1809-94)
Banking 6, Conversation 10, 11,
Ideas 5, Old Age 10, Parties 4,
Violence 8

Holmes, Oliver Wendell, Jnr.
(1841-1935)
Censorship 10, Faith 8, Liberty 9

Holtby, Winifred (1898-1935)
Insight 6

Holub, Miroslav (1923-98)
Persistence 8

Home, Lord (1903-95)
Aristocracy 5, Fishing 4

Homer (*fl. c.*750 BC)
Gifts 4, Transience 8

Hood, Thomas (1799-1845)
Change 13, Cooking 6, Poverty
13, Travel 8, Winter 3

Hoover, Herbert (1874-1964)
Fishing 3, Progress 10,
Teetotalism 2, United States 13,
War 15, Words and Deeds 7

Hope, A. D. (1907-2000)
Australia 8

Hope, Anthony (1863-1933)
Epitaphs 5, Thrift 2

Hope, Bob (1903-2003)
Banking 7, Golf 1

Hopkins, Gerard Manley
(1844-89)
Beauty 16, Birds 5, Creativity 6,
Despair 8, Environment 8, Human
Race 14, Mind 8, Oxford 3,
Pollution 8, Prayer 8, Silence 5,
Skies 7, Sorrow 9, Work 9

Hopkins, Harry Lloyd
(1890-1946)
Unemployment 4

Hopper, Edward (1882-1967)
Painting 16

Horace (65-8 BC)
Anger 6, Birthdays 2, Crises 12,
Death 15, Effort 8, Hope 9, Hosts
and Guests 6, Humour 10,
Mediocrity 3, Money 13,
Patriotism 11, Perfection 6, Praise
4, Present 8, Statistics 9, Style 6,
Teetotalism 3, Violence 9, Words
11

Hornby, Nick (1957-)
Cynicism 8, Fathers 3, Football 4

Horne, Donald Richmond
(1921-)
Australia 9

Horowitz, Vladimir (1904-89)
Musical Instruments 6

Housman, A. E. (1859-1936)
Alcohol 11, Army 12, Europe 12,
Nature 4, Past 10, Poetry 16,
Prejudice 7, Risk 3, Spring 5,
Thinking 11, Trees 9, Wind 2

Howe, Geoffrey (1926-)
Betrayal 8

Howe, Gordie (1928-)
Sports 8

Howe, Julia Ward
(1819-1910)
God 16

Howells, William Dean
(1837-1920)
Hosts and Guests 7, Tragedy 3

Hoyle, Edmond (1672-1769)
Winning 7

Hoyle, Fred (1915-2001)
Space 8, Universe 11

Hubbard, Elbert (1859-1915)
Apology 6, Genius 6, Life 14,
Lifestyles 16, Technology 16

**Hubbard, Frank McKinney
('Kin')** (1868-1930)
Money 14, Music 12, Revenge 8

Hudson, Richard (1948-)
see **Ford, John** and **Hudson,
Richard**

Hughes, Jimmy and **Lake,
Frank**
Army 13

Hughes, Langston (1902-67)
Racism 12, Rivers 5, 6

Hughes, Robert (1938-)
Australia 10

Hughes, Sarah (1985-)
Olympic Games 4

Hughes, Ted (1930-98)
Birds 6, Cats 3, Diaries 2, Horses
2, Imagination 7, In-Laws 4

Hughes, Thomas (1822-96)
Compromise 3, Cricket 4

**Hughes, William Morris
'Billy'** (1862-1952)
Painting 17

Hugo, Victor (1802-85)
Fame 11, Ideas 6

Hull, Josephine (?1886-1957)
Shakespeare 2

Hume, Basil (1923-99)
Dying 4

Hume, David (1711-76)
Beauty 17, Character 10,
Christianity 5, Clergy 2, Custom 3,
Human Race 15, Paranormal 6,
Self 15

Hunt, Leigh (1784-1859)
Conversation 12, Excellence 3,
Secrecy 15

Huntington, Samuel
(1927-2008)
International Relations 15, United
States 14

Hupfeld, Herman
(1894-1951)
Kissing 7

Hurd, Douglas (1930-)
Idleness 6

Hurston, Zora Neale
(c.1901-60)
Woman's Role 9

Hussein, Saddam
(1937-2006)
Gulf War 1, Iraq War 10

Hutcheson, Francis
(1694-1746)
Morality 8

Huxley, Aldous (1894-1963)
Achievement 11, Advertising 5,
Apology 7, Arts and Sciences 8,
Books 12, Bureaucracy 6,
Celibacy 3, Chance 6, Consistency
2, Critics 9, Experience 11, Facts
4, Human Nature 9, Leadership
10, Morality 9, Progress 11,
Propaganda 5, Revolution 12

Huxley, Julian (1887-1975)
God 17

Huxley, T. H. (1825-95)
Belief 9, Doubt 5, Goodness 10,
Inventions 13, Knowledge 15,
Logic 10, 11, Murder 7, Patience
5, Science 8, Science and Religion
6, Theory 6, Truth 15

Iacocca, Lee (1924-)
Friendship 21

Ibarruri, Dolores
(1895-1989)
Defiance 6, Liberty 10

ibn Hanbal, Ahmad
(780-855)
Women 18

Ibsen, Henrik (1828-1906)
Clothes 10, Disillusion 4, Human
Nature 10, Minorities 3, Strength
12

Ice-T (1958-)
Love 26

Ignatius Loyola, St
(1491-1556)
Gifts 5

Illich, Ivan (1926-2002)
Consumer Society 2, Possessions
10

Inge, Charles (1868-1957)
Ability 3

Inge, William Ralph
(1860-1954)
Argument 8, Education 13,
Human Race 16, Liberty 11,
Originality 8, Religion 6, Violence
10

Ingersoll, Robert G.
(1833-99)
Belief 10, Grammar 6, Nature 5

Ingham, Bernard (1932-)
Gossip 5, Government 13

Ingres, J. A. D. (1780-1867)
Drawing 2

Ionesco, Eugène (1912-94)
Civil Service 4

Irving, John (1942-)
Memory 12

Irving, Washington
(1783-1859)
Change 14, Speech 14

Isherwood, Christopher
(1904-86)
Writing 18

Issigonis, Alec (1906-88)
Committees 4

Ives, Charles (1874-1954)
Art and Society 3, Music 13

Izzard, Eddie (1962-)
Europe 13

Jackson, Jesse (1941-)
Protest 2, Race 6

Jackson, Mahalia (1911-72)
Self-Esteem 9

Jackson, Robert H.
(1892-1954)
Corruption 5, Trials 4, 5

**Jackson, Thomas Jonathan
'Stonewall'** (1824-63)
Duty 4, Warfare 5

Jacobs, Joe (1896-1940)
Boxing 4

Jagger, Mick (1943-) and
Richards, Keith (1943-)
Lovers 7, Protest 3

Jalal (1207-73)
Religion 7

James I (1566-1625)
Famous Poets 12, Smoking 5

James, Carwyn (1929-83)
Revenge 9

James, Clive (1939-)
Buildings 3, Grammar 7,
Television 6

Women 14, Mothers 5, Opinion 9,
Plagiarism 5, Quotations 7,
Responsibility 2, Sex 17, Sin 10,
Solitude 10, Sports 14, Suffering
12, Trees 11, Women 19, 20,
Words 15

Kissinger, Henry (1923-)
Crises 16, Loyalty 4, Power 14,
War 17

Kitchener, Lord (1850-1916)
World War I 13

Klee, Paul (1879-1940)
Colours 5, Drawing 3, Painting 19

Knight, Laura (1877-1970)
Drawing 4

Knox, John (*c.*1505-72)
Faith 9

Knox, Ronald (1888-1957)
Babies 5, Logic 12, Manners 7,
Opinion 10, Parties 5

Koestler, Arthur (1905-83)
God 19, Writing 21

Kohl, Helmut (1930-)
European Union 2

Koran, The
Goodness 12, Human Race 20,
Murder 9

Korb, Lawrence (1939-)
Gulf War 2

Kranz, Gene (1933-)
Failure 6

Kraus, Karl (1874-1936)
Government 16, Journalism 8,
Speed 6

Krishnamurti, Jiddu
(1895-1986)
Religion 10, Truth 16

Kristofferson, Kris (1936-)
Liberty 16

Kroc, Ray (1902-84)
Risk 4

Kronecker, Leopold
(1823-91)
Mathematics 11

Krutch, Joseph Wood
(1893-1970)
Cats 5, Summer 5

Kubrick, Stanley (1928-99)
International Relations 19

Kundera, Milan (1929-)
Animal Rights 7, Defeat 8, Power
15, Thinking 13, Vulgarity 3

Kuralt, Charles (1934-97)
Travel 11

la Bruyère, Jean de (1645-96)
Humour 11, Love 28

Laclos, Pierre Choderlos de
(1741-1803)
Happiness 13

Lacroix, Christian (1951-)
Fashion 3

la Fontaine, Jean de
(1621-95)
Eating 8, Fame 14, Secrecy 16

Lahr, John (1941-)
Advertising 7

Laing, R. D. (1927-89)
Guilt 6, Madness 5, Mental Illness
5, 6

Lake, Frank see **Hughes,
Jimmy** and **Lake, Frank**

Lamartine, Alphonse de
(1790-1869)
Human Race 21

Lamb, Charles (1775-1834)
Anger 8, Belief 12, Books 14,
Famous Poets 15, Gardens 9,
Gifts 7, Lending 2, Meeting 6,
Music 14, Pleasure 12, Singing
13, Smoking 7, Wordplay 5, Work
12, Worry 3, Writing 22

Lamb, Lady Caroline
(1785-1828)
Famous Poets 14

Lamming, George (1927-)
West Indies 1

Lamont, Norman (1942-)
Business 11, Government 17

Lampedusa, Giuseppe di
(1896-1957)
Change 18, Love 29

Landau, Lev (1908-68)
Space 9

Landers, Ann (1918-2002)
Parties 6

Landor, Walter Savage
(1775-1864)
Ireland 6

Lang, Andrew (1844-1912)
Statistics 10

Langer, Susanne (1895-1985)
Art 18

Langley, Noel (1911-80) and
Wolfe, Edgar Allan
Change 19

Lao Tzu (*c.*604-*c.*531 BC)
Beginning 7, Laws 13, Leadership

12, Self-Knowledge 10, Strength
13, Travel 12, Value 9

Larkin, Philip (1922-85)
Birthdays 3, Boredom 5, Church
5, Day 3, Disillusion 5,
Environment 10, Fiction 8,
Gardens 10, Innocence 7, Insight
7, Life 19, London 6, Love 30,
Parents 8, Poetry 18, Sex 18,
Work 13

la Rochefoucauld, Duc de
(1613-80)
Absence 4, Boredom 6,
Compassion 9, Friendship 25,
Gratitude 5, Greatness 5, Home 7,
Hypocrisy 3, Mind 10, Misfortunes
8, Relationships 16, Trust 8,
Unhappiness 5

Latimer, Hugh (*c.*1485-1555)
Persistence 9

Lauder, Harry (1870-1950)
Persistence 10

Laurel, Stan (1890-1965)
Cooperation 10, Problems 9

Laurier, Wilfrid (1841-1919)
Canada 14

Law, Andrew Bonar
(1858-1923)
Greatness 6

Lawless, Emily (1845-1913)
Famine 4

Lawrence, D. H. (1885-1930)
Autumn 7, Behaviour 10, Class 7,
Critics 13, Death 18, Design 3,
Fiction 9, Innocence 8, Insults 7,
Love 31, Pornography 3, Sex 19,
Shakespeare 5, Tragedy 5,
Twentieth Century 4

Lawrence, T. E. (1888-1935)
Choice 11

Lawson, Nigel (1932-)
International Relations 20

Lawson, Nigella (1960-)
Diets 5, Sports 15

Lazarus, Emma (1849-87)
United States 16

Leach, Edmund (1910-89)
Family 8

Leacock, Stephen
(1869-1944)
Advertising 8, Field Sports 1, Golf
2, Leisure 6, Reading 7

McLean, Don (1945-)
Famous Musicians 7
MacLeish, Archibald
(1892-1982)
Knowledge 19, Libraries 5, Poetry 20
McLeod, Fiona (1855-1905)
Solitude 11
McLeod, Irene Rutherford
(1891-1964)
Dogs 5
McLuhan, Marshall
(1911-80)
Advertising 10, Cars 8, Earth 5, Mental Illness 7, Mind 11, Names 13, Technology 17, 18, 19, Television 7
Macmillan, Harold
(1894-1986)
Africa 8, Economics 11, Morality 11, Political Parties 16, Politicians 9, Politics 23, Power 17, Progress 14
McNamara, Robert
(1916-2009)
Vietnam War 6, 7
McNealy, Scott (1954-)
Computers 9
MacNeice, Louis (1907-63)
Fate 7, God 22, Leisure 7, Marriage 21, Musicians 4, Pregnancy 4, 5, Similarity 7, Transience 10
McWilliam, Candia (1955-)
Children 13, Exile 4
Madison, James (1751-1836)
Government 22, Liberty 20
Madoff, Bernard (1938-)
Banking 9
Madonna (1958-)
Hair 2, Men 14
Maeterlinck, Maurice
(1862-1949)
Death 20
Magee, John Gillespie
(1922-41)
Air Force 4
Magna Carta (1215)
Human Rights 10, Justice 13
Magnusson, Magnus
(1929-2007)
Beginning 9
Magritte, René (1898-1967)
Familiarity 6, Painting 20

Mahaffy, John Pentland
(1839-1919)
Ireland 7
Maher, Bill (1956-)
Suicide 2
Mahler, Gustav (1860-1911)
Music 15, Senses 9
Mahy, Margaret (1936-)
Canada 15
Mailer, Norman (1923-2007)
Caution 8, Divorce 5, Emotions 10, Famous People 7, Fashion 4, Heroes 12, Homosexuality 7, Sex 20
Maine, Henry (1822-88)
Greece 3, Peace 15
Major, John (1943-)
Britain 5, Economics 12, Punishment 13
Malamud, Bernard (1914-86)
Determination 10, Friendship 27
Malcolm X (1925-65)
Peace 16
Mallarmé, Stéphane
(1842-98)
Chance 8, Disillusion 6
Mallory, George Leigh
(1886-1924)
Mountains 5
Mallory, John
Mountains 6
Malory, Thomas (d. 1471)
Royalty 11
Malraux, André (1901-76)
Art 19, War 22
Malthus, Thomas Robert
(1766-1834)
Life Sciences 14
Mancroft, Lord (1914-87)
Cricket 5
Mandela, Nelson (1918-)
Africa 9, Diplomacy 5, Forgiveness 9, Hatred 6, Poverty 17, Twentieth Century 5
Manifold, John Streeter
(1915-85)
Australia 13
Manikan, Ruby
Education 15
Mankiewicz, Joseph L.
(1909-93)
Danger 5
Manley, Mrs (1663-1724)
Readiness and Preparation 7

Mann, Herbie (1930-)
Jazz 5
Mann, Thomas (1875-1955)
Bereavement 11, Celebrations 4, Kissing 8, Speech 15, Time 17
Mansfield, Katherine
(1888-1923)
Famous Writers 15
Mao Zedong (1893-1976)
Politics 24, 25, Power 18
Maradona, Diego (1960-)
Football 7
Marchi, John (1948-2009)
Biotechnology 3
Marco Polo (c.1254-c.1324)
Travel 14
Marcy, William Learned
(1786-1857)
Winning 8
Marguerite d'Angoulême
(1492-1549)
Jealousy 5
Margulis, Lynn (1938-)
Earth 6
Marks, Leo (1920-2001)
Lovers 9
Marlborough, Sarah,
Duchess of (1660-1744)
Lovers 10, Sex 21
Marley, Bob (1945-81)
Defiance 8
Marlowe, Christopher
(1564-93)
Face 4, Love 34, Religion 11
Márquez, Gabriel García
(1928-)
Marriage 22, Necessity 5
Marquis, Don (1878-1937)
Delay 5, Honesty 9, Luck 7, Misfortunes 9, Optimism 6, Politicians 10, Teetotalism 4
Marshall, Arthur (1910-89)
Life 24
Martel, Yann (1963-)
Clothes 12
Martial (AD c.40-c.104)
Birthdays 4, Health 5, Relationships 19, Weddings 5
Martin, Dean (1917-)
Drunkenness 6, Teetotalism 5
Marvell, Andrew (1621-78)
Courtship 5, Executions 3, Gardens 11, Time 18

Marvell, Holt (1901-69)
Memory 15
Marx, Chico (1891-1961)
Kissing 9
Marx, Groucho (1890-1977)
Lesbianism 3, Names 12,
Prejudice 8, Reviews 4
Marx, Karl (1818-83)
Communism 9, History 10,
Philosophy 7, Religion 12, Society
10, Tradition 4
Marx, Karl (1818-83) and
Engels, Friedrich (1820-95)
Class 8, Communism 10
Mary, Queen (1867-1953)
Country 6, Sacrifice 7
Mary, Queen of Scots
(1542-87)
Ending 10
Masefield, John (1878-1967)
Boats 6, 7, Pregnancy 6, Sea 9
Mathew, James (1830-1908)
Justice 14
Matisse, Henri (1869-1954)
Painting 21
Matlovich, Leonard
(1943-88)
Homosexuality 8
Matthews, Cerys (1969-)
Wales 6
Maugham, W. Somerset
(1874-1965)
Censorship 13, Critics 14, Dying
6, Fate 8, Grammar 8, Hypocrisy
5, Laws 15, Love 35, Men and
Women 17, Money 16, Morality
12, Old Age 14, Parties 8,
Sacrifice 8, Suffering 15,
Tolerance 6, Wit 4, Words and
Deeds 8
Maupassant, Guy de
(1850-93)
Mind 12
Maxwell, James Clerk
(1831-79)
Science 10, Teaching 8
May, Theresa (1956-)
Political Parties 17
Mayakovsky, Vladimir
(1893-1930)
Men 15
Mazzini, Giuseppe (1805-72)
Nationality 5

Mead, Margaret (1901-78)
Cities 6, Mediocrity 5, Politics 26
Mead, Shepherd (1914-94)
Business 13
Medawar, Peter (1915-87)
Arts and Sciences 9, Ignorance 9,
Research 2
Medici, Catherine de'
(1518-89)
Propaganda 6
Medici, Cosimo de'
(1389-1464)
Forgiveness 10
Mee, Bertie (1918-2001)
Football 8
Megarry, Robert (1910-2006)
European Union 4
Mehmed II (1430-81)
Transience 11
Meir, Golda (1898-1978)
Pessimism 10, Woman's Role 14
Melba, Nellie (1861-1931)
Music 17
Melbourne, Lord
(1779-1848)
Art and Society 5, Certainty 5,
Foresight 9, Politicians 11,
Religion 13, Titles 3, Universities
10
Melville, Herman (1819-91)
Achievement 15, Censorship 14,
Sea 10, Universities 11
Menander (342-*c*.292 BC)
Lifestyles 19, Youth 12
Mencken, H. L. (1880-1956)
Bachelors 3, Birth Control 2,
Christianity 7, Compassion 10,
Conscience 7, Democracy 9,
Elections 11, Faith 10, Intelligence
8, Justice 15, Political Parties 18,
Problems 11, Science and Religion
8
Menuhin, Yehudi (1916-99)
Newspapers 9
Menzies, Robert Gordon
(1894-1978)
Australia 14
Mercer, Johnny (1909-76)
Optimism 7, Parting 12
Meredith, George
(1828-1909)
Certainty 6, Cooking 7, Nature 6
Meredith, Owen (1831-91)
Genius 10

Merrell, Jo Ann
Parents 9
Merrill, James (1926-)
Dictionaries 4
Merritt, Dixon Lanier
(1879-1972)
Birds 7
Metternich, Prince
(1773-1859)
Italy 3, Liberty 21, Politicians 12
Meynell, Viola (1886-1956)
Housework 7
Michals, Duane (1932-)
Photography 7
Michelangelo (1475-1564)
Perfection 7, Sculpture 4
Midler, Bette (1945-)
Present 9
Mies van der Rohe
(1886-1969)
Architecture 8, Simplicity 3
Mikes, George (1912-87)
Cooking 8, England 8, Sex 22
Mill, John Stuart (1806-73)
Discontent 6, Economics 13,
Happiness 15, Liberty 22, Opinion
11, Society 11
Millay, Edna St Vincent
(1892-1950)
Bereavement 12, Childhood 5,
Life 25, Memory 16
Miller, Alice Duer
(1874-1942)
England 9
Miller, Arthur (1915-2005)
American Cities 13, Business 14,
Causes 8, Effort 10, Newspapers
10, Organization 5, Relationships
20, Shopping 4, Suffering 16,
Suicide 3
Miller, Jonathan (1934-)
Sickness 8
Milligan, Spike (1918-2002)
Birth Control 3, Epitaphs 18,
Ireland 8, Money 17, Old Age 15
Mills, Irving (1894-1985)
Jazz 6
Milne, A. A. (1882-1956)
Absence 5, Birthdays 5, Christmas
8, Eating 10, Exercise 6, Food 12,
Golf 3, Knowledge 20, Likes 9,
Prayer 10, Thinking 15, Wind 4,
Words 17

Muir, Jean (1928-95)
Clothes 14
Muir, John (1838-1914)
Mountains 7
Muldoon, Robert (1921-92)
Australia 15
Muller, H. J. (1890-1967)
Human Race 23
Mumford, Lewis (1895-1990)
Generation Gap 5, United States 18
Munch, Edvard (1863-1944)
Painting 22
Murasaki Shikibu
(*c.*978-*c.*1031)
Memory 18
Murdoch, Iris (1919-99)
Flowers 8, Guilt 7, Love 37, Marriage 23
Murray, Les A. (1938-)
Cooperation 11
Murrow, Ed (1908-65)
Circumstance 10, Famous Politicians 18, Television 8
Mussolini, Benito
(1883-1945)
Punctuality 6
Muste, Rev. A. J. (1885-1967)
Love 38

Nabokov, Vladimir
(1899-1977)
Conformity 8, Death 22, Life 27, Railways 5, Reading 8, Sex 24, Teaching 10, Wit 5
Naidu, Sarojini (1879-1949)
Famous People 9
Naipaul, V. S. (1932-)
Life 28, West Indies 2
Napoleon I (1769-1821)
Army 16, Courage 11, England 11, Failure 7, France 10, Inventions 14, Money 18, Opportunity 4, Past 12, Sea 11, Sex 25, War 26, Woman's Role 15
Nash, Ogden (1902-71)
Advertising 11, Animals 15, 16, Appearance 9, Birds 8, Cars 9, Cats 8, Celebrations 5, Children 15, Cosmetics 3, Dogs 6, Employment 6, England 12, Environment 13, Family 9, Fathers 4, Food 14, Hatred 7, Holidays 3,
Houses 3, Husbands 9, Marriage 24, Middle Age 13, Parents 10, 11, Parties 9, Relationships 21, Senses 10
Navratilova, Martina
(1956-)
Tennis 5, Winning 9
Nehru, Jawaharlal
(1889-1964)
Capitalism 9
Nelson, Horatio, Lord
(1758-1805)
Ambition 11, Duty 8, Last Words 13
Nemerov, Howard (1920-91)
Inventions 15
Neruda, Pablo (1904-73)
Bereavement 14, Dying 7, Love 39, Lovers 11, Mexico 5, Warfare 6
Nesbit, Edith (1858-1924)
Parents 12, Pleasure 16
Neumann, John von
(1903-57)
Mathematics 13
Newbolt, Henry (1862-1938)
Cricket 6, Sports 17
Newman, John Henry
(1801-90)
Belief 15, Change 22, Conscience 8, Doubt 7, Perfection 8, Sin 13
Newman, Paul (1925-2008)
Faithfulness 9
Newton, Isaac (1642-1727)
Experiment 5, Inventions 16, Progress 15
Nicholas I (1796-1855)
Russia 8
Nicholson, Vivian (1936-)
Wealth 16
Nicias (*c.*470-413 BC)
Courage 12
Nicolson, Harold
(1886-1968)
Marriage 25, Political Parties 20, Royal Family 9
Niebuhr, Reinhold
(1892-1971)
Change 23, Democracy 10, Twentieth Century 6
Niemöller, Martin
(1892-1984)
Indifference 7, Liberty 23

Nietzsche, Friedrich
(1844-1900)
Chaos 3, Critics 17, Discontent 7, God 24, Human Race 24, Lifestyles 20, Morality 13, Problems 12, Suffering 17, Suicide 4, Wit 6, Women 26, Words 18
Nightingale, Florence
(1820-1910)
Medicine 11, 12
Nin, Anais (1903-77)
Fear 16
Nixon, Richard (1913-94)
Defeat 12, Guilt 8, Hatred 8, Presidency 9, 10, Vietnam War 8
Nizer, Louis (1902-94)
Self 20
Nkrumah, Kwame (1900-72)
International Relations 21, Liberty 24
Nobbs, David (1935-)
Careers 7
Noonuccal, Oodgeroo
(1920-93)
Australia 16, Race 9
Norquist, Grover (1956-)
Government 23
North, Christopher
(1785-1854)
Laws 16
Northcliffe, Lord (1865-1922)
Newspapers 11, Titles 4
Norton, Caroline (1808-77)
Death 23
Norworth, Jack (1879-1959)
Baseball 7
Nunn, Sam (1938-)
Homosexuality 10
Nyerere, Julius (1922-99)
Aid 4

Oates, Captain Lawrence
(1880-1912)
Last Words 14
Obama, Barack (1961-)
Ability 4, Fathers 5, Hope 11, Justice 16, United States 19
Obama, Michelle (1964-)
Education 16
O'Brien, Conor Cruise
(1917-2008)
Famous Politicians 19

Pollitt, Harry (1890-1960)
Heroes 13

Pollock, Jackson (1912-56)
Painting 24

Pompadour, Madame de (1721-64)
Revolution 18

Pompey the Great (106-48 BC)
Risk 5

Pompidou, Georges (1911-74)
Politicians 15

Pope, Alexander (1688-1744)
Administration 5, Apology 8, Aristocracy 10, Charity 5, Children 17, Circumstance 11, Conversation 18, Cynicism 10, Eating 11, Emotions 16, Food 17, Fools 11, Forgiveness 12, Futility 11, Gardens 12, Goodness 14, Happiness 17, Honesty 10, Hope 12, Hosts and Guests 9, Human Race 26, Intelligence 9, Knowledge 23, Opinion 13, Praise 7, Retirement 5, Science 15, Style 8, Teaching 11, Wealth 17, Words 20

Popper, Karl (1902-94)
Arts and Sciences 10, Liberty 28, Tolerance 7

Porter, Cole (1891-1964)
Country 7, Faithfulness 10, Love 41, Morality 14, Parting 14, Shakespeare 7

Potter, Beatrix (1866-1943)
Food 18

Potter, Dennis (1935-94)
Air Travel 6, Present 10, Religion 18

Potter, Stephen (1900-69)
Alcohol 16, Argument 14, Sports 20

Pound, Ezra (1885-1972)
Art and Society 6, History 12, Literature 6, Meaning 8, Middle Age 14, Music 20, Winter 4, Writing 26

Poussin, Nicolas (1594-1665)
Painting 25

Powell, Anthony (1905-2000)
Self-Esteem 12

Powell, Colin (1937-)
Gulf War 3

Powell, Enoch (1912-98)
Diaries 3, Politicians 16, Racism 14, War 29

Powell, John Wesley (1834-1902)
Exploration 8

Pratchett, Terry (1948-)
Advice 9, Alzheimer's 3, Conversation 19, Fantasy 5, Genius 11, Language 14, Reality 6, Self 24, Taxes 11

Preston, Keith (1884-1927)
Publishing 4

Price, Anthony (1928-)
Air Travel 7

Priestland, Gerald (1927-91)
Journalism 11

Priestley, J. B. (1894-1984)
Football 10, Relationships 22, Schools 7, Snow 4, World War II 13

Prior, Matthew (1664-1721)
Courtship 7, Medicine 14

Pritchett, V. S. (1900-97)
Books 20, Crime Fiction 5

Protagoras (c.485 BC)
Human Race 27

Proudhon, Pierre-Joseph (1809-65)
Possessions 12

Proust, Marcel (1871-1922)
Creativity 10, Evening 3, Greatness 7, Happiness 18, Heaven 2, Memory 20, Sickness 9

Publilius Syrus
Anger 10, Corruption 7

Pugin, Augustus Welby (1812-52)
Design 6

Pulitzer, Joseph (1847-1911)
Journalism 12, Newspapers 12

Pullman, Philip (1946-)
Fiction 12

Punch
Animals 17, Behaviour 13, Delay 6, Fat 5, Food 19, Mind 16, Prejudice 10, Tact 4, Thinking 18, Vulgarity 4

Pushkin, Alexander (1799-1837)
Deception 9, Russia 9, Winter 5

Putnam, Israel (1718-90)
American War of Independence 3

Puzo, Mario (1920-99)
Choice 12, Lawyers 5

Pyrrhus (319-272 BC)
Winning 11

Pythagoras (580-500 BC)
Strength 16

Quant, Mary (1934-)
Wealth 18

Quarles, Francis (1592-1644)
Discontent 8, Work 16

Quayle, Dan (1947-)
Mind 17, Space 12

Quiller-Couch, Arthur (1863-1944)
Excellence 4

Quine, W. V. O. (1908-2000)
Language 15

Rabelais, François (c.1494-c.1553)
Children 18, Last Words 16, Lifestyles 22

Rabin, Yitzhak (1922-95)
Peace 19

Racine, Jean (1639-99)
Hatred 10, Indecision 7, Lovers 14

Radcliffe, Paula (1973-)
Sports 21

Ralegh, Walter (c.1552-1618)
Ambition 13, Death 26, Emotions 17, Executions 5, Faithfulness 11, Sea 14, Time 21

Raleigh, Walter (1861-1922)
Examinations 6, Human Race 28, Quotations 9

Ramanujan, Srinivasa (1887-1920)
Mathematics 15

Randi, James (1928-)
Paranormal 7, Present 11

Ransome, Arthur (1884-1967)
Risk 6

Raphael, Frederic (1931-)
British Cities 6, Cities 9, Faithfulness 12

Raposo, Joe (1937-89)
Environment 14

Rather, Dan (1931-)
Patriotism 16

Ratner, Gerald (1949-)
Business 16
Rattigan, Terence (1911-77)
Class 10
Rattle, Simon (1955-)
Famous Musicians 8
Raverat, Gwen (1885-1957)
Class 11
Read, Herbert (1893-1968)
Army 18, Painting 26
Read, Piers Paul (1941-)
Sin 14
Reade, Charles (1814-84)
Causes 10
Reagan, Nancy (1923-)
Adversity 6, Presidency 12
Reagan, Ronald (1911-2004)
Alzheimer's 4, Character 15,
Leadership 15, Management 9,
Politics 29, Space 13, Terrorism 4,
Trust 9, Work 17
Reed, Henry (1914-86)
Army 19
Reed, Joseph (1741-85)
Corruption 8
Reeve, Christopher
(1952-2004)
Disability 8
Reger, Max (1873-1916)
Reviews 5
Reid, Keith (1946-)
Face 7
Reith, Lord (1889-1971)
Impartiality 2, Logic 13, Television
11
Remarque, Erich Maria
(1898-1970)
World War I 16
Renard, Jules (1864-1910)
Class 12
Rendall, Montague John
(1862-1950)
Television 12
Renoir, Jean (1894-1979)
Success 16
Renoir, Pierre Auguste
(1841-1919)
Painting 27
**Retz, Jean-François Paul de
Gondi, Cardinal de** (1613-79)
Management 10, Trust 10
Revson, Charles (1906-75)
Cosmetics 5

Reynolds, Joshua (1723-92)
Painting 28, Taste 7, Teaching 12,
Work 18
Reynolds, Malvina (1900-78)
Architecture 10
Reza, Yasmina (1969-)
Comedy 4
Rhodes, Cecil (1853-1902)
England 16, Last Words 17
Rhys, Jean (c.1890-1979)
Compassion 12, Famous People
10, Suffering 18, Women 28
Rice, Grantland (1880-1954)
Football 11
Rice-Davies, Mandy (1944-)
Self-Interest 9
Rich, Mike (1959-)
Gifts 9
Richards, Ann (1933-2006)
Speeches 12
Richards, Keith (1943-)
Drugs 12
Richards, Keith (1943-) see
Jagger, Mick and **Richards,
Keith**
Richardson, Justin (1900-75)
Famous Writers 17
Richardson, Ralph (1902-83)
Acting 4, Theatre 7
Richardson, Samuel
(1689-1761)
Love 42
**Richter, Johann Paul
Friedrich** (1763-1825)
Birthdays 6
Rifkin, Jeremy (1945-)
Europe 14
Rigg, Diana (1938-)
Gossip 8
Rilke, Rainer Maria
(1875-1926)
Art 22, Fate 9, Love 43,
Relationships 23
Rimbaud, Arthur (1854-91)
Life 30
Ritz, César (1850-1918)
Business 17
Rivarol, Antoine de
(1753-1801)
Languages 9
Robertson, George (1946-)
Balkans 4
Robespierre, Maximilien
(1758-94)

Human Rights 13
Robin, Leo (1900-84)
Wealth 19
Robinson, Anne (1944-)
Strength 17
Robinson, Sugar Ray
(1920-89)
Boxing 7
Rochester, Lord (1647-80)
Beginning 10, Cowardice 3,
Words and Deeds 9
Roddenberry, Gene
(1921-91)
Exploration 9
Roddick, Anita (1942-2007)
Cosmetics 6
Rodriguez, Sue (1951-94)
Suicide 6
Rogers, Richard (1933-)
Beauty 22
Rogers, Samuel (1763-1855)
Achievement 16, Marriage 26
Rogers, Will (1879-1935)
Cinema 17, Communism 11,
Heroes 14, Humour 15, Ignorance
10, Likes 10, Newspapers 13,
Taxes 12, Time 22, Weapons 11
Roland, Mme (1754-93)
Liberty 29
Rolland, Romain
(1866-1944)
Heroes 15
Rolle, Richard de Hampole
(c.1290-1349)
Class 13
Roosevelt, Eleanor
(1884-1962)
Self-Esteem 13
Roosevelt, Franklin D.
(1882-1945)
Books 21, Economics 15, Fear 17,
Human Rights 14, International
Relations 24, Peace 20, Political
Parties 24, Politicians 17, United
States 20, War 30, World War II
14, 15
Roosevelt, Theodore
(1858-1919)
Diplomacy 10, 11, Fathers 6,
Journalism 13, Language 16,
Presidency 13, United States 21
Rosa, Salvator (1615-73)
Silence 7

Saro-Wiwa, Ken (1941-95)
Last Words 18, Literature and
Society 5

Sarraute, Nathalie (1902-99)
Television 13

Sartre, Jean-Paul (1905-80)
Belief 18, Despair 10, Disillusion
9, Executions 6, Fathers 8, Futility
12, Habit 8, Hell 5, Liberty 31,
Literature and Society 6, Time 23

Sassoon, Siegfried
(1886-1967)
Army 20, 21, Disability 9, Singing
14

Satie, Erik (1866-1925)
Famous Musicians 10

Saunders, Cicely (1916-2005)
Dying 9, Sickness 10, Suffering 19

Sayers, Dorothy L.
(1893-1957)
Christianity 8, Pleasure 17,
Quotations 11

Scarfe, Gerald (1936-)
Drawing 6

Scargill, Arthur (1938-)
Parliament 11

Schelling, Friedrich von
(1775-1854)
Architecture 12

Schiller, Friedrich von
(1759-1805)
Fools 13, Originality 9, Secrecy
18, Wisdom 7

Schliemann, Heinrich
(1822-90)
Archaeology 5

Schnabel, Artur (1882-1951)
Famous Musicians 11, Musicians
6

Schoenberg, Arnold
(1874-1951)
Music 21

Schopenhauer, Arthur
(1788-1860)
Women 29

Schroeder, Patricia (1940-)
Famous Politicians 21

Schulberg, Budd (1914-2009)
Opportunity 6

Schulz, Charles Monroe
(1922-2000)
Happiness 20

Schumacher, E. F. (1911-77)
Business 18, Doubt 8, Economics
16, 17, Terrorism 5

Schumpeter, J. A.
(1883-1950)
Idealism 10

Schumpeter, Joseph Alois
(1883-1950)
Economics 18

Schurz, Carl (1829-1906)
Patriotism 17

Schwarzkopf III, H. Norman
(1934-)
Army 22

Schweitzer, Albert
(1875-1965)
Intellectuals 4

Schwitters, Kurt (1887-1948)
Painting 30

Scott, C. P. (1846-1932)
Journalism 14, Television 14

Scott, Robert Falcon
(1868-1912)
Courage 13, Exploration 10, Last
Words 19, Risk 7, Schools 8

Scott, Sir Walter (1771-1832)
Chance 9, Deception 10, Famous
Writers 18, Fools 14, Indifference
8, Patriotism 18, Scotland 11, 12,
Theatre 8, Women 30

Scottish Proverb
Toasts 3

Scott-Maxwell, Florida
Mothers 7

Searle, Ronald (1920-) see
Willans, Geoffrey and **Searle,
Ronald**

Seeger, Pete (1919-)
Experience 13

Segal, Erich (1937-)
Love 45

Sei Shōnagon (c.966-c.1013)
Enemies 10, Writing 27

Seinfeld, Jerry (1954-)
Newspapers 14

Selden, John (1584-1654)
Familiarity 8, Laws 17, Pleasure
18

Seldon, Arthur (1916-2005)
Government 27

Sellar, W. C. (1898-1951) and
Yeatman, R. J. (1898-1968)
Debt 7, Examinations 7, History
13, Schools 9

Semugeshi, Ezekiel
Genocide 6

Seneca ('the Younger') (c.4
BC-AD 65)
Adversity 7, Birth 5, Cooking 11,
Death 27, Debt 8, Ignorance 13,
Sorrow 13, Suffering 20, Teaching
13, Ways 5

Service, Robert W.
(1874-1958)
Promises 3, Strength 18, Time 24

Seward, William (1801-72)
Revolution 19

Sewell, Anna (1820-78)
Ignorance 14

Sexton, Anne (1928-74)
Earth 8, Fathers 9, Suicide 7

Shackleton, Ernest
(1874-1922)
Effort 13, Exploration 11

Shaffer, Peter (1926-)
Conformity 10, Culture 9

Shakespeare, William
(1564-1616)
Acting 5, Action 10, Adversity 8,
Ambition 15, Bereavement 17,
18, Bible 8, Careers 8, Character
16, Charity 6, Choice 13,
Circumstance 13, Cities 10,
Clothes 18, Compassion 13,
Conscience 9, Conversation 20,
Courage 14, Courtship 8,
Cowardice 4, Cruelty 10, Danger
6, Day 4, Death 28, 29, Defiance
10, Dreams 9, Drunkenness 8,
Dying 10, Eating 12, Effort 14,
Ending 12, Enemies 11, England
17, Epitaphs 20, Equality 12, Evil
13, Face 9, Failure 8, Faithfulness
13, Fame 18, Fate 10, Fear 19,
Flattery 5, Flowers 9, 10, Food 20,
Friendship 28, Futility 13, Future
18, Generation Gap 9, Goodness
15, Gossip 10, Greatness 9, Guilt
9, Hosts and Guests 10, Human
Race 29, Hypocrisy 6, Ingratitude
2, Insults 8, Jealousy 7, Lending 3,
Libraries 7, Life 32, 33, Love 46,
47, 48, Lovers 15, Madness 7, 8,
Marriage 27, Medicine 15,
Meeting 10, 11, Men 16,
Misfortunes 12, Murder 12, Music
22, Musical Instruments 7, Names
14, Nature 9, News 5, Night 5,

Country 8, Death 33, Food 22,
Heaven 3, Houses 4, Ireland 11,
Lifestyles 24, Marriage 30,
Mathematics 18, Minorities 6,
Prayer 12, Reviews 6, Singing 15

Smith, Tilly (1994-)
Disasters 5

Snagge, John (1904-96)
Sports 23

Snow, C. P. (1905-80)
Arts and Sciences 11

Snyder, Gary (1930-)
Economics 19, Simplicity 4

Socrates (469-399 BC)
Death 34, Knowledge 25,
Philosophy 10, Possessions 13,
Truth 19

Solzhenitsyn, Alexander
(1918-2008)
Censorship 20, Communism 12,
Evil 14, Power 22, Prison 5,
Propaganda 7, Suffering 23,
Twentieth Century 7, Work 21

Somerville, Edith Œ
(1858-1949) and **Ross, Martin**
(1862-1915)
Family 11, Hunting 6

Somoza, Anastasio (1925-80)
Elections 14

Sondheim, Stephen (1930-)
Air Travel 8, Optimism 9,
Transience 13, United States 23

Sontag, Susan (1933-)
Aids 3, Critics 20, Photography 9,
Pornography 5, Sickness 12

Soper, Donald (1903-98)
Parliament 13, Politics 30

Sophocles (c.496-406 BC)
Human Race 30, Life 36, Money
20, Sex 28

Soule, John L. B. (1815-91)
Exploration 12

Sousa, John Philip
(1854-1932)
Jazz 9

Southey, Robert (1774-1843)
Home 10, Winter 7, Youth 17

Spark, Muriel (1918-2006)
Christianity 9, Flowers 11,
Maturity 10, Parents 17, Schools
10

Sparrow, John (1906-92)
Dogs 8, Epitaphs 22

Spector, Phil (1940-)
Rock 7

Spencer, Herbert
(1820-1903)
Crime 9, Fools 15, Heroes 16,
Thinking 21

Spencer, Lord (1964-)
Press Photographers 4, Titles 7

Spencer, Stanley (1891-1959)
Painting 31

Spender, Stephen (1909-95)
Humour 16, Railways 6

Spenser, Edmund
(c.1552-99)
Rivers 9

Spice Girls, The
Ambition 14

Spielberg, Steven (1947-)
Cinema 18

Spinoza, Baruch (1632-77)
Insight 13

Spring-Rice, Cecil
(1859-1918)
Patriotism 20

Springsteen, Bruce (1949-)
Poverty 20, Success 18, Television
15

Spurgeon, C. H. (1834-92)
Lies 9

Squire, J. C. (1884-1958)
Drunkenness 9, God 28, Science
17

Staël, Mme de (1766-1817)
Insight 14, Opinion 15

Stalin, Joseph (1879-1953)
Communism 13, Death 35,
Gratitude 6, Literature and Society
7

Stanley, Bessie Anderson (fl.
1905)
Success 19

Stanley, Henry Morton
(1841-1904)
Meeting 12

Stark, Freya (1893-1993)
Women 33

Stark, John (1728-1822)
American War of Independence 4

Stassinopoulos, Arianna
(1950-)
Creativity 12

Stead, Christina (1902-83)
Greed 7

Steele, Richard (1672-1729)
Letters 7, Reading 13

Steffens, Lincoln (1866-1936)
Communism 14

Stein, Gertrude (1874-1946)
Danger 7, Disillusion 10,
Information 7, Last Words 21,
Literature 9, Self 27, United States
24, World War I 18

Steinbeck, John (1902-68)
Duty 11, Famine 5, Greatness 10,
Human Race 31, Insults 11,
Lifestyles 25, Pollution 12

Steinem, Gloria (1934-)
Woman's Role 19

Steiner, George (1926-)
Genocide 7

Steiner, Peter (1940-)
Internet 5

Stendhal (1783-1842)
Art and Society 8, Beauty 25,
Fiction 13

Stengel, Casey (1891-1975)
Baseball 8

Stephens, James (1882-1950)
Perfection 11

Sterne, Laurence (1713-68)
France 11, Love 49, Pleasure 19,
Pregnancy 7, Reading 14, Writing
31

Stevens, Wallace (1879-1955)
Beauty 26, Imagination 14,
Reality 8

Stevenson, Adlai (1900-65)
Famous People 11, Flattery 6,
Generation Gap 11, Political
Parties 25, 26, Politicians 19,
Science and Religion 12,
Speeches 15, Words 22

Stevenson, Anne (1933-)
Birds 10, Sea 15

Stevenson, Robert Louis
(1850-94)
Alcohol 17, 18, Books 24, Colours
6, Eating 14, Epitaphs 23, Food
23, Guilt 10, Lies 10, Marriage
31, Memory 22, Morality 18,
Sleep 9, 10, Travel 18, 19

Stewart, Donald Ogden
(1894-1980)
Relationships 24

Stewart, Martha (1941-)
Cooking 12

Poetry 27

Tubman, Harriet (*c*.1820-1913)
Determination 16

Tuchman, Barbara W. (1912-89)
War 36

Tucker, Sophie (1884-1966)
Wealth 22, Women 35

Tupper, Martin (1810-89)
Books 26

Turgenev, Ivan (1818-83)
Death 38, Emotions 18, Ideas 14, Insight 16, Nature 11, Prayer 15

Turgot, A. R. J. (1727-81)
Famous People 12

Turkle, Sherry (1948-)
Computers 10

Turner, J. M. W. (1775-1851)
Colours 7, Critics 22, Genius 13

Tusa, John (1936-)
Management 13

Tutu, Desmond (1931-)
Heaven 6

Twain, Mark (1835-1910)
Adversity 9, Anger 11, Asia 8, Awards 7, Books 27, Caution 10, Celebrations 7, Custom 6, Death 39, Dogs 11, Education 21, Facts 8, Familiarity 10, Food 24, Fools 16, Generation Gap 12, Golf 4, Goodness 19, Gossip 11, Hell 6, Human Nature 13, Human Race 35, 36, Indecision 8, Ingratitude 3, Inventions 19, Italy 4, Journalism 17, Lies 12, Manners 12, Men and Women 22, Mistakes 15, Morality 19, Mothers 8, Opinion 17, Originality 11, Prayer 16, Promises 5, Science 18, Style 11, Success 21, Temptation 9, Travel 21, Weather 12

Twiggy (1949-)
Middle Age 15

Tynan, Kenneth (1927-80)
Critics 23, Famous People 13, Worry 6

Tyndale, William (*c*.1494-1536)
Bible 9

Tyutchev, F. I. (1803-73)
Russia 10

Umar ibn Abd al-Aziz (*c*.682-720)
God 30

Unamuno, Miguel de (1864-1937)
Doubt 10, Science 19

Updike, John (1932-2009)
Adversity 10, Boredom 10, Britain 8, England 19, Fame 20, Parents 18, Physics 10, Rain 4, Theatre 11, United States 26

Ure, Midge (1953-) see **Geldof, Bob** and **Ure, Midge**

Ustinov, Peter (1921-2004)
Diplomacy 13, Famous Artists 5, Friendship 29, Humour 18, Leadership 17, Parents 19

Valéry, Paul (1871-1945)
Loneliness 6, Poetry 28

Vanbrugh, John (1664-1726)
Women 36

van Damm, Vivian (*c*.1889-1960)
Theatre 12

Vanderbilt, William H. (1821-85)
Business 24

van der Post, Laurens (1906-96)
Certainty 8

Van Dyke, Henry (1852-1933)
Hosts and Guests 11, Houses 5, Time 28

Vane, Henry (1613-62)
Executions 7

Vaneigem, Raoul (1934-)
Work 22

Van Gogh, Vincent (1853-90)
Value 13

Vaucaire, Michel
Guilt 11

Vaughan Williams, Ralph (1872-1958)
Music 25

Veblen, Thorstein (1857-1929)
Research 5

Vega, Lope de (1562-1635)
Theatre 13

Venturi, Robert (1925-)
Architecture 14

Verne, Jules (1828-1905)
Colours 8

Vespasian (AD 9-79)
Taxes 15

Vicious, Sid (1957-79)
Music 26

Victoria, Queen (1819-1901)
Birth 7, Defeat 13, Humour 19, Royalty 16, Woman's Role 22

Vidal, Gore (1925-)
Famous Artists 6, Famous Politicians 23, Punishment 16, Reality 9, Success 22

Vidor, King (1895-1982)
Marriage 32

Viera Gallo, José Antonio (1943-)
Political Parties 27

Villon, François (b.1431-after 1463)
Past 19

Virgil (70-19 BC)
Ability 6, Defeat 14, Experience 14, Farming 8, Gifts 10, Greed 8, Love 53, Sorrow 18, Time 29

Vitruvius (*fl*. 1st century BC)
Architecture 15

Voltaire (1694-1778)
Boredom 11, Censorship 23, Certainty 9, Change 26, Excellence 5, God 31, Government 30, Last Words 23, Leisure 9, Luxury 6, Moderation 9, Necessity 7, Optimism 10, Philosophy 11, Practicality 12, Prayer 17, Reputation 9, Tragedy 7, War 37, Ways 6, Work 23

Vonnegut, Kurt (1922-2007)
Character 18, Death 40, Lovers 17, Paranormal 9, Youth 18

Vreeland, Diana (1903-89)
Colours 9

Vyazemsky, Prince Peter (1792-1878)
Russia 11

Waite, Terry (1939-)
Terrorism 7

Walcott, Derek (1930-)
Africa 13, Creativity 13, Famine 6, Languages 11, West Indies 3, 4

Pessimism 9

Wilson, Sandy (1924-)
Courtship 11

Wilson, Woodrow
(1856-1924)
Democracy 13, Films 6,
International Relations 26,
Speeches 17, War 40

Windsor, Duchess of
(1896-1986)
Appearance 14

Winfrey, Oprah (1954-)
Education 25, Exercise 9, Luck 9

Winters, Shelley (1922-2006)
Theatre 14

Winterson, Jeanette (1959-)
Biotechnology 4, Clergy 8, God
33, Lovers 18

Wittgenstein, Ludwig
(1889-1951)
Body 20, Death 41, Language 18,
Last Words 24, Logic 16,
Philosophy 13, Speech 20,
Tragedy 8, Universe 14

Wodehouse, P. G.
(1881-1975)
Apology 9, Character 20,
Cooperation 14, Discontent 12,
Family 17, Field Sports 4, Golf 5,
6, Husbands 12, Scotland 16,
Surprise 6, Trust 13

Wogan, Terry (1938-)
Television 20

Wolf, Naomi (1962-)
Beauty 27, Fat 6

Wolfe, Edgar Allan see
Langley, Noel and **Wolfe,
Edgar Allan**

Wolfe, Humbert (1886-1940)
Journalism 19

Wolfe, Tom (1931-)
Fashion 10, Police 5, Self-Interest
10

Wollstonecraft, Mary
(1759-97)
Human Rights 16, Mind 22,
Parents 21, Woman's Role 25

Wolpert, Lewis (1929-)
Arts and Sciences 12

Wolstenholme, Kenneth
(1920-2002)
Ending 14

Wood, Victoria (1953-)
Intellectuals 6, Sports 25

Woodcock, George (1912-95)
Canada 20

Woods, Tiger (1975-)
Race 10

Woodward, Robert Burns
(1917-79)
Chemistry 4

Woolf, Virginia (1882-1941)
Critics 24, Diaries 8, Discontent
13, Eating 17, Famous Writers 22,
Friendship 30, Libraries 8,
Madness 9, Men and Women 27,
Misfortunes 14, Self 28, Writing
36

Woollcott, Alexander
(1887-1943)
Famous Writers 23, Pleasure 20

Wordsworth, Elizabeth
(1840-1932)
Goodness 24

Wordsworth, Mary
(1782-1859)
Letters 9

Wordsworth, William
(1770-1850)
Birds 13, Birth 8, Character 21,
England 21, Evening 4, Famous
Poets 22, Flowers 14, 15,
Generation Gap 13, Goodness 25,
Idealism 13, Imagination 15,
Leisure 10, London 8, Nature 14,
Originality 12, Poetry 29,
Revolution 22, Shakespeare 9,
Suffering 25, Transience 15, Youth
19

Worrall, Terry (fl. 1991)
Snow 5

Wotton, Henry (1568-1639)
Architecture 16, Bereavement 20,
Diplomacy 14

Wright, Frank Lloyd
(1867-1959)
Architecture 17, Cities 11, Luxury
7

Wu, Harry (1937-)
Prison 6

Wycherley, William
(c.1640-1716)
Critics 25

Wynette, Tammy (1942-)
Loyalty 6

Yamamoto, Isoroku
(1884-1943)
Warfare 10

Yāqūt (d. 1229)
Earth 11

Yeatman, R. J. (1898-1968)
see **Sellar, W. C.** and
Yeatman, R. J.

Yeats, W. B. (1865-1939)
Air Force 5, Chaos 5, Dance 11,
Death 42, Dreams 11, Dying 11,
Emotions 20, Excellence 6,
Friendship 31, Hair 6, Idealism 14,
Indifference 12, Innocence 11,
Ireland 12, Life 44, Love 56, Old
Age 19, 20, Opinion 18,
Perfection 13, Poetry 30, 31,
Problems 14, Solitude 14,
Suffering 26, Time 30

Yeltsin, Boris (1931-2007)
Europe 17, Russia 12

Yesenin, Sergei (1895-1925)
Pleasure 21

Yevtushenko, Yevgeny
(1933-)
Life 45

Young, Andrew (1932-)
Business 29

Young, Edward (1683-1765)
Fools 17, Self-Knowledge 12,
Sleep 13, War 41

Young, George W.
(1846-1919)
Teetotalism 7

Young, G. M. (1882-1959)
Publishing 6

Young, Neil (1945-)
Suicide 10

Zamyatin, Yevgeny
(1884-1937)
Thinking 23

Zangwill, Israel (1864-1926)
Christianity 14, United States 28

Zappa, Frank (1940-93)
Drugs 13, Journalism 20,
Similarity 11

Zeno (333-261 BC)
Speech 21

Zephaniah, Benjamin
(1958-)
Christmas 12, Poetry 32

Oxford Paperback Reference

The Concise Oxford Dictionary of Quotations
FIFTH EDITION
Edited by Elizabeth Knowles

Now based on the highly acclaimed sixth edition of *The Oxford Dictionary of Quotations*, this new edition maintains its extensive coverage of literary and historical quotations, and contains completely up-to-date material. A fascinating read and an essential reference tool.

The Oxford Dictionary of Political Quotations
Edited by Antony Jay

This lively and illuminating dictionary from the writer of 'Yes Minister' presents a vintage crop of over 4,000 political quotations. Ranging from the pivotal and momentous to the rhetorical, the sincere, the bemused, the tongue-in-cheek, and the downright rude, examples include memorable words from the old hands as well as from contemporary politicians.

'funny, striking, thought-provoking and incisive…will appeal to those browsing through it as least as much as to those who wish to use it as a work of reference'
Observer

Oxford Dictionary of Modern Quotations
Edited by Elizabeth Knowles

The answers to all your quotation questions lie in this delightful collection of over 5,000 of the twentieth century's most famous quotations.

'Hard to sum up a book so useful, wayward and enjoyable'   *Spectator*

The Oxford Dictionary of Literary Quotations
Edited by Peter Kemp

Containing 4,000 of the most memorized and cited literary quotations, this dictionary is an excellent reference work as well as an enjoyable read.

The Oxford Dictionary of Humorous Quotations
Edited by Ned Sherrin

From the sharply witty to the downright hilarious, this sparkling collection will appeal to all senses of humour.

Oxford Paperback Reference

The Concise Oxford Companion to English Literature
Margaret Drabble and Jenny Stringer

Based on the best-selling *Oxford Companion to English Literature*, this is an indispensable guide to all aspects of English literature.

Review of the parent volume
'a magisterial and monumental achievement'

Literary Review

The Concise Oxford Companion to Irish Literature
Robert Welch

From the ogam alphabet developed in the 4th century to Roddy Doyle, this is a comprehensive guide to writers, works, topics, folklore, and historical and cultural events.

Review of the parent volume
'Heroic volume ... It surpasses previous exercises of similar nature in the richness of its detail and the ecumenism of its approach.'

Times Literary Supplement

A Dictionary of Shakespeare
Stanley Wells

Compiled by one of the best-known international authorities on the playwright's works, this dictionary offers up-to-date information on all aspects of Shakespeare, both in his own time and in later ages.

Oxford Paperback Reference

The Kings of Queens of Britain
John Cannon and Anne Hargreaves

A detailed, fully-illustrated history ranging from mythical and pre-conquest rulers to the present House of Windsor, featuring regional maps and genealogies.

A Dictionary of World History

Over 4,000 entries on everything from prehistory to recent changes in world affairs. An excellent overview of world history.

A Dictionary of British History
Edited by John Cannon

An invaluable source of information covering the history of Britain over the past two millennia. Over 3,000 entries written by more than 100 specialist contributors.

Review of the parent volume
'the range is impressive . . . truly (almost) all of human life is here'
Kenneth Morgan, Observer

More Literature titles from OUP

The Oxford Literary Guide to Britain and Ireland
Edited by Daniel Hahn and Nicholas Robins

Explore the homes, haunts, and places of inspiration of your favourite writers from Jane Austen to Philip Pullman. Beautifully illustrated, it describes over 1,800 places of literary significance from across the British Isles.

Review from previous edition:
'The finest reference book of its kind: a brilliant and meticulous interweaving of anecdote and quotation . . . permanent magic'
The Times

The Oxford Companion to the Brontës
Christine Alexander and Margaret Smith

This Companion brings together a wealth of information about the fascinating lives and writings of the Brontë sisters.

'This book is a must . . . a treasure trove of a book'
Irish Times

The Concise Oxford Companion to Classical Literature
M. C. Howatson and Ian Chilvers

A lucid and fascinating guide to the literary heritage of the classical world.

Review of parent title (*The Oxford Companion to Classical Literature*):
'a volume for all seasons . . . indispensable'
Times Educational Supplement